Progress and Challenges of Nonfinancial Defined Contribution Pension Schemes

VOLUME 1

Progress and Challenges of Nonfinancial Defined Contribution Pension Schemes

VOLUME 1
ADDRESSING MARGINALIZATION, POLARIZATION, AND THE LABOR MARKET

*Robert Holzmann, Edward Palmer,
Robert Palacios, and Stefano Sacchi*

 **WORLD BANK GROUP**

Contents

Boxes

Figures

Tables

Preface

For many years, Italy was not as effective as Sweden and other countries in promoting abroad its pension reforms, in particular its nonfinancial defined contribution (NDC) scheme, introduced in 1995. Therefore, it was important that—following the two early NDC conferences held in Sweden in 2003 and 2009—the third conference took place in Rome in 2017.

Italy's 1995 pension reform introducing the NDC approach followed the 1992 parametric reform, which was a turning point in Italian policies. The issue of pension reform had been extensively discussed since the late 1970s, but no major action was taken until the early 1990s when changes became extremely urgent. Italy's pension system had three main problems: high and rising expenditure, inadequate labor market incentives, and chaotic distributional effects.

Pension expenditure, which had increased from 5 percent of gross domestic product (GDP) in 1960 to about 15 percent in 1992, was expected to increase further and get close to 25 percent of GDP by 2030. The contribution rate needed to cover private sector employees' benefits was set to increase from 44 percent in 1995 to 60 percent in 2025. The pension formula, the eligibility conditions, and the indexation rules granted rates of return that were considerably higher than the rate of growth of the social security tax base.

The lack of any link between the size of the pension benefit and the age of retirement was an incentive for the earliest possible retirement. In other words, there was a high implicit tax on continuing to work. This situation contributed to the low employment rates of older men and women. In addition, the segmentation of the pension system into several separate pension schemes, each one operating with its own rules, hampered the mobility of workers both between and within the public and private sectors.

There were also equity reasons for the reforms. The rate of return on contributions was extremely uneven across different groups of workers. It was usually higher for individuals with earnings rising toward the end of their careers. Inflation affected the relative value of retirement benefits.

The 1992 reform primarily addressed the sustainability issue. It deleted overnight about a quarter of existing public pension liabilities. The retirement age for old-age benefits was raised (over a 10-year period) from 55 to 60 for women and from 60 to 65 for men in private employment. The reference period for calculating pensionable earnings was lengthened from 5 to 10 years; for younger workers it was extended to the whole working life. The minimum number of contributing years for entitlement to an old-age pension was raised from 15 to 20. The reference index for the indexation of pension benefits was changed from wages to prices. The minimum number of years of contributions required for public sector employees to be entitled to a seniority pension was gradually raised to 35, a threshold previously applied only to private sector workers. By breaking the deadlock of Italian pension policy and immediately restraining expenditure increases, the parametric reform of 1992 set the conditions for better planned and more systematic changes.

The 1995 reform focused on incentives and distribution. Its design was a big step forward in both areas. The reform determined a shift from a defined benefit to a defined contribution system in which the notional accumulated contributions on individual accounts are transformed into an annuity at retirement. Italy moved toward homogeneous retirement rules and uniform rates of return. Although expenditure forecasts and the high level of contribution rates that would be needed to finance spending pointed to the need for further expenditure restraint, this was not the primary objective of the reform.

In contrast with other countries, in Italy the introduction of an NDC system came without an extensive debate about its merits and usefulness. Relatively little preparatory work was done, no major report was released to the public, and the pension formula was not immediately published. Maybe also because of that, the reform had some weak points:

- It envisaged a long and complex transitory arrangement: only those who started working after 1995 were fully under the new regime.
- It postponed the first revision of conversion coefficients until 2005.
- It envisaged a relatively low minimum retirement age (57 years).
- Self-equilibrating mechanisms were not fully adequate.

The reform represented a major step forward, but it was also somewhat incomplete, shifting some political tensions into the future. Moreover, little effort was made to explain the new pension rules to the public. This obviously reflected the lengthy transition. It is likely that the fact that the new rules were not well communicated or well understood reduced the positive impact on labor market incentives. It is possible that notional funding was also little understood by policy makers.

Some of these problems were tackled in the following years, when several changes were introduced, mostly to modify the eligibility requirements and other aspects applying to workers not fully under the new NDC regime. In 2011 the NDC rules for benefit computation were extended pro rata to all workers, starting from 2012. The statutory pension age was raised to 66 for all workers beginning in 2012. From 2013 onward, the statutory pension age was automatically indexed to increases in life expectancy. The fast tightening of eligibility criteria for retirement in a difficult macroeconomic context created some tensions. In recent years, some measures have been taken to allow disadvantaged groups of workers to retire earlier. Furthermore, more significant measures are now under discussion.

Two corrective mechanisms (the revision of retirement age and of the coefficients converting contributions into pensions) now work in parallel to offset the impact of increasing life expectancy.

Labor market trends are in line with reforms increasing retirement age. The employment rate among people ages 50–64 increased from about 41 percent in 2004 to 59 percent in 2017, and this rate is still gradually rising.

It would have been preferable to implement from the very outset a full NDC regime for all groups of workers and cohorts, but—in the end—Italy now has a sustainable and homogeneous pension system providing appropriate economic incentives. The longer you work and pay contributions, the better your pension will be.

In many ways, the challenges facing the Italian NDC system are similar to those of other countries with NDC systems.

The first issue is flexibility. The degree of flexibility in retirement is obviously a primary issue: What is the ideal age bracket for old-age pensions? One should also consider whether there should be flexibility in contribution rates (both up and down) and in the choice of the risks covered by the NDC scheme (for example, survivors' benefits). Obviously, solutions are now constrained by the need to limit expenditure growth in the short term.

Another issue is that of equity. Life expectancy at retirement is affected by education, income, occupation, and gender. Identical transformation coefficients for everyone induces a systematic redistribution of lifetime resources among different categories. If a correlation exists between longevity and lifetime income, the poorer groups of the population subsidize the richer groups. This is not exclusive to NDC systems, but in NDC systems the issue is more transparent, other redistributive mechanisms having been removed. Group-specific transformation coefficients might be a solution, but one should be careful about introducing new forms of fragmentation into the system.

Again on the equity side, one should consider the coordination of the NDC regime with welfare schemes. One has to avoid situations in which low-income earners do not get any return on their contributions. However, NDC schemes cannot be expected to prevent poverty in old age for the entire population. In Italy the issue was addressed with two main tools: supplementing the defined benefit pensions up to the so-called minimum level, and providing welfare pensions (*pensione sociale*) to the elderly poor. Only in recent years did Italy move toward a universal welfare scheme. By providing a framework for transparent distributional policy, the NDC scheme can easily be combined with a universal welfare scheme.

Another issue that may require policy attention is that of individuals with less than full careers. Younger cohorts entering late into the regular labor market may end up with insufficient contributions and relatively poorer pensions. Although this problem applies to any form of earnings-related pension scheme, it is highly visible in NDC pension schemes.

One should also evaluate whether the pace of adjustment to demographic changes and to economic shocks is adequate. If automatic adjustments are too slow, the rules will need to be changed, which might affect the credibility of the link between contributions and benefits.

In evaluating any change of the current rules, one should keep in mind that after the many reforms introduced since 1992, a certain stability in legislation may be necessary. People should perceive that the returns on their contributions are predictable and certain.

Finally, communication to the public is still an open issue. In recent years the efforts to inform the public have increased significantly, but further progress is warranted.

It has been heartening to see that the 2017 conference and the ensuing anthology address many of these issues at the conceptual, empirical, and policy level, thus offering food for thought for Italy and other countries.

Daniele Franco
State Accountant General, Ministry of the Economy, Italy

In June 1994, the Swedish government presented a bill to Parliament—prepared by the Working Group on Pensions—proposing a public nonfinancial defined contribution (NDC) pension scheme. This was to be accompanied by a public financial defined contribution (FDC) scheme and a minimum guarantee benefit at retirement. Both the NDC and FDC schemes are personal saving schemes in the sense that individuals forgo current personal consumption through their payment of contributions noted on personal accounts. And in both, the benefit received is based on the individual's account balance and life expectancy at the time of retirement. The 1994 reform provided universal longevity insurance to the whole of the Swedish population, placing the individual's role in saving for future retirement in the forefront.

The "simple" idea of an NDC scheme—although novel at the time—has numerous positive features. If carefully designed and introduced, it is a public pension scheme that delivers affordability and long-term financial sustainability that through its design manages the economic and demographic risks confronting all public pension schemes. The indexation (rate of return) of accounts and of pension benefits steers the scheme in the direction of economic balance and results in the sharing of ups and downs in economic growth between workers and pensioners. And the interaction of the benefit calculation with life expectancy constitutes a vital adjustment mechanism in addressing the financial pressures of a constantly aging population.

Sweden is still unique in going "all the way" in its NDC scheme design through two additional mechanisms. One is the maintenance of a reserve fund, within the pay-as-you-go-based NDC scheme, that distributes funded contributions over time between larger and smaller ("cyclical") generations, for example, those associated with baby boom or migration cycles. The second is the use of the solvency ratio, with a "balancing index" that adjusts liabilities to assets when the solvency ratio falls below unity. This is based on the sum of the explicit accounts of workers and the implicit accounts of pensioners, which are the liabilities of the provider—in the NDC case, the Swedish Pensions Agency—to participants. The assets in the context of the solvency ratio are the estimated value of future contributions and the market value of the reserve fund. From a macroeconomic standpoint, the Swedish NDC design strives to create autonomy from the state budget for the country's publicly provided universal longevity insurance scheme.

Sweden's NDC scheme is supported by a broad span of the political spectrum. When the original legislation was passed in 1994, it was supported by more than three-quarters of the members of Parliament. The NDC scheme today still has the active support of three-quarters of Parliament members, as represented by a contemporary cross-party working group on pensions that meets regularly to discuss Sweden's pension system. Of course, some fine-tuning has occurred, not the least in the technical application of the income index and balancing mechanism following the global recession of 2008–09.

Sweden sponsored the first conference on NDCs, which resulted in 2006 in the first of what has become a series of NDC anthologies published by the World Bank. The overriding aim of that first conference was to gather international experts to discuss the conceptual strength of the new NDC paradigm. The second two-volume NDC anthology (published in 2012–13) had a strong focus on maintaining financial stability and sustainability, including the Swedish accounting structure that underlies the calculation of the solvency (balance) ratio and the triggering of the balancing mechanism. It also added a focus on gender-specific issues.

This third anthology arose out of an October 2017 conference held in Rome in a joint effort with Italy. It moves the perspective toward a host of issues at the forefront of the current discussion in Sweden and, I believe, in many other countries. What are these issues, then? They include the importance of labor market policy that accommodates the dynamics of the labor market accompanying increasing globalization; the possible roles for pension policy in preempting and bridging the gender pension gap; the technical challenges of creating fair and sustainable annuities and how to deal with issues arising from socioeconomic differences in life expectancy; communication with participants; and much more.

Today's issues for countries' pension systems are a reflection of the larger dynamics of the socioeconomic foundations of modern societies and economies—education and skills attainment, spouses' time sharing, and formal labor market participation. They also give rise to consideration of strategies at the individual and societal level for recognizing and addressing changing technologies in all segments of the labor market. The challenges have always been great and will continue to be so. The current issues reflect an ongoing evolution. Hence, to do what we do within the area of pensions best, we need to bring together the worlds of policy and academia and to familiarize ourselves with, understand, and weigh how new knowledge gained from the experience of others and developments in research can help move our own and other countries forward. This was the overriding theme of the Rome conference and is the overriding theme of this third NDC anthology. We are pleased to have had the opportunity to share the responsibility for this undertaking with our Italian cosponsor and are grateful for the buy-in of the World Bank in this project.

In closing, I wish to thank the many academic scholars and experts from international organizations from around the world who participated in the creation of this publication. It is my belief that efforts of this nature are important for spreading knowledge and learning from the experience of others. This particular effort is an important contribution for countries that share the goal of providing affordable, financially sustainable, and adequate national pension schemes that cover the entire population.

Daniel Barr
Director General, Swedish Pensions Agency

Over the past decades, nonfinancial defined contributions (NDCs) emerged as a key tenet in global thinking about pensions. The inspiring and diverse perspectives of many thinkers have contributed enormously in enriching and advancing NDC policy and research.

This new anthology, alongside two preceding anthologies edited by Robert Holzmann and Edward Palmer, represents the most important intellectual effort for bringing together evidence on NDCs and pension reforms more broadly. Whereas previous anthologies were mostly concerned with the design and sustainability of NDC schemes, this new endeavor provides a stronger focus on the sufficiency of pensions under NDCs. Importantly, it also offers precious insights into the political economy of successful and failed NDC reforms. The richness of experiences presented in the ensuing pages will benefit both policy makers and the international agencies supporting them, including the World Bank and other actors.

The contributions enshrined in this anthology cover a wide and comprehensive array of topics from a theoretical, practical, and policy perspective. The studies' authors are well-known academics, policy makers, and practitioners, often combining more than one role at different times of their careers. Interestingly, the studies provide a variety of approaches to pension design and implementation that will be valuable for analysts and decision makers.

The completion of this comprehensive study on NDC pension schemes could not be more timely: the nature of work is changing and labor markets are evolving, leading to a profound rethinking of traditional Bismarckian social insurance arrangements.

Defined contribution systems (both financial and nonfinancial) have challenged the conventional wisdom on pension system design. Yet they have predominantly been perceived as alternatives to contributory pension schemes for wage employment. The challenge today is to develop more suitable systems to respond to the needs of workers in the new digital and gig economy, with labor markets increasingly expanding toward different forms of self-employment and more flexible jobs.

The pension systems of future generations will undoubtedly look different from those of the past. It is still a matter of debate whether this will expand or narrow the space for defined contribution schemes. The World Bank's vision and my own is one in which social insurance is extended to all workers independently of how they engage in the labor market. From this standpoint, governments have a key role to play in providing a basic level of pension to prevent large groups of the population from falling into poverty in old age. This, in turn, will leave a broad second level to individually financed social insurance covering primarily middle- and higher-income earners. Although this does not imply any preference for a specific financing model, the best fit will be the one that most closely links contributions with benefits. NDCs are potentially the best solution, as this anthology correctly argues, although not the only possible solution. In the years to come, we will probably witness a revival of the discussion about the comparative strengths of each approach to providing the best combination of low risk and high income replacement in old age.

Now more than ever we need the best available evidence to manage complex, diverse, and diversifying labor markets. This anthology not only lives up to such challenges but will provide a linchpin for a renewed debate on alternative approaches to pension policy making.

Michal Rutkowski
Senior Director, Social Protection and Jobs Global Practice, World Bank

Acknowledgments

This is the third anthology devoted to issues and challenges for universal public nonfinancial defined contribution (NDC) pension schemes. The anthology exists because of the contributions and incredible dedication of more than 70 academic scholars and institutional experts from all corners of the globe in seeing the project through to the end. Their generously provided time made this publication possible.

The project could have never been undertaken without the two key financial sponsors of the enterprise.

The first was the Italian sponsor of the conference in Rome in October 2017, the Istituto Nazionale per l'Analisi delle Politiche Pubbliche (INAPP), led by coeditor and colleague Stefano Sacchi, where the authors of the first drafts were gathered to present and receive feedback on papers—and interacted over the course of two days. INAPP's Massimiliano Deidda organized the event perfectly.

The second was the Swedish financial sponsor of the publication (that is, language and copy editing, layout, and typesetting and printing)—the Swedish Pensions Agency. To this end, we are especially grateful for the support of the agency's chief economist, Ole Settergren, also a third-time contributor.

In addition, we are grateful to the World Bank and its formal publishing program for enabling the publication of this NDC anthology. Its support provides an important gateway, enabling the two-volume work to reach scholars, institutional pension experts, and policy makers in both developed and emerging market economies. Robert Palacios, an experienced pension economist with a long legacy of work in emerging market economies and also a coauthor and coeditor, took the lead for the World Bank.

The quality of the project was enhanced by the generous efforts of 21 external international reviewers, and we are thankful to Tabea Bucher-Koenen, Elisa Chuliá, Erland Ekheden, Csaba Feher, Georg Fischer, Steven Haberman, Krzysztof Hagemejer, Alain Jousten, Jukka Lassila, Annamaria Lusardi, Andrew Mason, Alicia H. Munnell, Heikki Oksanen, Mike Orszag, Carmen Pagés, Joakim Palme, Eduard Ponds, Mauricio Soto, Viktor Steiner, Olle Sundberg, and Xinmei Wang. These external reviewers, together with the internal reviewers (that is, other authors) and the editors, were a critical part of the enterprise. The review process generated comments and suggestions for revision that substantially improved the quality of all chapters of the anthology.

Finally, we want to thank Amy Gautam for her skillful copy editing of the draft chapters and her experienced and superb management in putting the volumes together; Roberta Gatti, who reviewed the outcome of the project and gave the sign-off as Chief Economist for the Human Development Practice Group at the World Bank; and colleagues in the World Bank's publishing program—Jewel McFadden, Susan Mandel, and Yaneisy Martinez—for all their work and support in the many and very important steps of the final production of this publication.

About the Authors

Susanne Alm is an Associate Professor of Sociology at the Swedish Institute for Social Research (SOFI), Stockholm University. Her main research concerns the relationship between childhood living conditions and different aspects of social problems and social exclusion in adulthood, predominantly criminal offending, drug abuse, and housing eviction, but also poverty and long-term unemployment.

Jennifer Alonso-García has been an Assistant Professor at the University of Groningen in the Netherlands since July 2018. Previously she worked at CEPAR; University of New South Wales, Sydney; and Université Catholique de Louvain. Her research combines the areas of actuarial science and household, pension, and quantitative finance to study the design, risk sharing, and financing of funded and pay-as-you-go retirement income schemes. She is an expert on the fiscal sustainability and adequacy of nonfinancial defined contribution public pension schemes.

Nicholas Barr is a Professor of Public Economics at the London School of Economics and the author of numerous books and articles, including *The Economics of the Welfare State* (Oxford University Press, 5th edition, 2012), *Financing Higher Education: Answers from the UK* (with Iain Crawford; Routledge, 2005), and *Reforming Pensions: Principles and Policy Choices* (with Peter Diamond; Oxford University Press, 2008).

Mirko Bevilacqua is a researcher at Inarcassa (Pension Scheme of the Liberal Professions for Italian Engineers and Architects) and an Adjunct Professor of Economics and Statistics at University of Cassino and Southern Lazio, where he earned a PhD in economics in 2009. He formerly worked in the Research Department of the Swedish Social Insurance Agency.

María del Carmen Boado-Penas is a Senior Lecturer in Actuarial Mathematics at the University of Liverpool, U.K. She holds a PhD in actuarial science (Doctor Europeus) from the University of Valencia, Spain, and an MSc in quantitative finance. She has cooperated on pension projects at the Swedish Social Insurance Agency and at the Spanish Ministry of Labour and Immigration.

Tito Boeri is a Professor at Bocconi University. From March 2015 to February 2019 he was President of the Italian social security administration (INPS). He has been Scientific Director of the Fondazione Rodolfo Debenedetti since its inception and is Centennial Professor at the London School of Economics. He is the founder of the economic policy watchdog website, lavoce.info; on the editorial board of VOX Europe; and the Scientific Director of the Festival of Economics in Trento.

Boele Bonthuis has been an Economist at the Directorate for Employment, Labour and Social Affairs of the Organisation for Economic Co-operation and Development (OECD) since December 2016. Previously he worked at the Research Centre of the Deutsche Bundesbank (2013–16) and the Economics Directorate of the European Central Bank (2011–13). He holds a PhD in economics from the University of Amsterdam (2016) in the area of labor markets and pensions.

Sonia Buchholtz is an assistant in the Economics Department 1, Warsaw School of Economics, and a member of the Polish Pension Group. Her research interests include the economic and social activity of aging populations, pension economics, and economic policy.

Marcelo Abi-Ramia Caetano has a PhD in economics from Universidade Castelo Branco and a bachelor's degree in economics from Federal University of Rio de Janeiro. He was an IPEA Planning and Research Technician and Secretary for Social Security at the Ministry of Finance in Brazil. In 2019, he became General Secretary of the International Social Security Association in Geneva.

Agnieszka Chłoń-Domińczak is a Professor at the Warsaw School of Economics and Director of the Institute of Statistics and Demography. Her main research interests are generational economics and consequences of population aging, pension systems, labor markets, and life-course developments.

Rogério Nagamine Costanzi has a master's degree in economics from Universidad de São Paulo. He is a specialist in public policies and government management for the Brazilian government. He was Special Adviser to the Minister of Pension and Director of the Department of General Pension Regime.

Maria Cozzolino has been the Head of the Social Security Analysis Office in the INPS Research Department since 2015. Previously she was a Senior Economist at the Italian Ministry of Treasury (2013–15) and at several public Italian research institutes (ISAE and Istat from 1998 to 2012). Her research interests and main publications focus on welfare economics, pension systems, public finance, and microsimulation models.

Gustavo Demarco is the Pensions Global Lead at the World Bank. As a Lead Economist, he has led the World Bank's operations and policy dialogue on Pensions, Social Protection, and Labor across the Middle East and North Africa region for more than 10 years. He was a Program Leader for Human Development for the Arab Republic of Egypt, the Republic of Yemen, and Djibouti. He also led the pension capacity-building program at the World Bank Institute, including four editions of the World Bank's Pension Core Course and several regional events. Before joining the World Bank, he served at the Pension Supervision Authority of Argentina as Director of Operations and Planning. He was a core member of the Argentine pension reform team in the 1990s. Earlier in his career, he was Professor of Economics at the Universities of Córdoba, La Rioja, and Buenos Aires. He is the main author of or a contributor to seven books on economics and pensions. He has published several articles in specialized journals and contributed to World Bank publications on pensions, social safety nets, and social protection systems. He earned an economics degree from the University of Córdoba in Argentina. He did his doctoral studies at the same university and his postgraduate studies on development economics and planning at ECLAC (Economic Commission for Latin America and the Caribbean) in Chile.

Edoardo Di Porto is an Associate Professor at University of Naples Federico II. Currently on leave, he is working as a public manager at INPS–Direzione Centrale Studi e Ricerche. He is a CSEF Fellow (University of Naples Federico II) and an affiliated researcher at Uppsala University. His research focuses on public economics, urban economics, and applied econometrics.

Mark Dorfman is a Senior Economist with the Pensions and Social Insurance Global Solutions Group in the Social Protection and Jobs Global Practice of the World Bank. During his more than 30 years with the World Bank, he has worked on different areas of pensions, social security, aging, and financial markets in the South Asia, East Asia and Pacific, Sub-Saharan Africa, and Latin America and the Caribbean regions, respectively. He has directed the World Bank's Pensions Core Course since 2008.

Per Eckefeldt is currently Head of Sector in the Sustainability of Public Finances Unit in the Fiscal Policy and Policy Mix Directorate of the Directorate-General for Economic and Financial Affairs (DG ECFIN) at the European Commission in Brussels. Recent work includes carrying out long-term economic and budgetary projections for the European Union member states (*Ageing Report* and *Fiscal Sustainability Report*).

Erland Ekheden holds a PhD in insurance mathematics from Stockholm University. Since 2017 he has been the Chief Actuary at Pensionsmyndigheten (the Swedish Pensions Agency). He also worked as an actuarial consultant in life and pension from 2014 to 2017.

Eduardo Fajnzylber is a Professor of Economics and Public Policy at the School of Government of the Adolfo Ibáñez University in Chile. Until February 2009, he headed the Research Department at the Chilean Pension Fund and Unemployment Insurance Supervisory Agency, in charge of conducting theoretical and applied studies relating to the Chilean pension system and the individual accounts unemployment insurance program. His current research involves applications of econometric techniques to evaluate the impact of interventions on social security programs.

Elsa Fornero held the chair of Economics at the University of Turin, Italy (retired since November 2018). She served as Minister of Labor, Social Policies and Equal Opportunities in Italy's "technocratic" government (November 2011 to April 2013), and in this capacity conceived of and drafted the pension and labor market reforms. She is Scientific Coordinator of the Center for Research on Pensions and Welfare Policies (CeRP) and vice president of SHARE-ERIC (Survey of Health, Ageing and Retirement in Europe–European Research Infrastructure Consortium). Her research focuses on public and private pension systems and reforms, labor markets, population aging, household saving, retirement choices, life insurance, and economic-financial education.

Dennis Fredriksen earned a master's degree in national economics in 1988 and has been employed at the Research Department of Statistics Norway ever since. He has played a key role in the development, maintenance, and application of the dynamic microsimulation model MOSART.

Róbert Ivan Gál is a Senior Researcher at the Hungarian Demographic Research Institute, a Senior Extern at TARKI Social Research Centre, a Senior Fellow at the Social Futuring Centre, and an Affiliated Professor at Corvinus University, all in Budapest.

Bernd Genser was a Professor of Economics at the University of Konstanz in Germany, from which he retired in 2013. He holds an honorary doctorate from the University of Freiburg, Germany. From 2001 to 2005 he was Chairman of the Public Economics Committee of the German Economic Association and from 2002 to 2010 editor of FinanzArchiv/Public Finance Analysis. His main fields of research are theory of taxation, income and business taxation, international taxation, and tax harmonization.

Marek Góra is a Professor at the Warsaw School of Economics and Chair of Economics Department 1; a visiting Professor at the College of Europe; an IZA Research Fellow; the codesigner of the current Polish pension system; and the founder of the Polish Pension Group. He has publications in labor economics, pension economics, and social policy.

Sandro Gronchi is a Professor of Economics at Sapienza University of Rome, where he also taught Economics of Social Security for the master's program in Public Economics. In 2002, at the request of the Italian Ministry of Economy and Finance, he was appointed Temporary Lecturer at the ministry's newly founded School of Economics and Finance, and then consultant on social security issues to the President of the National Council for Economics and Labour. In the early 1990s he proposed an NDC reform program for the Italian pension system, and in 1995, he was appointed consultant to the government with the task of developing a bill for such a reform.

Igor Guardiancich is a Researcher in the Institute of Law, Politics and Development (DIRPOLIS) of the Sant'Anna School of Advanced Studies in Pisa and recently worked as a Senior Technical Officer on Social Dialogue in the Governance and Tripartism Department at the International Labour Organization. His main research interests are European social policy, welfare states in Central and Eastern Europe, and the political economy of transition and integration.

Erik Hernæs earned a master's degree in economics (Candidatus Oeconomices) in 1972. He was employed in the Research Department of Statistics Norway from 1972 until 1988 and has been employed at the Frisch Centre and its predecessors since. Since 2005 he has been project manager for analyzing the labor market effects of the Norwegian pension reform, mainly by econometric research based on administrative register data.

Erling Holmøy has an MSc in economics. He has worked in the Research Department of Statistics Norway since 1984, mainly with model-based analyses of supply-side policies, such as taxation and industry policy, and economic growth, including fiscal effects of population aging and migration.

Robert Holzmann is Governor of the Austrian National Bank and Member of the Governing Council of the European Central Bank (since September 2019) and Full Member of the Austrian Academy of Sciences (since 2016). He has held academic positions in Austria, Australia, Germany, and Malaysia; senior economist positions at the Organisation for Economic Co-operation and Development and the International Monetary Fund; and senior management positions at the World Bank, where he led the worldwide pension work. He has published 39 books and more than 200 articles on financial, fiscal, and social policy issues.

Anna Klerby is a PhD student at Örebro University and Dalarna University, Sweden. Her PhD work focuses on understanding gender inequality in terms of market failure in the context of cultural norms and values and identifying structural policy measures aimed at addressing these failures. For several years Anna has been consulting with local and regional governments in Sweden on how to perform gender analyses of their resource allocation, based on the gender budgeting method.

Bo Könberg was Swedish Minister of Social Insurance and Health from 1991 to 1994 and Chairman of the Swedish Working Group on Pensions, responsible for the Swedish 1994 pension reform. He was the Principal Investigator for the establishment of the Swedish Pensions Agency in 2010 and Chairman of the Board of the Pensions Agency from 2010 to 2015.

Irena E. Kotowska is a Professor of Demography, Warsaw School of Economics; Chair of the Committee on Demographic Studies and member of the Committee on Labour and Social Policy, both at the Polish Academy of Sciences; and a member of the Scientific Council on Statistics of the Central Statistical Office. Her main fields of research are population and economy; fertility, family, gender, and labor markets; population aging; demographic projections; population-related policy; and social policy.

Héloïse Labit-Hardy commenced work as a Senior Research Associate in the ARC Centre of Excellence in Population Ageing Research at University of New South Wales in September 2016. She completed her PhD at the University of Lausanne in the Department of Actuarial Science and graduated from the French Institut de Science Financière et d'Assurances. She works on mortality modeling, more specifically on longevity risk management, heterogeneity in mortality, cause-of-death mortality modeling, and morbidity.

Bo Larsson is a Swedish economist with expertise in public finance and financial economics.

Ronald Lee has an MA in demography from the University of California, Berkeley, and a PhD in economics from Harvard University. He has worked at Berkeley in demography and economics since 1979, after working eight years at the University of Michigan.

He works on macroeconomic consequences of population aging, intergenerational transfers, demographic forecasting, and evolutionary biodemography.

Vincent Leyaro is currently a Senior Lecturer in the Department of Economics of the University of Dar es Salaam in Tanzania. He was previously an Associate Economics Affairs Officer at the United Nations Economic Commission for Africa in Addis Ababa. He is also an External Research Fellow at the Centre for Research in Economic Development and International Trade at the University of Nottingham, U.K. He completed a PhD in economics at the University of Nottingham in 2010.

Maciej Lis is an Economist on the Ageing and Pensions Team in the Directorate for Employment, Labour and Social Affairs at the OECD. His work is focused on the cross-country comparison of pension systems using microsimulation tools. He contributed to the OECD's *Pensions at a Glance* and *Pensions Outlook* publications as well as to country-specific reviews of pensions. Before joining the OECD, he published papers on labor and health economics. He holds a PhD from the Warsaw School of Economics.

Bei Lu is a CEPAR Research Fellow located at the University of New South Wales Business School and a Research Fellow with Tsinghua University and Zhejiang University, China. Her research focuses on demographics, health, pensions, and population aging–related social welfare and economic issues. She has published in various journals.

Iga Magda is an Assistant Professor at the Warsaw School of Economics and Vice President of the Institute for Structural Research in Warsaw. Her work is centered on labor economics, in particular gender gaps, collective bargaining, wage and income inequalities, and family policies.

Poontavika Naka is a Lecturer in the Department of Statistics, Chulalongkorn Business School in Thailand. She holds a PhD in mathematical sciences, with a concentration in actuarial mathematics, from the University of Liverpool. Her research interests are focused on nonfinancial defined contribution pension schemes, health care financing, and mortality modeling.

Milton Nektarios is a Professor at the University of Piraeus, Greece, and former Governor of the Social Insurance Organization (1999–2004).

Kenneth Nelson is a Professor of Sociology at the Swedish Institute for Social Research (SOFI), Stockholm University. His specialty is research on the causes and consequences of welfare states and social policy. His most recent book is on generational welfare contracts, published by Edward Elgar.

Rense Nieuwenhuis is an Associate Professor of Sociology at the Swedish Institute for Social Research (SOFI), Stockholm University. He examines how family diversity and social policy affect poverty and economic inequality. His recent focus is on single-parent families, how women's earnings affect inequality between households, and family policy outcomes.

Sergio Nisticò is a Professor of Economics at the University of Cassino in Italy, where he is also Scientific Director of the Economic Research Center on Creativity and Motivations. He is the author of numerous publications.

Noemi Oggero is a PhD student at the University of Turin in Italy. She collaborates with the Center for Research on Pensions and Welfare Policies at the Collegio Carlo Alberto and has been a research associate at the Global Financial Literacy Excellence Center at George Washington University.

Robert Palacios is Global Lead for the Pensions and Social Insurance Group in the Social Protection and Labor Practice of the World Bank. From 1992 to 1994 he was a member of the research department team that produced the World Bank's influential volume on international pension systems, *Averting the Old Age Crisis*. He has worked in more than 30 countries across the world and has published on old-age poverty, health insurance, and a wide range of pension policy issues.

Edward Palmer is Senior Fellow at the University of Uppsala Center for Labor Studies in Sweden. He held professorships, first at Gothenburg University and then Uppsala University, while serving as Head of Research and Evaluation at the Swedish Social Insurance Agency, and in later years as Senior Advisor. He has worked extensively with governments of numerous countries as a consultant on pension reform.

John Piggott is Director of CEPAR, a major research center focused on population aging based at University of New South Wales, Australia, where he is Scientia Professor of Economics. He has published widely in the areas of pensions, retirement, and aging. He has worked extensively on the pension system in China and a range of other nations in the Asian region and has undertaken contract work for a range of international organizations, including the Organisation for Economic Co-operation and Development, the Asia-Pacific Economic Cooperation, the World Bank, the Asian Development Bank, and UNESCAP.

William Price is CEO of D3P Global Pension Consulting, a Program Leader and Advisory Board member of the Insurance and Pensions Program of the Toronto Centre for Global Leadership in Financial Supervision, and an Ambassador for the Transparency Taskforce. He has worked for the World Bank, U.K. Treasury, and U.K. Pensions Regulator and in collaboration with the Organisation for Economic Co-operation and Development and International Organization of Pension Supervisors. He has a master's degree in economics from University College London.

Riccardo Puglisi is an Associate Professor of Economics at the University of Pavia in Italy. His research interests are mainly in the fields of political economy and public economics, with a specific focus on the political and economic role of mass media.

Monika Queisser is Head of Social Policy at the Organisation for Economic Co-operation and Development in Paris.

Márta Radó is a Junior Researcher at the Hungarian Academy of Sciences CSS RECENS, a Junior Fellow at the Social Futuring Centre, and a doctoral candidate at Corvinus University of Budapest.

Ranila Ravi-Burslem leads customer strategy and proposition development for the small and medium enterprise (SME) market as Director of SME Solutions for Aviva in the United Kingdom. Previously she was Director of Marketing for the National Employment Savings Trust (NEST), where she was responsible for customer propositions and digital and customer insight.

David Robalino is a Senior Advisor for McKinsey and Professor of Public Finance at the American University of Beirut. He was the Manager and Lead Economist of the Jobs Group at the World Bank and Co-Director of the Labor and Development Program at IZA. His policy work and research focus on issues related to jobs, social insurance, and fiscal policies. He has worked in more than 60 countries around the world, providing advice to governments and international organizations.

Michal Rutkowski is a Senior Director for the Social Protection and Jobs Global Practice in the World Bank. In his World Bank career he has worked on issues of pensions, labor markets, social security, and social assistance. In the late 1990s he was Director of the Office of the Government Plenipotentiary for Pension Reform in Poland and coauthor of the pension reform package that shifted the system to defined contribution principles.

Anna Ruzik-Sierdzińska, PhD, is an Assistant Professor at the Warsaw School of Economics. Her areas of expertise include labor markets, pension systems, health economics, and social policy.

Stefano Sacchi is an Associate Professor of Political Science at LUISS University in Rome (on leave from the University of Milan). He is also President of the Italian National Institute for Public Policy Analysis in Rome.

Miguel Sánchez-Romero obtained his PhD in economics from Universidad Autónoma de Madrid. He was a Fulbright postdoctoral researcher under the supervision of Professor Ronald Lee at the Center on Economics and Demography of Ageing at the University of California, Berkeley (2008–10). He has worked as a researcher at the Max Planck Institute for Demographic Research in Rostock, Germany (2010–14). Since 2014 he has been a Senior Research Scientist for the Wittgenstein Centre for Demography and Global Human Capital; in 2018 he joined the Vienna University of Technology. He works on labor and demographic economics, intergenerational transfers, and computable general equilibrium models.

Will Sandbrook is Executive Director of NEST Insight, the in-house think tank of the National Employment Savings Trust (NEST) pension scheme. He has worked within the United Kingdom's pension reform agenda since 2004, including in policy and marketing roles within the U.K. government and, beginning in 2008, as Strategy Director of NEST Insight at NEST and now as Executive Director.

Ole Settergren is Director of the Research Department at the Swedish Pensions Agency. As an insurance expert at the Ministry of Health and Social Affairs (1995–2000), he proposed the automatic balance method of securing the financial stability of the new Swedish pension system. He also developed the accounting principles that have been used since 2001 in the *Annual Report of the Swedish Pension System* and was its editor from 2001 to 2007.

Otávio José Guerci Sidone has a master's degree in economics from University of São Paulo. He is a Federal Auditor of Finance and Control of Brazil's Ministry of Finance and General Coordinator of Technical Studies and Conjunctural Analysis of the Secretariat of Social Security in the Ministry of Finance.

Sandra Stabina has been the Director of the Social Insurance Department of Latvia's Ministry of Welfare since 2016. In 1996 she started work on the Latvian pension system and was part of the modeling team for long-term projections. She is a member of the European Union (EU) Economic Policy Committee Working Group on Ageing Populations and Sustainability, was involved in an EU-financed twinning project in Azerbaijan, and took part in the European Commission–organized technical mission in Tajikistan.

Nils Martin Stølen earned a PhD in national economics in 1993 and has been employed in the Research Department of Statistics Norway since 1982. Since 2005 he has been project manager for analyzing the effects of the Norwegian pension reform, mainly by using the dynamic microsimulation model MOSART.

Paweł Strzelecki, PhD, is an Assistant Professor at the Warsaw School of Economics and an economic expert at the National Bank of Poland. He is also a national expert in the Working Group on Ageing (European Commission). His work focuses on the demographic dimension of labor economics and on population projections.

Platon Tinios is an Assistant Professor at the University of Piraeus, Greece.

Andrés Villegas is a Lecturer at the School of Risk and Actuarial Studies and an Associate Investigator at the Centre of Excellence in Population Ageing Research, where he was previously a Research Fellow. He completed his doctoral studies at Cass Business School in London, focusing on the modeling and projection of mortality. His research interests include mortality modeling, longevity risk management, and the design of retirement income products.

Kent Weaver is a Professor of Public Policy and Government at Georgetown University and a Senior Fellow in the Governance Studies Program at the Brookings Institution. He has written extensively on both the politics of pension reform and the impact of pension system design features such as automatic balancing mechanisms, centrally administered defined contribution systems, and collective investment funds. He received his MA and PhD in political science from Harvard University.

Hernan Winkler is a Senior Economist in the Jobs Group at the World Bank. He is a labor economist, with a focus on technological change and the sources and consequences of poverty and inequality. His research has been published in peer-reviewed economics journals, including the *Review of Economics and Statistics* and the *Journal of Development Economics*. He holds a PhD in economics from the University of California at Los Angeles.

Yuwei Zhao de Gosson de Varennes is currently an Economist in the Analysis Division of the Swedish Tax Agency. Her research interest is in public economics. She holds a PhD from the University of Uppsala.

Bingwen Zheng is Director-General of the Center for International Social Security Studies at the Chinese Academy of Social Sciences, Beijing. He is a member of China's National Social Insurance Consultation Commission of the Ministry of Human Resources and Social Security and a member of the Advisory Committee of Major Decision-Making Experts of the China Banking and Insurance Regulatory Commission.

Abbreviations

ABM	automatic balancing mechanism
AI	artificial intelligence
APS	Pension Solidarity Component, Chile
ARR	average replacement rate
ASM	automatic stabilizing mechanism
ATP	Allmän tilläggspension, general supplementary pension
AWG	Ageing Working Group
BA	bilateral arrangement
BPU	basic pension unit
CEE8	Central and Eastern European 8 (Czech Republic, Estonia, Hungary, Latvia, Lithuania, Poland, Slovenia, Slovak Republic)
CPI	consumer price index
CR	contribution rate
DB	defined benefit
DC	defined contribution
DeSUS	Democratic Party of Pensioners of Slovenia
DTA	double taxation agreement
DWP	Department for Work and Pensions
EAP	East Asia and Pacific
EC	European Commission
ECA	Europe and Central Asia
ECB	European Central Bank
EC-EPC (AWG)	European Commission Economic Policy Committee Working Group on Ageing Populations and Sustainability
EU	European Union
EU-SILC	European Union Survey of Income and Living Conditions
FAZ	Frankfurter Allgemeine Zeitung
FDB	financial defined benefit
FDC	financial defined contribution
FUS	Fundusz Ubezpieczeń Społecznych, Polish Social Insurance Fund
GDP	gross domestic product
GPG	gender pay gap
GUS	Central Statistical Office, Poland
HFP	hypothetical future pension
HR	human resources

HRS	Health and Retirement Survey
ILFS	Integrated Labour Force Survey
ILO	International Labour Organization
IMF	International Monetary Fund
IPD	implicit pension debt
IT	information technology
IV	instrumental variable
KPST	Kosovo Pension Saving Trust
LAC	Latin America and the Caribbean
LC	Lee-Carter model
LCGLIG	life course gender labor income gap
LFPR	labor force participation rate
LFS	Labor Force Survey
LI	labor income
LO	Landsorganisationen
M&E	monitoring and evaluation
MA	multilateral arrangements
MOF	Ministry of Finance
MOHRSS	Ministry of Human Resources and Social Security
MPG	Minimum Pension Guarantee
MSOA	middle layer super output areas
NASEM	National Academy of Sciences, Engineering and Medicine
NDB	nonfinancial defined benefit
NDC	nonfinancial defined contribution
NEST	National Employment Savings Trust
NIS	National Insurance System
NKr	Norwegian kroner
NPS	National Pensions System
NRA	normal retirement age
NSP	New Solidarity Pillar
NTA	National Transfer Accounts
OA	old-age
OASDI	old-age, survivors', and disability
OECD	Organisation for Economic Co-operation and Development
ONS	Office for National Statistics
PAD	Palmer-Alho-Zhao de Gosson
PASIS	Assistance Pension, Chile
PAYG	pay-as-you-go
PB	pension base
PBS	Basic Solidarity Pension, Chile
PP	pension payments
PQA	pension qualifying amount
PQAC	Pension Qualifying Amount for Children, Sweden
PSL	Polish Peasants Party
RURPS	Rural and Urban Residents Pension Scheme
SES	socioeconomic status

SHARE	Survey of Health, Ageing and Retirement in Europe
SKr	Swedish kronor
SLD	Democratic Left Alliance, Poland
SME	small and medium-size enterprises
SPA	standard pensionable age
SSA	Sub-Saharan Africa
TATSI	total absolute tax subsidy indicator
TRR	theoretical replacement rate
UEPS	Urban Employee Pension Scheme
UN	United Nations
UPPS	universal public pension scheme
USAID	United States Agency for International Development
VAT	value-added tax
VSS	Vietnam Social Security
Zl	Polish zlotys
ZUS	Zakład Ubezpieczeń Społecznych, Polish Social Insurance Institution

CHAPTER 1

NDC: The Achievements and Challenges of Adulthood

Robert Holzmann and Edward Palmer

Introduction

The aim of this anthology is to provide new contributions to the collective knowledge of the issues and challenges of designing mandated and earnings-related universal public pension schemes (UPPS), in which a universal public nonfinancial defined contribution (NDC) scheme is one of four design options. In 1994 NDC left the crib and was taking its first steps in Sweden, Italy, and Latvia. A couple of years later a fourth sibling was born in Poland, with Norway eventually following in 2009. NDCs were born at a time when the academic and policy discourse was framed in terms of "public pay-as-you-go" versus "private funded," and all pay-as-you-go schemes were classified under what are now called universal public nonfinancial defined benefit (NDB) schemes.

At the time, mandated and earnings-related financial defined contribution (FDC) and financial defined benefit (FDB) schemes (that is, the so-called funded schemes) were also moving into the sphere of UPPS, with Chile's 1980–81 reform usually recognized as the first UPPS of this kind. Despite this, in the public pay-as-you-go domain, policy makers worked solely on NDB schemes until NDCs emerged in the mid-1990s.

In the world of NDB public pension schemes, the focus is on defining the conditions to be met for receiving a certain benefit. Obviously, the possible macroeconomic outcomes for a specified set of assumptions for the future development of important economic and demographic parameters of all public pension schemes are regularly evaluated. However, not until the arrival of NDCs was attention paid to the role of systematic design in creating long-term financial resilience.

Neither was the mission of the public pension scheme crystal clear. In the public rhetoric and minds of people, public social security was a tax transfer system. In fact, an NDC is a working-life savings scheme with the sole purpose of providing universal longevity insurance to the whole population. All working-age individuals pay the same percentage of their earnings into an individual account that earns an economic rate of return. At a chosen age of retirement, the balance on the individual account is transformed into a life annuity, determined by the average life expectancy of the individual's birth cohort at the individual's chosen age of retirement. The paradigm change is that this is an insurance scheme for all, based on nothing other than the principles of insurance for accumulation, annuity determination, and benefit disbursement.

NDCs' unique feature is a built-in design that achieves affordability, financial sustainability, and intergenerational fairness. NDCs achieve these goals through a combination of indexation based on the rate of growth of the contribution wage base—driven by the growth of the average wage and changes in the formal labor force—and the use of life expectancy in computing the benefit. The long-term dynamics of the system are thus determined by (a) the rate of growth of productivity (the wage rate) in the economy, and (b) the factors affecting the growth of the working-age population (fertility rates and net emigration) and individual labor supply decisions.

With individual accounts come transparent information on the interaction of individuals' decisions to work and pay contributions and their own roles in determining their future pension outcomes. Through transparent information, individual accounts promote both micro- and macroeconomic efficiency (that is, they provide an incentive at the margin to supply more formal labor), and by enhancing longer working careers aggregate gross domestic product (GDP) becomes higher. The accounts also communicate the message of fairness—a unit of money paid into the scheme gives the same pension rights to all participants. This design also explicitly separates the functions of a country's tax transfer system from its universal longevity insurance. The tax transfer mechanism becomes a separate policy issue, which by design can provide tax-financed add-ons to accounts, for example, for years in conjunction with childbirth, time devoted to tertiary education, or registered unemployment with compensation.

What ties the package together is the use of life expectancy in creating the benefit, and indexation of the minimum age at which a benefit can be claimed. At the micro level these two factors communicate the importance of postponing retirement with increasing life expectancy. At the macro level the adjustment of benefits to life expectancy under the NDC design promotes financial equilibrium, affordability, and long-run sustainability of a universal pension scheme with a fixed contribution rate. Individual accounts also provide the building blocks of an intertemporal financial budget constraint. And importantly, the ratio of system liabilities to assets creates a solvency ratio.

The counterfactual when NDCs entered onto the stage was a defined benefit (DB) promise with a multiplicity of possible designs. What DB schemes had in common in the mid-1990s and still have in common is the absence of a design that leads to an affordable universal public longevity insurance program with the same conditions for all—and with a transparent message emphasizing the importance of individuals' own roles in working and contributing to their own future pensions. In DB schemes, liabilities are typically brought in line with assets by applying politically painful ad hoc parametric adjustments—changing (breaking) the conditions of the DB promise. The most dramatic example during the last decade is the International Monetary Fund/European Union (EU) intervention in Greece to save the country from total economic collapse, in which adjustment of an overly generous and unaffordable pension scheme was first on the list of things to do. More recently, various countries have legislated crude balancing mechanisms for NDB schemes that all remain untested.

Against the background of these potential qualities of an NDC design, one would expect to find the emergence of a large number of systemic NDC reforms to countries' pension schemes, especially in Europe. Instead, the most recent Organisation for Economic Co-operation and Development (OECD) *Pensions at a Glance* (OECD 2018) and European Commission's *Ageing Reports* (European Commission 2018) document no new NDC reforms since the Norwegian reform in 2009, but instead a growing number of ad hoc parametric changes. For the editors of this and two previous anthologies, and as proponents of NDCs, this is a disquieting finding.

Many considerations may be behind the reaffirmed preference of policy makers for incremental parametric NDB reforms compared with systemic NDC reform in Europe and, generally, across the world. The following are the most important ones:

- The 2007–12 financial crisis in many parts of the world and the following repercussions may have made policy makers risk averse toward "experiments" with new designs.

- The delicate fiscal positions of many countries that undertook systemic FDC reforms prior to 2007 may have reduced the appetite for even more systemic reforms.

- International institutions broadly moved away from identifying best practices and appearing prescriptive—instead they now seem to favor country-specific parametric reforms.

- The OECD and the European Commission believe and pronounce that the steady string of parametric reforms of NDB schemes that took selective account of NDC design elements brought their member countries broadly onto a financially sustainable path, so that systemic reforms are not needed. The International Monetary Fund focuses primarily on short- and medium-term fiscal effects, not long-term systemic considerations. The International Labour Organization promotes parametric DB reforms because it appears to believe that a systemic defined contribution (DC) reform is out of the question. Pension experts at the World Bank remain largely committed to a systemic FDC but not NDC reform.

- Compared with parametric reforms, systemic reforms require a major effort—a new administrative apparatus and communication of a new narrative—whereas the political window of opportunity with new elections coming up soon is short and reform may be unpopular.

- A systemic NDC reform by the rulebook binds the hands of policy makers whose interests are primarily in the art of proposing the policy that buys the most votes in the next election.

So why produce—with the collaboration of about 90 policy researchers from around the world (70 authors and 20 reviewers)—another voluminous anthology of 31 chapters on the topic when the policy takers are so few? The main reasons are threefold and in line with the goals of the previous two anthologies (Holzmann and Palmer 2006; Holzmann, Palmer, and Robalino 2012, 2013):

The first reason is to periodically critically review and document the working of successful NDC schemes and to understand why some NDC reform attempts failed. Such a periodic review is important for any cross-country learning and must go beyond mere graphic presentations of cross-country data.

The second reason is to critically review design issues of NDC schemes that go beyond the basic NDC design structure and that may call for policy decisions. Such issues emerge from new conceptual insights, from new data analyses that shed light on previously unrecognized issues, or from existing issues no longer believed to be unimportant going forward. Examples of each of these items are as follows:

- *The important role of the basic benefit.* Under implementation of a systemic NDC or FDC reform, it very quickly becomes clear that the close link of contributions to benefits requires additional policy action because it leaves too many behind. A basic benefit is required not only for those who contributed nothing but also for those who for various reasons contributed not enough during their working lives. However, any such provision risks distorting the contribution-benefit link and hence the claimed incentive advantage of an NDC, so a skillfully designed adjoining of a basic benefit with the (N or F) DC pillar(s) is required.

- *Specific dimensions of family, gender, and the labor market.* The primary purpose of the universal mandate of public DC schemes—that is, NDC and FDC schemes— is to provide an adequate benefit for the large majority of participants when they retire from the labor force. But what are the appropriate social policy interventions to reduce or close contribution gaps further down the chain? Benefit gaps may arise from delayed entrance into the labor force of youth, the part-time work of mothers, forced layoffs from work created by constantly changing technology and globalization, and the need to reskill or redirect skills to more productive ends. The challenge is to address these gaps within the framework of pension policy, including supporting social and labor market policy, while keeping intact the design aspirations of fairness, efficiency, and sustainability. These topics are not unique to DC schemes; they are an aspect of all forms of universal pension schemes but are usually less transparent under DB designs.

- *Research in general, and particularly with regard to NDC schemes.* On one hand, such research can give rise to design and even conceptual issues that may call for redesign of particular details (for example, the design methods used for projecting life expectancy). On the other hand, with the increase in complexity, the NDC concept must be broken down into digestible bites for the uninitiated pension expert and layman.

- *The increasing cross-country information on high and often rising heterogeneity of longevity by socioeconomic characteristics, particularly lifetime income.* This topic has many ramifications. Most importantly it breaks the contribution-benefit link for individuals away from the average, leading to an implicit tax for the lower-income group that is higher the further they are from the average, and an implicit transfer in the opposite direction. Various chapters in this anthology examine the topic from different angles. The heterogeneity of life expectancy based on individual characteristics and circumstances is by no means a topic "only" for DC pension schemes; the ramifications of life expectancy differences are equally relevant for all but the most rudimentary current national DB schemes, although they are not as transparent as they become in the DC context.

The third reason for offering a new anthology is that even the best NDC design and implementation alone will not achieve the expected results if supporting conditions in other policy areas are not created. The most critical examples are the conditions in the labor market that affect formal labor force participation (that is, the coverage rate) and its regularity (that is, contribution density); a second labor market concern is the capacity of the older labor force to reskill into new technology and issues of geographic mobility and employers' age discrimination. Although it is easy to describe what is required to keep the elderly in the labor market (namely, being skilled, healthy, and motivated), the policies to establish these conditions are still broadly unknown.

The previous two anthologies (Holzmann and Palmer 2006; Holzmann, Palmer, and Robalino 2012, 2013) covered a lot of ground, but many issues emerged later or subsequently became more important. This third anthology aims to cover many of the new knowledge gaps.

The first section of this anthology begins by taking stock of the current status of NDC issues and challenges in five European countries that have introduced NDCs, and now have 20–25 years of experience behind them, and in one country (Greece) that introduced the NDC approach in one subscheme. The country chapters present and discuss country-specific designs, implementation details, and issues that have arisen along the road—as seen in the rearview mirror.

Two sets of important design issues receive specific attention in the anthology. The first is the design of the annuity—more specifically, the method employed to project the value of life expectancy used in the computation of the NDC annuity (and by definition, of other insurance annuities). The second is the issue of socioeconomic heterogeneity in life expectancy. The chapters on these topics identify and discuss the issues and weigh the relative merits of alternative approaches to addressing them.

The second set of chapters explores crucial topics such as the importance of the intersection of labor market and pension policy, family and gender, and the underlying design and integration of NDC with a second public pillar, usually an FDC component. One chapter addresses the overall system, bringing the voluntary pillar (usually a private or an occupational scheme, or both) into the overall picture.

A third set of chapters addresses the specificities associated with emerging market economies, using the future demography and economic framework of the young country of Tanzania as one example, and an emerging economic power (China) that is still weighing its options as another example.

A fourth set encompasses issues in administration, especially in the context of an increasingly mobile and global world of portability and taxation. In addition, three separate chapters address communication and cover Italy, Sweden, and the National Employment Savings Trust (NEST) in the United Kingdom, and another chapter describes the development of financial literacy in the DC world.

The "Overview of Chapters" section of this chapter offers a brief summary of each chapter in the anthology. "Main Conclusions and Next Steps" draws out the main lessons emerging from the 30 chapters, ponders the question of whether systemic NDC reforms are really required, and ends with proposed priorities for next steps.

Overview of Chapters

This section provides a brief overview of each chapter in both volumes. Chapters are presented under their corresponding theme headings to offer guidance on the overall anthology structure. The first theme heading of "Taking Stock" covers the five European reform countries—Sweden, Latvia, Italy, Poland, and Norway—and Greece, which recently undertook major reform efforts that included an NDC approach for a subset of occupational schemes.

Chapter 2 by Edward Palmer and Bo Könberg on the Swedish NDC scheme presents its development since 1994 as on track for success with room for reflection. Sweden was the first country to implement an NDC system. The journey began in 1992, when the Ministerial Working Group on Pensions set out the main ideas that led to a majority parliamentary decision in 1994. The decision led to the separation of disability and survivors' benefits from the public old-age pension scheme, and to an old-age saving scheme based on both NDC and FDC public components, both completely autonomous from the government budget. The chapter analyzes the underpinnings of the Swedish NDC scheme's financial stability, factors influencing the adequacy of benefits within the overall Swedish pension system, and the interplay of the NDC scheme with the public FDC scheme, the minimum pension guarantee, and the occupational schemes. Gender-based differences in labor market outcomes and individuals' behavior are both highlighted in the discussion of adequacy. The chapter also includes information on the December 2017 broad six-party political agreement on forthcoming legislation. Most important are (a) the increase in the minimum pension age from 61 to 64, from 2020 to 2026, and (b) its indexation to life expectancy thereafter. The chapter concludes with recommendations for additional improvements in the overall old-age pension system, based on its analysis of financial stability, adequacy, and the interaction of the NDC scheme with the guarantee benefits and the occupational schemes.

Chapter 3 by Edward Palmer and Sandra Stabina on the Latvian NDC scheme investigates its remarkable success under a decreasing labor force. Latvia's 1996 introduction of an NDC scheme was part of its post-Soviet transition to a market economy. Challenges included transforming acquired and documented Soviet "workbook" rights into NDC account values and honoring commitments to current and soon-to-be pensioners. A second transition shifted 6 percentage points of an overall contribution rate of 20 percent to a mandatory FDC scheme in 2001. Low fertility rates and steady emigration of the working-age population characterized the period 1997–2016. Despite a 20 percent decline in the working-age population, formal labor force participation increased from 70 percent to 90 percent, lifting the ratio of contributors to old-age pensioners from 1.6 in 1997 to 2.1 in 2016. Notably, both genders enjoyed an equally impressive increase in contribution density. Labor force and real per capita wage growth led to strong valorization of NDC accounts and eventually to adequate pensions for most retirees. Nevertheless, today about 30 percent still pay contributions on a minimum wage; at retirement this will translate into a minimum pension, a clear policy challenge. Latvia's NDC is predicted to maintain long-term financial sustainability, despite the diversion of contributions as the FDC scheme is phased in. It will be largely financed with earmarked reserves needed in the 2030s and 2040s. It maintains long-term financial balance from 2017 through 2070, despite a projected 50 percent decline in the total working-age population. Latvia's most important long-term policy challenge is to create domestic investments and economic growth that reward youth for remaining in the country.

Chapter 4 by Sandro Gronchi, Sergio Nisticò, and Mirko Bevilacqua on the Italian NDC scheme investigates its evolution since inception in 1995 and highlights remaining potholes. Starting with a reconstruction of the political context in which the 1995 Italian pension reform took shape, this chapter reviews the essential features of the 1995 and post-1995 legislation and assesses its fundamental shortcomings, including how life expectancy at retirement is used when initial pensions are determined. A straightforward theoretical discussion highlights both the targets and the instruments representing the hallmark of the NDC model. The contrast of such theoretical premises with the Italian legislation points out the shortcomings together with the necessary remedies.

Chapter 5 by Sonia Buchholtz, Agnieszka Chłoń-Domińczak, and Marek Góra traces the Polish NDC scheme and its success in the face of adversity since its inception in 1998. Poland's pension system faces multiple challenges. Population aging will accelerate in the coming decades. In contrast to Western European countries, Poland was uniquely challenged by a massive labor force exit that resulted from the use of retirement as a political sweetener (three times in the past four decades), leading to the rise of economic dependency of the retired generation. Transition from an NDB system to an actuarially balanced NDC+FDC system in 1999 mitigated the risk of a huge fiscal shortfall and of an unfair balance of interest between the working and retired generations. The new system transparently separated the income allocation and social functions, including redistribution. Numerous options for early retirement were also significantly limited. These features contributed to its success. However, the Polish system should be perceived as a case study of misuse for current political goals, ad hoc tweaks, and lack of completion (retirement age, occupational systems, and so on). Despite those weaknesses, the 1999 pension reform met its goals.

Chapter 6 by Nils Martin Stølen, Dennis Fredriksen, Erik Hernæs, and Erling Holmøy analyzes the Norwegian NDC scheme using the criterion of balancing risk sharing and redistribution. The main goal of reforming the Norwegian old-age pension system toward NDC in 2011 was to improve long-run fiscal sustainability. Improving labor supply incentives to increase the effective retirement age was another important aspect of the reform. Although strong concern for redistribution may work against the main principles of NDC schemes, maintaining much of the redistributive effects of the former public pension system was also an important concern. By exploiting administrative data for labor market participation and labor incomes by age and other characteristics, econometric analyses reveal the 2011 reform's significant effects on postponing retirement. Results from a dynamic microsimulation model, including a complete description of the Norwegian population and the pension system, suggest that the reform is expected to have substantial effects on old-age pension expenditures in the long run without any large negative distributional effects. Macroeconomic analyses indicate that the reform is likely to have a significant fiscal impact in the long run, and higher employment plays an important role in this respect.

Chapter 7 by Milton Nektarios and Platon Tinios critically reviews the recent Greek pension reforms under the heading of crises and NDC attempts waiting for completion. The current pension system in Greece relies almost exclusively on the state; it does not advance toward a multipillar system; and it remains staunchly pay-as-you-go and DB. The chapter claims that in a country struggling to exit a deep recession, the pension system must support the recovery—which is currently not the case. This chapter offers a radical proposal for change: (a) a new multipillar NDC and FDC pension system for all generations first insured after 1993, with contribution rates for primary pensions reduced by 50 percent; and (b) a transitional system for those first insured before 1993. The proposal's robustness is tested actuarially for the period up to 2060, building on demographic and economic projections prepared for the 2015 EU Economic Policy Committee Ageing Working Group, which were updated for macroeconomic and legislative developments. Though financing the legacy cost would be challenging, the results indicate that a radical pension reform, especially if implemented as part of an overall recovery package, could have much to recommend it. The chapter claims that rebuilding the pension system would regain the trust of Greek citizens, counteracting many established dysfunctions and setting the country on a more favorable growth trajectory.

Two chapters present conceptualization and communication efforts under the theme heading of "Conceptualization and Promotion."

Chapter 8 by Marek Góra and Edward Palmer offers a challenging conceptual view of NDCs, defining them as the generic old-age pension scheme. The chapter defines a UPPS as a government-mandated life-cycle longevity insurance scheme that transfers individual consumption from the working years to the retirement phase of the life cycle. It discusses the differences in four UPPS designs—DC or DB, and financial (F) or nonfinancial (N). Generally speaking, DC schemes are distinguished from DB schemes by their basic building block of individual accounts. The use of individual accounts ensures the important design feature of transparency—the "enabler" of economic efficiency—through the effects on marginal decisions to choose formal work over informal work or leisure and to postpone retirement marginally toward the end of the working life. The chapter examines additional criteria (fairness, financial sustainability, affordability, and adequacy), plus other design characteristics of interest in a comparative assessment. The conclusion is that the two UPPS-DC designs are superior to the two UPPS-DB designs. The difference in the relative rates of return of NDC versus FDC designs, together with uncertain demographic effects on future investment needs, speak in favor of a UPPS portfolio with both. UPPS-FDC involves additional risks and costs, but also provides positive effects through returns for individuals and the economy.

Chapter 9 by Robert Holzmann provides a complementary angle on the NDC approach by offering the ABCs of NDCs (that is, the basics of NDCs for the interested but not specialized reader). For example, the NDC approach features the lifelong contribution-benefit link of an FDC scheme but is based on the pay-as-you-go format. When starting an NDC scheme, the pay-as-you-go commitments of existing DB systems are best converted into individual personal accounts, allowing for a smooth transition while avoiding the very high transition costs inherent in such a move. An NDC approach implemented by the rulebook can manage the economic and demographic risks inherent in a pension scheme and by design creates financial sustainability. As in any pension scheme, the linchpin between financial stability and adequacy is the retirement age; in the NDC approach the individual retirement age above the minimum age is by design self-selected and by incentives should increase the effective retirement age in line with population aging. NDC schemes have become a strong competitor to piecemeal parametric reforms of traditional NDB schemes. Although frequent, the chapter claims that reforms of NDB schemes are far from transparent and usually too little and too late to create financial sustainability while providing adequate pensions for the average contributor. The chapter offers a nontechnical introduction to NDC schemes, their basic elements and advantages over NDB schemes, the key technical frontiers of the approach, and the experiences of countries with NDC schemes.

Two chapters investigate how basic pensions and NDC and FDC pensions can be provided in a socially effective and least distortionary manner under the theme heading of "Adjoining Zero Pillar with DC Schemes."

Chapter 10 by Kenneth Nelson, Rense Nieuwenhuis, and Susanne Alm analyzes the interaction between Sweden's guarantee pension and its universal public NDC and FDC pensions. Although Sweden's current pension system has been in place for roughly 20 years, no systematic analysis of its consequences on elderly incomes has yet been conducted. This chapter analyzes old-age incomes in Sweden from a pension policy perspective, focusing on both the economic position of elderly citizens and the redistributive effects of the pension system's different parts. The empirical analyses, based on micro-level administrative and survey data, show that median incomes among the elderly increased faster than prices, but fell short of the growth of earnings of the working-age population. With time, the income of the elderly grows increasingly more unequal among the elderly than among the working-age population. Single women, migrants, persons with only primary education, and people living on their own exhibit an especially precarious economic position in old age: their benefits are often insufficient to provide an income above the commonly accepted relative poverty threshold. The analysis shows that each successive cohort of these groups risks higher relative poverty than previous cohorts if enough attention is not given to increasing the ceiling with increases in the real earnings of the working-age population (that is, increasing the ceiling on the means-tested component of the zero pillar). The decline in the relative value of the guaranteed minimum pension vis-à-vis the real earnings growth of wage earners brings to the forefront the issues of indexation of the guarantee and the ceiling on means-tested housing benefits—that is, the basic safety net for pensioners. The authors conclude that the low take-up of housing supplements among the elderly and possible extensions of occupation pensions to groups of the Swedish labor market that lack collective agreements deserve further analysis directed toward raising the income of low-income pensioners.

Chapter 11 by Eduardo Fajnzylber analyzes how Chile's basic pension is integrated with its FDC scheme. In 2008, Chile undertook comprehensive reform of its pension system. The main change was the introduction of a New Solidarity Pillar (NSP) designed to eliminate the incidence of poverty among elderly adults. The NSP set a floor at about 40 percent of the minimum monthly income for the poorest 60 percent of the population by means of noncontributory benefits for people without pension rights and a solidarity top-up payment for people who have not accumulated enough own pension rights. The NSP represents a significant change for Chilean society, not only in terms of pension coverage but also through its effect on poverty reduction and lifetime income inequality. Its design features are also an important factor in reducing the pension-related gender gap. The increase in noncontributory benefits and its means-tested nature (which translates into an implicit tax on formal work), however, imply lower incentives for formal labor market participation. The chapter describes the NSP's main characteristics and its origins. The main results achieved during its first seven years of operations are presented, including coverage, fiscal cost, poverty reduction, and the role of the system in reducing the significant gender gap in pensions (GGP). Its effects on incentives to pay into the contributory system are discussed, as is the literature that has attempted to measure these effects. Finally, the main challenges facing the NSP and the implications for other countries under DC pension schemes are summarized.

Three chapters analyze the critical relationship of longevity—its expansion linked with rising heterogeneity—and pension system design and implementation under the theme heading of "The Challenges of Longevity."

Chapter 12 by Ronald Lee and Miguel Sánchez-Romero provides an overview on heterogeneity in longevity and pension schemes. Differences in life expectancy between high and low socioeconomic groups are often large and have widened in recent decades. In the

United States, this difference may now be as large as 10–14 years. Longevity gaps strongly affect the actuarial fairness and progressivity of many public pension systems, raising the question of possible policy reforms to address this issue. This chapter reviews the empirical literature on the longevity differences across socioeconomic groups and their impacts on lifetime benefits, considers how these impacts depend on four different pay-as-you-go pension structures (calibrated on the U.S. case), and discusses some policy options.

Chapter 13 by Edward Palmer and Yuwei Zhao de Gosson de Varennes identifies and discusses issues in creating annuities in NDC schemes. The first issue discussed is the choice between incorporating the rate of return into the annuity or incorporating it into the exogenous indexation. That choice results in a pensioner receiving more or less of a given lifetime income when young or when old. A second issue is the challenge of choosing a projection method for life expectancy that produces systematically unbiased estimates. The chapter presents an alternative to current projection models that largely eliminates systematic birth-cohort-pool deficits (or surpluses) and thus unintended inter-generational redistribution. A third issue is at what age the projection of life expectancy is to be fixed over the remaining lifetime of the annuity. The assessment involves reducing the risk of systematic bias and its consequences for finances and intergenerational fairness, in addition to what can be accomplished through a well-thought-out choice of projection model. The final issue discussed is the prevalence of socioeconomic heterogeneity within the insurance pool. The current picture, probable causes, and technical solutions are discussed against the backdrop of the ambition in NDC to separate out and deal exogenously with distributional issues.

Chapter 14 by Robert Holzmann, Jennifer Alonso-García, Héloïse Labit-Hardy, and Andrés Villegas analyzes the effects of heterogeneity in longevity on NDC schemes and presents proposals for redesign to neutralize the heterogeneity implications. Strong and rising empirical evidence across countries finds that longevity is highly heterogeneous in key socioeconomic characteristics, including income. A positive relationship between lifetime income and life expectancy at retirement amounts to a straight tax or subsidy mechanism when the average cohort life expectancy is applied for annuity calculation, as done under NDC schemes. Such a regressive redistribution and the ensuing labor market distortion bring into question a main feature of DC schemes and call for alternative benefit designs to compensate for the heterogeneity. The chapter explores five key mechanisms of compensation: individualized annuities; individualized contribution rates and account allocations; a two-tier contribution structure with one rate linked to average income and one rate linked to individual income; and two supplementary approaches under the two-tier approach to deal with the income distribution tails and the distortions above a ceiling and below a floor. Using unique data from England and Wales and the United States, the analysis indicates that both individualized annuities and a two-tier contribution scheme are feasible and effective and thus promising policy options, but only with a de-pooling of gender.

Two chapters explore the relationship between pension schemes and labor markets under the theme heading of "Accommodating Labor Market Change."

Chapter 15 by Robert Holzmann, David Robalino, and Hernan Winkler investigates NDC schemes and the labor market. DC schemes—whether financial or nonfinancial—are often considered superior to DB schemes in their ability to address labor market issues, particularly in encouraging formal employment and delayed retirement.

Conceptually, the assessment is based on superior incentives to work and save. Yet economic and social realities are more complex. Design and implementation issues may preclude DC schemes from living up to their promises. In addition, structural problems with labor markets can affect the performance of DC schemes. The chapter explores design and labor market conditions that potentially constrain DC schemes. It opens with a conceptual framework that contrasts the labor market shortcomings of typical DB schemes with the labor market promises of DC schemes. It then discusses the constraints that may affect the labor market performance of the latter. The chapter presents proposals to improve benefit design features and labor market policies that can promote formal employment and delayed retirement, while highlighting challenges and differences between advanced and emerging market economies. The chapter concludes that to achieve their conceptual potential, DC schemes require design innovations, including better integration of basic benefits and complementary labor policies that promote job creation in the formal sector and expand job opportunities during old age.

Chapter 16 by Róbert Gál and Márta Radó analyzes labor market participation and postponed retirement in Central and Eastern Europe. The chapter shows how the effective retirement age rose in eight countries of Central and Eastern Europe (the Czech Republic, Estonia, Hungary, Latvia, Lithuania, Poland, the Slovak Republic, and Slovenia) between the mid-1990s and the mid-2010s. It finds that the increase was fast enough to keep life expectancies at the effective retirement age practically unchanged. Every day an average worker of the region got closer to the effective retirement age by only 18.4 hours, instead of 24, because the effective retirement age was moving. In effect, the labor market absorbed all improvements in life expectancies in older working ages. The chapter also shows how the educational composition in older working age, specifically in the 55–64-year-old age bracket, improved over the same period, driving the growth of the effective retirement age. This relatively recent shift is traced back to human capital investments made decades before, specifically the spread of secondary education starting in the 1960s. Finally, the chapter shows that maintaining current life expectancies at retirement over the next 30 years requires less effort in terms of further raising the effective retirement age than what the region achieved in this respect in the past 15 years. This is because of improvements in education systems in recent decades that expanded tertiary enrollment among currently young cohorts. The authors suggest that further increases in the effective future retirement age can be expected, and that these may be sufficient to fend off most of the potentially negative effects of declining mortality.

Four chapters are devoted to the important yet underexplored interlinkages of family, gender, and pension benefits, dealt with under the theme heading of "Family and Gender."

Chapter 17 by Nicholas Barr provides a conceptual overview of gender and family. The chapter starts from the observed fact that women receive lower pensions than men, on average, and goes on to consider policies to address that fact. Women typically have lower wages than men, a greater likelihood of part-time work, and more career breaks, and thus generally a less complete contribution record. In addition, pension age may be lower for women and annuities may be priced using separate life tables for women. The chapter looks at three strategic ameliorative policy directions: policies intended to increase the size and duration of women's earnings and hence improve their contribution records; policies to redirect resources within the pension system, including for survivors and after divorce; and ways of boosting women's pensions with resources from outside the pension system.

Chapter 18 by Maciej Lis and Boele Bonthuis analyzes the drivers of the GGP by using evidence from the European Union Statistics on Income and Living Conditions and the OECD pension model. The chapter first explores recent trends and the drivers behind the GGP in Europe, focusing on countries with NDC schemes—Italy, Latvia, Norway, Poland, and Sweden. Based on these current gender gaps, the chapter relates the progressivity of pension systems and the coverage of child-care-related spells to the GGP. It shows that countries with NDC schemes do not stand out as a group compared with other European countries with regard to pension outcomes for women. Nevertheless, countries with NDC schemes differ significantly from one another. The choices of indexation of pensions in payment and survivors' pension options have an impact on gender inequalities. However, labor market differences seem to be the most important driver.

Chapter 19 by Agnieszka Chłoń-Domińczak, Marek Góra, Irena E. Kotowska, Iga Magda, Anna Ruzik-Sierdzińska, and Paweł Strzelecki investigates the impact of lifetime events on pensions for NDC schemes in Italy, Poland, and Sweden and the point scheme in Germany. Old-age pensions in NDC schemes reflect accumulated labor income over the life course. Thus, interrupted careers and other factors leading to low employment rates, particularly between men and women, will have a significant impact on pension incomes in NDC countries. Pronounced differences arise in the countries' labor market participation rates: high levels of employment in Germany and Sweden for both men and women contrast with low levels of employment in Italy and Poland. The latter two countries also have a large gender gap in labor market participation. Employment pathways are also different—career interruptions for women in Italy lead to very early withdrawal from the labor market, while in Sweden women transfer mainly to part-time employment. Lower employment rates and gender pay gaps are important causes of differences in expected pension levels, but differences also exist because of pension system design and demographic developments. The analysis confirms that employment paths contribute importantly to future pension incomes and their adequacy. The authors stress that current and future labor market and pension policies need to address this challenge. Prolonging working lives and reducing gender gaps in employment and pay, particularly for those at risk of interrupted careers, are key to ensuring decent old-age pensions in the future. The chapter concludes that instead of modifications that weaken the link between contributions and benefits, such as early retirement rules for women in Poland, prolonging working life is equally crucial for benefits in NDC (Italy, Poland, and Sweden) and point schemes (Germany), and in all four countries gender gaps need to be addressed through labor market policy.

Chapter 20 by Anna Klerby, Bo Larsson, and Edward Palmer explores with Swedish data the bridging of partner life-cycle earnings and pension gaps by sharing NDC accounts. Sharing of NDC accounts is implemented with nudging by making sharing the default. The transfer within the partnership embodied in sharing reduces the economic dependence of the caregiver spouse on the spouse with full market labor force participation by implicitly defaulting sharing of both informal home and formal market work. In addition, it reduces the implicit tax-financed subsidy to partnerships, where sharing is not the norm. The authors perform a logit analysis of the likelihood of receiving the guarantee benefit without and with account sharing given individual characteristics. This shows that the risk of taking up the guarantee benefit is much greater for women. The analysis shows that the risk of women needing a guarantee supplement is reduced from about 10 percent without the nudge into sharing to 5 percent with sharing. The analysis identifies several characteristics that increase the risk of needing a guarantee supplement: not being born in Sweden, lower education, and having a husband who is older—with the risk increasing in scale with an increase in the age gap.

Three chapters address critical NDC pension issues outside the developed world under the theme heading of "NDC Prospects in Emerging Market Economies."

Chapter 21 by Robert Palacios explores administrative requirements and prospects for universal NDCs in emerging market economies. Many public policies—from expanding health insurance coverage to collecting taxes—are impossible to implement (or at least to implement well) without adequate administrative systems in place. This is true for modern pension schemes and in particular for NDC schemes. Today these systems must be digital, yet most pension systems predate computerization and must find a way to bridge past and present to implement reforms. The shift from DB to NDC brings special challenges in recordkeeping. This chapter briefly reviews some of the administrative requirements of NDCs and offers a simple checklist for countries considering this type of reform. Its last section describes a universal NDC scheme that harnesses the modern digital infrastructure, including unique identification systems and digital commerce, that may allow developing countries to overcome the limitations of traditional contributory systems and their reliance on payroll taxes.

Chapter 22 by Bei Lu, John Piggott, and Bingwen Zheng investigates the potential expansion of the role of the NDC paradigm in the ongoing reforms of retirement provision in China. China has remarkably high nominal retirement coverage of its population, but issues of sustainability, equity, and governance are challenging and real. Furthermore, although many broad policy guidelines are set by the central government, jurisdictions at provincial, city, and sometimes even district levels have major control over implementation, covering administration, benefit rates, and other important retirement policy features. Retirement policy and provision, regardless of the approach adopted, are necessarily shaped by labor market experience. In China, heterogeneity is dramatic across provinces and between urban and rural settings—in development stage, cost of living, formalization level, and other characteristics. Interestingly, mature age life expectancy is remarkably uniform among formal sector workers at the time of retirement. Somewhat greater heterogeneity arises when membership of the Rural and Urban Residents Pension Scheme is considered, but mature age life expectancy varies by only a couple of years. The implications of a stylized NDC structure covering all three of China's major pension systems, calibrated to be actuarially fair to different contributing members, are examined in this chapter. Each scheme has a different contribution rate and retirement age, consistent with different life expectancies. A complementary social pension is also proposed. The chapter concludes that an increased presence of the NDC paradigm could raise aggregate welfare, especially in the large and growing Urban Employee Pension Scheme.

Chapter 23 by Bo Larsson, Vincent Leyaro, and Edward Palmer explores against the background of Tanzania whether an NDC public pension scheme can harness and transform the demographic potential of a young nation into a broad-based labor force and GDP engine of growth through investments in physical and human capital. With its real GDP growth of about 6–7 percent since the mid-1990s, Tanzania provides a relevant case study. The chapter combines (a) an NDC pension scheme with small increments in individual savings accounts and (b) a demographic NDC fund. The analysis shows how, as Tanzania's working-age population grows and the degree of labor force formality increases, the resulting double demographic dividend will fuel the country's growth. This is made possible through NDC participants' pension savings, which are transformed in part into domestic investments financed through government NDC bonds held by the NDC fund. In addition to funding future pensions for current workers and investments in human and physical capital, the analysis shows that scope exists to pay small pensions to the present generation of the relatively few above the age of 60. The authors claim that this should provide an additional incentive for the working-age generation to join the formal economy and participate in the pension scheme.

Four chapters explore the complex but little analyzed relationship between pension scheme performance and communication approaches under the theme heading of "Communicating with Participants."

Chapter 24 by Will Sandbrook and Ranila Ravi-Burslem presents the innovative communication approach of NEST in the United Kingdom. In 2011, 69 percent of U.K. employers in the private sector offered no workplace pension for their workers. In 2018, all U.K. employers offered a pension scheme meeting a set of legal standards, including the use of automatic enrollment, and with a mandatory employer contribution for employees choosing to remain enrolled. More than 9 million people have started saving into a workplace pension through auto enrollment. Set up as part of the reforms to introduce auto enrollment, NEST is a qualifying workplace pension scheme that any employer can use to meet its auto enrollment obligations. It was set up to serve those traditionally poorly served by commercial pension provision, and to ensure all employers had a high-quality, low-cost path to compliance. NEST is built around features tested and seen as important and motivating for potential members and employers. These features are underpinned by extensive research with future members and analysis of feedback from existing customers. This communications approach led to outputs such as NEST's "phrasebook" and "Golden Rules," with a major focus on providing reassurance that saving is a "good" thing and NEST will look after one's money. This approach was built on harnessing inertia and responding to behavioral biases in the target group, while recognizing that this same inertia means that many people will in practice have little or no interaction with NEST in the early years of their participation.

Chapter 25 by Elsa Fornero, Riccardo Puglisi, and Noemi Oggero investigates the role of information and financial literacy for socially sustainable NDC pension schemes. This chapter is centered on the complementary roles played by pension communication and information and financial literacy for a sustainable and equitable NDC system at both the micro and macro socioeconomic levels. It considers formal communication (typically in the form of personalized account statements) prepared by the national institution in charge of pension provision; informal dissemination (in the form of more general information provided by the media); and financial basic knowledge (pension literacy). The chapter presents new evidence on (a) public opinion about pensions in five European countries (France, Germany, Italy, Sweden, and the United Kingdom), both in a cross-country perspective and relative to other issues, as approximated by Google Trends data; (b) the relationship between measures of online search volume and coverage by traditional media (that is, national newspapers); and (c) the volume and framing of newspaper coverage for a specific reform (that is, the 2011 Italian reform). On the demand (users) side, the chapter considers pension literacy as a specific component of financial basic knowledge and as an ingredient to "make sense" of formal and informal pension information to improve personal decisions and as an element to increase the effectiveness of reforms.

Chapter 26 by Ole Settergren, María del Carmen Boado-Penas, Erland Ekheden, and Poontavika Naka presents Sweden's 15 years of communication efforts for the oldest NDC scheme. The chapter states that it is desirable for pension reforms and legislated rules to have the backing of the population or at least to be accepted by voters. One strategy that might contribute to such acceptance is to inform participants of the pension plan's logic, its rules, and its financial restrictions. With the objective of promoting the NDC and FDC components of the Swedish public pension commitment, the Swedish Pensions Agency is compelled by legislation to publish an annual financial "Orange" report. The report contains an actuarial balance sheet (global information) and examines the consequences for different scenarios on the solvency of the NDC scheme. Participants receive a personal yearly "Orange" letter that contains a statement of their own NDC and FDC balances, the change in the balance during the year, and (using standard assumptions about earnings and contribution growth and standardized rates of return) a projection of their future pensions. This chapter reports on the Swedish pension experience with communication with pension participants over the past decade, together with the main changes in information delivered to improve individuals' pension knowledge and help them make more informed and better decisions regarding labor force participation, savings, and retirement. The chapter also discusses how the confidence and understanding of both contributors and pensioners evolved over time.

Chapter 27 by Tito Boeri, Maria Cozzolino, and Edoardo Di Porto analyzes the challenges of setting up a communication package for the Italian NDC scheme. Since the beginning of the 1990s, the Italian pension system has been subject to several reforms, involving an increase in the minimum pension age and the transition from a DB to an NDC scheme. This was no smooth ride—the initial reform covered only new entrants, which meant that the two schemes ran simultaneously, increasing uncertainty. As a result, it was more or less impossible to provide general information; instead, what participants really needed was cohort-specific information. This led to confusion about rights and diluted the effectiveness of the NDC scheme's message. A very low level of financial literacy exacerbated this effect. In 2015, INPS (the Italian Social Security Institute) launched a project called "La mia pensione futura" ("My future pension") with the aim of giving all INPS-insured workers more precise information about their future benefits. The chapter analyzes the results of a survey carried out by INPS to evaluate the project's performance. The findings are encouraging—about 80 percent of respondents rate the INPS service as at least "very helpful." Even if 42 percent of the sample overestimates their future pension, 16–29 percent reveal a willingness to change their expectation on retirement income after receiving new information. This suggests that it is important for pension reforms to be accompanied by informative tools to provide individuals with incentives to reoptimize their retirement planning.

Chapter 28 by Igor Guardiancich, Kent Weaver, Mark Dorfman, and Gustavo Demarco investigates the constraints and drivers of the politics of NDC pension scheme diffusion. NDC schemes offer governments both desirable properties such as efficiency, fairness, and financial sustainability and an opportunity to reduce their exposure to blame when pension generosity is reduced through automatic stabilizers. Yet adoption of NDC schemes had ground to a halt by 2011. Moreover, several countries retreated from NDC implementation after legislation. The chapter claims that these patterns have several roots, including lack of support for NDCs from powerful international actors. The perceived rigidity of NDCs in reducing room for policy maneuver also decreases their appeal to politicians, compared with the degrees of freedom that can accompany, for example, a "point scheme," in which the value of points can be a political variable. In addition, substantial administrative capacity is required for correct implementation. In the EU, endorsement by EU institutions of alternative automatic, albeit untested, stabilizing mechanisms undercut the appeal of NDCs. Thus, while NDC-based reforms are likely to remain an important option for policy makers and a benchmark against which to measure alternative reforms, NDCs are unlikely to become the dominant pension design choice anytime soon.

The last two chapters introduce key aspects of the international dimension of NDC schemes under the theme heading of "Globalization: Portability, Taxes, and Private DC Supplements."

Chapter 29 by Bernd Genser and Robert Holzmann explores how in a globalizing world (N)DC and (N)DB schemes fare and compares their benefit portability and income taxation. Pensions and broader forms of retirement income do not stop at national borders. As part of globalization, individuals increasingly spend part of their working or retirement lives abroad but want to keep or move freely across borders their acquired rights, accumulated retirement assets, or benefits in payment. This raises the issue of the portability and taxation of cross-border pensions in accumulation and disbursement. The chapter addresses both portability and taxation issues from the angle of which type of pension scheme—DB or DC—is more aligned with globalization in establishing individual fairness, fiscal fairness, and bureaucratic efficiency. The chapter summarizes the limited literature on portability and taxation of cross-border pensions and concludes that the current taxation approach is unsustainable. It presents a proposal to move toward front-loaded taxation of pensions but with three payment options: immediate, deferred, and distributed across the pension cycle. The chapter shows that DC schemes tend to dominate DB schemes in all payment options except, perhaps, the distributed one, wherein a reduced rate is applied for the contribution, return, and disbursement phases. If the reduced tax rate across all three phases were to remain unadjusted, then DB and DC schemes would be equally easy to operate. The results apply for both FDC and NDC schemes but seem easier to achieve under the latter.

Chapter 30 by Will Price investigates design issues for private pension supplements to NDC schemes. This chapter reviews the factors that should guide the design of private-funded pensions to create a complete pension system alongside an NDC—or public—component. The fact that the proposals have more general applications does not reduce the importance of following those proposals when developing private pensions alongside the NDC pillar. A mix of public and private pensions is the most effective option for delivering the best combination of pension outcomes. Pension design should start with a vision for five core outcomes: coverage, adequacy, sustainability, efficiency, and security. Thinking through these outcomes helps guide choices for market structure, benefit type, contributions, investment strategy, and other factors such as the scope for international investment of assets. The governance, scale, and expertise of pension funds are critical to good investment and other outcomes. Regulators and supervisors should also focus on the five outcomes and then determine how best to mitigate risks to achieving them. NDC systems bring clarity and transparency to policy makers in the benefit formula in general, and the NDC payout formula can offer insights for improving payout options in funded pillars. The clarity on the NDC formula also means that the joint distribution of public and private pensions can be modeled. This is important because the precise NDC formula may have implications for optimal investment strategies for private pensions—given, for example, the negative correlation between real per capita GDP growth and equity market returns over long periods. Finally, NDC payout formulas may have broad applications in countries with weak annuity markets.

Chapter 31 reports on the observations and reflections of the Closing Policy Panel, with individual contributions by the then Brazilian State Secretary in charge of pensions (and now General Secretary of the International Social Security Association), *Marcelo Caetano*; the representative of the European Commission/ECOFIN, *Per Eckefeldt*; the former Swedish Minister responsible for the NDC reform, *Bo Könberg*; the OECD Division Head in charge of pension analyses, *Monika Queisser*; and the Senior Director of the World Bank in charge of pension issues, *Michal Rutkowski*. Their observations and reflections on the October 2017 Rome conference, at which first drafts of the papers were presented, offer interesting insights on institutional commonalities and differences regarding NDCs. The commonalities comprise the role of NDCs as a crucial analytical instrument and reform benchmark; the differences concern the role of NDCs as a systemic reform approach in the country context.

Main Conclusions and Next Steps

This final section summarizes the chapters' main conclusions to offer guidance for future analytical and policy work by we hope an increasing number of convinced but critical pension researchers and policy designers. It then addresses even more briefly the question of whether a systemic NDC reform is truly needed or whether emulating NDC elements in NDB schemes can do the job. Against these reflections, the last section contains suggested priorities for next steps.

TEN MAIN CONCLUSIONS

The 30 chapters yield 10 key conclusions. These supplement the seven main conclusions drawn in the opening chapter of NDC II (Holzmann, Palmer, and Robalino 2012).

(i) *NDCs' potential is reduced by design or implementation faults, or both.* The financial crisis of 2007–12 in Europe and many other parts of the world was an "elk test" for the stability of pension schemes across the world. Many newly started funded schemes' (FDC) reforms from the 1990s were reversed as governments struggled with fiscal issues and the financing of transition costs, but also because of incomplete preparation (such as in Argentina and Hungary). Insufficient attention to starting up with new workforce entrants, the associated difficulties with communicating the NDC narrative, and the complications of collecting contributions when the world was less electronically connected led to reversals of incomplete NDC reform attempts from the 1990s (such as in Mongolia and the Kyrgyz Republic) and thereafter. Yet the key European NDC reform countries did well, although Latvia and Sweden, Norway and Poland, and Italy can be broadly differentiated into three categories by their level of preparedness. In 2011, Italy required an accelerated transition to an NDC-type reform and still suffers from potholes in its evolution.

(ii) *NDCs work very well even under adverse circumstances if done by the rulebook.* The evidence is that a well-thought-out design and careful implementation, accompanied by communication of the narrative of the logic of the reform and broad political support, are the keys to success. The transition rule setting out the map from the past design to the future design should be seen as fair ex ante and prove to be so ex post. Once implemented, the government should ratchet up (not down) the information campaign and hold it at a continuously high level, making use of advanced information technology (electronic accounts) and knowledge-based marketing strategies, and taking full advantage of the transparency of information on individual accounts. The accounts are also a building block upon which to establish a reserve fund and financial stock-flow accounting. This provides the apparatus with which to foresee and deal with economic and demographic cycles.

(iii) *NDCs can easily be combined with FDCs.* A wide range of opportunity exists to split a targeted maximum contribution rate for an overall system design between NDC and FDC schemes. An NDC is a UPPS by definition. The FDC component can be a universal (mandated) complement to NDCs for contributions up to a specified ceiling or a separate component above the ceiling with a different rate. The FDC component(s) can be set up institutionally as public or privately managed schemes, with an occupational base or private individual base. The Scandinavian clearinghouse model has proven to be a cost-efficient organizational institution, while using the private sector to perform specific functions, in particular portfolio management.

(iv) *DC schemes dominate DB schemes for portability and international taxation purposes.* NDC and FDC schemes have strong comparative portability advantages compared with NDB and FDB schemes with respect to efficiency in portability within and between countries. An NDC account scheme has the advantage of being "there" (with interest) when it comes time for retirement, even if accountholders changed countries of residence many times during their active working lives. FDC schemes enable a simple transfer of money on personal accounts from one scheme's "home" to another. The latter assumes, of course, consistent and fair cross-border taxation rules, which is currently not the case. A proposed front-loaded expenditure-type income taxation with innovative payment options works under both a DB and a DC benefit structure but is much easier and transparent under the latter.

(v) *NDCs require a well-thought-out complement to address poverty.* Special efforts must be devoted to constructing a zero pillar to address poverty in old age. Some people will not have a career in the labor market that gives them an adequate earnings-based benefit. The role of the zero pillar is to compensate for this, but without unduly reducing the incentive to work toward one's own earnings-related benefit. The main options are a flat-rate guarantee, perhaps tapering off vis-à-vis the NDC (and FDC) benefit(s), and perhaps formulating a part or all of it as a means-tested supplement, which specifically captures the geographical spread of housing costs and other costs of living. Where countries can go wrong is in simply price-indexing the benefit(s) over a long period because the value of the benefit relative to an average wage will not keep up with real wage increases over time, pushing more into relative poverty—especially elderly widows.

Expanding the NDC design toolbox to include default sharing of pension accounts during a period in conjunction with parenthood is a way to reduce the relative poverty of divorced mothers during the working career and eventually in old age. Joint annuities constitute another tool that can be defaulted for retiring couples to reduce relative poverty among surviving spouses. Both measures shift society's costs of covering older single spouses—most often widows—from the anti-poverty benefit(s) to joint spousal pension income from pension rights attained through shared earnings.

(vi) *NDCs require social policy supplements in the form of tax-financed add-ons to accounts.* To address contribution gaps caused by childbirth, military conscription, periods of higher education, and other periods out of work for skilling or reskilling, NDC countries have created diverse credits such as for child care. Another policy used by NDC countries is to replace a percentage of earnings compensated for by social insurance, such as registered unemployment insurance connected with job-search activities, own sickness and sickness of one's child or children, and in some countries a period of lost earnings directly in conjunction with childbirth (that is, in addition to the child-care credit). For a person granted disability status during the working career, contributions can be calculated and paid on the basis of imputed lost earnings.

(vii) *NDCs require effective labor market policies to provide support for workers who cannot be easily helped solely by established market search mechanisms.* Most of the mobility in a labor force takes care of itself through formal job-search services or informal channels. For some groups in society this will not be sufficient, however: older workers experiencing unanticipated or forced job changes; persons with functional impairments who need support in getting into the labor force; older workers with little or no job-search experience; and school dropouts who are willing and able to improve education and learn new skills a little later in life. Immigrants will need accreditation of education, language skills, and on-the-job training to supplement necessary skills. Finally, job-search help is needed for those not familiar or comfortable with the country's normal networks and institutions. The goal of all activities here is to improve the chances of this relatively large number of special needs groups to integrate into the labor force.

(viii) *NDCs require modest redesign but strong labor market policy interventions to deliver on participation and later retirement goals.* The NDC concept is based on continuous labor force participation and payment of contributions during working life until self-selected retirement above a minimum retirement age. To make this happen requires some modest policy redesign around, say, the contribution payments made by the self-employed and innovations to address the tax- and subsidy-effects heterogeneity in longevity. Strong policy interventions in the labor market are required that favor formal labor market participation with high contribution density until voluntary departure from the labor market, also at a very high age. In both areas, important knowledge gaps remain. Although what is required to keep people on the labor market at higher ages is known (keeping them healthy, skilled, and motivated), the policies needed to make this happen are unclear.

(ix) *NDCs are confronted with three important annuity design issues that country experts and policy makers need to address.* The first choice is about exogenous or endogenous indexation of pensions as part of the annuity design. Introducing an expected rate of return allows for front-loading of benefits with planned price indexation thereafter. Getting the expected rate wrong or doing a mere price indexation thereafter creates additional distributional policy issues that are largely unnecessary if thought out well from the beginning. A second choice is finding an efficient method for projecting life expectancy that does not systematically under- or overestimate the actual outcomes during the 30 or more years a birth cohort spans in retirement. Most countries are choosing the easy way out—that is, projections are made based on the "period method," which leads to downward-biased estimates and continuous systematic deficits as the books are closed on successive annuity or benefit pools of birth cohorts. A third choice is about possible methods to correct for the tax- and subsidy-type effects of socioeconomic heterogeneity in life expectancy at retirement. This issue has not been on the radar screen of policy makers and the available policy options and their interactions are few and untested.

(x) *NDC schemes offer transparency on conceptual issues that are hidden in NDB schemes.* The various issues and design choices highlighted for NDC schemes also exist for NDB schemes but are typically ignored because the DB structure does not offer the same transparency into the analytical insights as DC schemes. This creates unique needs but also incentives for reflection and redesign under the NDC approach.

IS AN NDC REFORM TRULY NEEDED OR CAN INCORPORATING NDC ELEMENTS IN NDB SCHEMES DO THE JOB?

Over the past few decades many countries across the world introduced parametric reforms of their mostly traditional NDB schemes that are documented by the OECD for member countries (and, at times, beyond; OECD 2017, 2018), and for these and emerging market economies by the Federación Internacional de Administradoras de Fondos de Pensiones (FIAP 2018). Other information sources for parametric reform efforts are the U.S. Social Security Administration (undated) and AON Hewitt (undated), accessible online.

Over the period 1995 to 2009 the number of increases in the contribution rate of NDB schemes (57) dominated that of increases in the retirement age (18) and changes in the benefit formula and amount (28); comparable figures for 2009 to 2018 were 21, 29, and 33, respectively. Various recent changes in retirement age (for example, automatic indexation with life expectancy) and benefit formula (for example, stronger decrements and increments for earlier and later retirement or even decreases in the annual accrual factor) were inspired by the NDC scheme as a benchmark. This raises the question of whether a string of parametric reforms of NDB schemes that emulate NDC characteristics is sufficient to achieve the key reform objectives of financial sustainability, adequacy of benefits, affordability, labor market efficiency, and intra- and intertemporal fairness.

The publications by the OECD (2017, 2018) and European Commission (2018) suggest that both institutions strongly believe that most recent country reforms that adopted selective elements of NDC design were sufficient to provide financial sustainability while offering adequate pensions. For both institutions, future adjustments to their member countries' pension schemes will be needed—as is the case with any pension scheme—but these adjustments are expected to be minor and "only" corrective.

Based on the various chapters in this anthology, it is strongly hypothesized that the parametric reforms of the NDB schemes enacted so far are not enough to emulate an NDC reform. As a result, many more and drastic future parametric NDB reforms will be needed to move toward the reform objectives, but will still not reach them. This is because none of the NDB reforms subject the reformed schemes to a hard, intertemporal budget constraint with a dynamic design that responds to the economic and demographic environment (which in NDCs ensures a financially sustainable outcome). This is very visible even in the point schemes that claim proximity to NDC schemes. The emulated NDC features in NDB parametric reforms are too unsystematic and insufficient to achieve the expected NDC results. Moreover, the nontransparent character of NDB schemes disguises and is thus little able to address the crucial topics that emerge strongly in this anthology: the underestimation of changes in life expectancy and the treatment of rising heterogeneity of life expectancy.

These partly hypothesized and partly documented gaps in reform efforts and directions form the proposed direction of priorities and the next analytical work to guide policy makers across all public pension schemes. Many gaps remain but five stand out in importance, as presented next.

ANALYTICAL PRIORITIES AND NEXT STEPS

To grasp the financial sustainability of a pension scheme that is only partially or not at all prefunded, a comparison of annual flows—contribution revenue plus interest and benefit expenditure—is not enough and may actually be misleading. A sound assessment of financial sustainability requires a comparison of stocks—the estimated liabilities of benefits with the estimated assets, including the pay-as-you-go asset. Currently no international or transnational organization applies even longer-term comparable projections of revenues and expenditure flows to establish a first understanding of sustainability. The available pension expenditure projections as a percentage of GDP mostly do not reflect country realities. The envisaged System of National Accounts pension liability measures are still a work in progress, with estimation models of diverse quality. Nor is the revenue side developed for flows or stocks. Work in this area, including an assessment of the current stabilizing mechanisms' capacity under NDB and NDC schemes, should have priority and is planned for a future publication.

For both stock and flow estimates and both the expenditure and liability and the revenue and asset sides, unbiased estimates of the relevant life expectancies are key. These estimates are currently not available. Essentially all countries (including those with NDC schemes) use period table–based life expectancies for their sustainability calculations (if they are done at all) compared with the conceptually correct cohort-based life expectancies. For the latter, the Lee-Carter approach with various refinements has become the standard. Comparing the results of both approaches where official data exist (and also researchers' estimates) suggests differences of about 10–30 percent at retirement (or even higher). A new estimation approach of the cohort life expectancy documented in this anthology takes account of the accelerating improvements in mortality and issues a clear warning (Palmer and Zhao de Gosson de Varennes 2019): the results for Sweden suggest that the period method estimates for the most recently pensioned birth cohorts may be underestimated by about three years, and the same study shows similar gaps for all other OECD countries examined. This suggests major efforts are required across OECD and emerging market economies so that their statistical institutions provide less biased estimates of life expectancy across all relevant ages and these estimates are used to measure financial sustainability.

The high and increasing heterogeneity in life expectancy by socioeconomic characteristics is increasingly documented for developed economies but much less is known for emerging ones. The link between differences in life expectancy at retirement and lifetime income or accumulated retirement capital is crucial for the level of the initial annuity and intra- and intertemporal fairness of the scheme. First innovative research to document the scope of the tax and subsidy effects has been undertaken, and reform suggestions and estimations for how to address them in NDC schemes are developed in this anthology, but much more needs to be done at the level of country estimation and policy design.

The retirement age is the critical linchpin between adequacy and financial sustainability, and adequate formal labor force participation with high contribution density during earlier years is key to an adequate replacement rate. Both are challenges for the labor market in developed and emerging market economies alike. This anthology opens the discussion on the topic of the labor market in conjunction with NDC and FDC pension designs, and on the importance of designing the links to a DB-type income guarantee at retirement, but much more work in this area is needed. In this vein, an additional dimension was recently added on how the future of work will require de-linking the contribution payment from the employer (World Bank 2019). A less radical and perhaps more operational option would be to move the decision environment for contribution payment beyond classical employers, which are likely to remain important, and add the many current and future versions of self-employment to the research agenda.

Finally, the next policy research agenda should include an in-depth evaluation of the optimal link of NDCs (and other universal retirement schemes) with other pillars and the reform required for related programs, particularly disability, survivors', and long-term care benefits. This is a critical part of the proposed agenda for the future.

References

AON Hewitt. Undated. "Global Retirement Update." https://www.aon.com/human-capital -consulting/thought-leadership/leg_updates/global_reports/reports-pubs_global_retirement _update.jsp.

European Commission. 2018. *The 2018 Ageing Report: Economic and Budgetary Projections for the 28 EU Member States (2016–2070)*. European Economy—Institutional Papers 079. Luxembourg: Publications Office of the European Union.

FIAP (Federación Internacional de Administradoras de Fondos de Pensiones). 2018. *Parametric Reforms in the Public PAYGO Pension Programs. 1995–2018*. Santiago, Chile: FIAP.

Holzmann, Robert, and Edward Palmer. 2006. *Pension Reform: Issues and Prospects for Non-financial Defined Contribution (NDC) Schemes*. Washington, DC: World Bank.

Holzmann, Robert, Edward Palmer, and David Robalino, eds. 2012. *Nonfinancial Defined Contribution Pension Schemes in a Changing Pension World: Volume 1 Progress, Lessons, and Implementation*. Washington, DC: World Bank.

———. 2013. *Nonfinancial Defined Contribution Pension Schemes in a Changing Pension World: Volume 2 Gender, Politics, and Financial Stability*. Washington, DC: World Bank.

OECD (Organisation for Economic Co-operation and Development). 2017. *Pensions at a Glance 2017—OECD and G20 Indicators*. Paris: OECD Publishing.

———. 2018. *OECD Pensions Outlook*. Paris: OECD Publishing.

Palmer, Edward, and Yuwei Zhao de Gosson de Varennes. 2019. "Annuities in (N)DC Pension Schemes: Design, Heterogeneity, and Estimation Issues." In *Progress and Challenges of Nonfinancial Defined Contribution Pension Schemes: Volume 1 Addressing Marginalization, Polarization, and the Labor Market*, edited by Robert Holzmann, Edward Palmer, Robert Palacios, and Stefano Sacchi, Chapter 13. Washington, DC: World Bank.

United States Social Security Administration. Undated. "International Update." http://www .socialsecurity.gov/policy/docs/progdesc/intl—update//.

World Bank. 2019. *The Changing Nature of Work. World Bank Development Report 2019*. Washington, DC: World Bank.

PART I

Taking Stock

CHAPTER 2

The Swedish NDC Scheme: Success on Track with Room for Reflection

Edward Palmer and Bo Könberg

Introduction

In a series of steps beginning in the summer of 1992, Sweden transformed its three-pillar, universal defined benefit (DB) pension scheme into a three-pillar defined contribution (DC) scheme, with a DB minimum income guarantee at its foundation. The original reform proposal (Departementsserien 1992:89) was translated into English in 2017 ("A Reformed Pension System—Background, Principles, and Sketch"; see Swedish Ministry of Health and Social Affairs 2017).

A nonfinancial defined contribution (NDC) scheme is the centerpiece of Sweden's two plus zero-pillar universal public old-age pension commitment. Since 1999, the public component of the overall pension system has consisted of a tax-financed guarantee minimum pension as the zero pillar, an NDC[1] first pillar, and a financial defined contribution (FDC) second pillar. The guarantee minimum pension together with a means-tested housing supplement provide a basic income guarantee in old age for persons whose combined NDC and FDC pensions are too low to live on. The guarantee is means tested vis-à-vis the public NDC and FDC schemes. It is a fixed amount up to a ceiling and then gradually tapers off as the size of the overall pension benefit earned through the combined NDC and FDC components increases.

The public schemes are universal, which means that everyone in the workforce—employees, regardless of occupation or sector of employment, and the self-employed including farmers—is mandated to pay contributions into both public NDC and FDC schemes, the two first pillars of Sweden's overall pension system.[2] Contributions are paid on earnings throughout the working life without an age limit. In both schemes, individuals' contributions constitute their own account values, which are annuitized at retirement. In the FDC component of the public pension schemes, contributions are paid directly into FDC individual accounts for investment in financial market investment funds; in the NDC scheme they are noted on individual accounts and are the revenues that finance the pensions of current pensioners.

The one-to-one DC link between individual contributions and individual benefits creates fairness—in the sense that participants get what they pay for, with "interest." The DC construct is economically efficient because the contribution is not perceived as a tax—it is a contribution to one's own future pension. The use of life expectancy in computing

---

The authors are grateful to Erik Hernæs and Georg Fischer for suggestions generously provided on the first draft.

the benefit is economically efficient at the micro level because it creates incentives to work and pay contributions and at the end of the working career for younger generations to postpone retirement as life expectancy increases. It also contributes to efficiency at the macro level because the aggregate of all individual labor supply responses creates gross domestic product (GDP) growth.

The NDC revenues finance payment of benefits of current pensioners, while the contributions constitute individual "savings" noted on individual accounts (with "interest" through indexation). Individuals' contributions to NDC are individual contributions to longevity insurance. That becomes evident at retirement when individuals' account balances, divided by their life expectancy at retirement, create the flow of income to them for the rest of their lives. The money itself is transferred to the individual's birth cohort's aggregate sum of all individual account balances at retirement. This sum of money is intended to cover the payments to all individuals in the birth cohort throughout their remaining lives. This means that the remaining balance on the accounts of those who die earlier than the average retirement age finances the benefits of those who live longer than average.

Finally, note that the NDC framework ensures financial balance in the nonfinancial pension world. It does this through its basic construction, through indexation of accounts of workers and benefits based on the rate of growth of wages and the labor force. In Sweden, financial balance is ensured through a solvency ratio, wherein liabilities are adjusted for an estimated future solvency outcome of less than zero.

The final component of the overall pension landscape creates a complete picture of Sweden's pension system. In addition to the public NDC and FDC schemes, more than 90 percent of employees (80 percent of all workers) in Sweden have a quasi-mandatory[3] occupational (predominantly) FDC supplement that enhances the public NDC and FDC schemes under the ceiling on income for the public schemes, while the worker's occupational pension constitutes the entire pension for the portion of earnings above the ceiling for the public NDC and FDC schemes. Individuals can top up this three-pillar scheme with individual private insurance. Although earlier premiums paid up to a ceiling were tax deductible in the year in which they were paid and taxed when paid out, the tax deduction was recently abolished.

No redistribution occurs within the NDC or FDC collectives. Instead, the public mandatory NDC and FDC schemes are supplemented with redistributive components: nominal contributions are added for periods insured by other public (social) insurance programs—for unemployment, sickness, disability, care of sick children under 12 years of age, and compensated parental leave. Also, noncontributory credits are granted to parents (one at a time) for up to four years in conjunction with the birth of a child. Rights of this kind (which include rights for higher education) are financed with general tax revenues that are paid into the NDC fund(s) and directly into individual financial accounts in the public FDC scheme. Together with the guarantee, these social policy add-ons constitute the distributional components of the Swedish public pension system.[4]

This chapter has two goals. The first is to explain how the NDC works in the context of the Swedish NDC framework. The second is to identify and discuss issues arising in the context of the overall Swedish pension system after two decades of experience, focusing on the NDC component. The chapter begins with a brief history and overview of the Swedish pension reform.

Overview of Sweden's Pension System

The Swedish pension reform began with a sketch published in 1992 by the government-appointed Working Group on Pensions. The sketch outlined a proposal for the new pension scheme; the first legislation for the universal NDC[5] and FDC schemes was passed by Parliament in June 1994.

The first contributions to the individual accounts for the FDC scheme were made in 1995,[6] accompanied by the creation of personal NDC and FDC accounts, which were implemented in January 1999. The contribution rates are 16 percent and 2.5 percent, respectively. During the period 1996–98, NDC accounts were created for persons born in 1938 and later, based on contributions paid historically for the financing of the current DB scheme for the period 1960–98. Palmer (2006b) describes in detail the model used to create retroactive accounts on the basis of computerized individual wage and contribution information and retroactive child-care rights for the period 1960–98, together with other models of conversion to NDC accounts.

The watershed year for introduction of the Swedish NDC and FDC schemes was 1999. Starting in 2000, participants began to have electronic access to information on their personal NDC and FDC accounts. By logging into the system they can receive a personal dashboard picture, access structured information for all participating funds, and make their FDC fund choices.

Successively from 2000, the third major component of the overall Swedish pension system, individuals' occupational benefits, was integrated into this electronic personal information system (*Min Pension*). This step completed the process of making all components of individuals' pension portfolios transparent. The design of the information system enables individual calculations of expected total benefits based individually on chosen assumptions about earnings, rates of indexation and financial returns, and chosen retirement ages. It is hoped that this has increased the importance of individuals' choices in determining their pension outcomes.

THE TRANSITION FROM THE PREVIOUS REGIME INTO PUBLIC NDC AND FDC[7]

Personal NDC accounts were, as mentioned, created for persons born in 1938 and later, retroactively beginning with earnings data (already in the system's database). For the period 1960–94 individual accounts were created by applying a contribution rate of 18.5 percent. For the period 1995–98 a contribution rate of 16.5 percent was used. Since implementation of accounts in 1999 the contribution rate has been 16 percent. Personal FDC accounts began in 1995, with a contribution rate of 2.0 percent, which changed to 2.5 percent as of 1999.

The reform was introduced gradually, with a transition rule for cohorts born between 1938 and 1953. Participants in these cohorts receive benefits calculated on a pro rata basis (with changing weights of 1/20 per year, successively giving more weight to the new scheme over 20 years) based on the benefits they would have received from the old and new schemes.[8] The first pensions according to the new rules were paid out in 2001. The first birth cohort to reach age 65 in the new system was that born in 1938, whose members turned 65 in 2003. On January 1, 2020, the "transition" period will have come to an end.

The guarantee benefit, which can be claimed at age 65, was introduced in 2003 when the first of the transition cohorts turned 65. At the same time, the accounts of disability recipients (based on actual accounts before being granted disability status, and then a rule for calculating imputed earnings through age 64) received their new public pensions.

RULE-BASED NDC WITH IDENTIFIED SOURCES OF FINANCE AS THE GUIDING PRINCIPLE—INCLUDING FOR POLICY-MOTIVATED ACCOUNT "ADD-INS"

The principle behind the Swedish NDC and FDC schemes is that they should be completely rule-based and independent of ad hoc government interventions. Contributions are paid from government tax revenues to cover pension entitlements credited for earnings replacement in conjunction with unemployment, sickness and disability insurance, taking care of sick children under age 12, and statutory parental leave. In addition, the general budget finances contributions with a low amount per year for higher education, more for military conscription (when it existed), and, most importantly, for rights attached to the birth and early childhood of children (a maximum of four years per child).

HOW THE OCCUPATIONAL SCHEMES ENTER INTO THE OVERALL SWEDISH PENSION FRAMEWORK

At the time the reform was conceived, Sweden already had occupational supplements to the then universal public scheme (*Allmän tilläggspension*, or ATP) that was replaced by the reform. These supplements remained after the reform but their design was changed from DB to DC to coordinate them with the new public NDC and FDC schemes.

About 90 percent of all public and private sector employees are covered by quasi-mandatory occupational pension plans based on collective agreements between the unions and employers' confederations. These pension schemes, which are financed through employers' contributions, supplement the public NDC and FDC schemes. On average, the contribution rate is 4.5 percent on earnings below the ceiling—in addition to the 18.5 percent going to the public system, and 30 percent on earnings above the ceiling (up to a new ceiling—depending on the scheme). The occupational schemes also provide the entire benefit, based on contributions from earnings above the ceiling. Consistent with the public NDC and FDC schemes, these are also prefunded DC schemes, with a few small exceptions. The four major occupational plans are for blue-collar workers in the private sector, white-collar workers in the private sector, central government employees, and local government employees.

NO REQUIRED RETIREMENT AGE EXISTS—ONLY A MINIMUM AGE FOR CLAIMING A BENEFIT

The Swedish public pension scheme has no required retirement age. The rationale is that an economically efficient pension scheme is one that is neutral about individual decisions between work and "leisure," while at the same time the DC construction with the annuity grows as projected remaining life expectancy (for a given birth cohort) declines, yielding a higher benefit per year. This provides a "carrot" for postponing claiming the benefit.

Nevertheless, 61 is the minimum age at which public NDC and FDC pensions can be claimed. The guaranteed minimum pension benefit, however, cannot be claimed until age 65, which is also the age at which a disability benefit is replaced by an old-age pension benefit. The next age of importance is 67, at which time the employer has the right to discontinue a contract with an employee based only on age.

In December 2017, the six parties in the Pension Group (representing some 80 percent of members of parliament) reached a political agreement on revising these pension ages. This revision includes increasing in three steps the minimum age at which a pension can be claimed from age 61 to age 64 (2020–26). When the reform was legislated the age of the right to claim a guarantee pension was 65. This will be raised to 66.[9] The proposal also includes raising from age 67 to age 69 (2020–23), in two steps, the age at which employers have the legal right to lay off older workers or recontract them. The agreement also provides that after the changes, these ages will be indexed to life expectancy.

RETIREMENT BEHAVIOR OF SWEDES

At the beginning of the reform, about 90 percent of pensions were claimed before or at age 65. In 2015, the figure was still about 80 percent, but the distribution was around the mean age of 65. For example, 50 percent of persons born in 1950 who reached age 65 in 2015 claimed a benefit at age of 65, whereas 28 percent of persons ages 61–64 claimed it, and 22 percent claimed it when older than 65. The average de facto pension age hovered around 65 (the highest in the European Union [EU]) for the entire 15-year period with NDC, while the distribution around the average spread out in both directions after 2000.

For those who choose to retire at ages 61–64 (28 percent in 2017), it is possible, and not uncommon, to claim an "early retirement" occupational pension, also with, for example, a 25 percent public income component of the full early retirement pension. About 20 percent of workers retire after age 65.

The personal decision of when to claim NDC and FDC benefits can be an expression of rational behavior (Diamond 2003). Among the many individual circumstances that can influence decisions about retirement are those associated with the known life expectancy of the subgroups of the universal insurance pool. Zhao de Gosson de Varennes (2016) finds that 50 percent of Swedish exits from the labor force with an old-age pension follow the rule of thumb that people postpone claiming a pension or make an early claim if they have a group-based or "culturally conditioned" reason to do so.

In the context of Swedish pensions, the culture from 1960 of Swedes became "retirement at age 65"—in accordance with the then cultural norm of 65, which was viewed as the full pension age in the ATP (introduced in 1960), the forerunner to the NDC and FDC schemes. In practice this means that men, people with lower levels of education, and singles retire earlier. As it turns out, this may be a rational decision given that persons in these groups also have shorter life expectancies (Palmer and Zhao de Gosson de Varennes 2019). Another result of Zhao de Gosson de Varennes (2016) is that no strong empirical difference exists in the retirement age choices of foreign and native-born persons.

HAS THE DC DESIGN INFLUENCED OLDER WORKERS' EXIT FROM THE LABOR FORCE?

The nonfinancial DB scheme that Sweden's NDC replaced already had a schedule of decrements to benefits claimed before age 65 and increments for claims thereafter. Similar schedules are reflected in the anthology of countries examined in Gruber and Wise (1999).

As early as the 1990s, the Swedish tax and transfer rules pertaining to older workers supported decisions in the direction of working longer.

The question then is what happened to the pension age as the first NDC pensioners (born in 1938) turned 65 in 2003? Figure 2.1 shows the age of exit of men and women from the labor force with a pension from 1970 to 2013 for six European peers (excluding persons already on disability benefits).

Note the pronounced decline beginning in 1970 in the age at which workers claimed retirement benefits into the mid-1990s, including in Sweden. In the mid-2000s the trend reversed and the retirement age generally increased across Western Europe.

The announcement in 1994 in Sweden of the new NDC pension scheme legislation was accompanied by the launch of a new public narrative on what was reasonable to expect in the future. By 2003, when the first 65-year-olds covered by NDC claimed their pensions, the principle that healthy aging would require working longer was fairly well established, which became a part of the story.

Remarkable in figure 2.1 is that despite a good mark in the Gruber and Wise anthology regarding the overall economic "tax force" for retirement even before introduction of the NDC scheme, Sweden has remained at the top of the six countries since the first NDC benefits were granted in 2003. This could be ascribed to the introduction of the NDC—and the narrative developed around its introduction.

More generally, since 2000, when comparable statistics were first gathered by the EU, Sweden has had the highest labor force participation of all EU countries (EC 2018); about 85 percent of persons age 20–64 work, largely because of the high rates of labor-force participation of women and older workers (figure 2.1). Certainly, the evidence to date supports the contention that the NDC's introduction helped Sweden retain its leadership among the EU28 with respect to the continuous increase in older workers' labor force participation.[10]

FIGURE 2.1 **Average retirement age, select countries, 1970–2013**

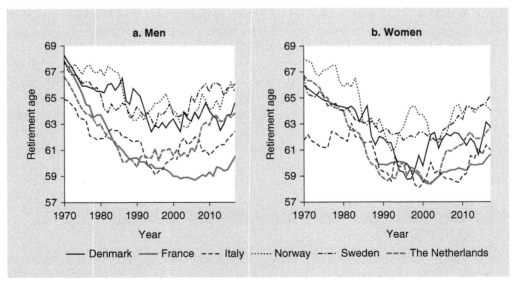

SOURCE: OECD Global Pension Statistics. Ageing and Employment Policies - Statistics on Average Effective Age of Retirement.

Long-Term Financial Sustainability
THE DESIGN OF NDC INHERENTLY WORKS TOWARD DYNAMIC SUSTAINABILITY

The foundation of an NDC's design can be expressed with reference to a simple formula summarizing the determinants of the financial status of a pension scheme. C is the contribution rate resulting from the ratio of expenditures to the revenue base, which for a pension scheme is the contribution base. The growth of the contribution base—which is the growth of per capita wages, w, multiplied by the number of contributors, L—is the pension scheme's "budget constraint." At the same time the total cost of pension payments is determined by the average pension per recipient, $\underline{p}$, and the number of persons receiving benefits, R. For the scheme as a whole this can be expressed by the following equation[11]:

$$C = \frac{\underline{p}}{\underline{w}} \times \frac{R}{L}. \tag{2.1}$$

A basic feature of NDC is that the contribution rate is the same for all persons within any specific birth cohort and over all future birth cohorts. This is also a precondition for long-term financial stability in the NDC framework. The macroeconomic contribution rate C was calibrated from the outset to a microeconomic counterpart that relates the average number of years of work of individuals—with the average wage—to the average number of years with a retirement benefit (Palmer 2013). Equation (2.1) can also be written in terms of nominal values. This means that the rate of inflation occurs in both the denominator as a component of nominal per capita wage growth and in the numerator as a component of the indexation of pension benefits.

The links to the economy and demography embodied in this simple relationship determine the dynamics of the ratio. All else equal, beginning in equilibrium, long-term financial stability in the system is maintained by indexing accounts and benefits to changes in both the per capita wage of contributors and their number, that is, $\Delta \underline{w} L$. The equilibrium setting of the system means that the contribution rate C is set for a specific outcome of R/L (which at the level of the average individual is the expected number of years with a benefit relative to the expected number of years in the labor force). What remains for a country starting an NDC scheme is the demographic starting "position" of the labor force resulting from the dynamics of the fertility rate and net migration.

From the point of view of long-term equilibrium, the ideal situation is that births fluctuate randomly around the population fertility rate of 2.1. If the fertility rate is systematically lower, so that the working-age population is declining, then compensation over time must come from net migration to the country. If net migration does not occur, the shortfall is corrected for by indexing the accounts of workers and the pensions of pensioners, through indexation that reflects the negative change in L. On the other hand, a rate higher than that necessary to reproduce the population leads to a "demographic dividend," which is passed on through indexation of personal accounts and pensions. In the Swedish scheme this component of the index (the dynamic development of the labor force) was left out. Instead, this process is regulated through the use of a solvency ratio and a balancing mechanism, explained in "The Suspenders of NDC—Sweden's Solvency Ratio and Balancing Index."

THE SUSPENDERS OF NDC—SWEDEN'S SOLVENCY RATIO AND BALANCING INDEX

Important in the context of the Swedish NDC scheme is that the rate of return is based solely on the growth of contributions (earnings) per capita, leaving out the impact of either positive or negative growth in the labor force, that is, in the factor L in equation (2.1). The risk of ignoring these impacts is that the labor force will decline, thereby shrinking the payment base, with no correction in the system's liabilities, which creates financial imbalance.

Sweden has been in the fortunate position of having maintained a fertility rate close to the 2.1 needed to reproduce the population—and hence the working-age population and labor force. The gap was filled for the last half-century through positive net migration to the country. The Swedish NDC scheme maintains financial balance without including changes in the labor force in its indexation. However, because a risk remains that Sweden may not always experience labor force growth, the Swedish NDC scheme is equipped with a solvency ratio—that is, the ratio of estimated assets to liabilities—that triggers a balancing index that reduces the valorization of liabilities when it falls below unity, until solvency is once again attained.[12]

System liabilities at any time are the accounts of contributors and the annuities granted pensioners. The system's contribution assets are estimated using the time a unit of money is in the system from the average time it was paid in until the average time it is expected to be paid out (the average life expectancy of all pensioners in the pension pool)—called turnover time. If there is a fund, as in the Swedish NDC scheme, then the fund's asset value at time t becomes an additional component of the total sum of the stock of assets. When the solvency ratio falls below unity, liabilities are adjusted downward by the resulting change in the balancing index,[13] which continues until balance is achieved again (Palmer 2013; Settergren 2001, 2013). Note that the solvency ratio calculated in this way also picks up other uncovered financial risks, such as possible systematic errors in the projection of life expectancy. Given this way of calculating assets, an increase in the average longevity of the entire pension pool increases the time a unit of contributions is in the overall pension pool at a given rate of return. This increases the liquidity (the time expected to pass before the unit of money is to be paid out), which given this rule for calculating assets also increases total assets.

The balancing index was triggered to effect on three occasions—2010, 2014, and 2015; figure 2.2 illustrates the development of the index used to valorize accounts of workers and benefits of pensioners, broken down into individual components. The income index is the rate of growth of per capita income (both below and above the ceiling on contribution-based earnings). In nominal terms then (that is, including the rate of growth of inflation), this is the rate of return on individual accounts, as long as the solvency ratio is greater than unity. If it falls below unity, then it is the balancing index that applies instead of the income index, which is reduced by the balancing index until solvency is once again achieved. Pensions are indexed (in the absence of balancing) with the income index, minus the 1.6 percent discount rate (an assumed rate of growth of productivity) that is factored into the calculation of the annuity. This means that pensions are indexed by the income index minus 1.6 percent plus the rate of inflation.

During 2002–17 real income per capita[14] grew at an average rate of 2.1 percent, leading to an average increment to the valuation of pensions of 0.5 percent per year above

FIGURE 2.2 **Indexation of NDC and transition benefits**

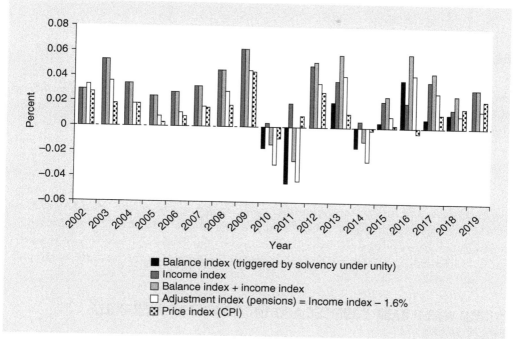

SOURCE: Data provided by the Department of Analysis, Swedish Pensions Agency.

NOTE: CPI = consumer price index; NDC = nonfinancial defined contribution.

the 1.6 percent already factored into the computation of the initial life annuity. In addition, during the same period, pensions were adjusted with the rate of inflation (consumer price index, or CPI), which was 1.2 percent per year.

CONSTRUCTION OF THE SWEDISH NDC ANNUITY

The Swedish NDC annuity is calculated based on the capital balance in the individual's NDC account at retirement, the individual's cohort life expectancy at the chosen age of retirement, and an assumed real rate of return of 1.6 percent per year, which front-loads the benefit. The rate of return of 1.6 percent derives from an assumed long-term rate of growth of productivity, and, consequently, real wage growth per capita. Going forward from the time of retirement, pensions are then revalued with a positive or negative indexation component based on the difference between 1.6 percent growth and the actual outcome, plus the rate of inflation. This results in a yearly supplement to indexation when real growth is greater than 1.6 percent, and a reduction in total indexation if real growth falls below this.

This calculation method shifts a portion of a given amount of pension capital forward to the beginning of the retirement period; that is, it front-loads the annuity. The overall result is that real indexation of Swedish NDC pensions is based on the rate of growth of per capita wage income after deducting the "norm" of 1.6 percent (which is already included in the formulation of the initial annuity). The difference between the actual per capita wage income index and 1.6 percent leads to a revaluation of the current year's annuity.

THE DEMOGRAPHICS OF FERTILITY AND MIGRATION—HOW SWEDEN ACHIEVED A CONSTANT RISE IN THE LABOR SUPPLY OVER MANY DECADES

The Swedish solvency ratio constantly counteracts financial insolvency. Nevertheless, the development of the fertility rate and net migration together determine the working-age population and the underlying demographics of a country's labor supply, and thus the dynamics of growth, together with the rate of labor productivity growth.

The two important demographic determinants of the labor force are the fertility rate and net migration. Migration into Sweden increased from the mid-1980s and grew strongly thereafter. Together, the relatively high fertility rate augmented by net immigration resulted in an increasing working-age population from the 1980s. The calculations performed for the European Commission's 2018 *Ageing Report* (EC 2018) assume the fertility rate will remain about 1.9 children per woman through 2060. Net migration is a policy parameter regulated since the 1960s to more than cover the remaining gap between the 2.1 children per woman needed to create positive growth in the working-age population, and hence, the labor force.

WORLD WAR II BABY BOOMERS AND THE DEMOGRAPHIC RIPPLES THEREAFTER

Sweden's first postwar baby boom occurred in 1943–49. With a fertility rate of 1.9, a little under the 2.1 rate needed to reproduce the population, the "deficit" compared with a historical fertility rate of 2.1 turned into a "surplus" through net migration to Sweden. Also, importantly, the original baby boom led to a second baby boom (the children of the first boomers) in 1965–75, and a third largely in 1989–93 (when their grandchildren were born). As the original baby boomers left the labor force in 2008–14 at age 65,[15] the overall labor force had absorbed two new generations of "offspring" baby boomers, thus maintaining an intergenerational demographic equilibrium. In fact, for several decades the labor force has grown thanks to the contribution of positive net migration to the country.

It is generally believed that Sweden maintained its long-term high fertility rate due to its generous family policy including highly subsidized preschool daycare and after-school activity centers and transfers to parents. The latter take the form of job security and paid leave with childbirth, reimbursed leave for care of sick children, and a general child allowance. In fact, the relatively high (ocular) correlation between the EU's top 10 countries with respect to fertility and (public and private) expenditures on preschool child care (table 2.1) suggests the importance of family policy for a country's fertility rates.

In summary, it is important to stress that the example of Sweden illustrates two points that can easily be missed in the baby boom discussions. A first baby boom can give rise to a succession of succeeding baby booms at 20–25-year intervals. In the context of Sweden, this, together with positive immigration to Sweden, has been sufficient to fill the dip between historical fertility gaps and to create overall dynamic long-run demographic equilibrium. In Sweden this has meant continuous growth in the labor force during the past half century. A final note in this context is the availability of

TABLE 2.1 **Fertility rates and spending on child-care services and early education**

Country	Fertility rate in 2020	Spending on child care and early education (% of GDP), 2011
France	2.0	4
Ireland	2.0	2
Sweden	1.9	6
United Kingdom	1.8	3
Norway	1.7	5
Finland	1.7	7
Belgium	1.7	14
Denmark	1.7	1
Netherlands	1.7	10

SOURCE: Fertility rate: ED 2016; Spending: OECD Family Database.
NOTE: GDP = gross domestic product.

child-care services (where families pay an amount that is subsidized, with a decreasing subsidy based on a means test) since the end of the 1960s. This has played a key role in supporting working parents, particularly mothers, and is easily linked to Sweden's successively high fertility rate. This policy has put Sweden among the leaders in the Organisation for Economic Co-operation and Development (OECD) in women's labor force participation, as illustrated in the previous discussion.

THE BOTTOM LINE ON FINANCIAL STABILITY IN THE SWEDISH NDC SCHEME—THE SOLVENCY RATIO AND BALANCING INDEX

Financial stability in the Swedish system is maintained through indexation, reflecting the degree of solvency. A solvency ratio of less than unity leads to a negative adjustment in the system's liabilities, and solvency ratio values greater than or equal to unity yield no adjustment. The balancing approach used in Sweden covers the risk of a declining labor force, but presently no rule exists for distributing excess liquidity. This issue is addressed in detail later, but the financial status of the Swedish NDC pension scheme is first reviewed.

In the Swedish NDC context the estimate of assets, called the contribution asset, is based on contributions paid in the nearest accounting period multiplied by the amount of time they are expected to remain in the scheme from the period of payment until the period in which they are to be paid out, called turnover time (Palmer 2013; Settergren 2001; Settergren and Mikula 2006; the Swedish Pensions Agency's annual report, *The Orange Report*, any year).

"Balancing"—that is, the process of bringing the value of liabilities back into line with the estimated value of assets—is triggered when the solvency ratio falls to less than unity. Liabilities are then devalued until a solvency ratio of unity is achieved. In years subsequent to the devaluation of liabilities (pension rights), after the circumstances that created a ratio of assets to liabilities less than unity corrects itself, an upside adjustment brings the system back on track with the per capita income index.[16]

The "risk" in the Swedish NDC balancing model is that no rule covers the circumstance for, for example, continuous strong positive growth in the labor force, all else equal, leading to an undistributed surplus that goes well beyond what can be considered a sufficient level of reserves. As Auerbach and Lee (2011) point out in a paper applying the Swedish model to U.S. data, an undistributed surplus, beyond what might be regarded to be a prudent reserve fund, leads to a decrease in welfare from funds not used for private consumption, as is the intention of the scheme.

Even with a basic scenario for growth of the labor force, the surplus in the Swedish NDC scheme can become very large. This is in fact what might currently be happening, as illustrated by the development of the solvency (balance) ratio (figure 2.3).

Figure 2.4 shows that the lowest "fund strength" in the base scenario—that is, the number of years of full pension payments the fund can cover—is expected to remain more or less steady at a value of about 4.5 until 2035 (Swedish Pensions Agency 2017, 52). Thereafter, according to both the baseline and optimistic scenarios, it "takes off." This is when the postwar baby boomers reach age 85 and older. Moreover, it continues upward, despite the entrance of children born to the postwar birth cohorts into the pension collective. Also note that the level of reserves of more than 4.5 is more than nine times greater than the lowest acceptable level mentioned in the 1994 proposal to Parliament.

According to the Swedish Pensions Agency (2017), revenues from contributions alone have not been sufficient to cover pension expenditures since 2008. Instead, a portion of the annual returns on the fund have been drawn upon to cover the flow deficit. However, this has still left a small but increasing yearly surplus that further enhances the size of the fund.

In summary, the most important macro issue for Sweden's NDC pension scheme is that no legislated procedure exists for dealing with the increase in the NDC fund if its growth exceeds the present baseline calculation (Figure 2.4), which the financial calculations of the Swedish Pensions Agency suggest is more or less inevitable. The question of the size of the fund was, in fact, examined by a committee in 2004, but no decision was taken on the basis of the committee's report.

FIGURE 2.3 **Sweden's balance (solvency) ratio under three scenarios, 2002–90**

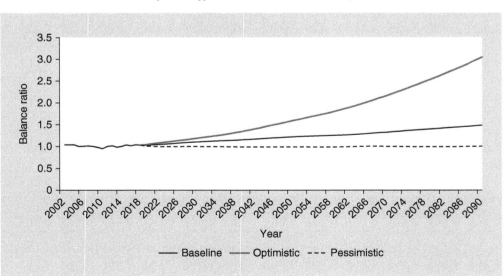

SOURCE: Data provided by the Department of Analysis, Swedish Pensions Agency.

NOTE: The balance ratio is defined as (contribution asset + buffer fund)/pension liability.

FIGURE 2.4 **Historical and projected size of the NDC reserve fund under three scenarios, 2002–90**

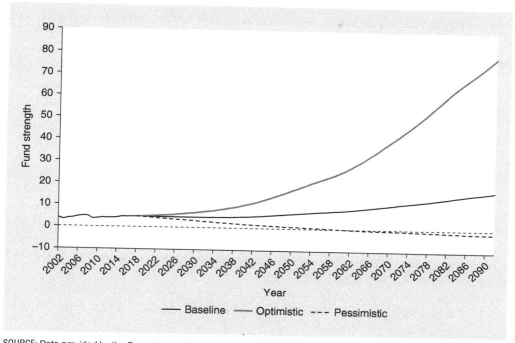

SOURCE: Data provided by the Department of Analysis, Swedish Pensions Agency.

NOTE: The size of the reserve fund (the y-axis) is the number of years of current pension payments that the reserve fund can cover at the specified time (the x-axis). NDC = nonfinancial defined contribution.

Three open issues regarding funding of the Swedish pension reform need to be resolved. The first is the absence of a rule to determine a prudent maximum size for a reserve fund surplus. The second the need for a rule to guide the Pensions Agency in determining how to distribute an unnecessarily large surplus to current and future retirees. The third issue, given the likely perspective of financial balance, with an increasing surplus in the funds, is that a modification of the balancing rule should be considered that allows the solvency ratio to fall to less than unity in recessions. In other words, why not allow the fund to act as a reserve to bridge over temporary recessions (which all recessions seen in modern times have been)?

A NOTE ON THE ORIGIN OF THE SWEDISH NDC RESERVE FUND

The assets held by the NDC reserve in 2016 were sufficient to cover four years of payments to current pensioners in that year. This came about because a decision was made in the 1950s to overfund the ATP scheme introduced in 1960. The following citation from the Parliamentary Bill from 1958 explains the motive (Parliamentary Bill No. 1958:55):

> The fund to be created in accordance with the proposed legislation of ATP would facilitate an equalization over time of the costs ... so that future contributions needed to cover the benefit payments could be less than they would otherwise be if contributions were not made to a fund.[17]

From the outset in 1960 until the 1990s, the ATP scheme was consciously "overfinanced." The goal was to build up a reserve fund to help finance the pensions of the Swedish World War II baby boom generation, born in 1943–49, for the period 2010–40. As a result of this decision, at the time of the introduction of the NDC scheme in 1999, the existing fund value was sufficient to cover four years and eight months of pension payments.

In conjunction with the introduction of the reform, about one-third of the total ATP fund was transferred to the state in 1999–2001 to cover the costs of transferring the financing of survivors' and disability insurance from the pension system to the state budget.

A SYSTEMATIC PROJECTION BIAS MAY UNDERESTIMATE NEW RETIREES' LIFE EXPECTANCY

Basing the NDC annuity on life expectancy at retirement is one of the important contributions to the financial stability and sustainability of pay-as-you-go NDC individual account schemes. In the Swedish NDC scheme, life expectancy is calculated from the average of observed age-related period mortality rates for persons 65 and older during the five years preceding the calculation period. The rationale for using this simple method is that it relates to published information. The measure is in fact legislated, to divorce the calculation from risk of political intervention.

Recent work for Sweden and nine other countries shows that a systematic demographic risk occurs in the state-of-the-art projections of life expectancy at the country level (Alho, Bravo, and Palmer 2013; Palmer, Alho, and Zhao de Gosson de Varennes 2018). Palmer and Zhao de Gosson de Varennes (2019) show that the simple method followed by the Swedish Pensions Agency to base the projection on a moving average of the preceding five years' period mortality statistics creates an even greater systematic underestimate.

The systematic bias in the projections is due to the accelerating rate of decline in the mortality of persons age 70 and older. The systematic bias arises because the period model used is a simple linear extrapolation method, whereas Swedish life expectancy is rising at an increasing rate. This was first documented in Alho, Bravo, and Palmer (2013) and explored in greater depth in Palmer, Alho, and Zhao de Gosson de Varennes (2018), who apply a new method developed, documented, and tested on 2,400 cohorts from eight countries,[18] including Sweden, beginning with cohorts born in the early 1900s and continuing until these cohorts have died out. The method was also tested based on still-living cohorts of persons who have become pensioners in present times.

The analysis shows that the Swedish life expectancy procedure increasingly underestimates the actual outcomes as the data examined approach current times. The estimation error is in fact 8 percent for birth cohorts that expired in the late 1970s, with evidence from still-living birth cohorts that the systematic error is continuing to increase in scale (Palmer and Zhao de Gosson de Varennes 2019).

This systematic deficit will be gradually absorbed through its negative effect on the balancing index. Palmer and Zhao de Gosson de Varennes (2019) estimate the effect on the pension fund to be close to 50 billion kronor for the recently pensioned cohorts born from 1937 to 1946. In addition, because the definition of assets includes life expectancy, the solvency ratio is affected. The estimate of the duration of time from the average age at which a krona is contributed is actually longer than that presently used. This implies that the value of the contribution asset—that is, the Swedish NDC pension system's total assets—is also underestimated. In summary, a new method that does not yield a systematic deficit should be adopted.

Adequacy

THE OVERALL PICTURE

The discussion of adequacy begins by taking a look at the OECD Pension Model for Sweden. The model is built up to see the replacement rates expressed as lifetime benefit payments as a percentage of lifetime earnings.

Table 2.2 shows the decomposition of how the individual components of the overall Swedish system contribute to the outcome. In OECD's *Pensions at a Glance 2015,* the average pretax pension replacement rate for mandatory public and mandatory private schemes for an average wage earner for the 34 OECD members is 52.7 percent. Table 2.2 is based on the same set of assumptions: the worker was born in 1950, entered into the labor force at age 20 in 1970, worked 45 years, and retired at age 65 in 2014. According to table 2.2, for these assumptions, the average Swedish wage earner's after-tax replacement rate is 64 percent. Of course, as life expectancy increases in the future, it will be important for individuals to work past age 65 to receive the same replacement rate. Note that the strong increase for higher wage and salary earners results from the higher contribution rate in the occupational based top-up for contribution-based earnings above the ceiling in the public NDC and FDC component of the overall system. (The "blip" is discussed in more detail below.)

According to forthcoming Swedish legislation (agreed on at the time of this writing), the minimum age at which a pension can be claimed will first be increased from the present age of 61–64 in steps during the period 2020–25. Beginning in 2026, the minimum age will be indexed to life expectancy, and is anticipated to result in a minimum pension age of 70 or more in 2060 if life expectancy continues to increase at the rate of about one year every ten years. This adds approximately four years for the average person's participation in the labor force before exiting with a pension. Assuming the occupational benefits follow the public pension schemes, the table in 2060 should yield a higher replacement rate than that in table 2.2 also because of the increase in the average age of exit.

TABLE 2.2 **Generic compensation rates for the overall Swedish pension system**
benefits compared to wage base for alternative wage levels

		Ratios				
Wage	Guarantee benefit	NDC benefit	FDC benefit	Occupational benefit (ITP)	All components together	
					Before tax	After tax
0.30	0.43	0.38	0.09	0.15	1.05	1.04
0.50	0.15	0.38	0.09	0.15	0.77	0.79
0.75	0.03	0.38	0.09	0.15	0.65	0.67
1.00	0	0.38	0.09	0.15	0.62	0.64
1.50	0	0.28	0.07	0.41	0.76	0.81
2.50	0	0.17	0.04	0.64	0.85	0.88

SOURCE: Based on the OECD model for Sweden. Originally published in Chłoń-Domińczak, Franco, and Palmer 2012.

NOTE: The first column is the ratio of alternative wage levels to the average wage. The remaining columns are the ratio of benefits to the contribution wage base. FDC = financial defined contribution; ITP = Swediish acronym for the collective pension agreement for private white-collar workers; NDC = nonfinancial defined contribution.

THE GUARANTEE BENEFIT LEVEL

The Swedish guarantee begins with a floor, above which it tapers off as it is means tested against the public NDC and FDC pensions. This is apparent in table 2.2. For a person with no earned pension rights from working, the guarantee is the entire benefit. For a person whose earnings are 30 percent of the average worker's earnings, the total compensation rate of 1.05 (the ratio of lifetime pension payments to lifetime earnings) is comprised of four components: a guarantee benefit constituting 43 percentage points, an NDC benefit constituting 38 percentage points, an FDC benefit constituting 9 percentage points, and an occupational benefit constituting 15 percentage points. For a person with earned pension rights from the equivalent of 50 percent of average earnings, the guarantee constitutes 15 percentage points, the total replacement rate from all sources. And it constitutes 3 percentage points of the replacement rate for a person with a combined public pension based on 75 percent of average lifetime earnings.

In 2003, when the first birth cohort of the reform (born in 1938) turned 65, almost 55 percent of pensioners had some amount of a guarantee pension supplement. In 2016, only 1 in 18 new pensioners (about 5 percent) had no public contribution–based NDC pension whatsoever, and 32 percent of all pensioners had a partial guarantee benefit at the bottom, according to statistics from the Swedish Pensions Agency. In the DC framework, the gender distribution of pension income reflects the distribution of earnings before retirement. This is reflected in turn in the fact that almost one-half of all retired women (48 percent) have a guarantee component in their overall benefit, whereas only 14 percent of retired men do.

Because the relative importance of the guarantee tapers off with increasing NDC and FDC benefits, although there are many recipients, the guarantee benefits account for a small share (4 percent) of total benefit payments to pensioners (table 2.3).

Both the guarantee and the housing allowance are tax-financed and paid through the government budget, as a component of social policy for persons age 65 and older. The discussion of the housing allowance is revisited in greater depth in "The Crucial Role of the Swedish Housing Allowance for the Relatively Poor Elderly."

THE "BLIP" IN THE OVERALL REPLACEMENT RATES

Returning to table 2.2, first note that the ceiling on earnings that generate contributions to the NDC (contribution rate of 16 percent), FDC (contribution rate of 2.5 percent), and typical occupational supplement below the ceiling (contribution rate of 4.5 percent)

TABLE 2.3 **Distribution of Sweden's total public pension expenditures in 2016**

	Billions of SKr	% of total
NDC, including transition pensions	282.3	91
FDC pensions	7.0	2
Guarantee benefits	13.4	4
Housing allowances	8.4	3
Total	311.1	100

SOURCE: Swedish Pensions Agency 2016; *Ekonomisk trygghet vid ålderdom*, Proposition 2016/17:1, Swedish Government Publication 2017 (http://www.regeringen.se/4a6b4d/contentassets/e926a751d9eb4c978c4d892c659ebc8e /utgiftsomrade-11-ekonomisk-trygghet-vid-alderdom).

NOTE: FDC = financial defined contribution; NDC = nonfinancial defined contribution; SKr = Swedish kronor.

is relatively low. Above the ceiling the occupational scheme constitutes the entire supplementary pension, typically financed by a contribution rate of up to 30 percent. In the theoretical replacement rate calculations performed by the OECD, FDC schemes are assumed to earn a real rate of return of 3 percent and the NDC scheme a rate of 2 percent.

Second, the average income earner has a replacement rate of 64 percent after tax, generated totally by contributions on earnings below the ceiling. However, the replacement rate increases as larger segments of an individual's earnings (and, thus contribution to the FDC scheme) rise above the ceiling for contributions to the public NDC and FDC schemes. This explains the "blip" in the overall result in table 2.2.

A clear way to reduce the scale of this blip would be to require the occupational schemes to adhere to the same overall contribution rate of some 23 percent, which is the contribution rate below the ceiling, to the same percentage both below and above the ceiling. Beyond this, it is nevertheless the case that the result is driven by the difference in the basic fundamentals, that is, the underlying differences between the rates of return.

Finally, why 30 percent instead of 23 percent? Apparently, people with higher earnings are willing to contribute a higher percentage of their earnings to their pension savings for the future—otherwise this rate would not have been negotiated, as in the end it is paid with forgone in-pocket earnings and current consumption. One can also argue that the outcome of FDC schemes depends on a much more volatile outcome for returns, with cyclical troughs that can last up to a decade (for example, the 1970s)—and who knows what the financial market will deliver in 40 years? And, finally, this chosen construction supports the premise that risk aversion decreases with increasing income.

Finally, the blip in table 2.2 is an unintentional design "accident," given that the transition of the occupational schemes from largely DB to largely DC occurred following the 1994 reform legislation—not at the same time. In fact, the last major occupational scheme to join the FDC club was that for private white-collar workers, about 10 years after the reform of public pensions. Clearly, this "kink" in the replacement rates for the overall pension system ought to be addressed by policy makers.

THE GENDER GAP IN PENSIONS

In 2014, the average pension for women was 77 percent of the average for men. If rights earned by women in conjunction with childbirth are added, the average pensionable income of women was 84 percent of the average pensionable income of men (Departementsserien 2016:19 p. 283ff). And the discrepancy is believed to remain well into the future (Swedish Social Insurance Inspectorate 2017). According to calculations in the latter report, persons working in municipal services—for example, care services for the elderly and functionally impaired, education, and social services—will continue to have the lowest pensions. This is, of course, a direct reflection of the generally low wages of persons (mostly women) working with care services provided by the municipalities.

Women's lifetime earnings from formal work are lower than men's for three reasons. The first is wage discrimination—that is, lower wages and salaries for the same work as performed by men. The second factor is that jobs in which women dominate the labor force—health care, child care outside the home, care of the aged and persons with functional disabilities, and education—generally have a lower average wage level than men's low-wage occupations. The third factor is that women choose to work part-time to a significant extent. Hence, although women work almost as many years as men, they work fewer hours per week over the whole working career.

The drivers can be viewed as "structural" factors associated with the traditional division of child care and work in the home, where women still perform more of these tasks than men according to time use studies performed by Statistics Sweden. The bottom line is that it is not, then, the pension system that is at fault. Instead it is a combination of discriminatory labor market structures and individual behavior, discussed in greater detail in Klerby, Larsson, and Palmer (2013, 2019).[19]

The results of Klerby, Larsson, and Palmer (2013, 2019) demonstrate that one or more of three possible policy reforms could satisfactorily address this issue: (a) enabling joint annuities—with the joint annuity as the default—for married and cohabiting couples in the public NDC and FDC schemes (Klerby, Larsson, and Palmer 2013); (b) sharing of accounts during a succession (up to 10–12 child-care years—or over a whole life [Klerby, Larsson, and Palmer 2019]); and (c) providing child-care-right account add-ons past the present age of four up until the youngest child reaches 10 or 12 years of age. The first two studies cited here calculate that both of the first proposals would replace a considerable cost for the tax-financed guarantee benefit and housing allowance. Last, but most importantly, these would considerably reduce the relative poverty of divorced women and those women who become single households in old age following the death of a spouse. The joint annuity is the obvious measure in the latter circumstance.

THE ECONOMIC STANDARD OF PENSIONERS

Regardless of which measure is chosen, only about 1 percent of persons age 65 and older live in "absolute poverty" (data last available for 2013). If the definition chosen for the low economic standard is 60 percent instead of 50 percent of the median disposable weighted household income, about 11.4 percent of those age 65 and older met this standard (in 2013). About 20 percent of single-person households age 65 and older (predominantly women) had a relative standard below 60 percent of the median disposable income of all persons, compared with only about 4 percent of households with two adults with at least one household member age 65 and older (Swedish Ministry of Finance 2015).[20]

In conclusion, note that the deterioration of the relative standard of persons age 65 and older compared with adult households under age 65 can be wholly attributed to a lower real rate of growth in pension income compared with wage income. This in turn reflects the fact discussed separately above that the Swedish NDC annuity is front-loaded with a rate of real wage indexation of 1.6 percent per year, and then supplemented with inflation indexation (which is neutral for the replacement rate) and the difference between the front-loading factor of 1.6 percent and the actual rate of change in the average wage rate. In addition, the guarantee and housing minimum benefits are indexed to the CPI, but real changes require ad hoc political decisions.

THE ROLE OF INDEXATION

"Overview of Sweden's Pension System" explains the indexation of accounts and benefits, including when the solvency ratio is negative and the balancing index is triggered. What is important here is that the method of creating the Swedish NDC[21] gives a constant annuity value throughout life, adjusted in the Swedish construction by (a) the actual difference on a yearly basis between the income index and assumed real rate of return of 1.6 percent, and (b) the rate of inflation.

Sweden's method of front-loading the NDC annuity with an assumption about the future rate of change in productivity and, thus, long-term real wage growth, redistributes individual capital balances to the initial years of a pensioner's life. This resonates well with the assumption that people would rather have more resources now and discount the future (that is, their time preference is biased toward present time). It is also an implicit redistribution from persons who live longer to those who have shorter lives, who generally speaking have lower lifetime income and pension balances when they become pensioners. This is discussed in greater depth in Palmer and Zhao de Gossson de Varennes (2019).

In closing, note that the Swedish guarantee granted initially to public pensions—which is means tested against the original public NDC and FDC benefits together—is price indexed. This means that, generally speaking, the Swedish pensioner's income is adjusted for inflation (with the CPI) through the NDC and guarantee benefits, but relative to the income of a contemporary wage earner, the pensioner's standard declines steadily throughout his or her life.

THE CRUCIAL ROLE OF THE SWEDISH HOUSING ALLOWANCE FOR THE RELATIVELY POOR ELDERLY

The Swedish means-tested housing allowance for pensioners, presented in the "Introduction," is designed to provide a sufficient income supplement to pensioners with a low-income standard—in early as well as later years.

According to information from the Swedish Pensions Agency, about 13 percent of all pensioners live in households receiving the means-tested housing supplement, attesting to its important role. This is especially the case for elderly singles, usually women, who are often younger than their male partners and live longer. A principal factor underlying the decline in the income standard of elderly single women was that neither the level of the guarantee nor the ceiling on the housing allowance was increased significantly, aside from a yearly CPI adjustment, during the period 2003–17. In this period the average rate of growth of real wages was well over 2 percent per year. This fact alone contributed to an increasing relative gap between low-income pensioners and the median income of the population (Nelsson, Nieuwenhuis, and Alm 2019).

Conclusions and Recommendations for Improvement

Several general conclusions emerge from this review of the Swedish NDC public pension system, encompassing the NDC scheme, the public FDC scheme, and the minimum income guarantee, as follows.

Financial stability. The Swedish NDC scheme is financially very healthy. The Swedish fertility rate is now (and has historically been) high, at about 1.8–1.9 children per woman. With positive net immigration, continuous growth in the working-age population has occurred, and Sweden's employment rates of both men and women are the highest in the EU (EC 2018), as is the average age of exit from the labor force with retirement.

Two caveats arise, however. The first is that it is difficult for immigrants to establish themselves in the Swedish labor market. The second is that women's average lifetime earnings—the basis for pension capital in DC schemes—is about 75 percent of men's, which is reflected in similar inequality in pensions. This reflects the gender gap in sharing of home care responsibilities and structurally determined gender wage discrimination—primarily in the difference in the average wage for women working in care and education compared with the average wage in male-dominated jobs.

Adequacy. The replacement rate in the NDC scheme for the career worker born in 1950 (age 65 in 2015) based expected lifetime benefits in relation to lifetime income at 64–65 percent. It increases to about 70 percent by working until age 68. This said, wage discrimination combined with women's decisions to work part-time while children are growing up risks them ending their lives in relative poverty with the death of a spouse or cohabiting partner. The pension system cannot make right all the wrongs of the labor market. Given this, one obvious recommendation for Sweden is to expand the scope of child-care pension supplements to an even higher age and introduce rules making it possible to share pension rights before and at retirement. In addition, Swedish politicians could improve the coverage and amount of the component of the overall minimum income, which constitutes the most important supplement to the income of elderly women who become single toward the end of life: this entails increasing the means-tested housing allowance that tops up the guarantee pension.

Minimum pension age. According to the agreement between six political parties, representing about 80 percent of the votes in Parliament in December 2017, the minimum pension age will be increased gradually from age 61 to age 64 during 2020–26; the age to claim a guarantee benefit from age 65 to 66 (2023); and the age at which employers have the right to lay off workers only because of age from 67 to 69 (starting with 68 in 2020). These ages will then be indexed to life expectancy. This provides a strong incentive for people to earn higher benefits by working longer, which yields a higher benefit at retirement.

Life expectancy projections. Research shows that the method presently used by the Swedish Pensions Agency—as well as pension administrations in many other countries—systematically underestimates the increase in life expectancy. A strategy must be developed to deal with this issue.

The NDC fund. Three rules need to be considered:

- Determination of the maximum fund size
- Given a maximum fund size, how the "surplus" should be distributed among participants
- Determination of a procedure to bridge over economic recessions and stock market drops, given that economic and financial market recovery is inevitable.

The FDC (premium pension) funds. The rules for participating funds need to become stricter and safer, to tighten practices and supervision to prevent fraud and misuse of pension savers' capital. This also means that the number of participating companies and the overall number of individual funds offered by companies will certainly be reduced.

Contribution rate. The de facto contribution rate to the combined public NDC and FDC schemes is not the original 18.5 percent, but slightly lower as a result of the use of pre- and post-tax adjustments. Increasing it to 18.5 percent would be to the advantage of all future participants, while creating medium-term liquidity, which could be taken into the picture if or when a correction in the life expectancy factor in computing annuities is considered.

Better coordination of public and occupational schemes. Better coordination would be accomplished in cooperation with labor market partners representing labor and management interests. The aims would be as follows:

- Straighten out the kink in the replacement rates (illustrated in table 2.2)
- Offer only single individual and joint life annuities, eliminating phased withdrawals (where they exist, that is, in the FDC scheme)
- Introduce the same contribution rate across occupational schemes for all levels of earnings.

This list is long and the numerous issues identified based on more than 20 years of experience can provide food for thought for countries introducing or improving their existing NDC (and FDC) public pension schemes.

Notes

1. Könberg, Palmer, and Sundén (2006) discuss the important enabling political backdrop of the Swedish pension reform. Many references to the specifics of the Swedish NDC pension scheme now exist, including Palmer (1999a, 1999b, 2002, 2006b, 2013); Settergren (2001, 2013); Könberg (2008) (which addresses the contention of the time that NDC is "old wine in new bottles"); Chłoń-Domińczak, Franco, and Palmer (2012) (which compares NDCs in Italy, Latvia, Poland, and Sweden); and Palmer (2013) (which discusses the equilibrium properties of a generic NDC).

2. This also includes people living in other countries commuting to work in Sweden or with previous earnings from work in Sweden, with significant numbers coming from adjoining Scandinavian countries, the Baltic states, and Poland.

3. Almost all employees in Sweden are covered by one of four major (and some minor) labor management agreements and, thereby, are covered by occupational supplements to the universal public commitment.

4. Note that contributions have an employee and an employer component, explained in more detail in "Overview of Sweden's Pension System."

5. At the time, Swedish pension experts had access to a 40-year-old report of the Swedish Pension Commission that advocated something similar to what has become NDC (Åkesson 1950), with individual accounts but only partially prefunded. Instead, the DB ATP scheme emerged and was introduced in 1960—tailor-made with a more generous and politically more attractive DB profile.

6. The money itself was invested in government bonds during the transition before 1999.

7. See Palmer (2006a) for a more detailed presentation of the Swedish transition procedure, as well as other alternatives, including those used in Latvia and Poland.

8. The ratio for persons born in 1954 was 100 percent; that is, they received the entire pension solely based on their individual account values. Persons born in 1953 received 95 percent of the NDC pension and 5 percent of the old system pension; those born in 1944 got 50 percent, and so on.

9. The agreement also encompasses an increase in the age for receipt of disability and unemployment insurance from 65 to 66 (2023).

10. A recent econometric study finds a significant effect of the reform on the retirement choice of men born in 1944, who reached age 65 in 2009 (Qi 2016).

11. See Palmer (2013) for a more exact mathematical presentation of NDC and its dynamics.

12. The technique legislated and employed is presented in the Technical Appendix to any annual *Orange Report* of the Swedish Pensions Agency.

13. In practice, the balancing index becomes an extra component of indexation when the mechanism is triggered.

14. Where the underlying income base for contributions from individuals and employers on their behalf is the NDC scheme's income base, which can differ from the national accounts' definition.

15. This is the age at which disability benefits are converted into old-age pension benefits and at which people can qualify to receive a guarantee benefit. In addition, because 65 was seen as a "normal" pension age before the introduction of the NDC and FDC account schemes, this norm was hard to erase from people's thoughts. In fact, despite clear information in the *Orange Letter*, many people (couples especially) choose to forgo the considerably higher pension they could receive by staying in the labor force another one or two years.

16. A similar effect can be achieved by indexing directly with the rate of change in the contribution database, but the adjustment process is likely to be much longer. See, for example, the simulations in Chłoń-Domińczak, Franco, and Palmer (2012).

17. The initial contribution rate was set so as to exceed the necessary financing of yearly pension payments. This overfunding continued into the 1990s. A study of the combined effects on private and public financial saving, by Markowski and Palmer (1979), found that the overfunding of the ATP scheme from 1960 to 1975 led to a 4 percent decline in private savings with an equivalent increase in public saving during the initial years. Note that in this way the baby boomers funded savings to cover their extra cost to the next generation.

18. Denmark, France, Italy, the Netherlands, Norway, Sweden, the United Kingdom, and the United States.

19. These factors are discussed for Sweden in greater depth in Klerby, Larsson, and Palmer (2019).

20. Table 3.1 from *Fördelningspolitisk redogörelse* is a yearly publication of the Swedish Ministry of Finance, presented regularly in conjunction with the government's spring budget.

21. Italy and Norway adopted the same model, albeit with a lower discount rate than Sweden's 1.6 percent.

References

Åkesson, O. A. 1950. "Allmän Pensionsförsäkring. Förslag Angivet av Pensionsutredningen." SOU 1950:33, Stockholm.

Alho, Juha, Jorge Bravo, and Edward Palmer. 2013. "Annuities and Life Expectancy in NDC." In *Nonfinancial Defined Contribution Pension Schemes in a Changing Pension World: Volume 2 Gender, Politics, and Financial Stability*, edited by Robert Holzmann, Edward Palmer, and David Robalino, 395–442. Washington, DC: World Bank.

Auerbach, Alan J., and Ronald Lee. 2011. "Welfare and Generational Equity in Sustainable Unfunded Pension Systems." *Journal of Public Economics* 95 (1): 16–27.

Chłoń-Domińczak, Agnieszka, Daniele Franco, and Edward Palmer. 2012. "The First Wave of NDC Countries—Taking Stock Ten Plus Years Down the Road." In *NDC Pension Schemes: Progress and Frontiers in a Changing Pension World: Volume 1 Lessons and Issues in Implementation*, edited by Robert Holzmann, Edward Palmer, and David Robalino, 31–84. Washington, DC: World Bank.

Diamond, Peter. 2003. *Taxation, Incomplete Markets and Social Security*. Cambridge, MA: MIT Press.

EC (European Commission). 2016. *Ageing Report 2015*. Brussels: European Commission.

———. 2018. *Ageing Report 2017*. Brussels: European Commission.

Gruber, Jonathon, and David A. Wise. 1999. "Introduction and Summary." In *Social Security Programs and Retirement around the World*, edited by Jonathon Gruber and David A. Wise, 1–37. Chicago, IL: University of Chicago Press.

Klerby, Anna, Bo Larsson, and Edward Palmer. 2013. "To Share or Not to Share—That's the Question." In *Nonfinancial Defined Contribution Pension Schemes in a Changing Pension World: Volume 2 Gender, Politics, and Financial Stability*, edited by Robert Holzmann, Edward Palmer, and David Robalino, 39–74. Washington, DC: World Bank.

———. 2019. "Bridging Partner Life-Cycle Earnings and Pension Gaps by Sharing NDC Accounts." In *Progress and Challenges of Nonfinancial Defined Contribution Pension Schemes: Volume 2 Addressing Gender, Administration, and Communication*, edited by Robert Holzmann, Edward Palmer, Robert Palacios, and Stefano Sacchi, Chapter 20. Washington, DC: World Bank.

Könberg, Bo. 2008. "The Swedish Model for Pension—New Wine in New Bottles." *Nordisk Försäkringstidskrift* 2/2008.

———. Edward Palmer, and Annika Sundén. 2006. "The NDC Reform in Sweden: The 1994 Legislation to the Present." In *Pension Reform—Issues and Prospects for Non-Financial Defined Contribution (NDC) Schemes*, edited by Robert Holzmann and Edward Palmer, 449–66. Washington, DC: World Bank.

Markowski, Aleksander, and Edward Palmer. 1979. "Social Insurance and Saving in Sweden." In *Social Security Versus Private Saving*, edited by George M. von Furstenberg, 167–222. Cambridge, MA: Ballinger Publishing Company.

Nelsson, Kenneth, Rense Nieuwenhuis, and Susanne Alm. 2019. "Sweden: Adjoining the Guarantee Pension with NDC." In *Progress and Challenges of Nonfinancial Defined Contribution Pension Schemes: Volume 1 Addressing Marginalization, Polarization, and the Labor Market*, edited by Robert Holzmann, Edward Palmer, Robert Palacios, and Stefano Sacchi, Chapter 10. Washington, DC: World Bank.

OECD (Organisation for Economic Co-operation and Development). 2015. *Pensions at a Glance 2015: OECD and G20 Indicators*. Paris: OECD Publishing.

Palmer, Edward. 1999a. "Exit from the Labor Force for Older Workers: Can the Swedish System Help?" *The Geneva Papers on Risk and Insurance* 24 (4): 461–72.

———. 1999b. "Individual Decisions and Aggregate Stability in the NDC System." National Social Insurance Board, Sweden.

———. 2000. "The Swedish Pension Reform Model. Framework and Issues." Social Protection Discussion Paper 0012, World Bank, Washington, DC.

———. 2002. "Swedish Pension Reform: Its Past and Future." In *Social Security Pension Reform in Europe*, edited by Martin Feldstein and Horst Siebert, 171–210. National Bureau of Economic Research. Chicago, IL: University of Chicago Press.

———. 2006a. "Conversion to NDCs—Issues and Models." In *Pension Reform—Issues and Prospects for Non-Financial Defined Contribution (NDC) Schemes*, edited by Robert Holzmann and Edward Palmer, 169–202. Washington, DC: World Bank.

———. 2006b. "What Is NDC?" In *Pension Reform—Issues and Prospects for Non-Financial Defined Contribution (NDC) Schemes*, edited by Robert Holzmann and Edward Palmer, 17–34. Washington, DC: World Bank.

————. 2013. "Generic NDC: Equilibrium, Valuation and Risk Sharing—With and Without NDC Bonds." In *Nonfinancial Defined Contribution Pension Schemes in a Changing Pension World: Volume 2 Gender, Politics, and Financial Stability*, edited by Robert Holzmann, Edward Palmer, and David Robalino, 309–42. Washington, DC: World Bank.

————. Juha Alho, and Yuwei Zhao de Gosson de Varennes. 2019. "Projecting Cohort Life Expectancy from the Changing Relationship between Period and Cohort Mortalities." Unpublished.

Palmer, Edward, and Yuwei Zhao de Gosson de Varennes. 2019. "Annuities in (N)DC Pension Schemes: Design, Heterogeneity, and Estimation Issues." In *Progress and Challenges of Nonfinancial Defined Contribution Pension Schemes: Volume 1 Addressing Marginalization, Polarization, and the Labor Market*, edited by Robert Holzmann, Edward Palmer, Robert Palacios, and Stefano Sacchi, Chapter 13. Washington, DC: World Bank.

Qi, Haodong. 2016. "Prolonged Working Life in Sweden—A Result of the Great Pension Reform?" In *Live Longer, Work Longer? Evidence from Sweden's Ageing Population*. PhD dissertation, Department of Economic History, Lund University, Lund, Sweden.

Settergren, Ole. 2001. "The Automatic Balancing Mechanism of the Swedish Pension System." *Wirtschaftspolitische Blätter* 2001 (4): 339–49.

————. 2013. "A Decade of Actuarial Accounting for the NDC Scheme in Sweden." In *Pension Reform—Issues and Prospects for Non-Financial Defined Contribution (NDC) Schemes*, edited by Robert Holzmann and Edward Palmer, 361–94. Washington, DC: World Bank.

————, and Boguslav Mikula. 2006. "The Rate of Return of Pay-As-You-Go Pension Systems: A More Exact Consumption-Loan Model of Interest." In *Pension Reform—Issues and Prospects for Non-Financial Defined Contribution (NDC) Schemes*, edited by Robert Holzmann and Edward Palmer, 117–48. Washington, DC: World Bank.

Swedish Ministry of Finance. 2015. Fördelningspolitisk redogörelse. Ministry of Finance, Government of Sweden, Stockholm.

Swedish Ministry of Health and Social Affairs. 2016. Departementserrien 2016:19. "Jämställda pensioner (Gender-equal pensions)." Swedish Ministry of Health and Social Affairs, Stockholm.

Swedish Ministry of Health and Social Affairs. 2017. "Departementsserien 1992:89. 1992. "A Reformed Pension System—Background, Principles and Sketch." Translation to English of Memorandum of the Pension Working Group. Translation of Departementsserien 1992:89. Swedish Ministry of Health and Social Affairs, Stockholm.

Swedish Pensions Agency. 2016. *Orange Report—The Annual Report of the Swedish Pension System*. Stockholm: Swedish Pensions Agency.

————. 2017. *Orange Report—The Annual Report of the Swedish Pension System*. Stockholm: Swedish Pensions Agency.

Swedish Social Insurance Inspectorate. 2017. *Women's and Men's Pensions: An Analysis of Gender Differences and Pension Dispersion Today and in the Future*. Report 2017:8. Stockholm: Swedish Social Insurance Inspectorate.

Zhao de Gosson de Varennes, Yuwei. 2016. "Private Information on Life Expectancy and Choice of Retirement Age in Defined Contribution Pension Schemes." PhD Dissertation, *Benefit Design, Retirement Decisions and Welfare Within and Across Generations in Defined Contribution Pension Schemes*. Economic Studies 157. Department of Economics, Uppsala University, Uppsala, Sweden.

CHAPTER 3

The Latvian NDC Scheme: Success under a Decreasing Labor Force

Edward Palmer and Sandra Stabina

Introduction

Before gaining its independence in 1990, Latvia was a state within the Soviet Union; as such its economy was integrated into the Soviet economy. The Soviet pension system Latvia inherited in 1990 was financially unsustainable and inappropriate for a market economy. The pension age was 55 for women and 60 for men, but the many exceptions based on special rights effectively reduced these to significantly lower ages. The issue of special rights for selected groups presented a challenge to fairness, and the low exit ages worked against affordability and long-term sustainability.

The number of persons for whom contributions were being paid fell by almost 50 percent between 1990 and 1994, whereas the ratio of pensioners to contributors increased by 67 percent (Fox and Palmer 1999). A new government took office in 1993; in early 1995 it decided to introduce a nonfinancial defined contribution (NDC) scheme—to be supplemented later with a financial defined contribution (FDC) scheme and with a minimum income guarantee for old-age pensioners. The Latvian NDC scheme was implemented, with a minimum guarantee at the floor of the system, on January 1, 1996, accompanied by a process to phase out the various special rights regimes. With the equalization of rights earned by a contribution of a given amount, the Latvian pension system began to progress toward a universal public pension scheme, with the same rules applying to all. This process included the equalization of pension ages to age 65 for both men and women, to be fully achieved by 2025.

Personal accounts constitute the basic building block of NDC and FDC pension schemes. The use of individual accounts communicates that individuals are saving for their own pensions. With the implementation of NDC in 1996, Soviet workbook logs became the basis for creating initial capital based on rights acquired before 1996.[1] From the outset, employees and the self-employed paid earnings-based contributions into the NDC scheme. The initial NDC contribution rate was 20 percent in 1996.

The authors are grateful for the suggestions generously provided by Herve Boulhol and Sonia Buchholtz on the first draft and by Ingus Alliks, State Secretary of the Latvian Ministry of Welfare, on all drafts.

When Latvia introduced its FDC scheme in 2001, the overall contribution rate of 20 percent was shared between the NDC and FDC components. Since 2017 the division has been 14 percent for the NDC and 6 percent for the FDC scheme. Together with a minimum pension, the mandatory NDC and FDC schemes constitute the overall universal public system, with the same rules for all. In addition to the public schemes, it is possible to contract private individual and occupational pensions, although these have yet to become prominent components of the overall pension landscape.

Social policy is pursued in the context of NDC through "add-ons" to individual accounts. Because add-ons are not supported by contributions from individuals themselves, they are instead financed with tax revenues from the state budget or other special social insurance budgets designated for this purpose. The Latvian NDC scheme contains a number of public policy add-ons. Examples are contributions granted and paid through tax revenues for insurance compensation for periods away from work owing to unemployment, sickness, and disability, and family benefits in conjunction with childbirth. In this way, distributional policy is added into the Latvian NDC scheme.[2]

This chapter presents an assessment and discussion of the development of the Latvian NDC over its first 20 years. It also provides a picture of what projected demographic and economic developments say about its financial sustainability and affordability in the half decade beginning in 2020. The story of the Latvian NDC begins in 1996 with a country in steady demographic decline low fertility rates and a high emigration rate. Despite this, labor force growth was positive because of the remarkable increase in the formal labor supply and the density of contributions in the first 20 years of the Latvian NDC.

The 2008–09 recession and its aftermath forced Latvia to revisit its 1995 decision to split the 20 percent contribution rate equally between the NDC and FDC schemes. This was an unaffordable decision from the very beginning given the commitments made to current pensioners and the financial reality. This unrealistically high division of the overall contribution rate was the result of a political decision that was never supported by calculations—a lesson learned the hard way.[3]

The analysis begins with a presentation of the underlying demographics and the projected development of the labor force. It then turns from an analysis of the first 20 years with NDC to an analysis of the financial sustainability and affordability of the NDC scheme going forward to 2070. The backdrop is an assumed continued decline of about 1 percent per year in the working-age population, leading to a similar decline in the labor force. At the same time the large pre-independence birth cohorts of pensioners begin to retire in the 2030s, accompanied by the continued financing of the growth of the FDC scheme.

Despite these financial challenges, the analysis shows that the NDC scheme is moving forward on a long-term equilibrium path, through continuous adjustments using the automatic stabilizers built into the valorization of accounts and indexation of benefits, and the life-expectancy component of the life annuity. However, the analysis also shows that extra revenues beyond those generated in accordance with the modelling assumptions of the European Commisson's *Ageing Report 2018* (EC 2018) will be needed during an interim period of 20–30 years beginning in 2030. The study identifies and assesses the possibilities of more optimistic development of the labor market—bolstered by policy designed to support increased labor force participation and continued high growth—and closes with a discussion of the financial options available to Latvia in the future. The final section analyzes the adequacy of benefits based on both empirical and theoretical replacement rates (TRRs).

Latvian Demographics and Labor Force Participation

THE FERTILITY RATE REBOUNDED IN THE 2000s FROM RECORD LOWS IN THE 1990S

Fertility rates within the present European Union (EU) were relatively high in the 1960s given economic stability, growth, and postwar optimism. The average fertility rate was 2.67 children per woman in 1960, following the baby boom of the 1950s, but by 1970 the rate had dropped to 2.31.[4] This decline continued, reaching 1.97 in 1980 and 1.79 in 1990. By the turn of the century, the average for all present EU countries together was less than 1.5 children per woman.

Latvia's total fertility rate hovered around 1.9–2.1 during the period 1950–84, staying close to but below the rate of 2.1 needed to reproduce the population. With the dissolution of the Soviet Union—accompanied by disruption of the economy, loss of jobs, and uncertainty about the future—and ensuing economic uncertainty, Latvia's fertility rate fell to about 1.2 in 1999 from about 2.0 at the time of independence from the Soviet Union. Beginning in 2000 it increased gradually to 1.7–1.75 in 2016 and 2017. According to the 2018 projections of the European Commission's Economic Policy Committee Working Group on Ageing Populations and Sustainability (EC-EPC [AWG]), Latvia will achieve a total fertility rate of close to 1.85 during the period 2020–70,[5] still less than the 2.1 rate needed to maintain a steady population size—and labor force.

THE WORKING-AGE POPULATION SHRANK FROM 1996 TO 2016 BUT THE LABOR FORCE GREW BECAUSE OF INCREASED PARTICIPATION

A second significant demographic event during the 20-year period from 1995 was the decline in Latvia's working-age population (that is, those ages 20–64) by about 20 percent (figure 3.1), the result of net emigration (EC-EPC [AWG]). The decline was largely within the age group 20–39. Despite this, the share of the working-age population participating in the labor force was about 11 percent higher in 2016 than in 1995 (figure 3.1).

Table 3.1 shows that the current projections for growth of the Latvia working-age population embody a close to 45 percent decline from 2016 to 2070.

The extremely low fertility rate throughout the period 1995–2015 will have a substantial negative impact on growth of the labor force through the 2030s, exacerbated by continued net emigration of younger workers. As a result of these two demographic forces, the working-age population is projected to fall from about 1.2 million persons in 2017 to 650,000 persons by 2060–70, despite an assumption of fertility rates of about 1.85 from 2020 onward.[6]

The obvious challenge for Latvia is to counter the continued outflow of working-age persons while at least maintaining and preferably increasing the present fertility rate. The latter could be promoted through family policies of better pre- and after-school public daycare, and earnings replacement for time away from work after childbirth.

FIGURE 3.1 **Development of Latvia's working-age population (ages 20–64) and contributing labor force, 1995–2015**

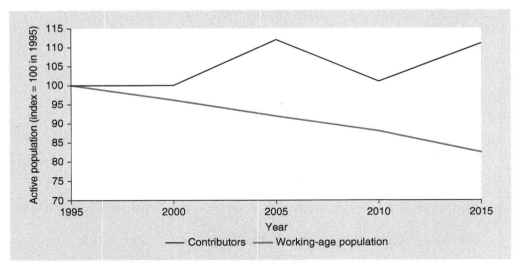

SOURCE: Department of Social Insurance, Latvian Ministry of Welfare.

TABLE 3.1 **Working-age population (ages 20–64), 2016–70**
thousands of people

2016	2020	2030	2040	2050	2060	2070
1,186	1,108	922	817	726	645	660

SOURCE: EC-EPC (AWG) 2018 projections for the *Ageing Report, 2018* (EC 2018).

AN INCREASING RATE OF PARTICIPATION IN THE FORMAL LABOR FORCE WAS ACCOMPANIED BY INCREASINGLY MORE CONTRIBUTORS PAYING CONTRIBUTIONS ON A REGULAR MONTHLY BASIS

For the purposes of this study, the Latvian State Social Insurance Agency performed a study of the monthly development of contributions from 1996 to 2016. The database was drawn from the entire working-age population—defined in this context as persons ages 15–63 from 1996 to 2016. Age 15 is the first possible age at which to become a contributor, and in 2016 age 62 and 9 months was the average age of exit.

All monthly contribution payments for all individuals born in the years 1953, 1961, 1971, and 1981 were examined to follow the dynamics of contribution payments of the cohorts born in 1953 and 1961, who were already working-age cohorts in 1996; the cohorts born in 1971, who were 25 years old when the NDC was introduced in 1996; and the 1981 birth cohort, which turned 15 in 1996. The 1981 cohort was the first to be completely covered by the Latvian NDC. The cohort born in 1953 retired in 2016, with an average exit age of 62.7.

The results (see annex 3A) show that contribution density increased dramatically in the period 1996–2016.[7]

- Contributions were paid at age 43 for 12 months per year by 72 percent of those born in 1953, by 78 percent of those born in 1961, and by 83 percent of those born in 1971. A similar pattern can be observed for persons age 35. About 69 percent of those born in 1961 paid a full 12 months of contributions at age 35, compared with 78 percent of those age 35 born in 1971 and 82 percent of those age 35 born in 1981.

- The assessment shows no strong gender differences, although about 2–4 percentage points more women than men pay all 12 months per year.

- By definition, these data say nothing about the level of contributions, and no systematic data exist to examine contribution amounts. However, for about 30 percent of all contributors, contributions are paid on an amount no greater than the minimum wage, according to information from the Ministry of Welfare, compiled by the Latvian State Social Insurance Agency.

- The overall conclusions regarding the development of the labor force in 1996–2016 are that (a) both the number of contributors and the number of months they paid contributions increased during Latvia's first 20 years with NDC, and (b) the increase in contributors and contribution density—months with paid contributions per contributor—more than outweighed the negative effect in the decline in the working-age population during the same period.

DEMOGRAPHIC DEPENDENCY RATIOS

A projected fertility rate of 1.85 and the continued net emigration of the younger population is reflected in the fall in the ratio of working-age persons to persons age 65 and older (that is, the demographic support ratio) from 4.2 in 2015 to 3.1 in 2060. More importantly for the system's finances, the population of Latvia (figure 3.2) and the number of persons available for employment (ages 20–64) relative to the number of persons age 65 and older (pensioners) (that is, the demographic dependency ratio) will decline from about 4.2 to about 2.2 in coming decades (figure 3.3).

FIGURE 3.2 **Latvian population projections, 2015–60**

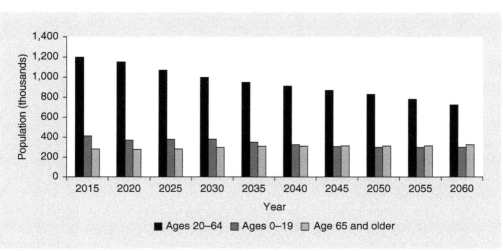

SOURCE: United Nations 2017.

FIGURE 3.3 Latvian demographic dependency ratios, 2015–60

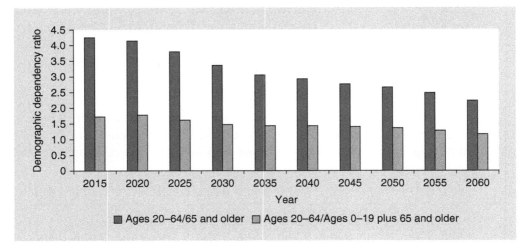

SOURCE: United Nations 2017.

If child dependents are also included, the decline in the ratio of the working-age population to persons age 65 and older and children together is equally dramatic—from about 1.75 to about 1.2 (figure 3.3). The projected decline in the labor force mirrors the demographic decline, as the next section shows. The economic dependency ratios are even higher.

Financial Sustainability of Latvia's NDC Scheme

By design an NDC scheme embodies dynamic adjustment of the pension system's liabilities.[8] This adjustment occurs through two mechanisms. One is the valorization of account values and indexation of pensions; the other is through application of the life expectancy factor in determining the amount of benefit to be paid out yearly over a retiree's lifetime. Using the EC-EPC (AWG) 2018 assumptions for Latvia, this section examines the long-term financial prospects for the Latvian NDC pension scheme for 2020–70.

GROWTH OF THE CONTRIBUTION WAGE BASE AND INDEXATION THROUGH 2016 IN LATVIA'S NDC AND PROJECTIONS FOR THE FUTURE

The analysis begins with a dissection of the growth rate of the nominal-valued contribution wage base. This is described by three parameters, $g + \lambda + p$, where g is the rate of growth of the real per capita contribution wage, λ is the rate of growth of the number of contributors, and p is the rate of growth of prices, measured by the consumer price index (CPI). These three factors are also the components of the valorization of Latvian NDC participants' accounts.[9]

According to new legislation in 2016, beginning in 2017 NDC benefits were to be indexed by $p + 0.50 \times (g + \lambda)$, which only partially covers the entire theoretically correct index $p + g + \lambda$, that is, the growth of the nominal wage-sum. This is still the case for persons with contributions of up to 30 years. But from 2018 the value of indexation for 30+ years is 0.60 for contribution years in the interval 30–39, and 0.70 for 40 or more contribution years. In the initial years, benefits were indexed solely using the change in CPI, but this was slowly changed to include a fraction of g + λ. However, from the outset the original goal was to increase the indexation of benefits to the full potential level, p + g + λ.

The terms λ and g are the two dynamic adjustment factors that work together to keep the NDC pension scheme on a long-term equilibrium gyrating around the fixed NDC contribution rate. The inflation rate has the well-known effect of maintaining the real purchasing value of accounts and pensions. Figure 3.4 plots the actual values of p, g, and λ through 2016 and projected values from 2017 through 2070. The projections shown in figure 3.4 are derived from the Latvian model, based on demographic and labor force participation assumptions provided by the EC-EPC (AWG). Several observations of importance emerge in connection with the dynamics shown in figure 3.4.

Figure 3.4 illustrates the dynamics of the NDC story; the results for financial stability and future contribution rates are discussed later in this chapter. To begin with, as already discussed, there was clear growth in employment (contributors) seen over the entire period. The dynamics of the development of contributors supports the contention that the DC scheme creates economic efficiency by providing a positive incentive for formal labor force participation. It is unknown to what degree the NDC design was responsible for the

FIGURE 3.4 **Rate of growth of real wage rate per capita and of contributors, and the rate of inflation, 1997–2070**

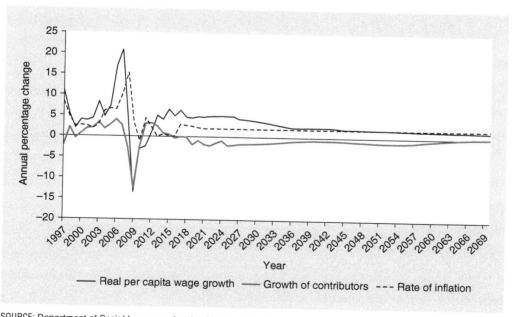

SOURCE: Department of Social Insurance, Latvian Ministry of Welfare.

NOTE: Based on actual values for 1997–2016 and projected values for 2017–70, using assumptions underlying the calculations performed for EC (2018). The rate of inflation is the deflator for wage growth.

strong increase in the number of contributors and to what extent this was just a natural result of the development of a formal market economy in the years following independence. Nevertheless, the role of the NDC accounts can be assumed to have been a part of the NDC scheme's success; that is, it must have tipped the scales in favor of supplying formal rather than informal labor in situations in which the option presented itself as an alternative.

Looking forward, as the small birth cohorts from 1995 to 2015 reach working age, they constitute a smaller group of potential workers in the decades beginning with 2020. And as already discussed, the younger cohorts are assumed to continue to opt for emigration from Latvia.

Second, the average rate of growth of real per capita wages was 4.9 percent over 1997–2016. Of course, the continued strong real wage growth seen in figure 3.4 is the result of steadily increasing productivity growth in Latvia and—with this—the development of a labor market with increasing long-term opportunities for new entrants, which means that the current projections for high emigration might be overly pessimistic.

Third, real wage rate growth of well over 2 percent is projected into the mid-2040s, and remains at about 2 percent thereafter. This results in a positive real wage-sum valorization of individual accounts and indexation of pensions around an average of 1.5 percent through the half century 2020–70. Despite the negative influence of the declining labor force—occurring because fertility rates are not sufficient (greater than 2.1) for population replacement and because of the added effect of the migration of younger workers from the country. The net result is lower increases in the valorization of worker accounts and indexation of pension benefits, compared with what "pure" wage indexation would yield without this adjustment—what is required to maintain financial stability.

Finally, two forces are at work in determining future prospects—a demographic effect and a labor supply effect. First it is the scale of the fertility rate that determines the number of new entrants into the labor force 15–25 years after birth. An increase in the fertility rate from the last observed value (2017) of 1.85 would improve prospects after about 2040 but cannot affect the size of the labor force until then. Of course, participation may continue to increase even more than projected. The obvious policy parameter that remains is increasing the age of labor force exit by increasing the minimum pension age beyond that prescribed by current legislation.

In summary, even with a large deduction for the negative labor force growth expected for 2020–70, full wage-sum indexation will yield positive real indexation to both NDC account holders and pensioners during the entire period.

THE MINIMUM RETIREMENT AGE IS SCHEDULED TO INCREASE IN THE FUTURE

The minimum age at which a pension can be claimed has been increasing since 2014 at the rate of three months per year and will reach 65 in January 2025. A pension age for both genders of 65 is in line with what is now the normal pension age in the EU. That said, some countries have already legislated increases to age 67 and many are considering or have legislated indexation of their minimum pension age to life expectancy.

Unisex life expectancy at age 60 in Latvia increased by 2.3 years from 1997 to 2017. This relatively rapid rate increase should be viewed in the overall context of accelerating increases in survival rates among 65- to 85-year-olds (Alho, Bravo, and Palmer 2013; Alho, Palmer, and Zhao de Gosson de Varennes 2019),[10] which is a strong indicator that this process is probably also at work in Latvia.

HOW THE FINANCIAL DEVELOPMENT OF THE NDC SCHEME WAS AFFECTED BY INTRODUCTION OF THE MANDATORY FDC SCHEME WITHIN A FIXED CONTRIBUTION RATE FOR BOTH OF 20 PERCENT

Moving from a pay-as-you-go to a prefunded pension system involves a transition period during which previous rights in the old pay-as-you-go pension scheme must be honored, while at the same time savings in the form of FDC contributions are channeled into FDC financial portfolios. The mechanism that originally made this transformation financially conceivable within the framework of a 20 percent contribution rate was the knowledge that the "baby boomers" of 1970–75 and 1980–85 would create a surplus in the NDC scheme for four decades after the turn of the century. Instead they sought work abroad.

The government's reform proposal in 1995 had three goals. The first was to share equally the 20 percent contribution rate between the NDC scheme to be introduced in 1996 and the FDC scheme to be introduced at a later date. The second was to reduce the overall contribution rate for social insurance expenditures from 38 percent in 1995 to 33 percent by 2003. The third was to begin wage indexation of pension benefits, also after 2002 (Fox and Palmer 1999). This combination of goals was too ambitious, however, as shown in a paper presented at the joint Swedish–World Bank NDC conference in 2003 and published in Palmer et al. (2006)—a total contribution rate of at least 24 percent would be required to cover total costs for both. The calculations performed in that study indicated, however, that NDC long-term sustainability could be maintained with a carve-out of a contribution rate of 6 percent for the new second pillar, retaining the overall contribution rate of 20 percent for the NDC and FDC schemes together. This effectively reduced the NDC contribution rate to 14 percent, while the pensions granted preceding the introduction of the FDC scheme were all based on an NDC rate of 20 percent. Furthermore, at the time these calculations were performed the strong flow of working-age emigrants beginning in the late 1990s had not really begun. Although emigration could be anticipated, the strength of the outflow and its duration were not anticipated.

Latvia introduced the FDC scheme in 2001 with a schedule aspiring to carve out one-half (10 percentage points) of the 20 percentage point NDC contribution rate for the FDC scheme. The initial contribution rate to the FDC scheme was 2 percent from 2001 to 2006, 4 percent in 2007, and 8 percent in 2008. The recession of 2009–11 hit Latvia particularly hard, however, with strong repercussions in the job market (see the relevant years in figure 3.4). The contribution base fell dramatically, with an accompanying drop of 33 percent in the wage-sum and thus contributions. To cover NDC expenditure commitments, the contribution rate to the FDC scheme was reduced to 2 percent in 2009–12. As the economy turned up, the FDC contribution rate was increased again to 4 percent in 2013 and 2014, to 5 percent in 2015, and to 6 percent in 2016—where it is scheduled to remain. This is thus the working premise for the financial sustainability analysis that follows.

HOW IS LATVIA MANAGING THE TRANSITION AND WHAT ARE THE PROSPECTS FOR THE COMING HALF CENTURY?

The total number of pensioners can be divided into three categories: persons who were already (Soviet) "old-law" pensioners when the reform was introduced in 1996; pensioners whose work records in the Soviet system through 1995 were converted into initial capital in individual accounts in the NDC scheme beginning in January 1996—that is, "transition rule" pensioners; and persons with their benefits computed solely from the new rules, in accordance with their account values in the NDC and FDC schemes (figure 3.5).

First note that old-law pensioners—persons granted benefits up through December 1995, some based on special conditions at ages as low as 40 and all women age 55—are mostly phased out by 2035. A second observation is that from 2045 on, pensioners with part of their total capital based on the transition rules begin to decline in number, and the number whose pensions are based completely on the new law (that is, NDC and FDC) begins to rise at an increasing rate.

THE PATH FOR NDC PENSION EXPENDITURES AND REVENUES MOVING TOWARD 2070

Figure 3.6 shows the projected development of pension expenditures expressed as a percentage of the contribution wage base. In 2016, the ratio of NDC expenditures to the contribution wage base was 13.3 percent, still less than the 14 percent contribution rate on individual income that gives rise to individual accounts. Note that FDC

FIGURE 3.5 **Distribution of pensions by pensioner type, 2016–70**

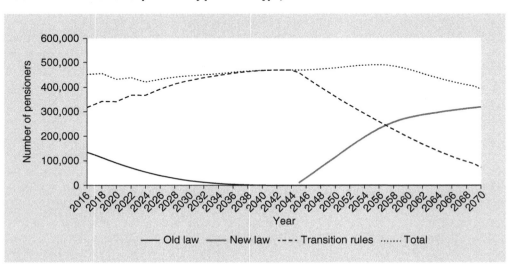

SOURCE: Department of Social Insurance, Latvian Ministry of Welfare. Projections are based on the assumptions underlying the calculations performed for EC (2018).

NOTE: Old-law pensioners, "transition-rule" pensioners, and pensioners with all rights earned in accordance with the 1996 reform (new law).

FIGURE 3.6 **Expenditures on pensions, 2016–70**

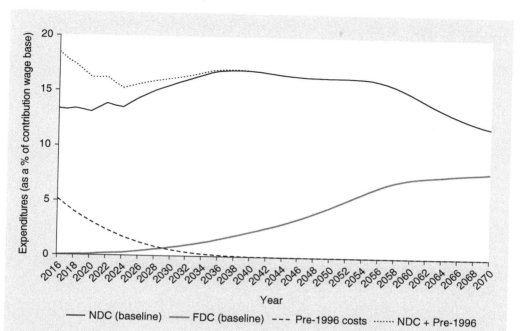

SOURCE: Department of Social Insurance, Latvian Ministry of Welfare. Projections are based on the assumptions underlying the calculations performed for EC (2018).

NOTE: NDC = nonfinancial defined contribution scheme; FDC = financial defined contribution scheme.

pension payments increase in strength from about 2030 at about the same time as the expenditures on pre-1996 benefits rapidly approach nil. Also noteworthy is the effect on expenditures of the large birth cohorts born before 1990 becoming pensioners beginning about 2035.

Figure 3.7 shows that the NDC scheme pension expenditures expressed as a percentage of the contribution wage base remain largely within a corridor corresponding to a contribution rate of 14–16 percent, moving into equilibrium at 14 percent in the 2050s. The predominant drivers are (a) the large birth cohorts of workers of the pre-1996 transition generation, (b) the small number of births (low fertility rates) after 1990, (c) strong net emigration of the working-age population in 1990–2020, and (d) expected strong net emigration through 2050.

The numbers behind the curves tell a clear story. In 2016, the ratio of NDC expenditures to the contribution base is 13.3 percent, that is, still well below the contribution rate of 14.0 percent. Finances still require a contribution rate of only 14.0 percent in 2025, but from here the ratio of expenditures to the contribution base climbs steadily to 16.7 percent in 2035. It begins to fall gradually beginning about 2040, reaching 15.0 percent in the early 2050s. The ratio gradually declines again to 14.0 percent in the late 2050s. In the end, and despite the assumed continuous fall in the working-age population from

FIGURE 3.7 **Expenditures on pensions—NDC and pre-1996, 2016–70**

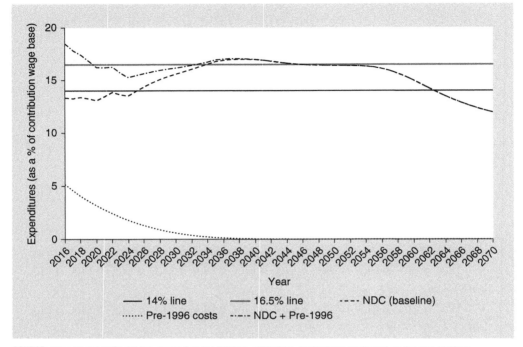

SOURCE: Department of Social Insurance, Latvian Ministry of Welfare. Projections are based on the assumptions underlying the calculations performed for EC (2018).

NOTE: NDC = nonfinancial defined contribution scheme.

2015 through 2070, the NDC pension scheme returns fully to equilibrium around 2060, with a ratio of NDC expenditures to the contribution base of only 12.0 percent as the last of the large prereform birth cohorts die out.

In summary, by the mid-2030s a contribution rate of about 16–17 percent will be required to finance NDC commitments if the "main" EC-EPC (AWG) 2018 assumption of an average 1 percent per year decline in the labor force from 2020 through 2070 becomes reality. Needless to say, the occurrence of an acute decline in the working-age population—especially during the period 2020–40—would keep the NDC scheme much closer to a 14 percent contribution rate through 2070. Generally speaking, the key issue for Latvia's pension policy going forward is to create a labor market that supports such a development. This is the topic of the next section.

HOW DOES LATVIA PLAN TO DEAL WITH THE PROJECTED DEFICIT IN REVENUES FOR THE PERIOD 2030–50?

Although Latvia has no explicit fund, the government—in this case the Ministry of Welfare—has an explicit framework of budgets for the various expenditures within the overall pension system and other areas of social insurance. At the time of this writing, in 2017, an overall amount of money equal to a contribution rate of 24.5 percent is budgeted for overall expenditures on pensions, including minimum pensions.

It is possible that the funds already available and those that will become available given present contribution rates will be sufficient to cover the 20-year deficit in revenues in 2030–50, which gradually declines with the present assumptions in the 2050s. The reason for optimism is that the assumptions underlying the projections for emigration of the working-age population may be much too pessimistic. Why is this?

A significant percentage of the projected deficit may be financed by an increase in the rate of participation—through a normal progressive increase in the average number of lifetime contribution years per person, all else equal, from the present assumption of 35 to 40–42 years by the beginning of the 2030s. Specifically, an increase to 42 years of work and contributions by about 2030 would increase the contribution base by 20 percent, thereby equalizing expenditures and revenues. Notably, the best performer in the EU (Sweden) was already at about 42 years for both men and women in 2016, with an average exit age slightly younger than 65. In addition, increases in the normal pension age beyond the presently legislated minimum pension age of 65—progressively to 68 by 2060—are in line with the projected increase in life expectancy at age 65. This creates more revenues from the contributions of those who continue to work and increases the liquidity of the NDC pension scheme. A third development that would generate more revenues is a more positive scenario for emigration over the coming half century, starting in the 2020s. This could be supported by a conscious policy to channel increasingly more resources from the second-pillar funds into both market-motivated and infrastructure investments, creating job opportunities and growth.

Adequacy of Benefits

The overall goal of the public pension system is to generate what is regarded to be a sufficient replacement rate deriving from the mandatory universal public pension commitment. Adequacy is defined by the average (actual) replacement rate (ARR) and the TRR under various assumptions, including before and after taxes. In the Latvian NDC framework, participants have to fulfill a qualifying condition of 15 years (to be increased to 20 in 2025) of contributions to qualify for an NDC benefit. Those who do not fulfill this criterion receive a minimum pension.

The replacement rate can be defined in several ways. Two definitions published in the European Commission's *Pension Adequacy Report* (EC 2015b) are the basis of table 3.2 and table 3.3, and are as follows:

Definition 1. The average replacement rate (ARR)

The ARR is calculated from all pensions (including survivors' pensions, and occupational and individual private plans). It is calculated as the median (pre-tax) sum of individuals' benefits for persons ages 65–74 in relation to the median (pre-tax) gross earnings per wage earner ages 50–59.[11] The ARR is shown in table 3.2. All other replacement rates in tables 3.2 and 3.3 are TRRs.

Definition 2. The TRR

The TRR is based on assumptions about the full-career worker and is calculated pre-tax (gross) and after tax (net). The hypothetical worker earns the average wage for 40 consecutive years from age 25 and retires at age 65 or at the country's standard pension age (denoted SPA in the tables). The assumed SPA for Latvia is age 62.

TABLE 3.2 **ARRs and TRRs for Latvia and selected European Union countries**

	(1) ARR Pre-tax 2013: Retirement at country's SPA[a]	(2) TRR Pre-tax 2013: LF=40 years to SPA[b]	(3) TRR After-tax 2013: LF=40 uninterrupted years to SPA[c]	(4) TRR After-tax 2013: LF=40 uninterrupted years from age 25 up to age 65[c]	(5) SPA in 2013[c]
Estonia	50	43	57	69	63
Latvia	48	47	65	72	62
Lithuania	49	41	53	66	M=62.7 W=60.6
Denmark	48	48	68	68	65
Finland	50	62	70	70	65
France	63	68	80	80	65
Germany	48	40	57	57	65.2
Sweden	60	69	69	69	65

SOURCE: The *2015 Pension Adequacy Report* (EC 2015b, Section 3.1.2).

NOTE: Average of men and women. ARR = average replacement rate; LF = labor force; M = men; SPA = standard pension age; TRR = theoretical replacement rate; W = women.

a. EC 2015b, Figure 3.1, page 125.

b. EC 2015b, Table 3.4, page 135.

c. EC 2015b, Table 3.2, page 118.

The hypothetical person is born in 1948 (a man) or 1951 (a woman) and retires in 2013 or 2021, respectively. For the TRR calculations for retirement in 2013, historical data are used. For calculations beyond 2013, the TRR calculations are based on historical data through 2013. Beginning in 2013, the EC-EPC (AWG) assumptions for real per capita wage, labor force growth, and inflation (2 percent) are used. The contribution rates used in the calculations are 14 percent (NDC) and 6 percent (FDC) beginning in 2016, together with the legislated rates going back in time. TRR calculations are performed separately for men and women because of their separate pension ages to 2025.

HOW LATVIA'S REPLACEMENT RATES COMPARE WITH THOSE OF OTHER EU COUNTRIES

The ARRs, which are based on actual empirical outcomes, are shown for Latvia and seven other EU countries in column (1) of table 3.2. Latvia's ARR is 48 percent, closely in line with that of all countries in the table except Sweden (60 percent) and France (63 percent).

Columns (2)–(4) of table 3.2 show the TRRs. Comparison of columns (2) and (3) shows that after-tax replacement rates are higher in Latvia than pre-tax replacement rates in all other countries except Sweden. The difference is 8–20 percentage points, with an 18 percentage point higher after-tax rate for Latvia.

A separate tax regime for pensioners proves to be important for Latvian pensioners: the after-tax effect on replacement rates in Latvia is second only to that in Denmark. Sweden is the only country in the table where the pre- and after-tax replacement rates are the same, reflecting the fact that earnings and pension income had largely the same tax rates in 2013. (Taxes on both wages and pensions have decreased since then.)

Together columns (3) and (4) in table 3.2 indicate that room remains to increase replacement rates by increasing the SPA from the present age to 65. The higher pension age boosts replacement rates in all three Baltic countries. The effect is due to two factors—higher contributions and actuarial adjustments in benefits deriving from the shorter length of longevity from an older age of retirement.

ASSUMPTIONS UNDERLYING THE CALCULATION OF THE EC-EPC (AWG) TRRs CALCULATIONS

Table 3.3 presents additional estimates based on historical data from before 2013, with more precise assumptions constructed on a country basis for the ages of entrance and exit and thus the length of average working careers. This is the group of assumptions also used for the macroeconomic calculations to 2060 in EC (2018). The assumptions regarding the ages of labor force entry and exit are from the cohort simulation model developed by the European Commission's Directorate-General for Economic and Financial Affairs.[12] These estimates are used to calculate the after-tax TRRs shown in table 3.3. Table 3.3 also provides information about the assumed career length, age of exit, and working life in years used in the calculations.

The last two columns in table 3.3 show that recently retired men and women in the Baltic states work and contribute considerably fewer years "today" than the 40 years assumed in the theoretical calculations in table 3.2. However, career lengths with exit at age 65 are expected to become considerably longer compared with career lengths for persons turning 65 in 2013, reflecting an increase in the minimum pension age and associated postponement in labor force exit with retirement for both genders to about 65 for both, combined with earlier entrance into the labor force. Given this increase in career length, compared with the actual career length in 2013 (column (3) in table 3.3), the TRRs for Latvian men and women are essentially the same as the results in column (4) in table 3.2. In other words, the EC-EPC (AWG) modelling motivates these outcomes based on increased working-career "profiles."

TABLE 3.3 **TRRs based on the EC-EPC (AWG) model of age of entry and exit into the labor force**

EU member state	(1) AWG TRRs based on career lengths and the exit age in column (2)		(2) AWG assumptions, years				(3) Actual working life in years (2013)	
			Exit age		Career length			
	M	W	M	W	M	W	M	W
Estonia	50.9	64.8	64.4	64.2	43.0	41.4	36.6	35.7
Latvia	73.8	70.9	64.6	64.0	43.0	40.8	35.0	34.6
Lithuania	53.3	54.7	62.8	61.9	40.6	38.1	34.1	34.2
Denmark	68.4	75.7	65.6	63.4	43.0	40.3	40.2	37.6
Finland	65.5	63.8	63.6	63.1	41.6	40.3	37.7	36.6
France	74.1	63.6	60.8	60.9	39.3	37.5	36.5	32.8
Germany	62.8	55.4	65.1	64.2	44.1	42.0	40.1	35.1
Sweden	75.1	70.5	65.8	64.5	44.8	42.7	42.1	39.6

SOURCE: *The 2015 Pension Adequacy Report* (EC 2015b, Section 3.1.2, table 3.3, page 121).

NOTE: TRRs are based on after-tax pension income and earnings. AWG = European Union's Economic Policy Committee Working Group on Ageing Populations and Sustainability; EU = European Union; M = men; TRR = theoretical replacement rate; W = women.

What can be concluded about adequacy from table 3.2 and table 3.3? First, the pre-tax ARR based on empirical data is 48 percent—on par with the other two Baltic states, Finland, Denmark, and Germany, but lower than that of Sweden and France. An explanation is that the replacement rates for the latter two countries are based on higher overall contribution rates, which in the case of Sweden also include a larger component of mandatory and occupational FDC pensions. Second, for Latvia, the pre-tax TRR is about the same as the ARR. However, the tax rate is important for the end result in Latvia. The after-tax TRR is 65 percent, with a pension age of 62, and 72 percent if the pension age is set at 65, everything else equal.

Finally, note that the exit-age assumption used for the EC-EPC (AWG)'s simulated ages of entrance and exit (close to age 65) also gives an after-tax replacement rate of 72 percent. The bottom line is, however, that achieving these replacement rates requires a working-career length of about 42 years (43 for men and 41 for women)—instead of the approximately 35 career years of new pensioners in 2013 for retirement at age 65. This will require both early entrance into the labor force and working longer.

Conclusions, Discussion, and Open Issues

Three important conclusions emerge in summing up the first 20 years of Latvia's NDC scheme, and two important outstanding issues need to be addressed.

The first conclusion is that the NDC scheme was successfully implemented and is both financially stable and sustainable. The transition to the NDC structure itself provided the framework for a paradigm shift in thinking. Pensions became a transfer of one's own resources from working years to financing consumption in retirement. The implementation process required managing the difficult transitional issues associated with rights acquired from the Soviet system, including phasing out a plethora of separate rights for "special" groups.

A second accomplishment was raising the pension age—officially from 55 for women and 60 for men, but in reality from much lower ages given the extensive scheme of special privileges in place in 1996. The NDC narrative contributed gradually to adjusting people's expectations about their working lives upward with increasing life expectancy. In 2017, the minimum pension age was 63 for both genders, with a scheduled increase to age 65 in 2025. This has two important effects. First, it provides an increase in the labor supply. Second, in comparison with a lower pension age, the process serves to increase the yearly amount of benefits as life expectancy increases, compared with what they would have been otherwise. Both of these outcomes result from the basic properties of NDC schemes, although indexation and the use of life expectancy in creating life annuities also interact to keep the system financially stable and affordable.

Third, the increase in participation in the formal economy and the strong increase in coverage from 1995 to 2017 was remarkable. The increase in coverage was instrumental in offsetting the strong decline in the working-age population during this period. Latvian pension reform has come a long way toward fulfilling its potential, but importantly, more remains to be accomplished. The next challenge is to increase the number of years worked of persons claiming a pension—from 35 in 2017 to more than 40 in the coming four decades.

The present assumptions underlying projections for the future embody an extremely pessimistic picture of the future development of the Latvian working-age population, despite a relatively high fertility rate of about 1.85 children per woman. This is due to the calculation assumption of strong net emigration of the working-age population at a rate of about 1 percent per year during 2020–70. A partial solution is for Latvia to use its financial pension funds to develop its infrastructure and more generally support home-market investments.

A final note is that if Latvia achieves and maintains balance in its demography and if this balance is also reflected in the demand for labor and accompanying labor force participation, the goal of neutralizing the negative effect generated through the declining labor force will be achieved. Under the current circumstances, however, the continuous downward pull of demography requires a continuous negative adjustment in the otherwise positive overall rate of return, and with present projections the process will continue through the period 2030–60. Nevertheless, despite the demographic projections, the NDC pension scheme's built-in dynamic adjustment process is leading to stable growth of pensions and can be considered a success.

ANNEX 3A

Increasing Coverage of the Latvian Working-Age Population Developed Hand-in-Hand With an Increase in the Density of Contribution Payments, 1996–2016

FIGURE 3A.1 **Persons paying contributions one or more months per year**

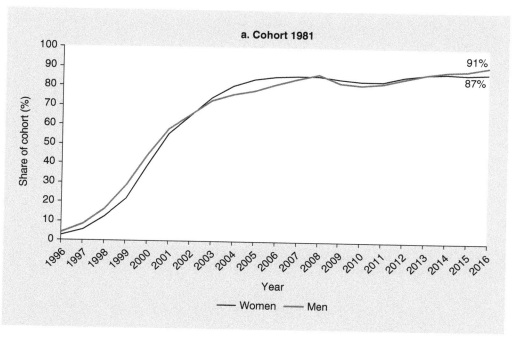

(continued next page)

FIGURE 3A.1 **Persons paying contributions one or more months per year (continued)**

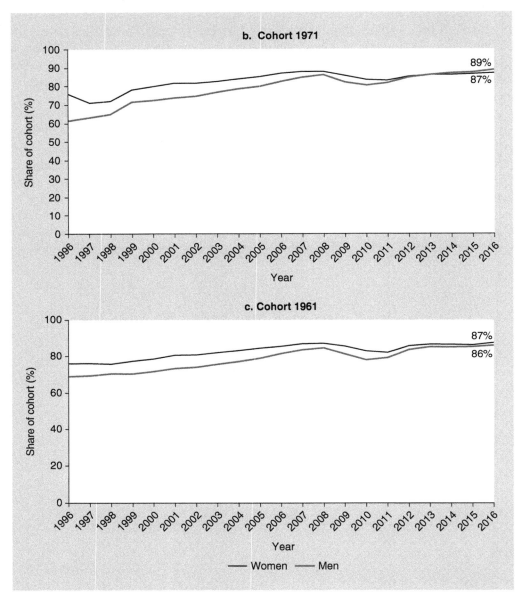

SOURCE: Latvian State Social Insurance Agency and Ministry of Welfare.

FIGURE 3A.2 **Density of contributions paid 1–12 months in the years 1996–2016**

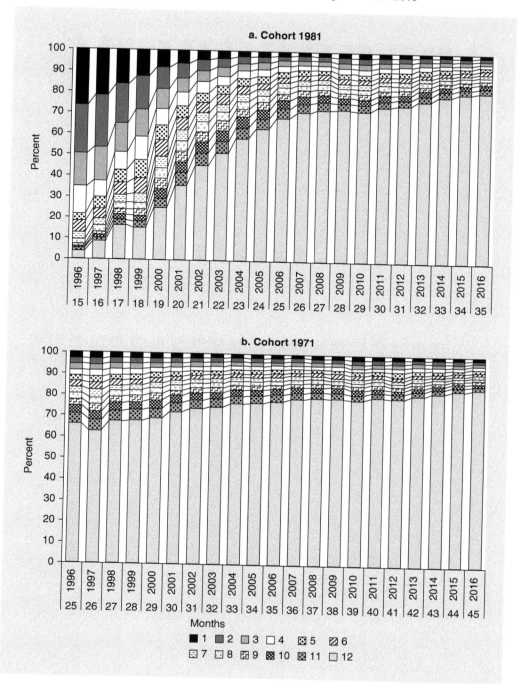

(continued next page)

FIGURE 3A.2 **Density of contributions paid 1–12 months in the years 1996–2016 (continued)**

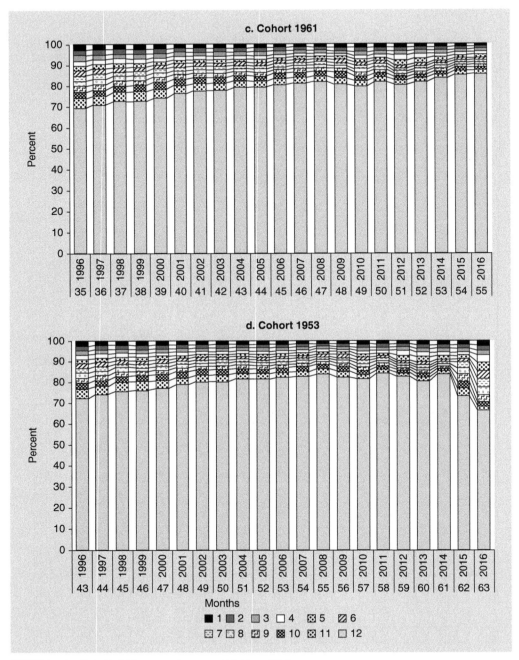

SOURCE: Latvian State Social Insurance Agency and Ministry of Welfare.

NOTE: The number below the years is cohort members' age that year.

Notes

1. The model used is presented in Palmer et al. (2006).

2. See the overview of Latvia, Italy, Poland, and Sweden in Chłoń-Domińczak, Franco, and Palmer (2012) for a more detailed discussion of Latvia in this context and a comparison with other NDC countries.

3. This is shown by calculations performed in 2001 and presented in Palmer et al. 2006.

4. The country data referred to in this discussion are EU data from the *Ageing Report, 2015* (EC 2015a, Table I.1.1, page 9).

5. According to the EC's projections performed in conjunction with the *Ageing Report, 2018* (EC 2018).

6. According to the 2018 round of EC-EPC (AWG) projections.

7. Note that the working-age population is defined as persons ages 15–64. Persons ages 15–19 are to a considerable extent still in education, although they may work part-time. Also, the minimum pension age for men was 60 at the outset and 55 for women, and these ages increased successively during 1996–2016.

8. The calculations presented in this section are those used for the Latvian Ministry of Welfare's calculations for EC (2018) based on the EC-EPC (AWG) assumptions.

9. See Palmer (2013) for a presentation of the underlying model.

10. The countries researched in these studies are Denmark, Finland, France, Italy, Japan, the Netherlands, Portugal, Norway, Sweden, the United Kingdom, and the United States.

11. The underlying data are from the European Union's Statistics on Income and Living Conditions database.

12. Box 3.3, page 20 of the *2015 Pension Adequacy Report* (EC 2015b) presents assumptions in greater detail.

References

Alho, Juha, Jorge Bravo, and Edward Palmer. 2013. "Life Expectancy and Annuities in NDC." In *NDC Pension Schemes: Progress and Frontiers in a Changing Pension World: Volume 2 Gender, Politics, and Financial Stability*, edited by Robert Holzmann, Edward Palmer, and David Robalino, 395–437. Washington, DC: World Bank.

Alho, Juha, Edward Palmer, and Yuwei Zhao de Gosson de Varennes. 2019. Unpublished.

Chłoń-Domińczak, Agnieszka, Daniele Franco, and Edward Palmer. 2012. "The First Wave of NDC Countries—Taking Stock Ten Plus Years Down the Road." In *Nonfinancial Defined Contribution Pension Schemes: Progress and Frontiers in a Changing Pension World: Volume 1 Lessons and Issues in Implementation*, edited by Robert Holzmann, Edward Palmer, and David Robalino, 31–84. Washington, DC: World Bank.

EC (European Commission). 2015a. *The 2015 Ageing Report: Economic and Budgetary Projections for the EU-27 Member States (2013–2060)*. Brussels: European Commission.

———. 2015b. *The 2015 Pension Adequacy Report: Current and Future Income Adequacy in the EU. Volume 1*. Brussels: European Commission.

———. 2018. *Ageing Report, 2018*. Brussels: European Commission.

Fox, Louise, and Edward Palmer. 1999. "Latvian Pension Reform." Social Protection Discussion Paper 9922, World Bank, Washington, DC.

Palmer, Edward. 2013. "Generic Equilibrium, Valuation, and Risk Sharing with and Without NDC Bonds." In *Nonfinancial Defined Contribution Pension Schemes: Progress and Frontiers in a Changing Pension World: Volume 2 Gender, Politics, and Financial Stability*, edited by Robert Holzmann, Edward Palmer, and David Robalino, 309–33. Washington, DC: World Bank.

Palmer, Edward, Sandra Stabina, Ingemar Svensson, and Inta Vanovska. 2006. "NDC Strategy in Latvia: Implementation and Prospects for the Future." In *Pension Reform through NDCs: Issues and Prospects for Non-Financial Defined Contribution Schemes*, edited by Robert Holzmann and Edward Palmer, 397–447. Washington, DC: World Bank.

United Nations. 2017. *World Population Prospects: The 2017 Revision*. New York: United Nations.

CHAPTER 4

The Italian NDC Scheme: Evolution and Remaining Potholes

Sandro Gronchi, Sergio Nisticò, and Mirko Bevilacqua

Introduction

In early 1995, after President Berlusconi resigned after not getting his parametric pension reform approved, a wide parliamentary coalition endorsed a "technical" government to lead the country in view of the general elections to take place no later than spring of 1996. The main task of the new cabinet, led by the former General Director of the Bank of Italy Lamberto Dini, was to pass a significant reform of the Italian pension system in due time, to overcome the financial difficulties implied by long-run projections.

A paper written by one of this chapter's authors, then an advisor to the Ministry of the Treasury, denounced the inequities of the earnings-related scheme while pointing out the remedy in what is now labeled the nonfinancial defined contributions (NDC) scheme (Gronchi 1994). The new scheme also promised to remedy long-run budget imbalances. The proposal circulated among experts and union leaders and also inspired a bill, presented in December 1994 by the majority of left-leaning representatives in Parliament, roughing out an NDC scheme. The Dini government explored these new ideas, appointing a reform working group that included the author of the above-mentioned paper. Although the group did not have to start from scratch, the government deadline was very tight.[1] This peculiar political context explains the shortcomings of Dini's reform, which have never been remedied.

For union members to endorse the radically new form of the pay-as-you-go (PAYG) system, its impact had to be delayed. Indeed, senior workers with a contribution record of at least 18 years were fully exempt, while those with a shorter record had to be concerned proportionally, with the weight of old rules depending on the ratio of the pre-1995 to the overall contribution period at retirement. Not surprisingly, the 1995 legislation did not produce any practical effect. The more recent 2011 Fornero reform fostered the transition with the provision that contributions paid in the system since 2012 produce pension credits according to NDC rules, independent of the aforementioned 18-year contribution record. Therefore, all pensions awarded since 2012 have an NDC component.

The authors are grateful to Agnieszka Chłoń-Domińczak, Robert Holzmann, Edward Palmer, and an anonymous referee for comments and suggestions.

Now that the Italian NDC is leaving the "waiting room," where it has remained trapped since 1995, identifying and remedying its shortcomings can no longer be deferred. In fact, Italy must now decide whether to "fully implement the NDC system or explicitly move to other solutions" (Franco and Sartor 2006, 484).

The main purpose of this chapter is to discuss the Italian system's shortcomings. It first summarizes the pension-related legislation since 1995 and presents current figures characterizing the Italian pension system.

Overview of Italy's Post-1995 Pension Legislation

One essential feature of Italy's post-1995 pension legislation is its instability. Moreover, the long transition mentioned above explains why frequent changes were passed by governments mainly concerned with retirement rules for workers exempt, fully or partially, from NDC rules.

The 1995 reform prescribed a 57–65 age interval for fully covered NDC workers (that is, those with a contribution record starting January 1, 1996), and confirmed a standard retirement age for pre-1996 workers at 60 for women and 65 for men. The pre-1996 workers were also allowed to retire earlier, starting at 57, provided they had contributed to the pension system for 35 years. Moreover, "seniority retirement" (regardless of age), very rooted in the Italian social security tradition, was confirmed and extended to post-1995 workers but the required contribution period was raised from 35 to 40 years.

After the 1996 general elections, the center-left Prodi government passed new measures mostly concerned with convergence of retirement rules for public employees toward those already established for the private sector.

Adequate pensions played a fundamental role in Berlusconi's 2001 electoral campaign, and the first law passed by his second government was meant to keep the promise of raising the minimum pension to €516 from €350. The minimum pension is a floor for earnings-related pensions that, if lower, are "integrated" up to the floor. This minimum pension will not survive the transition period, since the Dini reform ruled it out for full NDC pensions.

In 2004, according to the so-called Maroni reform, named after Berlusconi's Minister of Welfare, the required age for pre-1996 workers' early retirement with 35 years of contributions was raised from 57 to 60 as of 2008, to 61 as of 2010, and to 62 as of 2014. Surprisingly, such rules were also extended to fully NDC post-1995 workers. The standard retirement ages of 60 for women and 65 for men, regardless of the contribution period, were maintained for the former workers and also extended to the latter. In such a way, the 57–65 flexibility of the 1995 NDC scheme was completely lost. In the end, the seniority retirement after 40 years of contributions was preserved.

In summary, after Maroni's law all workers (both pre-1996 and post-1995) had three "exit channels": the first was based on age (60 or 65 depending on gender); the second was based on seniority (40 years of contributions); and the third was "mixed," requiring both 60 years of age and 35 years of contribution seniority. This third channel was relevant for men only since the first channel allowed women to retire at 60 regardless of seniority.

In 2007, after the center-left coalition won the 2006 general elections, Prodi's second government replaced the third channel with a different one, based on the concept of "quota," that is the sum of age and seniority. The required quota was set at 95 (with a minimum age of 59) to be raised to 97 (with a minimum age of 61) as of 2013. The required quotas (and minimum ages as well) were raised by one year for the self-employed. Prodi's 2007 law also updated the NDC divisors, which had to be done in 2006 by the Berlusconi government given that the 1995 reform established updating every 10 years. Indeed, the updating procedure envisaged in 1995 was not automatic but rather based on a troublesome political process that the Berlusconi government could easily escape (before the political elections). The Prodi law abolished this political process and established automatic updating every three years (instead of every ten).[2]

In 2008, the Prodi government resigned and Berlusconi won the elections once more. The most significant change in the pension legislation introduced in 2010 by the new Berlusconi government was indexation to longevity of the retirement ages required for the first exit channel mentioned above. The new cabinet remained in office until November 2011, when Berlusconi resigned under financial market pressure.

A technical government followed, led by the former European Commissioner Mario Monti. His new Minister of Welfare was Professor Elsa Fornero, who passed a radical reorganization of the chaotic Italian retirement rules, in addition to fostering the slow transition mentioned above. The main features of the 2011 Fornero law were as follows:

- Cancellation of Prodi's quotas
- Restoration of flexibility for fully covered NDC post-1995 workers within a longevity-indexed age interval of 64–67 as of January 1, 2019
- Gradual convergence for pre-1996 workers toward a unique longevity-indexed retirement age (regardless of gender and working category) of 67 years as of January 1, 2019
- Preservation of seniority retirement but with higher, longevity-indexed contribution records, different by gender, of 42 years and 3 months for women and 43 years and 3 months for men as of January 1, 2019.

The law also established updating of NDC divisors every two years (instead of every three) as of 2019.

Pension Expenditure: Structure and Evolution

Italy's 2017 expenditure on old-age, survivors', and disability (OASDI) pensions amounted to about €250 billion (14.5 percent of gross domestic product [GDP]), of which €197 billion (11.4 percent of GDP) was for old-age benefits, €39.5 billion (2.3 percent of GDP) was for survivors' benefits, and €13.5 billion (0.8 percent of GDP) was for disability benefits.[3] In January 2018, the number of disbursed OASDI benefits was about 17 million, 14 million of which went to former private employees or the self-employed, and the remaining 3 million to public employees. Overall OASDI revenues, generated by a 33 percent contribution rate, amounted to about €190 billion, covering only 76 percent of expenditures.[4] The remaining part was financed by the state.

Regarding adequacy, the average amount of the 12 million old-age pensions is €2,100 per month for public employees, €1,360 for private employees, and slightly less than €900 for the self-employed. The ratio of the average old-age pension to be received in retirement to average individual lifetime earnings is about 85 percent, 70 percent, and 50 percent, respectively, for the three categories of workers.

Note that all these figures have little to do with the NDC's effects, since fully NDC pensions are still few. Moreover, their levels are very low because of the short careers of beneficiaries.

According to official projections of the State General Accounting Office, in 2070 pension expenditure relative to GDP will return to the pre-2005 level (figure 4.1).[5] The main reasons are the increase in retirement age and the phasing out of the "baby boom" cohorts.

Nevertheless, it cannot be denied that because of Italy's demo-economic prospects, fully NDC pensions, starting on a large scale in the 2030s, will be lower than Italian retirees are now used to; thus, the number of those pointing to the NDC as the principal enemy of Italian retirees will probably increase at that time. They should understand that, in the absence of the NDC, sustainability should be ensured by some parametric adjustments affecting earnings-related pensions as well. In fact, the real "enemies" are demographic change and slowing productivity growth, while the NDC can only ensure that the necessary sacrifices are timely and fairly distributed. The expected increase of both life expectancy and the old-age dependency ratio for Italy are shown in figure 4.2.

FIGURE 4.1 **Italy's pension expenditure, 2000–70**

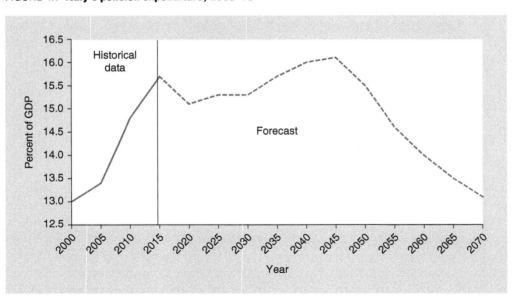

SOURCE: RGS 2018.

NOTE: GDP = gross domestic product.

FIGURE 4.2 **Life expectancy and old-age dependency ratio in Italy, 2017–65**

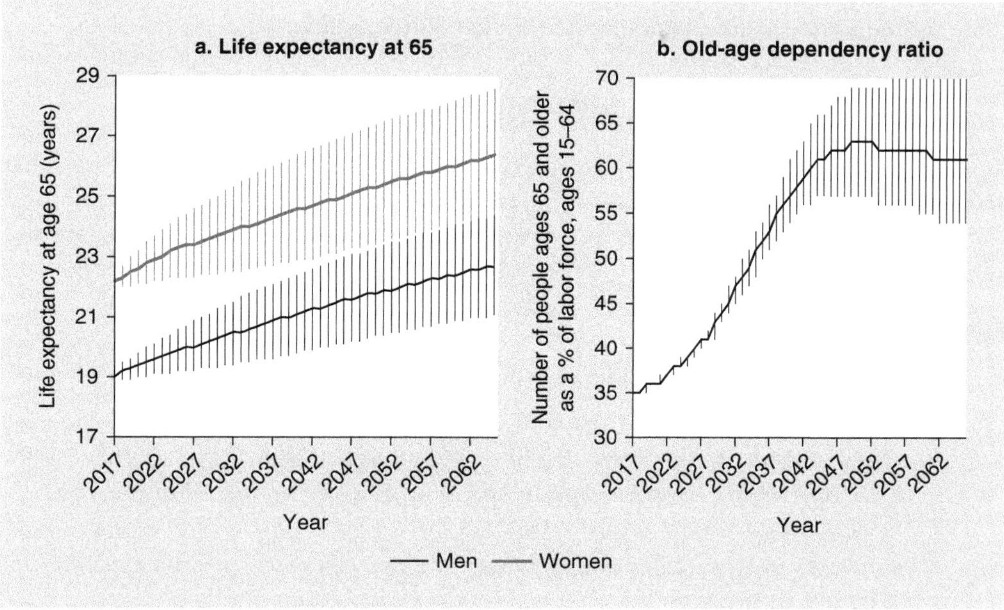

a. Life expectancy at 65 / b. Old-age dependency ratio

— Men — Women

SOURCE: Italian National Institute of Statistics (ISTAT) 2018.

NOTE: The lines show the median scenario; the vertical bars show the 90 percent confidence interval.

The "Last Call" for a Definite Choice

The NDC philosophy represents such a clear-cut cultural discontinuity that it took Sweden about six years of political debate and technical work to develop coherent legislation; and Swedish experts are still working on the many technical details that allow the new system to couple fairness and transparency with the automatic adjustments needed to keep pace with the country's ongoing demographic scenario.

Nothing of this sort took place in Italy. The short time the Dini government had available did not allow for a proper debate on the NDC's principles; after that, such a debate was not encouraged by the long transition mentioned above. The time has come for the political and cultural debate that Italy has deferred for so long. The rest of this chapter is intended to be a stimulus in this direction.

In the absence of a shared theoretical benchmark, both shortcomings and remedies are debatable. Thus, "NDC Principles" discusses the theoretical framework necessary to "disclose" them. "The Targets" identifies the NDC goals, or "targets" in Tinbergen's (1952) terminology. "The Instruments in Well-Behaved Economies" focuses on the technical tools, the "instruments" that allow those targets to be reached in "well-behaved" economies, where both the employment growth rate and longevity are constant over time. "Reality Is Not Well-Behaved" discusses how to adapt the instruments to the "real world," in which employment growth is not steady and longevity increases. "Shortcomings of the Italian NDC Scheme" contrasts such theoretical premises with the 1995 Italian legislation, pointing out the mistakes together with possible remedies.

NDC Principles

In a nutshell, the NDC is an old-age PAYG scheme based on interest-earning personal accounts in which money is deposited before retirement, in the form of contributions, and withdrawn later in the form of pension annuities. Interest is earned, both before and after retirement, according to a system rate chosen by the policy maker.

THE TARGETS

NDC pension schemes fulfil the following essential design principles[6]:

- *Fairness*, intended as "one-to-one correspondence," regardless of career patterns and retirement age, between lifelong withdrawals and deposits or, more precisely, as the equivalence between expected pension annuities and contributions including accrued interest on contributions
- *Sustainability*, intended as equality over time between yearly pension expenditures and yearly system revenues implied by the contribution rate fixed by the policy maker
- *Flexibility*, intended as the worker's free choice of retirement age at or above the minimum retirement age established by the policy maker.

Note that fairness implies the absence of any redistributive flows other than those from individuals who eventually live less than their life expectancy at retirement to individuals who live longer.

THE INSTRUMENTS IN WELL-BEHAVED ECONOMIES

This section identifies the instruments allowing the NDC to hit all three targets under constant longevity and employment growth.

Start with target 1. For the sake of simplicity, survivors are ignored; the analysis refers to an individual who retires on January 1, 2018, with an account balance of €100 and a life expectancy of 10 years. It is also assumed that pension annuities are awarded on January 1 each year and the system interest rate is constantly equal to 10 percent.

To show how the NDC must work after retirement to ensure fairness, start with table 4.1. Column (3) spreads the €100 account balance over life expectancy by cutting it into 10 €10 "slices," each one devoted to a different pension annuity. In fact, the first slice is withdrawn at retirement as the first annuity, while the others earn the interest shown in column (4) until they are withdrawn. The annuities, resulting from the sum of the account balance slices and the accrued interest, are shown in column (5). For example, the fourth slice earns €3.31 in three years until it is withdrawn on January 1, 2021, as the €13.31 (=10+3.31) fourth annuity. Finally, column (6) shows the annual indexation rate (that is, the rate at which annuities increase from each year to the following) resulting from the pension "time profile" in column (5). Note that the indexation rate is exactly equal to the system interest rate.

TABLE 4.1 **How NDC works after retirement for a standard pension profile**

Date (1)	Annuity number (2)	Balance spreading (3)	Interest earned (4)	Annuity payment (5)	Resulting indexation (%) (6)
January 1, 2018	1	10	n.a.	10.00	n.a.
January 1, 2019	2	10	1.00	11.00	10
January 1, 2020	3	10	2.10	12.10	10
January 1, 2021	4	10	3.31	12.10	10
January 1, 2022	5	10	4.64	13.31	10
January 1, 2023	6	10	6.11	14.64	10
January 1, 2024	7	10	7.72	16.11	10
January 1, 2025	8	10	9.49	17.72	10
January 1, 2026	9	10	11.44	19.49	10
January 1, 2027	10	10	13.58	21.44	10
		100		23.58	10

SOURCE: Original table.
NOTE: n.a. = not applicable.

Actually, the balance spreading in column (3) may also contemplate decreasing (rather than constant) slices. For example, one may want each slice s_i to be 1.5 percent greater than the next, such that slices 2 through 10 can be linked to the first one as follows:

$$\frac{s_1}{(1+1.5\%)^{i-1}} \quad i = 2, 3, \cdots, 10. \tag{4.1}$$

Since the sum of all slices has to exhaust the €100 account balance, the following equation must also hold:

$$\sum_{i=1}^{10} \frac{s_1}{(1+1.5\%)^{i-1}} = 100,$$

which implies that the first pension annuity (p_1), equal to the first balance slice, is computed as follows:

$$p_1 = s_1 = \frac{100}{\sum_{i=1}^{10} (1+1.5\%)^{i-1}} \tag{4.2}$$

while further annuities are still computed by adding interest to the first slice (that is, equation 4.1). In so doing, annuities can be expressed as:

$$p_i = s_1 \times \left(\frac{1+10\%}{1+1.5\%}\right)^{i-1} \quad i = 2, 3, \cdots, 10, \tag{4.3}$$

which implies the following indexation rate:

$$\sigma = \frac{p_i}{p_{i-1}} - 1 = \frac{1+10\%}{1+1.5\%} - 1 = 8.37\%. \tag{4.4}$$

The effects of this alternate balance spreading are reported in table 4.2.

Note how the new pension profile in table 4.2 differs from the "standard" one in table 4.1: the first annuities are higher whereas the later ones are lower. Thus, the new profile can be referred to as "front-loaded."

Equation (4.2) can be generalized as follows:

$$p_1 = \frac{B}{\sum_{i=1}^{n}(1+\delta)^{1-i}}, \tag{4.5}$$

in which B denotes the personal account balance at retirement, n life expectancy, and δ the "front-loading rate" established by the policy maker. The denominator of equation (4.5) is called the balance "divisor," which increases with life expectancy and decreases with the front-loading rate.

On the other hand, the "indexing rule" in equation (4.4) can be generalized as follows:

$$\sigma_t = \frac{1+\pi_t}{1+\delta} - 1, \tag{4.6}$$

in which π_t denotes the value that the system interest rate takes in year t.

Note that the choice described in table 4.1 implies that the divisor equals life expectancy at retirement, while the indexation rate in equation (4.6) equals the system interest rate. Note also that the policy maker can generate more front-loaded pension profiles by raising the value of δ, thus increasing the generosity of the computing rule in equation (4.5). Nevertheless, one should resist such a temptation since the indexation rate in equation (4.6) would risk becoming negative in real, or even nominal, terms. Moreover, "vintage pensions" would emerge; that is, the average level of pensions started in a distant year would become much lower than that of

TABLE 4.2 **How NDC works after retirement for a front-loaded pension profile**

Date (1)	Annuity number (2)	Balance spreading (3)	Interest earned (4)	Annuity amount (5)	Resulting indexation (%) (6)
January 1, 2018	1	10.68	n.a.	10.68	n.a.
January 1, 2019	2	10.53	1.05	11.58	8.37
January 1, 2020	3	10.37	2.18	12.55	8.37
January 1, 2021	4	10.22	3.38	13.60	8.37
January 1, 2022	5	10.07	4.67	14.74	8.37
January 1, 2023	6	9.92	6.05	15.97	8.37
January 1, 2024	7	9.77	7.54	17.31	8.37
January 1, 2025	8	9.63	9.13	18.76	8.37
January 1, 2026	9	9.48	10.85	20.33	8.37
January 1, 2027	10	9.34	12.69	22.03	8.37
		100			

SOURCE: Original table.

NOTE: n.a. = not applicable.

pensions started in a recent year. The phenomenon can cause social envy, a harbinger of expensive equalization that would further compromise both fairness and sustainability.

Both Italy and Sweden have chosen too high values for δ (1.5 percent and 1.6 percent, respectively). In this regard, the recent Norwegian choice of a 0.75 percent front-loading rate, inspired by the Swedish 2010 and 2011 negative indexations, went in the right direction (Christensen et al. 2012).

In view of the above, it can be concluded that reaching NDC target 1 is ensured by the following:

- *Instrument 1.* The first annuity is computed by equation (4.5), that is, by dividing the account balance at retirement by a divisor depending on life expectancy and a front-loading rate, possibly nil, established by the policy maker
- *Instrument 2.* The following annuities increase according to the rate in equation (4.6), which is obtained by subtracting the front-loading rate from the system interest rate.

Instruments 1 and 2 are also necessary for target 2. Nevertheless, they are not sufficient. In fact, it is evident that sustainability cannot be independent from the system interest rate, influencing both the account balances accumulated at retirement, hence new pensions according to equation (4.5), and the indexation rate of existing pensions according to equation (4.6). It has been proven (Gronchi and Nisticò 2006, 2008; Valdés-Prieto 2000) that target 2 is fulfilled by adding the following:

- *Instrument 3.* The system interest rate credited to personal accounts, both before and after retirement, equals the growth rate of the wage bill.[7]

As for target 3, it was shown that the NDC computes the first pension annuity according to equation (4.5), that is, by dividing the account balance at retirement by a divisor increasing with life expectancy n, which in turn decreases as retirement age increases. Therefore, workers who choose to retire at younger ages with a higher divisor "pay" for their longer benefits by receiving smaller annuities. Nevertheless, the policy maker has to define an interval of retirement ages since some physiological upper limit must exist (above which employers can impose retirement on their employees) while a lower limit is also advisable because too young retirement ages, implying low pensions, increase the risk of poverty among the elderly. All this can be achieved by adding the following:

- *Instrument 4.* The policy maker sets an interval of approved retirement ages and announces the corresponding divisors.

REALITY IS NOT WELL-BEHAVED

Instruments 1–4 can be fully effective for the specified NDC targets in well-behaved economies, that is, under the assumption that longevity is constant over time and employment grows steadily. Unfortunately, this is not the case in the real world, where longevity is rising sharply and employment growth shows irregular rather than cyclical patterns.

Cyclical changes in the employment growth rate do not prevent long-run sustainability, though they can produce temporary imbalances, which are positive (surpluses) when the employment growth rate increases and negative (deficits) when it decreases. This is why a sufficient buffer fund becomes a fundamental complement of instrument 2.

An additional problem implied by nonsteady employment growth is that the system interest rate during expansions is higher than during recessions. This may cause disparities both between and within cohorts. To stabilize the rate, the Swedish NDC scheme chose not to distribute the volatile "employment dividend" and to anchor the system interest rate to the more stable wage growth. Long-run sustainability is improved by temporary adjustments of the system interest rate through the automatic balance mechanism (Settergren 2003; Settergren and Mikula 2006).[8]

Increasing longevity, meaning that individuals born in a given year live longer than those born in previous ones, calls for divisors increasing by year of birth (that is, by cohort). In particular, divisors (different by retirement age) should be assigned to a cohort when it reaches the lower bound of the age interval required by instrument 4. Moreover, they should be based on the cohort's specific residual lives at ages included in the interval. Unfortunately, such data can only be ascertained after the cohort has expired and, therefore, they have to be estimated at the time when it starts retiring. Two choices exist.

The first one is to derive a cohort's residual lives from mortality tables specifically projected for the cohort itself. Under "perfect foresight," this choice would produce exact forward-looking divisors, ensuring perfect fairness. The second choice is to admit that perfect foresight is a chimera and simply derive cohort residual lives from the most updated usual period mortality tables, based on the observation for previous cohorts. This second choice produces obsolete, backward-looking divisors that are lower than they should be.[9]

Divisors' obsolescence does not allow instruments 1–3 to fully achieve targets 1–2 (fairness and sustainability). In fact, money withdrawn from personal accounts tends to exceed money previously deposited plus interest earned, while yearly pension expenditures tend to exceed corresponding contribution revenues. Note that perfect foresight does not prevent forward-looking divisors from producing imbalances. In fact, it has been proven that they produce "hypersustainability," that is, each year pension expenditures tend to be lower than contribution revenues (Gismondi and Gronchi 2008). Moreover, the lack of perfect foresight makes forward-looking divisors scarcely viable from a sociopolitical point of view. In fact, workers should accept having their pensions computed on the basis of possibly incorrect forecasted mortality tables.[10] Therefore, backward-looking divisors appear to be inevitable.

To minimize obsolescence (and thus to improve both fairness and sustainability), instruments 1–3 should be complemented with two recommendations. First, mortality tables should be updated in (almost) "real time." For example, the 2017 tables should be used in 2018 for computing divisors to be assigned to the cohort starting retirement in 2019. Second, the minimum retirement age should be as high as possible. In fact, obsolescence increases when retirement age decreases. In other words, younger coefficients are more obsolete than older ones.[11]

Shortcomings of the Italian NDC Scheme

This section contrasts the Italian NDC scheme with the required instruments discussed in the "NDC Principles" section. It starts with the indexation rule, which is quite different from that in equation (4.6).

PENSION INDEXATION

Computing rule in equation (4.5) and indexation rule in equation (4.6) are both fundamental since they "collaborate" in view of fairness (target 1), which is in turn a necessary condition for sustainability (target 2). Nonetheless, the Italian scheme applies the former but neglects the latter. In particular, it assumes 1.5 percent as the front-loading rate (δ) included in equation (4.5), while pensions are indexed to prices according to an elasticity that starts from unity for low-level pensions and decreases as the pension level increases. Such an indexation rule implies crediting to all account balances after retirement a rate of interest different from the system rate, which produces severe repercussions against both fairness and sustainability.

Fixing the problem, and hence involving in the indexation rule both the system interest rate and the front-loading rate, should be the occasion to lower the latter in line with the above-mentioned good practice started in Norway. In fact, the 1.5 percent front-loading rate would have implied negative indexation in the past 10 years.

SYSTEM INTEREST RATE

The Italian NDC scheme identifies the system interest rate as the growth of GDP, including profits and rents, rather than of the wage bill according to instrument 3 for target 2. Figure 4.3 shows that one should not take the similarity between the two rates for granted.

The circumstance that, as of 2002, the "mistake" implied crediting to all account balances an occasionally lower interest rate cannot be a good argument, since sustainability (target 2) has to be ensured in the long run.

DIVISORS

As discussed in the "Reality Is Not Well-Behaved," increasing longevity calls for divisors to be assigned, once and for all, to cohorts when they reach the minimum retirement age. The Swedish NDC scheme does exactly this.

Unfortunately, the Italian protocol is quite different. Starting January 1, 2019, divisors will be updated every two years (so far, every three) on the basis of the last available (most updated) standard period mortality tables, and applied to whomever retires within the following biennium, regardless of the year of birth. In this respect, the Italian divisors are of the conceptually wrong *erga omnes*[12] type.

Such a protocol produces disparities both between and within cohorts. On the one hand, it assigns different mortality rates to members of the same cohort who retire in different biennia. For example, the mortality rates imputed to Mr. White born in 1970 who retires in 2036–37 at 66–67 will be lower than those imputed to Mr. Brown born in the same year, who will retire in 2029–30 at 59–60. On the other hand, the same mortality rates are imputed to members of different cohorts who retire in the same

FIGURE 4.3 **Italy's wage bill versus GDP growth rate, 1996–2016**

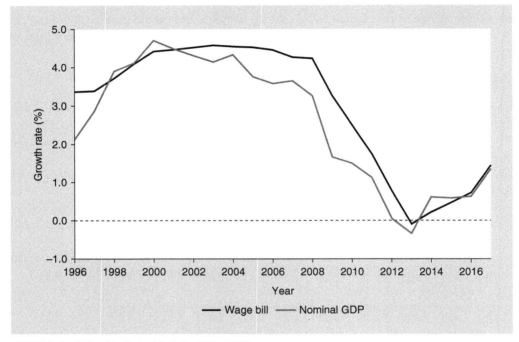

SOURCE: Italian National Institute of Statistics (ISTAT) 2018.

NOTE: GDP = gross domestic product.

biennium. For example, the mortality rates imputed to Mr. Green born in 1963 who retires in 2029–30 at 66–67 will be the same as those imputed to the already mentioned Mr. Brown.

Erga omnes divisors produce not only unfairness but also uncertainty, which, in turn, hinders personal planning and encourages early retirement. In fact, workers refrain from taking the risk that increasing divisors frustrate the sacrifice of prolonging work to obtain a higher pension.[13]

RETIREMENT RULES

According to the Fornero reform, as of January 1, 2019, the Italian NDC scheme will allow retirement at age 64, provided that contribution seniority is at least 20 years and the pension at least €1,268 per month. At age 67, the required pension amount drops to €679.5 per month, while 20 years seniority is still required. If these conditions (one or both) are not yet satisfied, retirement can be postponed until they are, up to the age of 71, when retirement is allowed regardless of seniority and pension amount.[14] These age requirements are automatically updated according to longevity evolution. Note that automatic updating is appreciable, since it accomplishes the recommendations in "Reality Is Not Well-Behaved." Other countries, including Sweden, will probably have to follow suit (Chłoń-Domińczak, Franco, and Palmer 2012, 68).

Requirements other than age (seniority and pension amounts) hinder flexibility (target 3). Removal of those barriers would also avoid prolonging work to the mentioned high ages, unparalleled in the rest of the world. Also note that restrictions on the freedom to choose apply to "weaker" laborers, that is, those with lower wages and career breaks.

As mentioned, the Fornero reform preserved the seniority pension for fully NDC (post-1995) workers, that is, the right to retire at whatever age after a given record of contribution years. Starting January 1, 2019, such a record will be 42 years and 3 months for women and 43 years and 3 months for men. Indeed, seniority pensions are alien to the NDC philosophy and clash with the idea of allowing flexibility within a preset age interval. They also exacerbate the problem of divisors' obsolescence in two ways.

On one hand, seniority retirees will get a significant premium from the backward-looking divisors being more obsolete for their younger ages. In fact, taking into account that until 2006 schooling was compulsory up to age 15,[15] as of 2019 the youngest seniority pensions will be awarded to women at about age 57 (15+42) and to men at about age 58 (15+43).

On the other hand, seniority pensions would conflict with recommendations in "Reality Is Not Well-Behaved" if Italy correctly adopts "cohort-exclusive" divisors (instead of *erga omnes*). In fact, their youngest retirement age (57) would precede the lower bound of the ordinary age interval (64–67), thus forcing early divisors' assignment.

DISABILITY AND SURVIVORS' PENSIONS

Discussion of the final drawbacks to the Italian NDC requires two premises. The first is concerned with the NDC being an exclusively old-age scheme. In other words, it is not compatible with the strong heritage of PAYG systems charging a unique contribution rate and awarding both old-age and disability pensions. In fact, such a unique rate should be credited to old-age personal accounts only partially. In so doing, the credited part would be able to finance old-age expenditures, while the rest could finance disability. Nevertheless, the contribution rate would be unique only nominally, in practice being the sum of the two. For the sake of transparency, it is preferable to split the system into different plans and let disability be financed through a different contribution rate. As an alternative, the disability plan could be "fiscalized" (that is, financed from general tax revenues) and disability allowances, possibly means-tested, awarded to citizens independent of their being workers. Following the Swedish model, such a plan should be charged to pay contributions on allowances (as if they were salaries) to the old-age plan. Contributions, in part paid also by the disabled, would be credited to old-age personal accounts and contribute to old-age pensions.

The second premise is concerned with survivors' benefits, which in principle can be included in the old-age NDC plan by increasing divisors to take into account the further annuities that are expected on the basis of survivors' ages. However, redistributive flows from single to married retirees and from similar-age to distant-age couples would take place, with negative effects on fairness (target 1). As an alternative, one could allow the choice between "one-head" divisors and "two-head" divisors, the latter ones based on survivors' ages. Despite its compliance with target 1, such a choice would put at risk sustainability (target 2), because of both moral hazard problems and the relevant database needed for correctly computing two-head divisors (Gronchi and Nisticò 2006). Following the Swedish model, a fiscalized survivors' program in charge of paying means-tested, and possibly temporary, allowances would avoid all such difficulties.

Italy's 1995 NDC reform failed to separate disability from old-age, while the 33 percent OASDI contribution rate is fully credited to old-age personal accounts. Thus, old-age pension expenditures will tend to absorb all OASDI contribution revenues (actually more than that because of increasing longevity), and disability expenditure will therefore produce chronic deficits.

As for survivors, the 1995 NDC reform preserved the tradition of conceiving of their benefits as a 60 percent continuation of old-age pensions. Sustainability (target 2) is safeguarded by computing divisors to consider the further annuities due to survivors according to their expected life and the probabilities that they will actually survive retirees.[16]

This chapter's authors have repeatedly recommended that survivors' pensions be transformed into allowances to be awarded by a separate fiscalized plan. The Italian political debate often discusses the hypothesis of thinning the wedge between wages and labor cost by shifting onto general tax revenues a portion of the contribution rate. Reforming survivors' benefits would allow Italy to reach such an aim while preserving fairness. Moreover, the same contribution rate would allow for more generous old-age pensions, or lower rates would allow the same pension levels. Also note that survivors' pensions, conceived of as automatic continuations of old-age pensions, tend to encourage Italian women not to participate in the labor market.[17]

Conclusions

Regardless of the form assumed by the PAYG system, the ongoing Italian demo-economic scenario will not allow future pensions to be as generous as in the past. A well-designed NDC scheme would have the merit of asking for the necessary sacrifices in a timely, fair, and transparent manner. However, it is common opinion that the NDC scheme itself is to blame for such sacrifices. Therefore, discussions are now widespread about whether it should be preserved as is. Proposals range from a guarantee to a basic pension to be financed by general tax revenues. Going back to the pre-Fornero period, low retirement ages are also on the agenda of the new Italian government. The proposers neglect to specify whether these proposals are compatible with the expected economic scenario and the outstanding public debt.

None of the fundamental shortcomings discussed in "Shortcomings of the Italian NDC Scheme" are on Italy's political agenda, as if Italian politicians are ignoring their fundamental importance. Thus, Italy would benefit from a general debate concerning the NDC philosophy and how it should be implemented by coherent legislation. Sweden did precisely this in the four years preceding its meticulous 1998 reform (Könberg, Palmer, and Sunden 2006). Such a debate would allow for an understanding to be developed of how a new reform could amend the 1995 mistakes and gaps such that Italy joins Sweden in being proud of its NDC scheme.

On the other hand, this chapter recognizes that within the permanently unstable Italian political landscape that precludes any long-term project, the poorly designed Italian pension system could at best remain as is, thus lending support to Tinbergen's premonition that "personal or institutional inertia and the tendency to maintain the existent … often impede the execution of a rational policy" (Tinbergen 1952, 76).

Notes

1. For a detailed reconstruction of Italian NDC antecedents, see Gronchi and Nisticò (2006, note 6).

2. The 2007 Prodi law did not change the awkward *erga omnes* (toward all) nature of the Italian divisor, discussed in "Divisors."

3. The figures reported in this section are taken from INPS (2018a, 2018b).

4. One-third (9 percent) of the rate is paid by employees, and the remaining two-thirds (24 percent) by employers. Such contribution rates are the same for workers in the labor force both before and after 1996.

5. The acronym RGS stands for the Italian name of the State Accounting Department (Ragioneria Generale dello Stato). Note that RGS's pension expenditures include social allowances. Because of the dramatic demographic prospects reported in figure 4.2, RGS's long-run projection might prove to be optimistic. For a detailed discussion of the underlying assumptions, see Andrle et al. (2018, 17–19).

6. The focus here is on the "undisputed" targets of the NDC scheme; Holzmann and Palmer (2012) discuss further possible benefits.

7. Gronchi and Nisticò (2008) proved that constant longevity and a constant employment growth rate (as assumed in the present section) are the only conditions under which instrument 3 can produce annual pension expenditures equal to the corresponding contribution revenues. In fact, the NDC indexing rule in equation (4.6) allows one to abandon Samuelson's (1958) and Aaron's (1966) further assumption that wages also (not only employment) grow at a constant rate.

8. Note that the balance mechanism reintroduces volatility to the system interest rate and, hence, disparities. However, the NDC disparities are negligible when compared with the structural ones generated by earnings-related schemes or even by the "point" schemes of the French and German type, as shown by Nisticò and Bevilacqua (2013, 2018) and Gurtovaya and Nisticò (2018a, 2018b).

9. For an assessment of the potential imbalances deriving from the use of period rather than cohort life tables, see Ayuso, Bravo, and Holzmann (2018). Palmer and Zhao de Gosson de Varennes (2019) provide a detailed account of how even cohort life tables tend to underestimate life expectancy.

10. For a discussion of how forecasting models tend to underestimate longevity, see Alho, Bravo, and Palmer (2013).

11. The problems connected with increasing longevity could be radically avoided with lump-sum payments of the entire account balance at retirement. More generally, it has been proven that both fairness and sustainability can improve by raising the front-loading rate (Gismondi and Gronchi 2008). Nevertheless, adopting such a measure should not be taken into consideration, given its negative impact on pension indexation (see the "Pension Indexation" section).

12. Latin for "toward all."

13. Note that the "cohort-exclusive" divisors tend to be more obsolete than the *erga omnes* ones. Therefore, it is of paramount importance to follow the recommendations pointed out in the "Reality Is Not Well-Behaved" section.

14. Actually, a contribution seniority of at least five years is still required.

15. As of 2006, schooling is compulsory up to age 16.

16. Survivors' benefits are subject to moderate means testing, which is roughly taken into account in computing divisors. This implies further redistributive flows (in addition to those from single to married retirees and from similar-age to distant-age couples), conflicting with fairness.

17. Despite the overall trend of reducing the gender gap of its labor force participation rates, Italy has the lowest women's participation rate in Europe (World Bank 2017). For a comprehensive review of the problems connected with survivors' benefits and work incentives for women, see James (2013).

References

Aaron, Henry J. 1966. "The Social Insurance Paradox." *Canadian Journal of Economics and Political Science / Revue canadienne d'Economique et de Science politique* 32 (3): 371–74.

Alho, Juha, Jorge Miguel Bravo, and Edward Palmer. 2013. "Annuities and Life Expectancy in NDC." In *Nonfinancial Defined Contribution Pension Schemes in a Changing Pension World: Volume 2 Gender, Politics, and Financial Stability*, edited by Robert Holzmann, Edward Palmer, and David Robalino, 395–436. Washington, DC: World Bank.

Andrle, Michal, Shafik Hebous, Alvar Kangur, and Mehdi Raissi. 2018. "Italy: Toward a Growth-Friendly Fiscal Reform." IMF Working Paper 18/59, International Monetary Fund, Washington, DC.

Ayuso, Mercedes, Jorge Miguel Bravo, and Robert Holzmann. 2018. "Getting Life Expectancy Estimates Right for Pension Policy: Period versus Cohort Approach." IZA Discussion Paper 11512, IZA Institute of Labor Economics, Bonn, Germany.

Chłoń-Domińczak, Agnieszka, Daniele Franco, and Edward Palmer. 2012. "The First Wave of NDC Reforms: The Experiences of Italy, Latvia, Poland, and Sweden." In *Nonfinancial Defined Contribution Pension Schemes in a Changing Pension World: Volume 1 Progress, Lessons, and Implementation*, edited by Robert Holzmann, Edward Palmer, and David Robalino, 31–84. Washington, DC: World Bank.

Christensen, Arne Magnus, Dennis Fredriksen, Ole Christian Lien, and Nils Martin Stølen. 2012. "Pension Reform in Norway: Combining an NDC Approach and Distributional Goals." In *Nonfinancial Defined Contribution Pension Schemes in a Changing Pension World: Volume 1 Progress, Lessons, and Implementation*, edited by Robert Holzmann, Edward Palmer, and David Robalino, 129–57. Washington, DC: World Bank.

Franco, Daniele, and Nicola Sartor. 2006. "NDCs in Italy: Unsatisfactory Present, Uncertain Future." In *Pension Reform: Issues and Prospects for Non-Financial Defined Contribution (NDC) Schemes*, edited by Robert Holzmann and Edward Palmer, 467–92. Washington, DC: World Bank.

Gismondi, Fulvio, and Sandro Gronchi. 2008. "Backward-looking and Forward-looking NDC Pension Schemes." *Journal of Public Finance and Public Choice* 26 (2–3): 93–108.

Gronchi, Sandro. 1994. "I rendimenti impliciti della previdenza obbligatoria: un'analisi delle iniquità del Sistema." In Ministero del Tesoro—Ragioneria Generale dello Stato, *Conti pubblici e Congiuntura Economica*, N.2 (reprinted, with modifications, in *Economia Italiana*, 1995, No. 1).

Gronchi, Sandro, and Sergio Nisticò. 2006. "Implementing the NDC Theoretical Model: A Comparison of Italy and Sweden." In *Pension Reform: Issues and Prospects for Non-Financial Defined Contribution (NDC) Schemes*, edited by Robert Holzmann and Edward Palmer, 493–515. Washington, DC: World Bank.

———. 2008. "Theoretical Foundations of Pay-As-You-Go Defined-Contribution Pension Schemes." *Metroeconomica* 58 (2): 131–59.

Gurtovaya, Vera, and Sergio Nisticò. 2018a. "Does the NDC Scheme Mimic the French Point System?" Applied Economics 51 (1): 117–30. doi: 10.1080/00036846.2018.1494805.

———. 2018b. "The Notional Defined Contribution Pension Scheme and the German 'Point System': A Comparison." German Economic Review 19 (4): 365–82.

Holzmann, Robert, and Edward Palmer. 2012. "NDC in the Teens: Lessons and Issues." In Nonfinancial Defined Contribution Pension Schemes in a Changing Pension World: Volume 1 Progress, Lessons, and Implementation, edited by Robert Holzmann, Edward Palmer, and David Robalino, 3–29. Washington, DC: World Bank.

INPS (Istituto Nazionale Previdenza Sociale). 2018a. Rendiconti Generali Dell'anno 2017. Rome: INPS.

———. 2018b. Statistiche in Breve. Rome: INPS.

ISTAT (Italian National Institute of Statistics). 2018. Il Futuro Demografico del Paese, 2017–2065. (May). ISTAT, Rome. https://www.istat.it/it/archivio/214228.

James, Estelle. 2013. "Gender in the (Non-financial) Defined Contribution World: Issues and Options." In Nonfinancial Defined Contribution Pension Schemes in a Changing Pension World: Volume 2 Gender, Politics, and Financial Stability, edited by Robert Holzmann, Edward Palmer, and David Robalino, 3–33. Washington, DC: World Bank.

Könberg, Bo, Edward Palmer, and Annika Sundén. 2006. "The NDC Reform in Sweden: The 1994 Legislation to the Present." In Pension Reform: Issues and Prospects for Non-Financial Defined Contribution (NDC) Schemes, edited by Robert Holzmann and Edward Palmer, 449–66. Washington, DC: World Bank.

Nisticò, Sergio, and Mirko Bevilacqua. 2013. "Notional Defined Contribution (NDC) Pension Schemes and Income Patterns." Economics: The Open-Access, Open-Assessment E-Journal 7 (2013–29): 1–24. http://dx.doi.org/10.5018/economics-ejournal.ja.2013-29.

———. 2018. "Some Notes on the Redistribution Inherent in the US Public Pension System." Contemporary Economic Policy 36 (3): 566–81.

Palmer, Edward, and Yuwei Zhao de Gosson de Varennes. 2019. "Annuities in (N)DC Pension Schemes: Design, Heterogeneity, and Estimation Issues." In Progress and Challenges of Nonfinancial Defined Contribution Pension Schemes: Volume 1 Addressing Marginalization, Polarization, and the Labor Market, edited by Robert Holzmann, Edward Palmer, Robert Palacios, and Stefano Sacchi, Chapter 13. Washington, DC: World Bank.

RGS (Ragioneria Generale dello Stato/State General Accounting Department). 2018. "Le Tendenze di Medio Lungo Periodo del Sistema Pensionistico e Sociosanitario." Ministry of Economy and Finance, Government of Italy, Report No. 19, Rome.

Samuelson, Paul Anthony. 1958. "An Exact Consumption-Loan Model of Interest with or without the Social Contrivance of Money." Journal of Political Economy 66 (6): 467–82.

Settergren, Ole, 2003. "Financial and Inter-generational Balance? An Introduction to How the New Swedish Pension System Manages Conflicting Ambitions." Scandinavian Insurance Quarterly 2/2003: 99–114.

Settergren, Ole, and Danne Mikula. 2006. "The Automatic Balance Mechanism of the Swedish Pension System." Journal of Pension Economics and Finance 4 (2): 115–38.

Tinbergen, Jan. 1952. On the Theory of Economic Policy. Amsterdam: North Holland.

Valdés-Prieto, Salvador. 2000. "The Financial Stability of Notional Account Pensions." Scandinavian Journal of Economics 102 (3): 395–417.

World Bank. 2017. World Development Indicators. https://data.worldbank.org/data-catalog/world-development-indicators.

CHAPTER 5

The Polish NDC Scheme: Success in the Face of Adversity

Sonia Buchholtz, Agnieszka Chłoń-Domińczak, and Marek Góra

Introduction

Designing and implementing a nonfinancial defined contribution (NDC) scheme in parallel with a financial defined contribution (FDC) scheme in a specific country context is challenging. The process of implementing new arrangements takes many years and faces many obstacles that are difficult to foresee. This chapter presents the Polish experience, focusing especially on (a) implementation experiences, particularly during the 2008–09 financial crisis; (b) links with the labor market; and (c) loose ends.

Implementation of an NDC+FDC pension system in Poland was a response to demographic, economic, and political developments faced by the existing system, particularly in the late 1980s and early 1990s. In only two decades, Poland's socioeconomic situation changed significantly. The Polish population went through a demographic transition, with a sharp decline in fertility rates and increasing life expectancy. Population aging accelerated quickly, with projections indicating even faster changes in the coming decades. Employment rates dropped after the economic transition, and high unemployment[1] became one of the most important issues for labor market policy.

The pension system inherited from the socialist era was not fit for the upcoming challenges. Many early retirement privileges (part of them granted to cushion the shock of the transition to a market economy), combined with the high level of pensions relative to wages, particularly after the revaluation in the early 1990s,[2] resulted in very high pension expenditures that were not sustainable, given the coming retirement of the postwar baby boom generation. The explosion of early retirement combined with the rising generosity of the pension system led to a dramatic increase in the social insurance contribution rate, up to 45.0 percent in the early 1990s compared with 15.5 percent in the previous decade. Attempts to introduce ad hoc changes deteriorated social trust in the pension system.

The need for systemic reform of the pension system became obvious in the late 1990s. The global climate for reforms was good. Encouraged by international institutions, a growing number of countries introduced reforms or considered reform options. Poland's ongoing transition included a wide range of institutional reforms. The new pension system

The authors acknowledge research support from the statutory research of the SGH Warsaw School of Economics. The authors are grateful to Paweł Strzelecki and anonymous reviewers for comments and suggestions.

was designed in 1996–97 and presented in the "Security through Diversity" report (Office of the Government Plenipotentiary for Social Security Reform 1997).[3]

While the previous system fostered the interests of the retired generation, the new system was designed to balance the interests of the retired and the working generations (Jabłonowski, Müller, and Raffelhüschen 2010). Poland's new pension system is gradually reaching maturity,[4] with the first benefits paid out beginning in 2009. The system weathered the global financial crisis of 2008–09, although it affected the pension system design.

Poland's NDC+FDC Pension System

This section presents the main principles of the old-age (OA) pension system in Poland, including the development of NDC accounts, benefit payments, and management of the social insurance system, in particular its OA component.

THE MAIN PRINCIPLES OF THE OA PENSION SYSTEM

The new OA pension system was introduced in 1999. All people born after 1948 were automatically switched into the defined contribution (NDC+FDC) system, while older people stayed in the old nonfinancial defined benefit (NDB) scheme. The implementation of the new OA system was not a parametric reform, but an exchange of the old system for a new one.

One of the most important features of the new pension system is the one-to-one link between contributions and pensions. It is entirely based on individual accounts of two types: an NDC account and an FDC account for each worker.[5] Both accounts play the same social role—income allocation over a lifetime. But the accounts are managed differently, which can generate different externalities, both positive and negative.[6] The initial split of the OA contribution (19.52 percent) was 12.22 percent NDC and 7.3 percent FDC. The rest of the social insurance contribution was separated and included disability and survivors', sickness, and work injury contributions, resulting in a total level of contributions equal to the prereform contributions. One of the assumptions of the new system is that the OA contribution will remain unchanged in the future, preventing further labor cost increases.

From the very beginning the NDC concept, as the generic OA pension system, played a crucial role and served as the organizing principle of the entire system. The OA system was separated from other social insurance components—disability and survivors', sickness, maternity, and work injury. Disability pensions are still based on the prereform defined benefits (NDB) formula. The attempt to harmonize benefit calculation in 2008 failed because of a presidential veto that was not overruled. After reaching retirement age, disability pensioners are transferred to the OA pension system. They receive OA benefits, topped up to the amount of the disability benefit they received before.

Individual accounts were introduced, comprising initial capital (that is, pension rights accrued in the previous system until the end of 1998, recalculated to the NDC account value) and new contributions paid since January 1999.

Other income redistribution instruments are separated as a part of tax-financed social security, including the minimum pension guarantee, as well as financing of the pension contribution for selected periods of labor market inactivity, such as maternity and child-care periods or unemployment benefits. The rationale for pushing redistribution out of the OA pension system is that the latter should be stable, while the former should respond flexibly to changing social needs.

For those whose benefits from NDC+FDC are less than the statutory minimum level, a top-up payment is financed from general government revenues. In recent years, the minimum pension rose faster than OA pensions, with the aim of protecting OA pensioners from poverty.[7]

A "mirror" regulation helping to focus the OA system on income allocation is the cap on contributions up to 30 times the average monthly wage.[8] Incomes above this threshold are contribution free. The cap serves as a limit for benefits from the mandatory system. Above this limit, workers should manage their income allocation themselves and there is no need to involve the public system in further income replacement. In the payout phase, benefits are subject to the personal income tax as well as health care contributions, according to general principles.

Although the NDC was at the center of the system design, the FDC was the most visible part of the new OA system. The FDC is a part of the public system, the management of which was contracted to the private sector.[9] NDC and FDC contributions generate liabilities in the same way, but they are treated differently in the public accounting system; this is not logical from the viewpoint of the public OA pension system (Góra 2014). As a result of the different treatment, public pensions channeled via the FDC increased explicit public debt, while the same amount of contributions going through the NDC did not. That was a clear motivation for politicians to change the proportions of both flows in favor of the NDC. Following the worsening situation in public finances after the 2008 financial crisis and short-term public finance needs, politicians decreased the share of the FDC contribution and redeemed government bonds comprising FDC assets, transferring pension rights to subaccounts in the NDC system. Although pension liabilities remain unchanged, explicit public debt seems smaller at the expense of rising implicit liabilities.

However, this decision did not change the essence of the system, namely that the present value of benefit flows equals the present value of contribution flows. In the long run, the discount factor for both the NDC and the FDC converges to the nominal gross domestic product (GDP) growth rate.[10] Given the NDC design, the change in proportions did not alter the main principles of the new system.

INDIVIDUAL ACCOUNTS IN THE POLISH PENSION SYSTEM

The public OA pension system collects the contribution rate of 19.52 percent of the individual wage. Currently, the contribution is divided between either (a) three accounts—NDC-1 (12.22 percent), NDC-2 (4.38 percent), and FDC (2.92 percent) for workers who decided to continue paying FDC contributions; or (b) two accounts—NDC-1 (12.22 percent) and NDC-2 (7.3 percent) for everyone else.

The part of the contribution that was initially a part of the FDC is recorded on the NDC-2 account, established in 2011, following the changes in the OA contribution split. In 2011, the contribution to the FDC account was reduced to 2.3 percent and the remaining 5 percent was transferred to the NDC-2 account. In 2015 the NDC-2 accounts were also credited with the value of redeemed government bonds from the FDC accounts. From 2015 the contribution to the NDC-2 accounts is also set at the current level—4.38 percent or 7.3 percent—depending on the decision of whether to put savings in the FDC part.

After the law changed in 2014, 10 years before the legal retirement age of 60 for women and 65 for men, assets from the FDC account are gradually transferred to the Social Insurance Fund (FUS) and recorded on the NDC-2 account. As a result, upon reaching the legal retirement age all pension wealth in the mandatory system is recorded on the NDC-1 and NDC-2 accounts. Annuities from the OA system are therefore fully paid from the NDC system.[11]

The NDC-1 and NDC-2 accounts differ in two respects. First, the rate of return in NDC-1 is the covered wage bill growth from the previous year, whereas in NDC-2 it is the average nominal GDP growth rate over the preceding five-year period. Although both rates can be justified, the use of two rates generates problems in managing the accounts as well as in informing participants about their account values. Second, the amount in the NDC-1 account of the deceased is not inherited (either by family members or the survivors in the insurance pool); instead the "inheritance gain" is (implicitly) used to finance liabilities from the actuarially imbalanced pre-1999 system. In contrast, the amount in NDC-2 is inherited. Although this feature is not logical for the NDC scheme, it was introduced to maintain social acceptance for the change. Politicians were able to shift contributions from the FDC to the NDC-2 account, but they did not want to change the individual inheritance rights of participants.

Additional voluntary private options to allocate more income for future pensions gradually developed. Since 1999 workers have been able to participate in employee pension plans. In 2004 and 2011 two forms of voluntary individual pension accounts were added: IKE (individual pension accounts) and IKZE (individual retirement protection accounts). However, fewer than 5 percent of workers participate in any of the instruments, for many reasons: no tradition of individual saving, limited long-term investment options, and lack of trust toward financial institutions. The financial crisis and changes in the pension system intensified this distrust. In 2018 the government proposed new auto-enrollment-based employee capital plans (Pracownicze Programy Kapitałowe—PPK) to boost additional savings for retirement consumption, but it is difficult to predict their impact on the increase of voluntary pension saving, planned for introduction in 2019.

An important principle of the new system was to increase workers' pension awareness. One of the key tools for achieving awareness was the distribution of individual account statements, which according to the initial assumptions were to be sent annually. However, because of the changes in the split of contributions, breaks in the delivery of statements occurred. Additionally, until 2017 the difficult language used in the statements made them incomprehensible. Since 2017 the statements have been significantly simplified and include (a) the amount of contributions paid to NDC-1, NDC-2, and FDC; (b) the total value of NDC-1 (including initial capital) and NDC-2; (c) the value of the hypothetical OA pension based on the current value of the NDC as well as their projected values, assuming the current level of contributions are paid until retirement.

Improving pension literacy is one of the most important challenges facing the Polish pension system. According to a 2017 Social Insurance Institution (Zakład Ubezpieczeń Społecznych [ZUS]) assessment, 82 percent of eligible workers plan to retire as soon as possible—despite the fact that one additional year of work would increase their benefits by about 8 percent. Simple and consistent communication is one of the key means of encouraging longer working lives and higher pension incomes in the future.

PENSION BENEFITS AND THE RETIREMENT AGE

The implementation of the NDC+FDC OA pension system required a change in the policy toward early retirement, one of the key reasons for actuarial imbalance in the former pension system. Given the rules of NDC+FDC, maintaining early retirement would lead to very low benefits. On the other hand, people were used to retiring early. The average effective retirement age was about 55 years for women and 59 years for men. No options for early retirement exist in the NDC system after 2008.[12] Limited early retirement resulting from hazardous and arduous conditions (following definitions developed by occupational health specialists) for those employed before 1999 is available through so-called bridging pensions (for about 2.5 percent of workers). Bridging pensions will eventually disappear after all eligible workers retire. Bridging pensions are outside the universal OA system and are financed from additional employers' contributions and taxes.

Options for early retirement for long service period at age 55 for women and 60 for men[13] were also removed from the OA system as of 2009. The outcome of these changes is shown in figure 5.1. The first pensioners from the new system retired in 2009 (women) and 2014 (men). This is also when the average retirement age for both sexes started to rise. Concurrently, the dominant age group of retirees shifted to 65–69 for men and 60–64 for women.

Delaying implementation of changes in the early retirement system, compared with the initial scenario, led to higher pension expenditures and state budget subsidies to the pension system. It contributed to the changes in the system introduced between 2011 and 2015, discussed in "The Minimum Retirement Age Is Scheduled to Increase in the Future."

One of the crucial factors affecting the level of benefits is the retirement age. An equal retirement age for men and women was among the key assumptions of the new pension system. The initial "Security through Diversity" proposal that equalized the retirement age at 62 was not supported by politicians. In 2012, the government initiated a gradual increase and equalization of the retirement age at 67 (at the pace of three months per year). However, in 2016, the new government reversed this change. As a result, in October 2017 the retirement age returned to 60 years for women and 65 years for men. The reversal of the retirement age increase resulted in an increased number of new pensions granted in 2017. Specifically, 417,000 people (of whom 62.8 percent were women) claimed benefits, a figure not observed in the past two decades (figure 5.1). The change will lead to a likely decline of the effective retirement age of women to about 60 years. This change should have significant consequences for the adequacy of pensions, particularly for women (Chłoń-Domińczak and Strzelecki 2013). Although this is a step backward, removal of early retirement is still a success.[14]

OA pensions are calculated by dividing the value of the sum of the NDC-1 and NDC-2 accounts by unisex life expectancy at retirement age.[15] The entire OA pension system focuses on income reallocation over a lifetime. Using universal unisex life tables implicitly reallocates between those living shorter lives and those living longer lives (that is, between men and women, and between those less educated and more educated), which is difficult to avoid in the public pension system. The life expectancy factor is announced annually by the Central Statistical Office (GUS), based on current cross-sectional data on mortality. This may lead to underestimation of life expectancy and overestimation of pension benefits (Knell 2016; Więckowska and Bijak 2009), which is partially offset by inheritance gains remaining in the system. Given this way of calculating benefits, the lower retirement age for women will lead to a rising gender pension gap and lower pensions for women.

FIGURE 5.1 **Inflow of new retirees by age and average retirement age, by sex, 1999–2017**

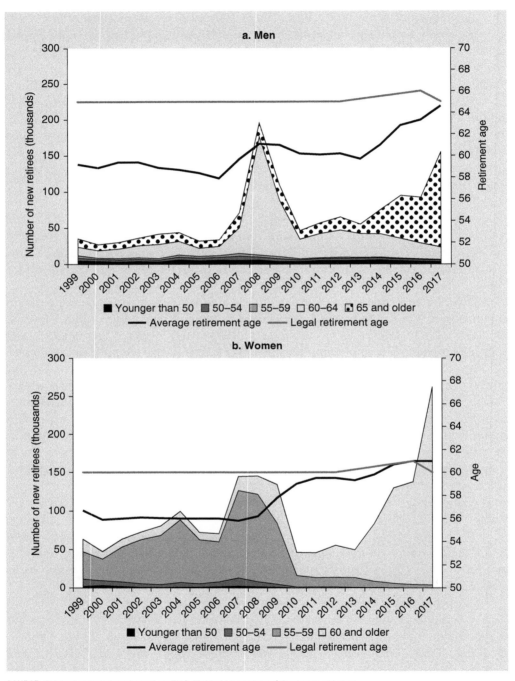

SOURCE: Original calculations based on ZUS (Zakład Ubezpieczeń Społecznych) data.

The worst outcome of lowering the retirement age is that a misleading signal is sent to the working generation. In the future, a rise in the retirement age is inevitable. Once it happens, the change will be much sharper, up to 67 or even higher. People will have to prepare for such a change, while politicians demotivate them.

ADMINISTRATION AND FINANCIAL ORGANIZATION OF THE SOCIAL INSURANCE SYSTEM IN POLAND

All parts of the social insurance system in Poland are managed by ZUS, a public entity responsible for collection of all types of social insurance contributions and for paying out all social insurance benefits. For that purpose, ZUS manages the following funds:

- The Social Insurance Fund (Fundusz Ubezpieczeń Społecznych—FUS), a state target fund and a part of the public finance system. The pension reform divided FUS into four parts: the OA pension fund, a disability and survivors' fund, sickness and maternity funds, and a work injury fund.

- The Demographic Reserve Fund (Fundusz Rezerwy Demograficznej—FRD), a buffer fund for the OA system. Initially, FRD was established from a part of social insurance contributions paid to FUS (since 2008, 0.35 percent), and since 2009 40 percent of privatization revenues have been paid into the fund. Between 2010 and 2014 FRD assets were used to finance the deficit in FUS (figure 5.2). At the end of 2016, FRD assets totaled Zl 21.8 billion (approximately €5.4 billion), compared to Zl 201 billion (approximately €48 billion) of total FUS expenditures.

- The Bridging Pensions Fund (Fundusz Emerytur Pomostowych—FEP), from which bridging pensions are financed. FEP was established in 2010. In 2016 total FEP outlays were Zl 519.7 million (approximately €123.7 million). Revenues from contributions were Zl 236.8 million (approximately €56.3 million) and the state budget subsidy was Zl 249.6 million (approximately €59.4 million).

Financial management of FUS and other funds is subject to annual assessment. First, the funds are reviewed by auditing companies, based on the premise of the Law on the Social Insurance System. ZUS and all funds are also reviewed by the Supreme Audit Office. The same law also obliges ZUS to prepare projections on expenditures and revenues for all parts of FUS. These projections cover a five-year period and are prepared annually. Every three years, ZUS also prepares a long-term (about 50 years) projection of revenues and expenditures of the OA part of the pension system. The reform project also included establishment of the National Actuary Office to supervise long-term liabilities created within the entire social security system. This element of the system has not yet been introduced and there is no political interest in doing so.

Overall, since the introduction of the new pension system, FUS has had a deficit ranging from 1.0 percent to more than 4.5 percent of GDP (in 2010). Most of this deficit is attributed to the overall imbalance between benefit expenditures and contribution revenues (figure 5.2). Since 2014, FUS has also received assets transferred from FDC. From 2010 on, because of the change in the proportion in OA contributions as well as the reduction of pension expenditures related to the shift to the new pension system, the subsidy declined to less than 3 percent of GDP.

FIGURE 5.2 **Polish social insurance system finances**

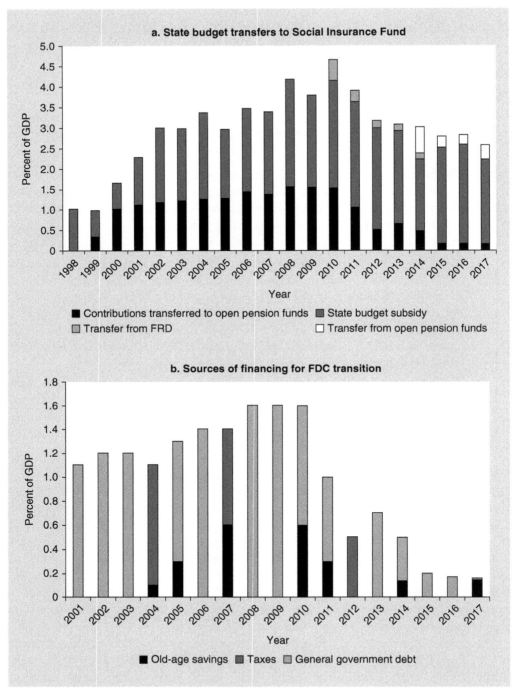

SOURCE: Original calculation based on ZUS (Zakład Ubezpieczeń Społecznych) data (panel b) (Bielawska, Chłoń-Domińczak, and Stańko 2017) with original update (panel a).

NOTE: FDC = financial defined contribution; FRD = Demographic Reserve Fund (Fundusz Rezerwy Demograficznej); GDP = gross domestic product.

FIGURE 5.3 **Decomposition of projected changes in the size of the population active in the labor force, 2020–50 relative to 2015**

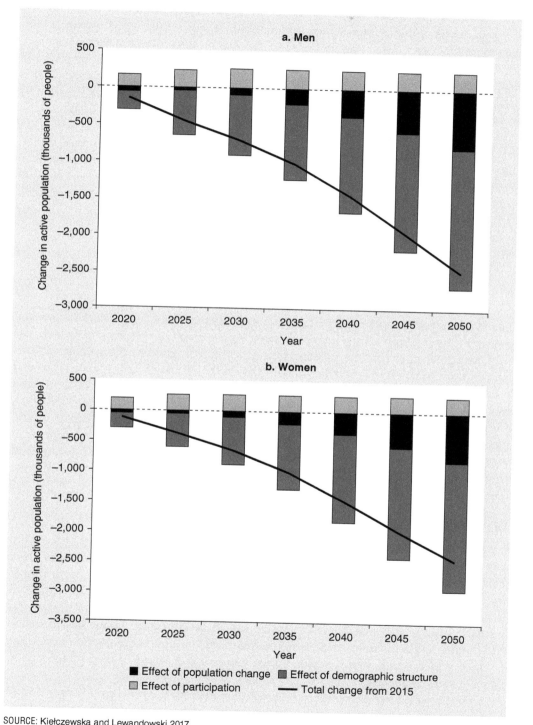

The financial projections prepared with the initial reform proposal assumed that the part of the transition costs related to the transfer of a portion of the contribution to the FDC system would be covered by the savings in the OA expenditures, that is, by reducing early retirement and lowering the pension indexation toward inflation. However, in reality, indexation was closer to wage growth and changes to early retirement were postponed. This means that in the past decades, annual pension expenditures usually increased in relation to GDP. Only in seven years between 2001 and 2017 did pension expenditures decline on a year-over-year basis. As a result, most of the transition costs were financed by an increase in the public debt (Bielawska, Chłoń-Domińczak, and Stańko 2017).

Projections published by ZUS indicate that the OA pension fund will remain in deficit. In the baseline scenario for the long-term projection, OA pension fund expenditures are expected to decline from 7.14 percent of GDP in 2017 to 6.12 percent in 2060, while revenues from contributions are projected to fall from 5.01 percent of GDP to 4.73 percent (ZUS 2016). The resulting deficit will drop from 2.13 percent of GDP to 1.40 percent. These developments are mainly due to long-term demographic and economic trends, discussed in the next section.

Demographic and Economic Short-Run Volatility and Long-Run Sustainability

Poland faces significant demographic and economic changes that will affect the short- and long-term sustainability of the pension system. As explained in the previous section, the NDC design ensures that the present value of benefits is equal to the present value of contributions paid. This is guaranteed mainly by the NDC rate of return, which is related to either the covered wage bill growth (in NDC-1) or GDP growth (in NDC-2). As a result, changes in gross productivity, driven by labor force size and human capital quality, affect both the wage bill and contribution revenues. Employment level and human capital also affect the potential GDP growth rate. This section presents recent developments in human capital formation. It also discusses the short-run volatility of the pension system, which is associated with the consequences of the financial crisis. Finally, it considers the long-term stability of the Polish pension system.

HUMAN CAPITAL IN POLAND

Poland is facing a twofold challenge. First, since the early 1990s, Poland has experienced very low fertility rates, which are now at their lowest levels. The current rate is lower than the European average, similar to other Eastern European countries. According to projections, the rate will remain below 1.5 children per woman for the next couple of decades. Second, at the same time, life expectancy is gradually rising; it is currently at the European average and increasing at a similar pace. As a result, total population as well as the working-age population are already declining and this trend is projected to continue for the next decades. Concurrently, the population older than age 65, including postwar baby boomers, is growing.

The projected trends have been intensified by migration. Since Poland's accession to the European Union (EU), emigration from Poland has increased significantly. GUS estimated that at the end of 2016 almost 2.5 million Poles lived abroad (GUS 2016a).

Post-accession migration amounted to a 3.3 percent loss in the working-age population (Kaczmarczyk and Okólski 2008). This includes in particular working-age men (4.4 percent), younger age groups, and individuals with higher education. The total estimated loss was 9.3 percent in the 25–29 age group and 8.8 percent in the 20–24 age group. The share of migrants was also higher among those with tertiary education (5 percent). Despite the increased flow of migrants from Eastern Europe (particularly Ukraine), the net effect remains negative. According to other estimates, changes in the age structure of the population are driving the projected decline in the labor force (figure 5.3) (Kiełczewska and Lewandowski 2017). By 2050, the total population active in the labor force is projected to decline by almost 5 million people.

To some extent, changes in labor force size will be offset by projected changes in individual labor productivity. Since the economic transition, participation of young people in tertiary education has increased significantly (Marciniak et al. 2013). According to Eurostat, between 1997 and 2015 the share of 30–34-year-olds with tertiary education more than tripled, rising from 13.5 percent to 43.4 percent. This share is expected to increase more in the coming years. This qualitative change will contribute to the steady increase in human capital in Poland until the 2030s (Stonawski 2014). Afterward, the quantitative impact will prevail and human capital will start to fall. Before 2050 it will return to the levels of the early 2000s.

THE IMPACT OF SHORT-RUN DISTURBANCES ON THE PENSION SYSTEM IN POLAND: LEARNING FROM THE ECONOMIC CRISIS

Economic growth remained positive during the 2008–09 crisis. However, the economic slowdown had an impact on the pension system, which was additionally affected by legislative changes.

Between 2008 and 2010, contribution revenues to the social insurance system relative to GDP first declined and then increased because of a combination of the reduction in the contribution rate for disability insurance (without a reduction in expenditures) proposed by the government before the elections in 2007, and the decline in wage growth during the slowdown. At the same time, the number of insured workers also decreased. Figure 5.4 (panel a) shows contribution revenues and expenditures by subfund. The decline in OA contribution revenues up to 2010 was driven by both the declining wage-fund-to-GDP ratio and the increase in the share of contributors covered by the new system with NDC+FDC accounts. After the change in 2010, OA contributions increased from 3.5 percent to 5.2 percent of GDP, in line with the increase in the part of OA contributions to the NDC scheme. The income from disability contributions dropped from 3.0 percent in 2007 to 1.7 percent in 2008 because of the reduction in the contribution rate, and increased again in 2012 and after, when it was raised again. Thus, a significant part of the FUS deficit in the period of economic slowdown (2008–10) resulted from the decision to reduce contributions regardless of the unbalanced fund. Even though the OA pension system was an autonomous part of the social security system, the government treated it as part of the entire social insurance system. As a consequence, the OA system bore the burden of covering the deficit resulting from lower disability fund contributions.

During the economic slowdown, expenditures on benefits rose in relation to GDP. The increase resulted from growth in the number of beneficiaries due to the larger inflow

FIGURE 5.4 **Expenditures and revenues of the social insurance system in Poland, 2001–17**

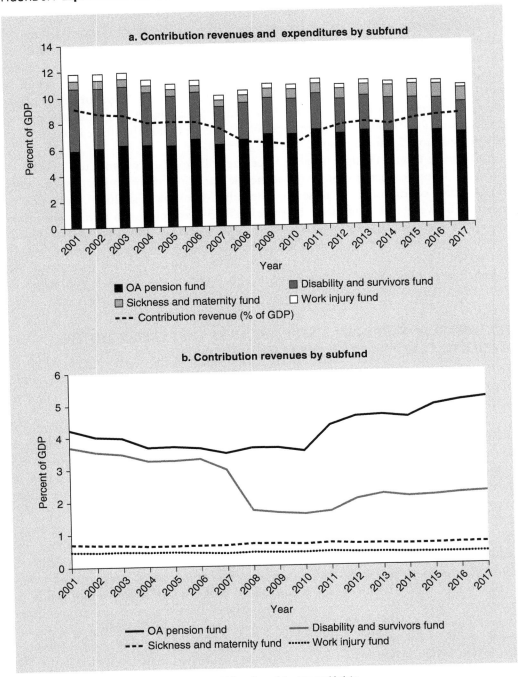

SOURCE: Original estimates based on ZUS (Zakład Ubezpieczeń Społecznych) data.

NOTE: GDP = gross domestic product; OA = old-age.

of early retirees and the regular indexation of benefits related to prices and part of wage growth. The former can be traced back to the early retirement reform described in the previous section.

The FUS deficit widened significantly between 2007 and 2010, coinciding with the overall deterioration in public finances. Over the same period, the general government deficit increased from 1.9 percent of GDP to 7.9 percent, much higher than the Stability and Growth Pact limit of 3 percent. At the same time, general government debt jumped from 45 percent of GDP to 54.9 percent.

Given this situation, combined with the upcoming parliamentary elections in 2011, the government introduced changes in the financing of the pension system that would lead to a reduction of the overall level of government subsidy to the social insurance system. As mentioned, FRD was used to finance some pension expenditures in 2010–14. Additionally, in 2010 the contribution rate for disability and survivors' insurance was increased slightly, partially reversing the decline from 2008. These measures were, however, not sufficient to avoid the risk of public debt exceeding the threshold of 55 percent of GDP. In comparison with other EU countries—especially these experiencing recession after the crisis in 2009—Poland's public finance situation was not very bad. The real problem was that the threshold of 60 percent debt established in the Polish Constitution, which would trigger the balancing of the government budget, was approaching relatively quickly. In response to this threat, the government decided that changes in the OA system would be easier than cutting expenditures or raising taxes. Another problem was the constant demand for bonds created by institutions that managed the FDC.

The changes were made in two steps. The first step, beginning in May 2011, included a reduction of the contribution to the FDC to 2.3 percent of wage, while 5.0 percent of wage was recorded on the newly established NDC-2 accounts, indexed to nominal GDP growth, averaged for four consecutive calendar years. Initially, the contribution to the FDC was planned to be gradually increased back to 3.5 percent, but this never happened.

The second step, undertaken in 2014, included the following:

- Transfer of FDC assets invested in government bonds (more than one-half of the total) to FRD and their redemption.

- Permanently reducing FDC contributions to 2.92 percent and making this part of the system voluntary. All workers contributing to FDC could choose to contribute either to private pension funds or to NDC-2. The latter was the default option. As a result, fewer than 2 million workers still have their contributions split between the NDC and the FDC.

- Introduction of the so-called slider mechanism: 10 years before retirement a fraction of one's assets is transferred to FUS and the value recorded on NDC-2.

The permanent reduction of contributions to the FDC since May 2011 reduced the general government debt by 0.6 percent of GDP in 2011. The one-off measure—transfer of Treasury bonds held by pension funds—accounted for a 5 percentage point drop in the debt-to-GDP ratio in 2014. Changes in the FDC contribution rate complemented with the voluntary character of participation led to a further reduction in transition costs to 0.3–0.4 percent of GDP (Bielawska, Chłoń-Domińczak, and Stańko 2017).

Overall, the long-term Ageing Working Group (AWG) projections in the subsequent Ageing Reports from 2009, 2012, and 2015 indicated that the key features of the new pension system led to the reduction in pension expenditures, compared with the baseline, despite a sharp increase in the projected dependency rate (European Commission DG ECFIN 2009, 2012, 2015). The forecasted decline in public pension expenditures is the smallest in the 2015 AWG report. However, if one takes into account the fact that full pension expenditures are attributed to the public part, the total 2060 pension expenditures projection remains stable (table 5.1).

This stability is achieved mainly in two ways: the benefit-ratio contribution shows that the level of individual benefits is linked to lifetime contributions and the coverage ratio, indicating the overall rise of the effective retirement age. Because the level of lifetime benefits depends on lifetime contributions, the recent reform lowering the retirement age means that in order to receive an adequate pension, people (especially women) will have to increase their years of participation and contribution amounts during the shorter period left before retirement. At the same time, the divisor in the benefit formula will increase because of longer life expectancy, resulting in smaller yearly payments. For these reasons, the reform constitutes a long-run risk for future adequacy. The results of the 2018 AWG indicate that projected pension expenditures by 2060 will be slightly higher compared with earlier projections. A significant shift also occurs in the decomposition of effects, leading to stabilization of pension expenditures. The impact of the benefit-ratio contribution increases, while the coverage-ratio contribution declines. This is a result of the reversal of the retirement age increase.

The main lesson from the economic slowdown is that for predominantly political reasons, the short-term perspective of the poor fiscal situation prevailed over the long-term perspective typical for the pension system. Furthermore, any deviation from the initial reform agenda leading to worsening fiscal outcomes increases the risk of fiscal adjustments to pension systems.

TABLE 5.1 **Long-term pension expenditures in Poland: Summary of Ageing Working Group projections**
percent of GDP

	2009	2012	2015	2018
Base year pension expenditures	11.6	11.8	11.5	11.2
Base year:	2007	2010	2013	2016
2060 public pension expenditures	8.8	9.6	10.7	11.1
2060 FDC expenditures	1.9	1.3	0	0
Total 2060 expenditures	10.7	10.9	10.7	11.1
	2007–60	2010–60	2013–60	2016–60
Change in pension expenditures	−2.8	−2.2	−0.8	−0.1
Dependency-ratio contribution	13.4	14.0	12.4	12.1
Benefit-ratio contribution	−7.1	−8.7	−5.2	−7.3
Coverage-ratio contribution	−6.3	−5.0	−5.2	−3.1

SOURCES: European Commission DG ECFIN 2009, 2012, 2015, 2018.

NOTE: The change in pension expenditures is the difference between projected 2060 public pension expenditures and base year pension expenditures. FDC = financial defined contribution. GDP = gross domestic product.

Labor Market Challenges

The NDC-based OA pension system balances the interests of the working and retired generations through the one-to-one link between contributions and benefits. For the working generation, this link means that in general the contribution rate remains stable irrespective of demographic developments. In other words, everyone receives an OA pension equivalent to what he or she paid in. Keeping contributions constant and not increasing them stimulates job creation and better remuneration of production factors supplied by the working generation. The NDC scheme is an automatic and neutral way to achieve this balance of interests.

LABOR MARKET IN POLAND: MAIN CHALLENGES FOR THE NDC PENSION SYSTEM

A strong link between benefits and lifetime contributions means that labor market performance is crucial, both for the sustainability of the pension system and for adequacy of individual benefits. Labor market policy should focus on longer working lives and higher productivity and wage levels. Four challenges the Polish labor market faces in the context of the pension system are described below.

(1) Low labor market participation is the reason for nonaccumulation of pension contributions.

While prime-age workers in Poland have employment rates similar to the EU average, workers older than 50 (men and women) are less frequently employed. In 2016 the gap in the 50–64 age group in employment rates exceeded 7 percentage points for men and reached 10 percentage points for women. Women's employment gap has remained stable since 2003, while for men it has decreased by one-half since 2004. Almost 75 percent of inactive women between 25 and 44 years old indicate that their inactivity is related to care responsibilities or other family obligations. In the oldest age groups, inactivity is related to poor health or receiving a pension.

According to a National Bank of Poland assessment, high inactivity exists among the 18–24 age group because of high participation in higher education (Gradzewicz et al. 2016). Combining studying and work is not as popular in Poland as in other EU countries.

The downward trend in activity among those 50 and older observed in the early 2000s resulted from preretirement allowances and benefits introduced to alleviate the consequences of structural changes in the economy. The rebound after 2004 and further after 2008 is attributed to the reduction of these options. The increase in labor market participation in the 50–64 age group was robust even during the global economic slowdown, not only in Poland. The reversal of the legal retirement age back to 65 (men) and 60 (women) is likely stop this trend, particularly for women.

According to the Labor Force Survey, almost one-fifth of the economically inactive declare that they would like to work. Gradzewicz et al. (2016) estimate that about one-third of them could start working. Boosting participation in this group could raise labor supply by 3.2 percent.

(2) Under fixed-term contracts, which are used excessively, paid work is reflected in accumulated contributions only partially or not at all, and the quality of jobs is lower.

According to GUS (2016a), in 2014 6.9 percent of all workers were working on the basis of fixed-term contracts; for 4.4 percentage points of them it was a main job. A similar level (4.2 percent) was estimated by the National Bank of Poland in 2016 (Saczuk, Strzelecki, and Wyszyński 2016). Both sources indicate that the decision on the type of contract was mainly involuntary (GUS: 80.2 percent; National Bank of Poland: 59.9 percent) and they would have preferred a regular labor-code contract, particularly those on commission contracts. Among the self-employed, 51.3 percent declared that employers forced them to designate themselves as self-employed. The quality of fixed-term jobs is significantly lower as measured by earnings, development opportunities, job security, job strain, or incidence of long working hours (Lewandowski, Góra, and Lis 2017). Those working in atypical forms of employment have limited social security coverage, either because their contributions are lower or, in the case of some civil code contracts, they are not covered at all (Chłoń-Domińczak, Sowa, and Topińska 2017).

Since 2002, the popularity of fixed-term contracts has increased significantly as a result of a modestly high labor tax wedge, a significant difference in privilege between regular and fixed-term contract workers, the possibility of omitting legal labor standards (minimum wage, overtime, safety standards, and so on), and other costs (Lewandowski et al. 2017). Legislative changes implemented in 2016 benchmarked the minimum social insurance contribution base (in the case of multiple contracts) to the minimum wage (Chłoń-Domińczak, Sowa, and Topińska 2017) and reduced the marginal benefit of using fixed-term contracts. However, they still have some strengths, such as ease of contract resolution. The legislation is believed to have raised the share of regular contracts (Saczuk, Strzelecki, and Wyszyński. 2016).

(3) Interruptions in the working career contribute in two ways: through nonaccumulation of pension contributions and by penalizing workers.

Interruptions in working careers usually happen when working arrangements are not flexible enough to be reconciled with personal commitments. One of the possible remedies in this respect is part-time work, which is a rare phenomenon in Poland compared with the EU average. With the exception of prime-age women, the trend was significantly downward for the past two decades (from 16.3 percent to 5.5 percent among men and from 23.0 percent to 11.3 percent among women in the 50–64 age group). Increasing the flexibility of the labor market without escalating the insider-outsider problem is difficult. There is no tradition of part-time work, and no incentives have been introduced to increase labor market supply. Employers are reluctant to create part-time jobs because of the high fixed cost of recruitment, training, and general management. It would seem that a tight labor market should change this segmentation.

(4) Informal employment is not reflected in contributions (unless individuals save on their own), while jobs are insecure and the ability to litigate own rights is extremely difficult.

No consensus exists regarding the scale and dynamics of informal employment in Poland. Schneider (2016) estimates its slow decline to 23 percent in 2016. Other sources (Ernst &Young 2016; GUS 2016b; Łapiński, Peterlik, and Wyżnikiewicz 2016) suggest it ranges between 12.4 percent and 19.7 percent. Estimates of the shadow economy are scarce, but more is known about unregistered employment—between 2004 and 2014 it decreased by more than one-half (from 9.6 percent to 4.5 percent). Unregistered employment is higher among men and individuals with vocational education and is concentrated in several sectors of the economy: agriculture, trade, hotels and restaurants, neighborhood services, and manufacturing (GUS 2016b). Reasons for taking up unregistered employment are inability to find a job (more than 60 percent), insufficient income (more than 30 percent), higher pay without a formal contract (more than 30 percent), and a too-high social insurance rate (more than 10 percent). For 60 percent of respondents it was a main job (GUS 2016b). According to Schneider (2012), more than one-half of the grey economy in Poland can be explained by labor-related factors. Given the relatively low tax compliance and the low efficiency of law enforcement, the incentives to move from informal to formal employment are low.

LABOR MARKET SEGMENTATION AND PENSION SUBSYSTEMS IN POLAND

The NDC system covers employees and the self-employed outside agriculture. Other subsystems in Poland include selected labor market segments, including farmers (Farmers Social Insurance Fund—KRUS—the largest subsystem), policemen and members of the armed forces (a noncontributory armed forces pension regime), and judges and prosecutors (a noncontributory pension scheme). Furthermore, since 2005, miners insured in ZUS have been covered by an NDB scheme based on the old system formula. These schemes are unbalanced actuarially, another source of long-term instability. Furthermore, their generosity hampers labor market mobility. In particular, as the European Commission stressed in 2017 in its European Semester Country Report, the existence of a separate pension regime for farmers is a fiscal burden (the subsidy to KRUS amounts to approximately 1 percent of GDP), a drag on labor mobility, and one of the causes of hidden unemployment in agriculture (European Commission 2017a). In light of these issues, the European Council and the European Commission in its Country Specific Recommendations continue to recommend aligning all pension systems with the general (NDC) framework (European Commission 2017b).

LABOR FORCE PARTICIPATION—LONG TERM OUTLOOK

These estimates are in line with the 2018 Ageing Report, which forecasts employment in the 20–74 age group to decline from 17.1 million in 2016 to 11.8 million in 2060 (European Commission DG ECFIN 2018). Extending working lives and increasing labor participation are two of the most important challenges the Polish NDC pension system and economy are facing. Future changes in the labor force will be driven mainly by demographic trends. Kiełczewska and Lewandowski (2017) estimate that cohort effects will increase participation rates because current prime-age and young people will have higher participation rates after reaching age 55 than their counterparts do today. This pattern is likely to occur because subsequent cohorts are better educated, and early retirement options were limited in the 2000s. The improvement in the labor force participation of older people will translate into 500,000 additional active individuals by 2050—a noticeable figure, but not nearly enough to offset the demographically driven reduction in the labor supply. Increasing prime-age women's labor participation is also important and should be targeted by labor market policies. If the gap in labor force participation between prime-age women and men were gradually halved by 2040 (in conjunction with an increase in the retirement age), labor supply would increase by 250,000 after 10 years, and by 500,000 after 20 years (Kiełczewska and Lewandowski 2017). This would also translate into longer working lives of women and, in turn, higher pension benefits.

POLICIES TO ENHANCE LABOR FORCE PARTICIPATION

A set of coordinated policies is required to significantly offset the demographically driven decline in the labor force. Extending working lives demands a return to the gradual increases in the legal retirement age, as well as improvements in the quality of the labor market for older workers. Results of the 2015 Survey on Health, Aging and Retirement in Europe show that Polish workers 50 and older are very frequently tired (either physically or because of routine tasks) or unsatisfied with their jobs, and they would like to retire as soon as possible (Chłoń-Domińczak, Holzer-Żelażewska, and Maliszewska 2017). Moreover, a lifelong learning policy is needed to increase the very low participation of adults in various forms of lifelong training, so that their skills are updated to meet the changing needs of the labor market. Working lives could also be extended by offering flexible retirement options for those who reach the minimum retirement age, for example, partial retirement, which was introduced for women with the increase in retirement age in 2014 but removed once the retirement age was lowered again to 60.

Raising the labor market participation of prime-age women requires introducing a set of coordinated family policies (Kotowska and Magda 2017). Such policies would include all the measures that assist both parents, facilitate their ability to combine work and family life, and allow for equal sharing of opportunities and responsibilities. Reconciling work and family life requires improved access to child-care facilities, especially for children under three, whose coverage is very low. Another recommended measure is to improve the accessibility and quality of daycare for school children and after-school support. A more coherent and flexible system of leave (maternity, paternity, parental, and family) is also recommended. Improving women's labor participation also requires labor market policy that facilitates equal partnership and incentives for fathers to share more of the care burden. Such a policy should encourage more women to stay in or return to the labor market, contributing to decreasing the gender pay gap, which itself will act as a strong incentive for both women's labor market participation and men's use of leave. Finally, progress in flexible working time patterns and improving job quality—for both men and women—will contribute to meeting family and labor market policy objectives. However, recent policies introduced by the government have the opposite impact, for example, the decline of the retirement age, increased cash transfers to families, and an increase in the school entry age to seven years, combined with removing mandatory preschool participation of five-year-old children.

The employment gap could also be partly filled by migration. Indeed, recent years saw an increased inflow of migrants to Poland. Gradzewicz et al. (2016) highlight that the share of companies that declared employment of at least one foreigner increased from 5 percent in 2010 to 13 percent in 2016 and to 30 percent in 2018 (Narodowy Bank Polski 2018). The increase was the largest among big companies, where four out of five foreign workers are employed. The share of migrants in total employment also increased. According to ZUS data, in the first quarter of 2018 foreigners amounted to some 3 percent of insured people. This feature stems from the quickly increasing inflow of migrants from Ukraine, particularly after 2014. The majority of this flow has a short-term or circulatory character, judging from the officially stated "expected" term of employment of migrants of up to six months (1.824 million in 2017), while employment based on work permits is less frequent (235,600 in 2017).

To summarize, the Polish labor market still needs policies that encourage more stable and longer working patterns that could contribute to slowing the expected employment decline and resulting low benefit levels. The NDC system remains neutral and financially stable, while the adequacy of benefits depends on long and productive employment careers over a lifetime.

Adequacy and Solidarity

Benefits paid out from the OA system based on the NDC reach the upper bound of the available average level of the expected value of benefits, given the contribution rate, the employment rate, and public sector expenditures. NDC benefits reflect the real demographic and economic situation, while NDB pensions are a result of a formula that might not be adjusted to this situation.

CURRENT AND FUTURE PENSIONS IN POLAND

Changes in the pension level are gradually observed with the increase in the number of NDC pensions in payment. The average level of NDC pensions granted since 2014 is close to the average OA benefit paid by the social insurance system and slightly less than 60 percent of the average wage in the economy (net of social insurance contributions) (table 5.2). The ratio between pensions and wages is gradually declining, as expected with the introduction of the new pension system.

The level of pension benefits in relation to wages will be lower for new entrants to the labor market, who will contribute throughout their entire careers to the new pension system. Reduction of the retirement age will further deepen this decline. According to projections of theoretical replacement rates (TRRs) in the 2018 Pension Adequacy Report (PAR), the net replacement rate for the average wage earner who started his or her career

TABLE 5.2 **Number and level of NDC pensions granted in 2014–17**

		2014	2015	2016	2017
Number of NDC pensions granted	(thousands of people)	132.1	208.2	216.2	404.3
Level of NDC pensions granted	(Zl)	1,975.53	2,037.29	2,055.99	2,097.08
	(% of average pension)	96.7	97.2	96.5	96.1
	(% of average wage)	59.8	59.8	58.2	56.2

SOURCE: Zakład Ubezpieczeń Społecznych (ZUS) 2017, 2018.

NOTE: NDC = nonfinancial defined contribution; Zl = Polish zlotys.

in 2016 at age 20 and will retire at the standard pensionable age (65 years for men and 60 for women with a career length of 40 years) is 44.7 percent for men and 37.8 percent for women (European Commission 2018). Therefore, because of their lower retirement age, women can expect pensions that will be about one-fifth lower than those of men. With deferred exit at age 67 with a 42-year career length, the net TRR increases to 47 percent. The pension system rewards postponing retirement decisions, an inherent feature of NDC systems.

The Pension Adequacy Report projections bear two important messages. First, the level of benefit that is affordable for the pension system, given the projected career length, will decrease relative to the average wage, if the legal retirement age is considered. Second, at the individual level workers can increase their expected pensions by postponing retirement.

Whereas the average NDC benefits result from the above-mentioned processes, their distribution needs further discussion. Table 5.3 shows future TRR levels depending on the wage. Low wage earners (those with income equal to or below two-thirds of the average) can expect a slightly higher pension relative to their wage because of the minimum pension guarantee. Those with high incomes (income rising from 100 percent to 200 percent of average over a lifetime) can expect replacement of about 30 percent of their final wage, which is related to the assumed wage profile, with peak earnings at the end of the working career. Those earning more than 250 percent of the average will also have relatively lower OA pensions because of the cap on contributions.

However, the projections are based on the unlikely assumption that the retirement age will remain 65 for men and 60 for women. The inevitable increase of that age will contribute to higher benefits. In an NDC+FDC system, that increase will be sharper than in traditional systems.

OA pensions are affected by career breaks. The Pension Adequacy Report provides projections of expected benefit levels for those with career breaks caused by periods of unemployment and childbirth. The TRR projections show a reduction in the expected pension level because the contributions for selected periods paid from the state budget are less than those implied by earnings in the base case.

However, reductions for career breaks of up to three years are not significant compared with the no-career-break scenario, which indicates that the redistribution mechanisms allow for adequate compensation of career breaks (table 5.4). A short career (one-half of the base case) leads to pension levels that are about one-half of those of full career workers.

TABLE 5.3 **Theoretical replacement rates (net) in 2056 by earnings level**
percent of last wage

	Wage level		
	Low	**Average**	**High**
40-year career ending at 65, men	44.9	44.7	33.2
40-year career ending at 60, women	38.0	37.8	28.1

SOURCE: European Commission 2018.

TABLE 5.4 **Theoretical replacement rates (net) in 2056 by earnings level**
percent of last wage

	Men's wage level		Women's wage level	
	Low	Average	Low	Average
No career breaks (from age 25 to SPA)	44.9	44.7	38.0	37.8
Career break: 3 years of unemployment	41.8	41.4	35.4	35.1
Career break: 3 years of child care	44.3	43.8	37.6	37.0
Short career (20 years)	23.6	23.1	20.1	19.7

SOURCE: European Commission 2018.

NOTE: SPA = standard pensionable age.

TABLE 5.5 **At-risk-of-poverty rate (percent) in Poland and EU-27 by age and sex, EU-SILC survey**
threshold: 60 percent of median income

		EU-27			Poland		
		2005	2010	2015	2005	2010	2015
Men	Total	15.7	15.7	16.9	21.3	17.4	18.1
	65–74	—	11.8	11.3	5.5	11.9	10.2
	75 or over	18.7	14.5	12.0	3.9	7.0	7.7
Women	Total	17.1	17.2	17.7	19.9	17.7	17.2
	65–74	—	16.2	14.0	10.1	18.5	15.3
	75 or over	23.6	20.5	17.8	7.0	15.1	12.5

SOURCE: Eurostat database.

NOTE: EU-27 = European Union 27; EU-SILC = European Union Statistics on Income and Living Conditions; — = not available.

OA POVERTY IN POLAND

Given the long-term transition from the old to the new NDC system, current OA poverty incidence is an outcome of the generosity of the previous pension system because most current pensioners receive benefits according to the former NDB formula.

Table 5.5 shows poverty rates in Poland and the EU-27 between 2005 and 2015. Poles ages 65 and older exhibit lower poverty rates than the total population. This demonstrates the relative generosity of the previous pension system, combined with the highly redistributive pension formula (Góra 2013). Relative poverty among the elderly increased in 2010 compared with 2005, mainly because of the high increase in the median income fueled by the high growth of wages until 2008. As a result, the total poverty rate declined with the growth of income from labor, while the poverty rate among pensioners increased, given that the indexation of pensions was less than the level of wage growth, and subsequently, median income growth. Women are at higher risk of poverty compared with men because their pensions are lower.

Discussion of Loose Ends

The Polish NDC system is currently close to reaching maturity—more than 18 years have passed since its implementation in 1999. When the current system was introduced, some issues remained unresolved. The implementation agenda foresaw gradual finalization of these outstanding issues. Today, some are still open and will require attention sooner rather than later.

One issue is the retirement age. The minimum retirement age for men and women remains different (a five-year difference), which will have consequences for future pensions and perception of the pension system. Chłoń-Domińczak and Strzelecki (2013) assess that such a difference in retirement age increases women's risk of receiving the minimum pension by more than 40 percent. Women's lower retirement age will exacerbate the gender pension gap.

Furthermore, the system remains rigid. No flexible retirement options exist for people older than retirement age, such as a partial pension. This can encourage retirement decisions that lower the age of those people who would like to continue working part-time and supplement their reduced labor income with a partial pension. In principle, the NDC system allows for such arrangements, but they need to be implemented.

Lower retirement ages and lack of flexible solutions are also combined with low pension literacy. The gradual shift to the new system means that many workers are still unaware of how the new pensions are calculated and of the impact of their lifetime contributions and retirement age on the final pension value. This also translates into very low levels of savings in voluntary pension accounts, despite existing fiscal incentives. Improving the pension education should be an important point in the pension policy agenda. In particular, the government should increase its efforts to educate citizens about the benefits of postponing retirement decisions, particularly if people plan to retire and continue working. Continuing to work increases the risk of low benefits when pensioners finish their labor market activity.

The NDC scheme is automatically sustainable at any minimum retirement age. However, if the age is low, benefits are also low. Even if people accept retirement in their sixties, they underestimate the needs they will face in their eighties. Increasing the minimum retirement age in the NDC is not a fiscal goal, as it was in the NDB. Instead, it is just a social goal. Perhaps this is also why it was so easily reduced.

Another loose end is the current complex structure of the NDC accounts, the result of political manipulation in the FDC account. Streamlining and simplifying their structure could improve system transparency, which to a large extent was lost through amendments made over the past decade.

In the area of benefits, coordination between the OA and non-OA components (particularly disability pensions) is unfinished. Disability pensions are still calculated according to the old NDB formula, which over time may lead to increased pressure to claim disability pensions before retirement age. An attempt to coordinate the two benefits was made in 2008, but the proposed law was effectively vetoed by the president.

The system is not fully universal. Some groups of active workers (miners, farmers, army, police and other uniformed services, and judges and prosecutors) are covered by different systems. As highlighted in European Commission (2017b), this is an obstacle for labor mobility as well as for coverage. This also applies to workers with nonstandard employment contracts, who have limited or no access to social insurance. Extending coverage to those groups is another important policy area to pursue.

Last, the system should be strengthened through recognition of pension liabilities in the form of NDC bonds. Given the changes in the NDC-FDC split, adequate recognition of pension liabilities could improve the credibility of the pension system. NDC account values are rather abstract for OA pension system participants. Moreover, many economists and politicians publicly state that the amounts on the accounts do not reflect any real value. Indeed, property rights related to NDC accounts are not well defined. Assets backing the accounts are not traded in financial markets. Therefore, it is quite natural that people have reservations about the accounts, which opens the door for political manipulation and unfair political as well as business tricks, such as introducing flat citizens' pensions not linked to lifetime earnings. Such ideas focus on potential short-term gains at the expense of long-term stability.

The real economic meaning of the pension system is the purchase of a share in future GDP financed by a corresponding share of current GDP (Góra 2013). The NDC reflects that deep nature (free of administrative details and ideological biases) and is the best among all types of OA pension systems (Góra and Palmer 2019). Issuing NDC bonds, the best bonds yielding a rate of return equal to nominal GDP growth, would not change anything in the real economy. However, if the bonds are formally issued they would be part of participants' property. Such bonds would not be perceived as politically dependent NDB promises. That would strongly contribute to pension education, which in turn would strengthen the OA system via public awareness. This particularly matters in current times, when political and business actors are tempted to manipulate the pension system even more than in times when the demographic dividend was still available.

Summary and Main Conclusions

Poland's NDC system is a success. Together with the FDC, it entirely replaced the previous, actuarially bankrupt NDB system. Moreover, the NDC system prevented the political manipulations around the FDC that started in 2009, and still continue, from ruining the stability of the OA pension system. The NDC system is designed to balance the interests of the working and retired generations. The system automatically adjusts to population changes and allows the different kinds of risks that pension systems face to be absorbed. The changes introduced over the past years did not change the foundation of the system but do impact the general public's perception of the system, as well as future adequacy levels.

Many challenges remain. First and foremost, population aging in Poland will accelerate as the bulk of people born in the postwar baby boom cohorts retire, while both the number of births and subsequently the number of young people reaching adulthood remain very low. This means that total employment is likely to decline, which will affect contribution revenues. Gradual adjustment of pension levels with implementation of the NDC scheme will not be sufficient to eliminate this effect.

Improving both the sustainability and adequacy of NDC pensions in Poland depends on labor market performance. Increasing coverage and participation levels are important, not only for the pension system, but for the Polish economy as a whole. Retirement age remains the key challenge for the OA system. Participants will have to retire later, otherwise the system will be balanced, but the social outcome of its functioning will not be satisfactory.

Notes

1. Góra and Rutkowski (1990) estimate from 25 to 75 percent disguised unemployment (depending on assumptions) in the late 1980s.
2. The revaluation of pensions was designed to compensate for the period of very high inflation. As a result of this process, between 1990 and 1994, the average pension to average wage ratio rose from 47.2 percent to 61.4 percent.
3. A summary of the assumptions of the new system is also presented in Góra and Rutkowski (1998).
4. Earlier experiences related to implementation of the pension system, as well as a broader description of the pension system's design, are included in Chłoń-Domińczak (2002); Chłoń-Domińczak, Franco, and Palmer (2012); Chłoń-Domińczak and Góra (2006); and Chłoń, Góra, and Rutkowski (1999).
5. Workers born between 1949 and 1968 could choose to use one or two accounts.
6. The concepts of NDC and FDC as presented in Góra and Palmer (2004) are used in this chapter.
7. In 2017 the gross minimum pension was increased to Zl 1,000 (€250).
8. In 2017 the government proposed removing the cap from the pension system. This regulation is expected to come into force in 2019.
9. Actually, the NDC could—and maybe should—be managed by a private firm.
10. The FDC can yield a higher rate of return than the NDC only if a country is able to exploit the rest of the world.
11. The government in 2017 announced proposed changes that include converting FDC accounts to voluntary retirement accounts, which may change this rule; however, details are not known yet.
12. Early retirement in the transition period was possible initially until the end of 2006, but because of political reasons the deadline was extended to the end of 2008.
13. In 2006, following the ruling of the Constitutional Tribunal, men born between 1946 and 1948 were given the option to claim early retirement.
14. In the new OA system, the statutory retirement age is also the lowest possible actual age (with few exceptions).
15. Because no information exists on past individual wages in the system, initial capital is computed on the basis of relevant documents submitted to ZUS. Calculation of initial capital is an ongoing process because of two main factors: (a) lack of awareness among workers of the necessity to claim their initial capital, and (b) difficulties in retrieving salary documents from companies that ceased to exist, which was quite frequent during the transformation.

References

Bielawska, Kamila, Agnieszka Chłoń-Domińczak, and Dariusz Stańko. 2017. "Retreat from Mandatory Pension Funds in Countries of the Eastern and Central Europe in Result of Financial and Fiscal Crisis: Causes, Effects and Recommendations for Fiscal Rules." Instytut Zarządzania Ryzykiem Społecznym, Warsaw.

Chłoń, Agnieszka, Marek Góra, and Michał Rutkowski. 1999. "Shaping Pension Reform in Poland: Security through Diversity." Social Protection Discussion Paper 9923, World Bank, Washington, DC.

Chłoń-Domińczak, Agnieszka. 2002. "The Polish Pension Reform of 1999." In *Pension Reform in Central and Eastern Europe. Volume I*, edited by Elaine Fultz, 95–205. Budapest: International Labour Organization.

Chłoń-Domińczak, Agnieszka, Daniele Franco, and Edward Palmer. 2012. "The First Wave of NDC Reforms: The Experiences of Italy, Latvia, Poland, and Sweden." In *Nonfinancial Defined Contribution Pension Schemes in a Changing Pension World: Volume 1 Progress, Lessons, and Implementation*, edited by Robert Holzmann and Edward Palmer, 31–84. World Bank: Washington, DC. http://dx.doi.org/10.1596/9780821388488—CH02.

Chłoń-Domińczak, Agnieszka, and Marek Góra. 2006. "The NDC System in Poland: Assessment after Five Years." In *Pension Reform. Issues and Prospects for Non-Financial Defined Contribution (NDC) Schemes*, edited by Robert Holzmann and Edward Palmer, 425–48. World Bank: Washington, DC.

Chłoń-Domińczak, Agnieszka, Dorota Holzer-Żelażewska, and Anna Maliszewska. 2017. *Polacy po 50-tce: Praca i Emerytura* [Workers after 50: Work and Retirement]. Ministerstwo Pracy I Polityki Społecznej, Warsaw. http://www.share50plus.pl/images/AnalitycznyRaportUzupeniajcy3.pdf.

Chłoń-Domińczak, Agnieszka, Agnieszka Sowa, and Irena Topińska. 2017. "ESPN Thematic Report on Access to Social Protection of People Working as Self-Employed or on Non-Standard Contracts Poland." (February). European Social Policy Network, Brussels. http://ec.europa.eu/social/BlobServlet?docId=17707&langId=en.

Chłoń-Domińczak, Agnieszka, and Paweł Strzelecki. 2013. "The Minimum Pension as an Instrument of Poverty Protection in the Defined Contribution Pension System—an Example of Poland." *Journal of Pension Economics and Finance* (April): 1–32.

Ernst&Young. 2016. "Szara Strefa w Polsce Rola Płatności Gotówkowych i Elektronicznych." Warsaw. https://www.ey.com/Publication/vwLUAssets/EY—Szara—strefa—prezentacja/$FILE/2016—04—05—Szara%20strefa—prezentacja.pdf.

European Commission. 2017a. "Country Report Poland 2017." Commission Staff Working Document, Brussels. https://ec.europa.eu/info/sites/info/files/2017-european-semester-country-report-poland-en.pdf.

———. 2017b. "Recommendation for a Council Recommendation on the 2017 National Reform Programme of Poland." COM(2017) 520 final, Brussels. https://ec.europa.eu/info/sites/info/files/2017-european-semester-country-specific-recommendations-commission-recommendations—-—poland.pdf.

———. 2018. *Pension Adequacy Report 2018: Current and Future Income Adequacy in Old Age in the EU. Volume 2—Country Profiles*. Luxembourg: Publications Office of the European Union.

European Commission DG ECFIN (European Commission Directorate-General for Economic and Financial Affairs). 2009. "The 2009 Ageing Report: Economic and Budgetary Projections for the EU-27 Member States (2008–2060)." European Economy 2, Brussels.

———. 2012. "The 2012 Ageing Report. Economic and Budgetary Projections for the 27 EU Member States (2010–2060)." European Economy 2, Brussels.

———. 2015. "The 2015 Ageing Report. Economic and Budgetary Projections for the 28 EU Member States (2013–2060)." European Economy 3, Brussels.

———. 2018. "The 2018 Ageing Report. Economic and Budgetary Projections for the 28 EU Member States (2016–2070)." European Economy Institutional Paper 079, European Commission, Brussels.

Góra, Marek. 2013. "Political Economy of Pension Reforms: Selected General Issues and the Polish Pension Reform Case." *IZA Journal of Labor & Development* 2 (1): 2. http://izajold.springeropen.com/articles/10.1186/2193-9020-2-2.

———. 2014. "Three Pension Issues: A Framework for Rethinking the Basics, an Economic Reinterpretation of the Concept of Public Debt, and the Impact of Pension Systems on Labour Mobility in the EU." Unpublished, ECFIN.

Góra, Marek, and Edward Palmer. 2004. "Shifting Perspectives in Pensions." IZA Discussion Paper 1369, IZA Institute of Labor Economics, Bonn, Germany.

———. 2019. "NDC: The Generic Old-Age Pension Scheme." In *Progress and Challenges of Nonfinancial Defined Contribution Pension Schemes: Volume 1 Addressing Marginalization, Polarization, and the Labor Market*, edited by Robert Holzmann, Edward Palmer, Robert Palacios, and Stefano Sacchi, Chapter 8. Washington, DC: World Bank.

Góra, Marek, and Michał Rutkowski. 1990. "The Demand for Labour and the Disguised Unemployment in Poland in the 1980s." *Communist Economies* 3: 325–34.

———. 1998. "The Quest for the Pension Reform: Poland's Security through Diversity." World Bank, Washington, DC.

Gradzewicz, Michał, Katarzyna Saczuk, Paweł Strzelecki, Joanna Tyrowicz, and Robert Wyszyński. 2016. *Badanie Ankietowe Rynku Pracy. Raport 2016*. Warsaw: Narodowy Bank Polski. https://www.nbp.pl/publikacje/arp/raport—2016.pdf.

GUS (Central Statistical Office). 2014. *Unregistered Employment in Poland in 2014*. Warsaw: Central Statistical Office.

———. 2016a. *Informacja o Rozmiarach i Kierunkack Czasowej Emigracji z Polski w Latach 2004-2015*. 1–5. Warsaw. http://stat.gov.pl/files/gfx/portalinformacyjny/pl/defaultaktualnosci/5471/11/1/1/szacunek—emigracji—z—polski—w—latach—2004-2014.pdf.

———. 2016b. *Pracujący w Nietypowych Formach Zatrudnienia [Working in Atypical Employment Forms]*. Warsaw: Central Statistical Office.

Jabłonowski, Janusz, Christoph Müller, and Bernd Raffelhüschen. 2010. "A Fiscal Outlook for Poland Using Generational Accounts." FZG Discussion Paper 47, Research Center for Generational Contracts (FZG), University of Freiburg, Breisgau, Germany.

Kaczmarczyk, Paweł, and Marek Okólski. 2008. "Demographic and Labour-Market Impacts of Migration on Poland." *Oxford Review of Economic Policy* 24 (3): 600–25.

Kiełczewska, Aneta, and Piotr Lewandowski. 2017. "Population Ageing and the Labour Supply in Poland up to 2050." In *Population Ageing, Labour Market and Public Finance in Poland*, edited by Piotr Lewandowski and Jan Rutkowski, 11–16. Warsaw: European Commission Representation in Poland.

Knell, Markus. 2016. "Increasing Life Expectancy and NDC Pension Systems." *Journal of Pension Economics and Finance* 17 (02): 170–99. http://www.journals.cambridge.org/abstract—S1474747216000226.

Kotowska, Irena E., and Iga Magda. 2017. "Family Policy and Labour Supply in Poland." In *Population Ageing, Labour Market and Public Finance in Poland*, edited by Piotr Lewandowski and Jan Rutkowski, 5–9. Warsaw: European Commission Representation in Poland.

Łapiński, Krzysztof, Marcin Peterlik, and Bogdan Wyżnikiewicz. 2016. "Szara Strefa w Polskiej Gospodarce w 2016 Roku." Gdansk Institute for Market Economics, Warsaw. http://www.ibngr.pl/content/download/2173/20176/file/Szara%20strefa%202016.pdf.

Lewandowski, Piotr, Marek Góra, and Maciej Lis. 2017. "Temporary Employment Boom in Poland—A Job Quality vs. Quantity Trade-Off." IBS Working Paper 04/2017, Warsaw.

Marciniak, Zbigniew, Ewa Chmielecka, Andrzej Kraśniewski, and Tomasz Saryusz-Wolski. 2013. "Self-Certification Report of the National Qualifications Framework for Higher Education."

Educational Research Institute, Warsaw. http://biblioteka-krk.ibe.edu.pl/opac—css/doc—num.php?explnum—id=702.

Narodowy Bank Polski. 2018. "Analiza Sytuacji Sektora Przedsiębiorstw Szybki Monitoring." Szybki Monitoring NBP (02), Warsaw.

Office of the Government Plenipotentiary for Social Security Reform. 1997. "Security through Diversity." Ministry of Family, Labor and Social Policy, Government of Poland, Warsaw.

Saczuk, Katarzyna, Paweł Strzelecki, and Robert Wyszyński. 2016. *Kwartalny Raport o Rynku Pracy w II Kw. 2016 r [Quarterly Report on the Labour Market, 2nd Quarter 2016]*. National Bank of Poland, Warsaw.

Schneider, Friedrich. 2012. "The Shadow Economy and Work in the Shadow: What Do We (Not) Know?" IZA Discussion Paper 6423, IZA Institute of Labor Economics, Bonn, Germany.

———. 2016. "Trotz Gegenläufiger Tendenzen (Anstieg Der Arbeitslosigkeit Und Der Flüchtlinge) Ein Rückgang Der Schattenwirtschaft (Des Pfusch) in Österreich in 2016." 1–11.

Stonawski, Marcin. 2014. "Kapitał Ludzki w Warunkach Starzeniach Się Ludności a Wzrost Gospodarczy." Kraków: Wydawnictwo Uniwersytetu Ekonomicznego.

Więckowska, Barbara, and Jakub Bijak. 2009. "Wpływ Zmiany Systemowej Na Wysokość Świadczeń Emerytalnych w Polsce." Problemy Polityki Społecznej (12), Warsaw.

ZUS (Zakład Ubezpieczeń Społecznych). 2016. "Prognoza Wpływów i Wydatków Funudszu Emerytalnego Do 2060 Roku [Projection of Revenue and Expenditure of Old-Age Pension Fund until 2060]." ZUS, Government of Poland, Warsaw.

———. 2017. "Ważniejsze Informacje z Zakresu Ubezpieczeń Społecznych. 2016 r. [Basic Information on Social Insurance 2016]." ZUS, Warsaw.

———. 2018. "Ważniejsze Informacje z Zakresu Ubezpieczeń Społecznych. 2017 r. [Basic Information on Social Insurance 2018]." ZUS, Warsaw.

CHAPTER 6

The Norwegian NDC Scheme: Balancing Risk Sharing and Redistribution

Nils Martin Stølen, Dennis Fredriksen, Erik Hernæs, and Erling Holmøy

Introduction

Norway's National Insurance System (NIS) was established in 1967 and is the first and most important pillar of the Norwegian pension system. In 2016 cash benefits from the central government to households from the long-term arrangements in NIS (old-age pensions, disability pensions, and survivors' pensions) amounted to more than 10 percent of gross domestic product (GDP) for mainland Norway. NIS is an integrated part of the central government and financed on a pay-as-you-go (PAYG) basis. Since 1967, the system has been based on defined benefits (DB).

Because of growing longevity and the large cohorts born after World War II approaching retirement age, it was evident toward the end of the 1990s that maintaining the original DB system for old-age pensions would lead to substantial growth in old-age pension expenditures in the coming decades. When NIS was established in 1967, there were about four persons in the labor force for each old-age and disability pensioner. In 2008 this ratio had fallen to 2.7. Without any reform, projections from Statistics Norway indicate that the ratio may decrease to 1.8 in 2050.

A Pension Commission was appointed in 2001 to discuss possible reforms of the NIS. The Commission report's (NOU 2004: 1) main suggestion was to reform the Norwegian old-age pension system toward a nonfinancial defined contribution (NDC) scheme, which had already been implemented in Italy, Latvia, Poland, and Sweden (see Chłoń-Domińczak, Franco, and Palmer [2012] for a survey). Two agreements in the Norwegian Parliament in 2005 and 2007 indicated that a broad majority supported a reform along the suggested lines, with some adjustments. The new system was approved by Parliament in the spring of 2009, and its main parts were implemented from January 1, 2011.

During the whole reform process, effects from different designs on total labor supply and old-age pension expenditures were calculated by the dynamic microsimulation model MOSART (see Fredriksen [1998] for documentation of an earlier version). Given the uncertainty regarding labor supply effects, assumptions made during the reform process were based on evaluations of the incentive structure in combination with possible

The authors acknowledge research support from the Research Council of Norway and are grateful to Olle Sundberg and Marek Góra for comments and suggestions, and to Birger Strøm for excellent research assistance.

effects from these changes discussed in the economic literature. By incorporating direct effects on pension expenditures and employment effects into a general equilibrium model, it was also possible to calculate possible direct and indirect effects on government revenues and other expenditures to sum up long-term effects on fiscal sustainability. Illuminating the necessity for the reform and possible effects of different designs may have made it easier to reach a political agreement in a situation in which public finances were exceptionally good in Norway.

Important elements of redistribution in the NIS from persons with high labor incomes (LI) to those with low LI are maintained in the new system. Possible horizontal distributional effects from different designs of the system were also analyzed during the reform process using the MOSART model. Because effects from the reform on replacement rates depend on the extent to which retirement is postponed, calculations of adequacy also had to be based on persons with given levels of incomes and assumptions regarding age of retirement. Such calculations are documented by Christensen et al. (2012).

A research project executed at the Norwegian Institute of Social Research and the Rokkan Centre (Ervik and Lindén 2014) found that the political process was of great importance for implementation of the reform. Representatives from the different political parties participated in the Commission, and the Centre–Right Wing Government up to 2005 and the following Social Democratic Government had a common understanding of why reform was necessary. In 2008, the Prime Minister of the Social Democratic Government succeeded in making a tripartite agreement with the Norwegian Confederation of Trade Unions and the Confederation of Norwegian Enterprises to incorporate a former early retirement scheme in the private sector as a supplementary pension in the new NDC system. Under the old early retirement scheme, it was possible to retire between age 62 and 67 with no consequences on the level of old-age pension benefits from the age of 67. This system obviously stimulated early retirement, conflicting with the main principles of the NDC system.

However, no final agreement was achieved between the government and public-sector trade unions to reach a similar solution during negotiations in 2009. Neither the early retirement scheme nor occupational pensions have been adapted to the new NDC system. Nonetheless, an agreement between the government and the trade unions regarding the main principles for this unsolved challenge was reached in the spring of 2018.

Norway's Pension System

As in many other countries, Norway's pension system is built on three pillars:

- The NIS
- Occupational pensions, including early retirement schemes
- Private savings (partly tax deductible) for future pensions

PUBLIC OLD-AGE PENSIONS

As discussed by Christensen et al. (2012) and not influenced by the reform, NIS is an integrated part of the central government budget and financed PAYG. Yearly expenditures do not have to be balanced by specific contributions, and pension expenditures are covered by general tax revenues. The system is thus nonautonomous and does not fulfill criterion 2 for an NDC system, as outlined by Börsch-Supan (2006, 35), who says that this kind of system should "include a mechanism that links the final balance with the demographic and macroeconomic environment." However, in Norway this criterion is fulfilled for the central government budget in general by the Fiscal Policy Rule, which states that in the long run over the business cycle, the use of petroleum incomes should be equal to the real return from the capital in the Government Petroleum Fund, estimated at 3 percent per year. In the new Norwegian pension system, no automatic mechanism stabilizes old-age pension expenditures other than the life-expectancy adjustment counteracting growing life expectancy.

In contrast to the Swedish system, which includes an automatic tightening because of demographic and macroeconomic developments other than growing life expectancy, Norwegian politicians must discuss to what degree the central government budget should be tightened by tax increases or by expenditures other than old-age pension benefits. A tightening mechanism like that used in Sweden would mean a much stronger tightening of old-age benefits in Norway in the coming decades than what will follow from growing life expectancy. Financing old-age pension expenditures PAYG has caused the present implicit contribution rate (CR) to be far lower than the accrual rate in the new system (see "How Latvia's Replacement Rates Compare with Those of Other EU Countries"). Norway is now moving away from an abnormal situation of a low ratio of old-age pensioners to persons in the working force. Small cohorts of old-age pensioners born in the period between the two world wars will now be replaced by large cohorts born in the decades after World War II. Strong growth in participation rates among women and high net immigration have also created a favorable ratio between the labor force and the number of old-age pensioners that cannot last.

Under the old system, old-age pensions could be claimed from age 67 and were tested against earnings until age 70, until a stepwise repeal of this test was imposed between 2008 and 2010. Under the new system, old-age pensions may be drawn partly or completely between the ages of 62 and 75, with actuarial adjustment and without any earnings test.

From accumulated entitlements at retirement age A, W_A, annual pension benefits for a cohort K retiring at that age are calculated by dividing by divisors $\Phi_{K,A}$ reflecting remaining life expectancy at that age. Calculation of divisors for a cohort is based on common mortality tables for men and women.

$$B_{K,A} = W_A / \Phi_{K,A} \tag{6.1}$$

in which:

$B_{K,A}$ = Annual pension benefits for persons from cohort K retiring at age A
W_A = Accumulated entitlements at age A
$\Phi_{K,A}$ = Divisors for persons from cohort K retiring at age A

The actuarial design reflected in equation (6.1) says that the account value of accumulated entitlements is divided by the number of expected years as retired. Early retirement leads to lower annual benefits because accumulated entitlements must be divided by more years. This is also the case when life expectancy increases for a given retirement age. Lower benefits when life expectancy increases may be counteracted by postponing retirement.

Statistical observations for the first years after the reform and econometric analyses based on these observations by Hernæs et al. (2016) show that the reform has already led to postponed retirement (that is, people are working longer).

To meet the criteria for NDC, the connection between pension entitlements and former LI is closer in the new system than in the old. Between ages 13 and 75, entitlements for old-age pensions in the new system are credited to individual accounts by 18.1 percent of annual LI up to a ceiling of 7.1 times the basic pension unit (BPU),[1] corresponding to approximately 120 percent of the average wage level. In addition to the ceiling for accumulation of entitlements, a guarantee pension of 2 BPU for singles and 1.9 BPU per person for couples is an important redistributive element.

The guarantee pension is means tested with benefits reduced 80 percent (not 100 percent) against income entitlements, so that even persons with small incomes will obtain a level of pension benefits somewhat higher than the minimum level (figure 6.1). The connection between annual pension benefits and former LI is shown for a single person with constant LI during a period of 40 years. Life-expectancy adjustments are not taken into consideration; thus, figure 6.1 represents the system for accumulation of entitlements. The ceiling on annual incomes for full accumulation of entitlements at 7.1 BPU in the new system compared with 6 BPU in the old means that persons in this interval especially gain from the change in the accumulation model. Because of high participation rates among women and a rather compressed distribution of LI in Norway, a large majority of yearly

FIGURE 6.1 **Annual labor incomes and annual pension benefits in Norway's old and new pension systems**

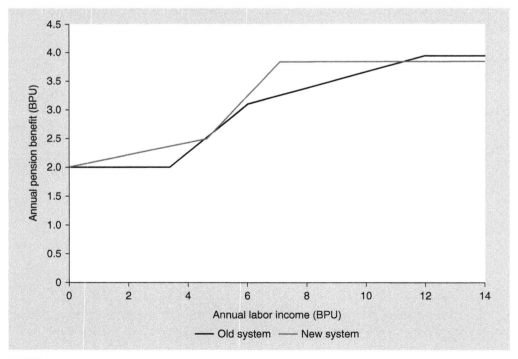

SOURCE: Original calculations.

NOTE: Figure is for a single person assuming constant labor income for 40 years. BPU = basic pension unit.

labor market income is in the interval 4.5–7.0 BPU. Like the Swedish pension system, Norway's system may be characterized as NDC with important elements of redistribution.

In the new system, pension entitlements during accumulation are indexed according to the average wage rate. After retirement, income pension in payment is indexed to the wage rate, but a fixed component of 0.75 percent per year is subtracted. The level of the guaranteed pension will be adjusted by growth in wages but reduced with higher life expectancy. In demographic projections from Statistics Norway, life expectancy at age 67 is assumed to increase by approximately 0.5 percent per year in the long run. Then the indexation of minimum pensions will usually be stronger than for ordinary pensions in payment.

Although the actuarial part of the new pension system was effective for all new retirements beginning January 1, 2011, a transitional arrangement was introduced to reform accumulation of entitlements. Persons born in 1953 or earlier will accumulate their pension entitlements according to the old system. In the group born from 1954 to 1962, pension entitlements will be partly calculated from the old system and partly from the new, with an increasing share; for example, pension entitlements for persons born in 1954 will be 90 percent based on the old rules and 10 percent on the new. Persons born in 1963 and later will earn their pension entitlements completely according to the new system. The Norwegian Labor and Welfare Administration developed a website from which everyone can have their pension benefits calculated for different assumptions about future wage level and retirement age.

DISABILITY PENSIONS AND OLD-AGE PENSIONS FOR THOSE FORMERLY DISABLED

Under the old system, disability pension and old-age pension were interconnected, and disability pensioners usually kept their pensions unchanged when they were transferred to old-age pension at age 67. About 10 percent of the population age 18–67 is on disability pension, and at age 66 about 33 percent of the new old-age pensioners are considered the former disabled. A new disability scheme was implemented in 2015. With this scheme, disability benefits are calculated as short-term benefits with a replacement rate of 66 percent and taxed like earnings.

Disability pensioners earn entitlements for old-age pensions based on the income they had before they were disabled. As in the old system, they will be transferred to old-age pensions at age 67. Because persons receiving disability benefits are not able to work after this age, to counteract lower pensions resulting from higher life expectancy, the government decided that the reduction in yearly benefits caused by growing life expectancy for a newly disabled person at age 67 should be only one-half of the reduction implemented for a former nondisabled person retiring at this age. Over time this more lenient life-expectancy adjustment for those who are formerly disabled will increase incentives for becoming qualified as disabled before obtaining an old-age pension. By 2018 the life-expectancy adjustment of old-age pensions for those formerly disabled is to be evaluated, considering whether nondisabled persons compensate for the life-expectancy adjustment by working longer.

SURVIVORS' PENSIONS

Survivors' pensions are also interconnected to the old system for old-age pensions. Given own income and the number of common children, a surviving spouse may get extra pension benefits depending on the accumulated entitlements of the deceased spouse. If the surviving spouse receives old-age benefits, he or she may also get a supplementary survivors' pension means-tested against his or her own entitlements for supplementary or income-dependent pension. Most surviving spouses are women, and normally their personal pension entitlements are significantly lower than the corresponding entitlements of their husbands.

OCCUPATIONAL PENSIONS

Occupational pensions in the central and local government sectors and a general old-age pension system existed before the NIS was established in 1967. Since then old-age, disability, and survivors' benefits from the central and local government occupational pensions have been coordinated with the corresponding benefits from the NIS, giving a total level slightly above what follows from government occupational pensions alone.

In the private sector, huge variation has existed in the occupational pension schemes with respect to benefit levels, duration of benefits, indexation, and whether the schemes are DB or defined contribution (DC). Before 2006 each company could choose whether to offer supplementary pensions to its employees, and many companies did not provide any occupational pensions at all. In general, benefits from occupational pensions in the private sector have been significantly less generous than the corresponding benefits in the public sector. Occupational benefits in the private sector are mainly supplementary and usually not coordinated with the NIS, although they are often designed to attain a certain total replacement rate. In 2006 a minimum level of supplementary pensions was made mandatory by law for all employees, and companies must at least pay 2 percent of wages exceeding 1 BPU into a DC pension scheme.

From 1973 to 2010 the retirement age for old-age pension benefits in the NIS was 67 years. To allow tired workers to retire before age 67 without using the disability pension scheme, an occupational early retirement scheme (AFP) was introduced in 1989 as a result of a 1988 tripartite agreement between the Norwegian Confederation of Trade Unions, the Confederation of Norwegian Enterprises, and the Norwegian government. By this agreement it became possible for wage earners in the private sector covered by the scheme to retire at age 66. The scheme was gradually spread to other collective agreements including the public sector, and the earliest possible retirement age was gradually reduced to age 62. All employees in the public sector and about 60 percent of those in the private sector are covered by an early retirement agreement.

Before the reform of the system for old-age pensions in the NIS in 2011, early retirement was possible with hardly any consequences for future benefits from the NIS after age 67. The early retirement scheme in the private sector was included and adapted to the new old-age pension scheme in the NIS as part of the pension reform in 2011. In the public sector, only a partial agreement was reached between the trade unions and the government during negotiations in 2009 on how to adapt the former early retirement scheme to the new system. Therefore, means testing of benefits from the early retirement scheme against LI between the ages of 62 and 67 from the old system has to date been maintained in the public sector, and retirement before age 67 has been of minor consequence for old-age benefits after age 67.

Labor Market Effects and Challenges

Labor supply is important for the level of pension entitlements and is also decisive for fiscal sustainability in the long run. One of the main aims of the Norwegian pension reform, like the former NDC reforms in Italy, Latvia, Poland, and Sweden, is to increase incentives for labor supply. Postponing retirement may have a double effect on fiscal sustainability because of a combination of lower pension expenditures and higher tax incomes. As discussed in Fredriksen et al. (2017), three kinds of employment effects may be expected because of the reform:

- Effects on working hours before retirement age caused by a closer connection between pension entitlements and LI with the new system
- Immediate effects on retirement
- Postponed retirement when life expectancy increases

EFFECTS ON WORKING HOURS

Changes in accrual of pension entitlements create a closer connection between pension entitlements and former earnings with the new system.

- The rule making entitlements dependent on the 20 years with highest LI is abolished.
- Whereas 40 years of accumulation were necessary to achieve full pensions with the old system, all years with LI may increase entitlements with the new.
- Whereas yearly income smaller than 1 BPU (equal to about one-sixth of average annual LI) does not produce any extra entitlements with the old model of accumulation, even small incomes count with the new system.
- Under the old system, incomes between 6 BPU (equal to average annual LI) and 12 BPU only produced one-third of full entitlements. Under the new system, full entitlements are accumulated up to yearly incomes of 7.1 BPU. Far more persons are in the interval 6.0–7.1 BPU than above 7.1 BPU.
- Under the old system, the special supplement for persons with low pension entitlements was means tested with benefits reduced 100 percent against income pensions. Under the new system, means testing of the guarantee pension against income pensions is reduced to 80 percent.

Stensnes (2007) estimates the labor supply incentives at the intensive margin under the old and new systems. According to his estimates, the reform implies that 1 NKr extra labor market earnings raises the present value of future pension benefits from 0.101 NKr to 0.157 NKr, on average. This corresponds to a 5.1 percent increase in the perceived effective wage rate. This estimate should be considered conservative, because it does not take into account that individual income dependency becomes more transparent and more similar between individuals in the new system. With a compensated labor supply elasticity of 0.5, the shift to the new pension system increases working hours before retirement by 2.5 percent.

IMMEDIATE EFFECTS ON RETIREMENT

Several studies find that labor supply is more elastic on the extensive than on the intensive margin (Chan and Stevens 2003; Gruber and Wise 2004; Heckman 1993; Immervoll et al. 2007). Through microsimulation, the analysis herein also accounts for heterogeneous retirement behavior. In the first econometric study of the effects of the Norwegian pension reform on retirement, Hernæs et al. (2016) find that the reform has a significant positive immediate effect on labor supply for 63-year-old workers in the private sector with access to the former early retirement scheme. The analysis compares the 1946–47 birth cohorts, who reached age 63 in the two years before the reform in 2010–11, with the 1949 cohort, who reached 63 in 2012. The results are in line with previous analyses of the effect of changes in the earnings test for those ages 67–69 in the Norwegian public pension system. First, there was an increase in the threshold (Hernæs and Jia 2013) and then there was the stepwise removal of the test over the period 2008–10 (Brinch, Hernæs, and Jia 2017), both of which significantly increased labor supply. Note that repealing an earnings test increases pension expenditures. However, Hernæs et al. (2016) find that tax revenues on increased earnings more than compensate.

In their analyses, Hernæs et al. (2016) exploit the fact that different groups of employees are affected in completely different ways by the reform. They divide employees, both pre- and postreform, into three main groups:

- Employees in the public sector who all have access to the former early retirement scheme (AFP)
- Employees in the private sector with access to AFP
- Employees in the private sector with no access to AFP, including the self-employed

Each of the three groups is further subdivided depending on whether its accumulated entitlements meet the requirements for claiming the new NIS pension at age 62. Between the ages of 62 and 67, early pension claiming is only allowed if the resulting public pension, after actuarial adjustment, at age 67 is calculated to be greater than the guaranteed NIS pension. Subdividing both pre- and postreform cohorts gives comparable groups, with different incentives from the reform. The postreform group with private AFP and the option of claiming the new pension at age 62 was not exposed to the confiscatory earnings test that was the case for the prereform group. This group's economic returns from work were much higher than those of the prereform group, and Hernæs et al. (2016) find significantly higher labor force participation and earnings. In the private sector, the postreform group entitled to AFP, but not eligible for early claiming of the new pension, was exposed both to the "carrot" (higher returns) and the "stick" (no early retirement) compared with the corresponding prereform group. Since its response was quite similar to the group for which only returns from work were higher, it seems that almost all the response was from the incentives, the "carrot." However, disability was also significantly higher in the postreform group. The postreform group with no access to AFP, but with enough entitlements to retire at age 62, experienced a reduction in access age because of the reform. Hernæs et al. (2016) find that the reform causes a small, but significant, reduction in employment and labor earnings for this group.

In the public sector, the old AFP has been preserved up to now, implying no changes in access age or in work incentives between age 62 and age 67. However, Hernæs et al.

(2016) find a small significant effect on employment and labor earnings for persons in this group with sufficient entitlements to be eligible for public pensions at age 62. Their interpretation of that finding is that some employees find it more attractive to continue in employment because it is also possible for employees in the public sector to combine employment with early payout from the social security pension.

EFFECTS CAUSED BY FURTHER GROWTH IN LIFE EXPECTANCY

Increasing life expectancy was not expected to have a large effect on retirement under the old system because the annual benefit was independent of the number of years as a pensioner. Under the new actuarial system, increased life expectancy is likely to lower annual benefits and increase retirement age through consumption smoothing (Bloom, Canning, and Moore 2004). The optimal response is then to trade some of the leisure increment for consumption, and postponing retirement is a probable response.

A relatively long period of observations after the reform is necessary to conduct empirical analyses of the effects of increased longevity on retirement age. About 30 percent of individuals will be unaffected by the changes in the early retirement incentives, given that they are disabled before age 62. Disability benefits will be replaced by old-age pensions at age 67 and disabled individuals cannot counteract the negative benefit effect of the life-expectancy adjustment by extending their working careers. The government has found it fair that the previously disabled to some extent should be sheltered from the default longevity adjustment in the new system; the benefit cuts implied by the longevity adjustment are therefore reduced by 50 percent for previously disabled old-age pensioners.

Also, when estimating possible effects of increased longevity on average retirement age, it is relevant to take into account that different groups may be affected differently. For those who work until they become old-age pensioners, it is assumed that 20 percent are so healthy that their delay of retirement equals the increase in life expectancy. For the remaining 50 percent working in the private sector, it is assumed that a delay of retirement is equal to two-thirds of the increase in life expectancy. This response neutralizes the benefit cut caused by the longevity adjustment. While assuming a minor response for the 30 percent working in the public sector, in sum these responses imply a 0.5 year delay of retirement for each year life expectancy increases ($0.5 \times 2/3 + 0.2 \times 1 + 0.3 \times 0 = 0.5$).

TOTAL EMPLOYMENT EFFECTS

From 2013 to 2060 the average remaining life expectancy for men and women at age 62 is expected to increase by about five years, from 22.8 to 27.6 years. Adding the immediate reform effect on retirement of 0.24 years and the effect that increases with remaining life expectancy, the average reform effect in 2060 equals $0.24 + 0.5 \times 5 = 2.74$ years for those who are not disabled at age 62. Also considering the positive effect on the participation rate for persons younger than 62, updated projections of the direct reform effect from 2016 indicate that the labor force in 2060 may be 276,000 persons, or 8.2 percent, larger under the new system than the old. This is a somewhat larger effect than reported in Fredriksen et al. (2017), caused mainly by stronger growth in life expectancy among men than previously assumed. In addition to the pension reform, net immigration to Norway is the main reason the total labor force is projected to grow by 856,000 persons, or more than 30 percent, from 2015 to 2060.

Fiscal Sustainability and Sensitivity for Demographic Development and Labor Supply

FINANCING OLD-AGE PENSION EXPENDITURES

As mentioned in "Norway's Pension System," expenditures of the public pension scheme are financed on a PAYG basis. Contributions and expenditures are integrated components of the entire central government budget. Because of the currently low number of old-age pensioners relative to the size of the labor force, the present expenditure rate is much lower than the accrual rate of 18.1 percent. Actual costs will probably not correspond to this number before population is assumed to stabilize after 2040. Figure 6.2 shows that the number of persons in the labor force relative to the number of old-age pensioners is expected to decrease from 3.9 in 2010 to 1.8 in 2060, based on the medium alternative in the population projections from 2016. The increasing old-age dependency ratio is partly caused by higher life expectancy, but even more importantly by the large cohorts born just after World War II retiring in the current and next decade, replacing much smaller cohorts born between the two world wars.

In a PAYG system in which public pension expenditures are financed by current tax revenues, the implicit CR defined by Disney (2004) may be a simplified measure of each member's contribution. Disney (2004, 270) defined the implicit CR for a public pension scheme as "the average rate (on earnings) that would be required to finance current spending on public pensions without budgetary transfers or the accumulation or decumulation of public pension funds." Under the standard PAYG formula, the implicit CR may be calculated as the ratio of public pension payments to LI. Gross pensions are taxed in Norway,

FIGURE 6.2 **Labor force compared with number of pensioners**

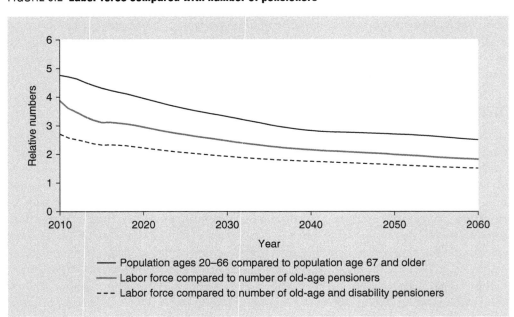

SOURCE: Statistics Norway.

but more leniently than LI, and therefore an appropriate implicit CR in accordance with the Disney definition may be formally calculated as

$$CR = \frac{PP}{(LI = \gamma \times PP)}. \qquad (6.2)$$

The right-hand-side numerator represents nominal public pension expenditures, and the denominator is the relevant tax base. The parameter γ represents the more lenient taxation of pension incomes compared with wage incomes and is approximated to about 50 percent under the current tax regime. The implicit CR can be interpreted as the tax rate sufficient to finance pension expenditures, assuming that the entire tax burden of pension expenditures falls on labor and pension incomes.

Average implicit CRs dependent on the pension system are presented in figure 6.3 for old-age benefits and the NIS, also including disability benefits and survivors' benefits. Under the old system, the implicit CR for old-age pensions would probably more than double from 2010 to 2060, from 10.7 percent to 23.6 percent. Under the new system, the implicit CR is estimated to increase to 17.2 percent in 2060. Longevity adjustment is the main tightening element of the new system. Larger birth cohorts born after World War II replacing smaller cohorts as pensioners is the main reason for the continued growth in the implicit CR toward 2040 under the new system. However, after 2040, further growth in the implicit CR is rather modest. As shown by figure 6.3, the implicit CR with the new system will be higher than with the old up to 2017. This is caused by a high rate of claiming of old-age pensions in the first years after the reform, by persons continuing to work. It follows from the actuarial design of the new system that those who claim pensions early will receive lower annual benefits.

FIGURE 6.3 **Implicit contribution rate for pension expenditures under Norway's old and new pension systems**

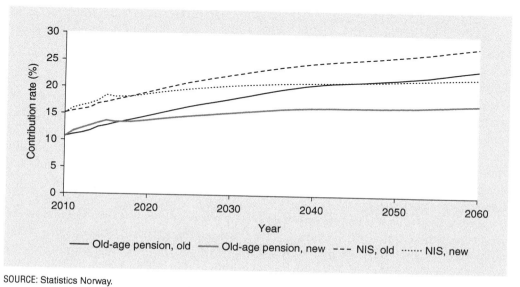

SOURCE: Statistics Norway.

NOTE: The implicit rate is the rate that would be required as a percent of the contribution base to pay for the expenditure. NIS = National Insurance System.

FISCAL SUSTAINABILITY

When claims on future benefits are not collaterized by real capital, and pensions are financed PAYG as part of general government finances, an isolated discussion about sustainability of the pension system is not of major importance. To ensure sustainability in public finances in Norway, politicians must decide whether increasing expenditures for old-age pensions caused by larger cohorts reaching retirement should be met by higher taxes or by tightening growth in other public expenditures. The question of fiscal sustainability is most properly analyzed using a general equilibrium model (see Fredriksen et al. [2017] for an example). The approach has much in common with the analysis by Coile and Gruber (2003) of effects on the budget balance of a U.S. Social Security reform. In both analyses, expansion of tax bases caused by stronger growth in labor supply is the most important general equilibrium effect.

The general equilibrium model used by Fredriksen et al. (2017) is calibrated to detailed National Accounts of 2010, and the development of the main macroeconomic aggregates is in line with observations until 2013. Demographic projections are taken from the medium alternative of the population projections from Statistics Norway (2014). As mentioned, growing life expectancy and the baby boom after World War II contribute to a strong increase in the old-age dependency ratio toward 2060. The increase is somewhat mitigated by net immigration, which was much higher after 2004 than in earlier years. Except from effects caused by the pension reform, it is assumed that both average future participation rates and working hours remain at their present levels in all population groups defined by gender, age, and education. For tax-financed production of individual services (child care, education, health services, and long-term care), the most recent observations of the gender- and age-specific ratios of users per capita are prolonged, whereas the corresponding service standards (defined as resources per user) in hospital services and long-term care are raised by 0.5 percent per year. This is far lower than the yearly growth up to the beginning of the 2000s. It is assumed that no improvements of standards occur in other individual tax-financed services.

The normalized fiscal gap is defined as the deviation between the simulated government budget deficit and the deficit consistent with annual use of petroleum revenues equal to the long-term expected real return of the Government Petroleum Fund relative to GDP for the mainland sector of the Norwegian economy. Figure 6.4 shows the normalized fiscal gap in the no-reform and the reform scenarios. The scenarios are basically identical until 2020. In this period the fiscal rule allows successive cuts in tax rates or increases in government spending under the assumptions used. After 2020 the no-reform scenario shows a continuous need for reversing the increase in government net expenditures. After 2035 the fiscal gap with the old system becomes positive, passing 8.7 percent of the projected mainland GDP in 2060. The increasing fiscal gap is caused by population aging after 2020 and the diminishing inflow of government petroleum revenues to the Government Petroleum Fund.

From figure 6.4 it is not evident that Norway needs a pension reform to avoid severe fiscal sustainability problems. The level of the fiscal gap is negative in all years until 2035, and the fiscal future for Norway looks much brighter now than when the pension reform process was initiated. At that stage the real oil price was expected to average less than one-half of the level assumed in this chapter. On the other hand, the figure still may serve as a fiscal motivation for the pension reform, because stronger growth in government expenditures than in the tax base after 2020 may undermine the government's finances. The political pressure to increase standards in tax-financed services may also be higher than assumed, and petroleum prices may be lower.

Figure 6.4 shows that the pension reform is likely to reduce growth in the fiscal gap significantly after 2020. The life-expectancy adjustment mechanism is the most important factor. Under the new system, the normalized fiscal gap goes from negative to positive in 2050 and reaches 2.8 percent in 2060. This is 5.9 percentage points lower than in the no-reform scenario. The slight increase in the fiscal gap in the first four years after implementation of the reform is due to the increase in early withdrawal of old-age pension benefits.

Sensitivity with respect to important assumptions are checked and documented in Fredriksen et al. (2017). Assumptions regarding longevity are very important for the tightening effects of the Norwegian pension reform. Because the reform almost neutralizes the effects on old-age pension expenditures from further increases in longevity, effects from altering longevity assumptions are much smaller than in the no-reform case. But higher longevity still causes higher growth in tax-financed health and care programs. Reform effects on the normalized fiscal gap are also checked for different assumptions about delayed retirement in the new system. These assumptions also seem to be significant for the fiscal gap. The close relationship between employment and most tax bases in the Norwegian mainland economy is the main reason.

FIGURE 6.4 **Normalized simulated fiscal gap under Norway's old and new public pension systems**

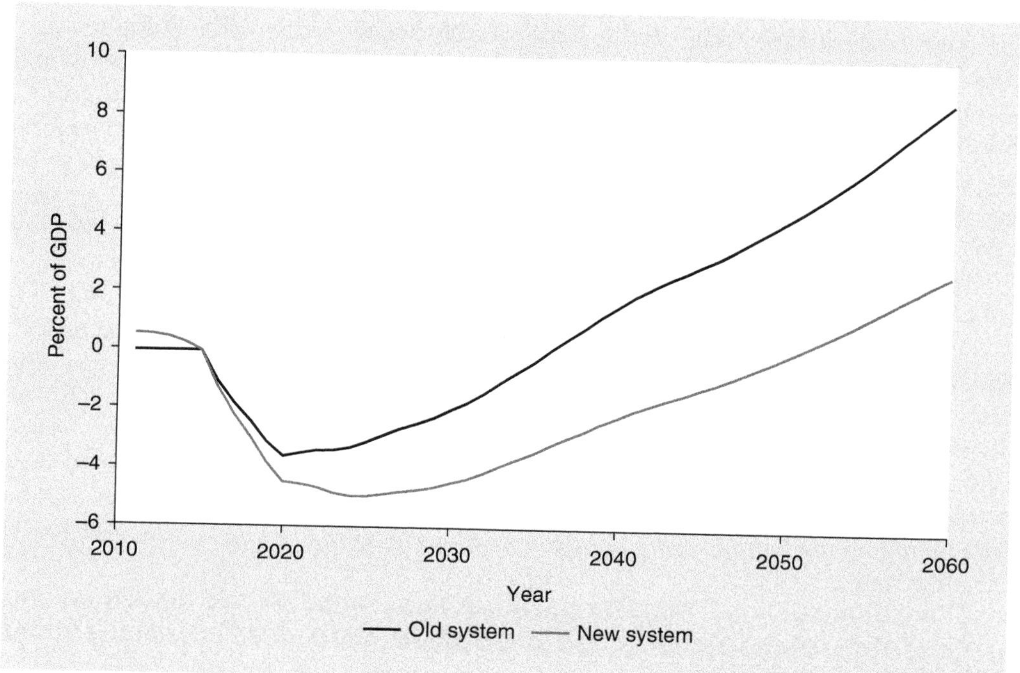

SOURCE: Fredriksen et al. 2017.

NOTE: GDP = gross domestic product.

Growth in real wages in all sectors in Norway normally follows growth in labor productivity in the manufacturing sector exposed to foreign competition. Pension entitlements are also indexed by wage growth. Fiscal sustainability is therefore not much affected by growth in real wages and productivity growth in private industry. Productivity growth in the public sector, however, has a positive effect on fiscal sustainability. Because a part of government expenditures is financed by returns from the Government Petroleum Fund, growth in real wages may even harm fiscal sustainability because the relative importance of the fund is reduced.

Adequacy and Distributional Effects

ADEQUACY

Whether reform toward an NDC system will influence adequacy of old-age pension benefits in the future as well as the distribution of incomes is highly relevant. These items were weighted heavily in the discussion of the Norwegian pension reform. It is not obvious that this concern is necessarily in great conflict with the criteria for an NDC system, and the Norwegian reform of 2011 may at least be characterized as a major step toward NDC compared with the old system.

To maintain adequacy in the pension system for persons with low incomes, a guaranteed pension of 2 BPU for singles (corresponding to approximately one-third of average LI) and at present 1.9 BPU for couples was established in the new system, at the same level as the minimum pension in the old system. Minimum pension benefits are not taxed, and the disposable income for minimum pensioners is presently somewhat below the European Union relative poverty measure of 60 percent of the country median. However, because of growing labor market participation among women during the past decades, the share of minimum pensioners is diminishing. The relatively high net immigration to Norway during the past decade may have an effect in the opposite direction. Immigrants' labor income is lower than that of natives (especially for women immigrating from Africa and Asia) and immigrants must be resident in Norway for 40 years to be entitled to a full minimum pension. The required number of residency years is lower for refugees. Because the guaranteed pension in the new system will be means tested against 80 percent of the income pension as presented in figure 6.1, this change will also result in a decreasing number of minimum pensioners.

Much of the discussion of distributional effects of the new pension system compared with the old has been limited to the accumulation rules and based on simplifying assumptions of a fixed level of income and 40 years of accumulation (recall figure 6.1). It is evident that persons with somewhat above-average income will gain from the reform before taking the life-expectancy adjustment and lower indexation of benefits in payments into account. Persons with low incomes may also gain from the new system of accumulation because minimum pensions were 100 percent means tested against income pensions with the old system.

In Christensen et al. (2012), replacement rates for the old and the new systems are compared at given wage levels, ages at withdrawal, and with 43 years of fixed labor income. Gross pension benefits in percentages of average wages are shown in figure 6.5, which illustrates that replacement rates in Norway's new pension system rise rapidly

FIGURE 6.5 **Gross total public pension benefits under Norway's new pension system by cohort, retirement age, and income level**

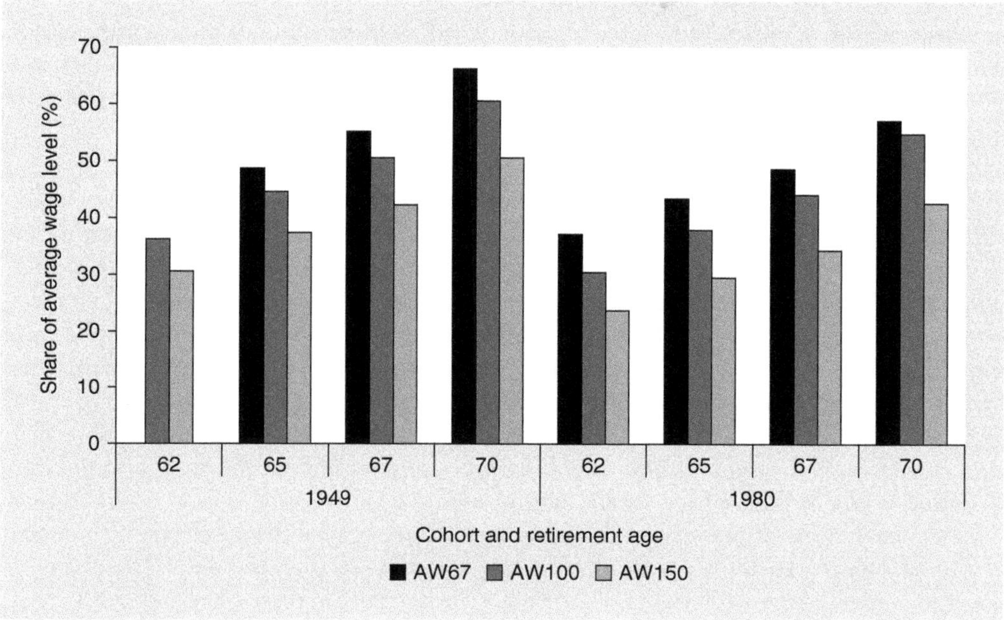

SOURCE: Christensen et al. 2012.

NOTE: The calculations assume a working career of 43 years, life expectancy of 84 years for persons born in 1949, and of 87 years for persons born in 1980. AW100 indicates 100 percent of average wage, and so on.

when retirement is postponed. For a person from the 1949 cohort with average wages, the replacement rate is about 36 percent for retirement at age 62 compared to 60 percent for retirement at age 70. Replacement rates decline as the average wage increases, caused by the guaranteed pension and the ceiling on annual pension-qualifying income. For a given retirement age, the replacement rates for the 1980 cohort are much lower, providing strong incentives to postpone withdrawal when life expectancy increases.

DISTRIBUTIONAL EFFECTS

Using the MOSART model, the distribution of old-age benefits between individuals is analyzed beyond the stylized calculations presented earlier. A microsimulation approach permits a more accurate description of the distributional consequences and opens the possibility of including behavioral effects. Even with this approach, it is convenient to restrict the analysis of distributional effects of the pension reform to pension benefits, leaving aside how the pension premiums paid by employees are distributed among individuals. The pension reform will also permit future lower taxes or a higher level of tax-financed government services than if the old system had been preserved. That is also likely to have distributional consequences that are not included in this analysis, given that their inclusion would necessitate speculative assumptions about future policy decisions.

In the first round of analyses presented in Christensen et al. (2012) and Fredriksen and Stølen (2014), the focus was on the horizontal distribution of old-age benefits from the new model for accrual of entitlements in 2050 (figure 6.6). By this limitation one can conveniently ignore indexation and actuarial adjustment through the flexible pension scheme. These elements of the reform have only small effects on the horizontal distribution of pension benefits. If distributional analyses are made after behavioral effects are included, these analyses will be a poor approximation of changes in welfare because they also reflect a voluntary shift in retirement ages.

A more favorable model for accrual of entitlements, before considering lower indexing of benefits than wage growth and adjustments for increasing life expectancy, means that no one seems to be worse off. Although figure 6.6 provides a good indication of horizontal distributional consequences, it is misleading regarding the level of entitlements. For the bottom two deciles the benefit level will improve somewhat, mainly because the old system applies 100 percent means testing of the special supplement against the income-based pension, whereas the guaranteed pension in the new system is means tested against the income pension at only 80 percent. Because of more favorable accrual of pension entitlements for unpaid child care, the improvement between the tenth and the thirtieth deciles is a bit larger for women than for men.

Accrual of benefits for old-age pensioners between the second and the fifth deciles is almost unaffected by the reform. The top five pension income deciles will experience an increase in entitlements, reflecting a somewhat increased accrual coefficient, and full accumulation of entitlements between 6.0 and 7.1 BPU with the new system,

FIGURE 6.6 **Estimated distribution of pension benefits in 2050 by income percentile and gender**

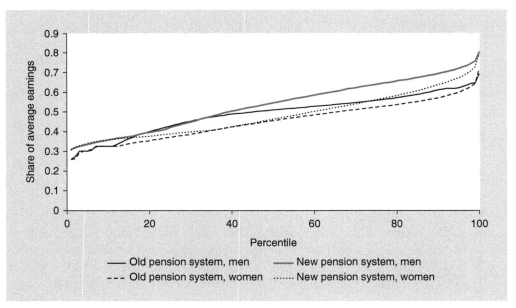

SOURCE: Fredriksen and Stølen 2014.

NOTE: Benefits are shown for a constant wage level before indexation and before exposure to the life-expectancy adjustment divisor.

compared with only one-third with the old. The improvement for these deciles is larger for men than for women.

Christensen et al. (2012) also present overall distributional effects from the old-age pension system, including behavioral effects, by calculating total old-age pension benefits over the period as pensioner relative to total lifetime earnings, by income group and gender. The comparison is based on simulated earnings over the life cycle for persons born during the 1990s and is illustrated for the old and new pension systems. Because of limited space, only a short summary is included in this chapter.

When the components for longevity adjustment and lower indexation of benefits in payment are included, everyone receives lower total benefits relative to total lifetime earnings. Although persons with high labor market incomes seem to lose less from the reform than persons with medium incomes (figure 6.6), the NIS for old-pension incomes is still highly redistributive over the life cycle. Total lifetime pensions are only about 20 percent of total lifetime earnings for men from the third decile and above and for women from the fourth decile and above. Because women live longer than men, and elements in the model for accrual of entitlements favor women, total pensions relative to total earnings are higher for women than for men for every level of earnings.

Because of the minimum pension benefit, average total old-age pensions were almost equal to average total earnings for both men and women in the first decile under the old system. With the assumptions made, this ratio was reduced to only 60 percent under the new system. However, for the calculations presented in Christensen et al. (2012), the previously disabled, who account for about 33 percent of the population at age 66, were assumed to be exposed to the same longevity adjustment as others, from age 67. Therefore, longevity adjustments for the previously disabled were reduced to one-half of the adjustment of others as a preliminary solution. A continuation of this arrangement will obviously create tension in the new system because it increases incentives to become qualified as disabled before age 67.

Analysis of distributional effects from the pension reform is further extended in Nicolajsen and Stølen (2016), who show that the results differ depending on how the effects are measured. One of the results is that total benefits over the period as old-age pensioner seem to be more equally distributed under the new system than under the old. The apparent conflict between distributional effects measured in this way compared with the results referred to above is caused by the fact that many men with high education and incomes from age 62 or older combined full-time jobs with partial withdrawal of old-age benefits after the reform in 2011. These men will be punished with lower annual benefits, and because men with high education normally have higher life expectancy than average, they will get lower total pension payments than if they postponed withdrawal.

Fredriksen and Stølen (2017) calculate distributional effects of the old-age pension system and the reform by comparing the total expected discounted contributions to the system with the expected discounted sum of benefits for every cohort born between 1910 and 2070. Figure 6.7 shows that the cohorts who established the PAYG system in 1967 experienced a substantial gain by letting future generations pay. With a positive net discount rate (the difference between the rate of interest and wage growth), the discounted value of contributions is higher than the future benefits for younger cohorts even if the amount of contributions is equal to the amount of benefits in fixed wage amounts. Because of the reform in 2011, future pension benefits will be tightened, but future contributions will also

FIGURE 6.7 **Net discounted value at age 62 for old-age pension benefits and contributions, all inhabitants**
net discount rate of 2 percent

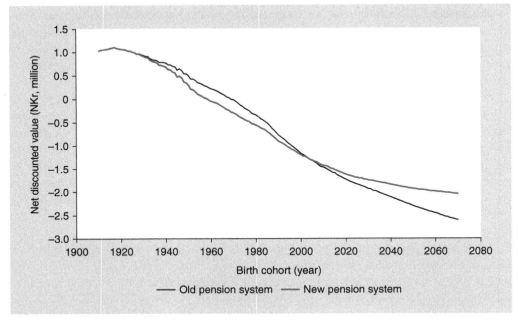

SOURCE: Fredriksen and Stølen 2017.

NOTE: NKr = Norwegian kroner, 2011 equivalent.

be reduced. With a positive net rate of interest, cohorts born between 1950 and 1980 are those who are most hurt by the reform, while cohorts born after 2000 gain.

Summary and Loose Ends

So far it seems that the reform of the Norwegian old-age pension system toward an NDC scheme in 2011 has successfully

- Improved long-run fiscal sustainability
- Created better labor supply incentives
- Maintained much of the redistributive effects of the former public pension system

The tightening components of the reform (the actuarial system with life-expectancy adjustments and lower indexation of benefits in payments than average wage growth) will obviously reduce growth in old-age pension expenditures. Econometric analyses also confirm that the reform has created better labor supply incentives. By eliminating the means testing of benefits in the former early retirement schemes against LI, the reform caused an immediate incentive to postpone retirement for those employed in the private sector. When life expectancy increases, the adjustment mechanism will obviously create incentives to postpone retirement, but much uncertainty still remains regarding the magnitude of this effect. This also means large uncertainty about effects on future tax incomes.

Even though the pension reform almost counteracts the further increase in life expectancy, the reform does not prevent a further increase of the fiscal burden of old-age pension expenditures. Large cohorts born after World War II replacing earlier small birth cohorts is the main reason. Expenditures for public health and care services will also increase with population aging. When public expenditures increase faster than the tax base, even Norway's solid public finances may meet sustainability problems. These challenges will be visible in the coming years when further growth in government services, or further tax cuts, must be reduced to fulfill the Fiscal Policy Rule.

According to the goals of the reform, adequacy of benefits is maintained if withdrawal of old-age pensions is postponed, counteracting the life-expectancy adjustment mechanism. Although the reform somewhat benefits persons with higher-than-average incomes, the main redistributive effects of the former pension system are maintained. And although cohorts born between 1950 and 1980 are those most hurt by the reform when comparing expected discounted value of pension benefits with expected contributions over the working period, the total effect on the distribution of lifetime incomes between cohorts is small.

Preserving important elements from the old occupational pension system for employees in the public sector up to now has been the main remaining challenge for the reform. A preliminary agreement between the government and the trade unions in the spring of 2018 about the main principles for adapting public sector occupational pensions to the reformed NIS indicates that this challenge may be solved. This agreement will increase incentives to postpone retirement for these employees and thus contribute to improved fiscal sustainability.

When about 40 percent of the Norwegian population is on disability pension at age 66, a more lenient system for life-expectancy adjustments may have significant effects on government expenditures and may create incentives to become qualified as disabled before age 67. This effect may be somewhat modified by lost entitlements for the early retirement supplement and no accumulation of entitlements for old-age pensions if one becomes disabled after age 62.

Note

1. The BPU is a measurement unit in NIS corresponding to about one-sixth of the average annual wage level for a full-time employee; it was indexed to about 94,000 NKr as of May 1, 2017.

References

Bloom, David, David Canning, and Michael Moore. 2004. "Health, Longevity and Optimal Retirement." Unpublished, Harvard School of Public Health, Boston, MA.

Brinch, Christian, Erik Hernæs, and Zhiyang Jia. 2017. "Salience and Social Security Benefits." *Journal of Labor Economics* 35 (1): 265–97.

Börsch-Supan, Axel. 2006. "What Are NDC Pension Systems? What Do They Bring to Reform Strategies?" In *Pension Reform: Issues and Prospects for Non-Financial Defined Contribution (NDC) Schemes*, edited by Robert Holzmann and Edward Palmer, 35–56. Washington, DC: World Bank.

Chan, Sewin, and Ann Stevens. 2003. "Do Changes in Pension Incentives Affect Retirement? A Longitudinal Study of Subjective Retirement Expectations." *Journal of Public Economics* 88: 1307–33.

Chłoń-Domińczak, Agnieszka, Daniele Franco, and Edward Palmer. 2012. "The First Wave of NDC Reforms: The Experiences of Italy, Latvia, Poland and Sweden." In *Nonfinancial Defined Contribution Pension Schemes in a Changing Pension World: Volume 1 Progress, Lessons, and Implementation*, edited by Robert Holzmann, Edward Palmer, and David Robalino, 31–84. Washington, DC: World Bank. https://openknowledge.worldbank.org/handle/10986/9378.

Christensen, ArneMagnus, Dennis Fredriksen, Ole Christian Lien, and Nils Martin Stølen. 2012. "Pension Reform in Norway: Combining NDC and Distributional Goals." In *Pension Reform: Issues and Prospects for Non-Financial Defined Contribution (NDC) Schemes*, edited by Robert Holzmann, Edward Palmer, and David Robalino, 129–54. Washington, DC: World Bank. https://openknowledge.worldbank.org/handle/10986/9378.

Coile, Courtney, and Jonathan Gruber. 2003. "Fiscal Effects of Social Security Reforms in the United States." Working Paper 2003–05, Center for Retirement Research at Boston College, Boston, MA. http://www.bc.edu/crr.

Disney, Richard. 2004. "Are Contributions to Public Pension Programmes a Tax on Employment?" *Economic Policy* 19: 267–311.

Ervik, Rune, and Tord Skogedal Lindén. 2014. "It Happened Here: The Role of Coordinative and Communicative Discourses in Justifying the Norwegian Pension Reform." Uni Research Rokkan Centre, Bergen, Norway.

Fredriksen, Dennis. 1998. "Projections of Population, Education, Labour Supply and Public Pension Benefits, Analyses with the Dynamic Microsimulation Model MOSART," Social and Economic Studies 101, Statistics Norway, Government of Norway, Oslo.

Fredriksen, Dennis, Erling Holmøy, Birger Strøm, and Nils Martin Stølen. 2017. "Fiscal Effects of the Norwegian Pension Reform—A Micro-Macro Assessment." *Journal of Pension Economics and Finance,* published online October 11, 1–36. https://doi.org/10.1017/S1474747217000361.

Fredriksen, Dennis, and Nils Martin Stølen. 2014. "Gender Aspects of the Norwegian Pension System." In *New Pathways in Microsimulation*, edited by Gijs Dekkers, Marcia Keegan, and Cathal O'Donoghue, 93–108. Farnham, UK: Ashgate.

———. 2017. "Life Time Pension Benefits Relative to Life Time Contributions." *International Journal of Microsimulation* 10 (2): 177–207. http://www.microsimulation.org/IJM/V10—2/IJM—2017—10—2—6.pdf.

Gruber, Jonathan, and David Wise, eds. 2004. *Social Security and Retirement around the World—Micro-estimation.* Chicago, IL: University of Chicago Press.

Heckman, James. 1993. "What Has Been Learned about Labor Supply in the Past Twenty Years?" *American Economic Review* 83(2): 116–21.

Hernæs, Erik, and Zhiyang Jia. 2013. "Earnings Distributions and Labour Supply after a Retirement Earnings Test Reform." *Oxford Bulletin of Economics and Statistics* 75 (3): 410–34.

Hernæs, Erik, Simen Markussen, John Piggott, and Knut Røed. 2016. "Pension Reform and Labour Supply." *Journal of Public Economics* 142: 39–55.

Immervoll, Herwig, Henrik Jacobsen Kleven, Claus Thustrup Kreiner, and Emmanuel Saez. 2007. "Welfare Reform in European Countries: A Microsimulation Analysis." *Economic Journal* 117: 1–44.

Nicolajsen, Stian, and Nils Martin Stølen. 2016. "Fordelingsvirkninger av Pensjonsreformen." *Søkelys på arbeidslivet, 33(1–2), 2016,* Universitetsforlaget, 24–44. (in Norwegian). https://www.idunn.no/file/pdf/66855636/spa—2016—01-02—pdf.pdf.

NOU 2004:1. *Modernisert Folketrygd. Bærekraftig Pensjon for Framtida.* The Ministry of Finance and Ministry of Social Affairs, Oslo (in Norwegian).

Statistics Norway. 2014. *Population Projections 2014–2100.* http://www.ssb.no/en/befolkning /statistikker/folkfram.

Stensnes, Kyrre. 2007. "Equity Versus Efficiency in Public Pension Schemes—Microsimulating the Trade-off." Discussion Paper 515, Statistics Norway, Government of Norway, Oslo.

CHAPTER 7

The Greek Pension Reforms: Crises and NDC Attempts Awaiting Completion

Milton Nektarios and Platon Tinios

The Crisis and the Current Structure of the Greek Pension System

Greece in 2018 is trapped in the deepest and longest recession of any developed country—longer and deeper than even the U.S. Great Depression of the 1930s. Output per capita is lower by one-quarter than precrisis levels, and earnings by one-third—the product of eight successive years of falling gross domestic product (GDP) after 2008. Ten years after the start of the country's economic woes, the most likely prospect is more stagnation (Meghir et al. 2017).

Pensions and pension reform were never far from the epicenter of this economic maelstrom. Pension reform was the first action of the first bailout (Law 3865/10) and destined to be the last of the third (Law 4472/17, prelegislated for January 2019). This busy reform scorecard was unable to prevent income insecurity among pensioners, evidenced in repeated cuts in pensions-in-payment.[1]

In 1997 an independent committee warned that the Greek pension system would collapse by 2007 unless it was drastically reformed. Trying to reassure public opinion, the head of the Confederation of Trade Unions retorted, "The social insurance system will collapse after the State Budget and the economy as a whole" (quoted in Paleologos 2014, 80). Indeed, the country resorted to a bailout less than 10 years later.

This chapter makes three strong claims about the causal link between pensions and the crisis. As for the past, the crisis would not have happened had pensions been reformed in time. As for the present, an exit from the crisis is prevented by side effects of the pension reform. As for the future, Greece's long-term prospects are being poisoned by an inappropriately designed pension system. The common thread is a political economy system that places the needs of pensions and pensioners uppermost, calling instead upon production to adapt.

These claims go beyond the quantitative observation that deficits linked to the pension system accounted for most of the fiscal deterioration behind bankruptcy. The microeconomic operation of the pension system is also examined. Benefits were decoupled from contributions, hampering the operations of pensions as insurance. Instead, they became an instrument of redistribution between occupational groups, encouraging a systematic shifting of the burden toward future generations. The lack of a clear link between

---

The authors are grateful to George Simeonidis (PhD candidate at the University of Piraeus) for excellent research assistance.

contributions and entitlements is termed "a lack of reciprocity" in a pension system. This chapter asserts that this lack of reciprocity is at the heart of the causal link between pensions and fiscal failure. Restoring reciprocity through systemic change should be the centerpiece of any meaningful reform if it is to lead the country out of the crisis.

"The Past: Pensions as a Mechanism for Disaster" examines how reform postponement fed the crisis in 2009–10. "The Present: The Bailout Leads to a New Pension System" surveys the cumulative results of the pension reforms undertaken during the crisis, from 2010 to 2018, before "The Future: Pensions and Long-Term Prospects" illustrates how the new postcrisis system is undermining future prospects. "'Pensions for the Young': A Radical Proposal to Exit the Crisis" outlines a bold new proposal to galvanize public discussion. The proposal is capable of breaking the impasse by making pensions serve the economy, rather than vice versa. Specifically, a proposed multipillar system is built around nonfinancial defined contributions (NDC) with a new prefunded second pillar; the break with the past is signaled by a boost to reciprocity but also a major reduction in contribution rates. In a country whose pension system demonstrably failed both the economy and those it was meant to serve, the proposal aims to regain the Greek public's trust.

The Past: Pensions as a Mechanism for Disaster

Outwardly, Greek pension system looks like that in many advanced economy systems based on pay-as-you-go (PAYG). The main pension provider, IKA, founded in 1934, was a direct contemporary of the U.S. Social Security system. Given that both were a reaction to the Great Depression, the two systems had many design similarities. In practice, however, the Greek system was governed with far greater laxity; for instance, the requirement for regular actuarial reviews was ignored for decades. Consequently, the system over the second half of the 20th century progressively fragmented. It did so in numerous dimensions—by occupational group; by pension tranche; and by cohort, within and between pension providers (Börsch-Supan and Tinios 2001; Panageas and Tinios 2017).

The combination of PAYG funding with fragmentation meant that the pension system severed its links with insurance and operated as a fiscal landmine: old-age support was exploited to secure privileges for different occupations—turning pensions into a key component of clientelistic politics. For example, the retirement age rule (65 years for men) was followed by only 15 percent of male applicants in 2006; the remaining 85 percent exploited various loopholes to retire much earlier. The system combined one of the highest pension expenditures in the Organisation for Economic Co-operation and Development (OECD) with the worst performance in old-age poverty alleviation (Börsch-Supan and Tinios 2001; Nektarios 2012; Panageas and Tinios 2017).The route to a good pension for many was either a shrewd choice of occupation or an ability to "play the system," rather than a long contribution history. The lack of reciprocity removed constraints on expenditure growth at the micro level, as groups tried to secure privileges and shifted costs onto consumers, taxpayers, or others. After the 1980s, expenditures were almost decoupled from system revenues—the difference was made up by ad hoc government grants, deficit finance, third-party taxes, and other devices shifting the burden of finance. These schemes removed constraints to expenditure growth at the macro level. Finally, notwithstanding the awareness that structural changes were overdue, pension reform proceeded in a piecemeal fashion, moving the system in the right direction but in small steps; this allowed intra-generational distributional issues to overshadow intergenerational equity (Tinios 2012a).

These structural issues created secular tendencies for expenditures to grow. In a frag-mented system with diverse degrees of generosity, the process of urbanization and the growth of the public sector gave rise to composition effects, raising total expenditures.[2] The system, still preoccupied with consolidation, was ill-prepared to meet the aging challenge, which appeared in the mid-1990s and accelerated in the 2000s. The inter-play of these tendencies was sufficient to anchor Greece in the European Union (EU) Ageing Working Group's (AWG) Reports from 2002 on as the EU state facing the greatest expected increase in age-related pension expenditures in the long term.[3]

How were these mechanisms connected to the debt bubble that finally burst in 2009? Structural deficits in the pension system had been endemic from the early 1980s. Policy makers were fully aware that structural reform was overdue. However, that reform was hard to implement and painful to discuss. While waiting for reform, all deficits were not financed by increasing system revenues, as that would have forestalled the pending reform on spending. They were, instead, seen as a "temporary phenomenon" and were financed largely by ad hoc government grants; these grants were originally not seen as a structural feature of the system, but as a kind of bridging finance of legacy costs. The last reform increasing contributions was passed in 1992; most changes affect-ing entitlements (age, system structure, privileges) were left for later. Unfortunately, the hoped-for entitlement rationalization was repeatedly announced and then postponed (notably in 1998, 2001, 2003, and 2008), and the "temporary measures" took on a permanent mantle.

In consequence, Greece before the crisis saw "half a reform," increasing contribu-tions in 1992. The more controversial other half of the reform that should have reduced entitlements kept being postponed. Because contributions were already felt to be too high, all expenditure increases were financed mainly by direct government grants. This became easier after entry into the euro area in 2001, when interest rates and external borrow-ing became cheaper, just as deficits were rising. On a wider political economy front, the evident reluctance to deal with an emblematic structural reform almost certainly stalled structural reform in other fields.[4]

Could meaningful pension reform have averted the crisis that broke in 2010? A prominent protagonist of the period, ex–Labour Minister Tassos Giannitsis, certainly thinks so. He calculated that cumulative grants to the pension system between 2001 and 2009 were €134 billion, representing 83.6 percent of the increase of the national debt. In the critical period 2006–09, central government expenditures on pensions accounted for 35.8 percent of the increase in the public sector deficit, when wages and salaries accounted for only 9.9 percent (Giannitsis 2016, 48–50, 60–61). To this direct effect should be added any indirect political economy effects of postponing other structural reforms (Featherstone and Papadimitriou 2008).

A common justification for public subsidies was that subsidies were dictated by social policy—the need to bolster low pensions. However, this confuses cause and effect: pensions were low because recorded careers were short. Short labor market participation, in addition to opportunities for early retirement, were caused by a high minimum pension that meant that a person on minimum earnings would be entitled to the same pen-sion between 15 and 23 years of work (Börsch-Supan and Tinios 2001). It is significant that a safety net for the general pensioner population did not exist; its introduction was prevented by the need to bankroll pensions.[5]

Counterfactuals can be treacherous—even if pension reform created fiscal space, the slack could have been taken up by other excesses. Nevertheless, discretionary pension increases indubitably played a direct part in the derailment after 2007, with rises in farmers', military, and civil service pensions almost 15 percent greater than inflation (Tinios 2010). In any case, Greek pension data are a well-known example of "Greek statistics"; data availability has become worse, not better.[6] A country that misgoverned its pension system to the extent seen in Greece would doubtless have succumbed to other problems.

Whatever the macro counterfactuals, the deeper microeconomic cause behind the fiscal debacle was ultimately that the Greek system, despite the logic of its foundation, had ceased to operate as social insurance. Individual entitlements bore little relation to personal contributions, while the principle of financial autonomy of pension providers was long forgotten. The lack of reciprocity at all levels meant that decisions at individual, system, and macroeconomic levels were made as if a budget constraint were absent. In that generational Ponzi game, burdens kept being shifted forward to the next generation. As many commentators realized,[7] it was only a matter of time before the pyramid collapsed. That collapse finally came in 2009–10.

The Present: The Bailout Leads to a New Pension System

The bailout period after 2010 introduced two key differences in the rules of the game. First, a strong new player entered, possessing an effective veto: the "Troika" (composed of the International Monetary Fund [IMF], the European Central Bank [ECB], and the European Commission), representing the creditors.[8] Blame avoidance and blame shifting became the order of the day on the part of governments. Second, a hard budget constraint was enforced for total pension expenditures. Because no borrowing was possible, any expenditure overruns, caused for instance by early retirements, could only lead to cuts in pensions already paid out (pensions-in-payment) (Lyberaki and Tinios 2012).

There was no doubt that pension reform would top the bailout reform agenda. There was keen awareness that the postponed reform should have been imposed without delay (IMF 2010). It was also clear that ironing out privileges and consolidation should be a key part of that reform. Because the bailout was ultimately financed by German taxpayers (themselves recovering from their 2003 pension reform), there was great sensitivity about comparisons—especially relating to retirement ages. In addition to dealing with consolidation ("problems of the past," or legacy issues), the reform would also have to deal with aging, which accelerated after 2010 ("problems of the future"). However, two difficulties arose that are largely absent in other pension reforms: (a) the reform had to be undertaken in a deep crisis without a functioning social safety net, which would need to be built up at the same time; and (b) macroeconomic adjustment had to occur. The crisis revealed that Greece was not as rich as it thought it was: GDP per capita compared with precrisis levels was down by 25 percent; if pensioners were to share in overall adjustment, it could only be accomplished through nominal cuts to pensions.[9] Seen a different way, any defined benefit (DB) pensions calculated on precrisis incomes would lead to relative incomes of pensioners far higher than before 2010. An equitable sharing of the pain of adjustment should have been placed on the political economy agenda.

Urgency by the creditors and lack of ownership by the authorities meant that reform took place in a sequence of confused steps, unfolding unsteadily between 2010 and 2018. The original law was supplemented by at least five other major reform laws, implemented over three bailouts by five governments, from all sides of the political spectrum. In addition to legislative changes, the process involved more than a dozen nominal cuts to pensions-in-payment, introduced under protest and presented as short-term fiscal fixes unrelated to the reform effort. The last major law was passed in May 2017; it preannounced further deep cuts to be implemented four months after the end of the last bailout, in January 2019 (Panageas and Tinios 2017; Tinios 2018).

In retrospect, the cumulative changes implemented over eight years amount to one of the most drastic parametric reforms of a PAYG system ever implemented. The end result, which will be fully complete in 2019, is characterized by three key features, amounting to wholesale abandonment of the status quo (Nektarios, Tinios, and Symeonidis 2018; Symeonidis 2017):

- A new two-tier DB system is applied to all—even retroactively to existing pensioners.
- The retirement age applicable to everyone not able to retire by May 2016 is 67 (62 for long service). In certain cases, this means step increases of up to 17 years.
- All separate (primary) pension providers, including civil service and military pensions, are consolidated beginning in 2017 into a single pension organization.

The drawn-out process that led to the ultimate result generated extra costs, though: as low pensions fell by less than earnings, a wave of early retirements, mostly of women, increased expenditures on a permanent basis. The repeated reneging on pension promises, typified by pension cuts, led to a diminution of trust in the pension system, which together with the fall in earnings encouraged falls in revenue. These drops were exacerbated by the fact that cuts repeatedly penalized long contribution records and favored short careers.

A cyclical process was repeated four times, in 2010, 2013, 2015, and 2017. The Troika, setting off the process, first pushed for decisive action to address fiscal problems; the government attempted to protect those close to retirement, favoring dual systems differentiating incumbents from new entrants. However, attempts to protect incumbents led to early retirement; because government grants to the pension system were strictly controlled, this increased cash shortfalls. These shortfalls were then addressed by cutting pensions-in-payment. Then new laws were enacted extending the application of the new system retroactively to categories of the population previously protected. While the precrisis practice was to affect only new entrants, the 2010 law applied new rules to all entitlements earned after 2011 by all those working. In 2016 new rules were applied to all new pension applications for the entirety of their careers (see box 7.1).

The vicissitudes and problems of syncopated parametric pension reform in the midst of a deep crisis are shown in the consistent rise of pension expenditures over the crisis period to levels unprecedented in advanced economies. The share of pensions in GDP, already high in 2009, increased to 18.3 percent in 2016 (figure 7.1). For comparison, the figure also shows the behavior of pensions in Germany and Italy, the two other EU countries challenged by aging.[10] The repeated pension cuts in Greece were insufficient to stem the rise in pensions, which were fed instead by a wave of early retirements. With private

BOX 7.1 **Recalibration of pensions-in-payment: A primer**

The fall in nominal GDP by one-quarter with the price level falling necessitated (for fiscal and for equity reasons) a downward adjustment of pensions-in-payment. Between 2010 and 2013, repeated ad hoc cuts were imposed using the sole criterion of pension size. The top administrative court decided that cuts before December 2012 were warranted constitutionally, on the grounds of fiscal necessity. In 2015, the same court reversed course, decreeing cuts that took place after 2012 were insufficiently justified and hence unconstitutional. So, the government legislated (Law 4387/16) that rather than calculating new pensions under old rules and then applying cuts, as done hitherto, all entitlements after May 2016 would be computed by applying new rules retroactively—as if the employee had always been subject to new rules. To comply with the court decision, the law decreed that all existing pensions would be recalculated under new rules by January 2019; any excess of pensions as currently paid over the recalibrated amounts was termed a "personal bonus," and was to be offset against any future rises and gradually abolished.[a]

A year later, and in the context of ensuring Greece would be able to meet future primary surplus targets, Law 4472/17 went a step further, positing that the personal bonus would be discontinued on January 1, 2019. It specified a maximum difference of 18 percent.[b] Any excess will be subject to the same offsetting process as before. The abolition of the personal bonus is important because it will affect low-income pensioners, who were mostly protected from previous pension cuts.[c]

In this way, a 90-year-old pensioner will be drawing in 2019 a pension as if she had contributed all her life into the new system. Widows, interestingly, will be hardest hit: the pension will be calculated as if the deceased had contributed all his life to the new system; survivors will be entitled to 50 percent of the direct beneficiary's hypothetical pension, rather than 70 percent; and they will not be entitled to the protection of the personal bonus cap.

On reflection, this unique recalibration exercise forcibly took entitlements approximately to where they would have been, had early warnings of pension unsustainability been heeded. But it did so by negating more than a generation's worth of solemn political reassurances that entitlements were "safe."[d] Seen as part of a larger aging narrative, Greece over the bailout period "telescoped" developments that normally span generations.

a. Using as a frame of reference the current value (that is, after cuts) rather than legal entitlements (before cuts) had the effect of "franking" all postcrisis cuts in pensions.

b. Any shortfall from the deficit reduction target of 1 percentage point of GDP would be taken by further cuts in auxiliary pensions.

c. Low pensions will also lose the protection of the dedicated means-tested pension supplement EKAS. They will be eligible for the less generous new "social solidarity income."

d. This process of recontracting did not affect retirement ages. Applications submitted before May 2016 are entitled to the lower retirement ages

sector employment taking the biggest hit, pensions appeared a safe haven out of the labor market[11] (Lyberaki 2018; Tinios 2018).

The fiscal problem was ultimately caused by a departure from reciprocity of pension benefits, possibly aided by a collapse of revenues during the crisis. This is obvious in the exceptionally high share of direct government finance: of the 18 percent spending

FIGURE 7.1 **Pensions as a percentage of GDP in Greece, Germany, and Italy, 2003–17**

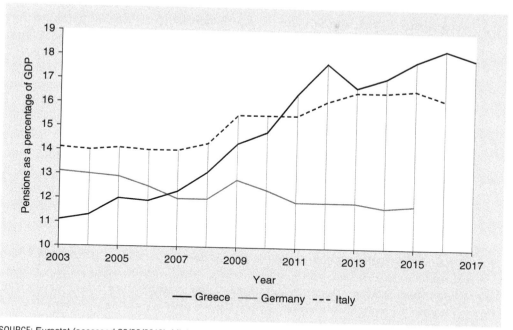

SOURCE: Eurostat (accessed 30/09/2018), Ministry of Labor (for 2016 on).
NOTE: GDP = gross domestic product.

on pensions, more than one-half (11 percentage points) came directly from government grants, rather than through contribution revenues (IMF 2017, 35[12]). Subsidies of that magnitude, mostly handed out on an ad hoc basis, negate the ostensive social insurance logic of the system. Regardless of the legal form, when more than 50 percent of income is unrelated to contributions, it is difficult to talk of "insurance."[13]

The new system that, according to official pronouncements, is to carry Greece to the mid-21st century is characterized by four key aspects[14]:

- *A new state first pillar system.* In a two-tier PAYG, DB pension system, the first tier is accessible to those with more than 15 years of contributions (€360 for 15 years, rising to €384 for 20 years). The second tier is proportional to years of contributions on a DB base, calculated on a nonlinear scale based on career average income.[15] Total replacement rates for minimum pay recipients are more than 80 percent for contributions from a 40-year career. An important feature is the low monthly pension ceiling (€2,000, when the ceiling for contributions is close to €6,000), which will discriminate against better-paid contributors.

- *Retirement age.* Retirement age rises to 67 for all who retire after May 2016 (62 for a full career), subject to a short transition period lasting to 2022. Exceptions remain for "Hazardous Occupations."[16] Retirement age is to be reconsidered every 10 years to match longevity increases. Work by pensioners is severely discouraged; undertaking any gainful employment means automatically forfeiting 60 percent of the pension.

- *Consolidation on the revenue side.* Beginning in 2017, all contributors are equated to salaried workers and pay the same contribution rates—26 percent for pensions only; total contributions for all risks rise to 38 percent for those entitled to separation payments. This entails a major change for professionals, the self-employed, and farmers (who were subject to an archaic system of voluntary insurance classes). All workers on nonstandard contracts, such as those in the sharing (gig) economy, were treated as pseudo-self-employed and equated to salaried workers. All subsidiary income accruing to employees (for example, for supplying services, or in a supplementary second job) is also fully subject to contributions. It was hoped that widening the contribution base would boost overall revenue. However, early indications are that disintermediation and avoidance have increased.[17]

- *Organizational consolidation.* All primary pension providers were folded into a single organization. In contrast to previous efforts to consolidate, which were accused of being merely decorative, the objective was to lead to uniform rules for entitlements, for revenues, and for administrative procedures. Fragmentation, the defining characteristic of the Greek pension system, was to be replaced by uniformity.[18]

The single exception to consolidation was the so-called auxiliary pensions.[19] These were retained in a separate state provider and were supposedly converted to NDC schemes. This is sometimes cited as a successful example of the application of NDC pensions in Greece. Because the reality is somewhat different, it is worth examining this claim in some detail.

All employees since 1983 had to pay a minimum of 6 percent of their salaries for auxiliary pensions to receive an additional second pension of about 20 percent replacement. That entitlement was otherwise indistinguishable from primary pensions: auxiliary pensions were compulsory, mandatory, PAYG, and DB; were provided by state bodies; and were equally prone to deficits. Nevertheless, the Greek government consistently tried to keep auxiliary pensions separate from primary pensions. The purpose was to retain the flexibility of being able to separately influence particular employment sectors.

Auxiliary pensions were thus excluded from the 2010 reform on the grounds that they ought not to receive public subsidies. This fiction created a major funding problem, "dealt with" in 2012 (Law 4052/12) by folding almost all auxiliary funds into one, the ETEA. Because some funds were generous and ran deficits and others were parsimonious and may have even been in surplus, unification resulted in extending the life of the spendthrift funds (representing influential groups, mostly in the civil service and in public enterprises). To prevent cross-subsidization, the 2012 law attempted to introduce strict reciprocity between contributions and pensions. It did so by applying the NDC principle retroactively to contributions from 2001. However, this decision was later overturned by stipulating that NDC would apply only after 2014. The main beneficiaries were the two most generous funds—customs officers and tax collectors—whose pensions could be paid for a few more years, using contributions from other occupations with less generous systems. This decision was confirmed by a later law in 2016 that specified that a DB system would be in operation for contributions paid between 2002 and 2016 and NDC would only be applied afterward. Characteristically, though, the first NDC pension was only issued in late autumn 2017, five years after the NDC system passed into law.

Getting one occupation to pay for the others in auxiliary pensions cannot balance the books for long. To stick to the story that auxiliary insurance is not bankrolled by the state, the "zero deficit clause" was inserted. Under this clause, if a deficit arises in one year, the balance is attained by cutting all pensions by an equal amount. Interestingly, pensions can only go down, and can never rise again (Zampelis 2013). The fact that NDC only existed on paper and all pensions paid were calculated on DB principles repaying the pre-crisis level of incomes—which were in any case actuarially overgenerous—deficits would be a virtually permanent fixture. Indeed, the zero deficit clause was applied in 2014, when pensions were cut by 5.3 percent.[20]

Auxiliary pensions thus remain a one-way bet downward. Given their rapid deterioration, they are no more than a pay-while-you-can, or even a pay-what-you-grab, system. The Committee of Experts formed by the government suggested in October 2015 that they should be incorporated into primary pensions.[21] This proposal was overruled and auxiliary pensions were retained, though contribution rates were increased temporarily by 1 percentage point, to 7 percent. Nevertheless, this tactic did not improve finances: higher auxiliary pensions were extensively cut in late 2016, while more cuts are expected in the future, including as part of the cuts preannounced for 2019 by Law 4472/17.

In consequence, after seven years of reform, the two questions of why separate auxiliary pensions exist and whether they will still exist in 10 years remain unanswerable. Appeal to the NDC principle was used, in practice, as a medium-term ploy to support some incumbents entitled to more generous auxiliary pensions. Actuarial reality predicts that this attempt is ultimately doomed; it will only succeed in postponing the final reckoning for a few years.

The Future: Pensions and Long-Term Prospects

According to pronouncements from the government, echoed by the institutions overseeing the bailout, the system to be in force in 2019 is the one that should see Greece through to 2060 and beyond (EC 2018). There is little doubt that many of the dysfunctional characteristics of the precrisis situation were put right. Yet it is also true to say that the reform chose continuity over systemic change: the new system relies exclusively on the state; it does not advance toward a multipillar system; and it remains staunchly PAYG and DB. Despite accusations that the system promotes a "neoliberal agenda" (Busch et al. 2013), it remains solidly within the logic of parametric change. Even if the system were imposed from the outside, the proposals mostly implemented the logic of the preceding discussions, shying away from systemic change.[22] The new system looks like a monolithic 1960s-style, state-run, PAYG system, currently under question in the advanced world.[23] The system still has the following faults:

- *Too generous.* Pension replacement, especially for low earnings, though lower than before, will still be at the top end of the EU for a full career.[24]

- *Too expensive.* Nonwage costs are high and will become higher. The increased emphasis on contribution revenues will prove a major drain on competitiveness.[25]

- *Too inflexible.* Little leeway is allowed for individual or sectoral differentiation. All are entitled to maximum protection and have to pay the necessary price. There is no possibility of opting out. Large groups of the population, such as the self-employed, are forced to overinsure to shore up current pensions of salaried workers.

- *Too statist.* Pensions are exclusively provided by the state, leaving very little room for other providers. High nominal replacement rates crowd out demand, while high state social insurance contributions (27–38 percent) crowd out supply. The insurance sector is still being actively discouraged from offering supplementary insurance cover, for example, by being barred from administering occupational funds.

- *Too opaque.* The new system eschews the transparency afforded by multipillar systems. Under the logic of PAYG finance, the increase in contributions is immediately available to bankroll incumbents; this generational transfer is hidden as an internal transfer. The opacity of the pension promise operates as another disincentive to contribute.[26]

However, the main problem arises from the way the 2010–18 reforms came about (Panageas and Tinios 2017). Those reforms dealt with (macro) fiscal problems, but ignored (micro) insurance aspects. The principal victim was trust in the ability of pensions to deliver income security. This trust was compromised by blame avoidance, and eroded by seemingly arbitrary pension cuts. High nonwage costs coupled with violations of solemn assurances undermined confidence, leaving younger contributors unable to distinguish between contributions and a punitive tax on work. Even if the pension promise is more viable (which is still to be demonstrated), it is therefore trusted less. Restoring trust should top any reform agenda.

An issue that has been overlooked is that pension entitlements proceed in tandem and compete with debt servicing of the national debt as claims on current production. The links between debt servicing and GDP growth are currently drawing attention, most notably in the context of GDP-linked bonds (Shiller 2018). The time structure of aging, whereby Greek dependency rates peak between 2040 and 2050, means that the rise in pension payments follows the peak in debt-service obligations and extends the problems created. This coincidence can potentially have dire effects on growth prospects.

A DB pension system of the type in force hands out pension promises redeemable in the distant future. In this way, future pensioners in a DB system are very similar to bondholders. Though they may be domestic residents, they are still external to the production process. Their interest lies in ensuring the promises they hold are honored; they do not care how. Pensions are senior to production. Indeed, external bondholders have similar concerns.[27] Both DB pensions and external debt mortgage future output; DB pensions could even be worse, because implicit debt may carry more fiscal and political uncertainty, for both the issuer and the holder, than explicit contractual debt.[28] In other words, a large DB system may well replicate in the future some of the conditions that led Greece to bankruptcy in the past, by encouraging irreconcilable claims on output.

In a country struggling to exit a deep recession, pension schemes need to help the recovery; this obligation is underlined by the central place of pensions in the processes that led to the crisis. Such schemes would be systems that redistribute the fruits of economic success after it has been earned, rather than mortgaging it in advance. Future pensioners must be encouraged to think and behave like shareholders, in partnership with production, rather than like external bondholders, in competition with other claims. These general arguments are reinforced in the specific case of Greece by four considerations of wider macroeconomic relevance:

- The size of the pension system is very large, both absolutely and relative to other public obligations—close to 18 percent of GDP and subject to upward risk because of demography and the consequent need for other aging-related expenditures, such as long-term care.

- Nonwage costs are very important as a determinant of competitiveness. Social insurance contributions, unlike value-added taxes, cascade tax obligations and directly hurt exports. A country such as Greece would benefit from a revenue-neutral reform shifting revenue out of payroll taxes. Export recovery propelled the exit of the other euro area countries; the failure of exports to rise, despite internal devaluation, makes Greece stand out (Arkolakis, Doxiadis, and Galenianos 2017).

- The dominant positions of the self-employed and the small business sector mean that applying employee-type contributions (up to 38 percent on net earnings) will be especially hurtful to competitiveness (Lyberaki and Tinios 2017).

- Growth is impeded by a shortage of savings. Greece has been, since 2006, dissaving in aggregate, as public sector surpluses are offset by private sector dissaving. In the absence of domestic savings, growth is reduced to hoping for foreign capital to flow in as a kind of deus ex machina. Pension systems are currently adding to dissaving (Haliassos et al. 2017).

The four macroeconomic considerations back the key claim of this chapter, that the current structure and size of the pension system (even after reforms) is preventing economic recovery. Indeed, it is possible to claim that without radical change in pensions, no recovery can prove lasting.

For Greece to exit stagnation, both the size of pension promises and the way they relate to the rest of the economy need to change. A proposal satisfying this condition systems thus have three features: First, it should provide a competitiveness shock—ideally by reducing nonwage costs. Second, it should alter how pensions relate to production. Defined contribution schemes do exhibit this key characteristic; their claims are contingent and not absolute. Third, it should be seen as a clean break with the (largely discredited) past. Contributory pension schemes should directly benefit participants; they must be used as aids to individual longevity planning, and not as "get-rich-quick" schemes on the part of some occupations or generations.

NDC systems satisfy these conditions. They deliver at an aggregate level by linking, in various ways, the technical rate of return to GDP growth. Prefunded defined contribution (DC) systems go one step further by directly involving the investment of pension reserves, providing a link visible to individuals.

The next section proposes and describes a system designed to meet the three requirements.

"Pensions for the Young": A Radical Proposal to Exit the Crisis

A radical proposal for change, actuarially costed, was first compiled in December 2016, and published in May 2018 (Nektarios, Tinios, and Symeonidis 2018). This proposal extended earlier suggestions to introduce a three-pillar system (for example, Nektarios 2008, 2012; Panageas and Tinios 2017). The proposal has three key characteristics (see box 7.2 for details):

BOX 7.2 Outline of the proposed three-pillar system for Greece

I. A new pension system for generations first insured after January 1, 1993. A three-pillar system can lead to an expected total earnings replacement rate greater than 60 percent.

A. First pillar: A single provider for all primary pensions on the nonfinancial defined contribution (NDC) principle

- Contribution rate is 10 percent (down from 20 percent today); the reduction could be phased in gradually.

- Pensions result from an NDC basis. Contributions cumulate in personal accounts, using a technical interest rate related to the rate of growth of GDP.[a]

- No specific safety net for pensions is envisaged; pensioners would be eligible for the new Social Solidarity Income that exists for the general population.

- Primary pensions corresponding to the period before the start of the system will be credited on a pro rata basis. There will be no right to an old system NDC auxiliary pension.

B. Second pillar: New mandatory prefunded supplementary pension system

- Contributions at 6 percent (replacing the current 7 percent to auxiliary funds).

- Credited to a personal account; funds invested professionally to build reserves.

- Pension entitlements are defined contribution.

- Opting out to occupational funds is allowed provided equivalent cover is secured. This encourages a sense of ownership.

C. Third pillar: Voluntary occupational pension funds

- Separation funds (together with their property) are transformed into occupational funds.

- Occupational funds allow for flexibility across employment sectors.

- The self-employed, nonunionized workers, or small enterprises can combine into open occupational funds.

II. The transition period: Guarantees for all who started work before 1993.
Outstanding commitments will be itemized and costed within six months, so that entitlements can be credibly costed and guaranteed and possible adjustments identified. Those currently working will receive a pension in two parts—one corresponding to pre-2017 service calculated as today (Law 4387/16), and one corresponding to new system rights earned. All preexisting primary and auxiliary funds will be consolidated. All entitlement changes legislated to 2017 will be fully implemented. Transition costs are reduced by the legislated cut in pensions due to take place in 2019. Government grants from general taxation will back the guarantees.

SOURCE: Nektarios, Tinios, and Symeonidis 2018.

a. NDC entitlements are calculated according to the formula used today for auxiliary pensions. This is not to imply that other alternatives are not feasible; however, using an existing method has the advantage of familiarity.

- It accords top priority to the immediate start of a new separate multipillar pension system based on full reciprocity for all who started working after 1992—that is, for virtually everyone under age 45 years.[29] A major reduction in contribution rates is combined with the immediate introduction of a separate, prefunded pension pillar. The system should be introduced as soon as possible—less than a year after the decision to go ahead.

- For older system participants (those who started working before 1993), it aims for the largest possible reassurance—that is, for a durable guarantee, financed out of general revenues—that pensions will not be cut again, for at least the next 20 years. The extent of the guarantee is deliberately left open, to not preclude the reconsideration of legacy costs; these costs could be further contained by measures such as alterations in the "Heavy and Hazardous" occupations schemes, or by providing incentives for those who retired early to return to employment.[30]

- It places a premium on transparency by electing the multipillar framework, where the roles of different kinds of actors and the extent of subsidization are subject to scrutiny and circumscribed. It also tries to keep separate insurance (income replacement) from safety net (social policy) factors. The latter should be transparent and subject to explicit rules.

The new proposal is calibrated to the specific needs of a macroeconomic recovery program for Greece. It focuses on regaining younger contributors' trust by stressing systemic breaks with the old, discredited, system[31]; it endeavors to keep the new system's operation "uncontaminated" to the maximum possible extent from transition and legacy issues. For the same reason, it seeks to start the new system as soon as possible by decoupling it from the financing of legacy costs. More important, and in sharp contrast to pension reform proposals in other countries, the proposal is not fiscally neutral—a central feature is an immediate reduction in contributions.

This bold reduction is intended to operate as a growth shock, and to form a prominent part of an overall recovery package.[32] Social insurance contributions are high and could have important disincentive and competitiveness effects. Recent changes widening the contribution base and extending the application of the system probably exacerbated an already problematic situation.[33] This reduction will combine with reciprocity in calculating entitlements to underline that a new leaf is being turned; new pensions must be seen to abide by a different logic from what pertained in the past. Finally, the creation of a stock of savings to finance domestic investment will address the chronic private savings deficit in the medium term and beyond.[34]

The proposal was tested actuarially, to the extent possible, for the period up to 2060 (Nektarios, Tinios, and Symeonidis 2018). Given inherent data and other limitations, such a quantification cannot be definitive. It should instead act as a reality check signposting areas of difficulties, but should, nevertheless, take the discussion forward.

The study built on demographic and economic projections prepared for the 2015 Economic Policy Committee Ageing Working Group exercise (EC 2015), updated for macroeconomic and legislative developments.[35] Table 7.1 computes assumed replacement rates for individuals retiring after a 40-year career at different times for the proposed system. These must be compared with total replacement rates of greater than 80 percent for the existing system: 74 percent primary (allowing for the flat-rate national pension) and about 8 percent auxiliary.[36] The proposed system gradually reduces replacement (because a larger portion of total pensions are derived from NDC), and makes it up by a greater reliance on a financial defined contribution (FDC) pension. When the new system is fully operational, first-pillar pensions (for which the public will be responsible) will be

TABLE 7.1 **Projected replacement rates for a full career under the existing and proposed Greek pension system, 2020–60**

| | First pillar NDC | Proposed system | | | |
| | | Second pillar | | Total | |
		3% return DC	4% return DC	3%	4%
2020 (%)	88	1	1	89	89
2030 (%)	83	6	6	89	89
2040 (%)	59	11	13	70	72
2050 (%)	33	18	21	51	54
2060 (%)	27	23	29	50	56

SOURCE: Original table.

NOTE: The existing system yields total replacement of greater than 80 percent (primary ≈ 70–74 percent; auxiliary 8 percent). Assumptions: 40-year career, retired at age 67, real wage increase 0.5 percent per year, 0.5 percent charge on second pillar contributions, annuity calculated over a 15.64-year expected period after retirement. DC = defined contribution; NDC = nonfinancial defined contribution.

about 30 percent. To this will be added funded supplementary pensions, to reach about 50 percent replacement if the return on capital is 3 percent. This type of return can provide a solid basis for individual pensions of the third pillar on a voluntary basis.

The new first and second pillars are self-supporting, meaning they are independent of government budget financing, and the third pillar will follow suit eventually. Government finance is restricted to compensation for contributions lost because of unemployment, parental leave, and military service[37]; government grants concentrate on financing legacy costs, insulating the new system to the extent possible. The second pillar will accumulate reserves, which are projected to amount to one-quarter of GDP (€50 billion) by 2030 and will rise more than 55 percent before 2060 (€400 billion). These figures make no allowance for impacts from incentives or from improving macroeconomic performance or faster reduction of unemployment.

The key problem is securing resources to pay the (reduced) pensions for the long transition period; the last legacy contributor will have retired by 2045. The actuarial study tried to approximate the funds needed as well as the financing gap that will be created by the reduction in contributions. Figure 7.2 shows the impact on primary pension deficits of reducing contributions by half (10 percentage points) plus redirecting 6 percent currently paying for auxiliary pensions to forming prefunded individual accounts. This is contrasted with the EPC projections of 2015 and 2018, corresponding to the second and third bailouts. The EPC incorporates all changes passed in 2017, including full allowance for the recalibration of pensions-in-payments, as well as increases in contribution rates. The 2015 projection would have introduced substantially the same system as the 2018 variant, but would have grandfathered incumbents. In this proposal, the deficit of 8.8 percent rises on impact to 10 percent. The relatively contained rise is due to (a) the problems of collecting contributions, and (b) the coincidence of the proposals with the legislated fall of pensions-in-payment to take place in 2019[38]; if comparison is made with the 2018 projection, the rise in deficits is larger, though probably overstated.[39] As NDC pensions fall in line with contributions, deficits fall, halving by the end of the projection period.

FIGURE 7.2 **Primary pension deficits for the proposal and 2015 and 2018 Economic Policy Committee projections, Greece, 2013–60**

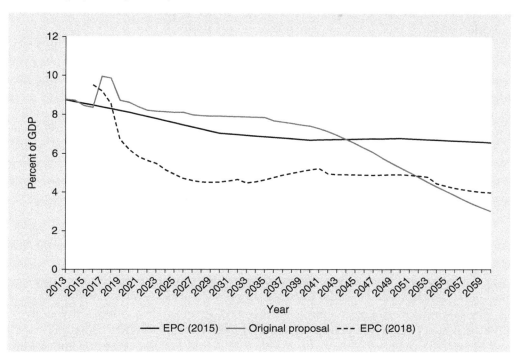

SOURCES: EC (2015, 2018); and original calculations.

NOTE: GDP = gross domestic product.

Part of the financing gap is due to the conversion of PAYG obligations of auxiliary pensions to prefunded DC supplementary pensions. This "implicit debt" is brought into the open and will stop growing. The second part is due to the reduction of contributions, essentially rebalancing the tax system away from distortionary taxes on labor, and reflects legacy costs. This interpretation is aided by the fact that the first pillar will be fully NDC, that is, 100 percent reciprocity. Further finance could be sought from targeted consolidation (for example, pension age increases on "hazardous occupations") or the use of new financial instruments to allow a more equitable spreading of the burden across generations.[40] Gradual introduction of the reduction in contributions[41] would ease fiscal problems but could subtract from the growth impact.

The deficit shown in figure 7.2 is thus, in a sense, an upper limit, and is the consequence of an attempt to keep the new system uncontaminated from legacy costs. For example, a larger PAYG component would increase current fiscal flows, but would increase the share of pensions in the steady state. This conundrum would have been dealt with in the past by promising now and planning to renege on promises a decade on, as part of a "reform by installments" (Tinios 2012a). This course of action would undermine confidence in the system and could risk negating key benefits of the reform. If generational rebalancing is needed, it would be better if it were discussed openly.

The rationale of this pension reform is squarely macroeconomic. This is obvious insofar as pensions are a large part of government finances, which must adhere to the fiscal limits agreed to with Greece's creditors. The proposal is to act as a growth shock, with an impact on employment, savings, tax collection, and investment. All these matters are dependent on the speed and extent of the reaction of the economy to falling insurance contributions.

The issue of how to "press reset" in the economy was approached in a unified proposal designed to deal simultaneously with the three major growth impediments of the economy: (a) the inability to finance investment while running 3.5 percent public surpluses, (b) a dysfunctional tax system, and (c) a top-heavy pension system.[42] Those three issues are held to condemn Greece to a permanently anemic growth path; the question is how to shift gears and switch to a higher growth trajectory. Thus, the features of this pension proposal were integrated into a macroeconometric dynamic model (Christodoulakis, Nektarios, and Theocharis 2018). The model examines how the economy reacts when 2 percent of public sector surpluses are redirected to private investment, combined with a gradual cut in insurance contributions and a revenue-neutral tax reform built around simplification. A pension reform of the type envisaged leads to employment increases, which translate to extra tax revenues and higher growth. This takes effect just as the growth-boosting impacts of the investment increase begin to wear out (after 2025). After the first decade, all nominal magnitudes are improved in the reform scenario.

An important issue is the elasticity of revenues following reductions in contribution rates, which depends on the impact on employment. This question is approached by Christodoulakis, Nektarios, and Theocharis (2018) through a comparative study of time series data in euro area pension systems. In four countries (Greece, Ireland, Portugal, and Spain), a reduction in the contribution rate would increase employment—a kind of Laffer curve. Greece has the sharpest reaction of any country studied: the long-term unemployment rate would fall by one-half, to 7.5 percent, compared with 15 percent without the reform. It is estimated that a 1.0 percentage point reduction in the contribution rate in the other euro area countries leads to a 0.77 percent increase in employment, whereas in Greece it is 1.1 percent. The model, nevertheless, uses the more conservative estimate. In this way, contribution revenues would rise to offset the biggest part of the fall in rates within the first decade. The macroeconomic model predicts that, without a pension reform, the impact of smaller surpluses will soon peter out. Its impact is magnified if it is combined with a pension and contribution reform of the type outlined.

Table 7.2 reproduces summary indicators of the scenarios investigated by Christodoulakis, Nektarios, and Theocharis (2018). Column (1) corresponds roughly to the anemic macroeconomic scenario presumed by the actuarial model. Though the actuarial model applies exogenous macroeconomic assumptions, these are derived endogenously in the model, which explains the absence of detailed replacement and fiscal figures in the original source. Column (2) includes the rise in investment plus the tax reform. Column (3) adds to that a reform like the one outlined; the difference is that contributions fall by 8 percentage points rather than 10, and this is implemented over a four-year period.

This radical proposal would have positive implications in five directions:

- *Pension protection.* A young contributor can be assured that 16 percent of contributions will lead to replacement of final salary exceeding 50 percent. If she contributes an additional 4 percent to an occupational fund, her replacement rate could reach 75 percent.

TABLE 7.2 **Simulated macroeconomic effects of three scenarios**

		(1) High contribution scenario	(2) High contribution without reform	(3) Reforms/low contributions[a]	Difference (3)–(2)
Employment (thousands)	2030	4,010	4,063	4,413	350
	2050	3,621	3,566	3,971	405
Unemployment (%)	2030	15.26	12.89	7.11	−5.79
	2050	15.23	14.29	7.82	−6.47
Pensioners (thousands)	2030	1,913	1,913	1,913	0
	2050	2,479	2,564	2,740	176
Personal disposable income (thousands €) 2017	2030	—	136	142	6
	2050	—	240	266	25
Fiscal balance (% GDP)	2030	—	0.91	1.23	0.31
	2050	—	1.78	3.06	1.28
Replacement rate (%)	2030	—	45.85	48.89	3.04
	2050	—	26.48	33.20	6.72
Average total pensions (€) 2017	2030	15,152	16,506	22,771	6,265
	2050	15,410	19,509	47,018	27,509

SOURCE: Chistodoulakis, Nektarios, and Theocharis 2018, 96.

NOTE: GDP = gross domestic product; — = not available.

a. Contributions are projected to fall to 12 percent gradually.

- *Viable state funding.* The new system has zero state subsidies. Extra finance is necessary for the transition period only for older workers and pensioners and will be provided in a transparent manner; the amounts are no larger than the burdens projected for the current system.

- *Aid to national debt restructuring.* The implicit debt due to pensions stops growing. The assurance and transparency will improve Greece's credit rating in financial markets. As new system reserves accumulate, Greece will find it easier to shift the composition of debt from external to internal.

- *New attitudes toward saving that promote generational solidarity.* The immediate reduction of contributions should free funds so that households and businesses can pay off part of their outstanding debts. Reciprocity could prove to be an incentive for saving.

- *An impetus for growth.* Halving social insurance contributions promotes competitiveness, improves work incentives, and helps saving. Success will be rewarded by growing pension reserves, but possibly also by the return of the new diaspora of young qualified people who left the country after 2010.

Conclusions

Greece's economic performance and troubles since 2010 are often compared to a tragedy. This comparison is more apt than many realize. Aristotle, analyzing classical tragedies in his *Poetics,* posited that the tragic hero goes through three stages: Hubris, thinking he can transcend rules laid by gods; this leads to Ate, a state of blindness to the impending catastrophe; and finally Nemesis, the punishment due to presumption.

This chapter's overview of pension reform would not surprise Aristotle. Greek governments ignored repeated warnings that aging necessitated restructuring pensions (Hubris). They kept postponing reform and invented novel ways to increase spending (Ate). When bankruptcy arrived, the people worst affected were those who had secured the most generous promises (Nemesis), bringing down the economy with them.

Greek tragedies have universal appeal because people recognize themselves in the tragic hero. In a similar way, the troubles of Greek pensions can be a type of warning of what lies ahead for any government that thinks that pension reform can wait indefinitely.

If pensions were responsible for this deep crisis, it follows that no exit will be viable if those same pensions continue unchanged. This chapter's proposal takes the dramatic challenge seriously: pensions, hitherto only renewing problems, must be used to provide solutions.

Notes

1. For a timeline see Panageas and Tinios (2017) and Tinios (2018).

2. Farmers' pensions were less than one-half those of the private sector. Public sector and civil servants' replacement rates were well above 100 percent.

3. But also, the one least concerned with correcting it; it was the only EU country not to send any projections in the 2006 round of AWG projections. See Tinios (2012b) for an analysis of how the EU Open Method of Coordination highlighted the unsustainability of Greek pensions, but was unable to overcome government complacency.

4. Greece is not the only country where pension reforms acquire systemic importance. The Juppé reforms of 1996 in France are probably the best known example.

5. The pension supplement EKAS played the role of a pensions-only safety net. It was introduced in 1996 to forestall generalized increases in minimum pensions. When incomes were rising before the crisis, EKAS expenditures played little role in expenditure increases.

6. "Greek statistics" became notorious in the misreporting of the 2009 public sector deficit. The Head of ELSTAT (Hellenic Statistical Authority) in charge of the recalculation is on record as saying the social insurance deficit was in reality 0.8 percent of GDP higher than originally reported.

7. Featherstone, Kazamias, and Papadimitriou (2001) examine a particular case in which an outspoken report on pensions was ignored and its key messages suppressed.

8. After the third bailout the Troika was transformed into a Quartet with the addition of the European Stability Mechanism.

9. In the 1990–93 adjustment, pensions were eroded by inflation by 25 percent. In the context of euro area monetary stability, this was not feasible.

10. Germany was reaping the benefits of reforms implemented in 2003. In Italy the financial crisis is seen to have exerted upward pressure on the share of pensions in GDP.

11. Increases were partly due to the denominator falling. With a 28 percent drop in GDP, a country that spends 12 percent of GDP will spend 16.5 percent of GDP. However, the crisis showed that levels of GDP were unsustainable; identifying precrisis GDP with normality begs a serious question.

12. The fragmentation and opacity of pension system finances imply that the exact numbers are subject to controversy. For example, how should one account for civil service pensions, for which no employer contribution was levied from the 1950s to 2017? Or the many funds for which employers had the legal obligation to cover all pension expenditures; in the case of some public enterprises, this was combined with large losses on their operating account.

13. The precrisis levels were not very different. In 2008 all contribution revenues amounted to 9.9 percent of GDP, the cost of civil service pensions to 1.8 percent of GDP, and all other non-contribution revenues (grants, third-party taxes, deficit finance) another 5.8 percent of GDP (Tinios 2010, 352–55). These grants were later proved to be underestimated by 0.8 percent of GDP.

14. Stergiou (2017) exhaustively covers legal aspects. For a critical economic reading, see Panageas and Tinios (2017).

15. Strictly, on all income since 2002, due to the absence of records. Given that that period encompasses the drop of 30 percent in earnings during the crisis, career average income will be larger than the previous situation, which was best five of the last ten years.

16. "Heavy and Hazardous" occupations were a feature of the precrisis system, encompassing more than 40 percent of all private sector retirees. Certain occupations (for example, hairdress-ers) were withdrawn in 2011. However, in a characteristic move, all incumbents with more than 10 years of contributions retained their rights.

17. Small firms and service companies have reportedly shifted their operations to Cyprus or Bulgaria to avoid contributions. A recurring problem is the lack of publicly available financial information.

18. However, two years on, consolidation is well behind schedule and is apparently causing major problems. One such problem is the delay in implementing the new (and far simpler) entitle-ment regulations.

19. These are also sometimes known as supplementary pensions, risking confusion with the European use of supplementary pensions to mean occupational pensions (of the second pillar).

20. No data justifying that figure were ever released, creating the suspicion that the cut warranted was larger. This, however, would only create pressure for bigger cuts in later years.

21. See Nektarios, Tinios, and Symeonidis (2018, 97). The Committee's recommendation echoes earlier proposals of Tinios (2015) and Nektarios (1997).

22. Tinios (2016) explains that the features of the reform are due to a failure of reform technology; oriented to solving the original issue of fragmentation (the problem of the past), it failed to address issues of the present (aging) and the future (technology, competitiveness).

23. Countries differ on whether to present reforms as systemic breaks. Countries where systems were seen as discredited (for example, in Eastern Europe and Latin America) stressed novelty. In others, reassurance was prioritized. That Greece chose continuity is itself interesting, and can be seen as an instance of denial.

24. Official pronouncements concur with this evaluation. An op-ed piece by the Employment Minister states that replacement rates will exceed 90 percent of final salary, while keeping total pension expenditures to 2040 (though not later) below the EU average (Achtsioglou 2018). No explanation is offered for the apparent paradox.

25. Precrisis contributions were high for traded sectors and low for nontraded services, agriculture, and the government. New contributions are levied on all categories of income as if everyone was a salaried employee. All gig economy work is treated as "hidden salaried employment" and is liable to 26–38 percent contributions.

26. Another little appreciated feature is that actuarial viability relies on consistent increases in the retirement age every decade. In EC (2018), this is set to rise from the current age 67–72 in 2050.

27. All pensions are bond-like. However, defined contribution and NDC pension entitlements are closer to GDP-linked bonds, which will pay more in favorable eventualities.

28. The argument that external debt represents a contractual obligation whereas pension promises rely only on moral obligations was proven to be facile when in June 2015 Greece preferred to pay monthly pensions at the expense of defaulting on an IMF payment, when the IMF was the senior legal creditor.

29. The choice of 1992 corresponds to a familiar criterion introduced by an earlier law (L2084/92) (Börsch-Supan and Tinios 2001).

30. Panageas and Tinios (2017) mention a number of possibilities, including a recall to the labor market of pensioners younger than certain ages.

31. The "brain drain" since 2010 has meant half a million mostly highly educated younger people emigrated in search of work. Enticing these people back to Greece should be a priority.

32. International discussions of Greek debt center on the need for debt relief as an aid to long-term prospects. If seen in this frame, financing the legacy cost of a growth-oriented pension reform out of a reduction in primary deficits could be interpreted as an acceptable form of debt relief.

33. So that, even if contributions are replaced by an increase in income tax, say, to an equivalent amount, there could be a welfare gain. See below for a discussion of contribution tax elasticities.

34. Private sector savings have been negative since 2007. The proposal must also be seen against the backdrop of needing to maintain very high public sector surpluses—3.5 percent of GDP to 2022 and 2 percent afterward. The extra private savings will be partly offset by the need to finance transition costs.

35. Nektarios Tinios, and Symeonidis (2018) catalogue data infelicities—for example, that the insured population is 2 percent larger than those employed, or that no data exist for the baseline. The EC (2015) projection did not allow for changes legislated or economic developments after the third bailout. Subsequent partial projections simulated the changes of 2015–17. The quantification combined all data available as of 2017 and attempted to safeguard consistency to the extent possible.

36. Exact replacement rates cannot be calculated because clarification is still needed. Nevertheless, official statements largely concur with this analysis. The minister is on record that Greek replacement rates remain at the top end of the euro area (Achtsioglou 2018). Because of the two-tier structure of the current system, replacement rates for low earnings are larger. Replacement rates do not allow for separation benefits.

37. A buffer fund could provide a cushion for revenues lost in recessions.

38. A mystery surrounds near-term pension projections. The official EC (2018) projection holds that pensions will fall by 3.8 percentage points of GDP (22 percent) from 2018 to 2020; the only plausible justification—the recalibration of old pensions—should account for a 1 percent fall only. This is an example of the kind of issues quantification can occasionally turn up.

39. Some aspects of the proposal, such as the abolition of insurance classes for the self-employed, are in common with the EC (2018) projection, but could not have been allowed in the projection exercise.

40. Panageas and Tinios (2017) explore analytically the use of recognition bonds to speed the introduction of the second pillar. These could be sold to the funds and treated as government consols—that is, amortized as the need arises to pay contributor benefits. This is a way to rationalize and plan for general revenue finance, which would have to happen in any case.

41. Equivalently, shifting contributions of the self-employed to an ad valorem basis could be phased in.

42. The proposal colorfully terms the three obstacles "the three dragons" guarding the exit to growth.

References

Achtsioglou, Efi. 2018. "The Difficult Equation of the Pension Problem." *Kathimerini Daily* March 11.

Arkolakis, Costas, Aristos Doxiadis, and Manolis Galenianos. 2017. "The Challenge of Trade Adjustment in Greece." In *Beyond Austerity: Reforming the Greek Economy*, edited by Meghir Costas, Christopher A. Pissarides, Dimitri Vayanos, and Nikolaos Vettas, 103–35. Boston, MA: MIT Press.

Börsch-Supan, Axel, and Platon Tinios. 2001. "The Greek Pensions System: Strategic Framework for Reform." In *Greece's Economic Performance and Prospects*, edited by Ralph C. Bryant, Nick Garganas, and George S. Tavlas, 361–443. Washington, DC: Bank of Greece and Brookings Institution.

Busch, Klaus, Christoph Hermann, Karl Hinrichs, and Thorsten Scholten. 2013. "Euro Crisis, Austerity Policy and the European Social Model: How Crisis Policies in Southern Europe Threaten the EU's Social Dimension." Friedrich Ebert Stiftung, International Policy Analysis, Berlin.

Christodoulakis, Nicholas, Milton Nektarios, and Harry Theocharis (with Christos Axioglou, Pavlos Kouris, and George Symeonidis). 2018. "Reset for the Greek Economy: How the Reduction of Taxes, Social Insurance Contributions and the Fiscal Surplus Leads to Growth, Employment and a Viable National Debt." diaNEOsis, Research and Policy Institute, Athens. https://www.dianeosis.org/wp-content/uploads/2018/02/Drakoi—Upd120218.pdf (in Greek).

EC (European Commission). 2015. *The 2015 Ageing Report: Economic and Budgetary Projections for the EU-27 Member States (2013-2060)*. Brussels, European Commission, Economic Policy Committee. http://ec.europa.eu/economy—finance/publications/european—economy/2015/pdf/ee3—en.pdf.

———. 2018. *The 2018 Ageing Report: Economic and Budgetary Projections for the 28 EU Member States (2016-2070)*. Brussels, European Commission, Economic Policy Committee. https://ec.europa.eu/info/sites/info/files/economy-finance/ip079—en.pdf.

Featherstone, Kevin, Georgios Kazamias, and Dimitris Papadimitriou. 2001. "The Limits of External Empowerment: EMU, Technocracy and the Reform of the Greek Pension System." *Political Studies* 49 (3): 462–80.

Featherstone, Kevin, and Dimitris Papadimitriou. 2008. *The Limits of Europeanization: Reform Capacity and Policy Conflict in Greece*. London: Palgrave.

Giannitsis, Tassos. 2016. *The Pension Problem and the Crisis*. Athens: Papazisis (in Greek).

Haliassos, Michael, Gikas Hardouvelis, Margarita Tsoutsoura, and Dimitri Vayanos. 2017. "Financial Development and the Credit Cycle in Greece." In *Beyond Austerity: Reforming the Greek Economy*, edited by Meghir Costas, Christopher A. Pissarides, Dimitri Vayanos, and Nikolaos Vettas, 251–305. Boston, MA: MIT Press.

IMF (International Monetary Fund). 2010. "Greece: Staff Report on Request for Stand-By Arrangement." IMF Country Report 10/110, IMF, Washington, DC.

———. 2017. "Greece: Selected Issues." IMF Country Report 17/41, IMF, Washington, DC. https://www.imf.org/en/Publications/CR/Issues/2017/02/07/Greece-Selected-Issues-44631.

Lyberaki, Antigone. 2018. "The Family, the Elderly and the Crisis." In *Ageing in the Crisis: Experiences from Greece*, edited by Fred Karl, 87–122. Zürich: Lit Verlag GmbH.

Lyberaki, Antigone, and Platon Tinios. 2012. "Labour and Pensions in the Greek Crisis: The Microfoundations of Disaster." *Südosteuropa. Zeitschrift für Politik und Gesellschaft* 60 (3): 363–86.

———. 2017. "Small Firms as a Blind Spot in Greek Austerity Economics." IDS Working Paper 491, Institute of Development Studies, Brighton, UK. https://www.ids.ac.uk/publication/small-firms-as-a-blind-spot-in-greek-austerity-economics.

Meghir, Costas, Chistopher A. Pissarides, Dimitris Vayanos, and Nikos Vettas. 2017. "The Greek Economy before and after the Crisis—and Policy Options Going Forward." In *Beyond Austerity: Reforming the Greek Economy*, edited by Meghir Costas, Christopher A. Pissarides, Dimitri Vayanos, and Nikolaos Vettas, 3–72. Boston, MA: MIT Press.

Nektarios, Milton. 1997. *Social Insurance for Greece*. Athens: Forum (in Greek).

———. 2008. *Pension Reform with Consensus and Transparency*. Athens: Papazisis (in Greek).

———. 2012. "Greece: The NDC Paradigm as a Framework for a Sustainable Pension System." In *Nonfinancial Defined Contribution Pension Schemes in a Changing Pension World: Volume 1 Progress, Lessons, and Implementation*, edited by Robert Holzmann, Ed Palmer, and David Robalino, 259–77. Washington, DC: World Bank.

Nektarios, Milton, Platon Tinios, and George Symeonidis. 2018. *Pensions for the Young: A Social Insurance System Focused on Growth*. Athens: Papazisis (in Greek).

Paleologos, Yiannis. 2014. *The 13th Labour of Hercules: Inside the Greek Crisis*. London: Portobello Books.

Panageas, Stavros, and Platon Tinios. 2017. "Pensions: Arresting a Race to the Bottom." In *Beyond Austerity: Reforming the Greek Economy*, edited by Meghir Costas, Christopher A. Pissarides, Dimitri Vayanos, and Nikolaos Vettas, 459–516. Boston, MA: MIT Press.

Shiller, Robert. 2018. "Introduction." In *Sovereign GDP-Linked Bonds: Rationale and Design*, edited by James Benford, Jonathan D. Ostry, and Robert Shiller, 5–11. London: CEPR Press.

Stergiou, Angelos. 2017. *Social Insurance Law*, 3rd ed. Athens: Sakkoulas Publishers (in Greek).

Symeonidis, George. 2017. "Forging a New, Solid Social Security System for Greece: The NTS Proposal." Paper presented at PBSS/IACA Colloquium, Cancun, June 4–7. http://actuaries.org/cancun2017/Papers/37.%20Georgios%20Symeonidis—Paper.pdf.

Tinios, Platon. 2010. *The Pension Problem: A Method to Decipher*. Athens: Kritiki (in Greek).

———. 2012a. "The Pensions Merry-Go-Round: End of a Cycle?" In *From Stagnation to Forced Adjustment: Reforms in Greece 1974–2010*, edited by Stathis Kalyvas, George Pagoulatos, and Harry Tsoukas, 117–32. London: C. Hurst & Co.

———. 2012b. "Pensions and the Lisbon Strategy." In *The EU's Lisbon Strategy: Evaluating Success, Understanding Failure*, edited by Dimitris Papadimitriou and Paul Copeland, 111–29. Basingstoke: Palgrave Macmillan.

————. 2015. "Off-the-Shelf Reforms and Their Blind Spots: Pensions in Post-Memorandum Greece." In *The Politics of Extreme Austerity: Greece beyond the Crisis*, edited by Roman Gerodimos and Georgios Karyotis, 66–76. London: Palgrave Macmillan.

————. 2016. "The Greek Pension Tragedy: A Case of Failure in Governance." Konrad Adenauer Stifftung, *Katoptron* 4. http://www.kas.de/wf/doc/kas—44877-1522-2-30 .pdf?160414150400.

————. 2018. "Pensioners and Pension Reforms during the Greek Crisis." In *Ageing in the Crisis*: *Experiences from Greece*, edited by Fred Karl, 25–45. Zürich: Lit Verlag GmbH.

Zampelis, Panos. 2013. "The New Method of Calculating Auxiliary Pensions and Separation Payments." *Review of Social Insurance Law*, NE: 35–50 (in Greek).

PART II

Conceptualization and Promotion

CHAPTER 8

NDC: The Generic Old-Age Pension Scheme

Marek Góra and Edward Palmer

Introduction

In all societies, people of working and childbearing age transfer economic resources to provide for the current consumption of their children and their parents, and for their own future consumption in old age. The resources they transfer consist of their unpaid non-market time and their labor market income. The latter occurs through abstaining from consumption (that is, saving) during the working phase of life to provide for consumption in old age. In a mature economy, the young save (pay contributions) and the old dissave (receive benefits), which is an exchange of financial and nonfinancial assets. As a consequence, paying for one's parents' consumption and paying for one's own consumption are almost the same.

This conceptual chapter begins with the universal need to allocate consumption over the life cycle from the working phase to the retirement phase. It is set in the paradigm that maximization of utility over a lifetime requires managing longevity risk, which—if done optimally—follows the principles of longevity insurance. The chapter presents the case for a universal public pension scheme, called a UPPS, as the universal life-cycle longevity insurance scheme for a nation. It assesses the relative strengths and weaknesses of four designs in achieving the UPPS life-cycle longevity insurance scheme: the end goal is provision of a fair, economically efficient, and financially sustainable UPPS.

The universe of possible pension schemes is assessed for four general UPPS designs, based on two sets of design properties: (a) defined benefit (DB) or defined contribution (DC), and (b) financial (F) or nonfinancial (N).[1] In all cases, payments of the current working generation are transferred over the life cycle into retirement income—and thus consumption possibilities—in old age. The chapter assesses to what extent these four alternative designs satisfy the criteria of fairness, economic efficiency, and financial sustainability.

The chapter begins by presenting the general economic rationale for a UPPS as a social contract mandated in a nation's laws. It then presents the four design choices: nonfinancial defined benefit (NDB), financial defined benefit (FDB), nonfinancial defined contribution (NDC), and financial defined contribution (FDC), a typology introduced in Góra and Palmer (2004). The arguments supporting the superiority of NDC and FDC

The authors are grateful to Robert Holzmann, Sergio Nisticò, Heiki Oksanen, and Michal Rutkowski for comments and suggestions.

over DB in the context of creating a UPPS are presented in depth. The end result is to establish whether NDC may merit the distinction of being the generic UPPS, which entails weighing each scheme's different strengths—and eventual weaknesses—in dealing with the economic, demographic, and financial risks confronting all UPPSs.

In the long term, the UPPS is thus an institutional structure whereby a claim on current gross domestic product (GDP) "pays" or is "traded" for a claim on future GDP (Góra 2013). This chapter deals with the design effects on the efficiency, fairness, and financial sustainability of this intertemporal transfer. The issues are analyzed outside the dichotomy of "pay-as-you-go versus funding" that—in this chapter's view—is misleading within the structure of the UPPS.

The chapter is divided into seven sections. "Distinguishing Features of Private and Public Pension Schemes" establishes the difference between the meaning of "private" and "public" in the pension design dialogue. "The Double Dichotomy of UPPSs" presents the double dichotomy—DB versus DC and nonfinancial versus financial—of UPPSs. "The UPPS Viewed as a Life-Cycle Longevity Insurance Scheme" presents the rationale for establishment of a UPPS as the universal life-cycle longevity insurance scheme. "The Design of the UPPS and How UPPS-DB and UPPS-DC Fulfill the Criteria of a Good Pension Scheme" presents a general framework for understanding the technical differences between the four UPPS designs and discusses and compares these differences. "NDC as the Generic UPPS" summarizes the assessment in terms of the criteria presented and discussed. "Conclusions" concludes.

Distinguishing Features of Private and Public Pension Schemes

UPPSs are macro pension schemes with micro properties, while private pension schemes are solely micro—by definition. This distinguishing property of UPPSs underlies the framing of the discussion of this chapter. Whereas individual private "micro" pension schemes by themselves are unlikely to interact significantly with the macro economy, a UPPS interacts with the macro economy by definition.

In a UPPS the public provider is responsible for the scheme, although some or all of the specific functions—that is, collection of revenues, account keeping, information to participants, financial portfolio management, and so on—can be performed by either public institutions or private firms. A major difference between private and public schemes involves where the legal (financial) responsibility lies. Traditionally, many DB UPPSs were intertwined financially with government budget transactions and the national debt. The emergence of DC UPPSs was driven by the need to create financial autonomy for the universal public pension commitment.

The Double Dichotomy of UPPSs

A UPPS design can be described by two characteristics—whether the scheme is nonfinancial or financial and whether it is DB or DC. This constitutes the double dichotomy presented in table 8.1. In a nonfinancial UPPS, the rate of return is determined by the return on nonfinancial human capital investments (the productivity of the labor force) and the labor supply that embodies these investments. In a financial UPPS, the rate of

TABLE 8.1 **Double dichotomy characteristics of UPPSs**

Direct determinants of the rate of return	UPPS-Defined Benefit (UPPS-DB)	UPPS-Defined Contribution (UPPS-DC)
Financial investments	FDB	FDC
Nonfinancial human capital investments and labor supply	NDB	NDC

SOURCE: Based on Góra and Palmer 2004.

NOTE: FDB = financial defined benefit; FDC = financial defined contribution; NDB = nonfinancial defined benefit; NDC = nonfinancial defined contribution; UPPS = universal public pension scheme.

return is the return on financial investments, which in an open market economy includes investments in domestic and foreign capital.

Irrespective of the design fairness of DB schemes that underlies the benefit rules used, all UPPS-DB designs have in common the absence of built-in mechanisms that steer them toward financial affordability and sustainability. The provider maintains financial sustainability through ad hoc adjustments. This approach is required by the fact that the DB design per se does not deal directly with the demographic, economic, and, in the case of UPPS-FDB, financial risks. This is the important distinction between UPPS-DB and UPPS-DC designs. In short, the dichotomy is discretion versus rules. "The Design of the UPPS and How UPPS-DB and UPPS-DC Fulfill the Criteria of a Good Pension Scheme" returns to a much more comprehensive discussion of the differences between UPPS-DB and UPPS-DC. However, "The UPPS Viewed as a Life-Cycle Longevity Insurance Scheme" first develops the rationale for the role of the UPPS as a life-cycle longevity insurance scheme.

The UPPS Viewed as a Life-Cycle Longevity Insurance Scheme

The discussion starts with the idea of the UPPS as a pure life-cycle longevity insurance scheme by considering the ramifications of the definition of saving, the definition of generic longevity insurance, and the rationale for universal longevity insurance.

THE ECONOMIC DEFINITION OF SAVING

Saving is a result of forgoing current consumption out of current income. The general motive for individuals to save is to provide resources for consumption in the future. Although it is not the only reason to save for the future, the most important reason in the life-cycle context to save is to provide for consumption when one is old and retired from the labor force. The act of paying contributions into a pension scheme performs the function of transferring individual consumption possibilities from the present into the future. The difference is the strength of the link on an individual basis. If the link is one to one, then even though participation is mandatory and thus unavoidable (why it is mandatory is argued later), it is not a tax by definition if one defines a tax as relinquishing income to the tax authority to provide general revenues that in the end may or may not return to the taxpayer. The intention of UPPS-DC is that the unit of money paid is a liability to be repaid with interest to the payee—which can be called forced saving.

In NDC and FDC frameworks, the transfer from the current period to the future is accomplished by using personal accounts that perform the function of a bank "savings account." What characterizes a UPPS is that the transfer of income is mandatory for everyone, and under the same rules for everyone, although it is the way of managing contribution flows that differs between nonfinancial and financial UPPSs—which follows from the discussion up to this point—and which will be alluded to several times hereafter.

LIFE-CYCLE SAVING THROUGH THE VEHICLE OF INSURANCE IN THE GENERIC UPPS SCHEME

The well-known reason for individuals to save by contracting into longevity insurance is uncertainty about how long they will live—explicitly, the risk of outliving one's resources in old age. In line with the life-cycle theory of consumption and saving, all rational individuals will also strive to achieve a steady level of consumption throughout their entire life cycle, referred to in the literature as consumption smoothing.

The rational choice for individuals is to contract longevity insurance to manage the risk of ending up with insufficient resources for consumption in old age. The underlying principle of insurance is, then, that those who end up living a shorter life than the average expected life contract by virtue of their participation in the insurance scheme to transfer the remaining money on their accounts to those who live longer lives. In the face of uncertainty about their individual longevity, this is an efficient individual strategy that also enhances the welfare of the entire group.

UPPS LONGEVITY INSURANCE IS WELFARE ENHANCING

Would everyone voluntarily join an insurance scheme, contribute regularly from the time they are young entrants into the workforce, and continue to save on a regular basis throughout their working lives, thereby accumulating the funds necessary to earn a benefit sufficient to finance adequate consumption in retirement? Most would probably not do this.

Generally speaking, people are shortsighted. They live for today and tend to forget their obligation to themselves to save for their own consumption tomorrow. The greatest risk for society is that the myopic segment of the population will discount future needs too heavily and start saving too late in life to create sufficient savings to cover at least basic consumption needs in old age.

A second reason is that some healthy people with sufficient work skills would nevertheless consciously choose to be free riders, which means that they expect the altruistic others to pay for them in old age. The logic of the UPPS is thus to save people from the unfortunate consequences of their own poor judgment, which also protects those who would make the right decisions from the negative economic consequences of those who would not. In addition, the UPPS can for some provide a positive incentive to work and contribute more than they otherwise would have. The conclusion is that overall economic efficiency and the welfare of (practically) all is increased by the creation of a UPPS.

THE UNIVERSAL PUBLIC PENSION SCHEME AS "THE" LIFE-CYCLE INSURANCE

Under the Rawlsian veil of ignorance, because of the absence of knowledge about one's personal outcomes in life, and where individual fates in life are distributed randomly, the claim can be made that economists' rational individual would do what is best and choose to join an insurance pool in which everyone is treated equally. Individuals' shared uncertainty about their own life expectancy when young provides the justification for all individuals in a nation to join together to form a national insurance pool. The universal scheme compels people to enter into the insurance scheme from the very outset of their working careers, reducing the long-term negative outcomes of myopia and free riding.

A straightforward criterion for participation is that everyone pays a certain percentage of income from employment or self-employment into the universal insurance scheme. The payments represent current savings that are set aside during working years to pay for future consumption during years of retirement. In this way, the life-cycle universal longevity insurance brings in the idea of individual consumption smoothing, creating a fair "Rawlsian" lottery of outcomes distributed around the average life expectancy of each participant's (for example, birth) cohort.

The Design of the UPPS and How UPPS-DB and UPPS-DC Fulfill the Criteria of a Good Pension Scheme

This section examines the four basic forms of UPPS design with reference to the following criteria for judging the micro and macro outcomes of a specific pension scheme, and within the context of three general categories of risk: economic, demographic, and financial. The criteria used in the comparison of schemes are transparency, micro and macroeconomic efficiency, intra- and intergenerational fairness, financial sustainability and stability, affordability, and adequacy. These are also assessed in terms of the basic function of the UPPS: to provide a life-cycle mechanism for converting individual savings, through contributions, to a universal (national) longevity insurance scheme with the same rules for all.

A GENERIC TECHNICAL FRAMEWORK FOR THE UPPS BASED ON THE LIFE-CYCLE MODEL WITH LONGEVITY INSURANCE

To illustrate the design consequences of the four life-cycle UPPS insurance schemes, this section begins with a generalized expression of the life-cycle model with longevity insurance as viewed at the individual level, that is, as the typical life-cycle saver might formulate his or her individual savings to provide for consumption in retirement.[2] It starts with the phase of the life cycle when individuals work and pay contributions to a UPPS. Individual, i, pays a certain percentage, c, of yearly earnings, W, during the working phase of the life of T years, and each year the accounts earn a rate of return α. The sum, or balance, of the individual's payments accredited with interest—valorization of some other origin—over T periods of contributing into the savings scheme at T is

$$K_{i,T} = \sum_{t=1}^{T} c_{i,t} W_{i,t} \prod_{t+1}^{T-1} \left(1 + \alpha_{i,t}\right) \tag{8.1}$$

in which year T can be seen as the last year of contributions into the saving scheme before the individual retires with a benefit based on the real situation that the money has been paid into the savings scheme. The whole purpose of the UPPS is to create a life-cycle savings vehicle for transferring individual resources from years of work to consumption during the remaining years of life. The important message of expression (8.1) is that individuals' decisions to work and contribute to their own savings in the UPPS insurance scheme also determine their consumption possibilities in old age. This is the principal message of the UPPS-DC design. The message is easy to communicate (that is, transparent) and easy to understand and accept as a fair outcome.

With the goal of achieving adequate and affordable pensions, the message of a good UPPS is that healthy individuals are ultimately responsible for contributing to their own life-cycle saving scheme. To the extent that they are not capable of doing this—for whatever reason—the UPPS is supplemented with a tax-financed minimum pension "floor." The one-to-one message of UPPS-DC stands in stark contrast to the dominant messages of pension politics underlying the post–World War II era and the generous UPPS-DB schemes that emerged—that could only become temporary pension schemes in a transition to a form of a financially intergenerationally sustainable UPPS.[3]

Moreover, in retrospect, there is little doubt that postwar generosity was made possible in the immediate two postwar decades by strong economic growth spearheaded by a postwar reconstruction boom together with a baby-boom labor force becoming working age in the mid-1960s. Sweden's UPPS-NDC scheme created in the 1990s was a response to Sweden's awakening to the long-term financial unsustainability of too generous rules regarding early exit (Palmer 1999) and more general system benefit design deficiencies of UPPS-NDB schemes, which generally do not maintain the one-to-one link between contributions and benefits, thereby leading to long-term financial difficulties. These are themes running through Palmer (2002, 2005).

Expression (8.1) is only half of the story, however. The second half is how the distribution of individual savings over the remaining life from the time of exit from the labor force with a retirement benefit is determined. This entails converting the accumulated capital balance (with the internal rate of return), K, into a stream of income (consumption) over the remainder of the individual's life. In the UPPS-DC framework this is done by constructing the yearly pension payment P as a life annuity (see Palmer and Zhao de Gosson de Varennes [2019] for a discussion of whether the rate of return should be included exogenously to the annuity, in the latter case in the form of periodic indexation):

$$P_{k,i,\tau} = \frac{K_{i,\tau-1}}{G\left[LE_k, \beta\left(LE_k\right)\right]} \tag{8.2}$$

in which k is individual i's birth cohort pool and LE_k is the cohort's average life expectancy from the year τ when the annuity is granted. Expression (8.2) converts the individual's savings K at retirement into a yearly payment based on a rate of return β and the individual's birth cohort's average life expectancy, LE_k. The role of the birth cohort pension pool is to create a sum of money—that is, the entire birth cohort's pension savings—that is distributed among individual participants in accordance with their actual number of years of life. This technical mechanism distributes the capital of those who die younger than average to those who live longer than average.

An important message of expression (8.2) is that the higher the individual's life expectancy at retirement, the lower the yearly benefit payment, and vice versa; that is, the distributional mechanism is "actuarially fair." Postponing retirement adds an additional year of contributions to K and also reduces the value of LE used in computing the yearly payment (that is, it results in a higher yearly payment).

Because the UPPS is a mandatory, universal insurance, the idea of discriminating on the basis of indicators of specific individual risk was eliminated from the outset on the basis of the social-value argument of the Rawlsian veil of ignorance. This by no means precludes the possibility of changing the final distribution of income through the general tax-transfer system, but it is a socially acceptable point of departure for the generic UPPS.

Summing up, this technical presentation of the life-cycle model of saving for old age to contract longevity insurance at retirement satisfies the basic criterion of accomplishing consumption smoothing over the life cycle. The longevity insurance is actuarially determined and as such is self-financing for the national pool of pensioners, and what individuals pay determines what they have available for consumption in retirement—that is, pensions are a direct reflection of individuals' allocation of their time during the working phase of their lives between market work and other activities.

The conclusion is that UPPS-DC fulfills the criteria set out in expressions (8.1) and (8.2) regarding the "saving" and insurance payout phases of the individual's life cycle. UPPS-DB schemes are not explicitly designed as in expressions (8.1) and (8.2). By virtue of its design UPPS-DC dominates UPPS-DB given the one-to-one relationship between individual lifetime contributions and benefits. And, if the design criteria of a UPPS-DB fully fulfill the criteria of expressions (8.1) and (8.2), then, in fact, it is instead a UPPS-DC design by definition. This conclusion is also important in the following discussions of the role of transparency in the determination of fairness and economic efficiency, and in the end the degree of affordability and long-term sustainability of a UPPS.

"THE" GENERIC UPPS IN THE CONTEXT OF THE TECHNICAL MODEL

From here on, this chapter presents the case that UPPS-DC is the optimum design of a UPPS and that UPPS-NDC is the generic version of financial or nonfinancial DC schemes, in the sense that UPPS-NDC brings the current elderly into the intergenerational transfer chain at the time the UPPS is started up. A UPPS-DC takes about 45 years from start-up for participants to achieve a benefit at retirement based on a full working career. Two factors favor the UPPS-NDC.

First, a UPPS-NDC design is an efficient intergenerational transfer mechanism that can harness the economic and demographic dynamics of emerging market economies—and demographic dividends (positive or negative) in general. The simple design vehicle of individual accounts accommodates all degrees of partial prefunding of a UPPS of intergenerational transfers. In other words, individual accounts consisting of explicit liabilities to today's workers make possible a transfer of consumption in real time today from the working-age population to the elderly. This can be done through a financial or a nonfinancial UPPS design—or something between these two alternatives.

An interesting design to think about in this context is a demography in which the working-age population is in an NDC equilibrium, but adopts a policy in which the population is increasing steadily because generous immigration rules or high birth rates—over decades—create reserves that accumulate until they are needed about 40–60 years later. This results in a substantial build-up of liquidity (funds).[4] The extreme example is introduction of an NDC in today's typical African nation. Larsson, Leyaro, and Palmer (2019) investigate how the UPPS-NDC design works in the context of a young population on its way toward demographic equilibrium and beginning with a largely informal labor market that begins to evolve into a formal market economy. Here the demographic dividend can be separated and invested through the vehicle of an NDC fund. The fund is invested in physical and human capital augmenting economic growth and development. What makes the emerging market economy an interesting real-world case is that a real option exists between consumption and investment of the funds. In the emerging market economy, the dynamically young population makes a transition from an informal to a formal market economy.[5]

In theory, the same principle can be harnessed in an economically developed society, which also has a range of options for distributing the dividend between consumption now or in the future. Even a mature economic society has the option of financing investment or consumption today generated by demographic dividends. An example is baby-boom generations whereby the second, third, and successive generations of offspring produce cyclical "booms" at intervals of, for example, 20 years or so.

Second, financial designs—that is, FDC (and FDB) schemes (private and public)—require government supervision because of the risk of mismanagement and fraud. Mismanagement entails systematic imprudent investment strategies and unmotivated costs for administration. Fraud entails unwarranted use of savers' funds for one's own gain. Supervision brings with it additional costs paid by the country's taxpayers, which in the case of a UPPS are the same persons as the savers and pensioners, even if these costs are seldom transparent for the participant. Since corruption is a real risk in financial dealings, this factor works against UPPS-FDC and FDB schemes.

UNIVERSAL FAIRNESS AND DISTRIBUTIVE SOCIAL POLICY

The one-to-one link between what individuals pay into the system during their working careers and what they get out of it in retirement is arguably an acceptable principle defining fairness of a UPPS. This statement, however, must be accompanied by the important qualification that social fairness also requires that society augment the universal life-cycle insurance scheme with a social income safety net that is deemed sufficient for those who because of various circumstances cannot provide for themselves.

Intragenerational fairness

With the building blocks of expressions (8.1) and (8.2), it is easy to understand that two persons coming from the same birth cohort who are employed at the same workplace doing work that yields the same hourly wage will be entitled to exactly the same expected pension benefit at retirement. If one works 10 percent more hours at this wage for the same number of years, then the result is a lifetime retirement benefit that is 10 percent higher.

Intergenerational fairness

In the same spirit, all else equal, if the wage rate increases by X percent over generations, the same formula (with a constant contribution rate) will yield an equivalent increase in pensions where the relationship of years of work and retirement maintains the same ratio over time (which is determined by the life-expectancy factor). In other words, the UPPS-DC rule—expressions (8.1) and (8.2)—defines a universal pension scheme that is fair within cohorts and over generations. This definition embodies the simplest combination of distributional rules—rules that aspire to do no more than fulfill every individual's need to save for an old age inevitably characterized by every individual's uncertain longevity.

Introducing distributional policy

The distinction between UPPS-DC and UPPS-DB schemes is fundamental. First, it has to do with creating rules regarding fairness that are transparent and can be accepted by general society as such. Second, it deals with the question of whether distributional rules should be internal or external to the UPPS. Proponents of UPPS-DB schemes point to the possibility of building distributional rules into the UPPS-DB design as its strength, whereas proponents of UPPS-DC believe that social policy should be exogenous, formulated as specific goals of policy and financed with general tax revenues.

Examples of exogenous goals are (a) externally tax-financed rights for care of children in conjunction with childbirth, and for higher education and skills training; and (b) contributions for periods covered by insurance for lost earnings caused by sickness, disability, and unemployment. All of these are universal rules in that they apply to all parents of newly born children, all persons in various types of higher education, or all persons who have lost days of earnings due to sickness, disability, or unemployment.

Making this transfer at the time of creating the liability into the individual account serves two purposes. The first is that by financing the transfer with "today's" tax revenues, the transfer is not pushed over to the coming generation to finance (this leads to intergenerational fairness). The second is that there is a greater chance that the individual will actually receive this benefit in a pension scheme where there is an actual and transparent individual account, because this makes it more difficult for the pension provider to shift the money in time, for example, from present workers to pensioners. In other words, by keeping the equivalence of rights through the vehicle of accounts, it is straightforward that the individual has a right to a future claim on consumption (GDP).

Finally, it is reemphasized that regarding the safety net for the poor elderly, whatever the cause of their poverty, that the strongest argument for holding the distributional rules outside the UPPS is the existence of a general-tax-financed minimum pension benefit available to all, with sufficient means testing, and also taking into consideration spouses' (co-habiting partners') economic resources.

In conclusion, the UPPS-DB design, regardless of its construction, fails to fulfill the one-to-one criterion of the universal life-cycle insurance scheme and is therefore inferior for two reasons. First, it is likely to be an inefficient model for income redistribution, compared with making redistribution an exogenous separate component of policy, steered by its own policy goals. Especially at the lower end of the earnings scale, the UPPS-DB redistributes money in the pension pool to spouses who are well-off themselves through their relationship with high income earners, that is, cases where a judgment based on combined economic resources would not approve such transfers. Second, all redistribution presumes a tax and a transfer.

The tax transfer mechanism can be implicit because of a nontransparent mechanism in the UPPS-DB context, or it can be an explicit, specific exogenous social policy as in the case of a UPPS-DC. In the DC case, the policy goal accomplished by putting policy-determined and explicit tax-financed "add-ins" (that is, transfers) into individual accounts. The DC approach is preferable on both an individual and a societal level, because it can be more successfully targeted toward prioritized needs that enhance the fairness of the overall UPPS.

To fulfill its basic purpose, a good UPPS needs to work efficiently and reliably over periods of time spanning generations of successive cohorts, with firm rules. On the other hand, social needs requiring redistribution change over time. A tax-financed policy can be easily adapted to these changes. The UPPS cannot simultaneously be an efficient life-cycle insurance and deal with the distributional issues associated with the many social policy needs that arise over time.

EFFICIENCY THROUGH TRANSPARENCY

The transparent account construction of UPPS-DC design opens the door for fulfilling another criterion—economic efficiency. The individual account design of DC schemes makes clear to everyone that they are pension savers. On the margin, this can be important to individual decisions regarding the tradeoff between formal work and the many alternatives. In principle the contribution should not be or be perceived as a tax. Instead, it should be perceived as an act of abstaining from consumption today (saving) in the working phase of the life cycle in exchange for a claim on future consumption (GDP) when retired.

In the UPPS-DC design this feature constitutes a positive incentive to choose work over time spent in other activities. This feature of UPPS-DC is efficient because it has either no effect or one that provides incentives to individuals to work more than they otherwise would have. In both less developed and developed market economies this may occur through choosing formal, market-based work rather than informal work. It may also entail choosing formal, market-remunerated work as opposed to work in the home. In both cases, the message focuses on the advantages of the yearly pension payment of postponed retirement rather than an earlier age of retirement.

Given timely and transparent information provided by the administration of the UPPS, individuals can easily see the advantage of remaining economically active longer. In a UPPS-DC design, increasing life expectancy means a smaller yearly pension (replacement rate) for the same number of years worked by previous birth cohorts—which provides an incentive to work marginally longer. This supports efficiency and by doing so works dynamically toward financial sustainability and affordability. All else equal, the UPPS-DB design implies some combination of "borrowing" from younger cohorts, increasing the DB pension age (ad hoc), increasing contribution rates or transfers from the government budget, or some combination of all of these.

Together with the one-to-one provision, the marginal effect of the narrative that life expectancy is an important determinant of the individual outcome is necessary to create both micro- and macroeconomic efficiency. Two elements are necessary: (a) the message transmitted through accounts, and (b) access to information about the individual outcomes of choosing work over informal activities and postponing exit from the labor force. In postponing exit, the design and the message it conveys can impact "everyday" economic decisions to allocate time between work and leisure. This property is supported by the knowledge that the contribution is personal savings for future consumption in old age, a belief that is easily conveyed by the annual development of the individual account. Because the aggregate effect is expected to be an overall positive incentive on labor supply at the margin, the result is an aggregate increase in the labor force and consequently GDP (that is, macroeconomic efficiency).

INTRA- AND INTERGENERATIONAL FAIRNESS

With the UPPS-NDC design all individuals in all living cohorts have universal life-cycle longevity insurance based on the same rules. The design itself embodies fairness both within a birth cohort and between cohorts over time because the same rules apply to all at any given time. More formally, expressions (8.1) and (8.2) apply to all cohorts over time in the context of NDC.

This is not the case for all UPPS-NDB designs. This is clear already from the information and examples in box 8.1. As opposed to this, the built-in redistribution of contributions between participants within the DB framework breaks with both the principle of

---

BOX 8.1 Definition of DC and DB schemes and their distinguishing features

The defined contribution (DC) design builds on a foundation of individual accounts, the accumulation of savings (through contributions) on these accounts, and the creation of a life annuity at retirement based on the individual's account balance and life expectancy at retirement.

No unique definition exists of what a defined benefit (DB) scheme is, other than its design does not fulfill the generic definition of a DC scheme. Examples of DB schemes are (a) the number of years of service and, for example, final salary; (b) the individual's salary during the best X of Y years; (c) a formula containing an "accrual" rate; or (d) a so-called point system based on the ratio of the individual wage to the countrywide average and a model for valuation of the points determined this way.

fairness and with the framework of the UPPS as universal life-cycle longevity insurance. Moreover, the UPPS-NDB internal tax-transfer mechanism is likely to be economically inefficient compared with a pure longevity insurance scheme (that is, NDC) augmented with an explicit tax-transfer minimum benefit and other explicit policy.

UPPS-NDB schemes are sometimes used to provide transfers—special rights—to specified occupational groups, financed by the revenues of the general collective of contributors, which runs counter to the universal insurance principle. The special privileges often have to do with early retirement with "a full benefit" or a higher benefit for the specified group—but unaccompanied by additional contributions from or on behalf of recipients. To the extent that the special rule regimes promote early retirement from the labor force, they are neither efficient nor fair.

Both nonfinancial and financial UPPS-DBs may seriously break the links between what people pay and what they can expect to receive. These breaks can occur because the links derived from expressions (8.1) and (8.2)—that is, the formal account link, or the liability of the provider—are soft links in the DB framework. In UPPS-FDB schemes this means money can be moved between cohorts when the provider misjudges the economic, demographic, and financial risks. Specifically, contributions of younger participants may be "borrowed" to cover benefit payments to contemporary pensioners, which, first, breaks the link between individuals' own contributions (savings) and future benefits. In addition, however, it is not always the case that development of the exogenous financial and economic environment enables repayment—which leads to a need to adjust liabilities downward by revising the conditions of the "defined" benefit actually paid.

A second deficiency of UPPS-DB designs (although there may be a life-expectancy factor in the DB formula) is that its function is usually not transparent. When this is the case, it is inefficient. In contrast, in the UPPS-DC design the life-expectancy projection is revised yearly and the consequences for retiring at alternative pension ages are made readily available by the provider. The high degree of transparency means that this information is more likely to be in the thoughts of the participant both as "the" retirement age approaches and thereafter promoting the rewards of postponed retirement compared with the "norm" at a lower age.

In closing, it is important to note that the UPPS-FDC design differs from the UPPS-NDC design with respect to the rate of return. In NDC schemes, one homogeneous rate of return is shared by all, but in the context of a UPPS-FDC institutional design, this is not necessarily the case. However, if there is more than one fund and well-advertised information on fund outcomes, competing investors are likely to achieve results that regress toward the mean—and this result may closely follow a world market portfolio rate of return. This suggests an underlying market-shared evaluation of the risks and yields of large financial portfolios. This picture means a world market rate for FDC funds, with small, random deviations around an age-adjusted mean, assuming all funds are characterized by life-cycle portfolio glide paths.

This final discussion suggests that although both UPPS-NDC and FDC schemes rest upon the same base (individual outcomes depend on labor force participation during the savings phase and life expectancy at retirement), NDC does not share the institutional risk associated with how policy makers determine (a) how individual participants are to be allocated to different participating funds in the UPPS-FDC participant fund managers, and (b) how annuity provision is accomplished in the UPPS-FDC context.

The bottom line is that UPPS-NDC schemes are generically fair, both in an intra- and intergenerational perspective, because they offer the same investment portfolio to all—the return is a single homogeneous valorization factor. In contrast, the risk of unequal portfolio investment outcomes for individuals in the same cohort and country may lead to a broad distribution around the average outcome with respect to FDC investment results, reducing intragenerational fairness. This risk is of course manageable by focusing on the institutional design of the UPPS-FDC scheme.

In summary, UPPS-NDC is intra- and intergenerationally fair—and the three other alternatives may come close one way or another (supplementary design or continuous ad hoc adjustments). Even a UPPS-FDC design does not necessarily deliver a fair outcome between individuals in the same generation (cohort), because the institutional setup may be flawed. This can occur when the institutional design focus is on enabling free choice, which has generally proven not to be a good design property, given that most participants are not financially literate and are not interested in becoming so. Research has shown that this group should be steered into a well-managed default portfolio or fund characterized by a mix of worldwide assets consciously chosen and combined through high-quality assessment of yields and risks. Many examples from around 2000 arise whereby faulty implementation of UPPS-FDC designs led to poor yields for suboptimally defaulted nonchoosers, inadvertently segmenting the UPPS pool of savers. The result of subop-timal institutional design has also been characterized by results well below the world-market index and with management costs that are much higher than in countries with efficient institutional designs.[6]

FINANCIAL SUSTAINABILITY, AFFORDABILITY, AND ADEQUACY
Financial sustainability

In macroeconomic terms the UPPS's total pension expenditures can be expressed as the product of the average pension $\bar{P}_t$ times the number of retirees R_t at time t. Likewise, the contribution wage base—the earnings that underlie the payment of individual contributions—is the product of the average wage $\bar{w}$ of all contributors L_t in the same period t multiplied by the number of contributors. The ratio of these two is the contribution rate needed to finance pensions at time t with the wage base generated in that period. In discrete time the ratio of pension expenditures to the wage base is

$$C_t = \frac{\bar{P}_{t-1}\left(1+g\right)_t\left(1+\lambda\right)_t\left(1+p\right)_t R(LE)_t}{\bar{w}_{t-1}\left(1+g\right)_t\left(1+\lambda\right)_t\left(1+p\right)_t L_t}. \tag{8.3}$$

This ratio communicates several messages. First, the ratio $\bar{P}_t/\bar{w}_t$ is the aggregate replacement rate. Second, R_t/L_t is the old-age dependency ratio. Third, under the assumption that the policy maker has chosen a contribution rate C based at the outset on a desired ratio of expenditures to revenues, C^*, C_t will oscillate around C^*. Moreover, C_t has a relationship to GDP that is fixed if the wage sum on which con-tributions are paid is a relatively fixed percentage of GDP (C^*_{GDP}). The economic dependency ratio is the critical component of expression (8.3). With increasing longevity at older ages, with a "fixed" pension age—including the DB concept[7] of a full-benefit or pension age—the message of "aging population" means two things. First, life expectancy is increasing at all ages in the age group 60 and older (including into the nineties). Second, countries need to adopt an effective policy to maintain a constant or growing labor force. The choice of UPPS design can contribute positively in this context, but only marginally. It is important to note that life expectancy is also increasing at ages younger than 60, and in most countries this is still an important positive factor determining the supply of labor.

Generally speaking, three strategies can accommodate aging populations while at the same time maintaining a targeted macro replacement rate: (a) increase the working-age population through family policy that supports a total fertility rate of about two children per woman in the population, (b) augment the working-age population through active (net) immigration policy, and (c) make life expectancy an explicit component of the UPPS pension formula, with the aim of providing a transparent incentive for healthy older workers to remain in the workforce to increasingly higher ages—together with indexing the minimum age at which a benefit can be claimed. A fourth mechanism to keep in mind that has implications for adequacy, affordability, and financial sustainability is the important role of transparent and efficient design, enabled by transparent individual accounts.

An important point regarding financial sustainability is that the indexation of benefits in the numerator of expression (8.3) is a process that begins with the accumulation of individual rights and continues through the life course of an individual. The overall index is the rate of return α in expression (8.1) and expression (8.4) below; and the rate of return β in expression (8.2). The component λ (see the discussion in conjunction with the presentation of expressions (8.1) and (8.2)) adjusts current and future benefits to both an increasing and a decreasing labor force—originating in an increasing or decreasing population or participation rate of a given population. As discussed above, a positive increase (positive value of λ—for example, in the form of a demographic dividend) can and in most cases should be funded, while it is important for a negative value to be included as a component of the indexation—working through α in expression (8.1) and β in expression (8.2). The latter stabilizes the UPPS in the face of demographically generated instability in the financial outcome of the UPPS.

In countries where the total fertility rate is chronically below two children per woman and net immigration is not sufficient to counter this low rate, the contribution base in expression (8.3) will experience a chronic decline in the labor force. The country may experience decades with a negative value of λ. In this case, it is necessary to valorize acquired rights or pension accounts and pensions in payment with an indexation formula including λ or to implement a solvency-ratio approach with continuous deflation of acquired rights and pensions in payment. Note that Sweden uses the latter approach to fund the demographic dividend arising from the combination of a fertility rate of close to 2.0 and policy leading to net immigration. If and when the labor force begins to recover, the outcome will yield a demographic dividend that can either be put into a reserve fund or distributed. The third option—ad hoc adjustments—is easily understood to be the worst approach, because the absence of transparency and built-in incentives is an inefficient way to deal with the situation, as already argued. Nevertheless, this is the approach

TABLE 8.2 **Distinguishing characteristics of UPPSs**

	Maintenance of affordability, financial stability, and sustainability in response to demographic and economic dynamics	
Determinants of the rate of return	Requires ad hoc interventions to modify the benefit promises, including implicitly reducing the commitment to younger generations to avoid breaking commitments to current pensioners	Automatic adjustment through the rate of return on accounts and benefits and life expectancy in the annuity calculation
Financial investments	FDB	FDC
Nonfinancial human capital investments and labor supply	NDB	NDC

SOURCE: Based on Góra and Palmer 2004.

NOTE: FDB = financial defined benefit; FDC = financial defined contribution; NDB = nonfinancial defined benefit; NDC = nonfinancial defined contribution; UPPS = universal public pension scheme.

most often used in the context of UPPS-DC designs. The dimensions of this discussion are summarized in table 7.2.

It is important to note the advantage of the UPPS-FDC design in this context, compared with the other three UPPS designs: it is constructed as an individual life-cycle insurance scheme that depends solely on the economic choices of individuals, other than mandated participation in the UPPS. As discussed under the topic of rates of return, this advantage of the UPPS-FDC design should nevertheless be weighed against the specific caveats regarding institutional design and the need for supervision.

Adequacy and affordability

In a UPPS-DC, at the micro level the replacement rate for the average contributor is determined by the average number of years worked up to retirement—in expression (8.1) this is years of work underlying the account balance at retirement, and the average life expectancy at retirement, that is, expression (8.2) (Palmer 2013). On an individual basis it is individual i's earnings history:

$$K_{i,\tau} = \sum_{i,t=1}^{t=\tau} \bar{w}_t \, L_{i,t} \, \prod_{t+1}^{\tau}(1+\alpha_t) \tag{8.4}$$

that matters in the context of expressions (8.1) and (8.2). To simplify the presentation, assume that the individual is an average wage earner. Yearly earnings are then determined by time worked, $\sum L_{i,t}$, which is simplified to the number of years worked, realizing that years may be part- or full-time in practice.

Regarding adequacy, it is obviously the individual's choice between work in the formal labor force versus informal, nonmarket-remunerated work and leisure time that determines the magnitude of the savings in expression (8.1) at retirement. Together with the average life expectancy of the individual's birth cohort at the chosen age of retirement, these determine the magnitude of the generic UPPS life-cycle insurance (that is, expressions (8.1) and (8.2)).

In summary, adequacy is intertwined with affordability—and both are dependent on financial sustainability as implicit in expression (8.3) and the discussion around it. The purpose of connecting the individual's results to an individual wage-based contribution is to support economic efficiency, the central line of argument up to this point. This is done most efficiently through use of a defined contribution rate and individual accounts, that is, UPPS-FDC and UPPS-NDC designs. The important challenge is to set the appropriate contribution rate from the outset—and in the DB context, defining an affordable benefit rule that yields an adequate benefit.

NDC as the Generic UPPS

This section summarizes the discussion in the preceding sections regarding four UPPS designs. It concludes with a discussion supporting the claim that UPPS-NDC is the generic UPPS.

ACCOUNTS, TRANSPARENCY, AND EFFICIENCY

All else equal, individual labor supply decisions ultimately determine the scale and distribution of outcomes of all UPPS designs of national, universal life-cycle longevity insurance schemes. This is what tips the scales in favor of UPPS-DC. UPPS-DC individual accounts provide a transparent framework for encouraging individual labor supply decisions at the margin between formal labor supply as opposed to informal work and leisure. The argument is as follows: accounts engender transparency, which together with the defined contribution—which is and is perceived as a contribution and unit saving but not a tax—transforms a unit of consumption today when young into a unit of consumption tomorrow when old.

SUMMARY OF THE ARGUMENTS FAVORING UPPS-DC OVER UPPS-DB

The transparent accounts of UPPS-DC support communication of the message that a full working life with contributions provides fair universal insurance against the risk of living much longer than the average person. Policy makers set the UPPS-DC parameters to provide an affordable and financially sustainable framework for a full working-life career. The message of an efficient UPPS is to communicate that it is individuals' years of work and contributions that determine the scale of the payout at the end of their working careers. A UPPS-DC is economically efficient because it provides incentives for this desired behavior, at the margin tipping the scale in favor of a longer working life and an "increasingly more adequate" pension, which also provides a benefit by encouraging marginal decisions that increase the nation's overall supply of labor.

In the UPPS-NDC design, with the DC foundation of transparent accounts and the accompanying contribution to efficiency, NDC works dynamically to "manage" demographic and economic risks through automatic stabilizers. NDC is thus financially stable and as a result an adequate pension—a function of one's own efforts—is by definition affordable under the same framework within and across cohorts. A UPPS-NDC is thus the benchmark for UPPS-NDB designs. Likewise, a UPPS-FDC, with its straightforward coupling of individuals' account values with the retirement annuity, is the benchmark for UPPS-FDB designs. It is worth emphasizing that the only way to increase the UPPS average replacement rate is through a reduction in the remuneration of economic activity of the working generation (today or tomorrow).

UPPS-FDC schemes enjoy the advantage of being financially sustainable by definition. Nevertheless, they are subject to considerable volatility and uncertainty regarding the future of the economy and financial markets. In a UPPS-NDC, financial sustainability is achieved through automatic stabilizers—that is, wage-sum indexation that adjusts for a declining working-age population and use of life expectancy, the latter being an advantage shared with a UPPS-FDC. A UPPS-NDC maintains a stable ratio of pension expenditures to GDP by automatically dealing with the macroeconomic demographic risks arising from low fertility rates and the subsequent decline in working-age population. The construction of the benefit—as an annuity based on the individual's balance in the NDC account and life expectancy at retirement—not only encourages postponed retirement, it also "balances" the effect on pensions of increasing life expectancy.

What characterizes UPPS-DB designs is that they encompass many sources of non-transparent redistribution between participants—whereas UPPS-DC designs provide a one-to-one link between forgone consumption (savings) today when working and consumption tomorrow in retirement. UPPS-DB designs either intentionally break with or have a higher risk of breaking with the criterion of intragenerational fairness; that is, some get less than and others more than what they pay for. It is particularly unfair and inefficient when a built-in redistribution works in favor of those working fewer years at the expense of those with longer working careers.[8] To the extent that such arrangements put financial stress on the pension scheme, this increases the risk of needing to use resources of the younger generation at the expense of intergenerational fairness. The automatic stabilizers of UPPS-NDC and the design of UPPS-FDC minimize the risk to intergenerational fairness by definition.

This chapter's assessment of the four UPPS designs—and how they fulfill the criteria of transparency, efficiency (encouraging desired behavior), intra- and intergenerational fairness, affordability, financial sustainability, and adequacy—concludes that a UPPS-DC performs better than a UPPS-DB on all counts. Proponents of the UPPS-DB design often argue that its virtue is that policy makers can craft different distributional rules, sometimes well-motivated but often not. In both cases they aim at goals here and today that adversely affect UPPSs' long-term generic goals. The UPPS framework and criteria presented here explicitly support the principle that all social distributional policy should be institutionalized separately from the UPPS in the context of the goals of a nation's tax-transfer policy, including the minimum income or pension guarantee for the elderly.

Summing up the general economic picture, a UPPS's overriding characteristic is that it covers, regardless of design, everyone in a country with the same set of rules.

The UPPS has two fundamental economic goals: (a) microeconomic—it provides an institutional mechanism meeting the need for individuals to transfer income over the life cycle from years of work to years of retirement, referred to as consumption smoothing; and (b) macroeconomic—in the perspective of a closed economy, it provides an institutional mechanism that in every period allocates current GDP between remuneration of production factors (labor and capital) and the financing of pensions. In the context of an open economy, the latter statement is modified to the extent that international assets share in pension portfolios.

To a significant extent the macroeconomic process surrounding pensions reflects the dynamics of the demographics of a country. Not yet addressed is how long-term demographics can be more precisely managed through funding in the context of the UPPS, the topic of the next section, which motivates the claim that a UPPS-NDC is the generic form of a UPPS.

UPPS-NDC AS THE GENERIC FORM OF A UPPS

This section asks the question, What is the best strategy for introducing a UPPS in a young, emerging market economy with a large informal labor force? The answer is NDC because as an account-based UPPS it can combine NDC with FDC, which is especially useful in the context of an emerging market economy, but also for using financial markets in conjunction with cyclically repeating booms of birth cohorts.

Begin with the case of an emerging market economy—which covers a majority of the world's population. Implementation of UPPS-FDC (or UPPS-FDB) takes 40 or more years. The full process of covering the entire working-age population as workers become formal members of the labor market and start paying pension contributions takes even more time. On the other hand, the contributions of the first generation of savers do not need to be converted into pensions fully until 15 or more years after retirement on average.

In the initial decades, a dual process will operate: in about 20 years the fertility rate will decline to about 2.1, while the economy will continue to formalize. Together, these two dynamics constitute the so-called double demographic dividend. The superiority of NDC in this context is that individual accounts allow the system to (a) keep track of the liabilities to contributors, and (b) provide a rate of return (Góra 2013). The liabilities can be used in part to finance minimum pensions to the current elderly. These can be transferred to an NDC fund that purchases NDC bonds. The NDC bonds are issued by the government for infrastructure, but also to finance private entrepreneurial capital investments. The bonds can, for example, be perpetuities, amortized in the future when needed to cover an increasing number of pensioners (Larsson, Layero, and Palmer 2019).

Another example is a reserve fund in a country that has a large baby-boom "generation," where their offspring and their offspring's children create repeated booms at intervals going forward in time (with an otherwise fairly constant fertility rate of about 2.1 children per woman). In this case the cyclical dividends are funded in the NDC reserve fund and drawn upon to finance the large generation when they become pensioners. Sweden is an example of a country that has done this (Palmer and Könberg 2019).

LOOKING BACK AT THE HISTORICAL DEVELOPMENT OF UPPSs SINCE WORLD WAR II

Note in closing that the pay-as-you-go ("public") versus funding ("private") nomenclature used in the pension world since World War II is based on a two-way distinction that fails to recognize that a public scheme can be either a nonfinancial or a financial DC. More generally, that nomenclature completely misses (a) the fundamental role of a UPPS in providing life-cycle longevity insurance, characterized by the criteria discussed herein; and (b) the distinction between UPPSs and the private schemes that emerge to provide

FIGURE 8.1 **The evolution of thinking on public pension schemes**

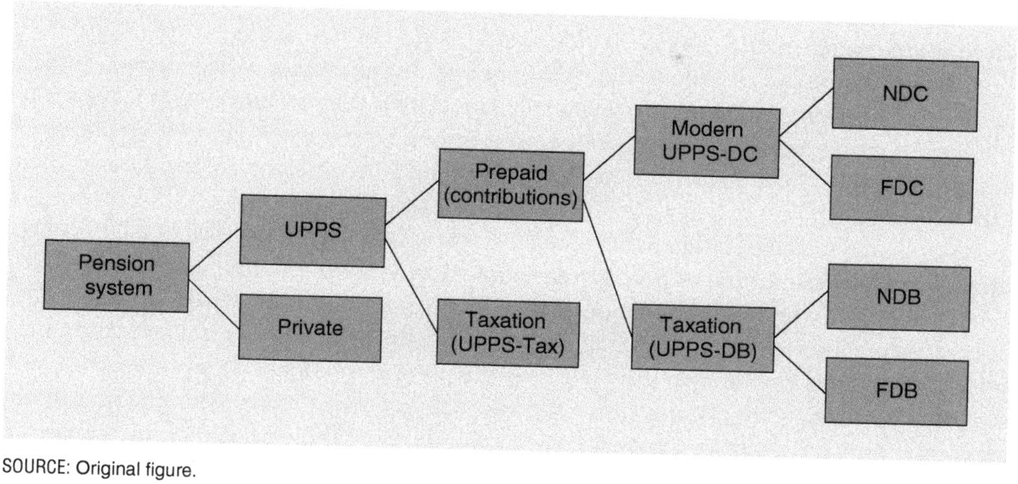

SOURCE: Original figure.

NOTE: FDB = financial defined benefit; FDC = financial defined contribution; NDB = nonfinancial defined benefit; NDC = nonfinancial defined contribution; UPPS = universal public pension scheme; UPPS-DB = universal public pension scheme–defined benefit; UPPS-DC = universal public pension scheme–defined contribution.

insurance for subgroups of the working population. Figure 8.1 illustrates the evolution of thinking on pension schemes as presented in this chapter.

This evolutionary path enabled fulfillment of the individual life-cycle model of consumption and saving in the context of providing universal longevity insurance to the population of a country. Progress has meant pursuing the properties of financial sustainability and affordability, economic efficiency, and intra- and intergenerational fairness—all properties believed by many, and hopefully most, to constitute a package of desirable properties of a UPPS—that together make and protect adequate universal public pensions over a continuum of cohorts and for the whole of a society.

Conclusions

A UPPS is a government-mandated life-cycle savings scheme that provides insurance covering the longevity risk in old age. It covers the entire population of a country with the same rules for all. In the long term, the UPPS is an institutional structure whereby a claim on current GDP "pays" or is "traded" for a claim on future GDP. From the individual point of view, this trade of individual claims on GDP in time is the microeconomic essence of the act of saving. In the macro perspective, these savings can be invested through the financial market or transferred to other individuals for the purpose of consumption.

One of the stimuli for writing this chapter was to replace the postwar dichotomy of pay-as-you-go (which implies "public") versus funding (which implies "private") with the double dichotomy of financial versus nonfinancial and DB versus DC. Why this goal? The answer is that the "old-school" nomenclature misses two fundamental points. First, a UPPS is publicly mandated universal life-cycle longevity insurance. Second, in today's world the double dichotomy can be easily defined with the four designs discussed in this chapter. The word "private" does not play any role in this context. The four relevant schemes are all publicly mandated and differ from each other through their designs. However, they may have functions that can be contracted out to privately managed companies, such as portfolio management.

In the context of the economic framework of this chapter, a UPPS design is "fully funded" if the design is inherently financially sustainable over generations. It is robust to changes in the exogenous demographic and economic parameters, and by virtue of its design "manages" these risks. This explains why UPPS-DC designs are superior to their DB counterparts. This is a key conclusion of this chapter, for even if UPPS-DB designs can provide the same level of benefits under a single set of exogenous risks, in a UPPS-DC (geared to a reasonable ratio of average years in work to years in retirement), the time-independent design "manages" the demographic and economic risks by balancing long-term assets and liabilities, thereby providing intertemporal financial equilibrium and autonomy from the government budget. And UPPS-DCs' long-term financial sustainability and economic efficiency are preconditions for affordability—and reduce the uncertainty of outcomes—not the least in comparison with the unaffordability and the uncertainty of outcomes of a UPPS-DB.

Although the raison d'être of the UPPS is to provide longevity insurance for all through individual contributions, the belief promoted here is that targeted prevention of poverty in old age is most efficiently dealt with through tax-transfer policy, rather than as a component clouding the basic function of the UPPS. Keeping policy outside frees policy makers to cope with the challenges of anti-poverty instruments where the needs can change with the times. In this spirit, countries that adopt UPPS-DC designs need to think through the construction of exogenous, tax-financed social safety nets or lowest means-tested, pension-level guarantees, and introduce policy-motivated, tax-financed account add-ins.

Both FDC and NDC schemes perform the basic function of a life-cycle longevity insurance scheme, transferring consumption from the working phase of the life cycle to the retirement phase, with a rate of return based on the growth of the economy. Both are transparent, economically efficient, fair, and financially sustainable by virtue of their design. The UPPS-NDC is nevertheless arguably the generic UPPS, since it focuses solely on the intertemporal transfer of consumption.

However, compared with a UPPS-NDC, a UPPS-FDC provides the opportunity to harness positive effects through high yields for individuals (if assets are successfully invested abroad), but an FDC also involves higher costs of administration, supervision, and a design that minimizes the risk of fraud.

Notes

1. Nonfinancial DC is presented in Palmer (2006, 2013); Palmer (2013) presents an alternative view regarding how the definition of the NDC "contribution asset" should be treated in the context of the conceptual rate of return. The term "nonfinancial defined contribution" as well as the NDC, FDC, NDB, FDB typology were introduced in Góra and Palmer (2004). The "nuts and bolts" of NDCs are presented in Holzmann (2019). For a broad perspective of issues and implementation strategies, readers are referred to the more than 80 individual studies on pensions contained in three anthologies: Holzmann and Palmer (2006); Holzmann, Palmer, and Robalino (2013); and this volume (Holzmann, Palmer, Palacios, and Sacchi 2019), which cover the development of NDCs and issues in creating and implementing NDCs.

2. This is the formulation of the individual life-cycle model underlying the discussion of the dynamic intergenerational model in Palmer (2013).

3. However, the immediate generosity of postwar DB schemes was clearly well-motivated by the necessity to provide adequate benefits to persons whose own prospects were severely restricted by two world wars separated by an extensive period of worldwide economic depression.

4. It is worth noting that in the mature UPPS, NDC with a buffer fund and FDC converge to a similar economic structure.

5. Prolonging large-scale informality is a challenge not only for pension systems. This important issue goes beyond the scope of this chapter.

6. Note that good examples of world-market index funds can cost 10–20 basis points, whereas many existing national UPPS-FDC funds cost 50–150 basis points, according to Organisation for Economic Co-operation and Development pension statistics.

7. Or more correctly rhetoric, since in reality it is systematically adjusted on an ad hoc basis.

8. For special cases, if a society decides that it is just, additional regulations outside the UPPS are more efficient than intra-UPPS solutions. A good example is the case of "bridging pensions" implemented in Poland in 2009.

References

Góra, Marek. 2013. "Political Economy of Pension Reforms: Selected General Issues and the Polish Pension Reform Case." *IZA Journal of Labour and Development* 2: 2.

Góra, Marek, and Edward Palmer. 2004. "Shifting Perspectives in Pensions." Institute for Labor Economics, IZA Discussion Paper 1369. IZA, Bonn, Germany.

Holzmann, Robert. 2019. "The ABCs of NDCs." In *Progress and Challenges of Nonfinancial Defined Contribution Pension Schemes: Volume 1 Addressing Marginalization, Polarization, and the Labor Market*, edited by Robert Holzmann, Edward Palmer, Robert Palacios, and Stefano Sacchi, Chapter 9. Washington, DC: World Bank.

Holzmann, Robert, and Edward Palmer. 2006. "The Status of the NDC Discussion: Introduction and Overview." In *Pension Reform—Issues and Prospects for Non-Financial Defined Contribution (NDC) Schemes*, edited by Robert Holzmann and Edward Palmer, 1–16. Washington, DC: World Bank.

Holzmann, Robert, Edward Palmer, and David Robalino, eds. 2013. *NDC Pension Schemes: Progress and Frontiers in a Changing Pension World: Volume 2 Gender, Politics and Financial Stability.* Washington, DC: World Bank.

Larsson, Bo, Vincent Leyaro, and Edward Palmer. 2019. "Harnessing a Young Nation's Demographic Dividends through a Universal NDC Pension Scheme: A Case Study on Tanzania." In *Progress and Challenges of Nonfinancial Defined Contribution Pension Schemes: Volume 2 Addressing Gender, Administration, and Communication*, edited by Robert Holzmann, Edward Palmer, Robert Palacios, and Stefano Sacchi, Chapter 23. Washington, DC: World Bank.

Palmer, Edward. 1999. "Exit from the Labor Force of Older Workers: Can the NDC Pension System Help?" *Geneva Papers on Risk and Insurance* 24 (October): 461–72.

———. 2002. "Is Swedish Pension Reform the Right Medicine for Aging Europe?" *Journal of Aging and Social Policy* 14 (1): 35–52.

———. 2005. "The Way Forward for European Pension Schemes." *Review of European Economic Policy* 40 (5): 268–73.

———. 2006. "What Is NDC." In *Pension Reform—Issues and Prospects for Non-Financial Defined Contribution (NDC) Schemes*, edited by Robert Holzmann and Edward Palmer, 17–34. Washington, DC: World Bank.

————. 2013. "Generic NDC: Equilibrium, Valuation and Risk Sharing—With and Without NDC Bonds." In *NDC Pension Schemes: Progress and Frontiers in a Changing Pension World: Volume 2 Gender, Politics and Financial Stability*, edited by Robert Holzmann, Edward Palmer, and David Robalino, 309–33. Washington, DC: World Bank.

Palmer, Edward, and Bo Könberg. 2019. "The Swedish NDC Scheme: Success on Track with Room for Reflection." In *Progress and Challenges of Nonfinancial Defined Contribution Pension Schemes: Volume 1 Addressing Marginalization, Polarization, and the Labor Market*, edited by Robert Holzmann, Edward Palmer, Robert Palacios, and Stefano Sacchi, Chapter 2. Washington, DC: World Bank.

Palmer, Edward, and Yuwei Zhao de Gosson de Varennes. 2019. "Annuities in (N)DC Pension Schemes: Design, Heterogeneity, and Estimation Issues." In *Progress and Challenges of Nonfinancial Defined Contribution Pension Schemes: Volume 1 Addressing Marginalization, Polarization, and the Labor Market*, edited by Robert Holzmann, Edward Palmer, Robert Palacios, and Stefano Sacchi, Chapter 13. Washington, DC: World Bank.

CHAPTER 9

The ABCs of NDCs

Robert Holzmann

Introduction: How NDC Emerged in the Pension Reform Process

The need for public pension reform is not a new issue. It emerged in Organisation for Economic Co-operation and Development (OECD) countries after the heyday of pension schemes' introduction in the 1950s and their expansion in the 1960s; the post–World War II economic boom was halted by the first oil-price shock in the 1970s and the change in the demographic foundation of pension schemes became visible then. The 1980s were characterized by the search for internal solutions to address pension schemes' perceived short-term financing gaps and longer-term demographic challenges, given the transition to lower fertility levels and increasing life expectancy. Then, the "reform" discourse was limited to interventions around adjustments to scheme parameters, such as reductions of the accrual rate, extension of the contribution-wage assessment period from the past few years to a longer period, changes in benefit indexation from wages toward prices, and increases in the contribution rate or budgetary transfers (Holzmann 1988). Little discussion at that time considered a continued increase in life expectancy and below-replacement fertility rates (and hence population aging without an end in sight). The focus was largely on the search for fixes to a one-time problem within the then almost universal nonfinancial (unfunded) defined benefit (NDB) scheme. Funded supplementary schemes emerged in a few, mostly Anglo-Saxon countries as voluntary occupational and personal schemes. Parametric adjustments to NDB schemes were typically implemented in a string of minor reforms that reduced the funding gap and economic distortions somewhat but did not lead to sustainability, that is, a state that does not require major future changes to keep the scheme financially afloat.

The vision of a more systemic reform approach was triggered internationally in 1981 by Chile. Chile's systemic reform of its universal pension system was the first worldwide to move from a traditional NDB scheme to a fully funded (financial) defined contribution (FDC) scheme. It introduced two major changes concurrently.

First, the reform moved from a DB scheme in which the benefit is well defined and the financing (contribution rate) is, in principle, the residual, to a defined contribution (DC) scheme in which the contribution rate is well-defined (fixed) and the benefit level depends on contributions paid, returns received, and life expectancy at retirement. The tight relationship between contributions and benefits was expected to offer much better incentives for labor supply decisions, including for formal labor market participation and

The author is grateful to Mercedes Ayuso-Gutierrez, Nick Barr, María del Carmen Boado-Penas, Elisa Chulia, Mark Dorfman, Elsa Fornero, José Antonio Herce, Sergio Nisticò, Edward Palmer, and John Piggott for comments and suggestions.

retirement age selection. Such improved labor participation incentives depend not only on the design of public pension schemes but also on occupational and voluntary pension schemes and on noncontributory social assistance. These needed to be appropriately designed or redesigned to support the expected lower labor market distortions (Holzmann, Robalino, and Winkler 2019).

Second, the Chilean reform moved from an unfunded scheme in which current revenues were used to finance current pension benefits to a fully funded scheme in which benefit obligations were to be fully backed by marketable financial assets. Because such a transition makes the implicit debt of an unfunded scheme explicit, realizing the expected results requires repayment of this implicit-turned-explicit debt by the current and future generations. The economic double burden of a repayment for current and future generations may potentially be prevented if such a pension reform creates reform externalities, including endogenous economic growth effects that go beyond those of higher saving and labor supply and may compensate for the additional taxes and lower public expenditure (Holzmann 1999). Empirical work suggests that such growth effects were created in Chile (Holzmann 1997).

This systemic reform and the move from NDB to FDC schemes created a reform dynamic that swept in the 1990s from Latin America over to the former transition economies in Central, Eastern, and Southern Europe and beyond. This move was substantially influenced by a seminal publication of the World Bank (1994). By 2011, 29 countries across the world had at least partially moved from NDB to FDC schemes in expectation that their financial and other pension problems (such as low contribution density and benefit coverage) would be solved (Holzmann 2013). As it turned out, many systemic reform countries underestimated the challenges of such a reform—at the level of creating an enabling financial market environment, at the level of expected financial market returns, and perhaps most importantly, at the level of financing the transition through a long-term tighter public budget with only temporarily higher explicit financial debt. As a result, a number of countries reversed their funding reform and abolished (for example, Argentina, Hungary) or substantially reduced (for example, Poland, Latvia) their funded pillar. Of course, the fallout of the 2008 financial crisis did not help.

Given the attraction of a DC approach but the challenges of funding change, two countries in Europe (Italy, Sweden) independently developed a systemic reform concept that moved from DB to DC but remained essentially unfunded: the nonfinancial (or notional) defined contribution (NDC) scheme. The vision of NDC began with Swedish legislation in 1994 that charted the map for a full-scale transition from the country's underfinanced NDB scheme to NDC, as discussed in Palmer (1999, 2000, 2002) and Könberg, Palmer, and Sundén (2006). Given that the Italian NDC reform of 1994 was implemented with long transition periods and was essentially only finished in 2012, the concept of NDC moved from Sweden to implementation in Latvia (Fox and Palmer 1999; Palmer et al. 2006) and Poland (Chłoń-Domińczak and Góra 2006), and later to Norway (Christensen et al. 2012). A few other countries attempted to introduce NDC schemes but failed in their efforts for a variety of reasons (the Arab Republic of Egypt, Mongolia, the Kyrgyz Republic, the Russian Federation) (Guardiancich et al. 2019). Other countries are still discussing an NDC reform (China, Greece, Kazakhstan).

For a long time it was thought that an unfunded DC scheme could not work, conceptually or operationally. But implementation in Sweden, Italy, Latvia, Norway, and

Poland since the mid-1990s—and successful operations ever since—have proved to the contrary. Thus, a systemic reform option emerged that promises financial sustainability under an unfunded scheme and a fixed contribution rate with incentives to address population aging through a self-determined increase in the retirement age in line with rising life expectancy. All NDB schemes have to do likewise to remain financially afloat, but an NDC scheme claims to offer better incentives and higher transparency. The emphasis on the labor market as a solution to population aging in the NDC approach is only on the surface a difference from FDC schemes. Fully funded schemes also need to build on this labor market mechanism to remain financially sustainable (unless they invest most of their assets internationally).

This chapter introduces the basics and key intricacies of NDC schemes. The target audience is not NDC experts but individuals knowledgeable about pensions who want to understand the key mechanisms and challenges of NDC schemes. Drawing heavily on Holzmann (2017b), the chapter uses simple technical language to convey the main concepts, issues, and possible solutions. Many of the intricacies around the NDC approach are addressed in two previous anthologies on the topic (Holzmann and Palmer 2006; Holzmann, Palmer, and Robalino 2012, 2013) and in this NDC III publication.

"The Basics of an NDC Scheme" sketches the basic features of NDC schemes that make them attractive and explains how they work. "What Can NDC Schemes Do Better than NDB Schemes?" compares the workings of the NDC approach to typical (traditional and reformed) NDB schemes. "Key Frontiers in Design and Implementation of NDC Schemes" outlines where more technical work is needed. "Country Experiences with NDC Reforms" briefly reviews international experience with NDC schemes or reform attempts in this direction while "Conclusions and Way Forward" concludes.

The Basics of an NDC Scheme

The basic conceptual structure of any NDC scheme is the consistent link between the individual level of its design, which promises a direct contribution-benefit link,[1] and the macroeconomic level, which promises financial sustainability while remaining essentially unfunded. Simply put, an NDC scheme is an individual savings account scheme in which individuals receive a common rate of return consistent with the financial sustainability of the scheme; at retirement they receive a benefit consistent with the remaining cohort life expectancy and anticipated interest and wage growth rates during their expected life.

At the individual level, an NDC scheme promises income smoothing and intragenerational equity because it creates a strong contribution-benefit link through the following characteristics:

- Individual accounts exist into which contributions of each individual (and those of his or her employer) are recorded based on a fixed contribution rate and the individual contribution wage.
- The individual account receives an annual rate of return established in the design.
- The initial benefit is based on an annuity calculation that itself is based on the account accumulation and life expectancy at retirement.
- During disbursement, annual indexation is the same notional interest rate.[2]

This pseudo-actuarial structure is appealing because of the following:

- The strict link between contributions and benefits creates transparency and possibly strong ownership of the approach: what you pay in you get out.
- It is thus broadly actuarially fair, so it offers incentives for formal labor market participation and delayed retirement.
- Despite this individual character, an NDC remains a social insurance scheme (that is, it pools risk across cohorts and generations) because it offers in any given year one rate of return for all and insurance against the uncertainty of death.
- By design, NDC schemes do not redistribute income across individuals, for example, from lifetime-poorer to lifetime-richer individuals in society.[3] Such redistribution can easily be added but needs to come from outside the scheme and external resources.

At the macro level, an NDC scheme promises intergenerational equity and financial sustainability through the following:

- A fixed contribution rate that broadly keeps the share of retirement income in gross domestic product (GDP) constant across generations
- Application of a rate of return consistent with the financial sustainability of the scheme
- Linking initial benefit level to remaining cohort life expectancy at retirement, thus adjusting benefit levels when relevant life expectancy changes
- A strong economic incentive to postpone retirement to address increasing longevity (and as an alternative and more precise mechanism to exogenously raising the legal standard retirement age)

These basic design features and implied qualities are based on a number of assumptions that are broadened and the challenges addressed in "Key Frontiers in Design and Implementation of NDC Schemes." The underlying assumptions are, however, the same as in the analysis of a typical NDB scheme. The latter serves as a benchmark to explore the qualities of an NDC scheme, discussed next.[4]

What Can NDC Schemes Do Better Than NDB Schemes?

NDC and NDB schemes share much in common, such as their unfunded character and that for solvency their liabilities need to be smaller or at most equal to their unfunded (pay-as-you-go [PAYG]) assets. These notional assets are the difference between the present values of future contributions over future benefits derived from these contributions. Beyond their commonalities, NDC and NDB schemes have a number of differences. This section presents NDC scheme features that dominate those of traditional and reformed NDB schemes (including point systems such as used in France and Germany).

A traditional NDB scheme exhibits a range of distortive features such as final salary benefits, no actuarial adjustment for advanced or delayed retirement start, and no adjustment for rising life expectancy. Parametric reforms of NDC schemes in recent years have tried to address such distortions and failings. A number of recently reformed NDB schemes emulate several of the features of NDC schemes, in particular lifetime averaging of income, indexing the standard retirement age to life expectancy, and actuarially motivated decrements and increments for earlier and later retirement. As discussed below, these aspects go some way but by themselves are insufficient to establish financial sustainability in an aging world. An NDB reform that fully mimics an NDC scheme is conceptually possible yet never done given the complexity and the need for repeated, complicated political decisions, rather than operating on "autopilot."

FINANCIAL LOGIC

The financial logic of an NDC scheme also applies to NDB schemes but is much easier and more transparently established under individual accounts. An NDC scheme's liability is immediately visible or easily calculated: the liability toward the working generation is the sum of individual accounts; the liability toward retirees is broadly the sum of individual annual pension amounts times remaining life expectancy (similar to an NDB scheme). In an NDB scheme, establishing the full public pension liabilities (that is, implicit debt, in particular for the working generation) is a complex task that only a few OECD countries are truly able to master. In an NDB scheme, the PAYG asset side is hardly ever considered.[5] As a result the solvency assessment of NDB schemes—traditional and reformed—remains with very few exceptions focused on short- to medium-term cash-flow deficits. The relevant policy angles for pension schemes to assess sustainability are, however, liabilities and assets.

AUTOMATIC ADJUSTMENTS TO PARAMETERS

An NDC scheme implemented by the rulebook offers many automatic adjustments to parameters that under NDB schemes require difficult discretionary political decisions. Key examples include the following:

- Legal changes in the standard and minimum retirement age are among the most difficult decisions for policy makers; for this reason, they happen mostly too little and too late. Various countries succeeded in indexing the retirement age with changes in a measure of life expectancy. This major accomplishment still falls quite short of the technically correct solution, because in all cases some projected period life expectancy (instead of the correct cohort life expectancy) is applied (Ayusa, Bravo, and Holzmann 2018), and in no instance does the indexed standard retirement age reflect the age at which the scheme would be sustainable. Furthermore, both with and without retirement age indexation, increases in retirement age face political resistance and implementation delays (even in the NDC country, Italy).

- In NDB schemes, earlier or later departure for retirement measured from the standard retirement age is (or should be) corrected with actuarial decrements or increments; otherwise, this creates major incentives for an early departure and significant redistribution and inequity among individuals. Many NDB schemes have increased their decrements and increments but only in a few instances do they reflect actuarially correct values; in no country are they revised when life expectancy changes.

In NDC schemes, these increments and decrements are implicit in the way the benefit is calculated and need no political decision. Because the benefit is calculated by dividing the accumulation at retirement (broadly) by the remaining cohort life expectancy of this age, any early retirement has both lower accumulation and a higher divisor, leading to a lower benefit level that includes the decrement. Delays in retirement work similarly, but in the opposite direction.

- In NDB schemes, increases in retirement age in line with life expectancy are an important necessary but not sufficient step. With an unchanged annual accrual rate, individuals increase their benefit beyond what actuarial calculations would suggest for financial solvency; that is, retirement age increases need to be accompanied by reductions in the accrual rate. This creates another political decision that is hardly ever made on time and to the correct level.

In NDC schemes, such a reduction is again implemented automatically as part of the benefit calculation and does not require a separate political decision.

MINIMUM RETIREMENT AGE

Incentives for working after the minimum retirement age in NDB and NDC schemes are likely to be different.

Full benefits in NDB schemes of the not-so-distant past were typically based on a specified maximum number of years of participating with contributions (for example, 30 or 40 years) and sometimes based on a highest income formula, or perhaps the last years of an earning career. This rewarded shorter careers and persons with steeper earnings curves. Others embodied redistributive features favoring lower-income groups. Both of these designs create incentives for earlier retirement. Even after a reform most NDB schemes do not impose truly actuarially fair decrements and increments for early and later retirement measured from the standard retirement age, thus favoring an early exit.[6]

An NDC scheme does not provide this incentive or distortion (because the intertemporal budget constraint remains linear across the life cycle). In NDC every incremental contribution leads to a proportional increase in the retirement benefit for everyone in the same birth cohort. Of course, some bunching of retirement decisions around the minimum retirement age in NDC schemes may still take place, possibly related to a signaling effect of the minimum retirement age to individuals, pressures by the employer, or people waiting to retire.

SEPARATING INCOME REPLACEMENT FROM REDISTRIBUTIVE CONSIDERATIONS

In an NDC scheme, the basis of income replacement is the individual's lifelong contributions to his or her personal account. Distribution is handled explicitly through a zero-pillar "social pension," or guarantee benefit, which is provided separately from the NDC scheme and is perhaps means-tested. The state can also contribute through tax-financed add-ons from the government budget. An example is contributions paid in conjunction with childbirth, which is a social policy–based transfer to the individual's personal account that constitutes a considerable supplement to the individual's total account value when the pension is calculated at retirement.

This is an important aspect for transparency. The NDC and NDB schemes' approaches differ in this regard. NDB schemes traditionally had strong redistributive features toward lower-income groups, albeit the outcome was often a reverse (regressive) redistribution. The redistributive objectives and outcomes are often opaque and special analysis is required to reveal the effects. In addition, redistributive features that are decided now, such as special supplements for women with children, have financial implications that are only incurred in the future (for example, when these women retire).

An NDC scheme is designed to be free of redistribution but allows for redistributive measures and social policy interventions. However, those interventions have to be explicitly introduced into the scheme and resources have to be provided when these liabilities are created, not when they are disbursed. The logic of the NDC scheme demands this up-front payment because only the contribution-based benefits are matched by the PAYG asset. Additional noncontributory commitments need to be financed now and kept in a reserve fund until disbursement. This avoids the creation of unfunded promises.

Possible social policy interventions may comprise the contribution payments to the NDC scheme on behalf of the individual during, for example, paid unemployment, maternity leave, and disability, by the corresponding other social security funds. Redistribution efforts may include a targeted or universal lump-sum contribution payment to individual accounts financed by general government revenues.

HETEROGENEITY IN LONGEVITY

Both NDB and NDC schemes are challenged by heterogeneity in longevity among socioeconomic groups. This phenomenon is increasingly documented among OECD countries—with regard to gender, lifetime income, education, and other characteristics (Ayuso, Bravo, and Holzmann 2017a).

In NDB schemes, a positive relationship between lifetime income and remaining life expectancy at retirement may be somewhat corrected by a progressive benefit structure (such as in the United States) but the correction is only approximate and inflexible; that is, as heterogeneity changes over time, the concomitant change in benefit structure is difficult to undertake.

In NDC and FDC schemes, a positive relationship between lifetime income and remaining life expectancy at retirement translates into a straight tax or subsidy mechanism with tax rates for the lowest income groups reaching 20 or even 30 percent in some countries, and subsidy rates for the highest income group reaching similar levels. To correct such taxes and subsidies and their distortionary effects, DC schemes may apply corrections at the time of annuitization by individualized life-expectancy estimates, or during the accumulation phase through differentiated contribution rates according to income level (Ayuso, Bravo, and Holzmann 2017b).

In an NDC scheme a simple way to correct for the positive relationship between lifetime income and life expectancy at retirement is a two-tier contribution structure: one share of the total contribution rate is applied to the average period income, while the remaining share is applied—as normally done—to the individual period income. With a total contribution rate of 20 percent, 2–5 percentage points when applied to the average income but recorded at the individual account seem sufficient to correct heterogeneity effects in most OECD countries. Any future change in heterogeneity can be reflected in periodic reestimations of the required contribution split while the overall contribution rate remains constant. Gender inequality in heterogeneity can be addressed by applying gender-specific life expectancies at retirement, an economically correct approach but likely politically difficult (Ayuso, Bravo, and Holzmann 2017b; Holzmann et al. 2019).

SURVIVORS' AND DISABILITY BENEFITS

Reforming partner survivors' and disability benefits is an important aspect of any pension reform. NDC schemes offer better prospects for accommodating this than NDB schemes, however reformed. The need for these programs' reform emerges as (a) women's labor force participation is approaching that of men's, and (b) disability has for decades been a separate risk from old age and thus should be addressed and priced separately (Holzmann and Hinz 2005).

Under an NDC approach, the separation of survivors' benefits is conceptually straightforward. For partner survivors' benefits, some transitional and time-limited DBs are needed, particularly if small children are concerned. Because accounts for one or both partners exist, the rights involved allow for splitting the amounts in a variety of ways, including on a mandatory or voluntary basis. For example, in the case of divorce, joint accumulations during the partnership or marriage may be simply split, and the process can be repeated under a new marriage and divorce. In case of survivorship, the surviving spouse may get some share of the deceased's accumulation that is added to her or his own account. In the presence of children, a time-limited DB may be paid that is dependent on the age and number of children. If both spouses opted for a joint annuity at retirement, the surviving spouse may be offered an actuarially adjusted annuity.

Because the disability risk is nowadays fully separated from the old-age risk, it can and should be separately priced and managed. The separate disability insurance becomes responsible for continuing to pay the full contributions to the NDC scheme if a disability risk (with and without rehabilitation) emerges. At a determined retirement age (for example, an indexed age somewhere between a minimum and a notional standard retirement age), the responsibility of the disability insurance stops and the old-age NDC scheme takes over.

Many variations of these approaches can be developed that treat survivors' and disability benefits separately from old-age benefits but seek an integration that minimizes distortions while delivering on social policy objectives.

HARMONIZATION OF SCHEMES

Harmonization of national sector pension schemes within the private sector and also between a private and a public sector scheme is on the reform agenda in many countries to reduce inequalities, to increase labor mobility, and to take care of unsustainable schemes. This is challenging among NDB schemes but conceptually and practically easy under an NDC personal account approach, in which the liabilities are transparent and easy to calculate.

Harmonizing national NDB schemes typically requires one sector scheme to take over the design of another general scheme. For new entrants to the labor market, the common rules apply while for all others, transitional arrangements are constructed. This can lead to transition periods of several decades, to which the complexity of smaller and larger follow-up reforms is added. This is often a technical and political challenge to design, implement, and sustain, given that inequalities are bound to surface.

The move from an NDB scheme and the harmonization of different NDB schemes into a single one may not take more than a year or so if individual records and the corresponding data management infrastructure are available. The approach essentially consists of (a) keeping benefits in disbursement untouched, (b) translating the acquired individual rights of insured workers into initial individual capital for the NDC accounts, and (c) starting the new common scheme with this initial capital, to which future contributions are added (Palmer 2006). To calculate the initial capital, assumptions about the applied discount rate need to be made, but thereafter the calculation and verification take a matter of days or weeks. This approach allows a smooth transition for everyone, from a person one day from retirement (hardly influenced by the new rules) to a two-week entrant to the labor market (hardly influenced by the old rules). Of course, without individual records and with insufficient data management infrastructure, the calculations are more difficult and time-consuming and development of the required infrastructure may take years. But this also applies to an NDB reform that aims to emulate an NDC scheme.

PORTABILITY

Portability of pensions across professions, sectors, and international borders is increasingly demanded in a world of rising labor mobility within and between countries.

For NDB schemes, portability arrangements have been established between countries in bilateral social security agreements (or directives within the European Union [EU] for all member states). They seem to work reasonably well where they exist between countries because they do not create mobility obstacles or financial advantages of one country over another, and are not too administratively cumbersome (Holzmann 2016a). However, bilateral agreements between NDB countries still create challenges because of differences in benefit calculations and retirement ages between jurisdictions. Absent such agreements, major portability issues will emerge in the case of long waiting periods (before becoming eligible) because individuals may not become eligible for any benefit in any country he or she works in given that the insurance periods are not totalized (that is, all insurance periods counted together).

Under an NDC approach, a waiting period is, in principle, not needed because one only gets out what one pays in (and if a waiting period exists, it is for administrative purposes and typically limited to one year or less). Thus, even in the absence of bilateral social security agreements, the right of exportability of benefits in the social security law is sufficient to establish portability for NDC benefits.

Within the European context, a common NDC approach would be analogous to the introduction of a value-added tax (which the predecessor of the EU spearheaded for

Europe and is implemented worldwide). The NDC approach would be a common concept that allows for country-specific NDC contribution rates (and thus differentiated room for funded and basic provisions) while facilitating portability across multiple borders within the EU. It would create a coordinated pan-European pension system without harmonization pressure (Holzmann 2006).

TAXATION OF CROSS-BORDER PENSIONS

Taxation of cross-border pensions remains an unaddressed issue of fiscal sustainability. The current OECD guidance on cross-border taxation of private sector pensions allocates the taxation rights to the residence country. This is also the basis for most double-taxation treaties between countries across the world. In view of the expenditure-type treatment of public pensions in most countries, the working country exempts contributions from taxation while taxing benefits during disbursement. Thus, the working country has to bear the tax expenditure of untaxed contributions while the residence country profits from the taxation of benefits. This creates fiscal disequilibria between countries, invites tax arbitrage, and is not sustainable in a world of rising labor mobility (Holzmann 2016b).

Addressing the cross-border taxation issue with NDB schemes under the existing international taxation rules is not impossible, but economists have given very little consideration to this question, to date the domain of tax lawyers. A conceptually simple solution is to move from a back-loaded taxation approach (at disbursement) to a front-loaded approach (at contribution payment and return receipt). This move would go against the general taxation direction over the past decades, but would be in line with recent policy changes in Australia and the United Kingdom.

A proposed alternative taxation approach exists that distinguishes between creation of the tax liability in a front-loaded system and its three main payment options: immediately when the liability is created, delayed (when leaving the country or receiving the pension), and equally phased across the three stages of contribution payment, return receipt, and benefit disbursement (Genser and Holzmann 2016, 2018). These payment options can be implemented under both NDB and NDC schemes but a review suggests that all three payment options are more easily implemented under an NDC approach (Genser and Holzmann 2019).

NDC, NDB, AND FDC: SELECT ISSUES

Distribution of survivors' dividend. In NDC schemes the question emerges, to whom does the accumulation of a deceased prior to retirement belong? Accumulations can be kept (without discussion) by the NDC scheme as is typically done by NDB schemes; they can be distributed among the same cohort survivors as is done in the Swedish NDC scheme; they can be used to finance mortality improvements (as proposed by Arnold-Gaille, Boado-Penas, and Godínez-Olivares 2016); they can help finance legacy costs; or they can simply be used to fill any reserve fund that exists. Whatever the approach, public discussion and a government position are called for.

Rationale for a reserve fund. Because an NDC scheme is unfunded, it cannot guarantee liquidity at all times, which calls for a liquidity fund (or else nominal benefits may need to be cut, public transfers received, or temporary credits taken). A reserve fund is an advisable addition to an NDC scheme for at least three reasons. The first is to smooth recessionary dips in the flow of revenues. The second is to deal with short-term demographic cycles. The third reason is to avoid sharp fluctuations in the rate of return within a single generation. However, large reserve funds to address large and protracted shocks may not be advisable (Holzmann, Palmer, and Robalino 2013). In any case, the hosting of redistributive measures and their upfront financing calls forcreation of a reserve fund that may accommodate all three rationales concurrently. Such considerations may also motivate a reserve fund for NDB schemes but there it is not part of the system logic and the experience with such funds has not been convincing.

Establishing the individual account logic. NDC and FDC schemes can complement each other. An NDC reform establishes a sustainable yet unfunded pension scheme and exposes individuals to the logic of a savings-type retirement benefit approach and a close contribution-benefit link. Once the enabling environment for funded provisions (such as financial infrastructure) and the budgetary provisions for the transition costs are established, an FDC scheme can be easily added to an NDC scheme or can replace it, at least partially.

Risk diversification. Furthermore, given that the rates of return of NDC (one rate that is closely linked to GDP growth) and FDC schemes (different rates by scheme) are not highly or even negatively correlated, splitting retirement provisions along NDC and FDC diversifies risk. The selection of the split will be codetermined by the much lower operating costs of an NDC scheme compared with typical FDC schemes.

Key Frontiers in Design and Implementation of NDC Schemes

Although a lot of thinking has gone into the development of NDC schemes, and academic research across the world has reduced the knowledge gaps, not all issues have been solved and new ones continue to be discovered. This section summarizes key issues and some proposed potential solutions.

HOW BEST TO PROXY THE NONFINANCIAL RATE OF RETURN

In an economic and demographic steady-state environment (that is, when all variables grow at a constant but not necessarily equal rate), a proxy for the nonfinancial rate of return is not needed, because the key variables all offer the same value for the implicit rate of return of an unfunded scheme: the growth rate of the labor force plus the rate of productivity growth. In such a setting this rate equals the growth rate of contribution payment or the growth rate of GDP, and the per capita growth rates of each of these aggregate variables are also equal.

Given the reality of economic and demographic shocks and measurement issues associated with each of these variables, it is not as easy to decide which variable is the best proxy for the rate that is expected to best guarantee financial sustainability (that is, the nonfinancial [notional] rate of return). Countries that established NDC schemes selected different rates, for different reasons: Italy chose the GDP growth rate, which may be on the generous side; Sweden selected per capita wage growth to offer some cushioning in front of an aging and perhaps shrinking workforce; Latvia, Norway, and Poland selected the growth rate of the contribution wage sum—the covered wage bill but with variance in scope (ceiling) and definition. The covered wage bill is the most consistent with the NDC model but has weaknesses in expanding and contracting environments of contribution coverage.

The rate of return that guarantees financial solvency can be theoretically calculated (when starting from equilibrium) from the growth rate of the PAYG asset[7] and the rates of return of the financial assets or the reserve fund. But how best to estimate the PAYG asset and its change is still under research, and the realized rates of return on the financial market may not express equilibrium values but reflect stochastic or biased outcomes in a highly complex market. Hence the theoretical construct is not very helpful in choosing an operational proxy.

A BALANCING MECHANISM: IS IT NEEDED AND WHAT SHOULD IT LOOK LIKE?

Neither an empirical variable (such as the growth rate of the contribution-based wage sum) nor any model-based estimate can claim to achieve financial sustainability of an NDC scheme without the need for any future corrections. The basic NDC mechanism consists of indexing accounts and pensions with the rate of growth of the nominal contribution wage base (that is, the base for contributions collected). This provides a steady adjustment that reflects three fundamentals: (a) growth of the real per capita wage, (b) growth of the contributing labor force, and (c) the rate of inflation. This generic NDC indexation, combined with the use of cohort life expectancy at retirement in computing the benefit, go a long way toward keeping the NDC scheme in long-term balance, not the least in the face of substantial long-run chronic declines in the labor force and low fertility. This is illustrated for Latvia in Palmer and Stabina (2019).

Nevertheless, any NDC scheme would be well-advised to consider a balancing mechanism that corrects the annual adjustment of accounts and pensions if a relevant difference between the scheme's liabilities and assets is detected. This is how the Swedish balancing mechanism works (Settergren 2013). Such a balancing mechanism should be designed to be automatic to remove politics from the mechanism and thus it has to determine when the mechanism is triggered, over how many years the correction is phased, and whether it applies symmetrically in both directions. Furthermore, a reserve fund (discussed below) may act as a mechanism to drag out an adjustment because the estimation of assets is still surrounded by conceptual uncertainties.

Interestingly, only one country—Sweden—has established an automatic balancing mechanism (ABM), with issues of its own (Barr and Diamond 2011; Palmer 2013). Norway relies essentially on its huge national wealth fund to guarantee sustainability (which some claim makes it consistent with a substantial "reserve"-funded system). The alternative is to rely on the general budget as a buffer reserve for temporary fluctuations, where again Latvia is an example, with a budgeted reserve. Italy made a further correction in 2012—but only because the scheme was poorly designed from the outset—a lesson in itself. A key requirement for an operationally relevant ABM is a good estimate of the assets that for NDC schemes comprise predominantly contribution (or PAYG) assets. The estimate used by Sweden based on cross-section data is the best approach available to date.

Academic research has produced a number of proposals for how best to select the account and benefit indexation variables to achieve sustainability or liquidity of an NDC scheme, or to correct through ABM approaches (for example, Gronchi and Nisticò 2008; Robalino and Bodor 2009; Boado-Penas and Vidal-Meliá 2013; Alonso-García and Devolder 2017). The translation into country practices is still to be done.

HOW BEST TO DEAL WITH THE LEGACY COST IN NDC INTRODUCTION

A reform that moves from an NDB to an NDC scheme typically fixes the long-term contribution rate below the previous cost-covering rate of the unsustainable NDB scheme. The difference between the short-term financing needs inherited from the old system and the long-term rate under the new system creates a transitory, albeit falling, revenue shortfall or legacy cost of, perhaps, decades, that needs to be financed. These legacy costs are conceptually similar to the transition costs of moving from an NDB and FDC scheme but smaller, because only the unsustainable part of the implicit pension liabilities is made explicit.

These legacy costs could be financed by levying a cost-covering contribution rate but allocating only the revenues from the long-term rate to the individual accounts; the rest would be an explicit tax. Such an approach risks undermining the credibility of the new scheme and the promise that one gets back what one contributed. Using an existing national wealth or reserve fund that can be tapped would be an option for countries that had such a fund before the reform (such as Sweden and Norway). In most OECD countries, one would have to use government transfers generated through reduced public expenditure or higher revenues to finance the transition. In emerging market economies such as China, the expansion in coverage may be able to cover the estimated legacy costs (Holzmann and Jousten 2013).

HOW TO SHARE THE LONGEVITY RISK WITH AND WITHOUT NDC BONDS

Using cohort life expectancy instead of period (cross-section) life expectancy is already a major contribution toward a sustainable NDC scheme. Because cohort life expectancy is based not only on estimations but also on projections of how age-specific mortality rates change over time, a higher level of uncertainty surrounds the estimated life-expectancy value. Yet these estimates cover only the "known unknown." Breakthroughs in medical science may lead to major reductions in mortality at higher ages; most changes will happen in the future at these ages when pensions are already in disbursement. How can the longevity risk in both cases be best shared among retirees and with the active population?

A distribution of the longevity risk within the NDC pool occurs through adjustments in the allocated rate of return and annual indexation of the pension benefits when different. The difference may happen with a front-loaded benefit scheme that assumes a rate of return and offers higher initial benefits and only, for example, price indexation thereafter. But many other possibilities and arrangements exist for how to share the longevity risk among retirees and contributors. These should be studied further.

One suggested way to share the longevity risk with the population at large is for the government to issue NDC bonds (Palmer 2013). An NDC bond transfers the residual risk (the risk of under- or overestimating cohort longevity) to the insurer—that is, the government. The NDC bond proposed is a nontradable instrument; that is, it is not for sale on the financial market. It is a contract between the government and NDC scheme participants that emulates the market contract underlying bond financing of government debt. The rate of return of the NDC bond is the NDC internal rate of return. Similar ideas about tradable longevity bonds for the risk management of occupational FDC and FDB schemes were not very successful, as their failed introduction in a few countries has demonstrated (Holzmann 2017a).

HOW TO ADDRESS MARGINALIZATION ON THE LABOR MARKET WITH AN NDC SCHEME

NDC schemes are a perfect consumption-smoothing instrument for full-time workers with few gaps in their working years; such workers may furthermore be covered by contributions from unemployment, sickness, or disability insurance programs. However, developments over the recent decade in OECD countries were often characterized by an increase in part-time employment, of which only part is voluntary and often applies to women; long spells of unpaid internships; a succession of temporary and lower-paid contracts; and an increase in the number and spells of unemployment.[8] During these periods, no or low contribution amounts are added to the individual account. Others may join the domestic labor market only late in their career as recognized refugees, economic migrants, or undocumented workers. For all these and other marginalized groups, an NDC scheme offers only modest benefits; and in the case of a public income guarantee for retirees, incentives to contribute to the scheme are limited.

How best to include marginalized groups in the NDC scheme while offering some income guarantee in old age is a key challenge. Should the government offer an ex post income guarantee that also tapers off as the NDC benefit increases? Or should the incentives for more contributions be created through ex ante interventions such as matching contribution payments by the government? Are two-tier contribution schemes—discussed above—an approach not only to address heterogeneity in longevity but also to address marginalization? Or should there be a mix of interventions to deal with related but different objectives and individual situations?

Various chapters in this book address issues and policy suggestions for how best to link the NDC approach and social policy interventions. NDC individual accounts provide an ideal basic building block for public policy regarding provision of pension rights in conjunction with public policy interventions that provide income and contribution support (for example, during periods of childbirth, retraining or reeducation in conjunction with disrupted careers or career changes, granting disability, and sharing rights between partners). NDC's advantage is that it provides the framework for transparent distributional policy because the resources have to be provided when committed. This compares well with similar attempts in NDB schemes where financing happens only at the time of disbursement while the effects on pension benefits at the time of decision are more difficult to determine.

HOW TO MARKET THE ADVANTAGES OF NDC SCHEMES TO POLICY MAKERS AND THE GENERAL PUBLIC

Despite the advantages of an NDC scheme compared with an NDB scheme, only a limited number of countries have introduced NDC schemes with variations, while a few more countries have introduced elements but not the full approach (discussed next). What could be the reason for this hesitation and the expressed preference for a sequence of late, insufficient, and parametric reforms to NDB schemes? And what can be done about it?

NDC schemes are poorly understood and communicated, and the population at large has only a limited understanding of economic and financial affairs. Significant improvements in these areas are critical for furthering better-designed pension schemes (Fornero 2015; Fornero and Prete 2017). The work on Sweden suggests that it is difficult to reach participants with NDC messages (Sundén 2013), and the messages provided may still be too complicated. Recent communication work under the voluntary and funded U.K. scheme National Employment Savings Trust is very innovative and promising (NEST 2017; Sandbrook and Ravi-Burslem 2019); the results may be useful for NDC schemes.

Many reasons may be raised to advance the advantages and desirability of NDC schemes. The fundamental one is that introducing an NDC scheme takes the politics out of pensions, an important achievement since policy makers usually do not want to be "lashed to the mast" (Brooks and Weaver 2006). If properly designed, an NDC scheme makes unsustainability fully visible and precludes postponement of the politically dicey adjustment. However, it should be made clear and publicly explained that an NDC scheme that disregards heterogeneity of longevity and marginalization is not a good deal for lower-income groups and that higher-income groups may lose compared to the status quo.

Various observers claim that recent NDB reforms in many OECD countries broadly achieved what an NDC scheme promises to do by introducing actuarially fair adjustments, automatic adjustments in retirement age based on life expectancy, and lifetime valorized career average wage bases. Such a claim, if often repeated and supported by recognized organizations, will reduce interest in an NDC reform. Although the claim of establishing financial sustainability through parametric reforms has undoubtedly reduced the attractiveness of a systemic NDC reform, it is doubtful these reforms have actually achieved their goals.

Country Experiences with NDC Reforms

Although conceptual considerations are relevant for the assessment and comparison of pension schemes, the experiences of countries with NDC reforms offer the actual proof. This section provides a brief overview of countries that implemented an NDC reform to a previous NDB scheme. It also highlights countries with near or lesser NDC reforms or those exploring this reform option. Several chapters in both volumes offer details.

COUNTRIES WITH NDC REFORM EXPERIENCE OR INTEREST

To date, five European OECD countries have implemented full NDC reforms, albeit with some variation[9]: Sweden (legislated in 1994, implemented gradually beginning in 1996, with full implementation in 1999), Italy (legislated in 1995, implemented in 1996, with reform measures and accelerated implementation in 2012), Latvia (legislated in 1995, implemented in 1996), Poland (legislated in 1998, implemented in 1999), and Norway (legislated in 2009, implemented in 2011). The variations across countries include the choice of proxy for the sustainable internal rate of return, the presence or absence of a balancing mechanism, the speed of transition, and the addition of a smaller funded pillar.

In the 1990s and 2000s, a few middle-income countries (such as Azerbaijan, the Kyrgyz Republic, Mongolia, the Russian Federation, Tajikistan, and Turkmenistan) adopted some NDC features in their pension schemes, but information on and assessment of the outcomes remain scant. Egypt legislated an NDC scheme in 2010 but the legislation was rescinded during the Arab Spring (Guardiancich et al. 2019). Implementation of an NDC scheme in a middle-income country is bound to raise new conceptual and operational issues about which the understanding and knowledge are currently very limited; Palacios (2019) and Lu, Piggott, and Zheng (2019) offer some insights. From Russia, it is known that the government moved to a point system, by some accounts because authorities could exercise more influence over pension benefits through valuation of points than they could under an NDC scheme.

A number of countries (or groups therein) across the world have expressed interest in the NDC approach to reforming their NDB schemes: Argentina (which reversed an FDC approach) and Uruguay in Latin America; various European countries such as Greece, Portugal, and Spain; and several countries in Asia, in particular China and the Islamic Republic of Iran (Lu, Piggott, and Zheng 2019). China has a two-tier contribution structure with province-specific attempts to fund individual contributions. Because this attempt has met with little success, the move from "empty accounts" to a formal NDC scheme is still under discussion in some parts of government.

REFORM LESSONS FROM NDC COUNTRIES

Overall, the lessons from the five European OECD countries with NDC reforms are positive. The four early adopters of the reform weathered the 2008 financial crisis and following years well, and no reform reversals were ever discussed. However, both Latvia and Poland, with their large prereform commitments, retrenched their funded ambitions because the transition costs of NDC and FDC proved to be too heavy a strain on the public budget. And Latvia and Sweden had to address the political challenge of negative account indexation during the early years of the crisis.

A review of the first 15 years of reform in the four early adopters (Italy, Latvia, Poland, and Sweden) suggests seven lessons (Holzmann and Palmer 2012). Six years later and with additional country information, the lessons remain broadly unchanged, but this NDC III publication adds three more lessons. NDC schemes broadly work pretty well, but room remains to make them even better if policy makers undertake the following:

- Follow the rulebook in design and implement fast transition options.
- Do not underestimate the technical requirements for NDC implementation, including individualized accounts and estimates for cohort life expectancies at retirement ages.
- If logistically possible, move immediately to NDC accounts and avoid parallel schemes and delayed implementation. The recommendation is to go "cold

turkey" and move straight from NDB to NDC schemes without transitional arrangements.

- Identify and finance the legacy costs in an explicit manner as they emerge, because they will have to be faced sooner or later. Ignoring such costs does not work, and not foreseeing an appropriate financing mechanism can be dangerous if unexpected shocks hit.

- Establish an explicit balancing mechanism to guarantee solvency in a transparent manner. Only Sweden implemented an automatic mechanism; all other countries have no explicit process. This is not good for the credibility of the scheme and risks leading to a significant government financial burden.

- Establish a reserve fund to cushion temporary shocks. This buffer helps provide liquidity and avoids too strong fluctuations of the rate of return within a generation. For larger and protracted shocks, a larger fund may not work and a better response may be to accept some differences in the notional interest rate within and across generations.

- Develop an explicit mechanism for sharing the systemic longevity risk. Such a mechanism can be simply a split of burden among retirees and with the contributor agreed to ahead of time. It may also include more sophisticated approaches once their conceptual dominance and operational implementation are established.

- Address head on the implications of NDC schemes for subgroups such as women, marginalized individuals, and marginal labor market participants through analysis and political discourse, and explore social policy options to address issues through an enhanced design and external financing that broadly keep the advantages of the scheme approach while taking care of these groups' needs.

- Explore, design, and implement early on reforms of benefit schemes that are closely linked with old-age income provisions, that is, survivorship, disability, and, perhaps, long-term care. Keeping the previous structure of these programs misses an opportunity for their needed reform and does not play to the advantages of NDC schemes.

- Explore early on in design and implementation the integration of other pension pillars with the NDC scheme: a zero pillar to take care of poverty concerns, a second-pillar provision of mandated and funded design, a third pillar of voluntary occupational and personal retirement saving efforts, and a fourth pillar that offers income support and services for the elderly.

- Explore early on the communication needs to explain the NDC approach and the communication means to keep individuals updated on their accounts, and invest in special education programs and tools.

Conclusions and Way Forward

The NDC pension scheme approach is the newest entrant to the small set of systemic pension reform proposals. Although just 25 years old, with even fewer years of implementation, the approach is doing well. The schemes in the five OECD countries that implemented the basic NDC approach in full are doing well overall by the key criteria of a pension scheme—adequacy, affordability, and sustainability. All of these schemes weathered the recent financial crisis relatively well, albeit the crisis demonstrated the importance of a complete design, including a balancing mechanism, a reserve fund, and preparation for the legacy costs of the reform.

The NDC scheme serves as a benchmark for other OECD countries that are undertaking only parametric reforms of their NDB schemes, because policy makers have started to understand that the NDC logic and constraints also apply to NDB schemes. The approach inspired a number of emerging market economies to implement elements of the NDC design, but little is known about the reported failings of such mixed schemes. The implementation of an NDC scheme has a number of institutional requirements that are not easily met by emerging market economies.

Despite the many advantages of the NDC approach compared with any NDB approach, few countries are actively preparing NDC reforms. This may be because the recent NDB reforms could broadly stabilize the short-term financing needs of the scheme while the longer-term financial unsustainability is beyond the time horizon of policy makers. It could be that the proponents of NDCs overestimated the ring of the efficiency and sustainability promises of the scheme while underestimating the importance of explicit features to take care of marginalized groups. It may also be that communication of the NDC concept and its actual working was insufficient to create a reform dynamic similar to that of the Chilean reform in the 1990s and 2000s.

Notes

1. The scheme is pseudo-actuarial because the derived and applied nonfinancial (notional) interest rate will differ from the one expected to be delivered by the financial market. Theoretically, in a dynamically efficient economy the financial market interest rate should be greater than the internal rate of return delivered by an NDC scheme; in reality this may not be the case.

2. In the general approach, in both annuity calculation and annuity indexation an imputed interest rate is used that needs to be deducted from the applied interest rate.

3. However, the NDC scheme tends to pay much higher replacement rates to lower-income groups with a flat earnings profile than to fast-rising career patterns; see Nisticò and Bevilacqua (2013).

4. For a technical presentation of a generic NDC scheme, see Palmer (2013).

5. Sweden developed a method to estimate the PAYG asset amount from cross-sectional data and compares this annually with the liability to determine solvency (Settergren and Mikula 2006).

6. The OECD's annual publication *Pensions at a Glance* (PaG) offers information about countries' status and reforms, including on increments and decrements for advanced and delayed retirement. The 2017 PaG publication (OECD 2017) addresses earlier retirement policy changes and table 2.2 of the OECD publication details the decrements and increments for each country. Although the number of NDB countries that introduced adjustments has increased, only a few countries have them close to their actuarial level; most are two-thirds or less. A comprehensive study to compare and assess countries' actual actuarial fairness is lacking.

7. The PAYG asset is the difference between the present value of contributions and related liabilities.

8. For simulations of the impact of unemployment spells on pension benefits in the Portuguese and Spanish pension schemes, see Bravo and Herce (2017).

9. For detailed information on NDC schemes in these countries since their start, see Chłoń-Domińczak, Franco, and Palmer (2012); Christensen et al. (2012); and chapters 2–5 in Volume 1 (respectively, Palmer and Könberg [2019]; Palmer and Stabina [2019]; Gronchi, Nisticò, and Bevilacqua [2019]; and Buchholtz, Chłoń-Domińczak, and Góra [2019]).

References

Alonso-García, Jennifer, and Pierre Devolder. 2017. "Sustainable Design of Notional Defined Contribution Scheme in a Continuous OLG Model." Unpublished, CEPAR, University of New South Wales.

Arnold-Gaille, Séverine, María del Carmen Boado-Penas, and Humberto Godínez-Olivares. 2016. "Longevity Risk in Notional Defined Contribution Pension Schemes: A Solution." *Geneva Papers on Risk and Insurance* 41 (1): 24–52.

Ayuso, Mercedes, Jorge M. Bravo, and Robert Holzmann. 2017a. "Addressing Longevity Heterogeneity in Pension Scheme Design and Reform." *Journal of Finance and Economics* 6 (10): 1–21.

———. 2017b. "On the Heterogeneity of Longevity among Socio-economic Groups: Scope, Trends and Implications for Earnings-Related Pension Programs." *Global Journal of Human Social Sciences–Economics* 17 (1): 33–58.

———. 2018. "Getting Life Expectancy Estimates Right for Pension Policy: Period versus Cohort Approach." IZA Discussion Paper 11512, IZA Institute of Labor Economics, Bonn, Germany.

Barr, Nicholas, and Peter Diamond. 2011. "Improving Sweden's Automatic Pension Adjustment Mechanism." *Issue Brief* 11-2, Center for Retirement at Boston College, Chestnut Hill, MA. http://crr.bc.edu/wp-content/uploads/2011/01/IB—11-2-508.pdf.

Boado-Penas, María del Carmen, and Carlos Vidal-Meliá. 2013. "The Actuarial Balance of the Pay-as-You-Go Pension System: The Swedish NDC Model Versus the U.S. DB model." In *Nonfinancial Defined Contribution Pension Schemes in a Changing Pension World: Volume 2 Gender, Politics, and Financial Stability*, edited by Robert Holzmann, Edward Palmer, and David Robalino, 443–80. Washington, DC: World Bank.

Bravo, Jorge, and José A. Herce. 2017. "Acerca de la influencia de las interrupciones en el empleo sobre las prestaciones por jubilación." Documento de Trabajo: N° 19/2017. Lisboa/Madrid: Instituto BBVA de pensiones.

Brooks, Sarah M., and Kent Weaver. 2006. "Lashed to the Mast? The Politics of NDC Pension Reform." In *Pension Reform: Issues and Prospects for Non-Financial Defined Contribution (NDC) Schemes*, edited by Robert Holzmann and Edward Palmer, 345–85. Washington, DC: World Bank.

Buchholtz, Sonia, Agnieszka Chłoń-Domińczak, and Marek Góra. 2019. "The Polish NDC Scheme: Success in the Face of Adversity." In *Progress and Challenges of Nonfinancial Defined Contribution Pension Schemes: Volume 1 Addressing Marginalization, Polarization, and the Labor Market*, edited by Robert Holzmann, Edward Palmer, Robert Palacios, and Stefano Sacchi, Chapter 5. Washington, DC: World Bank.

Chłoń-Domińczak, Agnieszka, Daniele Franco, and Edward Palmer. 2012. "The First Wave of NDC Reforms: The Experiences of Italy, Latvia, Poland, and Sweden." In *Nonfinancial Defined Contribution Pension Schemes in a Changing Pension World: Volume 1 Progress, Lessons, and Implementation*, edited by Robert Holzmann, Edward Palmer, and David Robalino, 31–84. Washington, DC: World Bank.

Chłoń-Dominczak, Agnieszka, and Marek Góra. 2006. "The NDC System in Poland: Assessment after Five Years." In *Pension Reform: Issues and Prospects for Non-Financial Defined Contribution (NDC) Schemes*, edited by Robert Holzmann and Edward Palmer, 425–48. Washington, DC: World Bank.

Christensen, Arne Magnus, Dennis Fredriksen, Ole Christian Lien, and Nils Martin Stølen. 2012. "Pension Reform in Norway: Combining an NDC Approach and Distributional Goals." In *Nonfinancial Defined Contribution Pension Schemes in a Changing Pension World: Volume 1 Progress, Lessons, and Implementation*, edited by Robert Holzmann, Edward Palmer, and David Robalino, 149–74. Washington, DC: World Bank.

Fornero, Elsa. 2015. "Reform, Inform, Educate: A New Paradigm for Pension Systems." In *The Future of Welfare in a Global Europe*, edited by Bernd Marin, 297–324. Farnham, UK: Ashgate.

Fornero, Elsa, and Anna Lo Prete. 2017. *Voting in the Aftermath of a Pension Reform: The Role of Financial Literacy*. CeRP Working Paper 171/17, Center for Research on Pensions and Welfare Policies, Torino.

Fox, Louise, and Edward Palmer. 1999. "Latvian Pension Reform." Social Protection Discussion Paper 9922, World Bank, Washington, DC.

Genser, Bernd, and Robert Holzmann. 2016. "The Taxation of Internationally Portable Pensions: An Introduction to Fiscal Issues and Policy Options." CESifo DICE Report 1/2016, CESifo, Munich.

———. 2018. "The Taxation of Internationally Portable Pensions—Fiscal Issues and Policy Options." In *The Taxation of Pensions*, edited by Robert Holzmann and John Piggott, 443–79. Cambridge, MA: MIT Press.

———. 2019. "Pensions in a Globalizing World: How Do (N)DC and (N)DB Schemes Fare and Compare on Portability and Taxation?" In *Progress and Challenges of Nonfinancial Defined Contribution Pension Schemes: Volume 2 Addressing Gender, Administration, and Communication*, edited by Robert Holzmann, Edward Palmer, Robert Palacios, and Stefano Sacchi, Chapter 29. Washington, DC: World Bank.

Gronchi, Sandro, and Sergio Nisticò. 2008. "The Theoretical Foundations of NDC Pension Schemes." *Metroeconomica* 58 (2): 131–59.

Gronchi, Sandro, Sergio Nisticò, and Mirko Bevilacqua. 2019. "The Italian NDC Scheme: Evolution and Remaining Potholes." In *Progress and Challenges of Nonfinancial Defined Contribution Pension Schemes: Volume 1 Addressing Marginalization, Polarization, and the Labor Market*, edited by Robert Holzmann, Edward Palmer, Robert Palacios, and Stefano Sacchi, Chapter 4. Washington, DC: World Bank.

Guardiancich, Igor, Kent Weaver, Gustavo Demarco, and Mark C. Dorfman. 2019. "The Politics of NDC Pension Scheme Diffusion: Constraints and Drivers." In *Progress and Challenges of Nonfinancial Defined Contribution Pension Schemes: Volume 2 Addressing Gender, Administration, and Communication*, edited by Robert Holzmann, Edward Palmer, Robert Palacios, and Stefano Sacchi, Chapter 28. Washington, DC: World Bank.

Holzmann, Robert. 1988. *Reforming Public Pensions? La Réforme des Régimes Publics de Pensions*. Paris: OECD.

———. 1997. "Pension Reform, Financial Market Development, and Economic Growth: Preliminary Evidence from Chile." *IMF Staff Papers* 44 (June): 149–78.

———. 1999. "On the Economic Benefits and Fiscal Requirements of Moving from Unfunded to Funded Pensions." In *The Welfare State in Europe*, edited by Mario Buti, Daniele Franco, and Lucca Pench, 139–96. Cheltenham, UK, and Northampton, MA: Edward Elgar.

———. 2006. "Toward a Coordinated Pension System in Europe: Rationale and Potential Structure." In *Pension Reform: Issues and Prospects for Non-Financial Defined Contribution (NDC) Schemes*, edited by Robert Holzmann and Edward Palmer, 225–65. Washington, DC: World Bank.

———. 2013. "Global Pension Systems and Their Reform: Worldwide Drivers, Trends and Challenges." *International Social Security Review* 66 (2): 1–29.

———. 2016a. "Do Bilateral Social Security Agreements Deliver on the Portability of Pensions and Health Care Benefits? A Summary Policy Paper on Four Migration Corridors between EU and Non-EU Member States." *IZA Journal of European Labor Studies* 5 (17): 1–35.

———. 2016b. "Taxing Pensions of an Internationally Mobile Labor Force: Portability Issues and Taxation Options." CESifo Working Paper 7515, CESifo, Munich.

———. 2017a. "La fase de percepción de los pagos de las pensiones: tendencias, problemas, principales desafíos y papel del gobierno." In *Ideas para una Reforma de Pensiones*, edited by Luis Carranza, Ángel Melguizo, and David Tuesta, 297–340. Capitulo 11. Lima: Universidad di San Martin de Porres.

———. 2017b. "The ABCs of Non-financial Defined Contribution (NDC) Schemes." *International Social Security Review* 70 (3): 53–77.

Holzmann, Robert, Jennifer Alonso-García, Héloïse Labit-Hardy, and Andrés M. Villegas. 2019. "NDC Schemes and Heterogeneity in Longevity: Proposals for Redesign." In *Progress and Challenges of Nonfinancial Defined Contribution Pension Schemes: Volume 1 Addressing Marginalization, Polarization, and the Labor Market*, edited by Robert Holzmann, Edward Palmer, Robert Palacios, and Stefano Sacchi, Chapter 14. Washington, DC: World Bank.

Holzmann, Robert, and Richard Hinz. 2005. *Old-Age Income Support in the 21st Century: An International Perspective on Pension Systems and Reform*. Washington, DC: World Bank.

Holzmann, Robert, and Alain Jousten. 2013. "Addressing the Legacy Costs in an NDC Reform: Conceptualization, Measurement, Financing." In *Nonfinancial Defined Contribution Pension Schemes in a Changing Pension World: Volume 2 Gender, Politics, and Financial Stability*, edited by Robert Holzmann, Edward Palmer, and David Robalino, 227–308. Washington, DC: World Bank.

Holzmann, Robert, and Edward Palmer (eds.). 2006. *Pension Reform: Issues and Prospect for Non-Financial Defined Contribution (NDC) Schemes*. Washington, DC: World Bank.

Holzmann, Robert, and Edward Palmer. 2012. "NDC in the Teens: Lessons and Issues." In *Nonfinancial Defined Contribution Pension Schemes in a Changing Pension World: Volume 1 Progress, Lessons, and Implementation*, edited by Robert Holzmann, Edward Palmer, and David Robalino, 3–29. Washington, DC: World Bank.

Holzmann, Robert, Edward Palmer, and David Robalino, eds. 2012. *NDC Pension Schemes in a Changing Pension World: Volume 1 Progress, Issues, and Implementation*. Washington, DC: World Bank.

———. 2013. *NDC Pension Schemes in a Changing Pension World: Volume 2 Gender, Politics, and Financial Stability*. Washington, DC: World Bank.

Holzmann, Robert, David Robalino, and Hernan Winkler. 2019. "NDC Schemes and the Labor Market: Issues and Options." In *Progress and Challenges of Nonfinancial Defined Contribution Pension Schemes: Volume 1 Addressing Marginalization, Polarization, and the Labor Market*, edited by Robert Holzmann, Edward Palmer, Robert Palacios, and Stefano Sacchi, Chapter 15. Washington, DC: World Bank.

Könberg, Bo, Edward Palmer, and Annika Sundén. 2006. "The NDC Reform in Sweden: The 1994 Legislation to the Present." In *Pension Reform: Issues and Prospects for Non-Financial Defined Contribution (NDC) Schemes*, edited by Robert Holzmann and Edward Palmer, Chapter 17, 449–66. Washington, DC: World Bank.

Lu, Bei, John Piggott, and Bingwen Zheng. 2019. "The Notional and the Real in China's Pension Reforms." In *Progress and Challenges of Nonfinancial Defined Contribution Pension Schemes: Volume 2 Addressing Gender, Administration, and Communication*, edited by Robert Holzmann, Edward Palmer, Robert Palacios, and Stefano Sacchi, Chapter 22. Washington, DC: World Bank.

NEST (National Employment Savings Trust). 2017. Communication Material. www.nestpensions .org.uk/schemeweb/nest/resources/communication-materials.html.

Nisticò, Sergio, and Mirko Bevilacqua. 2013. "Notional Defined Contribution (NDC) Pension Schemes and Income Patterns." *Economics: The Open-Access, Open-Assessment E-Journal* 7: 2013–29. http://dx.doi.org/10.5018/economics-ejournal.ja.2013-29.

OECD (Organisation for Economic Co-operation and Development). 2017. *Pensions at a Glance 2017: OECD and G20 Indicators.* Paris: OECD Publishing.

Palacios, Robert. 2019. "Administrative Requirements and Prospects for Universal NDCs in Emerging Economies." In *Progress and Challenges of Nonfinancial Defined Contribution Pension Schemes: Volume 2 Addressing Gender, Administration, and Communication*, edited by Robert Holzmann, Edward Palmer, Robert Palacios, and Stefano Sacchi, Chapter 21. Washington, DC: World Bank.

Palmer, Edward. 1999. "Individual Decisions and Aggregate Stability in a NDC PAYG Account Scheme." Unpublished.

———. 2000. "The Swedish Pension Reform Model: Framework and Issues." Social Protection Paper 0012, Pension Reform Primer, World Bank, Washington, DC.

———. 2002. "Swedish Pension Reform: Its Past and Its Future." In *Social Security Pension Reform in Europe*, edited by Martin Feldstein and Horst Siebert, 171–210. Chicago, IL: University of Chicago Press.

———. 2006. "Conversion to NDCs—Issues and Models." In *Pension Reform: Issues and Prospects for Non-Financial Defined Contribution (NDC) Schemes*, edited by Robert Holzmann and Edward Palmer, 169–202. Washington, DC: World Bank.

———. 2013. "Generic NDC: Equilibrium, Valuation, and Risk Sharing With and Without NDC Bonds." In *Nonfinancial Defined Contribution Pension Schemes in a Changing Pension World: Volume 2 Gender, Politics, and Financial Stability*, edited by Robert Holzmann, Edward Palmer, and David Robalino, 309–33. Washington, DC: World Bank.

Palmer, Edward, and Bo Könberg. 2019. "The Swedish NDC Scheme: Success on Track with Room for Reflection." In *Progress and Challenges of Nonfinancial Defined Contribution Pension Schemes: Volume 1 Addressing Marginalization, Polarization, and the Labor Market*, edited by Robert Holzmann, Edward Palmer, Robert Palacios, and Stefano Sacchi, Chapter 2. Washington, DC: World Bank.

Palmer, Edward, and Sandra Stabina. 2019. "The Latvian NDC Scheme: Success under a Decreasing Labor Force." In *Progress and Challenges of Nonfinancial Defined Contribution Pension Schemes: Volume 1 Addressing Marginalization, Polarization, and the Labor Market*, edited by Robert Holzmann, Edward Palmer, Robert Palacios, and Stefano Sacchi, Chapter 3. Washington, DC: World Bank.

Palmer, Edward, Sandra Stabina, Ingemar Svensson, and Inta Vanovska. 2006. "NDC Strategy in Latvia: Implementation and Prospects for the Future." In *Pension Reform: Issues and Prospects for Non-Financial Defined Contribution (NDC) Schemes*, edited by Robert Holzmann and Edward Palmer, Chapter 15, 397–424. Washington, DC: World Bank.

Robalino, David A., and András Bodor. 2009. "On the Financial Sustainability of Earnings-Related Pension Schemes with 'Pay-as-You-Go' Financing and the Role of Government Indexed Bonds." *Journal of Pension Economics and Finance* 8 (2): 153–87.

Sandbrook, Will, and Ranila Ravi-Burslem. 2019. "Communicating NEST Pensions for 'New' DC Savers in the United Kingdom." In *Progress and Challenges of Nonfinancial Defined Contribution Pension Schemes: Volume 2 Addressing Gender, Administration, and Communication*, edited by Robert Holzmann, Edward Palmer, Robert Palacios, and Stefano Sacchi, Chapter 24. Washington, DC: World Bank.

Settergren, Ole. 2013. "A Decade of Actuarial Accounting for the NDC Scheme in Sweden: Quantifying Change in the Financial Position of a PAG Plan." In *Nonfinancial Defined Contribution Pension Schemes in a Changing Pension World: Volume 2 Gender, Politics and Financial Stability*, edited by Robert Holzmann, Edward Palmer, and David Robalino, 392–91. Washington, DC: World Bank.

Settergren, Ole, and Buguslaw D. Mikula. 2006. "The Rate of Return of Pay-as-You Go Pension Systems: A More Exact Consumption-Loan Model of Interest." In *Pension Reform: Issues and Prospects for Non-Financial Defined Contribution (NDC) Schemes*, edited by Robert Holzmann and Edward Palmer, 117–47. Washington, DC: World Bank.

Sundén, Anika. 2013. "The Challenge of Reaching Participants with the Message of NDC." In *Nonfinancial Defined Pension Schemes in a Changing Pension World: Volume 2 Gender, Politics, and Financial Stability*, edited by Robert Holzmann, Edward Palmer, and David Robalino, 257–72. Washington, DC: World Bank.

World Bank. 1994. *Averting the Old-Age Crisis.* Washington, DC: World Bank.

PART III

Adjoining Zero Pillar with DC Schemes

CHAPTER 10

Sweden: Adjoining the Guarantee Pension with NDC

Kenneth Nelson, Rense Nieuwenhuis, and Susanne Alm

Introduction

The Swedish pension system received substantial international recognition when it was introduced in the mid-1990s. The earnings-related benefits, composed of the nonfinancial defined contribution (NDC) pension (*inkomstpension*) and the financial defined contribution (FDC) pension (*premiepension*), were left outside of the state budget, and established a direct link between what people pay during their working lives and the pensions they receive in retirement. Consequently, costs should not be passed on to future generations. Nonetheless, the system also included redistributive components intended to raise the incomes of the poorest elderly who were not able to allocate sufficient income-related contributions to secure an acceptable pension. These low-income targeted components, which consist of the guaranteed minimum pension (*garantipension*), the housing supplement (*bostadstillägg för pensionärer*), and social assistance (*äldreförsörjningsstöd*), were left in the state budget. Whereas the guaranteed minimum pension is tested only against the NDC and FDC schemes, social assistance and the housing supplement are means-tested more broadly vis-à-vis other income, including income from capital (or assets).

The new pension system has been in place for roughly two decades, which offers ample opportunity to study its effects on Swedish income distribution. This chapter applies a policy perspective on old-age incomes in Sweden, focusing on both the economic positions of elderly citizens and the redistributive effects of the pension system. It analyzes poverty trends among the elderly, as well as how income inequalities in old age have developed since introduction of the new pension system. Developments among the elderly are contrasted with those of the working-age population. The empirical analyses are based on the most up-to-date micro-level income data provided by Statistics Sweden. The data are from HEK (Hushållens ekonomi), which includes a sample of register data on incomes at the individual and household levels, coupled with survey data about household types and other characteristics of the sampled population. The total sample size varies across years and includes between 9,000 and 19,000 households annually. The sampling frame is at the individual level, to which household-level data from registers are later added.

The authors acknowledge the research support from the Swedish Research Council for Health, Working Life, and Welfare (2012-0995).

The reorganization of Swedish old-age pensions in the mid-1990s was largely motivated in politics by the aging of the population and the financial viability of the old system (Könberg, Palmer, and Sundén 2006). The ability to effectively control expenditures and provide incentives for long working careers by linking contributions to lifetime earnings was a clear advantage of the new system, including the prominent defined contribution (DC) components. However, one major challenge was how to balance concerns regarding financial and social sustainability in a DC framework. Whereas the former is related to costs and affordability of future pensions, the latter links to issues of low income, economic hardship, and inequality, as addressed in this chapter (Grech 2013, 2014). Financial sustainability was already high on the political agenda at the onset of the major pension reform in the late 1990s. Concerns regarding social sustainability are more recent, and have influenced the Swedish pension policy discourse only in the last few years. The Pensions Working Group, representing all parties in the Parliament when the new DC system was introduced, proposed that the instruments for regulating low income in old age—the guaranteed minimum income and the housing supplement—should be automatically indexed. It was finally decided that only the guaranteed minimum pension was to be indexed, and in this particular case only to prices.

Although the Swedish pension system survived its first two decades without any major changes, there have been some adjustments and smoothening of the automatic balancing mechanisms in the indexation of the income pension to economic developments and general income growth (European Commission 2018a). Despite these changes, which were intensified in 2010 and have continued stepwise, concerns remain that the incomes of current pensioners are falling behind average income growth (Social Ministry 2011). Other adjustments have primarily concerned the fully funded premium pension, including strengthened regulation and improved consumer protection. Additional steps in this direction are suggested, although they are not likely to significantly affect current pensioners.

The guaranteed minimum pension, paid to those with insufficient contributions; the housing supplement; and social assistance have been largely unchanged since their introduction. Nonetheless, low benefit take-up and inadequate indexation have recently raised concerns about the reemergence of old-age poverty and increased economic difficulties of elderly people with insufficient contributions for income-related pension benefits, including many women and elderly migrants (Social Ministry 2016). This chapter examines the consequences of almost two decades without any major reforms of minimum pension benefits, considered here to be essential components of a well-functioning pension system.

The chapter is divided into three sections. "Poverty" analyzes developments in low-end incomes among the elderly and identifies some underlying characteristics that increase the risk of being poor in old age. "Redistribution" addresses the issue of redistribution and analyzes the extent to which old-age pensions reduce poverty. It also provides an analysis based on synthetic cohorts of elderly people, thus illustrating how incomes and poverty risks change as pensioners are growing older. "Inequality" is devoted to the related, but somewhat broader, issue of income inequality, focusing first on developments since the mid-1990s, and second on the contribution of public pensions to income differences in old age. "Concluding Discussion" briefly discusses the results and concludes.

Poverty

Conceptualizing and measuring poverty is complex. Standard measures of poverty in rich countries typically apply a relative perspective on economic hardship and evaluate whether incomes are sufficient to maintain an average (or close to average) standard of living that in theory should allow people to participate in society (Townsend 1979). Figure 10.1 shows relative income poverty among the elderly (65 years and older) in Sweden for the period 1995–2013. As reference, the figure also shows poverty rates for the working-age population (18–64 years). Because relative income poverty is sensitive to the yardstick used to define when households are poor, different poverty thresholds are used, for each year expressed as certain fractions of the median equivalized disposable household income in the total population. People in households with incomes below 40 percent, 50 percent, or 60 percent of this median are considered relatively income poor. The higher poverty threshold is used by the European Commission to monitor social inclusion processes in member states (that is, the so-called at-risk-of-poverty threshold). To adjust incomes for economies of scale within households, household income is divided by the square root of household size. All analyses apply sampling weights.

At the 60 percent threshold, about 13 percent of those age 65 and older were at risk of relative poverty in 2013. This was almost on par with poverty in the working-age population. However, for most of the period, poverty (using the 60 percent threshold) was substantially higher among the elderly than in the working-age population, although relative income poverty among the elderly declines substantially at lower poverty thresholds. At the 50 percent poverty threshold, old-age poverty drops to 5 percent. At the 40 percent poverty threshold, less than 2 percent of the elderly are at risk. At these very low levels of income, poverty was lower among the elderly than in the working-age population throughout most of the observation period. Thus, in terms of more severe forms of economic hardship, elderly persons in Sweden seem to be rather well protected. This result corroborates other findings in the literature showing that the share of materially deprived people older than age 65 is very low in Sweden (Radoslaw and Asghar 2016). In terms of nonmaterial living conditions, not much research exists on the Swedish elderly. However, at least one recent study challenges common ideas in the international literature that loneliness is becoming more prevalent among the elderly (Dykstra 2009). In Sweden, no increase in loneliness among older people is found in the past two decades, nor do more recent elderly cohorts report loneliness to a greater extent than previous cohorts (Dahlberg, Agahi, and Lennartsson 2018).

Focusing on developments among the elderly over time, their relative income position has deteriorated quite substantially since the mid-1990s, irrespective of which poverty threshold is used for analysis. At the 60 percent poverty threshold, poverty among the elderly has almost doubled. Three periods with extraordinary developments stand out. The first one is the rise in old-age poverty between 1995 and 2000. Over these years, incomes in the working-age population increased more than twice as fast as those of the elderly. Whereas the equivalized median disposable income in the working-age population (18–64 years) increased by 19 percentage points, it increased by only 8 percentage points among those age 65 and older. As a consequence, the poverty threshold also increased much faster than old-age incomes, thus throwing a growing number of elderly people into poverty (table 10.1).

FIGURE 10.1 Relative income poverty in the elderly population and among those working age at various thresholds, 1995–2013

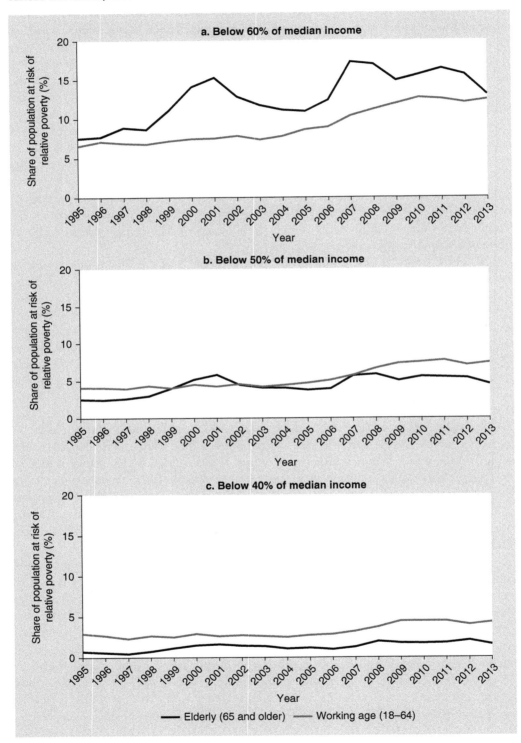

SOURCE: HEK (Hushållens ekonomi).

TABLE 10.1 **Median equivalized household disposable income in different age groups, 1995–2013**

	Total population		Elderly (65+ years)		Working age (18–64 years)	
	SKr	Percentage change	SKr	Percentage change	SKr	Percentage change
1995	121,289		100,433		129,278	
1996	123,329	1.7	102,396	2.0	130,965	1.3
1997	126,400	2.5	102,685	0.3	135,620	3.6
1998	128,398	1.6	103,759	1.0	137,736	1.6
1999	135,031	5.2	107,204	3.3	143,851	4.4
2000	142,352	5.4	108,367	1.1	153,325	6.6
2001	150,113	5.5	112,366	3.7	163,190	6.4
2002	156,968	4.6	119,509	6.4	170,770	4.6
2003	161,077	2.6	123,962	3.7	174,860	2.4
2004	165,861	3.0	127,164	2.6	179,754	2.8
2005	171,176	3.2	134,385	5.7	184,766	2.8
2006	179,507	4.9	138,961	3.4	194,309	5.2
2007	195,269	8.8	145,860	5.0	211,511	8.9
2008	203,187	4.1	154,065	5.6	220,357	4.2
2009	205,192	1.0	158,420	2.8	222,161	0.8
2010	210,219	2.4	162,978	2.9	228,164	2.7
2011	219,925	4.6	170,288	4.5	240,131	5.2
2012	225,067	2.3	176,256	3.5	244,547	1.8
2013	227,740	1.2	181,703	3.1	246,346	0.7

SOURCE: HEK (Hushållens ekonomi).

NOTE: SKr = Swedish kronor.

The second interesting result in figure 10.1 is the sharp rise in old-age poverty in 2007. This increase is most likely due to the introduction of an earned income tax credit, which raised the median income used in the calculation of poverty thresholds. The earned income tax credit does not apply to old-age pensions. After the introduction of the earned income tax credit in 2007, the equivalized median disposable household income in the working-age population increased by 9 percentage points in a single year, versus only 5 percentage points among the elderly. Despite the introduction and expansion of a special tax allowance for persons aged 65 and older, discussion is ongoing about the different tax treatment of earned income and pension income in Sweden. As of January 2018, taxes on old-age pensions were again reduced, and it is estimated that about 75 percent of the elderly will gain up to SKr 5,000 from this reform. All else equal, this lowering of taxes imposed on pensions will reduce relative income poverty among the elderly, although the exact redistributive consequences of the tax reform are difficult to assess at this stage.

The third conspicuous period in figure 10.1 is the decline in old-age poverty in the early 2000s, most noticeable at the 60 percent poverty threshold. Providing a solid explanation for this development is tricky. One tentative explanation is the rather substantial rise in unemployment in these years, which supposedly resulted in a slowdown of general income growth. Between 2001 and 2006, incomes among the elderly actually increased faster than in the working-age population (table 10.1). Whereas the equivalized median income among the elderly increased by 24 percentage points over these years, it increased by only 19 percentage points among those in their economically active years. According to Eurostat (the statistical agency of the European Union), the unemployment rate in Sweden increased from 5.8 percent to 7.7 percent between 2001 and 2005. Notably, when economic hardships declined among the elderly in the early 2000s, relative income poverty increased in the working-age population, from 7.5 percent in 2001 to 8.6 percent in 2005.

Relative income poverty only reveals how certain groups in society fare compared with the general population, irrespective of whether their incomes in real terms (that is, net of inflation) have in fact increased. The so-called anchored poverty rate provides a complementary account of developments in old-age incomes. It captures changes in poverty while keeping developments in living standards constant. Anchored poverty rates are particularly useful in periods of rapid economic transformation when the relative income position of poor people may be quite stable because of similar shifts in median incomes, but where low incomes have indeed changed, either as a result of economic growth or because of contraction (Atkinson et al. 2002).

Figure 10.2 shows the anchored poverty rate among the Swedish elderly (65 years and older) for the period 1995–2013. The poverty thresholds are set at 40 percent, 50 percent, and 60 percent of the equivalized median disposable household income in the total population in 1995. This median income is then updated for subsequent years according to movements in consumer prices. Thus, in this analysis, the poverty threshold is independent of changes in general income growth. It is only affected by movements in prices. The median equivalized disposable income among the elderly (65 years and older) in constant 1995 prices is also plotted, as is the similar median for the working-age population (18–64 years). The pattern is quite striking. Although relative income poverty increased among the elderly (figure 10.1), the anchored poverty rate declined substantially, particularly up to 2007, after which it remained more stable. The decline in the anchored poverty rate is most pronounced at the highest (60 percent) poverty threshold, but it is also visible at lower poverty thresholds. Between 1995 and 2013, the yearly increase in prices was about 1.2 percent. The corresponding yearly increase in median incomes among the elderly was about 3.6 percent (not shown). It can therefore be concluded that for the period 1995–2013, the purchasing power of the elderly improved. This is also illustrated by the sharp increase in the real value of median disposable income among the elderly. Notably, however, because the median income among those in working age increased even faster, the relative income position of the elderly deteriorated (as indicated earlier in the analyses of relative income poverty).

Poverty risks are not evenly distributed in society, neither in the total population, nor among the elderly. Figure 10.3 shows relative income poverty in different elderly groups, measured at the 60 percent poverty threshold in 2013. Because the scale of equivalence used in poverty measurement may affect the results, figure 10A.1 in annex A shows similar

FIGURE 10.2 **Anchored old-age poverty and equivalized median disposable income in different age groups, 1995–2013**

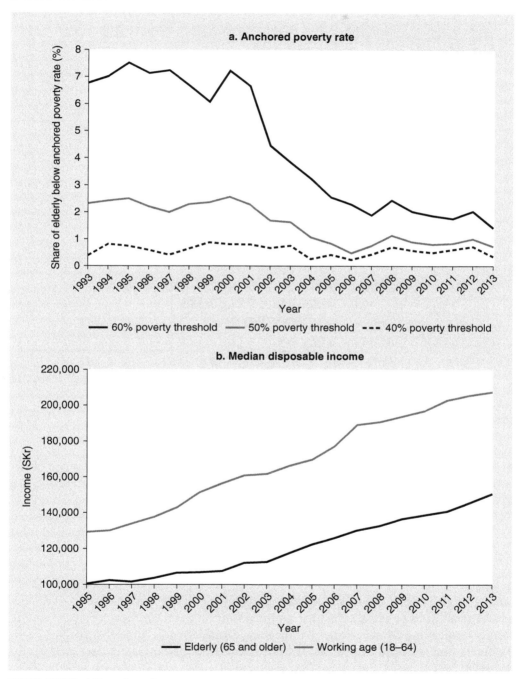

SOURCE: HEK (Hushållens ekonomi).

NOTE: In constant 1995 prices. SKr = Swedish kronor.

FIGURE 10.3 **Relative income poverty by household type, age, gender, education, and migration in the elderly population, 2013**
60 percent poverty threshold

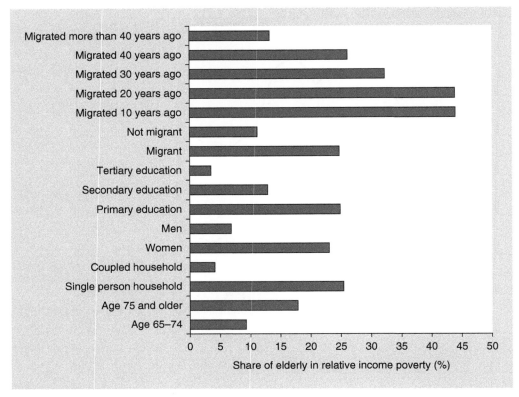

SOURCE: HEK (Hushållens ekonomi).

decomposed poverty rates using the modified Organisation for Economic Co-operation and Development (OECD) equivalence scale, instead of the square root of household size described earlier. The modified OECD scale was proposed by Haagenaars et al. (1994) and is the preferred equivalence scale of Eurostat. It assigns a value of 1.0 to the household head, a value of 0.5 to each additional adult member, and a value of 0.3 to each child. This change in equivalence scale hardly affects the interpretation of the results.

Relative income poverty is much higher among the oldest (75 and older) than among those age 65–74. Relative income poverty among the elderly is also concentrated among single persons. Slightly more than 25 percent of single persons age 65 and older are relatively income poor, compared with a poverty rate of less than 5 percent among elderly coupled households. Elderly women are in a particularly vulnerable position, with a poverty rate of about 22 percent. Relative income poverty among elderly men is substantially lower, about 7 percent. Observed gender differences in old-age incomes have brought about a discussion on the generosity (including indexation) of guaranteed pensions, incomplete take-up of housing supplements, and the role of survivors' benefits and other compensatory measures. The discussion is also centered on issues related to unequal pay and differences in working careers of men and women, which tend to spill over to the pension system and influence the formation of incomes in old age (Möhring 2014; Swedish Social Insurance Inspectorate 2017).

The results also clearly illustrate the role of education for old-age incomes, something that probably reflects differences in earnings and thus pension contributions during economically active years. Relative income poverty is almost doubled among elderly people with only primary education (about 25 percent), compared with those with secondary education (about 13 percent). Poverty drops even more among the elderly with tertiary education (about 3 percent). Another group with high poverty risks is elderly migrants, especially if they moved to Sweden as adults. More than 40 percent of the elderly who moved to Sweden in the latest two decades can be defined as relatively income poor. Notably, the relative income position of elderly migrants and those with more than 40 years of residence in Sweden is about 13 percent, and on par with the poverty rate of all elderly citizens.

The analysis does not capture the net contribution of each risk factor to old-age poverty, which can be calculated using a simple multiple regression framework. A multiple regression uses two or more variables and calculates their relative contribution in predicting the value of an outcome of interest. Figure 10.4 shows the beta coefficients of a linear probability model using old-age poverty (age 65 and older) at the 60 percent income

FIGURE 10.4 **Linear probabilities of relative income poverty in different elderly risk groups, 2013** 60 percent poverty threshold

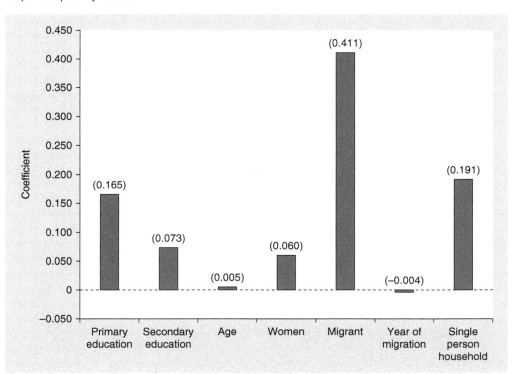

SOURCE: Original estimation based on HEK (Hushållens ekonomi) data.

NOTE: Unstandardized beta coefficients in parentheses. All coefficients are statistically significant at p<0.000. Elderly = age 65 and older.

threshold as the outcome of interest. The analysis is confined to 2013, and all coefficients are statistically significant at the 1 percent level. The value of each coefficient can easily be transformed into percentage points of change in probability by multiplying it by 100. The beta coefficient of primary education is 0.165. Thus, the probability of elderly people with only primary education being relatively income poor is 16.5 percentage points higher than those with tertiary education (the reference category).

In addition to education, migration background and household composition are also strongly associated with old-age poverty. Notably, the net effect of gender is much smaller in comparison, which is related to substantial overlaps between risk factors. Figure 10.5 therefore shows relative income poverty by gender in different elderly risk groups, using the 60 percent poverty threshold. Old-age poverty is indeed strongly gendered; the poverty rate of elderly women is much higher than that of elderly men across all identified risk factors. For example, whereas the poverty rate of elderly men hardly changes as they grow older (compare figure 10.3), the poverty rate increases substantially among elderly women. Also in terms of education, migration background, and household type, elderly women have substantially higher poverty risks than elderly men.

The observation that poverty risks among the elderly increase with age brings the issue of cohorts to the forefront of the analysis. Figure 10.6 shows the association between age and relative poverty separately for different elderly cohorts, using the 60 percent poverty threshold. The analysis is based on so-called synthetic cohorts (Deaton 1985; Shorrocks 1975), in which different cohorts are formed defined by year of birth and

FIGURE 10.5 Relative income poverty by gender in different elderly risk groups, 2013
60 percent poverty threshold

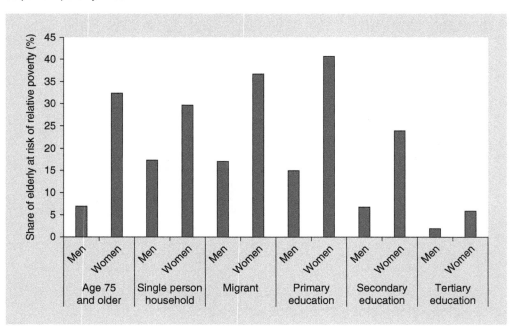

SOURCE: HEK (Hushållens ekonomi).

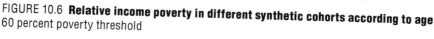

FIGURE 10.6 **Relative income poverty in different synthetic cohorts according to age**
60 percent poverty threshold

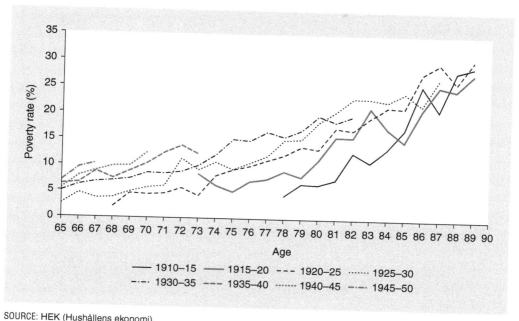

SOURCE: HEK (Hushållens ekonomi).

followed across successive waves of data. Although cohort membership is fixed over time, the same individuals are not followed as they grow older. Because the analysis is based on successive and independent cross-sections, the composition of each synthetic cohort may actually change over time, something that of course complicates interpretation of the results. Nonetheless, two findings are particularly noteworthy.

First, younger cohorts face consistently higher poverty risks than older cohorts. Thus, when cohorts reach retirement age, their poverty risks tend to be higher than those of the previous cohort. For instance, when the cohort born between 1925 and 1930 reached retirement age (65 years), about 2 percent were at risk of poverty. By comparison, about 6 percent were poor when they reached retirement age in the cohort born one decade later (between 1935 and 1940). These initial differences in poverty risks between cohorts at the onset of retirement are not recovered at later ages, but more recent cohorts quite consistently continue to face higher poverty risks than older cohorts.

Second, for each elderly cohort, poverty increases with age. The drivers of this relationship are complex. Notwithstanding that there may be compositional changes, figure 10.7 shows changes in different income components as a synthetic cohort of elderly people born between 1930 and 1950 is growing older. In addition to developments in household disposable income, the figure also shows changes in work income, the NDC pension, occupational pensions, the guaranteed minimum pension, as well as housing supplements and social assistance. It should be noted that this list of income components is not exhaustive. For ease of interpretation, capital income, private pensions, the FDC premium, and survivors' benefits are not included. Work income includes salaries and

FIGURE 10.7 **Developments in the income packages of a synthetic cohort born 1930–50 according to age**

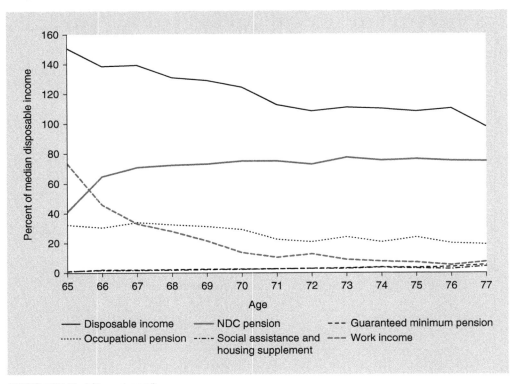

SOURCE: HEK (Hushållens ekonomi).

NOTE: Percent of median equivalized disposable household income in total population. NDC = nonfinancial defined contribution.

wages, as well as income from self-employment. The NDC pension category includes the supplementary pension (*tilläggspension*) paid to those born before 1954, and who have accumulated pension rights in the old system. The guaranteed minimum pension includes benefits paid to those born before 1938 and who were eligible for the people's pension (*folkpension*) in 2002. Each income component is shown as a percentage of median household disposable income. All incomes are adjusted for household size and composition using the same square root scale as above.

As expected, disposable income declines quite markedly as the cohort grows older. Before age 70, the decline in disposable income is mostly a result of a sharp reduction of work income, but also due to a decline in occupational pensions. In Sweden, people can choose how they want to receive their occupational pension. Although most pensioners choose to receive smaller lifelong payments, an increasing share of the elderly opt for a much shorter period, which typically increases payments during the first five or ten years of retirement (Hagen 2017).

After age 70, there is a slight, but noticeable, decline in the NDC pension, which is not fully compensated for by corresponding increases in the pension guarantee or the housing supplement (including social assistance). Notwithstanding compositional changes, it should be noted that the NDC pension is not fully indexed to the growth in average incomes. An amount corresponding to 1.6 percentage points is deducted from the annual percentage increase in the so-called income index, which is used each year by the pension authority to adjust the value of the NDC pension. Over time, there is thus a gradual erosion of the NDC pension vis-à-vis growth in average incomes. The deduction of 1.6 percentage points does not apply to the supplementary pension. The indexation of the NDC pension may also be discounted in periods of economic turmoil as a result of financial imbalances in the public pension system. In extreme situations, pensions may even be reduced. During the introduction of the new pension system, it was expected that this automatic balancing of the NDC pension would hardly ever be activated. However, the automatic brake in the Swedish pension system has already reduced NDC pensions on three occasions—in 2010, 2011, and 2014.

Insufficient indexation of the guaranteed minimum pension has resulted in quite a substantial erosion of benefits compared with general living standards. In this analysis, the low-income targeted character of the guaranteed minimum pension is likely to disguise much of this relative decline in benefits. It should therefore be noted that between 2003 and 2017, the guaranteed minimum pension for a single person increased by 16 percent (from SKr 6,852 per month to SKr 7,952 per month). By comparison, average gross salaries (according to the OECD) increased by 47 percent (from SKr 24,481 per month in 2003 to SKr 35,987 per month in 2017). In net amounts (that is, after taxes), the difference in the growth of the guaranteed minimum pension and average incomes is probably even greater because of the more favorable tax treatment of work income noted earlier.

The housing supplement has eroded as well, given that housing costs have increased faster than the ceiling above which no benefits are paid. In 2003, about 25 percent of beneficiaries of the housing supplement had rents above this ceiling. In 2017, this share increased to slightly more than 50 percent. In 2018, the government increased the ceiling, which is expected to lower the share to about 35 percent (Social Ministry 2018). This analysis lumps together the housing supplement and social assistance. However, it should be mentioned that the lion's share of incomes in this category is made up of the housing supplement for elderly people. In 2016, fewer than than 1 percent of Swedish pensioners received social assistance, the clear majority (about 93 percent) of whom are migrants with incomplete access to the minimum guaranteed pension and housing supplements (PROP. 2017/18:1). Social assistance for the elderly has increased somewhat faster than the minimum guaranteed amount, but it has still fallen behind the growth in wages. Between 2003 and 2017, social assistance for elderly persons increased by about 32 percent (from SKr 4,162 per month for a single person in 2003 to SKr 5,499 in 2013). The discussion above indicates that effective indexation of benefits is important to avoid eroded pension benefits. However, without panel data that observe incomes of the same person over time, it is difficult to analyze the extent to which indexation principles impair the effectiveness of the minimum guaranteed pension and other low-income targeted benefits to compensate for declines in other parts of the pension system.

Redistribution

This chapter's goal of providing a policy perspective on old-age incomes makes it reasonable to focus on the issue of redistribution. Conceptually, pension policies can redistribute vertically between the rich and the poor, and horizontally over the life course. Empirically, the analysis does not distinguish between these two forms of redistribution. The extent to which policy redistributes economic resources and reduces poverty is often assessed by comparing the shape of the income distribution before and after social transfers and benefits. To distinguish the effects of different types of policies, transfers and benefits are often ordered sequentially depending on at which stage of the distributive process from market to disposable income they are supposed to enter. The reduction in poverty is subsequently calculated at each step of the distributive process. Although intuitively powerful, this sequential method in poverty measurement and redistribution requires that transfers and benefits enter the distributive process in a natural order. Otherwise, the results may be very misleading (Nelson 2003).

Because the ordering of transfers and benefits in the distributive process is very difficult to achieve in this case, a simpler marginal method is used. Redistribution is assessed by deducting transfers and benefits from disposable income, after which the poverty rate is recalculated. For example, in the case of the NDC pension, this income component is deducted from disposable income and the poverty rate recalculated. Redistribution is assessed by inspecting the difference between the poverty rate of disposable income less the NDC pension and the poverty rate of disposable income. This procedure is repeated for each component in the transfer and benefit package. For the sake of simplicity, transfers and benefits are gross of taxes. It should be noted that neither the marginal nor the sequential method is additive. Depending on the interplay between transfers and benefits in the distributive process, the sum of each component may be lower or higher than the total reduction in poverty. Although there are more complex methods of assessing how different parts of the transfer and benefit package redistribute incomes and additively contribute to the total reduction in poverty (Nelson 2004), the marginal method serves the purpose of providing a first analysis of the relative importance of different income components. In the counterfactual analyses that follow, any behavioral effects that may appear in the absence of policy are not estimated.

Figure 10.8 shows the extent to which different types of transfers and benefits reduce old-age poverty. Data are from 2013 and redistribution is calculated by using a poverty threshold corresponding to 60 percent of the equivalized median disposable household income in the total population. The benefit and transfer package is divided into private pensions, occupational pensions, the NDC pension, the FDC premium pension, the guaranteed minimum pension, survivors' benefits, and housing supplements (including social assistance). Occupational pensions, the NDC pension, the guaranteed minimum, and housing supplements (including social assistance) are defined and measured similarly as above. The FDC premium is simply the fully funded component of the new pension system introduced in the mid-1990s, as noted above. Survivors' benefits are only paid to widows. The program was abolished in 1990 and is in the process of being phased out. For those currently receiving survivors' benefits, these will continue to be paid. Widows who got married before 1990 may still qualify for a survivors' benefit. All others, including men, may choose to add survivors' protection to their FDC premium pension, whereby

FIGURE 10.8 **Reduction of relative income poverty attributed to different income components by elderly risk group, 2013**
60 percent poverty threshold

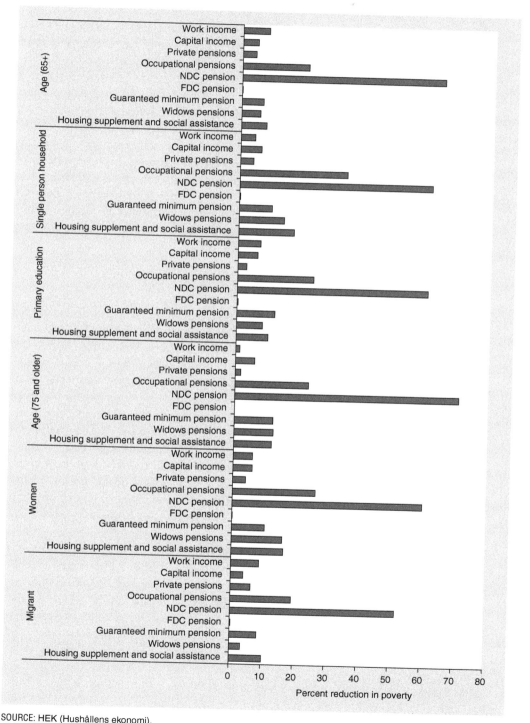

SOURCE: HEK (Hushållens ekonomi).

NOTE: FDC = financial defined contribution; NDC = nonfinancial defined contribution.

benefits are transferred from the deceased spouse to the survivor. Similar types of survivors' protection may be added to occupational and private pensions. Capital income includes earned interest and dividends, as well as capital gains and losses. Redistribution is assessed among the elderly as a whole, and separately for major elderly risk groups.

The single most important factor for income redistribution is the NDC pension. Without this component, and all else equal, old-age poverty would have been more than 60 percentage points higher. Occupational pensions come next with a reduction in old-age poverty of about 20 percentage points. The remaining transfers and benefits separately reduce poverty by less than 10 percentage points. Switching focus and analyzing poverty reduction in the old-age risk groups identified previously, it is clear that the guaranteed minimum pension, survivors' benefits, and the housing supplement (and social assistance) become slightly more important. Particularly, this pattern is apparent among elderly women and elderly single-person households. Notably, the guaranteed minimum pension contributes slightly less to poverty reduction among migrants compared with the other old-age risk groups. This result is likely due to the design of the guarantee, given that full benefits are only available for those with at least 40 years of residence in Sweden (from age 16). Three years of residence in Sweden are required to receive a partial guaranteed minimum pension.

Inequality

Although relative poverty is closely linked to the larger issue of inequality, the focus is very much on developments in low-end incomes. This section broadens the analysis and takes into consideration the distribution of incomes above the poverty threshold. Figure 10.9 shows Gini coefficients of disposable income from 1995 to 2013. The Gini coefficient is a measure of statistical dispersion commonly used in analyses of income inequality. Gini coefficients normally vary between zero and one (values greater than one may be observed if some people have negative incomes). Gini coefficients close to zero resemble situations of near-perfect equality, in which everyone has very similar incomes. A Gini coefficient of one reflects maximum inequality, where one person has all income. Income inequality is analyzed separately for the elderly (age 65 and older) and the working-age population (age 18–64). Because capital income has been a main driver of income inequality in many rich countries (Atkinson and Piketty 2007), including Sweden (Björklund and Jäntti 2011; Roine and Waldenström 2008), Gini coefficients of disposable income are shown before and after capital income.

Similar to developments in the working-age population, income inequality has increased among the elderly, particularly between 2003 and 2007. The rise in income inequality is not solely driven by changes in capital income, given that the Gini coefficient continues to increase after capital income is excluded from the analysis. However, the rise in income inequality is slightly less dramatic after excluding capital income. Even though changes in the distribution of capital income contributed to making the incomes of the elderly more unequal, the evidence thus shows the relevance of focusing on a broader set of income sources.

For most of the period, and especially after 2000, incomes (including those from capital) were distributed more unevenly among the elderly than in the working-age population. This age-related difference in income inequality also became more pronounced.

FIGURE 10.9 **Income inequality, 1995–2013: Gini coefficients of disposable income of elderly and working-age populations**

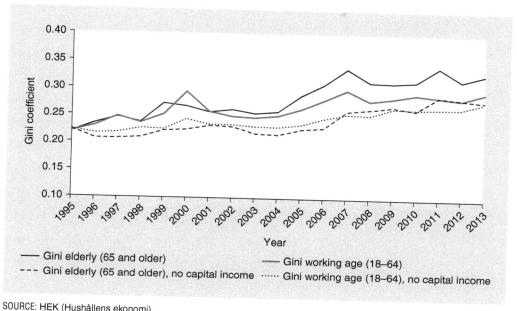

SOURCE: HEK (Hushållens ekonomi).

Income inequalities among the elderly and in the working-age population were quite similar in the mid-1990s. At the end of the period, in 2013, income inequality was clearly higher among the elderly than in the working-age population. Thus, income differences are reinforced in old age. To understand the drivers of these changes to inequality of old-age incomes, the section next analyzes the extent to which different types of incomes add to income inequality, or reduce income differences in old age.

Table 10.2 shows the contribution of different income sources to inequality of old-age incomes at three cross-sections: 2003, 2007, and 2013. Two measures are calculated: the concentration coefficient and the income share of each income source (expressed as percentages). Multiplying the concentration coefficient and the income share provides an impression of how each income source affects inequality (Kakwani 1977; Lerman and Yitzhaki 1985). The concentration coefficient shows the distribution of each income source when households are ranked from high to low according to disposable income. The concentration coefficient varies between minus one and plus one. Positive values indicate that the income source concentrates in the upper half of the income distribution, and all else equal increases inequality. Negative values show that the income source concentrates in the lower half, and—all else equal—reduces inequality. The income share simply shows the relative size of each income source in disposable income. A negative income share means that the component is deducted from disposable income (for example, applies to taxes). A change in the concentration coefficient will have more profound consequences for inequality the larger the share of an income source in disposable income, and vice versa.

TABLE 10.2 **Concentration coefficients and income shares of different income sources in the population age 65 and older (2003, 2007, and 2013), including and excluding capital income**

a. Including capital income

	Concentration coefficient			Income share (%)		
	2003	2007	2013	2003	2007	2013
Work income	0.74	0.69	0.71	11.3	13.1	17.1
Capital income	0.74	0.81	0.84	13.5	29.4	20.2
Public pensions	0.10	0.09	0.07	84.4	68.2	62.0
NDC pension	*0.19*	*0.16*	*0.11*	*69.7*	*59.1*	*55.7*
FDC pension	*0.42*	*0.36*	*0.29*	*0.0*	*0.1*	*0.7*
Survivors' benefit	*−0.26*	*−0.35*	*−0.35*	*4.7*	*3.1*	*2.2*
Guaranteed minimum pension	*−0.33*	*−0.38*	*−0.31*	*10.1*	*5.8*	*3.4*
Private pensions	0.55	0.50	0.42	9.6	8.0	7.4
Occupational pensions	0.48	0.45	0.44	19.3	17.7	21.7
Housing supplement (including social assistance)	−0.52	−0.60	−0.33	3.0	2.2	3.2
Taxes	0.36	0.41	0.43	−41.0	−38.6	−31.7

b. Excluding capital income

	Concentration coefficient			Income share (%)		
	2003	2007	2013	2003	2007	2013
Work income	0.76	0.76	0.72	12.8	17.4	20.7
Public pensions	0.10	0.09	0.07	95.6	90.0	74.9
NDC pension	*0.19*	*0.16*	*0.11*	*79.0*	*78.1*	*67.3*
FDC premium	*0.43*	*0.41*	*0.31*	*0.0*	*0.2*	*0.9*
Survivors' benefit	*−0.28*	*−0.38*	*−0.37*	*5.3*	*4.1*	*2.6*
Guaranteed minimum pension	*−0.34*	*−0.42*	*−0.30*	*11.3*	*7.7*	*4.1*
Private pensions	0.54	0.50	0.40	10.9	10.6	9.0
Occupational pensions	0.48	0.47	0.44	21.8	23.3	26.2
Housing supplement (including social assistance)	−0.44	−0.52	−0.24	3.4	2.9	3.9
Taxes	0.29	0.29	0.31	−44.5	−44.2	−34.7

SOURCE: HEK (Hushållens ekonomi).

NOTE: FDC = financial defined contribution; NDC = nonfinancial defined contribution.

The analysis begins by dividing disposable income into seven different components: work income, capital income, public pensions, private pensions, occupational pensions, housing supplements (including social assistance), and taxes (table 10.2, panel a). The results clearly show why income inequality has increased among the elderly.

Although the distributive profile of public pensions became more equalizing to disposable income (the concentration coefficient moved somewhat closer to zero), their share in disposable income decreased substantially. This decline in public pensions is particularly evident between 2003 and 2007 when the rise in income inequality among the elderly was pronounced. Meanwhile, other income sources with less egalitarian distributive profiles (larger positive concentration coefficients) increased their shares of disposable income, causing income inequality to rise. This particularly concerns developments in capital income, whose income share increased from 13.5 percent in 2003 to 29.4 percent in 2007. The decline in the income share of taxes between 2003 and 2007 is most likely associated with the substantial increase in capital income, which is taxed at a lower rate than work income.

Panel a of table 10.2 also shows a more detailed disaggregation of income inequality, focusing on different components of the public pension system. Similar to the previous analysis, the NDC pension, the FDC premium pension, survivors' benefits, the guaranteed minimum pension, and housing supplements (including social assistance) are separated. Because the guaranteed minimum pension and housing supplements (including social assistance) are pension- and income-tested, respectively, they obviously have distributive profiles that are more pro-poor than the NDC and FDC pensions (that is, the concentration coefficient is closer to zero or negative). Between 2003 and 2007, the guaranteed minimum pension and housing supplements (including social assistance) became increasingly targeted at elderly people with very low incomes (the associated concentration coefficients became increasingly negative). Considering the guaranteed minimum pension, it is evident that the equalizing effect of this change is circumscribed by a substantial reduction in the relative size of benefits.

The increased low-income targeting of the guaranteed minimum pension, as well as reductions in its income share, are most likely due to the insufficiency of price indexation in an overall economic context of real earnings increasing at about 2 percent per year, leading to a gradual erosion in the relative value of benefits, noted above. As a result, a larger share of elderly persons with low incomes is above the threshold used to determine eligibility for the guaranteed minimum pension. Data from the Swedish Pension Authority (Pensionsmyndigheten) show that the share of pensioners receiving the guaranteed minimum pension declined from about 42 percent in 2010 to 31 percent in 2017.

The FDC premium pension is currently such a small part of the public pension system that it hardly has an effect on inequality. Currently, the premium pension has a distributional profile that is less equalizing (has a larger concentration coefficient) to income inequality than the income pension, but this mostly reflects that there are still pensioners who retired before the premium pension came into force, or pensioners who have only been able to allocate a few years of contributions. It is reasonable to expect that the contribution of the premium pension to inequality will increase in the future, because a greater number of old-age pensioners will have allocated more funds within this component of the public pension system, and as a consequence the share of pension income contributed by the FDC pension will increase. However, since contributions to the premium pension are fixed at 2.5 percent of pensionable income for everyone (compared with contributions of 16.5 percent of income going to the NDC pension), it can be expected that the concentration coefficient of the FDC pension will decline. It already declined between 2003 and 2013. The pension premium will have fully matured in 2040, and in principle, its distributive profile should be more similar to that of the income pension, which includes benefits accrued in the old ATP (Allmän tilläggspension) system, later replaced by the mandatory public NDC and FDC premium pension.

Panel b of table 10.2 shows the same type of inequality decomposition by income source, but excluding capital income. The overall conclusion is analogous to the previous one. Income inequality among the elderly has increased, mainly because of a relative decline of public pensions, and a parallel increase in more unequal sources of income (now excluding capital income). Notably, both work income and occupational pensions now have substantially larger shares of disposable income, whereas the share of private pensions in total income has been quite stable. Tax deductions for savings in private pension funds were abolished in 2016, something that is likely to contribute to a decline in the share of private pensions in the future. The decline in the income share of taxes between 2007 and 2013 is most likely due to successive increases of the earned income tax credit each year between 2008 and 2011, combined with the introduction of a tax allowance for persons age 65 and older in 2009. The tax allowance for elderly persons was raised in 2010, 2011, and 2013.

Concluding Discussion

The major Swedish pension reform of the mid-1990s had multiple objectives, but the most important driving force behind the introduction of the new NDC scheme was financial (Könberg, Palmer, and Sundén 2006). The old pension system was on the verge of becoming unaffordable. Much has been written about the financial stability of the NDC component of the Swedish old-age pension system. This chapter instead focuses on social sustainability and the degree to which old-age incomes are equally distributed and higher than commonly applied poverty thresholds. Although old-age incomes are the result of complex processes that often operate over extended periods, the conclusions highlight three findings that add to the discussion about the social sustainability of the Swedish system of old-age pensions.

First, the income position of elderly persons in Sweden has become more precarious, although not because the incomes of pensioners have declined in real terms. Quite the contrary: median incomes among elderly persons have increased faster than prices. Yet incomes of the working-age population have increased even faster, and as a result the relative income position of the elderly has deteriorated. Although relative income poverty among the elderly resembles something like a rollercoaster pattern since the mid-1990s, the overall trend shows an increase.

The results are sensitive to the exact yardstick by which households are considered to be poor. In terms of more extreme levels of economic hardship (that is, incomes of less than 40 percent of the equivalized median disposable household income in the total population), elderly persons in Sweden are well protected. At these very low levels of income, relative poverty is actually lower among the elderly than in the working-age population. However, this pattern is reversed at higher poverty thresholds. At the 60 percent poverty threshold, a commonly accepted poverty threshold in the European Union, relative poverty has consistently been more widespread among the elderly than in the working-age population—throughout the whole observation period 1995–2013, and particularly toward the end.

Second, poverty risks in old age are not evenly distributed. Certain old-age sub-groups face exacerbated risks, including elderly single women, migrants, persons with only primary education, and people living on their own. The most important component in the disposable income of the elderly is the NDC pension, which also reduces poverty more substantially than other income components. Although the guaranteed minimum pension and housing supplements (including social assistance) become somewhat more important when the analysis focuses on particular old-age risk groups, it is evident that benefits are often insufficient to lift elderly households above commonly accepted poverty thresholds. Some indication also exists that the relative poverty risks increase for each cohort that reaches retirement age, something that obviously raises issues in relation to the social sustainability of the Swedish pension system. In particular, the erosion of the guaranteed minimum pension (vis-à-vis the development of wages), which has continued through both center-left and center-right political alliances, raises concerns. Perhaps more effort should be devoted to crafting an effective indexation of the minimum guarantee.

Third, the incomes of the elderly have become more unevenly distributed since the 1990s, reflecting a more general trend related to earnings. However, since the mid-1990s, income inequality has increased faster among those age 65 and older than among the working-age population. Much of this increase in income inequality among the elderly is due to a relative decline in the share of public pensions in total income, and corresponding increases in income sources that are distributed more unevenly. In addition to the increase of capital income as a major source of inequality in old age, the slow but pervasive increases of work income after (partial) retirement and the gradual rise of occupational pensions (for those who receive them) have also made old-age incomes more unequal.

Improvements in minimum pensions are high on the political agenda in Sweden. The parliamentary review group on the Swedish pension system (Pensionsgruppen) recently suggested several reforms to improve the lowest pensions, including increases in the guaranteed minimum pension and in housing supplements (Social Ministry 2018). These reforms certainly would strengthen the degree to which the Swedish pension system provides basic security in old age, and possibly would also reduce observed differences in poverty between population subgroups—including those defined by gender. Yet the suggested increases in the guaranteed minimum pension and housing supplements may not necessarily be sufficient remedies. Indexation principles are important to ensure that benefits are not eroded over the longer term. However, changes in indexation are not on the political agenda at the moment, and were not considered by the parliamentary review group. One important objective of the guaranteed pension, and to some extent the housing supplement, is to make sure that the poorest pensioners are not falling too far behind other income groups. Wage indexation is therefore a realistic alternative to price indexation or ad hoc political decisions to update benefits on a regular basis.

Another neglected issue concerns benefit take-up. Whereas eligibility for the pension guarantee is automatically assessed, the housing supplement for elderly persons suffers from an incomplete take-up of about 40 percent of those eligible for benefits. The take-up of social assistance for elderly persons is even worse, at about 20 percent, according to one inquiry (Riksrevisionen 2013). The reasons for this low take-up are not that well researched. Some indications suggest that many elderly people simply have too little knowledge about these programs. Other suggested reasons are failures in administration and stigma; the latter is more of an issue in relation to social assistance. Although estimates of benefit take-up should be treated with caution because of serious methodological difficulties, the results nonetheless warrant closer consideration in debates about old-age poverty.

Considering inequality in old-age incomes, it should be noted that about 10 percent of the Swedish workforce lacks collective agreements and is thus not covered by an occupational pension. Although greater coverage of occupational pensions would probably reduce some of the differences in old-age incomes, tax reforms could potentially reduce inequalities even further. Whereas the differential tax treatment of work and pension income will most likely disappear in the near future, there is no serious political discussion about changes in the tax treatment of capital income, or reforms to make occupational pensions compulsory, as suggested by Palmer and Könberg (2019). In Sweden, occupational pensions are generally considered to be outside the scope of political decision making, and instead subject to negotiations between the social partners.

The financial sustainability of the Swedish pension system is arguably essential for maintaining adequate provisions for current and future generations. Yet the importance of social sustainability should not be downplayed. Ensuring adequate incomes for all elderly people, without the better-off increasingly availing themselves of alternative private or occupational arrangements, would most likely increase popular support and willingness to contribute to the public system. Envisioned this way, social sustainability supports financial sustainability, promoting positive-sum solutions (Birnbaum et al. 2017). The generosity and accessibility of specific components in the pension system can of course be adjusted to achieve more desirable social inclusion outcomes in old age.

Because incomes in Sweden are growing more unequal at a rapid pace, as they are in the working-age population, the possibilities of pension systems with clear elements of direct contributions to deliver on a wider set of sustainability concerns need to be assessed repeatedly. A recent European Commission (2018b) projection of pension benefits in Sweden estimates that old-age poverty will continue to increase at a steady pace. Over the coming decades, and as a consequence of increased longevity, pension benefits in Sweden are expected to decline. The at-risk-of-poverty rate among the elderly is also expected to grow by an additional 8 percentage points, landing slightly above 25 percent of the Swedish elderly in poverty by 2070. An implicit remedy to this scenario is to postpone retirement by introducing measures that would increase the effective retirement age. However, without due consideration to inequalities in working conditions, this strategy of prolonging working careers may further accentuate the need to strengthen the redistributive components of the Swedish old-age pension system.

ANNEX 10A

FIGURE 10A.1 **Relative income poverty (60 percent poverty threshold) by household type, age, gender, education, and migration in the elderly population, 2013**
OECD modified equivalence scale

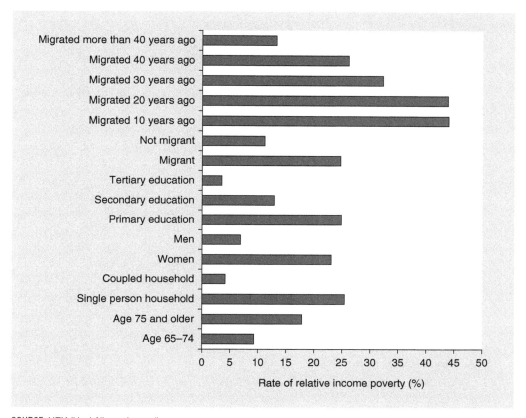

SOURCE: HEK (Hushållens ekonomi).

NOTE: OECD = Organisation for Economic Co-operation and Development.

References

Atkinson, Anthony B., Bea Cantillon, Eric Marlier, and Brian Nolan. 2002. *Social Indicators: The EU and Social Inclusion.* Oxford: Oxford University Press.

Atkinson, Anthony B., and Thomas Piketty. 2007. *Top Incomes over the 20th Century. A Contrast between Continental European and English-Speaking Countries.* Oxford: Oxford University Press.

Birnbaum, Simon, Tommy Ferrarini, Kenneth Nelson, and Joakim Palme. 2017. *The Generational Welfare Contract: Justice, Institutions and Outcomes.* Cheltenham: Edward Elgar.

Björklund, Anders, and Markus Jäntti. 2011. *Inkomstfördelningen i Sverige.* SNS Välfärdsrapport. Stockholm: SNS Förlag.

Dahlberg, Lena, Neda Agahi, and Carin Lennartsson. 2018. "Lonelier Than Ever? Loneliness of Older People over Two Decades." *Archives of Gerontology and Geriatrics* 75 (March–April): 96–103.

Deaton, Angus. 1985. "Panel Data from a Time Series of Cross-Sections." *Journal of Econometrics* 30 (1–2): 109–26.

Dykstra, Pearl A. 2009. "Older Adult Loneliness: Myths and Realities." *European Journal of Ageing* 6 (2): 91–100.

European Commission. 2018a. *Pension Adequacy Report 2018—Current and Future Income Adequacy in Old Age in the EU.* Volume 2. Brussels: European Commission.

———. 2018b. *The 2018 Pension Adequacy Report: Current and Future Income Adequacy in Old Age in the EU.* Volume 1. Brussels: European Commission.

Grech, Aaron G. 2013. "Assessing the Sustainability of Pension Reforms in Europe." *Journal of International and Comparative Social Policy* 29 (2): 143–62.

———. 2014. "Evaluating the Possible Impact of Pension Reforms on Elderly Poverty in Europe." *Social Policy and Administration* 49 (1): 68–87.

Hagen, Johannes. 2017. *Utbetalningstider i Tjänstepensionssystemet.* Stockholm: SNS Förlag.

Kakwani, Nanak C. 1977. "Measurement of Tax Progressivity: An International Comparison." *Economic Journal* 87 (345): 71–80.

Könberg, Bo, Edward Palmer, and Annika Sundén. 2006. "The NDC Reform in Sweden: The 1994 Legislation to the Present." In *Pension Reform—Issues and Prospects for Non-Financial Defined Contribution (NDC) Schemes*, edited by Robert Holzmann and Edward Palmer, 449–66. Washington, DC: World Bank.

Lerman, Robert, and Shlomo Yitzhaki. 1985. "Income Inequality Effects by Income Sources: A New Approach and Applications to the US." *Review of Economics and Statistics* 67 (1): 151–56.

Möhring, Katja. 2014. "Employment Histories and Pension Incomes in Europe. A Multilevel Analysis of the Role of Institutional Factors." *European Societies* 17 (1): 3–26. http://doi.org/1 0.1080/14616696.2014.934874.

Nelson, Kenneth. 2003. "Fighting Poverty: Comparative Studies on Social Insurance, Means-Tested Benefits and Income Redistribution." Dissertation Series 60. Swedish Institute for Social Research (SOFI), Stockholm.

———. 2004. "Mechanisms of Poverty Alleviation in the Welfare State. A Comparative Study of Anti-Poverty Effects of Non Means-Tested and Means-Tested Benefits in Five Countries in the 1990s." *Journal of European Social Policy* 14 (4): 371–90.

Palmer, Edward, and Bo Könberg. 2019. "The Swedish NDC Scheme: Success on Track with Room for Reflection." In *Progress and Challenges of Nonfinancial Defined Contribution Pension Schemes: Volume 1 Addressing Marginalization, Polarization, and the Labor Market*, edited by Robert Holzmann, Edward Palmer, Robert Palacios, and Stefano Sacchi, Chapter 2. Washington, DC: World Bank.

PROP. 2017/18:1. *Utgiftsområde 11. Förslag till statens budget för 2018. Ekonomisk trygghet vid ålderdom.* Stockholm: Finance Ministry.

Radoslaw, Antczak, and Zaidi Asghar. 2016. "Risk of Poverty among Older People in EU Countries." *ifo DICE Report* 14 (1): 37–46.

Riksrevisionen. 2013. *Bostadstillägg och äldreförsörjningsstöd till pensionärer—når förmånerna fram?* Stockholm: Riksrevisionen.

Roine, Jesper, and Daniel Waldenström. 2008. "The Evolution of Top Incomes in an Egalitarian Society: Sweden, 1903–2004." *Journal of Public Economics* 92 (1–2): 366–87.

Shorrocks, Anthony F. 1975. "The Age-Wealth Relationship: A Cross-Section and Cohort Analysis." *Review of Economic Statistics* 42 (2): 155–63.

Social Ministry. 2011. Efter 65—Inte Bara Pension. Ds 2011:42. Stockholm: Social Ministry.

———. *Jämställda pensioner?* Ds 2016:19. Stockholm: Social Ministry.

———. 2018. *Översyn av grundskyddet för pensionärer. Inriktning för ett nytt grundskydd.* Ds 2018:8. Stockholm: Social Ministry.

Swedish Social Insurance Inspectorate. 2017. *Kvinnors och Mäns Pensioner. En Analys av Skillnader och Spridning I Pensionsinkomster i Dag Och i Framtiden.* Rapport 2017:8. Stockholm: Swedish Social Insurance Inspectorate.

Townsend, Peter. 1979. *Poverty in the United Kingdom.* Berkeley, CA: University of California Press.

CHAPTER 11

Chile's Solidarity Pillar: A Benchmark for Adjoining a Zero Pillar with Defined Contribution Schemes

Eduardo Fajnzylber

Introduction to the Chilean Pension Scheme and the New Solidarity Pillar

The Chilean pension system has attracted the attention of the research community because Chile was the first country to replace a traditional pay-as-you-go (PAYG) scheme with a unique contributory pillar based entirely on individual savings accounts, managed by private fund managers (known as the AFP system).[1]

Before 2008, individuals with little or no pension rights could apply for an Assistance Pension (PASIS) or a Minimum Pension Guarantee (MPG). The PASIS program was targeted to poor individuals with no pension entitlements, providing a subpoverty benefit (as of 2008, US$110 per month) and subject to budget availability.[2] On the other hand, the MPG established a floor (equivalent to a monthly payment of US$222 as of 2008) for individuals with at least 20 years of contributions and personal income (wages or pensions) below the guaranteed level.[3] The MPG's combined restriction of minimum density and maximum income led to low coverage and a very limited poverty reduction effect.

In 2008, Chile enacted a new comprehensive pension reform that, among other changes, introduced a new poverty prevention pillar known as the New Solidarity Pillar (NSP). The reform replaced the above-mentioned programs with the NSP, a unique scheme that guarantees that all individuals in the 60 percent less affluent fraction of the population will have a guaranteed basic pension, regardless of their contribution history. This new program provides old-age and disability subsidies financed by general revenues.

THE NSP DESIGN
Eligibility requirements

To be eligible for NSP benefits, an individual must comply with five basic requirements[4]:

- *Age requirement.* Old-age recipients must be at least age 65; disability benefits are paid from age 18 to age 64 to individuals previously assessed by a disability commission as having permanent diminishment of their work capacity.[5]

The author is grateful to two anonymous reviewers for their comments and suggestions, and to Javiera Monreal for her excellent research assistance.

- *Armed forces.* Individuals who, at the moment of application, are participants or retirees of one of the armed forces' PAYG pension systems (CAPREDENA or DIPRECA) are not eligible for NSP benefits.

- *Residence requirement.* To qualify for old-age benefits, individuals must have resided in Chile for at least 20 years after the age of 20, and at least three of the five years before requesting the benefit. For disability benefits, individuals must demonstrate residence in the country for at least five of the six years before applying for the benefit.

- *Affluence test.* The affluence test is a form of means testing applied to assess whether a person's household belongs to the 40 percent richest fraction of the population. Currently, this test is based on a Pension Targeting Score (Puntaje de Focalización Previsional, PFP).[6,7] The score is constructed by combining the different sources of income for all members of the household of the applicant and dividing by an index of necessities, a function of the number of members in the household, their ages, and special needs conditions. Income sources include administrative information (such as covered wages, pensions, self-employment, and capital and property income), self-reported information (labor income), and imputed income (based on a measure of income-generating capacity).

- *Base pension.* To be eligible for old-age subsidies, the sum of all contributory pensions received by the applicant (the base pension) cannot exceed the maximum pension with solidarity complement (the Pensión Maxima con Aporte Solidario [PMAS], equivalent to approximately US$463 per month, as of September 2018).[8] Contributory pensions include old-age, disability, or survivors' pensions, either from the individual capitalization scheme or the previous PAYG programs (but not including the armed forces regimes). If a person is not yet retired at application time, an approximate pension is imputed based on his or her pension savings balance, age, potential beneficiaries, and life expectancy (a formula equivalent to a constant annuity).

Benefits

The NSP provides two types of benefits (both for either old-age or disability): a Basic Solidarity Pension (PBS) to eligible individuals with no other pension rights and a Pension Solidarity Complement (APS) to eligible individuals with positive pension rights (but with a base pension below the PMAS threshold).[9]

The schedule of subsidies is best described in figure 11.1, which presents solidarity subsidies and total pensions as a function of contributory pension entitlements (the base pension) for both old-age and disability benefits. The horizontal axis corresponds to the base pension, originated in the contributions made by the individual to a pension scheme (or survivors' benefits derived from a deceased spouse or parent). For pensioners of the PAYG regime, the contributory pension corresponds to the public pension paid by the pension scheme until death. For participants in the AFP scheme, the contributory pension corresponds to the pension currently being received or, for someone in the process of retiring, is calculated as an equivalent lifetime annuity based on the accumulated balance

FIGURE 11.1 **Subsidies and final pensions under Chile's New Solidarity Pillar**

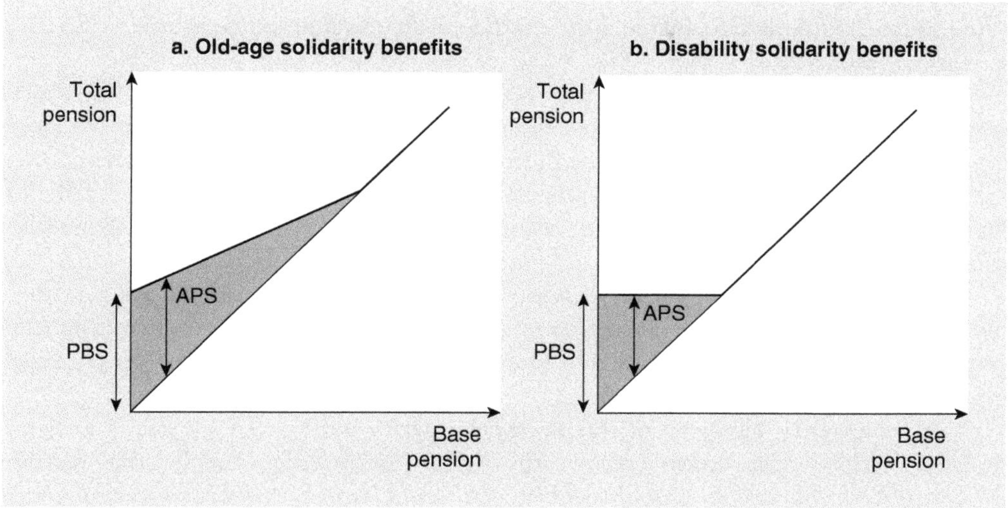

a. Old-age solidarity benefits

b. Disability solidarity benefits

SOURCE: Original figures.
NOTE: APS = Pension Solidarity Complement; PBS = Basic Solidarity Pension.

in the individual account. Survivors' pensions are also included in the concept of the base pension (they are added to the other pensions).

The vertical axis corresponds to the total pension that the individual would receive, given the benefit structure of the NSP. In the absence of subsidies, the total pension would be equal to the base pension and the relationship would lie on the 45-degree line. With the existence of the NSP, however, the total pension corresponds to the sum of the base pension and government subsidies. In particular, individuals who were not entitled to a pension under any pension retirement scheme (individuals with zero base pension) could be eligible—if they fulfill the other eligibility requirements—for the PBS, and their total pension would be equivalent to the PBS level.

Similarly, people who did accumulate pension rights but for whom the base pension lies below the PMAS level could be eligible for the APS, which would increase the pension level but in an amount lower than the PBS. The magnitude of this complement depends on the contributory pension: individuals with pensions close to zero would receive a complement similar to the PBS and participants with pensions close to the PMAS would receive a complement close to zero. Workers with contributory pensions above the PMAS would not be eligible for subsidies (for that reason, the benefit schedule lies on the 45-degree line when pensions are above the PMAS level).

The scheme was introduced gradually. In the first year, beginning in July 2008, the PBS was equivalent to US$138 and restricted to the 40 percent less affluent individuals. This benefit was increased to US$173 in July 2009, and covered up to the 45 percent poorest individuals. The final schedule of benefits was put in place in July 2011, covering up to the 60 percent poorest individuals.

The PMAS parameter was also gradually increased over time. Originally set at US$161 in July 2008, the PMAS was increased to US$276 in July 2009, US$345 in September 2009, and US$460 in July 2010, and set to its permanent level (US$587) starting in July 2011.

The 2008 law established that the PBS and the PMAS parameters would be maintained in real terms from July 2012 onward, with annual inflation adjustments (or more frequent adjustments if the accumulated inflation within a year exceeds 10 percent). As a result, all NSP benefits are inflation indexed. The only increase in real terms occurred in January 2017, when a law was passed that implied an extraordinary increase of the PBS level of 10 percent.

General tax provisions for the pension system are as follows: compulsory contributions and the financial returns earned by pension savings are tax-exempt but contributory pensions resulting from these contributions are subject to regular income tax. Benefits from the NSP are exempt from taxes.

Two particular elements of this design are worth noting: (a) the strong integration between the contributory system and the solidarity pillar, and (b) the concern for contributory incentives that this integration raises. Integration allows guaranteeing that everybody in the first three income quintiles will receive a pension equivalent to, at least, the PBS. If the benefit had been established as a top-up (as in the disability case), low-income individuals would have strong disincentives to contribute, because their retirement income would not increase with the number or amount of contributions. With the chosen design, old-age total pensions monotonically increase with self-financed savings; that is, every dollar saved always increases retirement income. An implicit tax is associated with the subsidy reduction as the pension increases, however: for every dollar of additional self-financed pension, the total benefit of an NSP beneficiary increases by only 66.3 cents (a 33.7 percent implicit tax rate). Whether this implicit tax actually affects workers' decisions is a subject of "A Literature Review of the Impact of the New Solidarity Pillar."

RECENT EVOLUTION OF THE NSP

Figure 11.2 depicts the recent evolution of NSP benefits. After the first two years of sharp eligibility expansion, the program gradually increased, reaching 1.15 million old-age beneficiaries in July 2017. Given the significant gender difference in contributory pension entitlements, most beneficiaries are women (63 percent), and in recent years, predominantly of the APS type (65 percent). Average benefits are gradually increasing over time (in real terms) and show no significant difference by gender.[10]

The APS provides a pension complement as a decreasing function of self-financed pensions. Figure 11.3 presents the distribution (as of September 2017) of APS beneficiaries and the APS's impact on the total pension as a function of gender and the number of contribution years. The average density of contributions is approximately 50 percent among Chilean workers, but as panel a of figure 11.3 shows, the distribution for women is more skewed to the left than that of men. As expected, the pension increase provided by the APS decreases with the number of contribution years, starting with 83 percent for women with fewer than 5 years (30 percent for men), and decreasing to 8 percent for individuals who contributed between 15 and 20 years.

FIGURE 11.2 **Old-age beneficiaries and average benefits, 2008–17 (July of each year)**

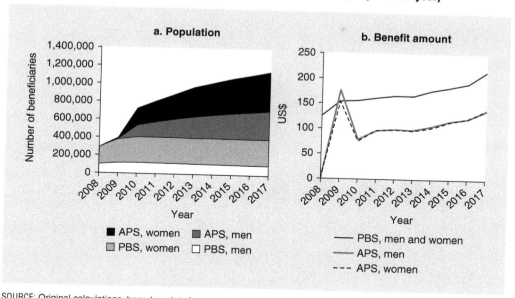

SOURCE: Original calculations, based on data from www.spensiones.cl.

NOTE: Amounts in U.S. dollars as of September 2017. Data are available in annex 11A. APS = Pension Solidarity Complement; PBS = Basic Solidarity Pension.

FIGURE 11.3 **Distribution of old-age pension beneficiaries and average benefits (with and without Pension Solidarity Complement) by gender and years of contributions**

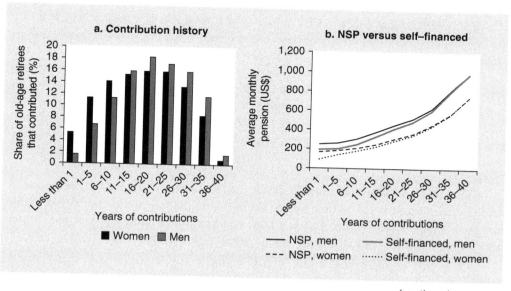

(continued next page)

FIGURE 11.3 **Distribution of old-age pension beneficiaries and average benefits (with and without Pension Solidarity Complement) by gender and years of contributions (continued)**

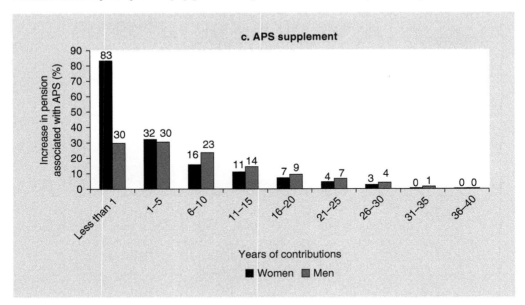

SOURCE: Original calculations, based on data from www.spensiones.cl.

NOTE: Amounts in U.S. dollars as of September 2017. ASP = Pension Solidarity Complement; PBS = Basic Solidarity Pension.

COVERAGE AND FISCAL PROJECTIONS

Given its design, the NSP should increase both the level and quality of pension coverage of the system as a whole. In terms of coverage level, the PBS should reach a vast segment of the population who did not participate in the formal contributory system and were not covered by the limited PASIS scheme.[11] At the same time, the APS allows a significant improvement in average pensions in the bottom part of the distribution.

Figure 11.4 shows an estimation of the reduction in the fraction of the population older than age 65 without pensions, associated with the introduction of the NSP. At the same time, the fraction of individuals with mixed financing (individual savings and state subsidies) would significantly increase as a consequence of the reform. Despite the NSP, a small fraction of the population remains uncovered, corresponding to individuals with no pension but other sources of income or wealth that would prevent them from qualifying under the affluence test.

The decision to introduce the NSP was made in a very particular context: pension-related public expenditure was starting to decline as a consequence of the 30-year transition from the previous system. This is a nontrivial matter; as figure 11.4 shows, the new benefits increase the state's significant role in pension financing.

Official projections suggest that introduction of the NSP only (without taking into consideration other benefits introduced by the reform) will imply over the next few years a gradual increase in public expenditure, going from 0.65 percent of gross domestic product (GDP) in 2010 to 1.2 percent of GDP by 2025.[12] However, it is important to remember that the NSP replaced other programs (the PASIS and the MPG) that would have incurred

FIGURE 11.4 **Coverage of Chile's pension system, with and without the New Solidarity Pillar**

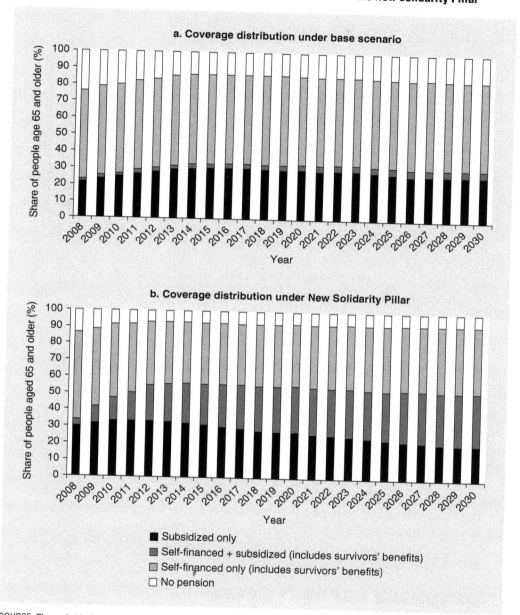

SOURCE: Figure 8.1 in Berstein et al. (2009).

their own public expenditures had the reform not been passed. The reform thus implied an "incremental" expenditure of approximately 0.3 percent by 2010 and 0.8 percent by 2025 (figure 11.5).

In summary, implementation of the NSP, with its character of entitlement guaranteed by law, implied a significant increase in the contingent liabilities of the Chilean state.

FIGURE 11.5 **Public expenditure (total and incremental) on Chile's New Solidarity Pillar**

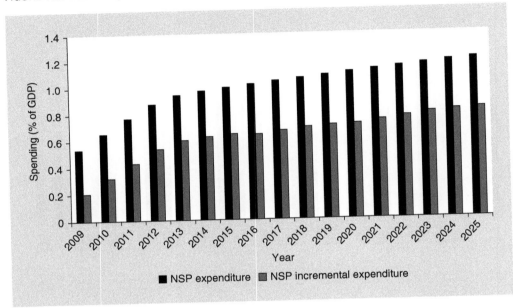

SOURCE: Original calculations based on Arenas de Mesa et al. (2008).

NOTE: GDP = gross domestic product; NSP = New Solidarity Pension.

A Literature Review of the Impact of the New Solidarity Pillar

First, by design, the NSP's effects may have multiple dimensions, the two most important being the potential increase in pension coverage and reduction of poverty among the elderly. Second, because of its income and substitution effects, it could also affect the incentives to work or at least to participate in the covered labor market. Third, being a large income redistribution program—mediated by the tax system—one would expect an effect on the income distribution of the Chilean population. In addition, because its design is gender-neutral (in contrast to the contributory pension pillar, in which benefits are actuarially calculated, differentiating between men and women), the NSP may help reduce the significant pension gender gap.

This section surveys the existing literature that has evaluated the different impacts of the NSP along different dimensions.

PENSION COVERAGE AND POVERTY REDUCTION

A study by CEEL (2017) analyzes the effects of the NSP on elderly life quality and poverty alleviation, using both quantitative and qualitative methods. Data from the CASEN 2015 survey and Round VI of the Social Protection Survey, linked with administrative contribution records,[13] were used to analyze the effects of the NSP on elderly income. Results show that 33.9 percent of the elderly receive income from the NSP—28.9 percent receive the PBS while the rest receive the APS—representing, on average, 26.5 percent of their monetary income (16.5 percent for men and 34.3 percent for women). For 8.9 percent of the elderly, the NSP constitutes their only income (5 percent for men and 12 percent for women). When considering only the first income quintile (constructed from per capita income at the household level, the indicator used for income poverty measurement), the data show that 65.3 percent of the elderly receive benefits from the NSP (59.8 percent from the PBS, 5.5 percent from the APS), which represents 56.7 percent of their monetary income; for 17.4 percent of them, NSP benefits constitute their only source of income. CEEL finds that the PBS is more frequently given to elderly persons who are not household heads, whereas older people who are head of the household more frequently receive the APS. Finally, some individuals from the fourth and fifth income quintiles also receive NSP benefits (18.3 percent and 8.2 percent, respectively). This could be a result of differences in the per capita income measure used for poverty measurement and the Pension Targeting Score used in the NSP affluence test (which uses an age-dependent measurement of income-generating capacity and includes administrative data on income and pensions).

To analyze how the cost of a consumption basket is modified when older people are part of the household and when income levels change (for example, when receiving benefits from the NSP), the CEEL studies use the most recent income and expenditure survey (the VII Encuesta de Presupuestos Familiares). For households from the first income quintile and made up of only (one or more) individuals older than age 65, the old-age consumption basket's monthly cost is worth an estimated US$300 (as of February 2017). The PBS is thus equivalent to 56 percent of the cost of this basket, and the average APS (approximately US$105, according to official statistics) represents a 35 percent share. When considering all income quintiles, the average PBS represents 17 percent of the monthly cost of the old-age consumption basket; the average APS represents 11 percent.

CEEL's results show that income poverty among the elderly is reduced from 14.1 percent (higher than the general estimated poverty rate of 11.7 percent) to 5.9 percent (of which 1.2 percent is extreme poverty) when income from the NSP is considered in the calculation. Similarly, using a multidimensional measure of old-age poverty, the reduction is from 28.3 percent to 19.2 percent through the NSP effects on the retirement indicator.[14] Nevertheless, the study suggests analyzing poverty among individuals and not households when possible, considering that only 9.3 percent of households comprise only people older than age 65.[15]

In summary, CEEL's study finds that the NSP constitutes an important source of income for the targeted population older than age 65, and that it greatly contributes to alleviating income and multidimensional poverty among them. This is also consistent with the general evaluation of the PBS, particularly for women: the qualitative analysis of the study shows that the NSP is positively evaluated across all socioeconomic strata, but especially by the lower ones.

LABOR INCENTIVE EFFECTS

Under the NSP design, the amount of noncontributory benefits decreases with the level of individuals' contributory efforts during their working lives, translating to an implicit tax on formal work.[16] Although special attention was given in the design of the new scheme to minimizing these adverse effects on incentives, the theory suggests that both the level of benefits and their gradual reduction, conditional on the level of the self-funded pension, could affect contributory participation: greater future wealth is likely to reduce the incentive to save in the present (the income effect); this effect is magnified by the fact that the future subsidy is partially reduced if the person saves more in the present (the substitution effect).

This section reviews the literature that has formally modeled these incentive effects and attempted to assess the empirical magnitude of their impact.

Attanasio, Meghir, and Otero (2011) estimate the impact of the 2008 pension reform on formal and informal labor market participation in Chile using two sources of longitudinal data: the Social Protection Survey and the Pension System Administrative Records. They estimate the relationship between pension wealth and accrual rate and labor market participation rates. Some of their outcomes of interest, before and after the reform, are changes in the distributions of pensions, the distribution of the pension gap between men and women, accumulated pension wealth, poverty levels among the elderly, the probability of contributing and the frequency of contributions, coverage of the system, men's and women's formal labor market participation, and the effects of having a child on labor force participation.

The study uses a difference-in-differences estimator to address the effect of expected pension wealth on labor market participation, exploiting the differential effects on individuals who belong to different birth cohorts and groups. To assess the long-run effects of the reform and effects for younger cohorts, they forecast a set of variables.

It is estimated that the reform increased self-financed pension wealth as well as the final pension. For workers retiring before 2015, self-financed pension wealth would increase on average by 0.6 percent, and the final pension by 15 percent on average. Attanasio, Meghir, and Otero (2011) find that the probability of contributing to the pension system decreased as a result of the reform, reducing formal labor market participation by about 4.1 percent for workers older than age 40. For female workers between ages 56 and 65, the reform reduces the probability of being formal by 3.2 percent, while for men of the same age range, the reduction is 2.8 percent. Finally, they find that the improvement in women's pensions has been 56 percent higher than that of men, significantly reducing gender inequalities.

Behrman et al. (2011) evaluate how Chile's 2008 pension system reform—specifically, the PBS—influenced economic outcomes (such as hours worked, self-reported health status, household expenditures, alcohol and cigarette consumption, health insurance, and ownership of consumer durables) for targeted poor households with at least one member age 65 or older. They also analyze two other sets of outcomes: if there are any changes in knowledge and receipt of these new transfers between 2006 and 2009.

Behrman et al. (2011) use data from the Social Protection Survey (waves corresponding to 2006 and 2009), linked with contribution data from the administrative database. They measure the "intent-to-treat" impacts of the PBS. The estimation strategy for transfers received and behavioral outcomes takes advantage of reported changes between the two years, along with discontinuities in the applicability of the reform, related to household members' age and the score in the means-testing instrument, the Ficha de Protección Social (FPS). They control for observed characteristics unaffected by the program. The measured impact is stated as a triple-difference estimator given that there are two eligibility criteria (age 65 or older and being poor) plus the time difference between 2006 and 2009. Regarding knowledge of the pension reform, because only the 2009 wave contains relevant information, they generate double-difference estimates using only data for that year (eliminating the "time difference" variable).

Results for pension reform knowledge and reports of transfers show that the poor are less well-informed than the nonpoor, but more likely to report receiving the PASIS or PBS targeted transfers. Regarding household transfers received, the 2008 reform positively and significantly impacts PASIS and PBS and total public transfers, but not private transfers, suggesting that little evidence exists of crowding out of private transfers. Targeted households received 2.4 percent more household annual income, with little evidence of a reduction in private transfers. Finally, for the impacts of the PBS on household behavior, results suggest that household welfare probably increased from a number of factors: higher expenditures on basic consumption (an increase of US$13 in annual expenditures on food, and of US$16 on medicine, for example), including health care; enhanced leisure time as a result of reduced hours worked (a reduction of 1.6 hours per week); and improved self-reported health.

However, the authors note that the results found are not quantitatively large and not significantly different from zero at a significance level of 5 percent (the two most significant coefficients are for self-reported health status, significantly nonzero at the 10 percent level, and hours worked per week, significantly nonzero at the 15 percent level). The authors mention that the short-run effects found are small, so follow-up analyses would be crucial to measure longer-run outcomes and to evaluate the evolution over time of the different effects and responses.

Encina (2013) estimates the effect of Chile's 2008 pension system reform over labor participation outcomes, such as months spent working, months in inactivity, months in unemployment, months with contributions (all measured as a percentage of total months in the labor history), and per capita income (measured in monthly Chilean pesos). To do so, she uses the Social Protection Survey (panel for years 2006 and 2009) and a difference-in-differences propensity score (nearest neighbor) matching estimation; the treated group comprised beneficiaries of the PBS in 2009, and the control group was selected by matching people who satisfied conditions for the reception of the benefit, but did not receive it in that same year. These conditions include being age 65 or older, belonging to the 40 percent poorest population, receiving the PASIS, and not receiving another pension.

In general, results show that beneficiaries of the PBS showed deeper withdrawal from the labor market, made lower contributions, worked less, and showed longer periods of inactivity. In detail, results find that the treated group increased months in unemployment by 2 percent, relative to the control group, and worked, on average, 8 percent fewer months than the control group in 2009. The treatment group also contributed 18 percent fewer months and spent 6 percent more months in inactive status, on average, all relative to the control group. Finally, no significant difference is found in per capita income; the treatment group increased per capita income by US$34 per month in 2009, which is considered a small effect compared with the poverty line.

The author concludes that the PBS is reducing incentives to participate in the labor market, which could explain the fact that people receiving the PBS do not have higher incomes: it seems that the new pension has a crowding-out effect, whereby the higher income of the PBS is compensated for by lower incomes from working activities. Using longer panel data and exploring the consumption patterns of PBS beneficiaries is suggested to analyze the effects of the PBS in more detail.

Wong (2016) analyzes the shift in the labor market between the formal and uncovered sector by exploiting the differential impact of the 2008 Chilean pension system reform on the relative attractiveness of formal- and uncovered-sector jobs for different subgroups of the population. The first subgroup consists of people who could reasonably expect that the 2008 pension reform would generate a jump in their implicit marginal tax rate on pension contributions from 0 percent to 29.4 percent. Based on the original benefit schedule, APS beneficiaries would expect to receive only 70.6 cents worth of incremental benefits from each dollar of contribution to their individual accounts. This is the largest subgroup. The second subgroup under analysis faced a drop in its implicit marginal tax rate, from 100 percent to 29.4 percent (as before the reform, for low-wage individuals who have slightly more than 20 years of pension contribution, additional pension contributions would not increase their total pension benefits; elimination of the MPG lowered the 100 percent implicit marginal tax rate to 29.4 percent), increasing incentives to work in the formal sector. These changes in the incentives to make pension contributions may significantly affect formal sector labor supply because the uncovered sector of self-employed and informal jobs had no mandatory pension contribution. Using data from the Chilean Social Protection Surveys (2006, 2009) linked to the administrative Social Security record, Wong estimates a difference-in-differences model with individual fixed effects (among other models, such as conditional logit estimators) for both subgroups separately.

Results from the difference-in-differences estimations show that the first subgroup is, on average, about 2.9 percentage points less likely to work in the formal sector after the reform. The second subgroup is found to be about 8 percentage points more likely to work in the formal sector after the reform. It is noted, however, that this cannot be precisely estimated given the small number of individuals in this subgroup. It is also found that formal sector labor supply responses are stronger among the young (younger than age 30) and people who are close to retirement (ages 55–59). No effect is found for people age 40–54. Finally, Wong (2016) concludes that although in a small subgroup of the population the 2008 Chilean pension reform eliminated certain perverse incentives for pension contribution behavior, it introduced a new disincentive to pension contribution behavior for a much larger subgroup.

Summarizing, empirical results are consistent with theoretical predictions in terms of labor market behavior, but the estimated impacts are relatively small, and the effect on total pension income seems to be positive, with little evidence of crowding out of private transfers.

INCOME AND GENDER INEQUALITY

The NSP is probably one of the largest income distribution policies to have been introduced in Chile in the past three decades.[17] The transparent and clearly targeted subsidy program is expected to modify the income distribution structure of the country, especially because the contributive pillar is essentially distribution-neutral (given that benefits are actuarially calculated as a function of savings balance, age- and gender-differentiated mortality tables, the presence of survivorship beneficiaries, and prospective interest rates). In addition, the NSP design (which is neutral to beneficiaries' gender) should reduce the significant pension-related gender gap. This section surveys some of the recent literature evaluating the distributional impacts of the introduction of the NSP.[18]

Fajnzylber (2012b) studies how two alternative approaches to pension design—a traditional PAYG scheme and the Chilean scheme based on individual accounts plus the NSP—affect the overall distribution of lifetime wealth.[19] Using administrative microdata, he simulates entire histories of income and benefits. As expected, no redistribution is found within the contributory pension scheme (individual accounts), but the inclusion of a solidarity component (financed by a fixed income tax rate) greatly reduces income inequality: the Gini coefficient diminishes from 0.499 (based only on lifetime income, without a pension scheme) to 0.462 when the AFP + NSP is put in place. The redistribution occurring through the pension system is in fact progressive. In contrast, the counterfactual defined benefits scheme has only a marginal impact in reducing income inequality but leads to a significant reduction in the gender income gap.

Joubert and Todd (2011) examine whether the reform to the pension system promotes gender equity and whether it might generate unintended behavioral responses by altering incentives to work and save.[20] They use longitudinal data from the Social Protection Survey, the Chilean supervisory authority for pension fund management, and data on the returns achieved by Chile's funds. The authors estimate a dynamic structural model of labor supply and household savings decisions that considers dimensions of individual heterogeneity, allowing them to capture the distributional aspects of the reform's impacts. The model incorporates uncertainty, incomplete information, and forward-looking behavior under a rational expectations assumption. Its parameters are estimated by the method of simulated moments using prereform data (based on 2004 and 2006 Social Protection Surveys), and forecasting for 2004, 2006 (in-sample), 2009, and 2014 (out-of-sample).

With this methodology, they simulate the differential, five-year-ahead impact of the reform on women's pension levels relative to men's, labor supply, poverty levels, contribution densities, participation in the formal sector, and age of effective retirement. They find that the reform will (a) greatly increase women's savings through the AFP system (increases of about 95 percent in the mean level of women's balances), reducing the gap between women's and men's pension benefits (a decrease of 7.7 percent in men's pension savings is also estimated due to the shift toward working in uncovered sectors); and (b) reduce poverty levels at older ages (but slightly increase poverty rates for younger age groups as a result of work disincentive effects). The reform also leads to a slight decrease in the density of contributions for women and men age 50 and older, which reflects changes in labor supply and labor force sector participation decisions. In other words, some negative behavioral responses are anticipated from the income effect: lower labor force participation at older ages and lower participation in the covered sector (which would result in lower contribution densities), for both men and women older than age 50. This reduced participation in the labor market, relative to the prereform scenario, would be particularly high in the covered sector and for women.

Fajnzylber (2012a) analyzes the four main factors that affect pension differences by gender in the context of the Chilean pension system: the accumulation of pension rights, retirement age, the type of pension, and differences in longevity. Using aggregate statistics and simulation results, the author evaluates the relative importance of these factors and how the different measures included in the 2008 reform (including the NSP but also a bonus per child and the suggestion to increase the legal retirement age to 65) affected this gap. The results suggest that introduction of a bonus per child can significantly raise pensions for women in the lower part of the pension distribution. The NSP will have a tremendous impact on all individuals with small pensions but especially among women, because they are more likely to be eligible for these benefits. Finally, a hypothetical increase in women's legal retirement age to 65 would have an important effect (9 percent on average), but would be especially important among women who are not eligible for the NSP.

Conclusions

Poverty prevention pension pillars are a fundamental part of any modern, diversified pension system, particularly in low- or middle-income countries, where pension coverage is usually inadequate (Holzmann and Hinz 2005). The extension of coverage by means of the contributory pillar is limited by the capacity of low-income households to make savings efforts for old-age protection and the tension created by the existence of an informal sector. Noncontributory benefits have proven to be an effective tool for extending social protection to the elderly population.

The NSP introduced in Chile in 2008 represents a relatively novel design for noncontributory benefits that tries to balance the tension between extending universal coverage while maintaining an affordable fiscal cost and minimizing the formal labor disincentive effects associated with government subsidies. In contrast with the implicit redistribution existing in traditional PAYG schemes or minimum pension provisions (usually available for individuals with a minimum number of contributions), subsidies provided by the NSP are transparent and clearly targeted to individuals who need it most. They also provide a means to compensate for gender differences associated with culturally assigned roles, labor market discrimination, or differential longevity.

The reviewed literature suggests that the NSP has played a significant role in extending pension coverage to the population that needs it most, reducing poverty levels (both in terms of income and from a multidimensional perspective) and reducing lifetime income and gender inequality, with only minor disincentive effects or crowding out of private transfers. The relatively small labor market effects are not so surprising, given that the new benefits replace an existing incentive structure (provided by the PASIS and the MPG) that also tended to discourage formal labor market participation.

These results are particularly important for countries with defined contribution pension schemes (of either a financial or nonfinancial nature), which tend to reproduce labor market distributional patterns into old-age income inequality.

Many unanswered questions should be taken into account when considering adopting a similar program in other contexts, such as how to provide sustainable financing, how to set the minimum pension level or the maximum pension eligible for subsidies, and which additional features to include to reduce the pension gender gap.

Introducing a noncontributory program like the NSP requires a sustainable fiscal effort from the government that should be maintained over the long run. A permanent source of income should be available to sustain the permanent source of fiscal expenditure. In the Chilean context, financing came largely from a gradual reduction in the transition cost associated with the 1980 reform that, by 2008, was starting to phase out. Alternative sources of financing could come from reducing fiscal imbalances in other pension programs (such as programs for civil servants) or redirecting resources from other assistance programs. Redistribution within the contributory program (which could be interpreted as an earmarked form of taxation) is also an alternative (when increased taxation is not an option), though the formality disincentives are likely to be more important in this case, because labor-related contributions usually affect the entire income distribution (in contrast with general revenues, usually more concentrated on more well-off individuals).[21]

An important design option is the level of the minimum benefit (in the NSP context, the PBS). As mentioned in the reviewed literature, this amount represents in many cases the main source of income in the household so its level should be high enough to ensure protection above the poverty line for the typical old-age household. But at the same time, setting it at too high a level results not only in higher fiscal costs but also in potentially greater disincentive effects associated with more important income and substitution effects.

Similarly, the maximum pension with solidarity complement (PMAS) determines the range of individuals covered by the program, the fiscal cost, and the extent of disincentive impacts (given by substitution effects): a higher PMAS implies reaching a larger share of the population, with a higher fiscal cost but at the same time a lower implicit tax rate. Its level should therefore take into account a country's fiscal capacity and the importance of extending solidarity benefits to the middle class.

Although the NSP played an important role in reducing the gender gap, it was not explicitly designed for that purpose. In fact, allowing for a differential PMAS value for men and women could have allowed the system to eliminate the gender gap associated with women's higher longevity, so that a man and a woman with the same savings balance and retirement age would receive exactly the same benefit.[23]

ANNEX 11A

TABLE 11A.1 **Beneficiaries and average benefits of the New Solidarity Pillar, 2008–17**

	Beneficiaries (as of July of each year)				Average benefit (as of July of each year, US$ of Sept. 2017)			
	PBS men	PBS women	APS men	APS women	PBS men	PBS women	APS men	APS women
2008	101,420	189,150	–	–	$125	$125	–	–
2009	117,124	261,334	4,882	8,395	$154	$155	$176	$153
2010	120,293	285,566	129,748	187,484	$156	$156	$78	$75
2011	118,793	286,810	169,626	232,716	$161	$161	$97	$97
2012	117,059	288,929	202,381	276,215	$166	$166	$99	$98
2013	113,823	286,900	237,441	327,498	$166	$166	$98	$97
2014	111,373	289,553	259,553	355,536	$176	$176	$106	$103
2015	110,438	289,446	281,099	387,145	$183	$183	$116	$115
2016	108,892	290,754	298,366	409,755	$191	$191	$121	$122
2017	107,824	291,786	316,011	434,836	$215	$215	$138	$139

SOURCE: Based on data available at www.spensiones.cl.

NOTE: APS = Pension Solidarity Complement; PBS = Basic Solidarity Pension.

Notes

1. AFP stands for Administradora de Fondos de Pensiones, a pension fund manager. A description of the Chilean pension scheme and the 2008 reform can be found in Berstein et al. (2009).

2. In contrast, the NSP is considered an entitlement for qualifying individuals. In the case of PASIS, eligible individuals could apply for benefits but their allocation would depend on the annual budget.

3. The contribution requirement corresponds to 240 months with paid contributions. It can also be complemented, among other cases, with periods receiving unemployment benefits, contributions made to the old PAYG scheme (for which no benefit has been paid), or periods of work in another country (subject to a bilateral social security agreement between the two countries). All local wages and pension income (including survivorship benefits) are considered in the assessment of the low-income requirement. This also excludes beneficiaries of the former PAYG scheme. The MPG had no citizenship or residence requirement.

4. Alternatively, when the system was put in place, beneficiaries of old-age or disability PASIS were automatically eligible for a Basic Solidarity Pension (old-age or disability, depending on the age) under the new scheme.

5. It is important to note that the legal retirement age in Chile is set at 65 for men and 60 for women. Among the recommendations made by the Pension Reform Commission that gave rise to the 2008 reform was to increase the pension age for women to equal that of men. Starting noncontributory benefits at age 65 (for both men and women) was meant as a signal that women should try to postpone retirement. This recommendation was not included in the reform bill.

6. A detailed description, in Spanish, of the PFP calculation procedure is presented in the Pension System Compendium of Regulations (Book III, Title V, Letter B, chapter IX), available on the pension supervising agency's website (www.spensiones.cl).

7. During the first two years of implementation, means testing was based on the Ficha de Protección Social, a means-testing instrument that calculates the vulnerability of the members belonging to a household based on information about their capacity to generate income, self-reported earnings, administrative data on pensions, and needs adjustments based on age and disability status.

8. To be eligible for disability subsidies, the base pension must be below the Basic Solidarity Pension (PBS).

9. The PBS is equivalent to approximately US$157 per month (as of September 2018).

10. In 2008, the first year of the reform, only PBS benefits were delivered. The relative increase of the APS is directly related to the gradual expansion of the PMAS.

11. The other noncontributory program present before the 2008 reform was the MPG. However, as mentioned earlier, its combined restriction of a minimum number of contributions and a maximum income level (including pensions) led to low coverage and a very limited poverty reduction effect.

12. These figures are calculated based on projections included in Arenas de Mesa et al. (2008). Estimations are based on an actuarial model that combines administrative data on the stock of retirees and population and labor market projections for the flow of future retirees. The model does not explicitly include endogenous reactions to the introduction of the NSP, nor does it conduct sensitivity analyses of some key parameters (such as returns, wage growth, or women's labor force participation). One of the key assumptions in these projections is that NSP benefits, following the rule included in the law that defined them, are kept constant in real terms (that is, inflation-indexed). This assumption, combined with positive real wage growth, implies that the average subsidies of beneficiaries would tend to decrease for younger cohorts. If, to the contrary, political or social pressure causes some real benefit increases over time, projected expenditures should increase at a faster pace than expected.

13. CASEN, the main household survey in Chile, collects data on education, health, living conditions, and different sources of income. It is the main instrument used to measure poverty and inequality. Following the U.S. Health and Retirement Survey, the Social Protection Survey was constructed to provide an understanding of individuals' participation in social protection

programs. It provides the possibility of linking individuals' self-reported answers to administrative data on contributions into the social security scheme.

14. The multidimensional poverty measure was introduced in Chile with the 2015 CASEN survey, including five dimensions: education, health, work and social security, housing and living environment, and access to social networks and social cohesion.

15. The authors suggest it would be important to develop an elderly consumption index and a specific multidimensional poverty index (MPI) for this group, considering some of the actual dimensions of the MPI do not apply for people over 65 years old.

16. A detailed analysis of the effect of noncontributory benefits on the labor market and formality decisions can be found in Valdés-Prieto (2008).

17. A general description of the context in which the 2008 reform took place (in contrast to the Argentinian pension reform in the same period) can be found in Rofman, Fajnzylber, and Herrera (2010). Fajnzylber and Paraje (2013) provide the Chilean demographic context and how public policy has been modified to take into account the increased relevance of the elderly in the general social protection system, including the introduction in 2005 of the health program known as the Universal Access with Explicit Guarantees (Acceso Universal con Garantías Explícitas, AUGE).

18. Earlier analysis of the gender impact of the Chilean pension system and the 2008 reform can be found in Berstein and Tokman (2005) and James, Cox Edwards, and Wong (2003).

19. The simulated PAYG scheme is based on the Chilean Social Security program, the largest defined benefits scheme before the 1980 reform that introduced the current defined contributions scheme: a 10-year minimum contribution requirement, an initial replacement rate (on average income over the past five years) of 50 percent, and an increase of 1 percent for every contributed year, with a 70 percent ceiling and a minimum pension equivalent to the PBS.

20. A more general treatment of this analysis can be found in Joubert (2015).

21. A reform bill sent to Congress in August 2017 proposes to create a new redistributive pillar, financed by a 2 percent increase in the pension contribution rate. The new contributions would finance a 20 percent improvement in the pension of current retirees (intergenerational redistribution), some redistribution between high-income and low-income participants (intragenerational redistribution), and longevity-related compensation for women's pensions, should they accept postponing their retirement until age 65. The government that took office in March 2018 is more keen on extending tax-financed subsidies, rather than redistributing within a contributory program.

22. This is particularly important in a context in which other options (like compulsory unisex tables or differentiated contribution rates) are not viable from a political or economic standpoint.

References

Arenas de Mesa, Alberto, Paula Benavides, Leonardo González, and José Castillo. 2008. "La Reforma Previsional Chilena: Proyecciones Fiscales 2009–2025." Estudios de Finanzas Públicas, Dirección de Presupuesto, Chile.

Attanasio, Orazio, Costas Meghir, and Alejandro Otero. 2011. "Pensions, Work, and Informality: The Impact of the 2008 Chilean Pension Reform." Unpublished, University College London, UK.

Behrman, Jere, Maria Cecilia Calderon, Olivia S. Mitchell, Javiera Vasquez, and David Bravo. 2011. "First-Round Impacts of the 2008 Chilean Pension System Reform." Population Aging Research Center Working Paper 33, University of Pennsylvania, Philadelphia, PA.

Berstein, Solange, Pablo Castañeda, Eduardo Fajnzylber, and Gonzalo Reyes. 2009. "Chile 2008: A Second Generation Pension Reform." Superintendence of Pensions, Chile, October.

Berstein, Solange, and Andrea Tokman. 2005. "Brechas de Ingresos entre Géneros: ¿Perpetuadas o Exacerbadas en la Vejez?" Working Paper 8, Chilean Pension Supervisor, Santiago, Chile.

CEEL (Centro de Encuestas y Estudios Longitudinales de la Pontificia Universidad Católica de Chile). 2017. "Evaluación del Pilar Solidario en el Financiamiento de la Canasta de Consumo, los Ingresos y la Pobreza Multidimensional de Hombres y Mujeres Adultos Mayores." Final Report, commissioned by the Consejo Consultivo Previsional and the Comisión de Usuarios del Sistema de Pensiones, Santiago, Chile.

Encina, Jenny. 2013. "Pension Reform in Chile: A Difference in Difference Matching Estimation." *Estudios de Economía* 40 (1): 81–95.

Fajnzylber, Eduardo. 2012a. "Gender Policy and Pensions in Chile." In *Nonfinancial Defined Contribution Pension Schemes in a Changing Pension World: Volume 2 Gender, Politics, and Financial Stability,* edited by Edward Palmer, Robert Holzmann, and David Robalino, 113–39. Washington, DC: World Bank.

———. 2012b. "Implicit Redistribution in the Chilean Social Insurance System." Working Paper 019, School of Government, Universidad Adolfo Ibáñez, Chile.

Fajnzylber, Eduardo, and Guillermo Paraje. 2013. "Chile." In *Más Allá de las Pensiones Contributivas: Catorce Experiencias en America Latina,* edited by Rafael Rofman, Ignacio Apella, and Evelyn Vezza, 159–98. Washington, DC: World Bank.

Holzmann, Robert, and Richard Hinz. 2005. *Old Age Income Support in the 21st Century: An International Perspective on Pension Systems and Reform.* Washington, DC: World Bank.

James, Estelle, Alejandra Cox Edwards, and Rebecca Wong. 2003. "The Gender Impact of Pension Reform." *Journal of Pension Economics and Finance* 2 (2): 181–219.

Joubert, Clement. 2015. "Pension Design with a Large Informal Labor Market: Evidence from Chile." *International Economic Review* 56 (2): 673–94.

Joubert, Clement, and Petra E. Todd. 2011. "How the Design of a Pension System Influences Old Age Poverty and Gender Equity: A Study of Chile's Private Retirement Accounts System." Working Paper, University of Pennsylvania, Philadelphia, PA.

Rofman, Rafael, Eduardo Fajnzylber, and Germán Herrera. 2010. "Reforming the Pension Reforms: Argentina and Chile." *CEPAL Review* 101: 83–106.

Valdés-Prieto, Salvador. 2008. "A Theory of Noncontributory Pension Design." Working Paper 335, Instituto de Economía Pontificia Universidad Católica, Santiago, Chile.

Wong, Boris. 2016. "Formal Sector Labor Supply Responses to the 2008 Chilean Pension System Reform." Unpublished, University of California San Diego, San Diego, CA.

PART IV

The Challenges of Longevity

CHAPTER 12

Overview of Heterogeneity in Longevity and Pension Schemes

Ronald Lee and Miguel Sánchez-Romero

Introduction

Health and longevity are among the most basic dimensions of human welfare. Unfortunately, in many countries in Europe, Latin America, and North America, individuals with higher socioeconomic status (SES) have been found to live longer and in better health than those with lower status, whether SES is measured by income, education, or occupation. Differences between high- and low-status groups are sometimes as great as 10–14 years of life expectancy. Furthermore, these differences have widened in recent decades. These widening differences are the most urgent matter for policy intervention. However, they also have secondary consequences with regard to the actuarial fairness and progressivity or regressivity of public pensions, and private sector financial products like annuities and life insurance. This chapter reviews the empirical literature on these longevity differences, considers their impact on lifetime pension benefits, discusses some broader economic implications, and considers some policy responses.

Conceptual Background

Life expectancy summarizes the average mortality experience in a population, but individual experiences vary considerably. Because this uncertain outcome has important implications for economic planning and well-being, both the private and public sectors have developed programs and financial products to reduce the risk of living longer than expected. Public programs include annuitized pensions, publicly provided health care, and publicly provided long-term care, among others. Private programs include annuities, life insurance, health insurance, and long-term care insurance.[1]

Differences in longevity ex ante and ex post are conceptually different. Ex ante differences arise from differences in the probability of death. Ex post differences in longevity reflect the random component of death outcomes, given the probabilities. Ex ante

Miguel Sánchez-Romero acknowledges research support from the European Union's Seventh Framework Program for Research, Technological Development and Demonstration under Grant Agreement No. 613247: "Ageing Europe: An application of National Transfer Accounts (NTA) for explaining and projecting trends in public finances." This project was also partly financed by the Austrian National Bank (OeNB) under Grant No. 17647. The authors are grateful to two anonymous reviewers and to Arda Aktas, Gretchen Donehower, Bernhard Hammer, Miguel Poblete-Cazenave, and Alexia Prskawetz for comments and suggestions.

differences in longevity can lead to issues of fairness in government programs or private financial programs. Ex post differences in age at death may result in large differences in benefits received but do not lead to issues of fairness and equity because pooling such risks is the purpose of insurance (NASEM 2015).

Ex ante differences in mortality challenge our concepts of fairness, given that risk sharing may on average involve a transfer either from those with shorter lives to those with longer (as in the case of annuities and annuitized pensions) or from those with longer lives to those with shorter (as in the case of life insurance). When ex ante differences in longevity grow larger, these transfers become larger. Additionally, if a public pension program has a redistributive goal, the shorter lives of low-income people can thwart the redistributive intent as has happened in the United States, for example (NASEM 2015).

Focusing on ex ante longevity differences in the public sector, NASEM (2015, 65) states:

> "policy makers would not worry about people with a lower life expectancy receiving lower lifetime benefits from national defense or clean air because there is no obvious time dimension: in any given year, people who are alive pay taxes and receive benefits. But for programs with a strong or explicit time and age dimension, where the ages at which taxes are paid and benefits are received differ significantly, the principle of equal treatment requires consideration of such differences."

TABLE 12.1 **The average ages over the life cycle of paying federal taxes and receiving federal benefits in the United States based on 2011 NTA data and U.S. life table age distribution for that year**

	Age
Total taxes	51.6
Total benefits	60.1
Selected benefits	
Social Security	72.5
Medicare	74.7
Medicaid, paid to nursing home	79.8

SOURCE: Original calculations based on National Transfer Accounts (NTA) data for the United States, which is accessible at ntaccounts.org.

NOTE: The NTA age profiles used here estimate all federal tax payments and all federal benefits received based on administrative data and survey data. NTA adjusts these age profiles so that when combined with population age distributions the implied total taxes and costs of benefits are consistent with totals in National Income and Product Accounts. Although benefits can be unambiguously assigned to a particular program, it is not possible to say which taxes are used to fund which program. The average age of taxes is calculated for the actual mix of kinds of taxes, including income tax, payroll tax, corporate taxes, and excise taxes, but excluding property taxes, which in the United States are levied at the local level, but not the federal. The numbers are the average benefits received at each age weighted by the probability of surviving from age 20 to that age.

Public pensions and long-term care are obvious examples of programs for which taxes or contributions are paid much earlier than the benefits are received. Because health care costs rise so strongly with age, they also fall in this category (table 12.1).

Social Security retirement benefits are received 21 years after taxes are paid (72.5–51.6). For Medicare, the difference is 23 years. For long-term care (nursing home care), the difference is 28 years. Of course, these are just the midpoints of broad distributions.[2]

The concept of ex ante longevity depends on the kind and amount of information that is used to estimate the systematic component of longevity variation. For starters, demographers typically estimate mortality differences and remaining life expectancy by age and sex. They might, in addition, estimate mortality by geographic location of residence or of birth, and perhaps by race or ethnicity, or for the foreign-born by country of origin and duration since arrival in destination country. Aside from age, each of these dimensions of variation could indeed lead to questions of fairness and equity. But the focus of interest in recent years has been different, with an emphasis on SES measured by educational attainment, by occupation, or by income, wealth, or labor earnings.[3]

It is well known that income distributions are becoming more unequal in many countries. As discussed later in this chapter, in many but not all countries, mortality and longevity differences have also been widening. While widening income distributions seem an obvious explanation for widening mortality differentials by SES, most empirical studies cannot shed light on this matter, because they measure income or education by quantiles, which do not reflect widening or narrowing of distributions.[4]

This chapter focuses on mortality and longevity differences by lifetime labor income, the measure used in NASEM (2015), Bosworth, Burtless, and Zhang (2016), and Waldron (2007), for example. It also sometimes considers mortality differentials by educational attainment, which are also widely used in the literature. The focus is on a particular kind of government program: public pensions. Many of the issues that arise, however, would apply equally to some kinds of private pensions or to other kinds of government programs, as suggested by table 12.1.

Empirical Evidence on Mortality Differences by Socioeconomic Status

METHODOLOGICAL ISSUES

Reverse causality. Since ill health reduces the ability to work it causes a reduction in labor income. The estimated association of mortality and contemporaneous labor income reflects causality running in both directions, biasing upward the apparent negative effect of income on mortality. Various methods for at least partially avoiding this problem have been proposed, and the recent approach of choice for the United States has been to use a multiyear average of income at midlife in relation to mortality at older ages (Bosworth and Burke 2014; Bosworth, Burtless, and Zhang 2016 NASEM 2015; Waldron 2007). Multiyear averages also avoid the problem that income in any particular year may not represent the normal circumstances of the individual. Another approach is to use educational attainment as the measure of SES (Manchester and Topoleski 2008; Olshansky et al. 2012); because education is typically completed in one's twenties, it is not affected by mortality in later life, and it is highly correlated with life expectancy and income. Chronic ill health dating back to childhood could affect both educational attainment and later adult mortality, so this does not solve the problem completely. After controlling for several factors, educational attainment is found to explain about 30 percent of the total difference in mortality by SES in the United States (Hummer and Hernandez 2013).

Households versus individuals. Many individuals live as couples in households, and presumably pool their income in some way. Bosworth and Burke (2014) sum the average midlife earnings of the individuals in a couple and divide by the square root of two, to allow roughly for returns to scale in household consumption.

Changing meaning of absolute measures over time. When considering mortality differences over long periods in which the general level of per capita income or educational attainment changes greatly (Goldring, Lange, and Richards-Shubik 2016), it does not seem advisable to use the absolute levels of these measures for individuals at different times in the same equation. The different absolute levels correspond to very different positions in their distributions at different dates. The literature on income and mortality typically uses income quantiles for each year in the analysis, for example, quintiles, deciles, or top and bottom halves of the income distribution (Waldron 2007). Similarly, high school graduation rates rose from less than 10 percent in 1900 to close to 80 percent by 1970 (Bound et al. 2015). Again, one way to partially address the problem is by using quantiles of the educational distribution rather than absolute levels attained, as done by Bound et al. (2015).

Quantile measures are not a panacea. Unfortunately, the use of quantiles for income or education answers different questions than those initially asked here. The quantile distribution does not change when the income distribution gets more or less unequal—the top quintile is always separated by the same distance from the bottom quintile, by construction. Whether the widening income distribution accounts for the widening mortality distribution, for example, can no longer be asked. Similarly, whether the relationship of mortality to the quantile distribution of income or education is linear is a different question than whether the level of income or education is linearly related to mortality.

DATA

Although data availability and limitations differ by country, some common cross-cutting issues are worth discussing. First, the public pension program may provide administrative data on earnings histories and deaths that are sufficient to analyze the relationship of mortality to labor earnings averaged over a number of years at midlife, as was done for the United States in the seminal study by Waldron (2007). But such data will be less meaningful in maturing systems that have been expanding the coverage of workers. In those cases, earnings histories will be incomplete for many people and it may not be known whether zeros and gaps are spells of nonwork or spells of uncovered work. Data from HRS- (Health and Retirement Survey) or SHARE- (Survey of Health, Ageing and Retirement in Europe) type surveys, which are often linked to public pension data on earnings histories, may greatly enrich the demographic, economic, and health information, but all the problems mentioned for the public pension earnings histories remain. In addition, the sample sizes are rather small, and the historical depth is severely limited by the timespan of survey cycles. Bosworth and Burke (2014) and Bosworth, Burtless, and Zhang (2016) are excellent examples of studies based on the HRS.

RESEARCH FINDINGS

A great deal of research has been done on the United States, using both educational attainment and income, and for both longitudinal (cohort) mortality and the more common cross-sectional (period) mortality measures (Bosley, Morris, and Glenn 2018; Bosworth and Burke 2014; Bosworth, Burtless, and Zhang 2015, 2016; Bound et al. 2015; Chetty et al. 2016; Dowd and Hamoudi 2014; Hummer and Lariscy 2011; Meara, Richards, and Cutler 2008; NASEM 2015; Waldron 2007, 2013). This research leads to two main robust conclusions. First, lower SES groups have substantially higher mortality than higher SES groups. Second, the mortality-SES gradient has gotten steeper in recent decades. For example, Rostron, Boies, and Arias (2010) find educational differences in period life expectancy at age 25 of 10–12 years for women and 11–16 years for men, with differences at age 65 of 5–8 years (for less than secondary school completion compared with more than university degree). (However, Bosley, Morris, and Glenn [2018] find little or no increase in disparities from 1995 to 2015 at ages 62–64 and older.) Results found in the NASEM (2015) using the HRS and average reported labor income at ages 40–49 are shown in figure 12.1. For the 1930 cohort, life expectancy at 50 (e_{50}) for the top quintile is 5.1 (= 31.7-26.6) years greater than for the bottom quintile. For the 1960 cohort the gap has grown from 5.1 to 12.7 years (= 38.8-26.1). The implications for the U.S. pension system are considered a bit later.

As discussed, education and income are both commonly used as measures of SES. Bosworth, Burtless, and Zhang (2016, 81–82) find that education and income do equally well individually in accounting for mortality differences, and whichever is used they find evidence of strong increases in the high-low gap. They also find that when both are included in the regression, both remain highly significantly associated

FIGURE 12.1 **U.S. male life expectancy at age 50 by midcareer average labor income quintile for birth cohorts of 1930 and 1960 (extrapolated)**

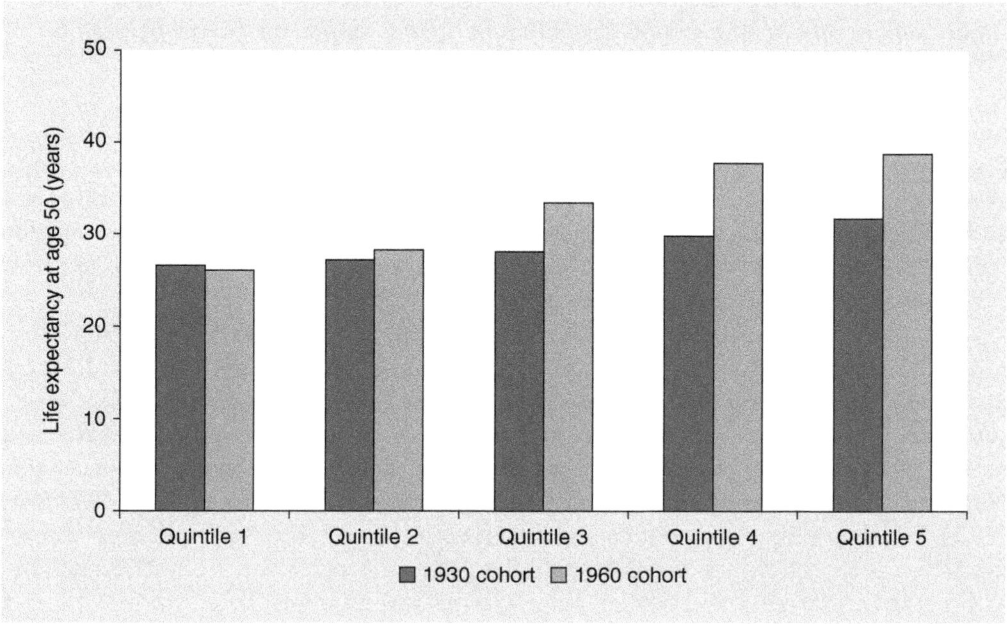

SOURCE: As estimated by NASEM (2015, 52).

NOTE: Birth cohorts survive past age 100, but for the 1930 cohort, death rates are observed only from age 62 in 1992 to 78 in 2008, and e_{50} is estimated by extrapolation of the trends in the fitted model. For the 1960 cohort, the entire estimate is by extrapolation since this cohort did not turn 50 until 2010, outside the sample range. Results are similar for Bosworth, Burtless, and Zhang (2016), who use the Health and Retirement the Survey through 2012 and also use the Survey of Income and Program Participation.

with mortality, so evidently neither one is sufficient to capture all the covariation of mortality with SES. This finding has implications for how policy might take SES into account.

For Europe and other Organisation for Economic Co-operation and Development (OECD) countries, the OECD (2016) report provides differences in life expectancy at 65 (e_{65}) between highly educated and least educated men and women of between one and seven years, with a median of three years for men and less for women. These differences are much less dramatic than for the United States, but they are not strictly comparable. The report also gives differences in e_{65} by high- versus low-income category for men and women in five countries, ranging from a low of two years in Chile to five years in Australia. Again, these are far less dramatic than the differences estimated for the United States. Methodological details are not given in the OECD report, so it is not clear how the methods may differ. The OECD report also finds that mortality differences by education have been widening, and for the one country with data this was also true for differences by income.

Some studies for Latin American countries report mortality differentials by SES. However, in Costa Rica the mortality gradient by SES is much flatter than it is in the United States, in part because higher SES individuals also have more unhealthy behaviors (Rosero-Bixby and Dow 2016).

Measuring the SES gradient to inform pension policy. To measure some sort of pure or net association (causal or not) of income or education with mortality, or to understand the pathways through which SES affects mortality, one would include other covariates such as marital status, geographic region of residence, disability status, biomarkers, health status, and so on. By doing so it is possible to greatly reduce the partial association of SES and mortality, because some of these variables are pathways through which mortality is affected. But for purposes of pension policy it does not matter how or why the SES-mortality association occurs, nor does the direction of causality matter (NASEM 2015; Pestieau and Ponthiere 2016). For policy purposes what matters is the strength and slope of association with income or perhaps education or occupation with controls only for age and sex. For this reason, many of the studies in the literature are not really relevant for policy purposes. Put differently, variables that are not candidates for inclusion in pension rules should not be included in the regression.

Is the relationship linear? Research for the United States has found a nonlinear relationship of mortality to educational attainment in recent decades. Until completion of secondary school, mortality declines slowly with educational attainment, then drops substantially for those who complete secondary school, and thereafter declines more rapidly with increasing education (Hummer and Lariscy 2011; Montez, Hummer, and Hayward 2012). For midcareer average income deciles in the United States, Waldron (2013, 25) shows that the slope remains negative all the way through the deciles—albeit less steep. It can be concluded that in the United States at least, the negative relationship between mortality and SES at older ages persists through the entire income and educational distribution, with some variation in slope. One implication emphasized by Waldron (2013) is that pension policies should not address differences in mortality by using some income threshold above which income variations are irrelevant. The relationship is continuous.

How the Growing Gap in Life Expectancy Affects Lifetime Benefits in the United States

The U.S. Social Security system is a mandatory, contributory defined benefit (DB) program. Retirement benefits are calculated based on the best 35 years of earnings. The payroll tax rate is constant up to an upper limit of US$128,400 earnings (in 2018), while the benefit formula is progressive. Individuals with low lifetime earnings have a marginal replacement rate of 90 percent; middle lifetime earnings of 32 percent; and high lifetime earnings of 15 percent. When a person retires before or after the normal retirement age (NRA), the monthly benefits are reduced or credited to keep the system actuarially fair.

The U.S. system is designed to redistribute from higher-income groups to lower-income groups. This is very different from nonfinancial defined contribution (NDC) systems, which are designed to provide benefits proportional to contributions, without redistribution on average. Yet the growing gap in life expectancy by SES poses challenges for both kinds of systems. NDC systems seek to treat all participants in an actuarially fair manner, but with ex ante differences in life expectancy and the use of a single life table to annuitize the contribution account for all individuals, the result is bound to be unfair. In the case of Social Security, higher-income participants with ex ante longer life receive benefits for more years than lower-income participants, undoing some or all of the intended progressivity of benefits on a lifetime basis.

This section reviews the NASEM (2015) study, which analyzed the effect on lifetime public pension benefits of the widening gap between longevity of those with higher and lower long-term labor income (figure 12.1). The design held constant all aspects of the life cycles across two simulations, varying only the mortality and survival according to the experience (actual and projected) of the 1930 and 1960 birth cohorts.[5] The results are shown in figure 12.2, in which present values are calculated with a discount rate of 3 percent (real). The difference between the high and low quintiles for men is US$103,000 for 1930 cohort mortality, rising to US$173,000 for 1960 cohort mortality. The high-low gap grows US$70,000 wider due solely to steepening of the mortality gradient. For women a similar calculation finds that the gap grows by US$48,000. While figure 12.2 shows only the effect on lifetime benefits, the effect on labor earnings is quite small because mortality during working years is low (see below for net total benefit results).

The NASEM report also estimated the impact of mortality change on "total" lifetime public benefits for the elderly, which included pensions; elder health care (Medicare); health care for low-income persons, including nursing home care (Medicaid); disability insurance; and Supplemental Security Income. Including all five of these programs raises the high-low gap even more, by US$132,000 for men and by US$152,000 for women. The changes in the net benefits (net of tax payments after age 50) are US$126,000 and US$154,000, respectively. These are very large effects.

The report also considers how certain policy changes would affect benefits. Perhaps of greatest interest here is a policy of raising the so-called NRA from 67 to 70, while leaving the early retirement age unchanged. Raising the retirement age is, of course, a form of benefit cut, and because the highest income quintile receives higher benefits as a reflection of its higher lifetime contributions, it also suffers a larger benefit cut in dollars if the retirement age is raised. For this reason, this policy change would reduce the pension

FIGURE 12.2 **Present value of U.S. lifetime pension benefits by income quintile under mortality regimes of the 1930 and 1960 birth cohorts**

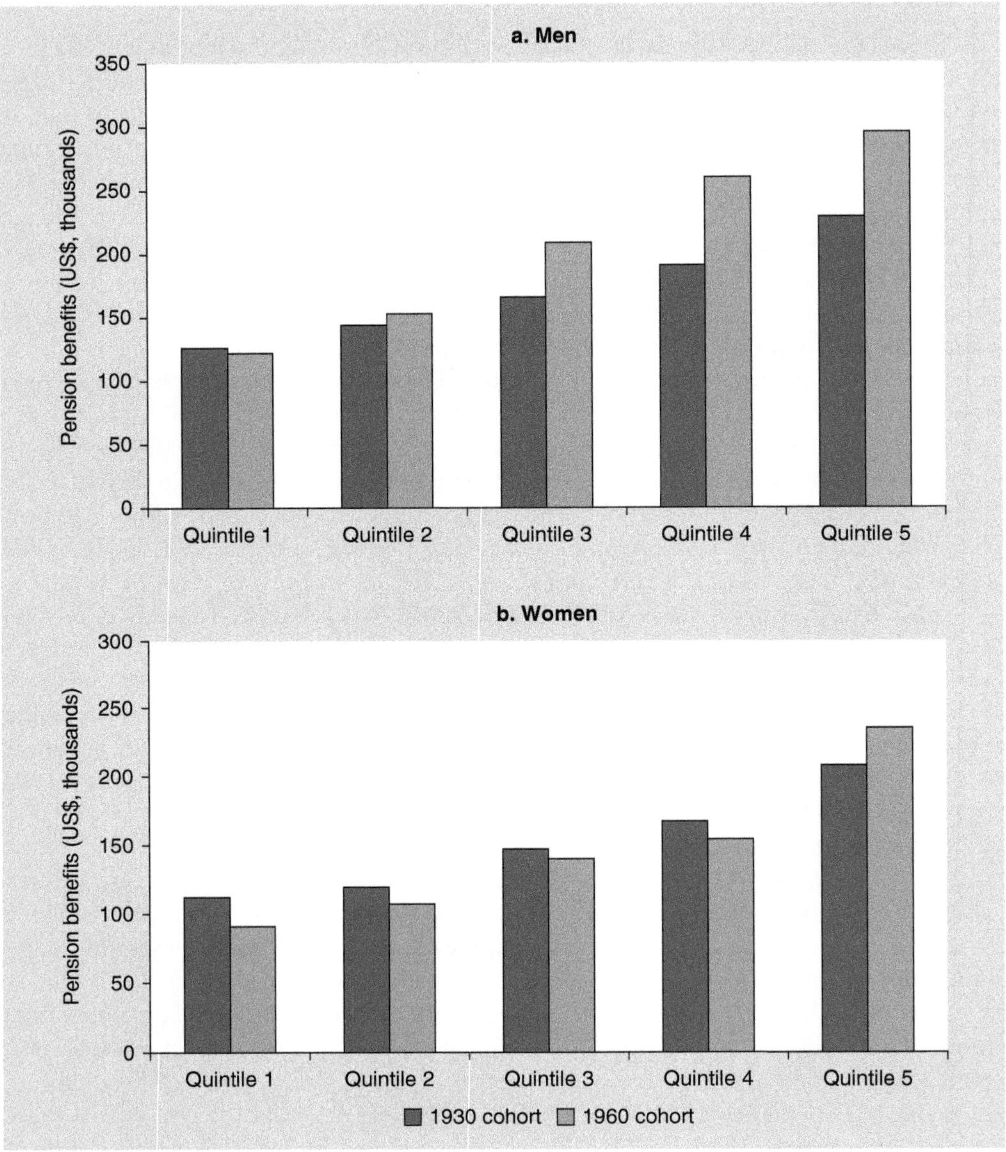

a. Men

b. Women

1930 cohort   1960 cohort

SOURCE: Data taken from NASEM (2015, 80, 82).

NOTE: In these simulations, everything including earnings histories is held constant except for the mortality regime and health. Discount rate = 3 percent.

benefit gap rather than increase it when measured in dollar terms. However, the size of the benefit cut relative to initial benefits is greater for the lowest income quintile than for the top quintile. Evaluated under 1960 cohort mortality, the cut is 24.4 percent for the bottom quintile of men versus 19.2 percent for the top quintile, and 16.6 percent versus 13.8 percent for women.[6]

General Equilibrium Issues

To better understand the impact of the increasing gap in longevity on lifetime pension benefits, it is convenient to compare the effects under four different pay-as-you-go (PAYG) pension systems. To take into account the behavioral responses of the different socioeconomic groups, this chapter develops a model in which individuals face an uncertain lifetime and decide about the number of years of schooling, the time devoted to work, and their retirement age. The information used in the model is based on the HRS and the NASEM (2015) report, from which cohort-specific life tables by income quintile are derived for the U.S. cohorts of 1930 and 1960 (figure 12.1). Moreover, the model is constructed to replicate the average lifetime Social Security benefits at age 50 (see figure 12.2), the average years of schooling, and the average retirement age by income quintile for men born in the United States in 1930.

The four different PAYG pension systems result from combining the following two characteristics. The first characteristic is whether (a) contributions are set a priori, known as defined contribution (DC), which implies that benefits will be adjusted to guarantee the sustainability of the pension system; or (b) in contrast, the benefit formula is defined a priori, known as DB, which implies that contributions are adjusted to guarantee the sustainability of the system. The second characteristic is whether the pension system (a) ex ante redistributes resources from high-income earners to low-income earners, herein called "progressive"; or (b) links the contributions paid during the working life to pension benefits in a one-to-one relationship by assuming a constant replacement rate, herein named "flat."

The model results are based on the following five assumptions:

- The model assumes a risk-free discount rate of 3 percent, similar to the one used in NASEM (2015); a stable population growth rate of 0.5 percent; and a growth rate of labor productivity of 1.5 percent per year. The implicit rate of return of the unfunded pension system is 2 percent, which is lower than the market discount factor.

- Individuals choose the number of years of schooling taking into account the existence of monetary and nonmonetary costs of attending school (Sánchez-Romero, d'Albis, and Fürnkranz-Prskawetz 2016).

- Individuals can retire at any time in the NDC systems and between 62 and 70 in the DB systems, similar to the U.S. pension system.

- Workers take into consideration that working is increasingly costly as the retirement period is squeezed. The marginal cost of continuing to work is proxied by the mortality rate (similar to Bloom, Canning, and Moore 2014) of the 1930 birth cohort.

- All individuals are assumed to understand that higher contributions today imply higher future benefits.[7]

In a DC system, the total number of pension points before retirement is equal to the pension wealth, whereas in a DB system the total number of pension points at retirement is used to calculate the "average indexed yearly earnings." To calculate a retiree's pension benefit in a DC system, the government transforms the pension wealth into an annuity using the average cohort-specific life table. The results from this simulation are labeled NDC (nonfinancial defined contribution). For comparison, the model also simulates the case in which the government has the cohort-specific life table for each income quintile, which is labeled NDC-CI (nonfinancial defined contribution–cohort-specific life tables by income quintile). This pension system is the benchmark against which all other pension systems can be assessed, since the NDC-CI corrects for differences in life expectancy across income quintiles. In the DB system, the government multiplies the average indexed yearly earnings by a replacement rate and then applies an adjustment factor for early or late retirement to determine the retiree's pension benefit. The replacement rate can be constant (labeled DB-Flat) or it can increase as the average indexed yearly earnings decline (labeled DB-Progressive). The last simulation corresponds to the U.S. Social Security system.[8] Finally, to consider actuarial fairness, the model implements for the DB system the penalties or rewards for early or late retirement established in the U.S. pension system for each birth cohort.

For the sake of comparison with the NASEM (2015) report, the analysis first calculates the present value of lifetime pension benefits at age 50 by income quintile and four different PAYG pension systems for the 1930 and 1960 birth cohorts.[9]

Figure 12.3 shows that for the 1930 birth cohort, the U.S. pension system (DB-Progressive) generates the lowest difference in lifetime pension benefits across income quintiles among the four pension systems analyzed. The difference between the top and bottom income quintiles is US\$101,000 (=US\$228,000–US\$127,000) in the DB-Progressive and US\$104,000 (=US\$237,000–US\$133,000) in the NDC-CI. Therefore, the DB-Progressive is the pension system with the greatest degree of progressivity. The highest discrepancy is obtained with DB-Flat, followed by the NDC. Specifically, workers in the lowest quintile could expect to receive US\$190,000 (=US\$316,000–US\$126,000) and US\$151,000 (=US\$267,000–US\$116,000) less than workers in the highest quintile in the DB-Flat and NDC, respectively.

Using the mortality rates for the 1960 birth cohort, the difference in lifetime pension benefits across income quintiles widens for all pension systems because of the further increase in the longevity gap. The difference in lifetime pension benefits between the top and bottom income quintiles doubles in the DB systems compared with the 1930 birth cohort, while this difference increases about 50 percent in the NDC systems. In addition, the model shows that once the longevity gap across income quintiles becomes excessively high, the U.S. pension system (DB-Progressive) does not redistribute income from top-income earners to low-income earners as well as the NDC-CI system does, even though the U.S. pension system is designed to be ex ante progressive. Indeed, in the DB-Progressive system workers in the lowest income quintile receive US\$203,000 (=US\$302,000–US\$99,000) less than workers in the top income quintile, whereas this difference is US\$154,000 (=US\$285,000–US\$131,000) in the NDC-CI system.

Table 12.2 shows the redistributive effects of each pension system in terms of rate of return. Remember that in a mature PAYG pension system with a stable population, the

FIGURE 12.3 **Present value of lifetime pension benefits by income quintile and pay-as-you-go pension system under mortality regimes of the 1930 and 1960 U.S. birth cohorts for men**

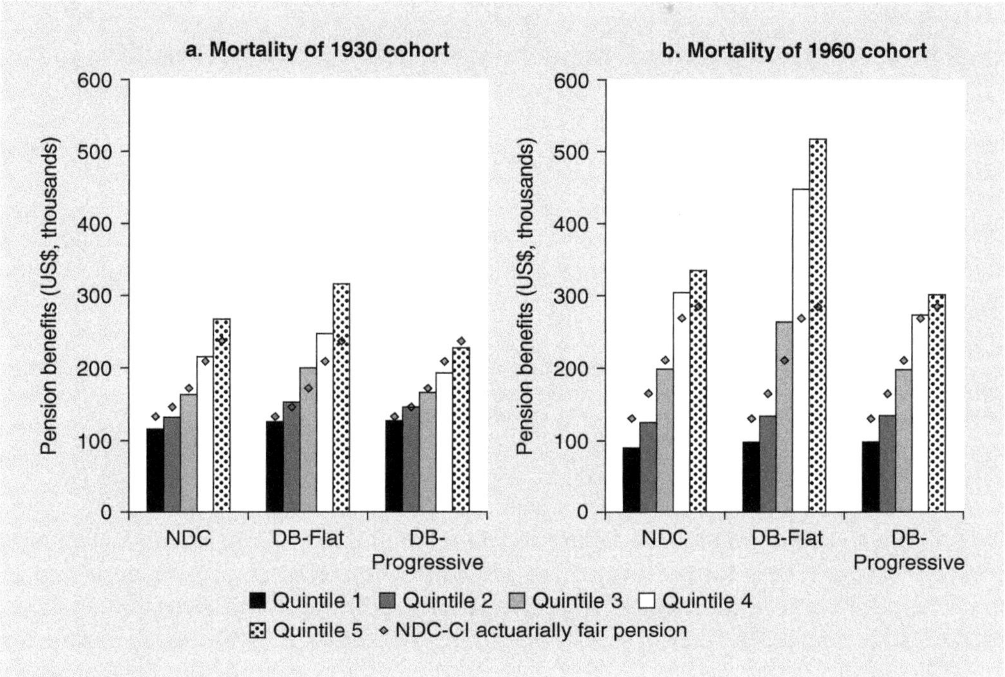

SOURCE: Original calculations.

NOTE: Risk-free market discount rate = 3 percent. Results for 1960 cohort are detrended by labor productivity growth. Pay-as-you-go pension systems: DC system using the average cohort-specific life table (NDC); DC system using the cohort-specific life table by income quintile (NDC-CI); DB system with a constant replacement rate (DB-Flat); and DB system with an ex ante progressive replacement rate (DB-Progressive). CI = cohort-specific life tables by income quintile; DB = defined benefit; DC = defined contribution; NDC = nonfinancial defined contribution.

implicit rate of return equals the rate of growth of the population plus the rate of growth of productivity for all income quintiles, or in this case 2 percent per year (Samuelson 1958). This rate of return is achieved by all income groups and mortality regimes under NDC-CI in which the pension system calculates the annuity using the mortality rate of each income group. However, in the NDC, DB-Flat, and DB-Progressive cases, lower income quintiles have an internal rate of return of less than 2 percent, while higher income quintiles have an internal rate of return greater than 2 percent. As a consequence, the redistribution goes from poor to rich. Moreover, this redistribution becomes more regressive when using more unequal mortality rates, such as those of the 1960 cohort. For the DB-Progressive case, which was designed to be redistributive from rich to poor, the system fails to reach this goal because of differential mortality by income quintile. Indeed, the expected return of a dollar contributed to the pension system by an individual born in 1960 who belongs to the bottom income quintile is 1.4 (=2.4–1.0) percentage points lower than the return received by an individual at the top income quintile.

TABLE 12.2 **Internal rate of return by income quintile and pay-as-you-go pension system, under mortality regimes of the 1930 and 1960 U.S. birth cohorts for men**

Pension system	NDC		NDC-CI		DB-Flat		DB-Progressive	
Birth cohort	1930 (%)	1960 (%)	1930 (%)	1960 (%)	1930 (%)	1960 (%)	1930 (%)	1960 (%)
Quintile 1	1.5	0.7	2.0	2.0	1.4	-0.3	1.8	1.0
Quintile 2	1.7	1.0	2.0	2.0	1.5	0.3	2.0	1.3
Quintile 3	1.8	1.8	2.0	2.0	1.8	1.6	2.1	2.0
Quintile 4	2.1	2.4	2.0	2.0	2.1	2.5	2.0	2.2
Quintile 5	2.4	2.5	2.0	2.0	2.6	2.8	2.1	2.4

SOURCE: Original table.

NOTE: Pay-as-you-go pension systems: DC system using the average cohort-specific life table (NDC); DC system using the cohort-specific life table by income quintile (NDC-CI); DB system with a constant replacement rate (DB-Flat); and DB system with an ex ante progressive replacement rate (DB-Progressive). CI = cohort-specific life tables by income quintile; DB = defined benefit; DC = defined contribution; NDC = nonfinancial defined contribution.

Public pension systems also distort decisions about labor, education, and consumption, which may cause further inequality. This distortionary effect can be measured as the difference between the value of the extra pension points and the social contribution paid from an additional hour of work (Auerbach and Kotlikoff 1987; Sánchez-Romero and Fürnkranz-Prskawetz 2017; Sánchez-Romero, Lee, and Fürnkranz-Prskawetz 2018). If the value of the extra pension points generated from an additional hour of work is less than the social contribution paid, workers view their contribution as an implicit tax on labor income, which leads to a reduction in labor supply and hence to a fall in consumption. Of course, the opposite effects occur when the value given to the extra pension points from an additional hour of work is greater than the social contribution rate paid.

Table 12.3 shows the implicit tax rate (negative number) or implicit subsidy rate (positive number) by income quintile and PAYG pension system for U.S. male cohorts born in 1930 and 1960. A worker born in 1930 with an income that belongs to quintile 3 faces an implicit tax of 6.1 percent from his contribution to the DB-Progressive system.[10,11] The implicit tax on a worker born in 1930 with an income that belongs to quintile 3 is 2.6 percent in the NDC, 2.1 percent in the NDC-CI, and 3.1 in the DB-Flat system. Table 12.3 provides three important results. First, given that the assumed market discount factor is higher than the implicit rate of return of the PAYG system, all the numbers are negative. As a consequence, individuals view their contributions as an implicit tax (Auerbach and Kotlikoff 1987; Börsch-Supan 2006). Second, in the NDC and DB-Flat cases, the system penalizes short-lived and poor workers more than long-lived and rich workers. Third, the NDC-CI system produces very equal tax rates across all five quintiles, because the distortion is due solely to the differences in retirement age. This last result suggests the value of introducing reforms in the direction of applying cohort-specific life tables for different socioeconomic groups, as proposed by Ayuso, Bravo, and Holzmann (2017) and explored for further policy options in chapter 14.

TABLE 12.3 **Implicit tax rate (negative number) and implicit subsidy rate**
positive number on labor by income quintile and pay-as-you-go pension system under mortality regimes of the 1930 and 1960 U.S. birth cohorts for men

Pension system	NDC		NDC-CI		DB-Flat		DB-Progressive	
Birth cohort	1930 (%)	1960 (%)	1930 (%)	1960 (%)	1930 (%)	1960 (%)	1930 (%)	1960 (%)
Quintile 1	−3.2	−5.1	−2.1	−2.1	−4.1	8.7	−5.0	−6.9
Quintile 2	−2.9	−4.5	−2.1	−2.3	−3.9	−7.8	−4.5	−6.2
Quintile 3	−2.6	−3.1	−2.1	−2.5	−3.1	−4.9	−6.1	−6.6
Quintile 4	−2.0	−1.7	−2.2	−2.7	−2.3	−1.9	−7.6	−7.6
Quintile 5	−1.3	−1.4	−2.4	−2.8	−1.0	−0.8	−7.2	−7.3

SOURCE: Original table.

NOTE: − signals a tax and + signals a subsidy. Values calculated at age 50. Pay-as-you-go pension systems: DC system using the average cohort-specific life table (NDC); DC system using the cohort-specific life table by income quintile (NDC-CI); DB system with a constant replacement rate (DB-Flat); and DB system with an ex ante progressive replacement rate (DB-Progressive). CI = cohort-specific life tables by income quintile; DB = defined benefit; DC = defined contribution; NDC = nonfinancial defined contribution.

Policy Options

This section considers some policy options for addressing the negative effects of the increasing gap in life expectancy by SES on PAYG pension systems. An important result already shown is the necessity of accounting for the mortality differential by SES. Indeed, with an increasing longevity gap by SES, the pension system that does not account for the differential mortality will become ex post highly regressive. Here, the pros and cons of different reforms are analyzed along three dimensions: (a) benefits, (b) contributions, and (c) the socioeconomic variables to be used for differentiating across groups.

BENEFITS

Redesigning the benefit formula to cope with different ex ante life expectancies can be accomplished by adjusting the annual benefit or by modifying the retirement age for each socioeconomic group (which amounts to the same thing).

In the presence of ex ante differences in life expectancy, an actuarial adjustment of the pension benefit—based on the average cohort life table—penalizes those with low life expectancy and favors those with long life expectancy. In this context, is desirable that the actuarial adjustment should be specific for each socioeconomic group. If this policy is not feasible, another approach would be to apply the actuarial adjustment of the most disadvantaged group for retirement before the NRA, and after the NRA the actuarial adjustment of those with the highest life expectancy.

An alternative option in a DB system for reducing the polarization of the present value of lifetime benefits is to change the replacement rate (figure 12.3). In a DB-Flat system, moving to a replacement rate that varies by SES (DB-Progressive) would be desirable. For example, the annual benefit rate could be adjusted when mortality changes or differs so as to keep constant the ratio of present value of lifetime benefits to present value of contributions, or the implicit rate of return. In an NDC system, equity would be improved by applying the life table specific for each socioeconomic group or using a different effective interest rate for each socioeconomic group.[12]

CONTRIBUTIONS

Some of the negative consequences of the increasing gap in life expectancy by SES are strengthened at the contribution side. Low socioeconomic groups enter the labor market earlier and face greater unemployment risk, especially late in their working lives, than high socioeconomic groups. Hence, when the pension benefit formula gives a greater weight to contributions late in the working life, the pension system tends to polarize even more the present value of lifetime benefits across socioeconomic groups. To avoid this polarization, pension systems should calculate the pension benefits using both all the years contributed and the total amount contributed to the system. Similarly, pension systems that index past contributions less than the growth of the labor force in real efficient units (known as the Aaron-Samuelson condition) also give more weight to late contributions.[13] Therefore, PAYG pension systems should also use the implicit rate of return of a PAYG system as the indexation, or capitalization, factor for past pension contributions.

Whether pension benefits should be financed not only through contributions but also through taxes is also increasingly debated. This strategy has three major drawbacks. First, any tax will have a negative effect on labor income and thus on the implicit tax or subsidy (Sánchez-Romero, Sambt, and Fürnkranz-Prskawetz 2013). Hence, the implicit tax may also rise rather than fall. Second, if the marginal tax paid by long-lived and wealthy workers is lower than the marginal tax paid by short-lived and poor workers, then shifting the finaning toward taxes will generate a higher distortion. Third, workers will find it more difficult to link their contributions to their pensions. At the same time, for some countries in special circumstances (such as a very large informal sector and highly unequal distribution of income), other considerations may dominate.

SOCIOECONOMIC VARIABLES

To implement some of the recommended policies, to constructing cohort–life tables by SES. In this regard, Ayuso, Bravo, and Holzmann (2016) provide an overview of the suitability of different socioeconomic indicators for capturing the difference in life expectancy. In addition, OECD (2016, 2017) reports data for many countries on differences in mortality rates by education, occupation, and lifetime earnings. In principle, the choice of a socioeconomic indicator should be based on two major criteria: (a) it should capture the strength of the increase in the life-expectancy gap, and, conveniently, (b) it should not change over time. For instance, occupational group is an indicator that captures the increasing gap in longevity, as has been found in several countries (Burström, Johannesson, and Diderichsen 2005; Luy, Di Giulio, and Caselli 2011; Luy et al. 2015). However, the use of the occupation group as an indicator is more controversial than education and income level, given that individuals can have several occupations over their working lives, which can produce an adverse selection effect (Pestieau and Racionero 2016).[14]

Sex is an indicator that does not change over time. However, looking at age-profiles of consumption and labor income estimated for the NTA/AGENTA[15] project, small differences in consumption and large differences in labor income by gender are observed, which suggests a significant pooling of resources among household members

(Istenič et al. 2016). Under such a circumstance, it is then logical to use a unisex life table to pool the risk of the household, rather than at the individual level. Nevertheless, the increasing relative importance of different household types and individualistic lifestyles creates a need for finding new solutions and raises very difficult questions about gender-specific mortality differences. Education is also somehow problematic because pensions may have a positive impact on education (Sánchez-Romero and Fürnkranz-Prskawetz 2017) and education has a positive impact on life expectancy (Lleras-Muney 2005). Therefore, before a pension reform in which the use of cohort–life tables by SES is introduced, to avoid unexpected adverse selection effects, the impact that the pension system may have on the socioeconomic indicator must be accounted for.

Notes

1. Health and long-term care insurance primarily deal with uncertainty about the relevant costs, but individuals also face the risk of outliving their savings and these unexpected costs greatly raise this risk—the total risk is an interaction of the two.

2. This issue of fairness of public programs has a mirror image, illustrated by public education. Public education is received in childhood and paid for many years later through taxes. Those with ex ante high mortality are less likely to survive to pay the taxes that fund it. To complain about the resulting inequity would require a hard heart indeed.

3. One might go further and consider variation in self-assessed health, disability status, health biomarkers, and the individual genome. These possibilities are not entirely fanciful, since an OECD (2016) report raises the possibility of using this sort of information to set retirement age or replacement rate. This chapter focuses mainly on the more traditional dimensions of SES.

4. It might also seem obvious that if socioeconomic differences in longevity have been widening, then variation in longevity must also be increasing. In fact, this is not the case, and in some populations the variation in longevity (conditional on surviving childhood) has declined in recent decades, even as SES differentials widened (see Tuljapurkar [2011], here and for the rest of the paragraph). This happens because the component of variance arising from differences in longevity between SES groups has indeed been growing, but at the same time the component arising from variance within SES groups has been falling. The first might be loosely referred to as ex ante variation (between groups identified by observable characteristics) and the second as ex post variation (within groups).

5. In addition to mortality, health was permitted to vary across the simulations in a way that is consistent with the mortality differences. This matters very little for this simulation of retirement benefits, but is quite important for the case of public health and disability insurance (NASEM 2015).

6. Other useful calculations are provided in the literature. For example, in the OECD (2016, 198) report, the ratio of years in retirement to contribution years is 0.38 for the bottom income quartile in the United States in 2011 but is 0.46 for the top quartile. In France, this same ratio varies from 0.41 for manual workers to 0.49 for higher managerial and professional workers. To maintain the same ratio in 2011 as held in 1979 in the United States, the lowest income quartile would have to work 2.7 years longer, but the highest quartile would have to work 5.4 years longer, twice as great an increase. The necessary changes for France from 1987 to 2011 for the highest and lowest occupational groups are very similar to these figures for the United States.

7. The mechanism works as follows: By contributing to the pension system, individuals gain pension points that entitle them to receive a pension benefit upon retirement. Pension points are capitalized (or indexed) by the population growth rate plus the productivity growth rate. The amount of pension points earned each period depends on whether the system is DC or DB. In a DC system, the pension points earned each period are equal to the contribution paid, whereas in a DB system the pension points are equal to the yearly pension benefit accrual.

8. Retirement benefits are calculated based on the best 35 years of earnings, which are indexed to increases in the average national wage, divided by 420 to obtain the "average indexed monthly earnings" (AIME). Applying a progressive benefit formula with three segments with marginal rates of 0.90, 0.35, and 0.15, AIME is transformed into the "primary insurance amount" (PIA). PIA is the benefit a person would receive if she or he retires at the NRA. The average replacement rate for the average income earner is 41.67 percent.

9. The social contribution rates are 11.2 percent and 11.9 percent when assuming the mortality of the 1930 and 1960 birth cohorts, respectively. For the sake of comparison across pension systems, the two NDC systems assume the same social contribution rate obtained for the U.S. pension system (DB-Progressive).

10. Alternatively, given that the social contribution rate faced by the 1930 birth cohort is 11.2 percent, a worker belonging to this cohort considers that 46 percent (= [11.2 percent– 6.1 percent]/11.2 percent) of each dollar contributed at age 50 is invested in a savings account (saving share), while 54 percent (=6.1 percent/11.2 percent) is taxed (tax share). Similar interpretations can be given to all other numbers.

11. The implicit tax in the DB-Progressive case is higher than in all other pension systems because the replacement rate decreases as the average indexed yearly earnings increase.

12. The first option is a priori better because it clearly accounts for differences in life expectancy. But if differences in life expectancy are correlated with other characteristics, such as the number of offspring, which influences the intrinsic return of the PAYG system, using a different effective interest rate by socioeconomic group could also be used to reduce the difference in the present value of lifetime benefits across socioeconomic groups. Indeed, policies that link pension entitlements to the quantity and quality of offspring have been proposed several times in the literature (Demeny 1987; Fenge and Meier 2005; Sinn 2004).

13. An indexing factor lower than the growth of the labor force in real efficient units raises the implicit tax for young workers at the expense of producing an implicit subsidy for old workers. For example, consider a worker who earns exactly the average labor income and contributes to a pension system with a flat replacement rate of 50 percent and an indexation factor of zero percent (in constant terms). If the implicit rate of return of the PAYG system is 2 percent, the contribution paid at age 30 will increase less rapidly than the total wage bill of the economy. As a consequence, when the individual retires at age 65, the additional pension benefit entitlement from the contribution at age 30 will be close to $25 (= 0.5\ exp\{(0 - 0.02)\ (65 - 30)\})$ percent of the average income of a worker rather than 50 percent.

14. An alternative is the use of health indicators as instruments for measuring the gap in life expectancy by SES. Some of these health indicators are smoking and drinking habits, body weight index, grip strength, disability status, and genome, among others. However, to avoid adverse selection, one might exclude smoking and drinking habits and, to some extent, body weight. The genome qualifies as a suitable indicator, but only 25–30 percent of the mortality gradient is due to exogenous factors such as genetic background (Christensen, Johnson, and Vaupel 2006). Hence, additional indicators are necessary.

15. The EU-funded AGENTA project (www.agenta-project.eu; AGENTA = Ageing Europe—An Application of National Transfer Accounts for Explaining and Projecting Trends in Public Finances), which relies on the NTA methodology (see www.ntaccounts.org), measures how the difference between consumption and labor income of each age group is financed through the ownership of assets, public transfer, and private transfers. The data explorer wittgensteincentre .org/ntadata contains monetary and nonmonetary age profiles by age and sex for 25 European countries.

References

Auerbach, Alan J., and Laurence J. Kotlikoff. 1987. *Dynamic Fiscal Policy*. Cambridge: Cambridge University Press.

Ayuso, Mercedes, Jorge M. Bravo, and Robert Holzmann. 2016. "On the Heterogeneity in Longevity among Socioeconomic Groups: Scope, Trends, and Implications for Earnings-Related Pension Schemes." IZA Discussion Paper 10060, Institute of Labor Economics, Bonn, Germany.

———. 2017. "Addressing Longevity Heterogeneity in Pension Scheme Design." *Journal of Finance and Economics* 6 (1): 1–24.

Bloom, David E., David Canning, and Michael Moore. 2014. "Optimal Retirement with Increasing Longevity." *Scandinavian Journal of Economics* 116 (3): 838–58.

Börsch-Supan, Axel H. 2006. "What Are NDC Pension Systems? What Do They Bring to Reform Strategies?" In *Pension Reform: Issues and Prospects for Non-Financial Defined Contribution (NDC) Schemes*, edited by Robert Holzmann and Edward Palmer, 35–56. Washington, DC: World Bank.

Bosley, Tiffany, Michael Morris, and Karen Glenn. 2018. "Mortality by Career-Average Earnings Level, Actuarial Study No. 124." Social Security Administration Office of the Chief Actuary, Woodlawn, MD.

Bosworth, Barry, and Kathleen Burke. 2014. "Differential Mortality and Retirement Benefits in the Health and Retirement Study." Working Paper 2014-4, Center for Retirement Research at Boston College, Boston, MA.

Bosworth, Barry, Gary Burtless, and Kan Zhang. 2015. "Sources of Increasing Differential Mortality among the Aged by Socioeconomic Status." Working Paper 2015-10, Center for Retirement Research at Boston College, Boston, MA.

———. 2016. "Later Retirement, Inequality in Old Age, and the Growing Gap in Longevity between Rich and Poor." Brookings Institution, Washington, DC.

Bound, John, Arline T. Geronimus, Javier Rodriguez, and Timothy A. Waidmann. 2015. "Measuring Recent Apparent Declines in Longevity: The Role of Increasing Educational Attainment." *Health Affairs* 34 (12): 2167–73.

Burström, Kristina, Magnus Johannesson, and Finn Diderichsen. 2005. "Increasing Socio-Economic Inequalities in Life Expectancy and QALYs in Sweden 1980–1997." *Health Economics* 14 (8): 831–50.

Chetty, Raj, Michael Stepner, Sarah Abraham, Shelby Lin, Benjamin Scuderi, Nicholas Turner, Augustin Bergeron, and David Cutler. 2016. "The Association between Income and Life Expectancy in the United States, 2001–2014." *Journal of the American Medical Association* 315 (14): 1750–66.

Christensen, Kaare, Thomas E. Johnson, and James W. Vaupel. 2006. "The Quest for Genetic Determinants of Human Longevity: Challenges and Insights." *Nature Reviews. Genetics* 7 (6): 436–48.

Demeny, Paul. 1987. "Re-linking Fertility Behavior and Economic Security in Old Age: A Pronatalist Reform." *Population and Development Review* 13 (1): 128–32.

Dowd, Jennifer B., and Amar Hamoudi. 2014. "Is Life Expectancy Really Falling for Groups of Low Socio-Economic Status? Lagged Selection Bias and Artefactual Trends in Mortality." *International Journal of Epidemiology* 43 (4): 983–88.

Fenge, Robert, and Volker Meier. 2005. "Pensions and Fertility Incentives." *Canadian Journal of Economics/Revue Canadiense d'Economique* 38 (1): 28–48.

Goldring, Thomas, Fabian Lange, and Seth Richards-Shubik. 2016. "Testing for Changes in the SES-Mortality Gradient When the Distribution of Education Changes Too." *Journal of Health Economics* 46: 120–30.

Hummer, Robert A., and Elaine M. Hernandez. 2013. "The Effect of Educational Attainment on Adult Mortality in the United States." *Population Bulletin* 68 (1): 1–15.

Hummer, Robert A., and Joseph T. Lariscy. 2011. "Educational Attainment and Adult Mortality." In *International Handbook of Adult Mortality,* edited by Richard G. Rogers and Eileen M. Crimmins, 241–61. New York: Springer.

Istenič, Tanja, Ana Šeme, Bernhard Hammer, Aleša Lotrič-Dolinar, and Jože Sambt. 2016. *European NTA Manual.* Vienna, Austria: AGENTA Public Deliverable, Vienna Institute of Demography.

Lleras-Muney, Adriana. 2005. "The Relationship between Education and Adult Mortality in the United States." *Review of Economic Studies* 72 (1): 189–221.

Luy, Marc, Paola Di Giulio, and Graziella Caselli. 2011. "Differences in Life Expectancy by Education and Occupation in Italy, 1980–94: Indirect Estimates from Maternal and Paternal Orphanhood." *Population Studies* 65 (2): 137–55.

Luy, Marc, Christian Wegner-Siegmundt, Angela Wiedemann, and Jeroen Spijker. 2015. "Life Expectancy by Education, Income and Occupation in Germany: Estimations Using the Longitudinal Survival Method." *Comparative Population Studies* 40 (4): 399–436.

Manchester, Joyce, and Julie Topoleski. 2008. *Growing Disparities in Life Expectancy.* Washington, DC: United States Congressional Budget Office. http://purl.access.gpo.gov/GPO/LPS93373.

Meara, Ellen R., Seth Richards, and David M. Cutler. 2008. "The Gap Gets Bigger: Changes in Mortality and Life Expectancy, by Education, 1981–2000." *Health Affairs* 27 (2): 350—60. doi: 10.1377/hlthaff.27.2.350.

Montez, Jennifer Karas, Robert A. Hummer, and Mark D. Hayward. 2012. "Educational Attainment and Adult Mortality in the United States: A Systematic Analysis of Functional Form." *Demography* 49 (1): 315–36.

NASEM (National Academy of Sciences, Engineering and Medicine). 2015. *The Growing Gap in Life Expectancy by Income: Implications for Federal Programs and Policy Responses.* Committee on the Long-Run Macroeconomic Effects of the Aging U.S. Population Phase II. Washington, DC: National Academies Press.

OECD (Organisation for Economic Co-operation and Development). 2016. "Fragmentation of Retirement Markets due to Differences in Life Expectancy." Chapter 6 in *OECD Business and Finance Outlook 2016.* Paris: OECD Publishing. doi: http://dx.doi.org/10.1787/9789264257573-11-en

———. 2017. *Preventing Ageing Unequally.* Paris: OECD Publishing. doi: http://dx.doi.org/10.1787/9789264279087

Olshansky, Jay S., Toni Antonucci, Lisa Berkman, Robert H. Binstock, Axel Börsch-Supan, John T. Cacioppo, Bruce A. Carnes, et al. 2012. "Differences in Life Expectancy due to Race and Educational Differences Are Widening, and Many May Not Catch Up." *Health Affairs* 31 (8): 1803–13.

Pestieau, Pierre, and Gregory Ponthiere. 2016. "Longevity Variations and the Welfare State." *Journal of Demographic Economics* 82: 207–39. doi:10.1017/dem.2016.4.

Pestieau, Pierre, and Maria Racionero. 2016. "Harsh Occupations, Life Expectancy and Social Security." *Economic Modelling* 58: 194–202.

Rosero-Bixby, Luis, and William H. Dow. 2016. "Exploring Why Costa Rica Outperforms the United States in Life Expectancy: A Tale of Two Inequality Gradients." *Proceedings of the National Academy of Sciences of the United States of America* 113 (5): 1130–37.

Rostron, Brian L., John L. Boies, and Elizabeth Arias. 2010. "Education Reporting and Classification on Death Certificates in the United States." Vital and Health Statistics Series 2, Number 151, DHHS Publication No. (PHS) 2010–1351.

Samuelson, Paul. 1958. "An Exact Consumption-Loan Model of Interest with or without the Social Contrivance of Money." *Journal of Political Economy* 6: 467–82.

Sánchez-Romero, Miguel, Hippolyte d'Albis, and Alexia Fürnkranz-Prskawetz. 2016. "Education, Lifetime Labor Supply, and Longevity Improvements." *Journal of Economic Dynamics and Control* 73: 118–41.

Sánchez-Romero, Miguel, and Alexia Fürnkranz-Prskawetz. 2017. "Redistributive Effects of the US Pension System among Individuals with Different Life Expectancy." *Journal of the Economics of Ageing* 10: 51–74.

Sánchez-Romero, Miguel, Ronald D. Lee, and Alexia Fürnkranz-Prskawetz. 2018. "Redistributive Effects of Different Pension Structures When Longevity Varies by Socioeconomic Status in a General Equilibrium Setting." Unpublished.

Sánchez-Romero, Miguel, Jože Sambt, and Alexia Fürnkranz-Prskawetz. 2013. "Quantifying the Role of Alternative Pension Reforms on the Austrian Economy." *Labour Economics* 22 (C): 94–114.

Sinn, Hans-Werner. 2004. "The Pay-as-You-Go Pension System as Fertility Insurance and an Enforcement Device." *Journal of Population Economics* 88: 1335–57.

Tuljapurkar, Shripad. 2011. "The Final Inequality: Variance in Age at Death." In *Demography and the Economy*, edited by John B. Shoven, 209–221. Chicago, IL: University of Chicago Press for the National Bureau of Economic Research.

Waldron, Hilary. 2007. "Trends in Mortality Differentials and Life Expectancy for Male Social Security–Covered Workers, by Socioeconomic Status." *Social Security Bulletin* 67 (3): 1–28.

———. 2013. "Mortality Differentials by Lifetime Earnings Decile: Implications for Evaluations of Proposed Social Security Law Changes." *Social Security Bulletin* 73 (1): 1–37. http://ssrn.com/abstract=2217432.

CHAPTER 13

Annuities in (N)DC Pension Schemes: Design, Heterogeneity, and Estimation Issues

Edward Palmer and Yuwei Zhao de Gosson de Varennes

Introduction

When they emerged in the mid-1990s, nonfinancial defined contribution (NDC) schemes constituted a new way of thinking about the construction of the benefit in a universal public pension scheme. Individuals pay contributions to the public NDC scheme that are registered on personal accounts that receive a yearly rate of return. The rate of return is the rate of growth of the wage base upon which contributions are based. Contributions are paid to the scheme and noted on the individual's personal account throughout a lifetime working career until the individual claims a benefit after reaching the minimum pension age. The benefit received—in technical terms, the life annuity—is calculated as the individual's account balance divided by a divisor that depends on the average life expectancy of the individual's birth cohort—and possibly even a long-run assumed rate of return (that is, a discount rate).

This chapter presents and discusses policy issues that arise in the formulation of the annuity. Four aspects of annuity creation are examined in four separate sections of this chapter.

Construction of the annuity. It is a given that the annuity includes projected life expectancy at the annuitant's chosen age of retirement. There are options that need to be considered in how the rate of return enters into the picture, however. The choice is between (a) including the rate of return endogenously together with life expectancy in the construction of the annuity, (b) basing the annuity solely on life expectancy complemented with exogenous yearly indexation, or (c) using a mixed version. What are the micro and macro implications for the distribution of pension pool payments over the life of a cohort of pensioners in the pension pool?

The importance of getting the projection of life expectancy right. Fulfillment of the NDC conditions of financial sustainability and intergenerational fairness require that the value for life expectancy used in formulation of the annuity does not systematically over- or underestimate life expectancy, viewed over a continuous series of birth cohorts. This section identifies issues, illustrates the outcomes of model choice, and identifies the basics of best practice projection methods.

The authors are grateful to Robert Holzmann, Nico Kielman, and Ronald Lee for comments and suggestions in various phases of the work.

Variable annuities. What is gained—and lost—by recalculating the annuity at regular intervals based on new projections of life expectancy? One way to minimize the projection error is to reestimate and recalculate annuities up to a fixed age of, for example, 80–85. This section identifies the policy issues viewed against the background of the effects on individual and distributional outcomes within the pension cohort.

Socioeconomic determinants of life expectancy in the context of creating the annuity. There is mounting evidence of an increasing gap in life expectancy between persons with lower and higher lifetime earnings. This gap reflects directly on the outcomes of pensions in all the various forms of earnings-related pension schemes, and not the least defined contribution (DC) schemes—both financial (FDC) and nonfinancial (NDC) ones. Secondary markers of this phenomenon are education and occupation, and in the gender dimension the gap between a low-income and a high-income man can be twice the gap between a low-income and a high-income woman. This section identifies the policy issues arising from these characteristics of the pension pool and discusses the pros and cons of various proposals for dealing with these issues in the construction of the annuity pools.

The chapter ends with a general summation of the main policy lines developing from the issues discussed.

The NDC Annuity

The points of departure in formulating an annuity model are (a) the total capital balance on an individual's account at retirement, (b) an estimate of the life expectancy of the average member of the individual's birth cohort at an age relevant for claiming a pension, and (c) an assumed future rate of return. This section addresses the issues involved in integrating the rate of return into the construction of the annuity to create ex ante an affordable benefit that also maintains long-term financial sustainability.

THE BASIC ANNUITY FORMULA

The annuity is a function of the known individual account balance at the individual's chosen age of retirement and projected values of two factors. The first factor is the cohort-based average life expectancy, LE, for cohort k (person j's birth cohort) at retirement. The second is the internal rate of return, α, computed over the length of average life expectancy.

The account balance is the sum of the individual's contributions up to time τ accredited with a yearly return based on the scheme's internal rate of return before the time of retirement. The amount on balance at the end of the period before retirement, $K_{\tau-1}$, is divided by an annuity factor, G. The annuity factor includes the average life expectancy at the chosen pension age projected for individual j's birth cohort and a rate of return α (to be discussed), where $\alpha = 1$ if the entire rate of indexation is left outside and applied ex post on a yearly basis. This gives the initial value of the annuity, P_τ, for the jth person:

$$P_{j,t} = \frac{K_{j,t-1}}{G\left[LE_k,\ \alpha(LE_k)\right]} \tag{13.1}$$

"Projecting Life Expectancy" is devoted to the calculation of life expectancy. This section focuses on the rate of return in the NDC context and the pros and cons of different "models" for distributing it over time—either endogenously within the calculation of the annuity or exogenously through its external regular indexation.

POLICY CONSIDERATIONS REGARDING THE RATE OF RETURN TO BE INCLUDED IN THE ANNUITY CALCULATION

In an FDC scheme, the rate of return on the savings transferred to the pool of pensioners is the nominal financial rate earned on the investment of this money in the financial market; that is, it consists of two components—the real rate of return (r^*) and the rate of inflation (p). Even in a financial scheme it is quite possible to set $\alpha = 1$ and to index the annuity with, for example, a moving average of yearly returns. This is a straightforward way to deal with the uncertainty in the discount rate, as determined by the rate of return.

In an NDC scheme, the rate of return is the internal rate of return, determined by the growth of the nominal contribution wage base (W), which can be broken down into three components: (a) the rate of growth of the real wage per capita (w), (b) the rate of growth of the number of contributors that underlies this wage growth (λ), and (c) the rate of change in prices used to deflate the nominal wage to obtain the real wage—that is, the consumer price index (CPI), or "p." In an NDC scheme, the overall rate of return is thus $(1 + w)(1 + \lambda)(1+p)$, whereas it is $(1 + r)(1 + p)$ for an FDC scheme.

To begin, it is difficult to argue in favor of including the rate of growth of the number contributors (λ) in the computation of the annuity, principally because the determinants are subject to factors that are extremely difficult to project. The rate of growth of the contributing labor force is determined by three factors: (a) the total fertility rate over an average of years two decades earlier, (b) a country's current net immigration of prime working-age population, and (c) individuals' formal supply of labor and demand for their labor.

Generally, it is highly arguable that periods of positive growth in the labor force can and should be used to build up reserves that later on can be used to neutralize the effects of negative labor force growth on indexation, when indexation is based on the wage sum. In periods with a declining labor force—for example, caused by fertility rates of less than 2.1 or net emigration of the working-age population—the normal population-driven cyclical development of the reserves can cushion the need to adjust pensions downward, owing to short-term variation. With a demography with continuously low fertility and net migration from the country (such as that characterized by Southern, Central, and Eastern Europe since the mid-1990s), positive reserves can only develop through increases in the density of contributions of a declining population (see, for example, Palmer and Stabina [2019]). In the context of emerging market economies, this is clearly possible because of the combined forces of economic and population-driven growth in the workforce—the mechanism is explained in Larsson, Leyaro, and Palmer (2019) and for more developed economies in the European Union (EU) in Palmer and Stabina (2019).

Alternative values of α can be considered potential candidates for inclusion in the annuity. One alternative is to set $(1 + \alpha) = (1 + w)(1+p)$ and another is to set $(1 + \alpha) = (1 + w)$, where both of these alternatives exclude the factor $(1 + \lambda)$, as just discussed. The latter is the alternative adopted by the three NDC countries—Italy, Norway, and Sweden. Sweden complements this design feature with an exogenous correction mechanism that accounts for the difference between the norm (the long-term expected value of the return in the formulation of the annuity) and the actual yearly outcome, which then becomes an additional component of exogenous indexation. The argument for leaving out the rate of inflation is as strong because it is a difficult parameter to estimate and is more easily introduced exogenously (that is, after it has occurred). Finally, the remaining alternative is to set $(1 + \alpha) = 1$, which means that the rate of return is not included at all in the annuity. In this case, yearly annuity payments are based solely on the individual's capital balance at retirement divided by life expectancy, and indexation of the yearly annuity payment is performed exogenously on a regular basis.

For the purpose of illustration, figure 13.1 assumes an estimate of the rate of per capita real wages $(1 + w)$ of 1.5 percent per year, and with 2 percent inflation, a rate of $(1 + w)$ $(1 + p) = 3.5$ percent. For comparison, the payment profile of the annuity is also calculated excluding the rate of return, but with each yearly payment indexed (exogenously) with the same assumed yearly rate of return—as it occurs. By including the rate of return in the annuity—with a fixed payment per payout period—the annuity redistributes the time path of payments from the final half of the average life to the first half, and implicitly from those with longer-than-average lives to those with shorter-than-average lives.

THE PAYMENT PROFILE OVER TIME: A DISTRIBUTIONAL ISSUE

The distributional issue emerging in figure 13.1 is worth pondering. To begin with, moving a larger percentage of a given sum of money to consumption when younger accords with the belief that people may generally derive greater utility from having a larger part of a given sum of money to consume now rather than later.

On the other hand, leaving the indexation outside the creation of the annuity and instead indexing benefits exogenously on a yearly (regular) basis has one obvious advantage: by increasing with the rate of growth in the real wage of all contributors, the relative value of benefits to wages remains essentially unchanged over time. In addition, it results in relatively more income for consumption of goods and services toward the end of life for the very elderly. For those for whom this is the only source of income, this can be important. Figure 13.1 also demonstrates that shifting pension lifetime income to a pensioner's younger years (front-loading payouts) increases the risk of relative poverty in old age.[1] This underscores the importance of an accompanying means-tested minimum income guarantee for pensioners.

FIGURE 13.1 **Considerations regarding the rate of return underlying the annuity**

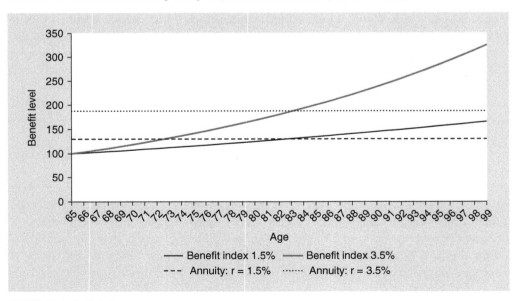

SOURCE: Original calculations.

NOTE: Initial benefit of 100 at age 65 with given life expectancy. Inflation = 2 percent. Two cases: real return of 1.5 percent and nominal return of 3.5 percent. r = rate of return.

THE RISK FOR THE INSURER

Returning to the payout phase of FDC pension schemes, because of the uncertainty about the financial rate of return over the 30 or more years of life of the members of the pension pool, it is prudent to invest in safe assets with low yields. In addition, the annuity provider will keep a large portion of the pension pool balances as secure reserves to hedge against unfavorable outcomes for the insurer—despite having made very conservative assumptions about the life expectancy of the annuitant's cohort and the future rate of return.

Obviously, considerable uncertainty exists about the rates of growth of the real per capita wage, the growth of the contributing labor force, and the rate of inflation. In the context of the universal public NDC pension scheme, the obvious way to avoid this risk is—at most—to include only a portion of the expected rate of growth of productivity in the computation of the annuity, where 1.5–2.0 percent is considered relatively high, leaving the rate of growth of the labor force and rate of inflation exogenous to the annuity computation.

In summary, the reasoning here speaks in favor of either (a) leaving the rate of return completely outside the creation of the annuity, or (b) including a conservative long-term estimate together with a rate of return adjustment index to even out deviations from this "norm." In NDC schemes the adjustment index, the price index, and the labor market index should be used on a regular (for example, annual) basis through continual ex post indexation. This is particularly important in the context of exposure to continuous population deflation (for example, a chronically low fertility rate) that is not compensated for by positive labor force growth (for example, through net immigration). Countries with continuous net labor force growth can create a demographic reserve as a buffer against an anticipated cyclical downturn (instead of transferring the dividend directly to current pensioners).

THE ROLE OF LIFE EXPECTANCY IN CREATING AFFORDABLE, SUSTAINABLE NDC PENSIONS

Life expectancy is one of the key parameters of NDC schemes, entering the picture in five important ways:

- Together with individual account balances, it determines the amount of a yearly pension.

- Knowledge of the effect of increasing life expectancy provides individuals with incentives to postpone retirement.

- Participants' awareness and behavioral adjustment to changing life expectancy at the micro level increase the amount of the yearly benefit payment over what it would have been if participants exited the labor force earlier.

- The macro result of individuals' postponing retirement is an improvement in the labor supply and the economic dependency ratio.

- Life expectancy is used for automatic indexation of the minimum pension age.

Finally, life expectancy—together with the average number of years the participant is in the labor force—is a determinant of the time an amount of contributions is in the system before it has to be paid out (the turnover time). All else equal, increasing life expectancy means a longer turnover time—which increases the system's liquidity, reflected as an increase in the present value of assets in the solvency ratio (Palmer 2013). Although to date only Sweden has an automatic balancing mechanism based on a Swedish style solvency ratio, with the projection of contribution assets based on the duration of time the average contribution remains in the system. This is an important technical aspect of life-expectancy projections in the construction of the Swedish style solvency ratio.

Projecting Life Expectancy

DIFFERENT APPROACHES TO PROJECTING LIFE EXPECTANCY

By definition, no method for projecting uncertain outcomes of life expectancy ex ante can avoid producing errors. In the case of projecting mortality rates, the linchpin of life-expectancy modeling, the survival of some cohorts will be overestimated and that of others underestimated. The goal of modeling is that the errors should be random with an expected value of zero over a large number of projections. However, systematic underestimation leads to a systemically increasing deficit, financial unsustainability, and an unfair transfer of debt to coming generations.

This section assesses projection methods currently used with the help of current literature and reports on a new estimation approach that promises better estimates of life expectancy at retirement that, however, suggest their major underestimation by the current dominating approaches—period and cohort models.

THE PERIOD METHOD FOR PROJECTING LIFE EXPECTANCY

Countries quite commonly do not use sophisticated statistical projection procedures in making official projections of life expectancy. Instead, there is a long legacy of using straightforward period statistics based on mortality rates by age in the most recent year—or a moving average of such calculations for a series of years (Bengtsson et al. 2018). This procedure is referred to in the literature as the period method.

The period method yields the average length of remaining life at a given age, assuming that people are going to experience the same age-specific mortality rates observed in the transition from each age x to age x+1, beginning with the most recent year one can observe from the actual data. The obvious problem with this method is the "risk" that the decline in mortality rates systematically speeds up over a series of decades (or slows down). The result of an accelerating process is that life-expectancy estimates based on the period method are biased toward underestimation.

Using birth cohort data for 1900–2014 obtained from the Berkeley Mortality Database, Alho, Bravo, and Palmer (2013) and Alho, Palmer, and Zhao de Gosson de Varennes (2019) examine the development of cohort mortality from age 40 and older of 10 countries (Denmark, Finland, France, Italy, Japan, the Netherlands, Norway, Portugal, the United Kingdom, and the United States). Although the profiles of countries vary over the more than a century of birth cohort data examined, what the data show is that declining mortality for older age groups is prevalent from the 1960s or shortly thereafter for all the countries examined.

Using a five-year moving average of period data, Alho, Palmer, and Zhao de Gosson de Varennes (2019) show that the period method systematically underestimates the remaining life expectancy at age 65 of the 1,600 completely deceased cohorts that could be followed to age 99 up to 2014 for cohorts turning age 65. For Sweden, this method yields an error that is as high as 8 percent for the last cohort that turned 65—which was in 1979—and that had expired completely in 2014. Applying the period method to data for cohorts turning age 65 from 1980 and forward in time (that is, younger cohorts that had not yet reached age 99 in 2014) suggests that the gap between projections and outcomes using the period method is increasing as we approach present time. For Sweden, illustrated in a comparison of methods toward the end of this section, the period method underestimates life expectancy from age 65 by on average 8 percent for the cohort that was 65 years old in 1975; that is, the birth cohort 1910 for all countries examined.

THE STATISTICAL APPROACH FOR COHORT MODELING—THE LEE-CARTER MODEL AND ITS VARIANTS

In 1992, Lee and Carter published what was to become known as the Lee-Carter (LC) model, and a new era of stochastic modeling of mortality and life expectancy arose. The 1992 LC model interprets the log-transformed age-specific mortality at a certain period with two age-dependent parameters and one time-dependent parameter. The model has only one period effect, which means that the underlying assumption is that the rate of change in mortality is time-invariant, as explained in Girosi and King (2007). Although the LC model has proven to be superior to the period model, it is not flexible enough to fully capture the development of mortality that became evident in the decades beginning in the 1960s and 1970s, according to the historical data examined by Alho, Bravo, and Palmer (2013).

Many attempts were made to improve the original LC model in the years following its publication in 1992 (Booth, Maindonald, and Smith 2002; de Jong and Tickle 2006; Hyndman and Ullah 2007; Lee and Miller 2001; Li and Chan 2007; Wilmoth 1993). However, the model extensions of these and other LC variants do not explicitly address the restrictive assumption of time-invariant change in mortality identified by Girosi and King. To the authors' knowledge, the single exception is Booth, Maindonald, and Smith (2002), who attempt to deal with the time invariance issue by fitting the model with an "optimal estimation period." This has the obvious drawback of having worked for a single (and best) period but not a large number of periods and for a sample of countries.

Booth and Tickle (2008) compare the model improvements of Lee and Miller (2001), Booth, Mainland, and Smith (2002), Hyndman and Ullah (2007) using data for 10 countries. They find that the newer variants of the LC model reduced the mean error of log death rates as compared with the original LC model. However, a word of caution is that lower mean errors of log death rates do not necessarily translate into lower errors viewed ex post (after the cohort has died) in projecting life expectancy over a period of 35 or more years—which this chapter's work focuses on.

In a study commissioned by the U.S. Office of the Government Actuary, Waldron (2005) analyzes official U.S. long-term mortality projections as well as projection models used by several European countries. She concludes that regardless of the choice of procedure, ex post evaluations reveal systematic underestimation of expected lifespans. In a series of studies, Alho, Bravo, and Palmer (2013), Zhao de Gosson de Varennes (2016a, 2016b), Palmer and Zhao de Gosson de Varennes (2018), and Alho, Palmer, and Zhao de Gosson de Varennes (2019) analyze data from 10 countries that cover the period 1900 to 2014. They find that the degree of systematic underestimation escalates with the accelerating improvements that have characterized the mortality profiles of cohorts born since the 1950s. Alho, Palmer, and Zhao de Gosson de Varennes (2019) find that for Sweden the underestimation of cohorts born during 1935–44 using the period model is most likely to be more than 10 percent and that the scale of the error is increasing.

THE DATA ANALYTICAL PERIOD-COHORT APPROACH: THE PALMER-ALHO-DE GOSSON (PAD) MODEL

Alho, Palmer, and Zhao de Gosson de Varennes (2019) present a new projection method for life expectancy, the Palmer-Alho-de Gosson model (PAD model). The PAD model is a "data analytical period-cohort" approach. Its unique feature is that no underlying assumption is made about the rate of change in mortality. Instead, the rate is used as a key parameter for the purpose of the projection because it is what links the period mortalities with the cohort mortalities.

Annex 13A contains a formal mathematical description of the model. An intuitive explanation of the method follows. Assume that the task is to project the remaining life expectancy for those who turned 65 years old in year *t*, and the data at hand are the age-specific mortality rates for all ages between 65 and 99 from 1900 to 2014, which was the case in the study that underlies the empirical results summarized in this section. The projection for any year *t* in this period is made by performing the following steps:

Step I. A sequence of empirical rates of change in mortality of past cohorts is obtained by using the observed period and cohort mortalities using the second formula in annex 13A, called the PAD model.

In this example, the rates of change in mortality for the cohorts who turned age 65 from 1900 to 2014 are derived using their empirically observed cohort mortality. Note that for the cohorts that turned 65 from 1900 to 1979, the actual rate can be computed because they have completed their lifespans up to age 99 by 2014. For the later cohorts beginning with those that turn 65 in 1980, only a quasi-empirical rate using incomplete cohort information can be calculated. However, these rates can still be valuable for the purpose of the projection because they provide the most recent information of how mortality has been changing. Alho, Palmer, and Zhao de Gosson de Varennes (2019) present alternative ways of using these "partial" empirical rates. This section continues with the description of the model of a full cohort (that is, a cohort with no remaining survivors).

Step II. The rate of change in mortality of the projection cohort is extrapolated based on the series of empirical rates derived in the first step.

A robust extrapolation method should be chosen to perform this step. The first question is whether to use a sophisticated statistical method (for example, an autoregressive integrated moving average [ARIMA] model) or a simple extrapolation based on the average rates during the last X number of years. The obvious limitation with ARIMA modeling is that it requires a long time series of about 40 years or more, data that are generally not available in most countries. A second and related question is whether the extrapolation should be based on a long or a short historical time series. Obviously, a short time series from the nearest preceding periods bases estimates on the most recent information. At the same time, it may be wrongly influenced by short- or medium-term and temporary divergence from a longer trend in mortality.

Zhao de Gosson de Varennes, Palmer, and Alho (2016) and Alho, Palmer, and Zhao de Gosson de Varennes (2019) test four extrapolation methods, including three simple extrapolations with (a) the most recent year (PAD-1), (b) 20 years (PAD-2), (c) 5 years (PAD-3), and (d) ARIMA modeling (PAD-4).

Step III. The projection of cohort mortality—and life expectancy—is then calculated with the observed period mortality and the extrapolated mortality rates estimated in the previous step.

In Alho, Palmer, and Zhao de Gosson de Varennes (2019), the data-analytical period-cohort method, as described in the above three steps, is examined in considerable detail using data for eight countries from as early as 1900. The authors compare the PAD model with the four different extrapolation methods, with the LC model for 1,600 entirely expired cohorts from eight countries: Denmark, France, Italy, the Netherlands, Norway, Sweden, the United Kingdom, and the United States. The ex post evaluations show that the longer estimation method (PAD-2 with a 20-year memory) and the ARIMA method (PAD-4) deliver the smallest out-of-sample errors for already expired cohorts for all countries and show practically no tendency toward either systematic over- or underestimation, whereas the two other alternatives are systematically biased toward underestimation, as the preceding discussion suggests is to be expected.

A COMPARISON OF THE PERIOD MODEL, THE LC MODEL, AND THE PAD MODEL FOR CONTEMPORARY BIRTH COHORTS

The ex post evaluations for expired birth cohorts examined in Alho, Palmer, and Zhao de Gosson de Varennes (2019) and summarized above end with the birth cohorts that turned 65 in 1979. The interesting question is, What can be said about the life expectancy of those birth cohorts that have turned age 65 since 1979? To answer this question, these more recent birth cohorts were also examined. They consisted of an additional 1,000 individual cohorts from the eight countries. Together these provide a possible picture of the mortality dynamics of current cohorts—possible because the youngest cohorts still have a good portion of their lives to live—and it will not be long until accelerating improvements in mortality lead to longer life expectancy even in persons ages 85–99. To shed some light on this, life expectancy for these cohorts is estimated using the available information and the projections compared with the known outcomes as these cohorts age from 1980 through 2014. These projections constitute what is called the ex ante evaluation in the following discussion.

The results of the analyses in Zhao de Gosson de Varennes, Palmer, and Alho (2016) and Alho, Palmer, and Zhao de Gosson de Varennes (2019) are summarized as follows. First, the period, LC, and PAD (2 and 4) models all estimate a continuous increase in remaining life expectancy at age 65 and older for all birth cohorts from the eight countries. However, the PAD models almost always yield higher projections than the LC model. The exceptions are a few cohorts from the U.S. data.

To relate this result to an NDC public pension scheme, Sweden is chosen as an example. The alternative projection models are applied to persons who turned age 65 in the years 2001–14. The results are shown in figure 13.2.

FIGURE 13.2 **Projected cohort remaining life expectancy at age 65 for Swedes who turned 65 in 2001–14**

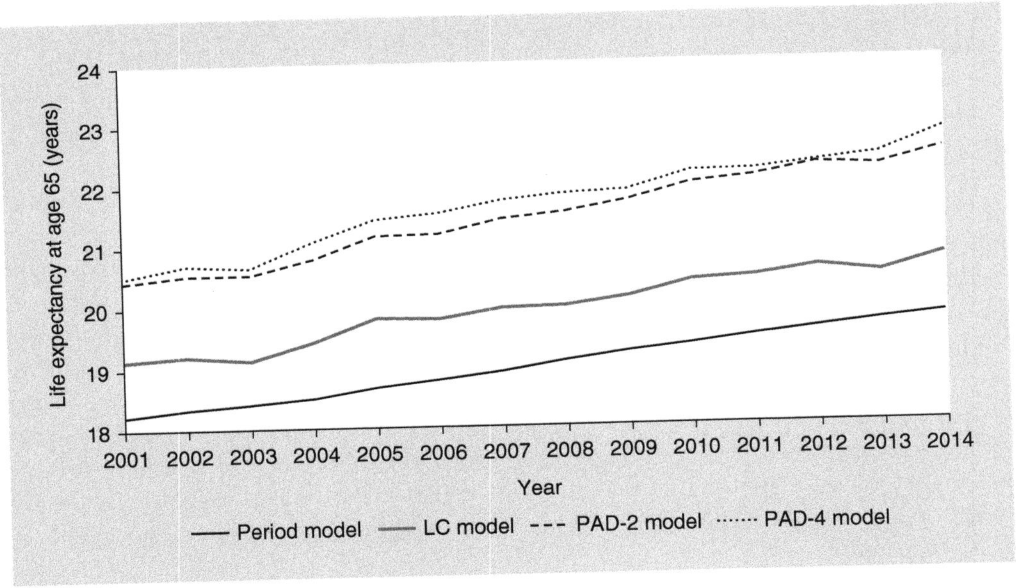

SOURCE: Alho, Palmer, and Zhao de Gosson de Varennes 2019.

NOTE: LC = Lee-Carter; PAD-2 = Palmer-Alho-de Gosson-20 years; PAD-4 = Palmer-Alho-de Gosson-ARIMA. ARIMA = autoregressive integrated moving average.

The results in the figure give a clear warning signal. The acceleration in the rate of decline in mortality is causing not only demographers (for example, Statistics Sweden) but also practitioners to systematically underestimate the rate of increase in life expectancy. In addition, the strength of the systematic underestimation is increasing with more recent new entrants into the pension pool who turned 65 years old in 2001–2014. A conservative estimate of the uncovered cost is that the current Swedish NDC pension scheme can expect accumulated deficits of about SKr 95 billion for the 10 recently pensioned cohorts born from 1938 to 1947 (Palmer and Zhao de Gosson de Varennes 2018). At the same time, the substantial increase in life expectancy creates long-run financial liquidity because the overall payment period is stretched out over longer lives.

POLICY IMPLICATIONS

The conclusions from theoretical literature (Girosi and King 2007) and empirical research results—and especially the empirical results in the succession of studies by Alho, Bravo, and Palmer (2013) and more recently Alho, Palmer, and Zhao de Gosson de Varennes (2019)—are as follows:

Public pension administrations that are responsible for providing DC annuities need to move toward more sophisticated projection models backed by evidence that the methods they employ are not systematically downward biased under the present conditions of steadily improving mortality rates from age 65.

The period model should be abandoned as a projection model for public pension schemes. Given that the assumption of time invariance in the rate of change in mortality is believed to be fulfilled, the LC model works well. However, the empirical evidence shows that the data seldom fulfill this assumption. A more prudent approach would be to adopt a PAD procedure incorporating more available cohort information into the database used for extrapolation, which the PAD procedure suggests is at least as good as the LC model or better. All the country studies underlying the research behind the PAD model improve the likelihood of more accurate and systematically unbiased estimates of the life expectancy of countries' pools of pensioners.

The consequence of choosing a projection method that systematically underestimates life expectancy is that this undermines financial sustainability and generates transfers of debt to the younger generation. This breaks with the underlying principle of intergenerational fairness in NDC schemes.

Variable Annuities: What Is Gained and Lost by Recalculating the Annuity at Regular Intervals Based on New Projections after the "Normal" Retirement Age?

Current practice in calculating benefits or annuities in public DC pension schemes—including all current NDC schemes—is to use a once-and-for-all projection of remaining life expectancy at the "normal" pension age. This practice needs to be reconsidered given that mortality in older ages is declining at an accelerating rate in many developed countries and is moving up into the older age groups. This is a main result of Alho, Bravo, and Palmer (2013), which also examines aging in Japan, the leading larger nation in aging.

An alternative strategy would be to periodically adjust the annuity (that is, the stream of yearly benefits) with revised projections of mortality or remaining life expectancy up to a certain ceiling age (for example, 80 or 85 years old). A variable annuity is similar to adding a new negative factor into the indexation of annuities as the pensioner ages. This sort of approach was suggested by Piggot, Valdez, and Detzel (2005) and Valdez, Piggott, and Wang (2006) for private insurance (but not in conjunction with the PAD model). Alho, Bravo, and Palmer (2013) illustrate its application (without the PAD method of creating the database) in a public NDC pension scheme.

A variable annuity construction means that the risk of deficits caused by underestimation of life expectancy is reduced at the expense of those who survive to the next revision point. This also implies redistribution within the insurance pool from those who live longer to those who live shorter lives.

Alho, Bravo, and Palmer (2013) demonstrate the expected result that reprojecting remaining life expectancy brings the estimations closer to actual outcomes, using the LC model as the underlying projection method. Zhao de Gosson de Varennes (2016b) evaluates the variable annuity construction starting at age 65 using the PAD model, comparing results with a fixed annuity at age 65 based on an LC projection, evaluates with 208 cohorts from Denmark, France, Italy, the Netherlands, Norway, Sweden, the United Kingdom, and the United States. In the variable annuity model life expectancy is reprojected up to age 85 using the PAD database and extrapolation models PAD-2 and PAD-4. Table 13.1 shows that the variable annuity scheme always reduces the ex post projection error compared with the fixed annuity scheme with the same projection model. All reduce the size of financial deficits.

Adjusting annuities with new projections of cohort remaining life expectancy to reduce the uncertainty (error) in projections results in a clear improvement in financial stability. The conclusion regarding intra- and intergenerational fairness is that there are both pros and cons involved with the shifting of financing within the pension pool by introducing a variable annuity up to a ceiling age of, for example, 80 or 85. The adjustment of individual younger cohorts' pensions is spread out among many participants, whereas the adjustment is "heavier" per capita for the older cohorts. This causes some loss in the expected utility (consumption) of the oldest, compared with the alternative of an annuity fixed at an earlier date (Zhao de Gosson de Varennes 2016b). At the same time, however, those who gain are a third party (that is, the younger cohorts), because the transfer of whatever remaining debt there might be is lower. If a reserve fund is established, as was indicated in "The NDC Annuity" section, then it is likely that this fund would buffer against fluctuations.

Finally, this observation does not suggest that "the" benchmark age for the pension system should not be indexed to life expectancy. The explicit and transparent presence of life expectancy in the calculation of NDC pensions is a key factor in the automatic stability generated by public NDC pension schemes. And, generally speaking, against the backdrop of continuously increasing life expectancy, it is important to periodically adjust (through indexation) both the minimum pension age as well as the age at which life expectancy is fixed after some number of revisions.

TABLE 13.1 **Variable and fixed annuities: Average size of financial deficits with new projections at five-year intervals up to age 85**
percent of the total capital of a cohort annuity pool

	Fixed annuity with PAD-2	Fixed annuity with PAD-4	Variable annuity with PAD-2	Variable annuity with PAD-4
Denmark	3.64	1.42	1.97	0.91
Norway	1.60	2.66	1.28	0.95
Sweden	3.69	1.98	2.47	0.67
France	1.84	4.36	0.77	0.50
Italy	1.78	5.65	1.49	1.69
Netherlands	3.14	4.35	1.87	0.49
United Kingdom	1.44	5.91	1.24	1.38
United States	2.51	10.33	3.41	0.98

SOURCE: Zhao de Gosson de Varennes 2016b.
NOTE: PAD-2 = Palmer-Alho-de Gosson-20 years; PAD-4 = Palmer-Alho-de Gosson-ARIMA. ARIMA = autoregressive integrated moving average.

Socioeconomic Determinants of Life Expectancy in the Context of Creating the Annuity

Recall that NDC is a longevity insurance that reflects the life-cycle earnings of participating individuals: "You get what you pay for, with interest." The DC principle is economically efficient because it rewards formal work in the labor market, which in a universal public pension scheme must be the basis upon which pension rights are attained if the universal scheme is to be viewed as fair. From this perspective, NDCs are both intra- and intergenerationally fair. A logical corollary is that a country's income distribution policy is preferably pursued through social measures exogenous to the (N)DC scheme design that are created for specific events, such as childbirth, unemployment, sickness, and disability.

What are the ramifications of knowledge of socioeconomic differences in life expectancy within this framework? "Higher Life Expectancy Accompanies Higher Income, Higher Education, and Choice of Occupation" presents an overview of the evidence of the correlation between socioeconomic factors and life expectancy. "Gender Differences in Income, Life Expectancy, and NDC Annuity Construction" addresses gender as a separate issue and discusses the reasoning behind the use of unisex life expectancy, in the perspective of gender income inequality. "Other Approaches to Dealing with the Socioeconomic Gap in Life Expectancy in Creating (N)DC Annuities" discusses the pros and cons of some technical approaches proposed in the literature to redistributing pension pool resources, given that this is the chosen policy. "To What Extent Does Unisex Pooling Level the Gender Playing Field?" addresses the question of whether gender pooling is a sufficient policy for dealing with the gender gap in pensions, which is largely due to the gender gap in earnings.

HIGHER LIFE EXPECTANCY ACCOMPANIES HIGHER INCOME, HIGHER EDUCATION, AND CHOICE OF OCCUPATION

The existence of socioeconomic gaps in life expectancy is by now a well-documented phenomenon. A large number of empirical studies show significant gaps in life expectancy associated with individuals' positions in the income distribution, their level of education, and their occupation. The general picture is that individuals with higher incomes, higher education, and professional and white-collar jobs can expect to live longer. This is a feature of life expectancy in countries with relatively high Gini coefficients, such as the United States (Gini = 0.4), but also characterizes Western European countries, with generally more equitable income distributions (Gini about 2.5–3.0). This section begins with a selection of empirical studies that illustrate the evidence predominantly from the United States, Germany, and Sweden.

The discussion begins with two comprehensive studies of U.S. data. The first is the National Academies of Sciences, Engineering, and Medicine (2015) study of U.S. data, which provides a comprehensive overview of the issues and empirical evidence focusing on the relationships between life expectancy and the distribution of income. The overall conclusion of this study, based on a considerable body of empirical evidence, is that a gap in life expectancy is associated with income (and education) and that it has been increasing over time. The picture is characterized by at best static life expectancy in the lower income deciles, with increasingly longer life expectancy as one moves up the percentiles of the income distribution.

The second study is that of Chetty, Stepner, and Abraham (2016), who analyze a sample of 1.4 billion person-year observations for individuals age 40–76 residing in the United States. The study focused on explaining the gaps in life expectancy associated with income in the United States. The database also includes 4.1 million male deaths and 2.7 million female deaths. One of this study's many interesting results is that the richest 1 percent of women live on average 14.6 years longer than the poorest 1 percent of woman and the richest 1 percent of men live on average 10.1 years longer than the poorest 1 percent of men.

In addition to their main finding that low average life expectancy is strongly correlated with low income, Chetty, Stepner, and Abraham (2016) show two other factors stand out: low-income communities with a higher share of immigrants and with higher levels of government spending on social programs, such as public health, have a higher average life expectancy than low-income communities with fewer immigrants and less government spending on social welfare. For the population as a whole, life expectancy for individuals in the lowest income quartile was significantly correlated with lifestyle risk factors such as smoking, use of narcotics, and obesity; however, Chetty, Stepner, and Abraham (2016) find no significant correlation—either positive or negative—with access to medical care, physical environmental factors, overall relative income status of the local community, or the local labor market.

No other study matches that of Chetty, Stepner, and Abraham (2016) in breadth of data collected on explanatory factors. However, numerous other country studies support the conclusions of these two U.S. studies. For example, using German data, Reil-Held (2000), Klein and Unger (2002), and Lampert, Kroll, and Dundelberg (2007) find that the difference in life expectancy from birth between the lowest and highest income groups is 8.4 years among women and 10.8 years among men. Also using German data, Kroh et al. (2012) find a difference in life expectancy at age 65 between low- and high-income individuals of 3.5 years for women and 5.3 years for men.

Using Swedish data for 1970–2007, Eriksson et al. (2014) find that income inequality in life expectancy, already notable at age 35, increased during the period studied, primarily driven by improvement for high-income persons. These results agree with the other available studies of country data.[2] Finally, a Swedish study from Statistics Sweden (2016) finds that already at age 35 the difference in life expectancy between the highest and lowest income group is eight years for men and four years for women. Coupling this result to the most significant factor found in Chetty, Stepner, and Abraham (2016) (that is, lifestyle factors), it is perhaps not a far stretch of the imagination to claim that men are more disposed to take on negative lifestyle habits at early ages—where the prime habits in many countries are still alcohol, substance abuse, smoking, and the absence of regular exercise.

From these and other studies, the chain linking education to occupation to earnings appears to represent different aspects of the same situation—often starting with low or discontinued education. In a study of Swedish white- and blue-collar workers, Zhao de Gosson de Varennes (2016b) finds a clear occupational gap between the life expectancy of "nonmanual" and "manual" workers, whereby education is the most important factor in the Swedish context as early as age 40 and continuing to age 60. Similar results are found by the U.K. Office for National Statistics based on life expectancy at age 65 in England and Wales; and for Finland, the data indicate the occupational gap has remained unchanged for some time (van Raalte, Martikainen, and Myrskylä 2014).

Summing up, gaps in life expectancy are strongly correlated with income. Being in the lower income percentiles is characterized by stagnant life expectancy, while life expectancy is generally higher for persons in higher income percentiles. The empirical evidence suggests this is a global phenomenon, at least within the community of highly developed economies for which there are data and analysis of these data.

GENDER DIFFERENCES IN INCOME, LIFE EXPECTANCY, AND NDC ANNUITY CONSTRUCTION

A point of departure here is that equal treatment of the genders requires the use of unisex life expectancy in universal public pension schemes, and for that matter, logically, all pension schemes. This is in fact prescribed by the EU for all of its members. The economic rationale for using unisex life expectancy is straightforward: doing so transfers the accumulated balances of all participants in the pool of pensioners—usually segmented in practice by birth cohort—from the generally richer "class" of men who have shorter lives as pensioners to the generally poorer "class" of women who live longer lives.

Sweden provides an example. A study performed by the Swedish Pensions Agency (2016) divides earnings data for the entire working-age population into five income classes, with each income group also divided by gender. The main result is that 80 percent of the population in the lower-income groups is composed of women. This means that the unisex life-expectancy divisor counteracts the regressive profile of the gender income distribution at all levels. The Swedish Pensions Agency's report also identifies low-income men with the lowest income as the biggest "double losers"—with on average low pensions and low life expectancy.

Before proceeding, consider what lies behind the gap in the yearly earnings of women and men. To begin with, the gender wage gap (that is, the average difference between the yearly remuneration of working men and women) is 14 percent for Organisation for Economic Co-operation and Development (OECD) countries.[3] This does not account for the gender difference in the allocation of time to participation in the formal labor force, attributable to time devoted principally to child care up to adolescence. The Swedish pension gender gap (in 2013) based on the average of all pensioners—just the public pension and excluding the minimum pension guarantee—was 33 percent.[4] With a gender wage gap somewhat better than the OECD average hovering around 10 percent, this suggests a gap component of about 20 percent, representing less time devoted to work in the formal labor market.

Using NDC individual accounts from 1960, Klerby, Larsson, and Palmer (2019) study the NDC pension accounts of spouses giving birth to at least one child for mothers born between 1955 and 1970, with NDC account data for the period 1960–2012. They find a seemingly fixed pattern for the development of contributions noted on NDC accounts following the birth of the mother's first child. Not surprisingly, a large earnings gap with respect to the female spouse's yearly earnings begins with the birth of the first child and then falls gradually from age 2 of the first child up to age 4, about when the second child is born. This gives a period of about six years of coverage of lost contributions from earnings by the tax-financed birth-related child care rights (claimed almost exclusively by mothers). From this point the earnings gap between the mother and her spouse declines, reaching a steady state at about 20 percent (on average) until the second child has reached age 12, about 17 years after the birth of the first child.

The authors attribute this steady-state earnings gap to parents' revealed preference for devoting a portion of the couple's time to care for children at home well into adolescence—behavior well in line with established cultural norms, but it is the mother who supplies the larger part of unpaid care labor at home. On this basis they argue in favor of making account sharing between parents (including the tax-financed child-care contributions paid from the state budget) the default option in the universal public NDC (and FDC) schemes.

In summary, computing the annuities in universal public DC schemes using unisex life expectancy makes sense. It results in a redistribution within the pension pool from men with predominantly higher incomes (and pension balances at retirement) and shorter lives to women with lower incomes (and pension balances at retirement). Because a substantial portion of the gender income gap is attributable to structural cultural factors— occupational gender wage discrimination and women's part-time work during child-rearing years—the use of unisex life expectancy contributes to evening out the income outcomes; but this is only a second-best policy given that it is contingent on the gender difference in life expectancies. With convergence of men's and women's life expectancies, this form of redistribution would cease, although the earnings and pension gaps would remain.

OTHER APPROACHES TO DEALING WITH THE SOCIOECONOMIC GAP IN LIFE EXPECTANCY IN CREATING (N)DC ANNUITIES

To reduce the unintended redistribution caused by the socioeconomic gaps in life expectancy, Nalebuff and Zeckerhauser (1985) propose creating a separate pension plan for each (identifiably homogeneous) life-expectancy group. Bommier, Lerous, and Lozachmeur (2011); Esö and Simonovits (2003); Esö, Simonovits, and Toth (2011); and Simonovits (2006) derive a benefit-age rule under which information available for individuals enables the application of individual-related retirement ages. They show that this can dampen unintended inefficient redistribution and improve overall social welfare—of course, one might add, given that the rule is fair and representative.

Putting all other considerations aside, an obvious drawback arises in calculating annuities with individualized projections: doing so requires extensive administration— much of which is sensitive and may not be forthcoming—and presumes that a reliable and manageable statistical procedure exists for "allocating" the individualized life expectancies to create fairly segmented subgroups within the birth cohort pool. In addition, this detailed process may still lead to biased outcomes (among other things because of asymmetric information and adverse selection), and, generally, there is no easy check on the fairness of the procedures chosen until a large number of cohorts have passed through the 35- to 40-year process to the cohort's extinction.

A more practical approach is to segment the universal NDC pension pool into occupational groups. Occupational groups have a fairly strong link to both education and income, where income is the most dominant identifier of heterogeneity. This makes sense if a country already has unions with occupational affiliations that are more or less all-encompassing. Some countries already have this sort of institutionalized segmentation (for example, Denmark and the Netherlands) but most do not on any meaningful scale. Zhao de Gosson de Varennes (2016b) examines theoretically and demonstrates numerically with Swedish data the potential effects on intra- and intergenerational redistribution of a "blue-white" collar segmentation of the population. She finds that de-pooling the

NDC scheme by occupation can reduce the intragenerational transfer from the blue- to the white-collar occupations by about 5 percent. On the other hand, occupational groups tend to be gender-dominated. For example, occupations with predominantly female workers (of which there are many examples) could no longer benefit from substantial transfers from men within the insurance pool.

Given a decision to segment, Holzmann et al. (2017) show that a total absolute tax and subsidy indicator can be used to compare the extent to which alternative segmentation designs reduce distortions. For example, these authors show that "de-pooling life expectancy by gender reduces distortions/improves efficiency, but further increases the gap between men's and women's pension levels." The study also demonstrates that a two-tier contribution structure (as in the Republic of Korea) is able to eliminate most of the heterogeneity effects with a simple and adjustable process as heterogeneity develops. Ayuso, Bravo, and Holzmann (2017a) present a tax-subsidy mechanism for redistribution within the pension pool and explore alternative policy designs to apply to the new pension cohorts during accumulation. Examples are individualized life expectancy and a two-tier contribution rate structure.

In summary, options and "quasi-options" to using unisex life expectancy are presented herein. The simplest is the quasi-option of segmenting the population into occupational groups at retirement. This implies implicit gender segmentation as well as segmentation by level of education—by separating male-dominated from female-dominated occupations, higher-income from lower-income occupations, and the higher educated from the lower educated. Institutionally, this is the smooth alternative to implement, but it not only relinquishes but in fact runs against the goal of reducing the gender gap in pensions through the use of unisex life expectancy.

TO WHAT EXTENT DOES UNISEX POOLING LEVEL THE GENDER PLAYING FIELD?

This section asks the question, "Does unisex pooling level the gender playing field in the end?" The bottom line is that the use of unisex life expectancy embodies an aggregate transfer from men as a group—with higher average income but shorter lives—to women with longer lives but on average lower income, but it does so in the aggregate. The answer therefore is that although it does this on an aggregate average basis because women's long life expectancy dominates men's, it will not set right all the "wrongs" on an individual basis.

Given the same average gender gap in earnings before constructing the annuity using unisex life expectancy, if life expectancy is exactly the same for both genders, then the lifetime pension gap between genders will remain unaffected. The conclusion is that although unisex life expectancy reduces the pension gap, the gap will remain as long as men's average lifetime earnings continue to be significantly higher than women's.

Taking a simple example, with the population divided equally between men expected to live 18 years on average and women 22 years, the unisex life expectancy factor is 20 years, and provides a 10 percent higher yearly benefit for all women than putting men and women into separate pools. Importantly, this simple example also illustrates the basic difference between a nonfinancial defined benefit (NDB) scheme (for example, the German or French point system) and an NDC scheme (for example, the Swedish, Latvian, or Norwegian schemes), which uses unisex life expectancy by virtue of its construction. For the same population, aggregate sum of lifetime contributions, and internal rate of return, NDC with unisex life expectancy contributes toward leveling out the gender income (that is, pensions) gap, whereas no such built-in mechanism exists in the NDB context.

Taking this one step further, continuing to use Sweden as an example, work by Klerby, Larsson, and Palmer (2019) finds that the pension account of a Swedish mother born in 1970 reflects an estimated average earnings gap of 20 percent vis-à-vis the father of her child and somewhat more for the Swedish standard of almost two children per mother. The gap originates in time with the birth of the mother's first child. The statistical evidence suggests it can be attributed to the culturally determined preference of parents for one of them (predominantly the mother) to be away from work part-time and at home to care for children up to adolescence (with two children this means a period of about 17 years from the birth of the first child)—where the father is predominantly the full-time worker in the formal labor market.

With a Swedish gender earnings gap of about 20 percent on average and a four-year gap in gender life expectancy, the 10 percent unisex life-expectancy factor bonus is a significant step forward in creating gender earnings equality on average for all mothers. But by no means does it deal directly with the cause of the earnings—and consequently pension— the earnings gender gap. It will give some individuals too large a "bonus" and others too small a bonus. The drawback of relying on unisex life expectancy to reduce the earnings gap is that it does not deal directly with the ex ante reasons for why women have lower income than men on average. If the life-expectancy gap were to disappear, the earnings gap would still remain.

Two pension policy measures can set things straight. The first is (default) sharing of (N)DC pension accounts during a period of shared parenthood. The second is creation (by default) at retirement (of the youngest partner) of a joint annuity at retirement. This is a specific insurance product based on joint income and individual life expectancies, in which the surviving spouse (usually the female partner) receives more than a 50 percent share (for example, 60–65 percent) of the couple's total pension income at the death of the other partner. Both of these social policy measures redistribute pension rights within the domain of the family, instead of indirectly transferring an implicit tax on all men in the pension collective to finance a general transfer to women who have been parents, including both those women who shared informal care time with their partners and those whose division of home care of children was lopsided. Unisex life expectancy is thus a weak second best as a measure for sharing, and it lacks the possible efficiency of sharing of accounts in providing an increased incentive for equal sharing of time between care in the home and work in the formal labor market.

The knowledge that life expectancy is stagnant at the lowest income levels and increases with the level of education and income is another issue. The signal comes at early ages—age 30 and perhaps earlier—as discussed in "How Best to Proxy the Nonfinancial Rate of Return" in chapter 9. This illustrates the importance of national and community policies focusing on education and occupational training in the first two decades of life and renewed opportunities later in life, together with a focus on acquiring and renewing skills to meet the demands of the labor market, in which social support and institutions have an important role to play. This brings to the table the key issues brought out in Chetty, Stepner, and Abraham (2016) regarding lifestyle and longevity, underscoring the need for conscious public health interventions and community services.

Finally, the evidence is overwhelming of the importance of, first, recognizing and, second, dealing through public health efforts the lifestyle issues underlying the low life expectancy of low-income individuals—observable in the data as early as ages 30–40. Unfortunately, the absence of public health policy initiatives for addressing these issues is all too notable.

Conclusions

This chapter presents and discusses issues regarding the policy choices that have to be made in determining the construction of the NDC annuity in four areas. All have to do with the criteria of a good universal pension scheme and the backbone of NDCs—affordability, financial sustainability, and intra- and intergenerational fairness. An important message is that the topics of this chapter are not all "simply" technical issues; they also have sociopolitical ramifications. The key conclusions from each section follow.

CONSTRUCTION OF THE ANNUITY AND OPTIONS FOR INCLUSION OF THE RATE OF RETURN

This section weighs the advantages and disadvantages of inclusion of the rate of growth of productivity (as discussed in the initial section of the chapter on the construction of annuities) in the ex ante calculation of the NDC annuity. The case is made for including a conservative estimate of future long-term productivity growth (that is, per capita real wages) in the ex ante creation of the annuity—accompanied by an ex post "Swedish" adjustment index based on the difference between actual per capita real wage growth and the "norm" included in the annuity divisor. In addition, the rate of inflation index should be used on a regular (for example, annual) basis as part of the ex post indexation.

With chronic negative labor force growth, this negative growth component must be factored into the overall indexation (usually only reducing the scale of positive indexation), for which the ex post model is preferable. In countries with consistently positive labor force growth, a demographic reserve fund can be established to buffer both recessionary and cyclical events. Finally, the Latvian model (Palmer and Stabina 2019) of dealing with economic dips originating from deeper recessions provides an example of how short bouts of (potentially) negative indexation can be smoothed.

UNBIASED ESTIMATION OF COHORT LIFE EXPECTANCY

Generally speaking, two criteria for determining the choice of projection method are that (a) the expected value of projection errors over a succession of birth cohorts is zero, and (b) the method chosen delivers the highest degree of accuracy as measured by the variation around the mean of outcomes. That is, the estimator that comes closest to projecting the actual outcomes (has the lowest random errors) is the most preferable, given that it neither systematically over- nor underestimates ex post outcomes.

With evidence from eight (and in two additional) countries, "Projecting Life Expectancy" shows empirically that mortality rates have generally declined at an accelerating rate through age 85. Judging from the example of Japan, this process can be expected to continue even higher up into the nineties. The challenge for projection methods is to capture this upward movement. This chapter shows that the two methods frequently used by public agencies to project life expectancy at standard retirement ages—the period model and the LC model—systematically underestimate life expectancy at retirement. A third model, the PAD model, developed by Alho, Palmer, and Zhao de Gosson de Varennes is presented. This model uses the changing relationship between period and cohort mortalities as the basis for projections. It is presented and the three models are compared with the period and LC models using Swedish data. The conclusion from the literature—illustrated by the Swedish example—is that the period model is not appropriate for projecting life expectancy for the purpose of constructing the NDC (or FDC) annuity. Neither is the LC model because it presumes a time-invariant rate of change in life expectancy and as a result is likely to lead to systematically underestimated life-expectancy projections. On the other hand, strong evidence is presented that supports the use of the more general PAD model.

A VARIABLE ANNUITY?

This section examines the consequences of not fixing the value of life expectancy to be used in the fixed annuity as early as age 65. Of course, this argument will become partially self-fulfilling as countries index pension ages to life expectancy. However, a variable annuity, recalculated at specific ages with reforecasted remaining life expectancy, is similar to adding a new factor into the indexation of annuities, shifting the cost burden more in the direction of those who live longer. It can be argued that adequate means-tested minimum income supplements—financed with general tax revenues—can compensate for marginal increases in poverty in old age for single pensioners (consisting of an increasing proportion of women as the cohort ages).

SOCIOECONOMIC HETEROGENEITY IN LIFE EXPECTANCY?

National statistical agencies and researchers are finding an increasing gap in life expectancy with respect to income. Life expectancy is almost stagnant in the lowest income deciles, but increases progressively up into the higher income deciles. The empirical evidence demonstrates that the gap reflects level of education, occupation, and the resultant income, and the differences are traceable back to as early as age 30, whereas the predominant cause of early death often has to do with lifestyle factors.

The pension outcomes observed reflect the many underlying structural socioeconomic characteristics that contribute to individuals' life-cycle labor market outcomes. Well-recognized ways to address stagnant life expectancy for the least economically well-off are policies aimed at achieving full participation in secondary education, promoting new skills learning in support of job mobility, and targeting lifestyle health issues through better public health programs, also from younger years.

Most importantly, the gender dimension enters into the discussion of income and life expectancy. This dimension has to do with the fact that women are overrepresented in the lower income quintiles—given structural differences in the density of their labor force participation and the unequal gender division of nonmarket household activities, particularly caring for young children, and labor market gender wage discrimination.[5]

Use of unisex life expectancy goes approximately halfway toward narrowing the pension gender gap—from about 20 percent to about 10 percent. And, for example, if the Swedish life-expectancy gap of four years were to disappear, the income gender gap in the overall pension collective would still remain.

In conclusion, if the goal is to even out the distribution of shares of the pension pool between men and women the best pension policy measures would be to (a) mandate default sharing of pension accounts between spouses who are parents from the birth of the first child, and (b) mandate default joint annuities, together with unisex life expectancy. This has the desirable effect of evening out the difference in income between spouses and, thus, between genders. These measures work through reducing the earnings gap, and by definition the gender pension gap. These are not the only measures needed, however. The empirical evidence emerging from large-scale studies in the United States shows that the gap in life expectancy has a great deal to do with negative individual lifestyle habits and the availability of important community services in this context. Given this, a technical solution is to use a tax-transfer procedure to redistribute money within the pension pool. Above all, the literature suggests that policy focusing on the factors underlying the determination of life-expectancy outcomes at earlier ages could go far toward reducing the causes of low life expectancy among the economically worse off.

ANNEX 13A
A Formal Description of the PAD Model

To formalize the model, the notation is first defined.
Age-specific mortality rate at age x and year t is given by

$$m_{x,t} = \frac{D_{x,t}}{N_{x,t}}$$

in which $D_{x,t}$ is the number of deaths at age x and year t, and $N_{x,t}$ is the corresponding population at risk.

The starting point of the analysis is a calendar year, t, and only ages from some x up to the highest age w are considered. The set of relevant period mortality rates for year t is

$$M_{x,t} = \{m_{x+z,t} : z = 0, 1, \ldots, w - x\}.$$

The set of cohort mortality rates starting at $t + 1$ is

$$M^c_{x,t+1} = \left\{ m_{x+z,\, t+1+z} : z = 0, 1, \ldots, w - x \right\}.$$

The average rate of change in mortality of the cohort can be expressed by the relationship between the period and cohort mortality as follows:

$$\xi_{x,t} = \frac{1}{w - x + 1} \sum_{z=0}^{w-x} \frac{\ln\left(m_{x+z,t}\right) - \ln\left(m_{x+z,\, t+1+z}\right)}{z + 1}.$$

Suppose then that the year $t = T$ is the last year for which period mortality data are available, or known, $M_{x,T}$. The cohort mortality rate, $M^c_{x,T}$, can be predicted in terms of the cohort rate of change in mortality and the period mortality rates:

$$\hat{m}_{x+z,\, T+1+z} = m_{x+z,\, T} \, \exp\left(-(z+1)\hat{\xi}_{x,T}\right)$$

where $\hat{\xi}_{x,T}$ is the predicted value of $\xi_{x,T}$. This gives, as a byproduct, an estimate of the period mortality, $M_{x,T+1}$, so the procedure can be repeated using those estimates and the predicted value $\hat{\xi}_{x,T+1}$ to obtain a forecast for mortality in $M^c_{x,T}$. In this manner, forecasts for $M^c_{x,T+k}$, $k = 0, 1,\ldots$ can be obtained iteratively.

Once the predicted values of $M^c_{x,T+k}$, $K = 0, 1,\ldots$ are available, remaining life expectacies in age $x + z$, $z = 0, 1,\ldots w - z$ can be computed with the usual methods.

INCOMPLETELY OBSERVED COHORTS AT JUMP-OFF TIME

What remains is to formulate the specific model for incorporating information from the predicted life expectancy of birth cohorts that immediately preceded the cohort under study. For example, to estimate life expectancy during the interval $x = 65$ and $w = 99$ at year t, the last cohort with full empirical age-specific mortality is 65 years old at year $t - 35$. For those cohorts that are age 65 between year $t - 34$ to $t - 1$, only partial empirical information of age-specific mortality is available. However, this additional cohort information can still be used. The feasibility of applying linear weights to the observed rates of change in mortality of these adjoining but still incomplete cohorts is examined (that is, $\tilde{\xi}_{x,t}$, and the projected rates of decline $\hat{\xi}_{x,t}$ for all $t \in [t - 34, t - 1]$). In other words, the weight given to the observed rates of decline of the first incomplete cohort at $t - 34$ is 34/35, and the weight decreases to 1/35 for the latest incomplete cohort. The weight given to the projected rate of decline of the first incomplete cohort is then 1/35 and increases gradually to 34/35 for the latest incomplete cohort. Formally, the average rate of change of incomplete cohorts can be written as

$$\xi_{x,\,T-z} = \frac{z}{w-x}\tilde{\xi}_{x,T-z} + \frac{w-x-z}{w-x}\hat{\xi}_{x,T-z}, \; for \; all \; z \in [1, w-x].$$

Notes

1. In a study assessing the causes of relative poverty among single elderly women in Sweden, Nelsson, Nieuwenhuis, and Alm (2019) and Palmer and Könberg (2019) stress the overall importance of the Swedish means-tested minimum income housing cost guarantee for the elderly in this context.

2. Ayuso, Bravo, and Holzmann (2017b) and Zhao de Gosson de Varennes (2016b) also contain recent and extensive overviews of the literature on socioeconomic heterogeneity in life expectancy, supporting the line of thought presented here.

3. Using data available from 2014 to 2017. https://data.oecd.org/earnwage/gender-wage-gap .htm.

4. Using data available from 2014 to 2017. https://data.oecd.org/earnwage/gender-wage -gap.htm.

5. Proponents of unisex life expectancy rest their case on the fact that women's longer lives result in an automatic transfer from male to female participants in the pension pool, which reduces the pension gap.

References

Alho, Juha, Jorge Bravo, and Edward Palmer. 2013. "Annuities and Life Expectancy in NDC." In *NDC Pension Schemes: Progress and Frontiers in a Changing Pension World: Volume 2 Gender, Politics, and Financial Stability*, edited by Robert Holzmann, Edward Palmer, and David Robalino, 395–436. World Bank: Washington, DC.

Alho, Juha, Edward Palmer, and Yuwei Zhao de Gosson de Varennes. 2019. "Projecting Cohort Life Expectancy from the Changing Relationship between Period and Cohort Mortalities." Unpublished.

Ayuso, Mercedes, Jorge Bravo, and Robert Holzmann. 2017a. "Addressing Longevity Heterogeneity in Pension Scheme Design." *Journal of Finance and Economics* 6 (10): 1–21.

———. 2017b. "On the Heterogeneity in Longevity among Socioeconomic Groups: Scope, Trends, and Implications for Earnings-Related Pension Schemes." *Global Journal of Human Social Sciences-Economics* 17 (1): 33–58.

Bengtsson, Tommy, Nico Keilman, Juha Alho, Kaare Christensen, Edward Palmer, and James W. Vaupel. 2018. "Introduction." In *Old and New Perspectives on Mortality Forecasting,* edited by Tommy Bengtsson and Nico Keilman, 1–22. Max Planck Institute of Demography. Basel, Switzerland: Springer International Publishing.

Bommier, Antoine, Marie-Louise Lerous, and Jean-Marie Lozachmeur. 2011. "Differential Mortality and Social Security." *Canadian Journal of Economics* 44 (1): 273–89.

Booth, Heather, John Maindonald, and Len Smith. 2002. "Applying Lee-Carter under Conditions of Variable Mortality Decline." *Population Studies* 56 (3): 325–36.

Booth, Heather, and Leonie Tickle. 2008. "Mortality Modeling and Forecasting: A Review of Methods." *Annals of Actuarial Science* 3 (I/II): 3–44.

Chetty, Raj, Michal Stepner, and Sarah Abraham. 2016. "The Association between Income and Life Expectancy in the United States, 2001–2014." *JAMA* 315 (16): 1750–66.

de Jong, Piet, and Leonie Tickle. 2006. "Extending Lee-Carter Mortality Forecasting." *Mathematical Population Studies* 13 (1): 1–18.

Eriksson, Karin, Markus Jäntti, Lena Lindahl, and Jenny Torssander. 2014. "Trends in Life Expectancy by Income and the Role of Specific Causes of Death." Working Paper 8/2014, Swedish Institute for Social Research, Stockholm University, Stockholm.

Esö, Péter, and András Simonovits. 2003. "Designing Optimal Benefit Rules for Flexible Retirement." Technical Report 1353, Northwestern University, Evanston, IL.

Esö, Péter, András Simonovits, and János Toth. 2011. "Designing Benefit Rules for Flexible Retirement: Welfare vs. Redistribution." *Acta Oeconomica* 61 (1): 3–32.

Girosi, Federico, and Gary King. 2007. *Understanding the Lee-Carter Mortality Forecasting Method.* Santa Monica, CA: Rand Corporation.

Holzmann, Robert, Jennifer Alonso-García, Héloïse Labit-Hardy, and Andrés M. Villegas. 2017. "NDC Schemes and Heterogeneity in Longevity: Proposals for Redesign." Revised paper presented at the Third International Conference on Nonfinancial Defined Contribution Pension Schemes, Rome, October 5–6.

Hyndman, Rob J., and Shahid Ullah. 2007. "Robust Forecasting of Mortality and Fertility Rates: A Functional Data Approach." *Computational Statistics and Data Analysis* 52 (10): 4942–56.

Klein, Thomas, and Riner Unger. 2002. "Aktive Lebenserwartung in Deutschland und in den USA." *Zeitschrift fur Gerontologie und Geiatrie* 35: 528–39.

Klerby, Anna, Bo Larsson, and Edward Palmer. 2019. "Bridging Partner Life-Cycle Earnings and Pension Gaps by Sharing NDC Accounts." In *Progress and Challenges of Nonfinancial Defined Contribution Pension Schemes: Volume 2 Addressing Gender, Administration, and Communication,* edited by Robert Holzmann, Edward Palmer, Robert Palacios, and Stefano Sacchi, Chapter 20. Washington, DC: World Bank.

Kroh, Martin, Hannes Neiss, Lars Kroll, and Thomas Lampert. 2012. "Menschen mit Hohen Einkommen Leben Länger." Tech. Rep. 38, DIW, Working Paper, German Institute for Economic Research, Berlin.

Lampert, Thomas, Lars Kroll, and Annlena Dundelberg. 2007. "Soziale Unterschiede in Dermrtalitt und Lebenserwartung." *Aus Politik und Zeitgeschichte* 42: 11–18.

Larsson, Bo, Vincent Leyaro, and Edward Palmer. 2019. "Harnessing a Young Nation's Demographic Dividends through a Universal NDC Pension Scheme: A Case Study of Tanzania." In *Progress and Challenges of Nonfinancial Defined Contribution Pension Schemes: Volume 2 Addressing Gender, Administration, and Communication*, edited by Robert Holzmann, Edward Palmer, Robert Palacios, and Stefano Sacchi, Chapter 23. Washington, DC: World Bank.

Lee, Ronald D., and Lawrence Carter. 1992. "Modeling and Forecasting the Time Series of U.S. Mortality" *Journal of the American Statistical Association* 87: 659–71.

Lee, Ronald D., and Timothy Miller. 2001. "Evaluating the Performance of the Lee-Carter Method for Forecasting Mortality." *Demography* 38 (4): 537–49.

Li, Siu-Haang, and Wai Sum Chan. 2005. "Outlier Analysis and Mortality Forecasting: The United Kingdom and Scandinavian Countries." *Scandinavian Actuarial Journal* 2005 (3): 187–211.

Nalebuff, Barry, and Richard J. Zeckerhauser. 1985. "Pensions and the Retirement Decision." Working Paper 1285, National Bureau of Economic Research, Cambridge, MA.

National Academies of Sciences, Engineering, and Medicine. 2015. *The Growing Gap in Life Expectancy by Income: Implications for Federal Programs and Policy Responses*. Committee on the Long-Run Macroeconomic Effects of the Aging U.S. Population-Phase II. Committee on Population, Division of Behavioral and Social Sciences and Education. Board on Mathematical Sciences and Their Applications, Division on Engineering and Physical Sciences. Washington, DC: National Academies Press.

Nelsson, Kenneth, Rense Nieuwenhuis, and Susanne Alm. 2019. "Sweden: Adjoining the Minimum Pension with NDC." In *Progress and Challenges of Nonfinancial Defined Contribution Pension Schemes: Volume 1 Addressing Marginalization, Polarization, and the Labor Market*, edited by Robert Holzmann, Edward Palmer, Robert Palacios, and Stefano Sacchi, Chapter 10. Washington, DC: World Bank.

Palmer, Edward. 2013. "Generic NDC: Equilibrium, Valuation and Risk Sharing with and without NDC Bonds." In *Nonfinancial Defined Contribution Pension Schemes in a Changing World: Volume 2 Gender, Politics, and Financial Stability*, edited by Robert Holzmann, David Robalino, and Edward *Palmer*, 309–33. Washington, DC: World Bank.

Palmer, Edward, and Bo Könberg. 2019. "The Swedish NDC Scheme: Success on Track with Room for Reflection." In *Progress and Challenges of Nonfinancial Defined Contribution Pension Schemes: Volume 1 Addressing Marginalization, Polarization, and the Labor Market*, edited by Robert Holzmann, Edward Palmer, Robert Palacios, and Stefano Sacchi, Chapter 2. Washington, DC: World Bank.

Palmer, Edward, and Sandra Stabina. 2019. "The Latvian NDC Scheme: Success under a Decreasing Labor Force." In *Progress and Challenges of Nonfinancial Defined Contribution Pension Schemes: Volume 1 Addressing Marginalization, Polarization, and the Labor Market*, edited by Robert Holzmann, Edward Palmer, Robert Palacios, and Stefano Sacchi, Chapter 3. Washington, DC: World Bank.

Palmer, Edward, and Yuwei Zhao de Gosson de Varennes. 2018. *Pensionsystemens Demografiska Utmaningar*. Stockholm, Sweden: SNS Förlag.

Piggott, John, Emiliano A. Valdez, and Bettina Detzel. 2005. "The Simple Analytics of Pooled Annuity Funds." *Journal of Risk and Insurance* 72 (3): 497–520.

Reil-Held, Anette. 2000. "Einkommen und Sterblichkeit in Deutschland: Leben Reiche Inger?" Discussion Paper 504, Department of Economics and Statistics, Mannheim University, Mannheim, Germany.

Simonovits, András. 2006. "Optimal Design of Pension Rule with Flexible Retirement: The Two-Type Case." *Journal of Economics* 89: 197–222.

Statistics Sweden. 2016. "Life Expectancy and Mortality of Different Socioeconomic Groups." *Demographic Report* 2016: 2, Statistics Sweden, Government of Sweden, Stockholm.

Swedish Pensions Agency. 2016. "Longevity and Group Income." (*Livslängdsanalys för olika inkomstgrupper*). Pensionsmyndigheten: Stockholm.

Valdez, Emiliano A., John Piggott, and Liang Wang. 2006. "Demand and Adverse Selection in a Pooled Annuity Fund." *Mathematics and Economics* 39 (2): 251–66.

van Raalte, Alyson A., Pekka Martikainen, and Mikko Myrskylä. 2014. "Lifespan Variation by Occupational Class: Compression or Stagnation over Time?" *Demography* 55 (1): 73–95.

Wilmoth, John R. 1993. "Computational Methods for Fitting and Extrapolating the Lee-Carter Model of Mortality Change." Technical Report, Department of Demography, University of California, Berkeley.

Waldron, Hilary. 2005. "Literature Review of Long-Term Mortality Projection." *Social Security Bulletin* 66 (1): 16–30.

Zhao de Gosson de Varennes, Yuwei. 2016a. "Benefit Design, Financial Risk and Inter-Generational Transfer in NDC Pension Schemes." In *Benefit Design, Retirement Decisions and Welfare within and across Generations in Defined Contribution Pension Schemes*, edited by Yuwei Zhao de Gosson de Varennes, 49–72. Uppsala, Sweden: Uppsala University.

Zhao de Gosson de Varennes. 2016b. "Socioeconomic Differences in Life Expectancy, Unintended Intra and Inter-Generational Transfers in DC Pension Schemes." In *Benefit Design, Retirement Decisions and Welfare within and across Generations in Defined Contribution Pension Schemes*, edited by Yuwei Zhao de Gosson de Varennes, 111–48. Uppsala, Sweden: Uppsala University.

Zhao de Gosson de Varennes, Yuwei, Edward Palmer, and Juha Alho. 2016. "Projecting Cohort Life Expectancy Based on Its Rate of Change in Mortality." In *Benefit Design, Retirement Decisions and Welfare within and across Generations in Defined Contribution Pension Schemes*, edited by Yuwei Zhao de Gosson de Varennes, 13–48. Uppsala, Sweden: Uppsala University.

CHAPTER 14

NDC Schemes and Heterogeneity in Longevity: Proposals for Redesign

Robert Holzmann, Jennifer Alonso-García,
Héloïse Labit-Hardy, and Andrés M. Villegas

Introduction

Strong and growing empirical evidence shows that longevity is highly heterogeneous in key socioeconomic characteristics, including income status. Ayuso, Bravo, and Holzmann (2017b) review the literature on the main socioeconomic dimensions of heterogeneity in longevity, their past development, and likely future trends. This international evidence, currently available only for advanced economies, suggests that heterogeneity in longevity arises across many socioeconomic dimensions, is often sizable, is becoming more prevalent, and shows few signals of abating in the near future.

The scope and trend of such heterogeneity in longevity regarding measures of lifetime income create a major concern for providers of lifetime annuities—namely, private insurance companies under voluntary and mandated financial defined contribution (FDC) schemes, and the rising number of countries that did or plan to adopt a nonfinancial defined contribution (NDC) scheme. Under an NDC approach, the initial pension benefit (lifetime annuity) is calculated at retirement by broadly dividing the notional account accumulations by the remaining (average) cohort life expectancy (see chapter 9 for a primer on NDCs). When heterogeneity based on socioeconomic characteristics exists in the remaining life expectancy, some individuals profit at the expense of others in the social insurance pool. If life expectancy is positively correlated with lifetime income and with the level of accumulation, lower-income groups lose and higher-income groups profit from a common risk pool and application of a common life-expectancy measure.

From a policy design perspective, socioeconomic heterogeneity in longevity with regard to income or other individual characteristics breaks the tight contribution-benefit link considered the signature feature of an NDC scheme: what you paid in you get out—not less and not more. Breaking the link creates tax wedges that the reform from nonfinancial defined benefit (NDB) to NDC schemes aimed to eliminate. Such heterogeneity wedges also exist in NDB schemes beyond those created by explicit or implicit redistribution mechanisms, but with the benefit formulas in NDB schemes, they are less visible. In an NDC scheme, one can more easily calculate the tax or subsidy wedge created by

The authors acknowledge research support from the ARC Center of Excellence in Population Ageing Research (grant CE110001029). They are grateful to Ronald Lee and Steve Haberman for their excellent comments and suggestions.

the heterogeneity in life expectancy at retirement, which has implications for individuals' decisions regarding formal labor supply and retirement age. Hence, if shown to be significant, left unaddressed, the risk associated with heterogeneity in life expectancy is threefold, given that it reduces the strength of the link between contributions and benefits, renders an increase in retirement age as the key approach to deal with population aging regressive and less powerful, and creates an unfair redistribution, an outcome the NDC approach seeks to eliminate.

This chapter explores in depth key policy options for addressing heterogeneity in longevity in NDC schemes. Some options are outlined by Ayuso, Bravo, and Holzmann (2017a); this chapter deepens the analytical and empirical framework. "Scope of the Issue and Policy Implications" investigates the scope of the heterogeneity issue by using much more fine-grained data for the United States and England and Wales and estimating the distributions, not just point estimates, of the tax and subsidy mechanism. "A Formal Framework to Present Alternative NDC Designs" presents alternative NDC designs to address heterogeneity within a common analytical framework. "Empirical Application and Exploration" applies this analytical framework to the disaggregated data of "Scope of the Issue and Policy Implications" to gain a better understanding of feasibility, additional data needs, and empirical indications. "Summary and Next Steps" summarizes and outlines suggested next research steps.

Scope of the Issue and Policy Implications

Although establishing a high quality statistical database on mortality data on heterogeneity in longevity by various socioeconomic dimensions are increasingly available in advanced economies, the disaggregated link between life expectancy and the socioeconomic characteristics of lifetime income remains the exception. Where data do exist, they are typically not suitable for examining this link. However, such disaggregated estimates across the whole income strata are critical to guiding policy design options. The first part of this section presents estimated disaggregated information on the scope and distributional patterns of characteristics underlying heterogeneity in life expectancy based on data from the United States and England and Wales. The second part uses this information to estimate the disaggregated tax and subsidy effects of socioeconomic heterogeneity in life expectancy for these countries with regard to their measure of lifetime income. The section ends with a brief discussion of the policy implications of these estimates.

SCOPE AND DISTRIBUTION OF HETEROGENEITY IN LIFE EXPECTANCY

Individual lifetime incomes and the corresponding mortality data for a whole country are complex to establish and thus rarely available. Indeed, an estimation of lifetime income and cohort life expectancy requires combining various sources of data (such as tax declarations and death certificates). However, to gauge the relationship[1] between lifetime income and life expectancy, related information was obtained for the United States and England and Wales, as follows.

United States

Chetty et al. (2016) use federal income tax and Social Security records to investigate the relationship between lifetime income and life expectancy in the United States. This chapter uses their data[2] to estimate life expectancy at age 65 by income percentile. The available data comprise mortality rates and population counts for the United States by gender and income percentile for ages 40–76 and calendar years 2001–14. In this data set, income is approximated by yearly pretax household earnings adjusted to 2012 dollars using the consumer price index.[3] Full details of the data collection and sources can be found in Chetty et al. (2016).[4]

To estimate period life expectancy at age 65 by income percentile ranks 1–100, gender-specific life tables by income percentile are constructed using a Gompertz-type generalized additive model linking log mortality rates to age, income percentile rank, and calendar year.[5] Figures 14.1 and 14.2 illustrate the estimated relationship between income and period life expectancy at age 65. Here, nominal lifetime income values correspond to the sum of gender-specific, yearly pretax household earnings between ages 20 and 64, with earnings from ages 20–40 assumed to be equal to earnings at age 40.[6]

Figure 14.1 indicates that in a percentile view of the income distribution, the link to life expectancy is broadly linear except in the lowest percentiles, and less pronounced in the highest percentiles. If mapped to the real income measure in dollars, the relationship to life expectancy is strictly concave, with the strongest curvature where most household incomes are situated.

FIGURE 14.1 **U.S. period life expectancy in 2014 at age 65 by household income percentile**

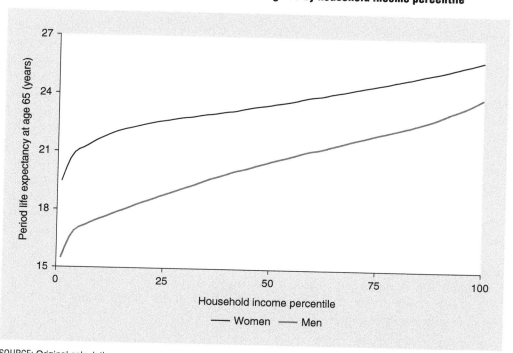

SOURCE: Original calculations.

FIGURE 14.2 **U.S. period life expectancy in 2014 at age 65 by nominal household income**

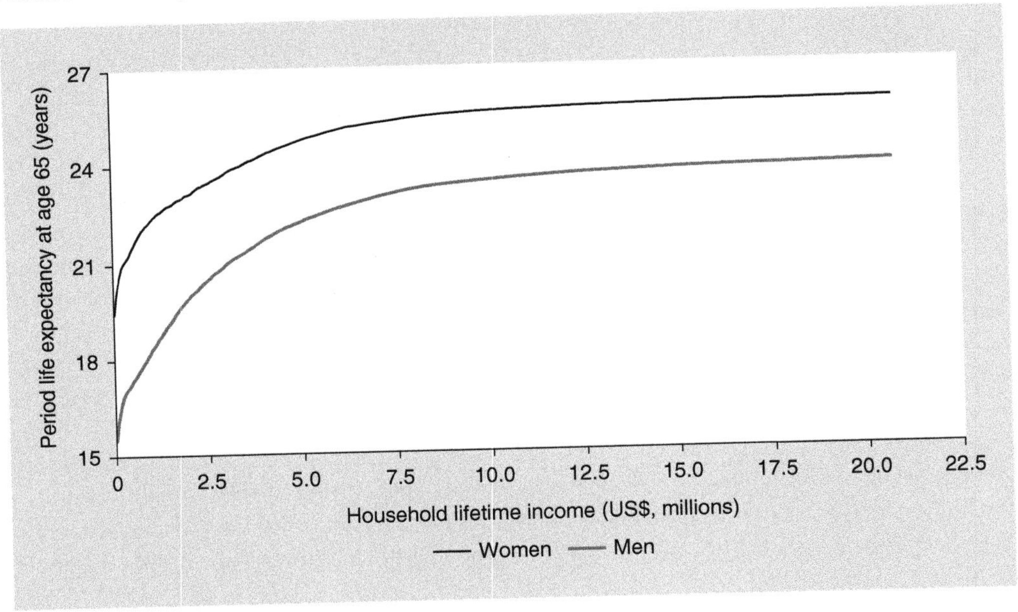

SOURCE: Original calculations based on Chetty et al. (2016).
NOTE: The top income percentile is omitted for scaling purposes.

England and Wales

England and Wales has no data set linking a measure of individual lifetime income to life expectancy. Instead, area-level measures are used to approximate this relationship. In particular, the analysis uses income and mortality data for middle layer super output areas (MSOA) in England and Wales, which are statistical geographies used by the Office of National Statistics (ONS). The available data comprise ONS estimates of the total (gross) weekly household income at the MSOA level for the financial year ending 2014,[7] number of deaths,[8] and midyear population estimates[9] by gender and MSOA for 2015 and for ages 50–89. To approximate period life expectancy at age 65 by income percentile rank 1–100, MSOAs are first aggregated into household income percentiles, and then gender-specific life tables by income percentile are constructed using a Gompertz-type generalized additive model linking log mortality rates to age and income percentile rank.[10] Figure 14.3, panels a and b, shows the estimated relationship between income and period life expectancy at age 65. In panel a of figure 14.2, nominal lifetime income values correspond to the sum of the gender-specific annual incomes between ages 20 and 64, which were approximated using the distribution of pretax mean income by age and gender for the 2015 financial year as reported by the United Kingdom's HM Revenue and Customs department.[11,12]

In comparing the results for England and Wales and the United States, it is important to bear in the following mind:

- Income "percentiles" for England and Wales refer to percentiles of average income in local areas and not to percentiles of individual incomes. Because individuals in an

FIGURE 14.3 **England and Wales period life expectancy in 2015 at age 65 by individual income percentile**

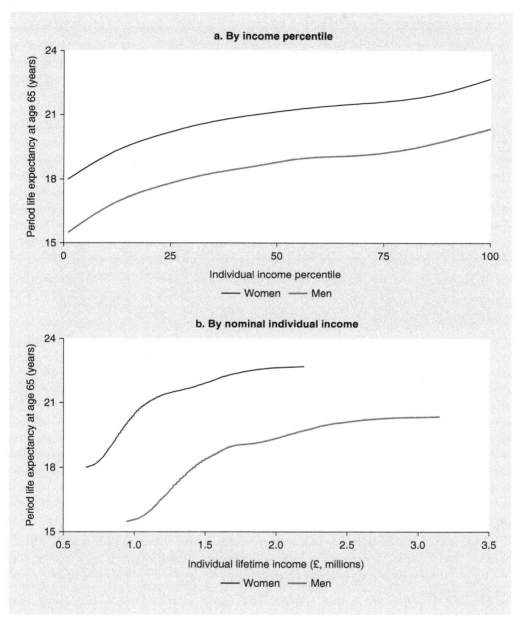

SOURCE: Original calculations based on Office of National Statistics data.

area will have additional heterogeneity, the actual distribution of individuals' incomes is likely to be more spread, as seen in the U.S. data, for instance. Furthermore, unlike the U.S. data, the England and Wales data will include contextual effects of geographic inequalities that could account for part of the association between income and mortality.

- Income in England and Wales is associated with individual income, whereas for the United States it is associated with household income. Using household income statistics instead of individual income may lead to misestimation of income by gender. This explains the greater disparity in income by gender observed in England and Wales as compared with the United States.
- The income axis for England and Wales is much more compressed than that for the United States, even when considering household versus individual income, and £ versus $ units.

HETEROGENEITY IN LONGEVITY AS TAX AND SUBSIDY MECHANISM: CONCEPT AND ESTIMATES

The redistributive effect of heterogeneity in longevity can be easily assessed by translating the outcomes on benefit levels into a tax and subsidy mechanism (Ayuso, Bravo, and Holzmann 2017b). The approach is similar to translating differences in money-worth ratios below and above one into tax or subsidy rates.

The general framework is based on an individual contributing tc of her contribution base y^{k} [13] between age x_0 and retirement age x_r to an NDC pension scheme, where the accumulated contributions at retirement age x_r are denoted $Y_{x_r}^{k}$. The superscript k represents her lifetime income characteristics. These contributions earn a notional rate of return i and yield accumulated capital equal to $AK^{k}(tc)$ at retirement:

$$AK^{k}\left(tc\right) = tc \times \sum_{j=0}^{x_r - x_0 - 1} y_{x_0 + j}^{k} \left(1 + i\right)^{x_r - x_0 - j} = tc \times Y_{x_r}^{k}. \qquad (14.1)$$

Upon retirement, the notional capital is transformed into an initial pension $P_{x_r}^{k}$ by dividing the accumulated capital $AK^{k}(tc)$ by an annuity factor a^{k} equal to the life expectancy of the cohort when the precharged indexation coincides with the discount rate.[14] The annuity factor can be individualized or can be based on the average life table of the cohort. In the latter case, the superscript k is specified to equal a. The annuity factor depends on the probability of surviving to age $x_r + j$ after retirement, denoted as $_{j}p_{x_r}^{k}$

$$a^{k} = LE^{k} = \sum_{j=0}^{\omega - x_r - 1} {}_{j}p_{j=0}^{k}, \qquad (14.2)$$

where ω is the last possible surviving age.

The difference in mortality becomes more explicit whenever the pension wealth or pension liability $PW_{x_r}^{c,k}$ is calculated. Indeed, pension wealth depends on the observed mortality for an individual with characteristics k, even when the pension is based on an average annuity:

$$PW_{x_r}^{c,k} = P_{x_r}^{c} LE^{k} = AK^{k}\left(tc\right) \frac{LE^{k}}{LE^{c}}. \qquad (14.3)$$

The pension wealth formulae presented above put forward two key concepts when dealing with heterogeneity. The first superscript, c, indicates the annuity factor used to calculate the pension at retirement. In practice, this is commonly based on the average life table of the population, despite observed differences in mortality.[15] The second superscript, k, indicates that the individual experiences a distinct mortality that depends on lifetime income, education, and other socioeconomic characteristics. It follows from the expression that pension wealth at retirement equals accumulated notional capital if the pension is based on the individual's life expectancy.

Following this framework, the implicit tax or subsidy rate t^k for the individual with lifetime income characteristics k can be calculated as

$$t^k = \frac{\text{Pension wealth}}{\text{Accumulated notional capital at retirement}} - 1 = \frac{PW_{x_r}^{c,k}}{AK^k(tc)} - 1. \qquad (14.4)$$

A positive value of t^k represents a subsidy, because the liability in the system exceeds the accumulated contributions paid. This indicates that the individual will receive on average t^k percent more than she has contributed. On the other hand, a negative t^k represents a tax, given that the realized liability is lower than the liability in the NDC books.

To clarify the distributional effects, the current design of a typical NDC (and for that matter, an FDC) pension scheme is presented. The pension at retirement is calculated with the average life table, although the pensioner will have a different mortality experience on average according to her lifetime income characteristics k. In this case, the tax (subsidy) t^k, which can be positive or negative, is represented as follows:

$$t^k = \frac{PW_{x_r}^{a,k}}{AK^k(tc)} - 1 = \frac{\dfrac{AK^k(tc)}{LE^a}LE^k}{AK^k(tc)} - 1 = \frac{LE^k}{LE^a} - 1. \qquad (14.5)$$

The individual receives a subsidy if $LE^k > LE^a$, that is, if she belongs to a category that lives on average longer than the total population. This typically corresponds to individuals with higher lifetime incomes. However, those who belong to a category that lives shorter than the total population on average will bear an implicit tax because of the difference in life expectancy.

For several advanced economies, Ayuso, Bravo, and Holzmann (2017a, 2017b) offer a number of point estimates of tax and subsidy rates that typically reflect the tertiles or quintiles of the income distribution. The data in figures 14.1 and 14.3 are used to estimate the whole distribution across all percentiles for the United States and England and Wales, respectively. The results, presented in figures 14.4 and 14.5, lead to the following observations:

- Given the known higher average life expectancy of women when applying a common average annuity factor—as is the case in social security schemes—all women above the 12th income percentile in the United States (16th percentile in England and Wales) receive a subsidy, while all men below the 73th income percentile in the United States (86th percentile in England and Wales) pay a tax.

- The tax rate of men can be as high as 30 percent for the lowest percentile in the United States (whereas it is below 20 percent in England and Wales), and the subsidy rate for women can reach as high as 18 percent in the United States (15 percent in England and Wales).

- Both men and women in the lowest 10 percent of income in both countries are particularly hit by a high tax rate of heterogeneity that is likely to affect their decisions regarding formal labor market participation and the scope of labor market supply.

FIGURE 14.4 **U.S. tax and subsidy rates by household income percentile**

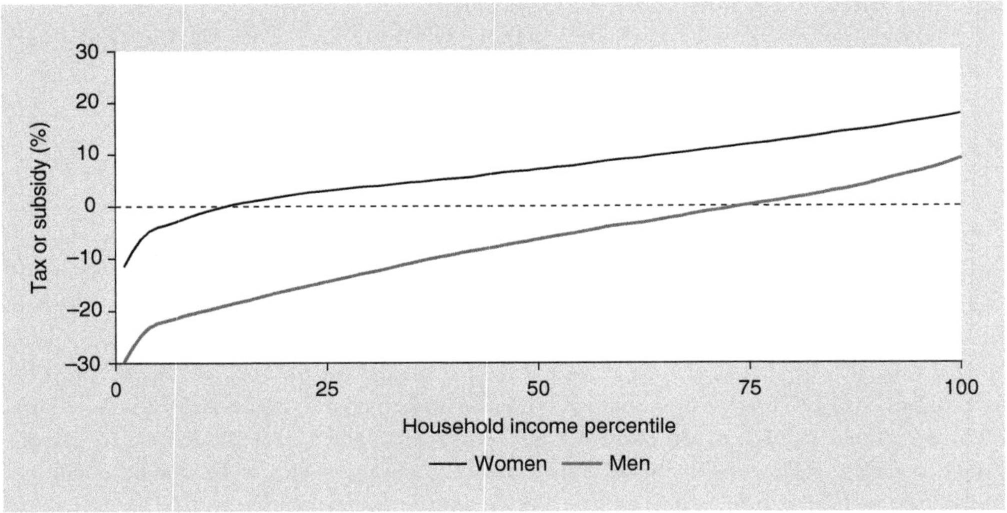

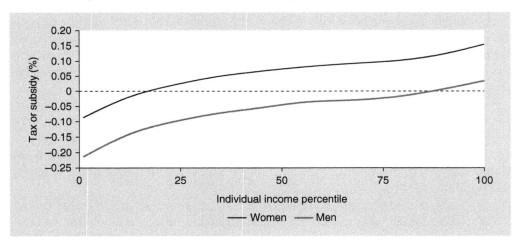

SOURCE: Original calculations based on Chetty et al. (2016).

FIGURE 14.5 **England and Wales tax and subsidy rates by individual income percentile**

SOURCE: Original calculations based on Office of National Statistics data.

IMPLICATIONS FOR SCHEME DESIGN AND PENSION REFORM

A relevant and rising scope of heterogeneity in longevity—particularly linking higher life expectancy at retirement with higher accumulations at retirement—has major implications for scheme design and pension reform. The implications of this trend apply specifically to the reform movement in recent decades from defined benefit (DB) to (financial or nonfinancial) defined contribution (DC) schemes to establish a closer contribution-benefit link and to address population aging by increasing the retirement age in line with increasing life expectancy. If relevant heterogeneity in longevity is left unaddressed in the design and implementation of DC schemes, their underlying design and reform rationale may be called into question. This section thus focuses on three main concerns with NDC schemes; the arguments apply roughly for FDC schemes as well.[16]

First, the beauty of NDC schemes is their simplicity and claimed fairness: there is no tax wedge because what you paid in you get out with a rate of return, and this is what constitutes your account at retirement and goes into the determination of your yearly benefit.[17] Any redistributive considerations are transparent, with external financing that happens at the time the commitment is made, not when it is disbursed. This approach contrasts with NDB schemes, in which some redistribution is part of the design but most of it is implicit, creating a tax and subsidy wedge often of unknown size and with unknown effects on distribution, financing, and scheme participation. With sizable socio-economic heterogeneity and thus sizable tax and subsidy effects for the distribution of income in the pension pool, the transparency of NDC schemes enables the policy maker to devise counter measures, which is the topic pursued here.

Second, NDC schemes promise a linear intertemporal budget constraint in which the choice of retirement age depends only on the linear resource constraint and individual preferences for consumption and leisure. Minimum and standard retirement ages, in principle, lose their relevance in an NDC scheme, except for dealing with some behavioral restrictions by individuals in their decision making. Because life expectancy at retirement continuously increases (for most but not all socioeconomic groups), individuals will receive a lower benefit at any given retirement age, which is expected to provide them with incentives to postpone retirement to smooth their lifetime consumption. This is the case when life expectancy is assumed to be homogeneous. However, if individuals realize that the initial benefit is calculated by applying an average cohort life expectancy, even though they have a better assessment of their own longevity, their retirement decision risks being different. Both the poor and the rich have an incentive to retire as soon as possible—that is, shortly after the minimum retirement age fixed by all NDC countries—because the poor cannot expect to live so long, and the rich can maximize their subsidy.

Last, a critical rationale for reforming NDC schemes is the transparency of their redistributive processes, as alluded to earlier. With stark heterogeneity, the envisaged distributive neutrality under NDC schemes does not hold. This means that redistributive interventions in the context of NDC schemes would ideally also take this into consideration. This calls for a clear understanding of the magnitude of heterogeneity and the design alternatives to address it, and a full understanding of how external redistributive interventions will affect individuals with life expectancies that deviate from the applied common average.

A Formal Framework for Presenting Alternative NDC Designs

This section presents five alternatives to the design of the pension paid at retirement, by modifying either the annuity rate or the contribution rate. The government can intervene either at retirement or during accumulation. Three designs are analyzed that deliver a tax or subsidy of zero when life expectancy is known with certainty. However, in practice, individual-specific improvements and aggregate mortality risk raise the need to perform approximations, as presented in Designs 3, 4, and 5.

Design 1 considers individualized annuities. Design 2 individualizes the contribution rate during the accumulation phase instead of paying individualized annuities. As an approximation, Design 3 splits the total contribution rate tc to accrue both a social and an individualized pension. The contribution split suggested in Design 3 works very well only as long as the relationship between life expectancy and lifetime income is broadly linear (in percentile or log income) across the whole income strata, so Designs 4 and 5 address heterogeneity when this linearity is not the case. Design 4 deals with the upper tail of the established longevity-income link and explores the extent to which caps on contributions paid into the individual account but not on contributions levied on income and wages can address deviations for the highest income group. Design 5 explores the extent to which individualized contribution rates that build on the two-tier design structure are needed to address deviations for the lowest income group.

DESIGN ALTERNATIVE 1: INDIVIDUALIZED ANNUITIES

The most effective way to reduce the distortionary effects of heterogeneous mortality—as defined in equations (14.4) and (14.5)—is to pay pensions that depend on the individualized mortality experience instead of using the average mortality rate. If everyone pays the contribution rate tc, the tax or subsidy is reduced to zero:

$$t^k = \frac{\dfrac{AK^k(tc)}{LE^k}LE^k}{AK^k(tc)} - 1 = 0. \tag{14.6}$$

DESIGN ALTERNATIVE 2: INDIVIDUAL CONTRIBUTION RATES—VERSIONS A AND B

An individual approach during the accumulation stage can be achieved in two ways. The first one considers that everyone pays the same rate tc whereas the contribution allocated into the individual notional account is adjusted by differences in life expectancy. A second approach consists of allocating the average notional contribution rate while collecting an individualized contribution rate tc^k that is adjusted for heterogeneity. Both approaches lead to a zero tax and subsidy component but to different allocation and benefit levels at a given retirement age, which may lead to different retirement incentives.

In version 2a, participants pay $tc \times y^k$ but are credited $tc \times y^k \dfrac{LE^a}{LE^k}$ to ensure actuarial fairness. The accumulated capital then becomes $AK^k(tc) = tc\dfrac{LE^a}{LE^k}Y^k_{x_r}$. Indeed, individuals who live longer than average are credited a lower amount than they have contributed to correct for the additional years during retirement. This adjustment also increases the replacement rate for those with a lower life expectancy, facilitating their early withdrawal from the labor force. Upon retirement, the pension is calculated based on the average life table. In this case, the realized liability corresponds to the one present in the books and the tax or subsidy becomes zero:

$$t^k = \frac{\dfrac{tc \times \dfrac{LE^a}{LE^k}Y^k_{x_r}}{LE^a}LE^k}{tc \cdot Y^k_{x_r}} - 1 = 0. \tag{14.7}$$

Alternatively, in version 2b, participants pay the individual contribution rate, $tc^k = tc \times \dfrac{LE^k}{LE^a}$, which is related to their life expectancy. If they live longer (shorter) than average they pay more (less) into the pension system. However, they are credited an amount corresponding to the average contribution rate tc. Their accumulated capital at retirement therefore coincides with expression (14.1) and the replacement rate is equal across the different categories. If the pension is calculated with the average life table, the tax or subsidy becomes zero:

$$t^k = \frac{\dfrac{tc \times Y^k_{x_r}}{LE^a} LE^k}{tc \times \dfrac{LE^k}{LE^a} Y^k_{x_r}} - 1 = 0. \tag{14.8}$$

DESIGN ALTERNATIVE 3: TWO-TIER CONTRIBUTION SCHEMES WITH FLAT AND INDIVIDUALIZED CONTRIBUTION RATES—VERSIONS A AND B

This alternative works at the accumulation stage and assumes that pensions paid during retirement are based on the average annuity. To reduce the distortions, individuals pay a total contribution rate tc equal to the one in Design 1. However, the contribution rate is further split between a social contribution sc and an individual contribution nc. The rights of the individual depend on the two-tier split: the social contribution sc accrues rights on the median salary y^a, whereas the individual contribution nc accrues pension rights on the individualized contribution base y^k. The accumulated capital at retirement is then given as follows:

$$AK^k(sc, nc) = \sum_{j=0}^{x_r - x_0 - 1} \left(sc \times y^a_{x_0 + j} + nc \times y^k_{x_0 + j} \right) \times (1 + i)^{x_r - x_0 - j}$$
$$= sc \times Y^a_{x_r} + nc \times Y^k_{x_r}. \tag{14.9}$$

The two-tier allocation can be rewriten to highlight the redistribution as follows:

$$sc \times y^a_{x_0 + j} + nc \times y^k_{x_0 + j} = tc \times y^k_{x_0 + j} + sc \times \left(y^a_{x_0 + j} - y^k_{x_0 + j} \right).$$

An individual earning less than $y^a_{x_0 + j}$ receives an additional pension right equal to $sc \times \left(y^a_{x_0 + j} - y^k_{x_0 + j} \right)$, whereas someone earning more than the reference level sees her accrued rights decrease by $sc \times \left(y^a_{x_0 + j} - y^k_{x_0 + j} \right)$. The split between the social and individual contributions needs to be made at a cohort level to jointly reduce the distortions caused by the differences in life expectancy. A way to achieve this goal is to minimize on a cohort basis the squared difference between the pension $P^k_{x_r}(tc)$ from Design 1 based on the unique contribution rate tc and an individualized annuity, denoted as P^k_1 for an individual k, and the pension $P^a_{x_r}(sc, nc)$ based on the split contribution rate and the average annuity, denoted as P^k_2 for simplicity (Design version 3a):

$$\min \sum_{k \in I} \left(P^k_1 - P^k_2 \right)^2 = \min \sum_{k \in I} \left(tc \times \frac{Y^k_{x_r}}{LE^k} - sc \times \frac{Y^a_{x_r}}{LE^a} - (tc - sc) \frac{Y^k_{x_r}}{LE^a} \right)^2. \tag{14.10}$$

It can be shown that the optimal social contribution sc^* is then equal to:

$$sc^* = tc \times \frac{\sum_{k \in I} \frac{Y_{x_r}^k}{LE^k}\left(LE^k - LE^a\right)\left(Y_{x_r}^k - Y_{x_r}^a\right)}{\sum_{k \in I}\left(Y_{x_r}^k - Y_{x_r}^a\right)^2}. \tag{14.11}$$

In this case the tax rate (4) is:

$$t^k = \frac{\frac{AK^k(sc,nc)}{LE^a}LE^k}{AK^k(tc)} - 1 = \frac{sc \times Y_{x_r}^a + nc \times Y_{x_r}^k}{(sc+nc) \times Y_{x_r}^k}\frac{LE^k}{LE^a} - 1 = \left(1 + \frac{sc}{tc}\left(\frac{Y_{x_r}^a}{Y_{x_r}^k} - 1\right)\right)\frac{LE^k}{LE^a} - 1. \tag{14.12}$$

If $Y_{x_r}^k > Y_{x_r}^a$ and $LE^k > LE^a$, then it is unclear whether a tax or subsidy arises, since the first part of equation (14.12) would be less than 1 and the life expectancy ratio would be greater than 1.

Alternatively, in version 3b, the difference in replacement rates is minimized instead, yielding:

$$\min \sum_{k \in I}\left(\frac{P_1^k}{y_{x_r-1}^k} - \frac{P_2^k}{y_{x_r-1}^k}\right)^2. \tag{14.13}$$

The optimal social contribution sc^* is then equal to

$$sc^* = tc \times \frac{\sum_{k \in I}\frac{Y_{x_r}^k}{LE^k}\left(LE^k - LE^a\right)\left(\frac{Y_{x_r}^k - Y_{x_r}^a}{(y_{x_r-1}^k)^2}\right)}{\sum_{k \in I}\left(\frac{Y_{x_r}^k - Y_{x_r}^a}{y_{x_r-1}^k}\right)^2}. \tag{14.14}$$

In this case the mathematical expression of the tax rate (14.4) coincides with the one presented in equation (14.12). However, it will differ in its magnitude because the split between the total contribution in a social and individual contribution will differ.

A tax or subsidy rate of zero can be achieved by either individualizing the annuity or the contribution rate. However, as an approximation, implementing a two-tier contribution scheme can help reduce the distributionary effects of current typical NDCs. If the contribution rate tc is split into (a) a social contribution rate sc accruing rights on the median salary, and (b) an individual contribution rate nc accruing rights on the individual salary, then the tax or subsidy rate can be reduced. Setting the tax rate in equation (14.12) to zero derives a link between individual life expectancy as a function of average life expectancy and the relationship between individual and median lifetime income. The closer the empirical link to this functional relationship, the lower the tax or subsidy would be.

$$LE^k = LE^a\left(\frac{tc \times Y^k}{tc \times Y^a + nc\left(Y^k - Y^a\right)}\right). \tag{14.15}$$

FIGURE 14.6 **Actuarial fairness under heterogeneous life expectancy in a two-tier contribution scheme for alternative contribution rate splits**

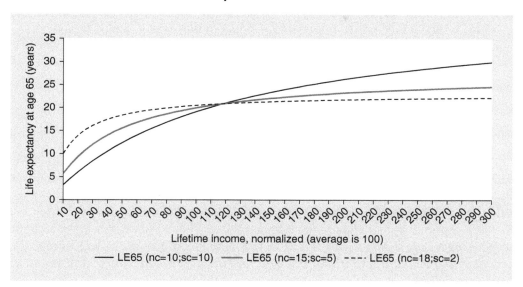

SOURCE: Original calculations based on equation (14.15) with average life expectancy at age 65 of 20.88 years in England and Wales and average lifetime income of £1,183,902.

NOTE: LE65 = life expectancy at age 65; nc = individual contribution rate; sc = social contribution rate.

Figure 14.6 presents the implied relationship between life expectancy and lifetime income for three pairs of individual and social contribution rates. The higher the social contribution rate relative to the individual rate, the more Design 2 is able to compensate for the higher heterogeneity of longevity that is linked to lifetime income inequality. The concave curvature of this relationship is consistent with empirical observations (discussed in "Scope of the Issue and Policy Implications").[18]

DESIGN ALTERNATIVE 4: TWO-TIER CONTRIBUTION SCHEME (DESIGN ALTERNATIVE 2A) WITH CAPS ON THE CONTRIBUTIONS

This alternative seeks to complement Design 2a with the two-tier contribution system when the relationship between lifetime income percentile and life expectancy is not concave in the upper tail (as highlighted with U.S. data in figure 14.1, panel a): In this case the highest income group gains overproportionally in life expectancy to all other groups and the effect cannot be corrected by the two-tier scheme alone. As before, the total contribution rate is split into a social contribution sc and an individual contribution nc. However, the individual and social contribution base is capped for accumulation purposes. In this case, the accumulated capital at retirement $CAK^k (sc,nc)$ is

$$CAK^k (sc,nc) = \sum_{j=0}^{x_r-x_0-1} \left(sc \times y^a_{x_0+j} + nc \times \left(y^k_{x_0+j} + \left(Cap - y^k_{x_0+j} \right) 1_{y^k>Cap} \right) \right) \times (1+i)^{x_r-x_0-j}$$

$$= sc \times Y^a_{x_r} + nc \times CY^k_{x_r}. \tag{14.16}$$

This expression indicates that accumulated capital at retirement consists of the following two parts: the social contribution sc applied to the accumulated average wage $Y_{x_r}^a$ plus the individual contribution rate nc applied to the accumulated capped individual wage $CY_{x_r}^k$. If the individual earns more than the cap, the contribution allocated to the individual account remains constant at the cap level.

In this case, the tax is given as follows:

$$t^k = \frac{\dfrac{AK^k(sc,nc)}{LE^a}LE^k}{AK^k(tc)} - 1 = \frac{sc \times Y_{x_r}^a + nc \times CY_{x_r}^k}{(sc + nc) \times Y_{x_r}^k}\frac{LE^k}{LE^a} - 1. \qquad (14.17)$$

The cap varies substantially across countries, ranging from median income (thus fully covering only 50 percent of the insured) to a multiple of the average income (thus fully covering 90 percent or even 95 percent of the population). The scope of coverage below the ceiling often has historical reasons and is codetermined by the role of supplementary pensions for those above the ceiling. Historically, the cap did not take account of hetereogeneity. However, differences in longevity could inform the selection of the ceiling. If those in the upper 5th or 10th percentile deviate upward in their life expectancy from an empirically established concave pattern for the large majority of the population, then such a ceiling selection under a Design 4 approach would make sense. How well the Design 4 approach is able to correct for such a deviation needs to be investigated in a country setting.

DESIGN ALTERNATIVE 5: TWO-TIER CONTRIBUTION SCHEME (DESIGN ALTERNATIVE 3A) WITH INDIVIDUALIZED CONTRIBUTION RATES

Design 5 blends Design alternative 3a, that is, a two-tier contribution rate structure—with Design alternative 2b, that is, an individualized total contribution rate. The individual pays an individual contribution rate tc^k but credits the total contribution rate under a social and individual contribution rate split. The individual contribution rate tc^k is a proportion α of the total contribution rate tc, calculated such that the contributions made result in actuarially fair benefits. Upon retirement, the accumulated capital is transformed into a pension with the average life table. The tax is then given as

$$t^k = \frac{sc \times Y_{x_r}^a + nc \times Y_{x_r}^k}{(sc + nc) \times \alpha \times Y_{x_r}^k}\frac{LE^k}{LE^a} - 1.$$

It follows from the expression above that the proportion α that adjusts the total contribution rate needs to be chosen as

$$\alpha = \frac{sc \times Y_{x_r}^a + nc \times Y_{x_r}^k}{(sc + nc) \times Y_{x_r}^k}\frac{LE^k}{LE^a}$$

to achieve a zero tax or subsidy, that is, an actuarially fair pension scheme ($t^k = 0$). Consistent with Design 3, it is not straightforward to determine whether the correction to the contribution rate α will be higher or lower than 1, increasing or decreasing the contribution rate accordingly.

A second and more operationally oriented Design alternative 5b seeks to complement the two-tier Design 3 for the lowest tail of the income distribution. As figures 14.1 and 14.3 for the United States and England and Wales suggest, the lowest 5 percent of the population's estimated life expectancy seems below even that of the established concave curvature of a two-tier approach. If this were the case for the most marginalized insured, compensation through the social contribution share would not be sufficient to establish broadly actuarial neutrality.

Empirical Application and Exploration

This section offers some empirical evidence for the effectiveness of the policy options in reducing the effects of heterogeneity. To compare among policy options, a total tax measure is applied to aggregate the individual tax and subsidy rates across the available percentile data of lifetime income and the related period life expectancies at age 65. For this aggregate average measure, the absolute values are used so that tax and subsidy rates are added up across the full income spectrum at retirement; both taxes and subsidies are an indication of fairness distortions. This total absolute tax and subsidy indicator (TATSI), defined as the averaged sum of the absolute values of the individual tax and subsidy rates, is fully comparable across all policy options.

Two policy options are explored: individualized annuities and the two-tier contribution scheme. Both appear empirically, politically, and operationally feasible. The individual contribution Design 2 that would be applied during the accumulation phase is left out, because it raises a number of operational and policy issues. For data and space reasons, the alternatives that deal with the tails of the distribution are also omitted. When presenting Designs 1 and 3, the current situation, denoted Design alternative 0, is the benchmark.

DESIGN ALTERNATIVE 0: ALMOST STATUS QUO

Starting with the results of TATSI for Design alternative 0—the benchmark—two rate estimations are explored: the rate for pooled life expectancy and the rate when life expectancies between men and women are separated, that is, the individual tax and subsidy rate is calculated based on gender-specific average life expectancy. Table 14.1 summarizes the results.[19] In separate pools the average taxes match the average subsidies that make the nominal tax rate zero[20]; in joint pools men pay taxes that are subsidies to women (first row). Calculating the average taxes and subsidies in absolute terms reveals the distortions in both joint and separate pools (second row). Aggregating the nominal taxes and subsidies across genders gives a tax rate of zero (third row) but not when absolute values are aggregated (fourth and last row), which is the average of the results in the second row.

Table 14.1 indicates for England and Wales a TATSI of 6.91 percent for the traditional joint pool of both genders. The gender-specific tax and subsidy rates differ slightly between women and men, being higher for men because the difference between the highest tax and subsidy is larger. Applying separate pools reduces the gender-specific absolute rate significantly for women, but little for men. The TATSI value for England and Wales is reduced to 4.64 percent, or by one-third. The results for the United States are similar in the direction of change but with altogether higher values. The joint pool value of 8.59 percent

TABLE 14.1 **Design alternative 0—Aggregate tax and subsidy rate indicators for England and Wales and the United States**

	England and Wales				United States			
	Joint pool (%)		Separate pools (%)		Joint pool (%)		Separate pools (%)	
	Women	Men	Women	Men	Women	Men	Women	Men
Nominal tax and subsidy rate	6.02	−6.02	0.00	0.00	7.05	−7.05	0.00	0.00
Absolute tax and subsidy rate	7.34	6.48	4.28	5.00	8.02	9.16	4.73	8.31
	Total		Total		Total		Total	
Nominal tax and subsidy rate (%)	0.00		0.00		0.00		0.00	
TATSI (%)	6.91		4.64		8.59		6.52	

SOURCE: Original table.
NOTE: TATSI = total absolute tax and subsidy indicator.

is reduced through separate pooling to 6.52 percent, or by almost one-quarter. These results suggest that risk pool separation could be a critical ingredient for the reduction of TATSI in countries, but it is not sufficient.[21]

DESIGN ALTERNATIVE 1: INDIVIDUALIZED ANNUITIES

In many existing annuity markets, annuity rates are derived using age and gender as the only rating factors, ignoring any socioeconomic variation in mortality. However, in more advanced markets such as the United Kingdom, the importance of considering differential mortality for the valuation of pension liabilities and the pricing of annuities has been recognized. Lifestyle and socioeconomic mortality profiling is common in the U.K. bulk annuity market and is increasingly being used in the pricing of individual annuity products and in the valuation of pension portfolio liabilities (Gatzert and Klotzki 2016; Richards 2008; Ridsdale and Gallop 2010). Variables used by insurers and pension providers in estimating an individual's mortality include postcode, salary, pension, smoking status, and occupation. As illustrated in Madrigal et al. (2011) and Richards, Kaufhold, and Rosenbusch (2013), such variables are typically considered using generalized linear models or survival models applied to large and detailed data sets of historical individual mortality. Life expectancy per lifetime income over the years would lead to better estimated impacts of alternative pension designs over generations.

Here it is hypothesized that public institutions running NDC schemes at a national level would be able to produce such data: estimates for lifetime income along the income distribution—for example, for each percentile—and the corresponding estimated period or cohort life expectancy, and differentiated by gender. Estimations by the National Academies of Sciences, Engineering, and Medicine in the United States in 2015 offer a possible approach in addition to the data sets for the United States and England and Wales applied previously. The estimation of individual life expectancy for individuals within a percentile cohort may be enhanced by other socioeconomic characteristics such as education and geography if considerations of magnitudes and relevance suggest so.[22]

A much simpler approach is followed here. It seeks to measure by how much TATSI is reduced compared with the starting position—Design alternative 0—if the life expectancy of a percentile (compared with the untreated estimate) is estimated through a simple life expectancy–lifetime income relationship. Two specifications are explored:

Quadratic $$LE_k = a + b \times Y_k + c \times Y_k^2$$

Logarithmic $$LE_k = a + b \log Y_k$$

Figure 14.7, panels a, b, c, d, e, and f, illustrate the observed and approximated link between life expectancy and lifetime income—for joint and separated gender pools—for England and Wales and the United States, respectively. As the figures clearly show, the individualization of annuities works broadly well when the gender pools are disaggregated. The simple quadratic specification does a reasonable job of approximation for England and Wales, as does the logarithmic specification for the United States.

Table 14.2 presents the data behind figure 14.7. The mere approximation of individual life expectancy in the joint pool brings a moderate reduction in TATSI for the United States and a slight deterioration for England and Wales. However, when the pools are separated by gender, even simple individualization of annuities leads to a reduction in TATSI in the United States compared with the gender-separated value in table 14.1, from 6.52 to 4.12; the reduction is even stronger in England and Wales, from 4.64 to 0.95 (that is, by about 80 percent). Note that as opposed to table 14.1, where the nominal tax and subsidy rate is exactly 0 percent, in table 14.2 the nominal tax and subsidy rate is not exactly 0 percent. This results from a negligible approximation (model) error induced by the regression.

DESIGN ALTERNATIVE 3: A TWO-TIER CONTRIBUTION SCHEME

The other promising approach to reducing the distortionary effects of heterogeneity in longevity in an NDC scheme is to introduce the two-tier contribution approach presented in "A Formal Framework to Present Alternative NDC Designs." Carving out a social contribution rate sc under a total contribution rate of 20 percent (the assumed rate for the exploratory calculations) and linking this rate to the average, not the individual income or contribution base, offers this correction. It creates a tax for those with incomes greater than the average that counteracts the subsidy they receive from living longer than the average, and vice versa for those below the average.

Table 14.3 presents the estimated social contribution rate for alternative policy specifications as in equation (14.11). Essentially one can calculate separate social contribution rates under common life expectancies, common social contribution rates under gender-separated life expectancies, and separate social contribution rates under gender-separated life expectancies. The results indicate that the magnitude of the social contribution rate is moderate. It remains less than 4 percentage points out of 20 percent (a share of lower than one-fifth).

FIGURE 14.7 **England and Wales: Observed and approximated life expectancies; United States: individualized annuities**

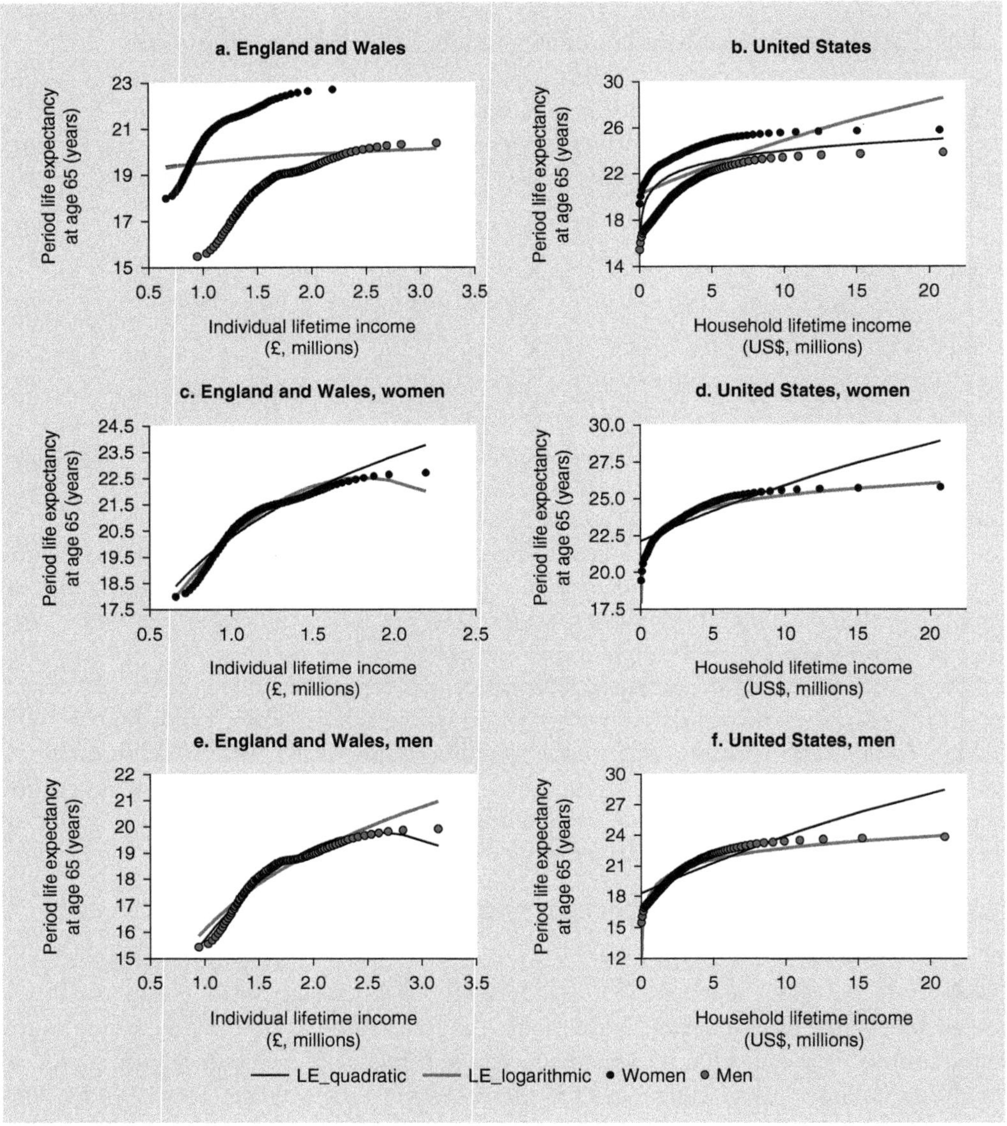

SOURCE: Original calculations.

NOTE: LE = life expectancy.

Figure 14.8, panels a, b, c, and d, present again the observed life expectancies for both England and Wales and the United States, but this time with the approximated life expectancies implied by the two-tier scheme (as in equation (14.15)) and based on the estimated social contribution rates from table 14.3. The approximations presented differ by the choice of the social contribution rate (common across both genders [CSC] or gender-separated [GSC]); in all cases, life expectancies are separated by gender (GLE). The casual observation suggests that the approach works broadly well, particularly when the genders are separated.

TABLE 14.2 **Individualized annuities—aggregate tax and subsidy rate indicators**

	England and Wales				United States			
	Joint pool (%)		Separate pool (%)		Joint pool (%)		Separate pool (%)	
	Women	Men	Women	Men	Women	Men	Women	Men
Nominal tax and subsidy rate	6.47	−6.47	0.00	0.00	7.28	−7.26	0.00	0.04
Absolute tax and subsidy rate	7.44	6.59	0.88	1.02	7.36	7.33	1.09	7.16
	Total		Total		Total		Total	
Nominal tax and subsidy rate (%)	0.00		−0.01		0.03		−0.03	
TATSI (%)	7.01		0.95		7.34		4.12	
	Quadratic		Quadratic		Logarithmic		Logarithmic	

SOURCE: Original table.

NOTE: TATSI = total absolute tax and subsidy indicator.

FIGURE 14.8 **Observed and approximated life expectancies—two-tier contribution scheme**

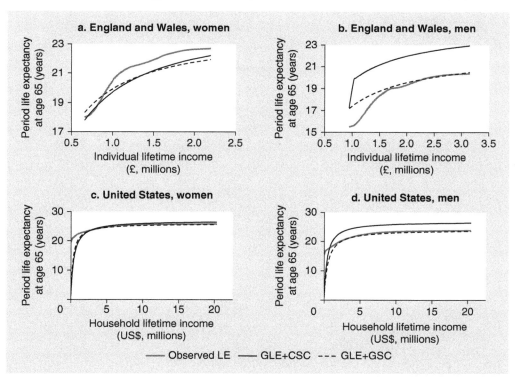

SOURCE: Original calculations.

NOTE: CSC = social contribution rate across both genders; GLE = life expectancies by gender; GSC = social contribution rate separated by gender; LE = life expectancy.

Figure 14.9, panels a and b, map the approximated life expectancies into the tax and subsidy space to see how well and for which percentiles the two-tier scheme succeeds in keeping TATSI close to the zero tax line. Here, proximity in the lines is not the issue, but how close the TATSI approximations are to the zero tax rate axis.

Table 14.4 translates the data for figure 14.9 into the TATSI values.

The results in table 14.4 signal that for England and Wales a two-tier scheme does a reasonable job in reducing TATSI values under Design alternative 0—the starting value

TABLE 14.3 **Social contribution rates for alternative specifications**

England and Wales		United States	
Common life expectancy (%)			
sc population	0.58	sc population	2.45
sc women	1.15	sc women	3.16
sc men	0.34	sc men	1.70
Separate gender life expectancies (%)			
sc population	3.21	sc population	2.56
sc women	2.58	sc women	1.89
sc men	3.42	sc men	3.09

SOURCE: Original table.

NOTE: sc = social contribution.

FIGURE 14.9 **Observed and approximated total absolute tax and subsidy indicator**

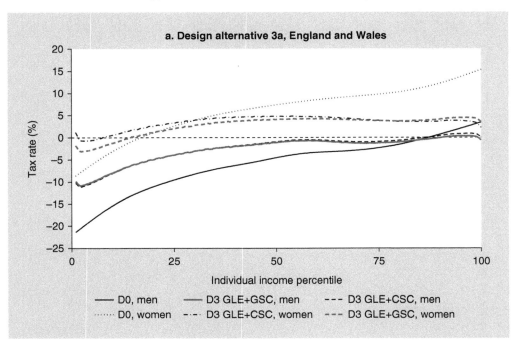

(continued next page)

FIGURE 14.9 **Observed and approximated total absolute tax and subsidy indicator (continued)**

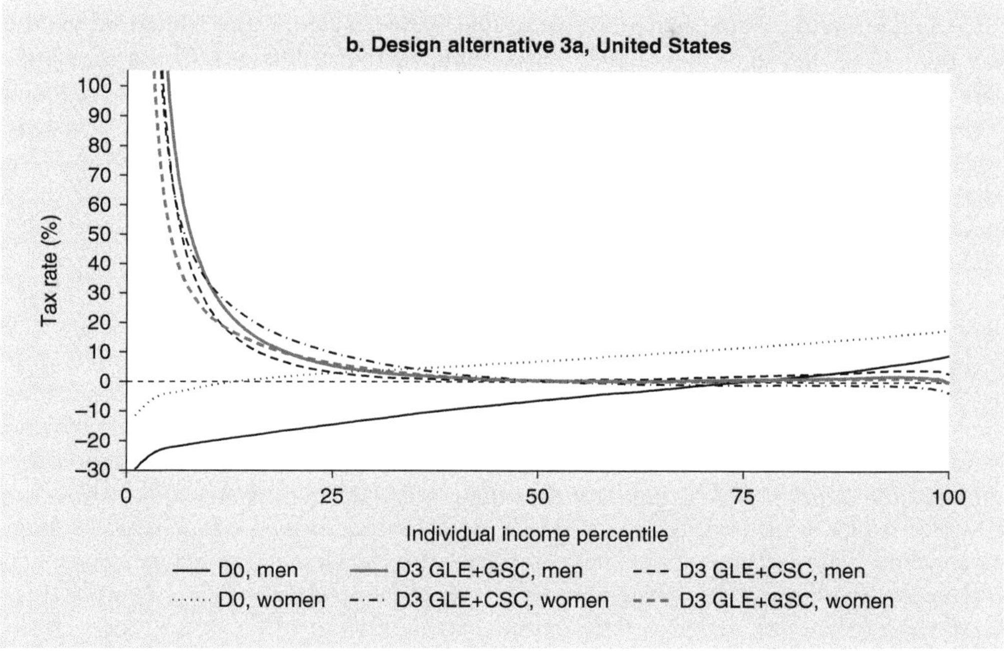

b. Design alternative 3a, United States

SOURCE: Original calculations.

NOTE: D0 = Design alternative 0; D3 = Design alternative 3; CSC = social contribution rate across both genders; GLE = life expectancies by gender; GSC = social contribution rate separated by gender; LE = life expectancy.

TABLE 14.4 **Two-tier contribution scheme—aggregate tax and subsidy rate indicators**

	England and Wales				United States			
	Separate pool (%)		Separate pool (%)		Separate pool (%)		Separate pool (%)	
	Women	Men	Women	Men	Women	Men	Women	Men
Nominal tax and subsidy rate	3.41	−2.52	2.74	−2.68	27.15	30.35	20.04	36.61
Absolute tax and subsidy rate	3.47	2.67	3.23	2.72	28.07	30.35	20.04	36.61
	Total		Total		Total		Total	
Nominal tax and subsidy rate	0.89		0.05		57.49		56.64	
TATSI	3.07		2.98		29.21		28.32	
	Pooled sc		Separate sc		Pooled sc		Separate sc	

SOURCE: Original table.

NOTE: sc = social contribution; TATSI = total absolute tax and subsidy rate indicator.

of table 14.1. The TATSI value is more than one-half compared with that of joint pooling but only one-third compared with that of separate gender pooling. Hence, most of the reduction results from separate pooling. The lifetime income approximations via the two-tier scheme add some, but altogether moderate, further reductions. This design alternative for England and Wales, however, is dominated by the option of gender-separated individualized annuities. Interestingly, little difference arises between pooled or separately calculated social contribution rates. Recall, however, that the lifetime income measure for England and Wales is based on small area measures of income and not individual income measures as in the U.S. data; this might account for part of the difference in effectiveness of the two-tier scheme between the two countries.

The latter result also applies for the United States, but TATSI increases to a multiple of the starting value and is much greater than that seen in the individualized annuity design alternative. Furthermore, in the United States, the result for TATSI differs little between the joint and the separate gender pool. This outcome is due to the high subsidies the lowest 20th percentile receives under a two-tier contribution option—both men and women. The lowest income decile in the United States has both low income and low contribution density, which translates into these very high subsidy rates. For the other 80 percent of the insured, the tax and subsidy rate under a two-tier scheme is about ±1 percent or less and thus almost perfect. Hence, for the United States a two-tier NDC scheme could address three policy objectives with one instrument: a close contribution-benefit link for the vast majority of the population, elimination of the distortionary effects of heterogeneity in longevity for this population, and major old-age income support for those in the lowest income percentiles.

The United States actually already has a very progressive benefit structure that limits the replacement rate for individuals at the ceiling to about 36 percent, while offering a replacement rate of more than 100 percent for the lowest income percentiles. This is an avenue to explore in future research.

Summary and Next Steps

Increasing international evidence shows that heterogeneity in longevity is high and relevant for policy outcomes. It is hypothesized that this heterogeneity negatively affects pension schemes' performance, including recently reformed schemes that moved toward DC to improve the contribution-benefit link. Heterogeneity in longevity risks undoing this link. The transparency of DC schemes with respect to the link between the initial benefit and average life expectancy at retirement makes the resulting distortions even more relevant.

This chapter moves the analytical and policy discussion forward, using two country data sets that are able to present the whole distribution space on the link between life expectancy and measures of lifetime income. These data for the United States (provided by Chetty et al. [2016]) and England and Wales (self-constructed from national data) allow analysis of the tails of the income distribution, where the distortions are highest. Building on the tax and subsidy conceptualization of heterogeneity in longevity, access to the distribution of data over all lifetime income percentiles allow construction of aggregate measures of distortions. TATSI (total absolute tax and subsidy indicator) can be applied to alternative policy designs to compare their capability to reduce the distortions.

Alternative designs are modeled under a common framework and include individualized annuities; individualized contribution rates or account allocations; a two-tier contribution structure with socialized and individual rate structures; and two supplementary approaches under the two-tier approach to deal with the distribution tails, and the distortions above a ceiling and below a floor.

This chapter uses these new data to explore the two most promising design alternatives: individualized annuities and the two-tier contribution approach. Compared with the status quo, both design alternatives succeed in reducing tax distortions. This happens through the approximation of the observed individual life expectancy with estimated individual life expectancy, and perhaps more importantly by disaggregating life expectancy by gender when the calculations are made. Applying the two-tier contribution scheme in the United States may improve efficiency and the redistributive outcome over the current progressive tax-benefit approach, but the relevant comparative analysis has not yet been done.

De-pooling life expectancy by gender reduces distortions and improves efficiency, but further increases the gap between men's and women's pension levels because of a not-yet-eliminated gender wage gap and continued reduced income prospects for women with children. This begs the question of whether gender pooling is the best instrument for addressing the gender pension gap or whether it would be better addressed through some combination of (a) direct labor market policies to reduce the wage gap, (b) social policies to compensate for the contribution loss due to childbearing and rearing, or (c) an annual splitting of contributions between partners to balance labor market outcomes. A direct approach may allow appropriate pension design to efficiently separate allocative and redistributive considerations. However, such arguments may only matter outside the European Union.[23]

The next steps for this research are to address the following:

- Access or construct similar life expectancy and lifetime income data for other countries and improve on lifetime estimates, and investigate the link to other heterogeneity characteristics, particularly education. This would improve the estimates and make them even more policy relevant.

- Explore empirically the full set of policy alternatives developed and presented, and develop new ones. In particular, deeper investigation of the tails of the distribution is required.

- Empirically compare results across countries to better understand what may simply be a statistical issue or artifact, or whether issues exist beyond heterogeneity that require policy interventions.

Notes

1. It is worth highlighting that this chapter is only interested in the degree of association between lifetime income and life expectancy, and does not make any claims about the causal effects of income on mortality.

2. Available at https://healthinequality.org/data/; in particular, data from online Table 15 are used.

3. For those who filed tax returns, Chetty et al. (2016) define household earnings as adjusted gross income plus tax-exempt interest income minus taxable Social Security and disability benefits. For those who did not file a tax return, they define household earnings as the sum of all wage earnings and unemployment benefits. Note that household income statistics differ by gender because the effect of single-individual households.

4. An alternative U.S. data set for exploration is that developed by the National Academies of Sciences, Engineering, and Medicine (2015). However, this data set is not publicly available.

5. Mortality rates beyond age 76 were extrapolated using a variant of the method of Coale and Kisker (1990) under the assumption that mortality rates at age 110 are equal to 0.7.

6. The available data include pretax earnings by age (x), year (t), and income percentile (k), $y^k_{x,t}$, for years 2001 to 2014 and ages 40 through 65. To obtain income by age and income percentile, y^k_x, the data for all years are pooled and smoothed by age using a cubic smoothing spline.

7. https://www.ons.gov.uk/employmentandlabourmarket/peopleinwork/earningsandworking hours/datasets/ smallareaincomeestimatesformiddlelayersuperoutputareasenglandandwales.

8. https://www.ons.gov.uk/peoplepopulationandcommunity/birthsdeathsandmarriages/deaths /adhocs/ 006416lowersuperoutputarealsoadeathregistrations2015.

9. https://www.ons.gov.uk/peoplepopulationandcommunity/populationandmigration /populationestimates/ datasets/lowersuperoutputareamidyearpopulationestimates.

10. Similar to the U.S. case, mortality rates beyond age 89 were extrapolated using a variant of the method of Coale and Kisker (1990) under the assumption that mortality rates at age 110 are equal to 0.7.

11. https://www.gov.uk/government/statistics/distribution-of-median-and-mean-income-and -tax-by-age-range-and-gender-2010-to-2011.

12. For each gender, the income at age x for someone in income percentile k is approximated by

$$y^k_x = y_x \frac{w^k}{0.01 \sum_{i=1}^{100} w^i} \text{, where } w^k \text{ denotes weekly household income for income percentile}$$

k and y_x the gender-specific annual income for someone age x in England and Wales.

13. The contribution base does not always coincide with salaries. Indeed, the pension schemes in some countries only accrue rights up to a certain level of earnings, the remainder not being considered for benefit accrual purposes.

14. The expression of the annuity could be generalized to consider indexation rates that differ from the discount rate. However, this analysis abstracts from this to obtain intuitive and tractable results. The authors acknowledge that a general annuity could be also be a tool for dealing with mortality heterogeneity.

15. Because the distribution of the differences is not symmetric, the choice of the average matters. Typically, the arithmetic average is selected even though the median would be the better choice.

16. For a broader discussion of heterogeneity in longevity and pension systems and reform, see Whitehouse and Zaidi (2008); for a discussion of the implications for funded pensions, see OECD (2016); and for suggestions for how to address heterogeneity in longevity in the German point system, see Breyer and Hupfeld (2009).

17. NDC accounts before retirement are typically not inheritable and the assets of the early deceased are distributed to the insurance pool of the survivors. This creates distortions in the presence of mortality differentials between ages 20 and 65 as well as after age 65. These minor distortions are ignored in the following discussion.

18. In Ayuso, Bravo, and Holzmann (2017a) a linear relationship between individual life expectancy and lifetime income position is explored. It is derived by equating the tax and subsidy rate under current design for heterogeneous life expectancy with the subsidy and tax rate of a two-tier approach under homogeneous life expectancy.

19. For the following estimations, the observed data used are the smoothed mortality data for both England and Wales and the United States. Using the raw data would not make any difference in scope and conclusions.

20. Despite individual tax and subsidies, on average the tax is equal to zero because of the assumption of the annuity being equal to the average life expectancy, which is calculated based on the individual experience across the whole income spectrum.

21. For European Union countries, separate pooling for pricing and benefit design was barred as discriminatory by the European Court of Justice as of December 2012 (Court of Justice of the European Union 2011).

22. For references and recent use of area-level deprivation measures to quantify mortality inequalities for England, see Dunnell et al. (2018) and Mayhew, Harper, and Villegas (2018).

23. In 2011, the Court of Justice of the European Union ruled out the possibility of using individuals' gender to assess their risk profile on discrimination grounds (Court of Justice of the European Union 2011).

References

Ayuso, Mercedes, Jose Bravo, and Robert Holzmann. 2017a. "Addressing Longevity Heterogeneity in Pension Scheme Design." *Journal of Finance and Economics* 6 (1): 1–24.

———. 2017b. On the Heterogeneity in Longevity among Socioeconomic Groups: Scope, Trends, and Implications for Earnings-Related Pension Schemes." *Global Journal of Human Social Sciences-Economics* 17 (1): 33–58.

Breyer, Friedrich, and Stefan Hupfeld. 2009. "Fairness of Public Pensions and Old-Age Poverty." *FinanzArchiv/Public Finance Analysis* 65 (3): 358–80.

Chetty, Raj, Michael Stepner, Sarah Abraham, Shelby Lin, Benjamin Scuderi, Nicholas Turner, Augustin Bergeron, and David Cutler. 2016. "The Association between Income and Life Expectancy in the United States, 2001–2014." *Clinical Review and Education Special* 315 (16): 1750–66. https://doi.org/10.1001/jama.2016.4226.

Coale, Ansley J., and Ellen Kisker. 1990. "Defects in Data on Old Age Mortality in the United States: New Procedures for Calculating Approximately Accurate Mortality Schedules and Life Tables at the Highest Ages." *Asian and Pacific Population Forum* 4: 1–31.

Court of Justice of the European Union. 2011." Taking the Gender of the Insured Individual into Account as a Risk Factor in Insurance Contracts Constitutes Discrimination." Judgment in case C-236/09. Press Release No. 12/11, March 1.

Dunnell, Karen, Colin Blakemore, Steven Haberman, Klim McPherson, and John Pattison. 2018. "Life Expectancy: Is the Socio-Economic Gap Narrowing?" Longevity Science Panel, London.

Gatzert, Nadine, and Udo Klotzki. 2016. "Enhanced Annuities: Drivers of and Barriers to Supply and Demand." *Geneva Papers on Risk and Insurance—Issues and Practice* 41 (1): 53–77. https://doi.org/10.1057/gpp.2015.21.

Madrigal, Ana M., Fiona E. Matthews, Deven Patel, Andrew Gaches, and Steven Baxter. 2011. "What Longevity Predictors Should Be Allowed for When Valuing Pension Scheme Liabilities." *British Actuarial Journal* 16 (1): 1–38.

Mayhew, Les, Gillian Harper, and Andrés M. Villegas. 2018. "Inequalities Matter: An Investigation into the Impact of Deprivation on Demographic Inequalities in Adults." International Longevity Centre, London.

National Academies of Sciences, Engineering, and Medicine. 2015. "The Growing Gap in Life Expectancy by Income: Implications for Federal Programs and Policy Responses." Committee on the Long-Run Macroeconomic Effects of the Aging U.S. Population-Phase II. Committee on Population, Division of Behavioral and Social Sciences and Education. Board on Mathematical Sciences and Their Applications, Division on Engineering and Physical Sciences. National Academies Press, Washington, DC.

OECD (Organisation for Economic Co-operation and Development). 2016. "Fragmentation of Retirement Markets due to Differences in Life Expectancy." In *OECD Business and Finance Outlook 2016*, 177–205. Paris: OECD Publishing.

Richards, Stephen. 2008. "Applying Survival Models to Pensioner Mortality Data." *British Actuarial Journal* 14 (2): 257–303.

Richards, Stephen, Kai J. Kaufhold, and Susanne Rosenbusch. 2013. "Creating Portfolio-Specific Mortality Tables: A Case Study." *European Actuarial Journal* 3 (2): 295–319. https://doi.org/10.1007/s13385-013-0076-6.

Ridsdale, Brian, and Adrian Gallop. 2010. "Mortality by Cause of Death and by Socio-Economic and Demographic Stratification 2010." Paper for the International Congress of Actuaries 2010, Cape Town, South Africa, March 7–12.

Whitehouse, Edward, and Ashgar Zaidi. 2008. "Socio-Economic Differences in Mortality: Implications for Pensions Policy." OECD Social, Employment and Migration Working Papers 71, OECD Publishing, Paris. http://dx.doi.org/10.1787/231747416062.

PART V

Accommodating Labor Market Change

CHAPTER 15

NDC Schemes and the Labor Market: Issues and Options

Robert Holzmann, David Robalino, and Hernan Winkler

Introduction: Background, Issues, and Structure

Defined contribution (DC) schemes—whether unfunded or funded—are typically considered superior to defined benefit (DB) schemes in their ability to address many issues, including their capacity to encourage formal labor force participation and employment (and therefore increase the density of contributions), and later retirement in an aging population. A higher rate of formal labor force participation is expected through the one-to-one contribution-benefit link, which reduces the tax wedge: individuals get back what they paid in, with a sustainable rate of return; not less but also not more. In addition, in a world of continuously rising life expectancy, a DC benefit based on remaining life expectancy is expected to encourage later retirement, because individuals receive a lower benefit for a fixed retirement age (that is, the actual or notional account values at retirement are essentially divided by expected remaining life expectancy at any selected retirement age). Yet economic and social reality is more complex, and design and implementation issues may preclude DC schemes in general, and nonfinancial defined contribution (NDC) schemes in particular, from living up to their promise. Initial and enabling labor market conditions also matter and may be different for emerging market (middle-income) and advanced (high-income) economies. For many low-income economies, the enabling conditions for an NDC scheme may simply not exist and are difficult to establish.

An important issue is the provision of minimum income support for the elderly. A budget-financed minimum income guarantee to all elderly (a social pension) is considered a necessary complement of any DC scheme for social, economic, and political reasons. Yet such a provision breaks the close contribution-benefit link of an NDC scheme, provides incentives to reduce labor supply, and encourages informality and early retirement. Another element to take into consideration is the lack of proper skills among the elderly that would allow them to delay retirement and continue working. Other structural issues can also compromise the performance of NDC schemes—for instance, the heterogeneity in longevity that makes the scheme less interesting for lower-income individuals, who have shorter life expectancies; behavioral biases that affect retirement and savings decisions; and institutional capacity to manage DC schemes.

The authors are grateful to Carmen Pagés and Stefano Sacchi for pertinent comments and suggestions.

This chapter identifies key design features of NDC schemes that can affect formal labor market participation, contribution densities, and incentives for delayed retirement, including the architecture to guarantee a minimum income to the elderly. The chapter also discusses the types of integrated labor policies and programs that countries need to consider to enable the proper functioning of an NDC scheme and how these likely vary between emerging market and advanced economies. The chapter offers a framework for policy analysis and selective recommendations but does not offer a fully developed and comprehensive set of policy proposals.

"Promises, Shortcomings, and Constraints of NDB and NDC Schemes for Formal Labor Market Employment and Retirement Decisions" opens with a conceptual framework that contrasts the labor market distortions induced by typical nonfinancial defined benefit (NDB) schemes with the labor market promises of NDC schemes; it then highlights the constraints that can affect the latter's performance. This provides the conceptual background and benchmark for the discussion of NDC design features that can promote formal participation and employment ("NDC Schemes and Formal Labor Force Participation and Employment"), and for the labor market policy discussion to allow the elderly to work longer ("NDC Schemes and Delayed Retirement"). Both of these sections first present key NDC design features and labor market policy proposals, and then highlight differences in realities in advanced and emerging market economies. "Conclusions and Next Steps" summarizes the implications for NDC design and labor market policy actions and suggests next steps.

Promises, Shortcomings, and Constraints of NDB and NDC Schemes for Formal Labor Market Employment and Retirement Decisions

Two preconditions must be met to ensure broad coverage, adequate pensions, and financial sustainability in mandatory pension schemes: (a) high formal labor force participation and employment, and (b) long working careers. Other key objectives of a pension system may be achieving equity and risk sharing within and between generations. Alternative pension schemes can affect the labor market in different ways and are affected differently by labor market dynamics. (N)DB schemes are considered to be less supportive of higher labor force participation, formal employment, and adequate retirement decisions than (N)DC schemes.[1] At the same time, the performance of both mandatory DB and DC schemes is affected by the structure of labor markets. When farm work and own-account work are more prevalent than wage employment, or when firms have few incentives to invest and create jobs and workers few incentives to take them, the performance of mandatory systems can be compromised. Hence, the design of the pension scheme is not enough. Policy makers also need to address constraints that affect the structure and performance of the labor market.

This section starts out by highlighting the conjectured advantages of NDC schemes compared with the documented pitfalls of traditional as well as reformed NDB schemes in delivering high formal labor force participation and delayed retirement.

It next outlines behavioral and other constraints that may impede the achievement of labor market objectives even under a well-thought-out and well-implemented NDC scheme; this calls for new policy interventions. The section ends by sketching key labor market limitations that need to be overcome for NDC schemes to deliver on their labor market promises.

CONSTRAINTS OF NDB VERSUS NDC SCHEMES

The promises of an NDC scheme regarding labor market participation are best seen in comparison with the widely reported drawbacks of traditional NDB schemes. Although many NDB schemes underwent reform in recent years, mostly in the direction of NDC schemes' operations, none of these NDB reforms were able to fully replicate the characteristics of an NDC scheme.[2]

NDB schemes are said to reduce formal employment and distort retirement decisions for a number of design reasons, particularly the following:

- The absence of a close link between contributions and benefits creates a tax and subsidy wedge that risks distorting labor demand and supply decisions. This tax wedge is typically implicit, changes over an individual's life cycle and between groups, and is strengthened through explicit and implicit redistributive interventions. More generally, the interaction of DB schemes with noncontributory arrangements may create implicit taxes and subsidies on formal and informal jobs that depend on the earnings profile of workers (Pagés, Rigolini, and Robalino 2014).

- The mandated contribution rate is too high in many countries for the savings preferences of a significant part of the population, making participation less attractive for both low- and high-income earners.[3]

- The lack of sufficient adjustments for earlier and later retirement creates incentives for retirement at the earliest possible age. It contributes to a tax force that keeps labor force participation of elderly low (Gruber and Wise 1998). Gruber and Wise's graph, enriched by the comparable data point for Austria, offers a powerful message about the importance of actuarial design for labor force participation around the retirement age (figure 15.1).

- Increasing the standard retirement age (that is, the age at which full benefits are received) in line with rising life expectancy requires repeated politically difficult decisions. Even if indexed using some measure of change in life expectancy, the approach typically remains imperfect because the wrong remaining life expectancy is applied (period instead of cohort), the decision is often delayed, and concomitant changes such as a reduction in annual accrual rates are not undertaken.

- NDB schemes are less supportive of labor mobility across sectors and between countries. Their redistributive character often leads to very long waiting periods that increase the tax character of the contributions, and bilateral social security agreements are required to establish totalization.

FIGURE 15.1 **The link between unused labor capacity and the "tax force to retire"**

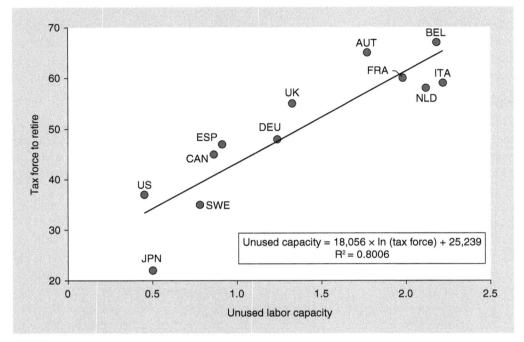

SOURCES: Original based on Gruber and Wise (1998); and Hofer and Koman (2006).

NOTE: "Tax force to retire" is the sum of the implied tax rates on continued work beginning at the earliest retirement age running through age 69, which is a measure of the tax incentive for early retirement.

In contrast, the move toward an NDC scheme promises a number of features that reduce distortions on formal labor market participation and employment and retirement decisions:

- The strongest possible contribution-benefit link, which reduces most or all of the implicit taxes and subsidies (except one that may emerge through the difference between a risk-adjusted higher financial market interest rate and the internal rate of return), which should foster labor market participation and formal employment.

- A linear intertemporal budget constraint for individuals that makes the retirement decision smooth and dependent only on individual preferences and own resources (that is, NDC eliminates the kinks with clustering of retirement decisions around specific age or contribution levels), which should make way for an automatic increase in the effective retirement length as life expectancy increases, given that individuals receive a lower initial benefit if they retire younger than the previously envisaged retirement age.

- A lower, mandatory contribution rate, often envisaged under an NDC reform of a former NDB scheme, which should facilitate higher formal labor force participation and later retirement (assuming that a less distortionary way than contributions to finance the legacy costs can be found; Holzmann and Jouston 2013).

- Easier labor mobility, because notional accumulations can be easily carried across jobs and geographic locations and are not subject to complex and tedious bilateral social security agreements (Holzmann 2017b; Holzmann and Koettle 2015).

Clearly, the NDC system needs to recognize that (a) many low-wage workers may not be able to accumulate enough contributions to finance an adequate pension during retirement, and (b) because of transitions between inactivity, unemployment, and formal and informal employment, not all workers are able to have full careers. This calls for minimum pension guarantees or matching contributions (or both) to promote retirement accumulations. Both can distort labor markets although, presumably, in more controlled and predictable ways than in the case of DB systems. For example, consider the following:

- Subsidies can take the form of universal or means-tested benefits or front-loaded provision through matching contributions. Depending on their design, they will generate income and substitution effects that affect labor supply and retirement decisions. For instance, universal pensions have an income effect and strong empirical evidence shows that they can induce early retirement (Bertrand, Mullainathan, and Miller 2003). Because they do not have a substitution effect, they do not distort the decision to move from a low-paying to a high-paying job, or from a formal to an informal job. Means-tested social pensions will have an additional substitution effect and distort choices between formal and informal jobs, for instance, if eligibility only applies to those who do not participate in contributory systems or those with a level of income or pension below a certain threshold (that is, there is 100 percent marginal tax rate on the subsidy after a given level of income). To address the incomplete participation of marginal workers on the labor market, NDC schemes are induced to offer encouragements for formal labor force participation through temporary matching contributions, lump-sum contribution transfers (for example, for migrant workers), and so on.[4] Although they may be designed to improve participation and contribution density, they may affect formal early retirement decisions through either their design or merely their income effect.

- As in FDC schemes, the initial pension benefit is determined essentially by the accumulation at retirement and life expectancy at this age. Low-income individuals (who exhibit markedly lower life expectancy in all countries) can easily see that the approach is a bad deal for them; thus, they avoid formal labor force participation and resist an increase in the retirement age.

CONSTRAINTS BEYOND MANDATED SCHEMES' DESIGN

Even the most well-designed NDC schemes are confronted with constraints and distortions outside their making but likely heavily influenced by them. The most common problem is that the mandate to participate in the scheme can, depending on workers' preferences and unconstrained behaviors, become an implicit tax that the NDC approach aims to minimize. Recent policy research stresses the effects of incomplete information and behavioral biases that may preclude scheme participation from happening or render retirement decisions not based on design incentives as envisaged. The main considerations are as follows:

- The many other risks individuals are exposed to and the incompleteness of financial markets in emerging market and even advanced economies make contributions to an NDC scheme unattractive. The more relevant these other risks are and the more incomplete the financial markets, the less attractive is any future annuity promise by any mandated or even voluntary scheme (Davidoff, Brown, and Diamond 2005; Holzmann and Hinz 2005).

- The existence of other risk management instruments (such as family as a risk pool and general poverty-oriented public provisions) reduces the incentives for paying for a public annuity even if it is fully credible and actuarially fair (Kotlikoff and Spivak 1981).

- The total costs of formality (such as licenses, taxes, the social insurance bundle, and so on) increase the costs of contributing, even to a perfect DC scheme for both employers and employees, and encourage informality (Almeida and Carneiro 2012).

- The credibility of government and social security institutions is often low (a factor that could also apply to a newly introduced or reformed NDC scheme, with consequences for formality and contribution efforts).

- Even in advanced economies, individuals complain about the lack of information about the working of NDC and NDB schemes, their economic basics, and the level of financial literacy. How best to offer the information about DC design and financial status of individual accounts is still unknown, and the role of financial literacy and the effectiveness of financial education remain under-researched (Holzmann 2014).

- Behavioral limitations (such as hyperbolic discounting, loss aversion, and behavioral biases) may also apply to NDC schemes (Frölich et al. 2014). In turn, proposed instruments to overcome these limitations will have to be added to the NDC design. This may include the nudging effect of a life expectancy–indexed standard retirement age under an NDC approach as a signaling device, albeit only a formally indexed minimum access age is likely needed, while the rest can be left to individual decision. The same applies to the need for an improved decision environment for contribution payments for part-time employees and the self-employed (Delarue 2013).

THE NEED FOR COMPLEMENTARY LABOR MARKET INTERVENTIONS

Even perfectly designed NDC schemes and policies that are able to address the key constraints highlighted previously will not be sufficient to generate the desired labor market effects of high formal labor force participation and employment and delayed retirement. Other types of government interventions are required to address some of the following problems facing emerging market economies and high-income countries:

- Technological advances are changing the demand for different types of skills (from manual and repetitive to analytical and interpersonal) and changing the world of labor. Even if the introduction of new technologies such as robots and artificial intelligence (AI) brings opportunities to create new products and therefore new types of jobs, disruptions in the labor market will still affect certain workers' capacity to participate in NDC schemes. New technologies are also increasing the prevalence of self-employment and reducing the share of wage employment (Gentilini et al., forthcoming).

- Related to the above, more rapid technological change may result in skills becoming obsolete at a faster rate, a phenomenon that will be exacerbated in rapidly aging countries. The existence of market failures in the provision of lifelong learning by firms and educational institutions implies that the level of human capital acquisition throughout the life cycle is suboptimal. Furthermore, some strands of education, such as apprenticeship programs, favor early labor market integration and higher wages, an advantage that is getting lost at higher ages to those with a more general education (Hampf and Woessmann 2017).

- The continued existence of mobility barriers across jobs, occupations, and geographic locations contributes to labor market disruptions, and thereby impedes the ability of workers to contribute constantly to pension savings.

- Many countries are still struggling to accelerate the rate of employment creation in the formal sector, which depends on firm dynamics (creation, growth, and destruction). Evidence indicates that most jobs are created by new firms, but insufficient firm entry is observed across middle-income countries. At the same time, few firms survive beyond five years and those that do may not grow. Although countries are generally expanding employment in line with their labor force growth, many of these jobs are in low-productivity, informal activities (Merotto, Weber, and Aterido 2017).

- Many or all high-income countries are struggling with the increasing marginalization of part of the labor force caused by less secure entry points when young (short-term contracts, low or no pay, and little or no on-the-job-training), part-time work, numerous unemployment spells when middle-aged, and downgraded job offers or unemployment when older. For most or all market emerging economies, stubborn informality is the rule rather than the exception for many reasons, including inadequate social and labor market policies.

- In many emerging market economies, large gender gaps in labor force participation and wages create additional challenges. When women face barriers to labor force participation and employment (driven by, for instance, a lack of child-care services and maternity leave benefits, social norms, or regulations), countries need to implement gender-specific policies to improve women's labor market outcomes.

- The existence of lagging regions in poor countries implies that even when the macroeconomic context and the overall business environment are conducive to job creation, only those individuals in the leading urban areas may benefit.

- Institutional failures can generate health and education systems that are not able to keep the elderly healthy, skilled, and motivated to stay in the labor market. Employers may also fail to offer quality jobs to the elderly. To be healthy, skilled, and motivated is claimed as a necessary condition to extending labor force participation in old age in line with increasing life expectancy (Holzmann 2013).

The following two sections focus on this set of policy challenges for advanced and emerging market economies: first addressing scheme design issues, then labor market issues.

NDC Schemes and Formal Labor Force Participation and Employment

The previous sections identify formal labor force participation and employment with high contribution densities as one crucial element for a successful NDC scheme. "Key NDC Design Suggestions and Other Policies to Improve Labor Market Outcomes" discusses the types of NDC design issues that need to be (re-)considered to achieve these outcomes, as well as the role of macro and regulatory, labor, and sectoral and regional policies. The next two subsections highlight broad trends in demographic, labor market, and pension scheme outcomes and identify labor market policy issues that need to be addressed in advanced ("The Reality of Advanced Economies") and emerging market economies ("The Reality of Emerging Market Economies").

KEY NDC DESIGN SUGGESTIONS AND OTHER POLICIES TO IMPROVE LABOR MARKET OUTCOMES

NDC schemes are relatively simple in design, yet to deliver on their promises the transition from an NDB system needs to follow certain rules (Holzmann 2017a, 2019; Holzmann and Palmer 2012). "Key NDC Design Suggestions and Other Policies to Improve Labor Market Outcomes" first presents the relevant lessons drawn from the limited number of NDC countries with broadly successful and less successful experience before moving to the labor market side.

Key NDC implementation lessons

- Do not pick and choose some NDC design features while otherwise staying within the inherited NDB scheme.[5] Doing so will not create the expected labor market incentives or the expected pension benefit advantages. Hybrid schemes have not proved to be successful.

- Before launching the individual account system, ensure that the demanding administrative requirements are in place, including individual identifiers, an information and communication technology (ICT) and payment system, and methods to establish and apply cohort life expectancies at relevant retirement ages (Palacios 2019).

- Establish the NDC logic as quickly as possible (that is, no lengthy transitions with parallel NDC and NDB schemes; no contribution financing of any legacy costs; no uncertainty about the balancing mechanism in case of economic or demographic shocks; and so forth). Any of these deviations or even delayed introduction after mishaps risks diluting the expected labor market incentives and credibility of the scheme.

Key design challenges for NDC schemes

NDC schemes need to be able to address four key issues: (a) how to minimize implicit taxes resulting from heterogeneous life expectancies that can reduce participation among low-income and low-skilled workers; (b) how to ensure a minimum level of income for workers who might not be able to contribute enough; (c) how to extend coverage to the informal sector, particularly farmers and self-employed workers; and (d) how to design sustainable survivors' and disability pensions without discouraging participation. Possible innovations to address these issues include the following:

- *Heterogeneous life expectancy.* The increasing availability of data on heterogeneity in longevity suggests a strong and positive link between lifetime income position and life expectancy that seems to increase over time (Ayuso, Bravo, and Holzmann 2017b). Such heterogeneity is equivalent to a tax and subsidy mechanism when applying an average cohort life expectancy for the calculation of the pension benefit at retirement: low-income groups pay a tax that can reach 30 percent and more, while high-income groups receive a subsidy of similar magnitude (Ayuso, Bravo, and Holzmann 2017a). To correct for such distortions a number of options are available. One promising option is a two-tier contribution approach that allocates under an overall total contribution rate one share of contribution payments to the individual account according to the average and the remainder according to individual income. Hypothetical NDC calculations using U.S. and U.K. social security data suggest that one-fifth or less of the social contribution rate as part of the total contribution rate would be sufficient to address most of the longevity heterogeneity effects (Gál and Radó 2019; Holzmann et al. 2019).

- *Low-income workers and incomplete careers.* The proper integration of minimum pension guarantees and anti-poverty programs (zero pillar) with the NDC scheme to minimize labor market distortions is a key challenge. The best options are still unclear and limited country experience exists regarding how well the current zero provisions are working (Fajnzylber 2019; Nelson, Nieuwenhuis, and Alm 2019; Palacios 2019). Some general principles can be considered, however: (a) transfers should be explicit and financed through a reallocation of general revenues or increased nonpayroll taxes; (b) transfers should be universal or allocated based on means (not where people work); and (c) when targeted on the basis of means, claw-back rates should decrease gradually, generating low marginal tax rates (Ribe, Robalino, and Walker 2012).

- *Self-employed and small-scale employers.* Worldwide experience with small-scale employers, farmers, infrequent workers, and the self-employed suggests that these groups cannot be easily integrated into a pension scheme even if it is actuarially fair (for example, an FDC or NDC scheme). For the self-employed this may be due to different cash flow needs while active and investing, but also when inactive and running down own assets. In addition, the income of these groups can be subject to frequent fluctuations, which makes it difficult to commit to a period, fixed payment based on a fictional income. Changing the contribution payment taking into consideration these fluctuations can improve incentives to contribute. This was shown, for instance, in experiments with fishermen in Africa that allowed for infrequent payments (at the time when the catch is sold) through the purchase of contribution vouchers (Delarue 2013). Again, general principles that can be followed when considering innovations are that (a) it is important to separate the problem of identifying, registering, and enrolling workers from the problem of providing incentives to contribute; (b) new ICTs massively reduce the cost of identifying and enrolling workers; (c) new ICTs facilitate and reduce the cost of financial transactions and facilitate the collection of contributions; and (d) financial and nonfinancial incentives can motivate people to save, according to some evidence (Akbaş et al. 2016).

- *Survivors' and disability pensions.* The design of survivors' and disability benefits under the typical NDB scheme has typically proven to be not conducive to enhanced labor force participation and delayed retirement. Carrying these benefit programs over to an NDC approach without reform risks continued or even worsened labor market distortions. This risk calls for their reform in particular, given that reform innovations exist for both survivors' and disability benefits that promise to render them much more labor market neutral.

Main labor market policy challenges and options

The goal of productive formal employment for the active population is a challenge for all countries in the world. The traditional approach is to treat jobs as a byproduct of economic growth. Countries simply need to promote investment and improve allocative efficiency by fixing market and government failures in product, capital, and labor markets. Indeed, in general, when economies grow they create jobs. And when no distortions exist in the allocation of resources—labor and capital—those jobs are created in the sectors and economic activities where they generate the most value. Thus, over time, jobs tend to move from low- to higher-productivity sectors, from rural to urban areas, and from informal to formal activities. These "structural transformations" then contribute to lift people out of poverty and increase standards of living. To achieve this, countries must have in place the right macroeconomic policies to ensure stability and reduce uncertainty; a business environment (including appropriate infrastructure) that reduces transactions costs and promotes competition and entrepreneurship; governance and the rule of law to enforce contracts and the possibility to earn appropriate returns on investments; education and health policies to have healthy workers with the right skills; and labor policies to reduce friction in the labor market, improve matching, and protect workers from abuse and exploitation (MILES framework[6]; Banerji et al. 2008). Because the agenda is complex, proposals have been made to identify the most binding constraints to investments and economic growth (Haussmann, Rodrik, and Velasco 2005).

In practice things are difficult. Identifying binding constraints remains an art more than a science. Governments usually push several policy agendas at the same time, and which reforms go through depends more on political opportunities (the political economy of reforms) than rigorous economic analyses (Tommasi and Velasco 2007). The reality is that even in countries such as Chile, Georgia, Mexico, and Uganda, which excelled in adopting key structural reforms and promoting investment and growth, the performance of labor markets did not necessarily improve. Yet without guidance on what is believed to prevent employment creation with productivity growth, the result is often a laundry list of analyses and proposals that are difficult to agree on, implement, and assess. One approach is to hypothesize the specific key binding constraints for a country based on preliminary analyses and good economic intuition and substantiate them with detailed empirical analyses thereafter (see Bodor and Holzmann [2016] for Saudi Arabia). Another approach is to have a general hypothesis and develop policies accordingly.

The latter approach characterizes the hypothesized presence of job externalities that create a gap between social and private rates of return on investments (World Bank 2012). One externality (labor externality) emerges in the presence of high inactivity, unemployment, and underemployment, when the market price of labor deviates from its social opportunity cost. The other externality (social externality) appears when jobs generate value beyond that appropriated by the employer and the workers. For instance, youth who work learn on the job, build their human capital, and make other workers in the economy more productive; women who have a job have fewer children and invest more in their human capital; and jobs for certain population groups can contribute to social stability (Robalino and Walker 2017). These externalities imply that private investments that are efficient from a social point of view may not take place. The World Bank has proposed a new policy direction that offers a sophisticated set of interrelated policy actions under the new jobs strategy approach (box 15.1).

BOX 15.1 New policy directions in the labor market

Jobs strategies versus growth strategies. Countries should start to rely more on jobs strategies (different from growth strategies) with specific objectives in terms of (a) accelerating the rate of job creation in the informal sector of the economy, (b) improving the quality and earnings associated with informal jobs, and (c) helping workers move from unemployment or inactivity into jobs or from low- to higher-productivity jobs. Macro and regulatory policies, labor policies, and sectoral and regional policies can then be mapped to these outcomes and inform priorities for taking jobs externalities into account.

Macro and regulatory policies. Beyond having the right business environment and governance arrangements, ensuring investments in infrastructure, and reforming education and technical and vocational education systems, two challenges arise from a jobs perspective: (a) how to prioritize reforms (for example, which are the binding constraints if the focus is job creation in the formal sector), and (b) how to balance the economic costs and benefits of economic transformations taking into account social externalities related to jobs. For example, the optimal path of fiscal adjustment in highly indebted countries might be more gradual when job losses are factored in. A similar gradual approach might be needed when implementing policies to promote trade liberalization, eliminate restrictions on capital flows, or change the relative prices of tradable versus nontradable goods.

Labor policies. Labor regulations and active labor market policies have an important role in dealing with labor market failures and jobs externalities. To that end, however, it is necessary to rethink their design. Labor regulations need to be more efficient at protecting workers, including in the informal sector, while internalizing the social costs of jobs destruction and reducing distortions that constrain the creation of formal jobs. This implies allowing firms to manage human resources as long as there is proper advance notice for dismissal, considering different approaches to guarantee a minimum level of income and ensure a fair distribution of value added between wages and profits, strengthening unemployment benefit

(continued next page)

> **BOX 15.1 New policy directions in the labor market (continued)**
>
> systems while reducing the agency of employers, and enforcing core labor standards and adequate working conditions by relying more on civil society and less on labor inspectors.
>
> *Sectoral regional policies*. These policies are fundamental to addressing jobs externalities. They involve using public resources to crowd-in private investments in particular sectors and regions conditional on job creation or improvement in the quality of jobs. The programs themselves are not new and include various types of entrepreneurship programs (incubators or startups for high-end entrepreneurs or support to subsistence entrepreneurs), programs to support small and medium-size enterprises, extension programs in the agriculture sector, and value chain development programs. The programs, however, need to be adapted to maximize their impact on jobs. Issues to be considered include adopting modern personal identity mechanism, monitoring and evaluation, and profiling systems to register and track beneficiaries and better understand the constraints they face; rethinking selection mechanisms to focus on investments with the highest potential to affect jobs outcomes or internalize jobs externalities; and, beyond addressing issues related to access to finance (when needed), introducing explicit subsidies that reduce the gap between social and economic rates of return.
>
> SOURCE: Robalino and Walker 2017; Robalino, Romero, and Walker 2019.

Coordinating policies

Whatever the approach, coordination across government entities is critical. Although government heads like to call the Minister of Labor when the labor market underperforms, this minister may actually have the least influence on labor market outcomes. As suggested by both the MILES framework and the World Bank jobs strategy, it is critical to coordinate policies because of the following:

- The experience in country after country suggests that the labor market–relevant ministers in a government hardly ever talk to each other about how best to achieve employment outcomes. Being united in a panel discussion on labor market performance convened by international organizations might be the first time they talk to each other on the topic (Banerji et al. 2008). This reflects the widespread lack of, or any clear coordinating mechanisms and institutions among the key policy players.

- The experience for emerging market economies at least suggests that the Minister of Social Affairs (in charge of pension reform), the Minister of Labor (in charge of labor market reforms), and the Minister of Finance or Economy or head of the central bank (in charge of or part of financial sector reform) generally have high but largely unspecific expectations about what each can bring to the table and they hardly ever talk to one another about expectations and possible deliverables (Holzmann, Mackellar, and Repansek 2009).

- The lack of policy interaction within the government is reflected in the scarcity of rigorous impact evaluations of policy interventions across much of the world. Few labor market interventions and even fewer pension reform interventions have any kind of rigorous monitoring and evaluation (M&E) that could be used to improve their performance over time. The impression is that emerging market economies with World Bank and other multilateral institutions' support may have—in general—a higher level of rigorous M&E than do advanced economies.

- Nonetheless, some recent examples exist of countries that have been able to coordinate the preparation of multisectoral jobs strategies or the implementation of integrated jobs operations. They all involved the creation of an intergovernmental body, such as a multiministerial steering committee, chaired by a strong ministry (for example, Finance) or the Prime Minister's Office. In Tunisia, for instance, the government is implementing a multisector investment project to promote value chain development and job creation. The project is co-managed by the Ministries of Finance, Industry, Labor, and Social Affairs. Similarly, in Bangladesh, the government designed and is implementing a jobs strategy that involves several ministries and sectors.

THE REALITY OF ADVANCED ECONOMIES

This section presents a few figures and tables with key trends and issues in formal labor force participation. It also highlights policy trends as well as policy gaps to support high formal labor force participation in advanced economies.

Figure 15.2 presents demographic trends for selected high-income countries (Germany, and Japan, and the United States) with actual data for the period 2010–15 and projections thereafter. Actual data signal the falling share of births and rising share of deaths as determinants of population growth, and the growing role of net immigration. The projections keep the share of births broadly constant but gradually increase the share of deaths. The projected fall in net migration is not model based but a technically and politically convenient assumption by the United Nations that net migration between all countries will eventually become zero (Ayuso, Bravo, and Holzmann 2015a). The rich world is moving to a demographically stagnant or shrinking future, a phenomenon that even record-high rates of net migration will be unable to counteract (Ayuso, Bravo, and Holzmann 2015b).

Figure 15.3 presents the trends over the past 25 years in labor force participation in high-income countries. The total rate stabilized as the rise in women's participation compensated for the fall in men's. This is in line with demographic trends. Similarly, the contributor ratio toward the old-age pension scheme in table 15.1 signals broad stability (across the observed shorter period) with some moderate variations. The differences between countries are noticeable but not sizable and largely expected. Yet in all countries they suggest that old-age pension coverage or contribution regularity is incomplete.

Beyond these selective and incomplete figures and tables, and consistent with the literature, various pension and labor market issues emerge. Three are discussed here,

FIGURE 15.2 **Contribution of births, deaths, and migration to population growth in high-income countries**

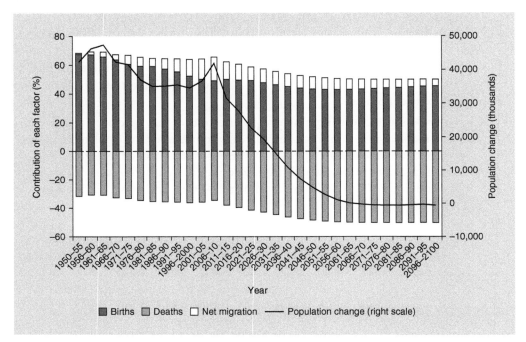

SOURCE: Original elaboration based on data from the United Nations, Department of Economic and Social Affairs, Population Division (2017). World Population Prospects: The 2017 Revision, DVD Edition.

selected because they harbor critical policy issues for which the conceptual and empirical guidance is very thin:

- Although increasing the number of immigrants can increase the size of the working-age population, it cannot stop the process of demographic aging (Bussolo, Koettl, and Sinnott 2015). Moreover, when it comes to the role of unmanaged immigration for the financing of the pension scheme and other social programs, there are two key questions: First, what is the likelihood of unskilled, and often illegal economic migrants, integrating sufficiently into the labor market of sophisticated economies to pay taxes and contributions, when even low-skilled nationals have difficulty doing so? Second, what is the impact on an NDC-type scheme of middle-aged yet labor market-fit migrants who are offered an old-age minimum income guarantee (given that this combination makes contributions akin to taxes)?

- Formal pension scheme coverage typically increases with countries' income and development level but not necessarily at the same pace. Yet the expectation was once that eventually and with sufficiently high income, essentially all countries would have full pension coverage. This was not the case before the 2008 financial crisis, and indications suggest that coverage may have peaked in Organisation for Economic Co-operation and Development (OECD) countries toward the end of

FIGURE 15.3 **Labor force participation in high-income countries**

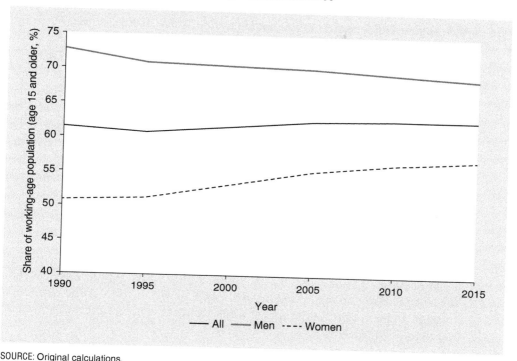

SOURCE: Original calculations.

TABLE 15.1 **Old-age contributor ratio**

| | Percent of working-age population | |
| | 2000–14 | |
	Earliest	**Latest**
Australia	70	70
Czech Republic	66	67
Israel	66	70
Japan	76	79
Korea, Republic of	51	52
Latvia	63	71
Portugal	60	59
Singapore	46	45
Slovenia	60	64

SOURCE: Data from International Labour Organization (ILO) Social Security Department.

NOTE: This indicator reflects the extent to which the current working-age population is protected in old age. It is calculated as the number of current contributors to a social security institution providing benefits in old age as a proportion of the working-age population. This version of the old-age demographic protection ratio might slightly understate the future level of protection, because some of those affiliated, but currently not actively contributing to an old-age pension scheme, might still build up sufficient entitlements during working age. The year 2000 is the earliest and 2014 the latest year for which there is data, but the data do not start at 2000 or end at 2014 for every country.

the last century (Holzmann 2003). Since then labor market marginalization has reportedly increased. And the arrival of industry 4.0, robots, and AI is expected to further increase contributory marginalization. What does this mean for future coverage and how can this be best handled by NDC schemes?

- Over the past decades a number of countries moved toward FDC and NDC schemes and most traditional NDB schemes underwent reforms of diverse depth. This development calls for empirical analyses of differences in the labor market and scheme participation and their changes over time. Can such differences be established or have they been smoothed over by other scheme characteristics? Or are the differences between DC and reformed DB schemes actually irrelevant? The answers matter significantly for reform design. Encouraging reports on positive NDC labor market effects are seen in chapters 2, 3, 5, and 6 discussing the experiences of Latvia, Norway, Poland, and Sweden.

With regard to the policy trends and reform gaps in the pension and labor market area, the following observations are noteworthy:

- The information base suggests that both NDB and NDC reforms were mostly undertaken for reasons of financial sustainability, with only limited concern for labor market interactions and outcomes. The elimination of the tax wedge through a closer contribution-benefit link seems of concern to economists but less so to policy makers.
- Concerns are increasing about the marginalization and precarious position of a subset of the population and the implications for future pension rights (under NDB and NDC schemes alike), but limited interest or even legislated actions exist to correct the resulting low contribution density during active life, for example, through matching contributions and other promising mechanisms. Any corrections undertaken typically happen ex post. Is this due to the different effectiveness of interventions, merely reflecting budgetary shortsightedness?
- Over the past two decades, zero pillar arrangements expanded and essentially all high-income countries now have such an instrument. Yet this was done with little concern for distortion-minimizing integration with earnings-related schemes and the impact on labor market outcomes.

THE REALITY OF EMERGING MARKET ECONOMIES

This section also presents key trends and issues in formal labor force participation, and highlights policy trends as well as policy gaps to support high formal labor force participation, but this time in emerging market economies. The focus is on countries in the Europe and Central Asia (ECA), Latin America and the Caribbean (LAC), and East Asia and Pacific (EAP) regions, or a subset of those countries depending on data availability.

Panels a–c of figure 15.4 present the components of demographic change with the same period of observed data (until 2010–15) and projected data thereafter. Although commonalities driven by slowing fertility rates and reduced mortality rates exist among the regions, differences also arise. In both LAC and EAP the demographic transition is still in full swing; in ECA the transition is long over. The projected negative population change in LAC and EAP starts in the second half of this century, but has already occurred

FIGURE 15.4 **Contribution of births, deaths, and migration to population development by region**

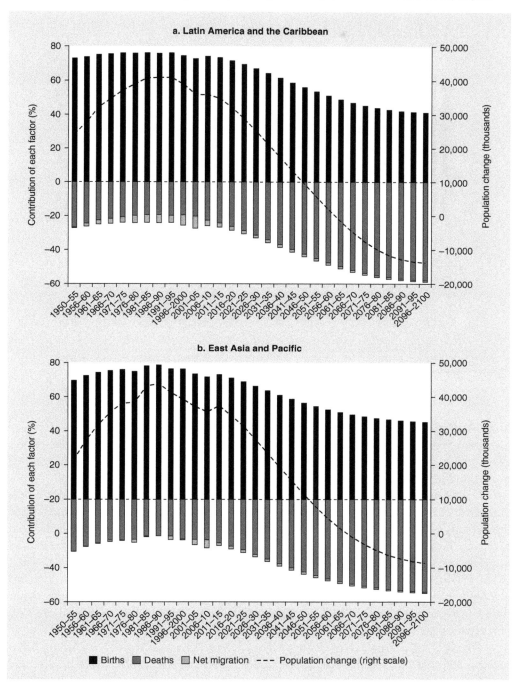

(continued next page)

FIGURE 15.4 Contribution of births, deaths, and migration to population development by region (continued)

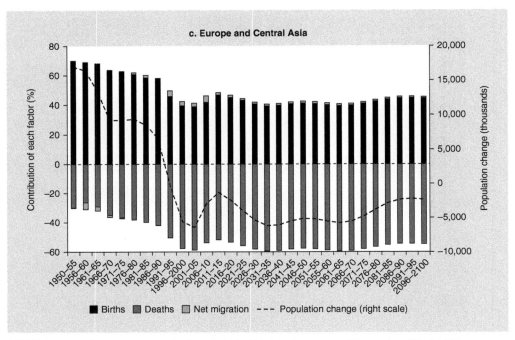

SOURCE: Original elaboration based on data from the United Nations, Department of Economic and Social Affairs, Population Division (2017).

in ECA. Both LAC and EAP are net migration contributors, while in ECA net migration went from positive to negative. The negative net migration and negative population growth were stark in a number of ECA countries—for example, Latvia and Bulgaria lost more than one-quarter of their populations.

Panels a–c of figure 15.5 present the regions' labor force participation trends. These data are difficult to obtain, so the figures for ECA cover only Poland, Romania, the Russian Federation, and Turkey, and for EAP only the Philippines and Thailand. Hence the data may not be representative. The data suggest lower labor force participation rates than typically expected in OECD countries in all regions, with the highest rates in EAP (that is, the Philippines and Thailand). No noticeable trend of increase is observed for men and women combined in any of these regions. The same applies for men alone, with major differences between the regions. The density of coverage is lower for women but a rising participation trend for women is observed.

Figure 15.6 compares a measure of benefit coverage across regions, including high-income countries as a benchmark. The figure shows the main differences in coverage across the regions of emerging market economies, although their per capita income is broadly similar. ECA has the highest coverage rate, which came down from very high rates during the early years of economic transition with a small increase thereafter. LAC follows with a lower rate but a noticeable increase during the most recent 15 years. The lowest rate but also the highest change is observed for EAP. Overall, a major coverage gap exists in all

FIGURE 15.5 **Labor force participation rates by gender in different regions**

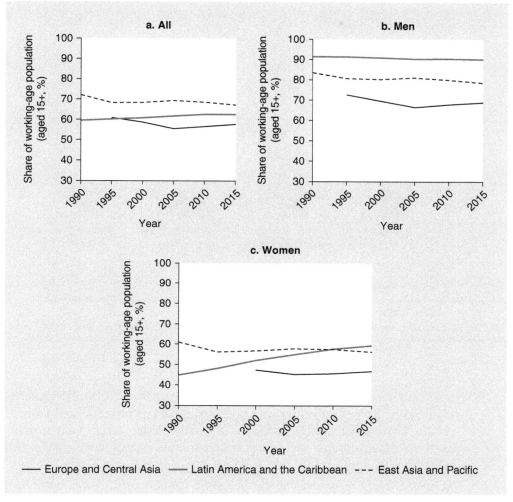

SOURCE: Original elaboration based on data from ILOSTAT (for Latin American and the Caribbean and East Asia and Pacific) and OECD.stat (for Europe and Central Asia).

emerging market regions. This presents a major challenge for all existing pension schemes and would also challenge even a perfectly designed and implemented NDC scheme.

Beyond these figures and based on a rich literature on the topic, many issues emerge, including the following:

- The strong emigration from a number of ECA countries puts major stress on their pension systems, because contributors in best working age are leaving the country. Some may return during their active age (such as Poles leaving the United Kingdom); others may move to other European countries; and some may return after retirement. Although this causes little problem for individuals and their portability of acquired rights and benefits disbursement, it creates challenges for the cash flows of these countries' pension schemes and for the calculation of the

FIGURE 15.6 **Old-age contributor ratio, 2000 and 2014**

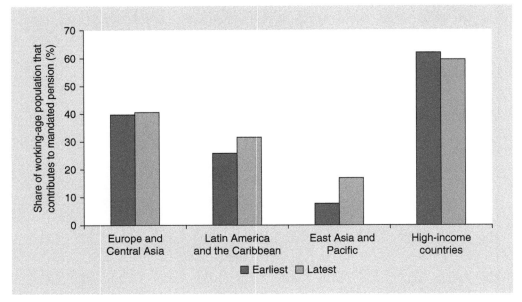

SOURCE: Data from the International Labour Organization (ILO) Social Security Department. See http://www.ilo.org/dyn/ilossi/ssimain.home?p_lang=en.

NOTE: The year 2000 is the earliest and 2014 the latest year for which there is data, but the data do not start at 2000 or end at 2014 for every region.

sustainable (notional) rate of return when an NDC scheme is involved and the cross-country flow of workers is sizable. However, the experience of Latvia, which lost almost one-third of its labor force in the past two decades, strongly suggests that the NDC approach is well able to master a shrinking workforce (Palmer and Stabina 2019).

- Old-age coverage increased but still has room to grow before reaching that of high-income countries (which themselves are dealing with a decrease). In addition, the relevant studies illustrate a continued low contribution density for lower- and at times higher-income groups in these countries. Under a pure DC scheme this would result in very low benefit levels in retirement. Currently benefit gaps are handled with ex post top-ups on low benefits once received, and with the introduction of zero pillars in many emerging market economies. This is laudable but risks aggravating the coverage problem because the tax wedge between the formal and informal sectors is increased (Levy 2008; Pagés, Rigolini, and Robalino 2014).

With regard to policy trends and reform gaps for the pension and labor market, the following comments are made:

- Many pension policy reforms were undertaken or attempted in the 1990s and 2000s in LAC, ECA, and Central (Kazakhstan, the Kyrgyz Republic, and Mongolia) and East Asia (the Republic of Korea, China) to address short- and long-term financial sustainability through introduction of funded DC pillars that were partially reversed thereafter. The reversal was often fiscal in view of sizable transition costs. As in high-income countries, coverage and labor market issues played a very limited role in the reform process in emerging market economies.

- Informality remains a problem in emerging market economies in LAC and EAP, and became an issue in ECA with the transition. The discussion in LAC reflects the view that expanded basic provisions plus high costs of formality create a tax wedge that makes informality a rational choice (Levy 2008). In Asia, the mandated but unfunded character of public provisions is claimed to be an obstacle to formalization. The preference for funded provisions mixed with reservations about social security institutions remains high there.

- Pension policy is mostly developed with little regard for and understanding of labor market issues. Pension staff in social security institutions and related ministries typically have little information about the labor market connection and issues. The relevant policy makers hardly talk to each other and those technically in charge of pension reform have a limited understanding of labor market challenges and limited guidance on how to handle them.

NDC Schemes and Delayed Retirement

Many of the labor market inadequacies and distortions during early and middle working life carry over into the labor market for older workers. In addition, specific labor market issues exist for the elderly that are likely to affect their retirement decisions. "Key NDC Design Suggestions and Main Labor Market Policy Actions and Options" offers key NDC design and labor market policy issues and options for delaying retirement in line with increasing life expectancy and broader population aging. Many circumstances risk undoing the promised neutrality of NDC schemes with regard to retirement decisions. The next two subsections present trends in labor force participation of the elderly and effective retirement ages, and explore the extent to which the design and policy issues are reflected in policy discussions and interventions in advanced ("The Reality of High-Income Economies") and emerging market ("The Reality of Emerging Market Economies") economies.

KEY NDC DESIGN SUGGESTIONS AND MAIN LABOR MARKET POLICY ACTIONS AND OPTIONS

The close contribution-benefit link of an NDC scheme promises not only a low or no tax wedge for labor supply decisions it also promises to create a linear intertemporal budget constraint for an individual so that retirement depends only on his or her preferences for consumption and leisure and the shadow price of leisure (that is, the wage rate). In consequence and in principle, it is not necessary to set any retirement age, benefit receipt can be mixed with continued labor market participation in any combination, and the delay in retirement in line with the increased life expectancy should be smooth and welfare optimizing.

Key NDC design issues for retirement delay

The concept of an individual linear intertemporal budget constraint established by an NDC scheme is presented in figure 15.7. The budget constraint measures lifetime labor supply when moving from E—the entry point to the labor market—to the left on the leisure axis L. The angle is the wage rate, or the opportunity cost of leisure. The realized labor earnings buy one a consumption bundle C. Depending on his or her preferences for leisure and consumption, an individual chooses a point on the linear intertemporal budget constraint (solid line), and thus retirement age R.

The left-hand panel of figure 15.7 presents a situation in which the standard retirement age R_s happens to be the welfare optimal choice A on the intertemporal budget constraint. The choice A, however, may also emerge under a somewhat different preference set if after the standard retirement age the intertemporal budget constraint has a kink, caused by, for example, a lower wage rate from this age onward.

The right-hand panel of figure 15.7 presents an individual with a much lower wage rate who has access at minimum retirement age to guaranteed income that lifts his or her intertemporal budget constraint to point B and keeps it constant thereafter (the wage rate for further labor supply is assumed zero). This shift in the intertemporal budget constraint is the result of a redistributive process during the retirement years. As a result, most preference sets will make B an individually optimal selection. If the individual has a very low life expectancy that moves the consumption axis toward the minimum retirement age, then withdrawal from the labor market before the minimum retirement age may be optimal (and the mandated contributions act as a mere tax).

FIGURE 15.7 **Intertemporal budget constraint and selection of the retirement age**

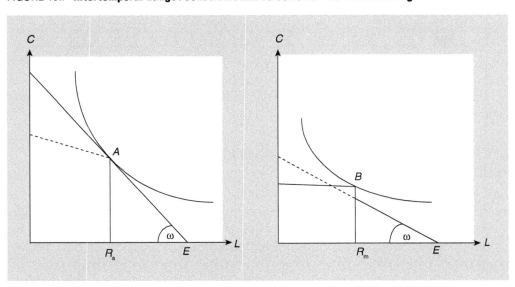

SOURCE: Original figures.

The following briefly illustrates some of the considerations that may undo the linearity of NDC schemes and instead establish kinks around the minimum or standard retirement age:

- The tax treatment of earnings and pensions matters. With high social security contributions and high marginal tax rates on active income, net (consumption) income before and after retirement may not be too different and thus labor supply may fall to zero as soon as the minimum benefit access age is reached.

- Access to occupational pensions is typically contingent on withdrawal from a firm's labor market. Lacking alternative job opportunities in other firms or being offered lower wage rates makes full withdrawal at the first possible moment attractive.

- A number of family events can shift preferences and encourage earlier retirement, including a spouse's withdrawal from the labor market (and the increase in joint leisure utility) or the need or opportunity to care for grandchildren (for example, because of absent child care institutions—a frequently cited early retirement argument in Italy).

- Interactions with other social programs such as access to or loss of survivors', disability, or health care benefits at a specific age may affect early retirement—for example, substituting government-subsidized health care for self-financed private provisions is one such scenario.

- For lower-income groups, minimum income guarantees or top-ups from a certain age onward may lead not only to a kink but to a jump in the intertemporal budget constraint, making this retirement age a rational choice (as in the right-hand panel of figure 15.7).

- For individuals with lower life expectancy, the left axis moves to the right, making earlier retirement preferences rational and the choice of the earliest possible moment optimal. Such a preference is strengthened by a front-loading of NDC benefits, which offer higher initial benefits for lower indexation thereafter (as very transparently done under the Swedish NDC scheme).

These and other circumstances that undo the linearity of the individual intertemporal budget constraint and risk bringing the retirement decision forward suggest that the design of minimum or standard access rules, the redesign of other social programs, and the availability of rewarding job opportunities are ever more critical as life expectancy increases and people are expected to postpone retirement. The following are only some of many possible benefit redesign considerations:

- In view of the importance of the minimum access age to NDC benefits for retirement decisions, its indexation with some measure of remaining life expectancy seems required.

- Retirement and take-up of benefits may not be granted at minimum access age to individuals with insufficient own accumulations; the rules may ask for accumulations or annuity equivalents of at least a guaranteed minimum income level. In this case a higher (and life expectancy–indexed) access age to a guaranteed minimum income needs to be selected; this can be a notional standard retirement age or a higher selected access age.

- Low-income individuals are likely to have a lower life expectancy, which needs to be taken into consideration when deciding on the first two design proposals.

- Although the standard retirement age loses, in principle, any meaning under an NDC approach, selection of a notional standard retirement age and its indexation to the related cohort life expectancy may be crucial as a signaling or nudging device.

KEY LABOR MARKET POLICY CHALLENGES AND OPTIONS

The key policy challenge is to make society understand that population aging is (a) a very new development for mankind—it started only about 250 years ago in advanced economies, (b) expected to continue without end in sight, and (c) likely the most important socioeconomic change since the beginning of mankind—at least as significant as climate change and its consequences (Holzmann 2013). As a result, the concomitant increase in retirement age will stay and must be proactively addressed. This calls for an appropriately structured system of retirement programs as well as innovative, far-reaching, and well-implemented labor market policies.

Outlining the full scope of required policy changes in the labor market and other key policy areas is well beyond the scope of this chapter (see Börsch-Supan 2003; Holzmann 2013; Piggott and Woodland 2016). A few pertinent policy considerations and options around the labor market are offered here:

- The right regulatory framework for an economy is quite likely crucial to keeping individuals healthy, skilled, and motivated but knowledge regarding how to design the regulations is lacking. What can be done to provide individuals with incentives to follow a healthy lifestyle throughout their lives? This is important for extended labor force participation but also to address the health costs of an aging society and to make longer life more enjoyable. To this end, the empirical knowledge of effective programs is very limited as is the political willingness to implement them (except, perhaps, by some European green parties). Similar knowledge gaps apply to the relevant skills enhancements for an older workforce. Lifelong learning is popular in political speeches but the conceptual and empirical foundation for effective programs remains weak given that rigorous M&E is essentially absent (OECD 2005; European Commission/EACEA/Eurydice 2015). Empirical research has found some strategies to keep older workers motivated (such as changing one's job and work environment, including colleagues), but employers must have the right incentives to offer the elderly jobs.

- For employers to have incentives to offer jobs to older workers, suggestions include the following:

  o Revise the strict protection rules for the older workforce seen in most countries, which can be counterproductive for new hires.

  o Review the seniority principle of wage setting, which periodically incrementally raises wages for workers simply because they are getting older; instead move to a productivity-oriented wage-setting process that keeps older workers competitive.

- Offer more contract flexibility with an elderly workforce to overcome asymmetric skills. The present inflexible policy may explain why employers in some OECD countries have problems keeping older workers in their workforce beyond retirement age, while at the same time they are highly reluctant to hire unfamiliar older workers.

- Whatever progress can be made at shifting the age-skill profile upward, the mix of skills is changing with age and needs to be accommodated by work assignments to the profit of all. Known approaches include the following:

  - Redefining the role of the elderly. Firms in advanced economies in this area (such as Finland and Germany) have started to change the work process for elderly workers on the production line or to move them into mentor positions for younger workers, with reportedly measurable success.[7]

  - Accommodating a preretirement job change, for example, through reassignment within the unit or changing to a new employer or self-employment. For employees in enterprises and administration, retirement at the highest job level will need to be a feature of the past.

THE REALITY OF HIGH-INCOME ECONOMIES

This section highlights trends and issues in retirement age, and policy trends as well as policy gaps to support increasing retirement age in high-income countries.

Figure 15.8 presents the trend in labor force participation of individuals age 65 and older for select high-income countries for the past 25 years. A clear change can be seen from the decades-long trend of ever-decreasing labor force participation of the elderly for both genders. This trend is mirrored in the decreased effective average retirement age from a larger data set of rich OECD countries since 1970 (figure 15.9). The retirement age came down from levels of over 68 years for men to as low as 63 years in 1996 and 1997 before rising after the 2008 financial crisis to 64.5 years in 2014. The same happened for women, for whom the retirement age is one year lower.

This development is likely the result of increases in the legal retirement age and the introduction of decrements (increments) for earlier (later) retirement; it may also be influenced by the reduction in public generosity as well as periodic stock market disturbances; and it may be codetermined by the retirement of baby boomers, which often left skill gaps that employers were willing to cover by keeping elderly workers employed longer.[8]

Despite this positive trend, some remaining issues include the following:

- In most but not all advanced economies an increase in labor force participation of the elderly and in effective retirement ages took place. This explains the moderate change seen since the end of the 1990s, which reflects the average of both leaders and laggards. Hence a number of other advanced economies still have to act to reverse current trends.

- For those countries that substantially increased their effective retirement age, two related but distinct questions emerge:

  - Was the increase sizable enough to compensate for the intermediate increase in life expectancy at this age? For the three front-running countries with increases

FIGURE 15.8 **Elderly labor force participation in high-income countries (Germany, Japan, United States), 1990–2015**

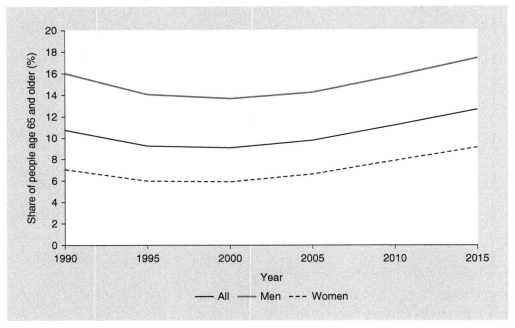

SOURCE: Original elaboration based on data from OECD.stat.

FIGURE 15.9 **Effective average retirement age in high-income Organisation for Economic Co-operation and Development countries, 1970–2014**

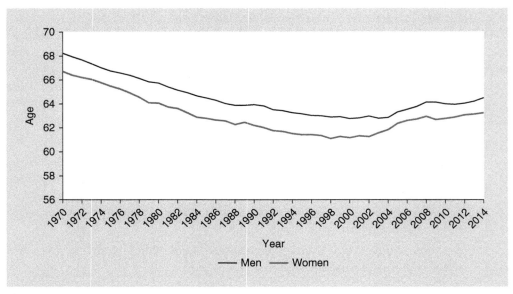

SOURCE: Original elaboration based on data from OECD.stat.

of 3.3–4.2 years between 1996 and 2014, this was quite likely the case. Life expectancy at birth increases by about 2.5 years per decade, and at retirement by about 1.5 years. Thus, the current effort of the large majority of high-income countries was insufficient if only to catch up with recent increases in life expectancy.

   o Did the trend in effective retirement age lead to financially sustainable schemes? Given the answer above, this does not seem to be the case (even assuming adjustments in the benefit level and more). This calls for further legal action for retirement age, benefit reforms, or introduction of an NDC scheme.

- Similar to the increase in labor force participation mentioned previously, the empirical issue stands about whether NDC or FDC schemes have been more successful at increasing the effective retirement age than reformed or unreformed NDB schemes. The available data do not allow this question to be answered.

With regard to the policy trends and reform gaps for the retirement age and labor market participation of the elderly in advanced economies, the following observations are suggested:

- Essentially all OECD countries have started to increase the retirement age of men and women, but often with long implementation periods (OECD 2017). Some countries have started to index the standard retirement age to changes in life expectancy. In most countries this approach will not be sufficient to establish financial sustainability because the starting age is too low, the effort too timid, or no commitment to reducing the accrual rate is undertaken.

- Most countries use an estimate of period life expectancy and its expected changes to anchor their retirement policies instead of the methodologically correct esti-mate of the cohort life expectancy. There is strong empirical evidence from countries that produce and publish both estimates that period life expectancy at retirement underestimates the cohort life expectancy by 30 percent and more (Ayuso, Bravo, and Holzmann 2018).

- There is only limited public recognition that population aging is here to stay, that a continuous increase in the legal and effective retirement age is the first-best option to address it, and that the mandated pension scheme and overall pension system need to be made population aging–compliant.

- With regard to the elderly in the labor market, significant differences arise between country approaches, from a purely market-driven one (as in the United States—you take the job that you get) to a government and social partner–driven one (as in Finland).

- There is no understanding of the need for a comprehensive reform approach that addresses each of the potential binding constraints for delayed retirement—from redesign of the disability pension and minimum income guarantee to labor mar-ket reforms that offer capabilities and opportunities for elderly workers.

- No advanced economies have a systematic approach to keeping the elderly healthy, skilled, and motivated, and to increasing the incentives (decreasing disincentives) of employers to offer jobs to elderly workers. And no international inventory exists with which to compare and rigorously assess the applied approaches.

THE REALITY OF EMERGING MARKET ECONOMIES

Figure 15.10 presents the labor force participation rate of individuals age 65 and older for the regions and countries presented in "The Reality of Emerging Market Economies." Three observations stand out:

- In all three regions the labor force participation rate at age 65 and older is broadly constant or falling. The latter is the case for ECA, whose rate is now lower than the OECD average.
- For all three regions the starting value in 1990 was well above that of high-income countries. In LAC and EAP the rate still remains well above the rate of these countries.
- In LAC the rate remains broadly high for men, but there is a slight increase in the rate from much lower levels for women.

FIGURE 15.10 **Elderly labor force participation in different regions by gender, 1990–2015**

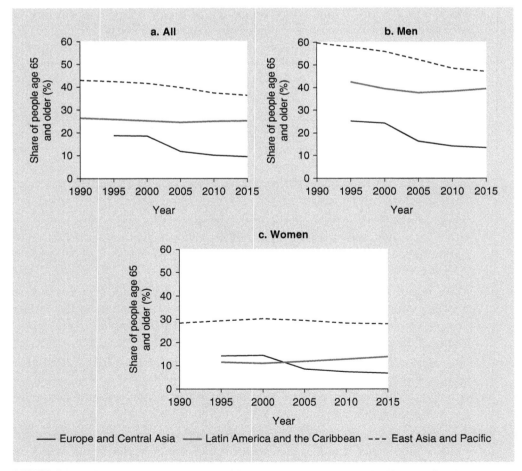

SOURCES: Original elaboration based on data from ILOSTAT (for Latin America and the Caribbean and East Asia and Pacific) and OECD.stat (for Europe and Central Asia).

Figure 15.11 presents complementary information on the effective retirement age for a subset of countries in LAC and ECA and in China. The results are broadly but not fully consistent and not easily explained except by different country examples:

- For LAC (covering Brazil, Chile, and Mexico) the retirement age for both genders is falling from very high levels, with fluctuations across the period from the early 1970s to 2014.

- The information for China suggests an essentially constant effective retirement age for men of about 66 years. For women the data suggest an increase in waves.

- The data for ECA countries (Bulgaria, Croatia, Latvia, Lithuania, Poland, Romania, and Turkey) show an OECD-type profile, with a fall and a subsequent rise after the end of the 1990s. The increases since its lowest value are higher than the average for high-income OECD countries. The recent increase in effective retirement age was able to compensate for the rise in life expectancy (Gál and Radó 2019).

FIGURE 15.11 **Effective average retirement age in Latin America, China, and Europe and Central Asia by gender, 1970–2014**

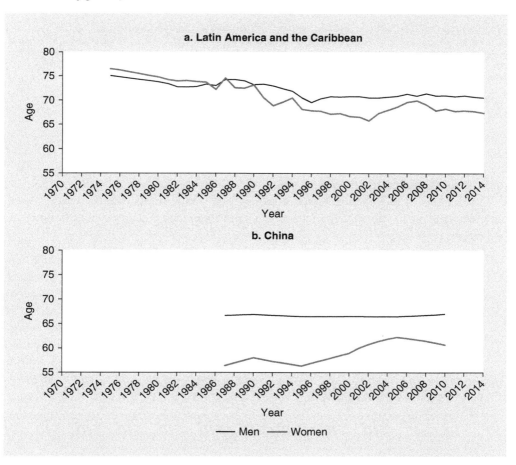

(continued next page)

FIGURE 15.11 **Effective average retirement age in Latin America, China, and Europe and Central Asia by gender, 1970–2014 (continued)**

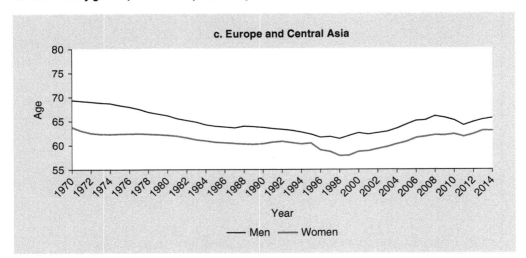

SOURCES: OECD estimates based on the results of national labor force surveys, the European Union Labour Force Survey, and, for earlier years in some countries, national censuses.

NOTE: The average effective age of retirement is calculated as a weighted average of (net) withdrawals from the labor market at different ages over a five-year period for workers initially age 40 and older. To abstract from compositional effects in the age structure of the population, labor force withdrawals are estimated based on changes in labor force participation rates rather than labor force levels. These changes are calculated for each (synthetic) cohort divided into five-year age groups.

The analytical issues raised are the same as those for high-income OECD countries, in particular the questions of (a) whether the re-increase in ECA countries was sufficient to compensate for the progress in life expectancy, and (b) whether the increase was linked to the type of pension reform introduced.

With regard to policy trends and reform gaps for retirement age and labor market participation of the elderly in advanced economies, the following observations are suggested:

- Emerging market economies have seen only a slow policy drive to increase the legal retirement age: in some it is under discussion, in a very few it has been legislated. Although experts strongly recommend an increase in the retirement age among countries in EAP, only Korea, Japan, and Singapore have made progress in this area (World Bank 2016). In ECA, many countries (for example, Bulgaria, the Czech Republic, Estonia, Hungary, Latvia, Poland, Romania, Slovenia, and Turkey) are gradually increasing the retirement age as well as restricting eligibility or lowering benefit levels for early retirement (Bussolo, Koettl, and Sinnott 2015).

- Emerging market economies seem to have even less of an understanding than advanced economies that population aging is here to stay, and that the overall pension system thus needs to be made population aging–compliant.

- Proposals in these countries for increasing the legal and effective retirement age are typically rejected by the "lump of labor fallacy" position and views that the current elderly (compared with those in advanced economies) are less fit and less skilled to work longer.

- Emerging market economies may have even higher heterogeneity in longevity than advanced economies. This creates an even starker challenge for the redesign of benefit schemes and minimum pension age and guarantees.

- Emerging market economies seem to have no understanding of and hence no comprehensive or systematic approach for policies to keep the elderly healthy, skilled, and motivated, and to increase the incentives (decrease the disincentives) of employers to offer jobs to elderly workers.

Conclusions and Next Steps

This chapter analyzes the constraints that NDC schemes face in living up to their promise of creating strong incentives for formal labor force participation and high contribution density, and for delaying retirement in line with rising life expectancy. These constraints include design and implementation issues, behavioral shortcomings that affect retirement and savings decisions, and structural problems in labor markets that affect the share of wage employment and work opportunities during old age. Despite these constraints, FDC and NDC schemes remain the most promising earnings-related pension systems for addressing not only population aging but also the impact of new technologies (robots and AI) on labor markets.

This chapter discusses design and redesign features and labor market policies needed for NDC schemes to fully deliver the expected labor market outcomes. Labor policies, in particular, are likely to differ between advanced and emerging market economies, taking into consideration structural differences in labor market conditions.

Low formal labor force participation and contribution density remain an issue in emerging market economies, and marginalization and fragmentation in the labor market has reemerged as an issue in advanced economies. In their separate contexts these two situations create a huge challenge for benefit design and social and labor policies to find the right balance between assistance and work incentives. Or it calls for a completely new thinking around the individual account design.

In a world of continual population aging, the extension of working life is considered the most adequate response, and NDC schemes offer the most promising instrument for achieving this extension. Yet public recognition of these two issues is limited in advanced economies and essentially nonexistent in emerging market economies. Benefit design issues remain largely unresolved, and the required policies associated with the labor market for the elderly are, for the most part, terra incognita.

These challenges are not unique to NDC schemes. They apply equally to FDC schemes as the main mandated or supplementary pillar. But the argument still holds that both NDC and FDC schemes can address the demographic and labor market challenges better than any NDB or FDB scheme, however well reformed. What is missing is an integrated approach to the design of DC schemes, social and family policies, and labor market policies to improve the performance of pension systems and achieve better labor market outcomes.

Notes

1. The discussion of whether NDC or financial defined contribution (FDC) schemes provide better labor market responses is not yet closed. Conceptually, FDC schemes with higher financial rates of return should dominate NDC schemes with lower notional rates of return. Empirically, however, it is unclear if this is the case. Emerging market economies typically see much higher wage growth than the rate of return of decentralized or centralized pension funds, except perhaps in the past in Chile.

2. For a primer on NDC schemes, and a stylized comparison between NDB and NDC schemes, see Holzmann (2017a, 2019).

3. This point may also apply to not-well-designed-and-implemented NDC schemes in which the contribution rate pays for the legacy costs from the old NDB scheme, or if the mandate to save is simply too high.

4. See Palacios (2019) and Palacios and Robalino (2019) for a discussion of a universal NDC scheme.

5. This prescriptive-sounding summary builds on the chapters in NDC I, II, and III publications. For the refined and extended 10 key messages and lessons, see Holzmann (2017a, 2019).

6. MILES stands for Macroeconomics, Investment, Labor Market, Education and Skills, and Social Protection and thus the five key areas that may harbor the constraints to productive employment. Hence low labor force participation and high unemployment may emerge from any of these demand and supply areas, which should be identified and addressed.

7. See Ilmarinen (2005) for an early review of issues and Finnish approaches, and read the success story on "BMW 2017" and changes made to the production line to support an aging labor force (Bauer and Mauermann 2010).

8. For a first analysis of the German development of elderly men's and women's labor force participation, see Börsch-Supan and Ferrari (2017).

References

Akbaş, Merve, Dan Ariely, David A. Robalino, and Michael Weber. 2016. "How to Help the Poor to Save a Bit: Evidence from a Field Experiment in Kenya." IZA Discussion Paper 10024, Institute of Labor Economics, Bonn, Germany.

Almeida, Rita, and Pedro Carneiro. 2012. "Enforcement of Labor Regulation and Informality." *American Economic Journal: Applied Economics* 4 (3): 64–89.

Ayuso, Mercedes, Jorge Bravo, and Robert Holzmann. 2015a. "Revisión de las proyecciones de población: Más allá de los convenientes supuestos sobre fertilidad, mortalidad y migración." Instituto BBVA de Pensiones, *Documento de Trabajo N° 11/2015*. Madrid: BBVA.

———. 2015b. "Revisión de las proyecciones de población, Parte 3: Respuestas de la política demográfica al envejecimiento de la población: Familia, mercado laboral y migración." Instituto BBVA de Pensiones, *Documento de Trabajo N° 14/2015*. Madrid: BBVA.

———. 2017a. "Addressing Longevity Heterogeneity in Pension Scheme Design." *Journal of Finance and Economics* 6 (1): 1–24.

———. 2017b. "On the Heterogeneity in Longevity among Socioeconomic Groups: Scope, Trends, and Implications for Earnings-Related Pension Schemes." *Global Journal of Human Social Sciences-Economics* 17 (1): 33–58.

————. 2018. "Getting Life Expectancy Estimates Right for Pension Policy: Period versus Cohort Approach." IZA Discussion Paper 11512, Institute of Labor Economics, Bonn, Germany.

Banerji, Arup, Robert Holzmann, Pierella Paci, Carmen Pagés, Stefano Scarpetta, and Milan Vodopivec. 2008. "Miles to Go: A Quest for an Operational Labor Market Paradigm for Developing Countries." World Bank, Washington, DC.

Bauer, Nikolaus, and Helmut Mauermann. 2010. "How BMW Is Defusing the Demographic Time Bomb." *Harvard Business Review* 88 (3): 99–102.

Bertrand, Marianne, Senhil Mullainathan, and Douglas Miller. 2003. "Public Policy and Extended Families: Evidence from Pensions in South Africa." *World Bank Economic Review* 17 (1): 27–50.

Bodor, Andras, and Robert Holzmann. 2016. "GCC Labor Markets: Challenges and Policy Options." *Gulf Affairs 2015, Labor Market Dynamics in the GCC States* 1: 30–31.

Börsch-Supan, Axel. 2003. "Labor Market Effects of Population Aging." *Labour*, Special Issue 17: 5–44.

Börsch-Supan, Axel, and Irene Ferrari. 2017. "Old-age Labor Force Participation in Germany: What Explains the Reversal among Older Men? And What about the Steady Increase among Older Women?" NBER Working Paper 24044, National Bureau of Economic Research, Cambridge, MA.

Bussolo, Maurizio, Johannes Koettl, and Emily Sinnott. 2015. *Golden Aging: Prospects for Healthy, Active, and Prosperous Aging in Europe and Central Asia*. Washington, DC: World Bank.

Davidoff, Thomas, Jeffrey R. Brown, and Peter A. Diamond. 2005. "Annuities and Individual Welfare." *American Economic Review* 95 (5): 1573–90.

Delarue, Antoine. 2013. "Using Prepaid Contributions to Cover Mobile Workers in Cape Verde and Tunesia." In *Matching Contributions for Pensions*, edited by Richard Hinz, Robert Holzmann, David Tuesta, and Noriyuki Takayama, 261–74. Washington, DC: World Bank.

European Commission/EACEA/Eurydice. 2015. *Adult Education and Training in Europe: Widening Access to Learning Opportunities*. Eurydice Report. Luxembourg: Publications Office of the European Union.

Fajnzylber, Eduardo. 2019. "Chile's Solidarity Pillar: A Benchmark for Adjoining Zero Pillar with DC Schemes." In *Progress and Challenges of Nonfinancial Defined Contribution Pension Schemes: Volume 1 Addressing Marginalization, Polarization, and the Labor Market*, edited by Robert Holzmann, Edward Palmer, Robert Palacios, and Stefano Sacchi, Chapter 11. Washington, DC: World Bank.

Frölich, Markus, David Kaplan, Carmen Pagés, Jamele Rigolini, and David Robalino, eds. 2014. *Social Insurance, Informality, and Labour Markets: How to Protect Workers While Creating Good Jobs*. Oxford, UK: Oxford University Press.

Gál, Róbert, and Márta Radó. 2019. "Labor Market Participation and Postponed Retirement in Central and Eastern Europe." In *Progress and Challenges of Nonfinancial Defined Contribution Pension Schemes: Volume 1 Addressing Marginalization, Polarization, and the Labor Market*, edited by Robert Holzmann, Edward Palmer, Robert Palacios, and Stefano Sacchi, Chapter 16. Washington, DC: World Bank.

Gentilini, Hugo, Philip Okeef, Truman Packard, Robert Palacios, David Robalino, and Indhira Santos. Forthcoming. "Social Protection and Jobs in a Changing World of Labor." Jobs Group, Working Paper, World Bank, Washington, DC.

Gruber, Jonathan, and David Wise. 1998. "Social Security and Retirement: An International Comparison." *American Economic Review* 88 (2): 158–63.

Hampf, Franziska, and Ludger Woessmann. 2017. "Vocational vs. General Education and Employment over the Life Cycle: New Evidence from PIAAC." *CESifo Economic Studies* 63 (3): 255–69.

Hausmann, Ricardo, Danny Rodrik, and Andres Velasco. 2005. *Growth Diagnostics*. Cambridge, MA: John F. Kennedy School of Government, Harvard University.

Hofer, Helmut, and Reinhard Koman 2006. "Social Security and Retirement in Austria." *Empirica* 33 (5): 285–313.

Holzmann, Robert. 2003. "A Provocative Note on Coverage in Public Pension Schemes." In *The Three Pillars of Wisdom—A Reader on Globalization, World Bank Pension Models and Welfare Society,* edited by Anton Tausch, 85–99. New York: Nova Science Publisher.

———. 2013. "An Optimistic Perspective on Population Aging and Old-Age Financial Protection." *Malaysian Journal of Economic Studies* 50 (2): 107–37.

———. 2014. "Participation in Mandated and Voluntary Social Risk Management Arrangements: The Role and Limits of Financial Education and Other Interventions." In *Social Insurance and Labor Markets: How to Protect Workers While Creating Good Jobs,* edited by Markus Fröhlich, David Kaplan, Carmen Pagés, Jamele Rigolini, and David Robalino, 147–79. Oxford, UK: Oxford University Press.

———. 2017a. "The ABCs of NDCs." *International Social Security Review* 70 (3): 53–77.

———. 2017b. "Do Bilateral Social Security Agreements Deliver on the Portability of Pensions and Health Care Benefits? A Summary Policy Paper on Four Migration Corridors between EU and Non-EU Member States." *IZA Journal of European Labor Studies* 5 (17): 1–35.

———. 2019. "The ABCs of NDCs." In *Progress and Challenges of Nonfinancial Defined Contribution Pension Schemes: Volume 1 Addressing Marginalization, Polarization, and the Labor Market*, edited by Robert Holzmann, Edward Palmer, Robert Palacios, and Stefano Sacchi, Chapter 9. Washington, DC: World Bank.

Holzmann, Robert, and Richard Hinz. 2005. *Old-Age Income Support in the 21st Century: An International Perspective on Pension Systems and Reform*. Washington, DC: World Bank.

Holzmann, Robert, and Alain Jouston. 2013. "Addressing the Legacy Costs in an NDC Reform: Conceptualization, Measurement, and Financing." In *NDC Pension Schemes in a Changing Pension World: Volume 2 Gender, Politics, and Financial Stability*, edited by Robert Holzmann, Edward Palmer, and David Robalino, 277–304. Washington, DC: World Bank.

Holzmann, Robert, and Johannes Koettl. 2015. "The Portability of Pensions, Health, and Other Social Benefits: Concepts and Issues." *CESifo Economic Studies* 61 (2): 377–415.

Holzmann, Robert, Landis Mackellar, and Jana Repansek, eds. 2009. *Pension Reform in South-Eastern Europe: Linking Pension Reform with Labor and Financial Market Reforms*. Washington, DC: World Bank and Ljubljana: Center for Financial Excellence.

Holzmann, Robert, and Edward Palmer. 2012. "NDC in the Teens: Lessons and Issues." In *NDC Pension Schemes in a Changing Pension World: Volume 1 Progress, Issues, and Implementation*, edited by Robert Holzmann, Edward Palmer, and David Robalino, 1–29. Washington, DC: World Bank and Swedish Social Insurance Agency.

Holzmann, Robert, Jennifer Alonso-García, Héloïse Labit-Hardy, and Andrés M. Villegas. 2019. "NDC Schemes and Heterogeneity in Longevity: Proposals for Redesign." In *Progress and Challenges of Nonfinancial Defined Contribution Pension Schemes: Volume 1 Addressing Marginalization, Polarization, and the Labor Market*, edited by Robert Holzmann, Edward Palmer, Robert Palacios, and Stefano Sacchi, Chapter 14. Washington, DC: World Bank.

Ilmarinen, Juhani. 2005. *Toward a Longer Working Life. Ageing and the Quality of Worklife in the European Union.* Helsinki: Finish Institute of Occupational Health.

Kotlikoff, Laurence J., and Avia Spivak. 1981. "The Family as an Incomplete Annuities Market." *Journal of Political Economy* 89 (2): 372–91.

Levy, Santiago. 2008. *Good Intentions, Bad Outcomes.* Washington, DC: Brookings Institution.

Merotto, Dino, Michael Weber, and Reyes Aterido. 2017. "Jobs Diagnostics Facts and Findings." Jobs Group Working Paper, World Bank, Washington, DC.

Nelson, Kenneth, Rense Nieuwenhuis, and Susanne Alm. 2019. "Sweden: Adjoining the Guarantee Pension with NDC." In *Progress and Challenges of Nonfinancial Defined Contribution Pension Schemes: Volume 1 Addressing Marginalization, Polarization, and the Labor Market*, edited by Robert Holzmann, Edward Palmer, Robert Palacios, and Stefano Sacchi, Chapter 10. Washington, DC: World Bank.

OECD (Organisation for Economic Co-operation and Development). 2005. *Promoting Adult Learning.* Paris: OECD Publishing.

———. 2017. *Pension at a Glance.* Paris: OECD Publishing.

Pagés, Carmen, Jamele Rigolini, and David Robalino. 2014. "Social Insurance, Informality and Labor Markets: How to Protect Workers While Creating Good Jobs." In *Social Insurance, Informality and the Labor Markets*, edited by Markus Frölich, David Kaplan, Carmen Pagés, Jamele Rigolini, and David Robalino, 8–27. Oxford: Oxford University Press.

Palacios, Robert. 2019. "Administrative Requirements and Prospects for Universal NDCs in Emerging Economies." In *Progress and Challenges of Nonfinancial Defined Contribution Pension Schemes: Volume 2 Addressing Gender, Administration, and Communication*, edited by Robert Holzmann, Edward Palmer, Robert Palacios, and Stefano Sacchi, Chapter 21. Washington, DC: World Bank.

Palacios, Robert, and David Robalino. 2019. "Integrating Social Insurance and Social Assistance Programs for the Future World of Labor." Social Protection Discussion Paper. World Bank, Washington, DC.

Palmer, Edward, and Sandra Stabina. 2019. "The Latvian NDC Scheme: Success under a Decreasing Labor Force." In *Progress and Challenges of Nonfinancial Defined Contribution Pension Schemes: Volume 1 Addressing Marginalization, Polarization, and the Labor Market*, edited by Robert Holzmann, Edward Palmer, Robert Palacios, and Stefano Sacchi, Chapter 3. Washington, DC: World Bank.

Piggott, John, and Alain Woodland. 2016. *Handbook of the Economics of Population Aging*, Volume 1A. Amsterdam: North Holland.

Ribe, Helena, David Robalino, and Ian Walker. 2012. *From Right to Reality: Incentives, Labor Markets, and the Challenge of Universal Social Protection in Latin America and the Caribbean.* Washington, DC: World Bank.

Robalino, David, Jose Manuel Romero, and Ian Walker. 2019. "Allocating Matching Grants for Private Investments to Maximize Jobs Impacts." Unpublished, World Bank, Washington, DC.

Robalino, David, and Ian Walker. 2017. "Economic Analysis of Jobs Investment Projects." Guidance Note, Jobs Group Working Paper 7, World Bank, Washington, DC.

Tommasi, Mariona, and Andres Velasco. 2007. "Where Are We in the Political Economy of Reform?" *Journal of Policy Reform* 1 (2): 187–238.

World Bank. 2012. *World Bank World Development Report 2013: Jobs.* Washington, DC: World Bank.

———. 2016. *Live Long and Prosper: Aging in East Asia and Pacific.* Washington, DC: World Bank.

CHAPTER 16

Labor Market Participation and Postponed Retirement in Central and Eastern Europe

Róbert I. Gál and Márta Radó

Introduction

The last phase of the demographic transition brings low fertility and low mortality. The resulting age structure loses its pyramid shape, and more resembles a cylinder. The population ages. The median age person of the eight Central and Eastern European countries discussed in this chapter (from north to south Estonia, Latvia, Lithuania, Poland, the Czech Republic, the Slovak Republic, Hungary, and Slovenia, referred to hereafter as CEE8) will grow 9.0 years older, from 39.4 years to 48.4 years, between 2015 and 2045.[1] This chapter focuses on one of the two drivers of this aging process: falling mortality.

Whereas in the past gains in life expectancy were concentrated in infancy and childhood, resulting in higher youth dependency, recent improvements are skewed to older ages (Eggleston and Fuchs 2012). Such a development would raise the old-age dependency ratio should the demarcation age between the active section of the life cycle and old age be fixed. This chapter demonstrates that this is not the case, at least not in the CEE8. It shows that the effective age of retirement, a key driver of the demarcation age in question, increased fast enough throughout the region to keep life expectancy at the effective retirement age constant.

Perhaps unusual for an analysis of pension developments, the potential causes are not sought in pension policies but in past investments in human capital. Empirical evidence is used to make a case for connecting recent developments in pensions with historical developments in education. "Life Expectancy at the Effective Retirement Age" supports the following statements with empirical evidence:

- The average age of leaving the labor market (the effective retirement age or exit age) increased over the past two decades in the CEE8 region as a whole and separately in its constituting countries.

- Over the same period, life expectancies at the effective retirement age remained practically unchanged. Consequently, general gains in life expectancies in higher active ages were absorbed almost fully by the labor market.

The authors acknowledge the research support, both intellectual and financial, from the Social Futuring Center of Corvinus University, Budapest. The authors are grateful to Michael Boissonneault, Robert Holzmann, Carmen Pages-Serra, Joakim Palme, and András Simonovits for comments and suggestions.

- This improvement was made possible by a replacement process. The educational composition, and the resulting labor market durability, of the 55–64-year-old population changed during the period discussed here. New retirees today are different from the then-new retirees two decades ago.

- This development was preceded by the spread of secondary education in the CEE8 nations in the 1960s and 1970s.

- A simple projection of completed education of cohorts currently in active age predicts further improvements in the educational composition of future retirees. This in turn suggests room for increasing the standard pensionable age and consequently the effective retirement age. Even if the speed of growth of the exit age slows from the annual 2.8 months seen in the past 15 years to 1.7 months per year over the next 30 years, the increase will be suficient to keep life expectancies at the effective retirement age constant.

"Robustness of the Results" discusses the key methodological choices. "A Wider Context" shows that the CEE8 region is not unique in its increasing effective retirement age and stagnating life expectancies at that age. It briefly discusses the method of characteristic ages applied here versus the widely used predetermined demarcation ages, such as the age of 60 or 65, between the active age and old age. Also, the approach is embedded in related research on the causes and effects of mortality decline. The conclusions are optimistic but realizing the outcome is far from automatic. The "Limitations" section lists some potential obstacles, such as misguided policies that would retrench the growth of the effective retirement age even for better-educated cohorts, as well as the margins of the educational hierarchy and the formal labor market. Even if the average level of education increases, those with poor education and those evading contribution payment will face poverty in old age.

Life Expectancy at the Effective Retirement Age

This section discusses developments in the CEE8 countries. It first demonstrates that the effective retirement age (the average age of leaving the labor market, or the exit age) increased over the past 20, and indeed mostly the past 15, years.

INCREASED EFFECTIVE RETIREMENT AGE OVER THE PAST 20 YEARS

Based on five-year age group data of the Organisation for Economic Co-operation and Development (OECD) on population and labor market participation, the estimation follows a formula by Latulippe (1996).[2] Estimates for five-year intervals between 1996 and 2016 are presented in figure 16.1 (and the complete yearly time series in annex 16A), separately for the Central European and the Baltic nations. For convenience, the Central European group is split by the geographical position of each capital city (that is, whether it is east or west of Vienna).[3]

In the five countries for which data are available for the entire period of two decades (the Czech Republic, Estonia, Hungary, Poland, and the Slovak Republic), the growth of the average effective retirement age was 4.3 years over 20 years. The process started to accelerate around the turn of the millennium. In the past 15 years, for which data for all countries discussed here are available, the exit age increased 3.5 years, or 2.8 months per year, indeed rather quickly.

FIGURE 16.1 **Average age of leaving the labor market in Central and Eastern Europe, 1996–2016**

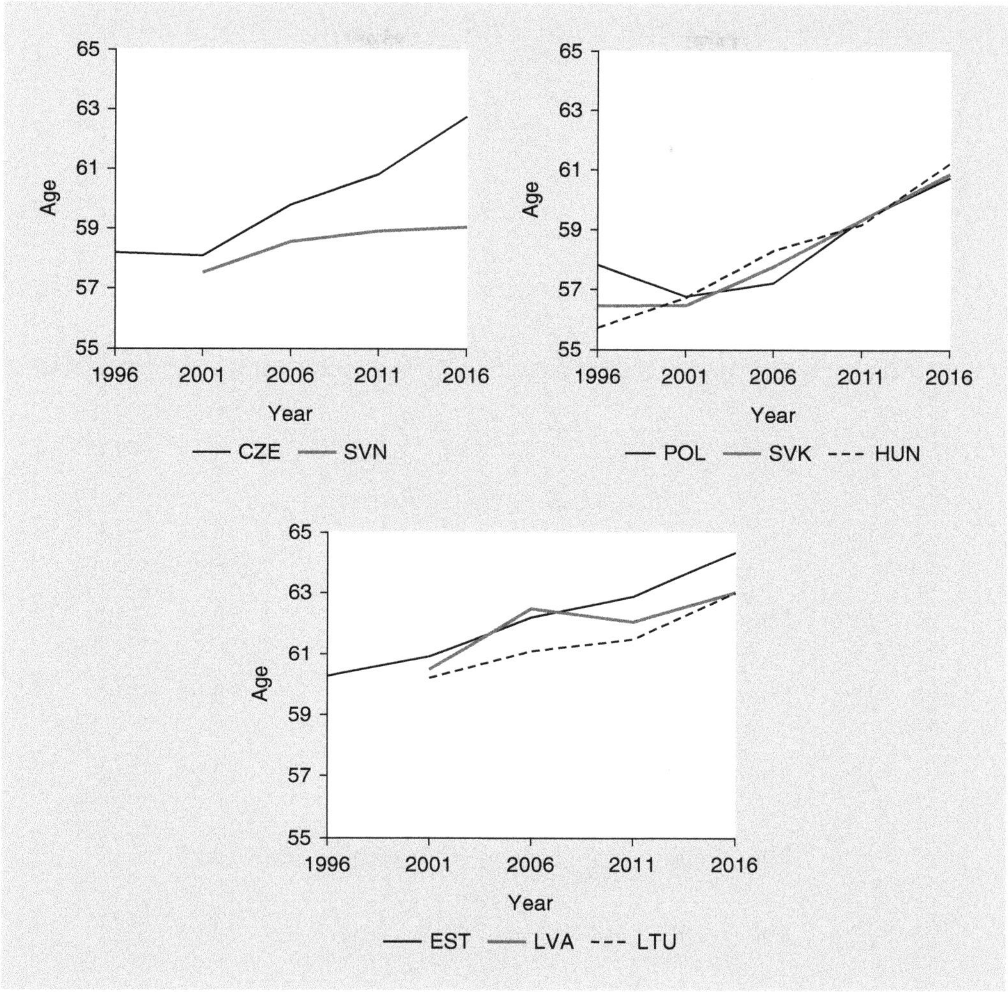

SOURCE: Original calculations based on OECD data on population and labor market participation.

NOTE: Country codes: CZE = Czech Republic; EST = Estonia; HUN = Hungary; LTU = Lithuania; LVA = Latvia; POL = Poland; SVK = Slovak Republic; SVN = Slovenia.

UNCHANGED LIFE EXPECTANCIES AT EXIT AGE

The estimated age distribution of people leaving the labor market can also be used as weights, this time not for exit ages but for life expectancies. The weighted average of life expectancies of people retiring at various ages can be used to estimate the duration of retirement (figure 16.2).[4] The estimates show that during the same period when the effective retirement age grew rapidly, life expectancies at retirement remained practically unchanged. In the five countries for which information is available for all five points in time, the average retirement duration was 20.1 years in 1996 and 20.3 years in 2016. This hides an increase in the beginning, between 1996 and 2001, to 20.9 years and a decline after 2011. For the region as a whole, data are available only from 2001 (2002 in Latvia).

FIGURE 16.2 **Expected duration of retirement in Central and Eastern Europe, 1996–2016**

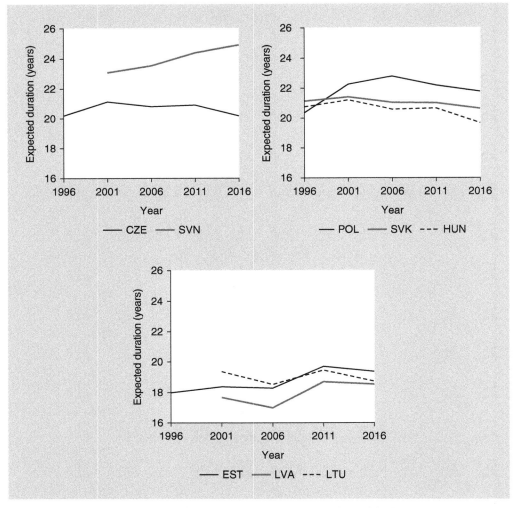

SOURCE: Original calculations based on OECD data on population and labor market participation.

NOTE: Country codes: CZE = Czech Republic; EST = Estonia; HUN = Hungary; LTU = Lithuania; LVA = Latvia; POL = Poland; SVK = Slovak Republic; SVN = Slovenia.

In 2001 the eight-country average was 20.6 years versus 20.5 years in 2016. Gains of growing life expectancies in older working ages were absorbed by the labor market.

IMPROVED EDUCATIONAL COMPOSITION OF NEW RETIREES

One reason for the ease with which the retirement of older working-age people could have been postponed is the rapid improvement in the educational composition of new retirees. Panel a of figure 16.3 shows how this process took place between the second part of the 1990s and the mid-2010s. Simple instead of population-weighted averages are used because the focus is institutional systems rather than populations. At the first timepoint for which data are presented by Eurostat, 1996–98, 46 percent of the 55–64-year-old age group had

FIGURE 16.3 **Composition of 55- to 64-year-olds in Central and Eastern Europe by highest level of education, actual values for 1996/1998–2016 and projections for 2026–46**

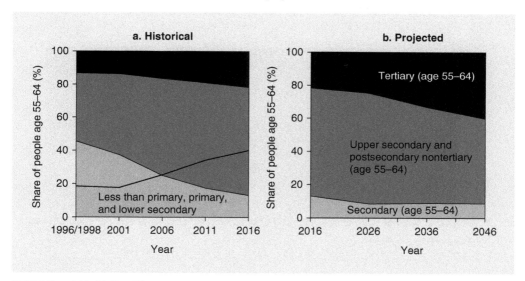

SOURCE: Eurostat (edat_lfse_03).

NOTE: Simple averages of period data. The first timepoint is 1996 for Slovenia, 1997 for Hungary and Poland, and 1998 for the Czech Republic, Estonia, Latvia, Lithuania, and the Slovak Republic. Educational composition of the 55–64-year-old age group in 2026, 2036, and 2046 is based on the actual educational composition in 2016 of the 45–54-year-old, 35–44-year-old, and 25–34-year-old age groups, respectively.

lower secondary education or less (code 0–2 by the International Standard Classification of Education, ISCED). This group contains those who had no education at all, or started but never finished primary school, or finished only that, as well as those who completed lower vocational school. By 2016 the rate of such people among the 55–64-year-old age group decreased to 13 percent. Over the same period the rate of upper secondary and postsecondary nontertiary degrees (ISCED 3–4) (that is, people holding more or less an equivalent of a *matura,* an *abitur,* or a *baccalauréat)* grew from 41 percent to 65 percent and the rate of tertiary degrees (ISCED 5+) nearly doubled, from 13 percent to 22 percent.

The figure makes a strong case for the connection between changing educational composition and higher exit age. Accordingly, people retired later because they were better educated than those who left the labor market two decades before. Especially important is the decrease in the share of the group with the lowest education. Recent retirees preserved better health up to a higher age and they possessed employable skills—so they could more easily stay longer in the labor market.

IMPROVED EDUCATIONAL COMPOSITION OF NEW RETIREES ESTABLISHED BY HUMAN CAPITAL INVESTMENTS DECADES BEFORE

The improvement in the average effective retirement age was preceded by investments in human capital many decades before (figure 16.4). Figure 16.4 is a leftward extension of figure 16.3, that is, back in time to the 1950s. Two curves are added to show how the share of selected levels of education of the retiring age groups (presented as shaded areas) looked when they were still young, in their twenties. Developments in the shaded areas

FIGURE 16.4 **Composition of 55- to 64-year-olds in Central and Eastern Europe by highest level of education, 1950–2010, and share of 20- to 29-year-olds by selected educational attainments, 1950–75**

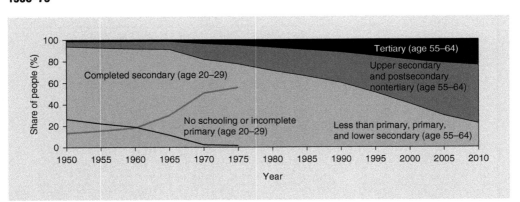

SOURCE: Original calculations based on Barro and Lee (2013) for 1955–65 and Lutz, Butz, and KC (2014) for 1970–2010.

NOTE: Simple averages of period data.

(as well as in panel a of figure 16.3) are mirrored by the two curves. In particular, the dashed line shows how the problem of no schooling or incomplete primary schooling almost disappeared during the quarter-century between 1950 and 1975 but especially after 1960. Its rate started at 26 percent of the then 20–29-year-old age group in 1950; it was still 19 percent in 1960 but dropped to 1 percent by 1975. People with no schooling or incomplete primary school are a subgroup of the ISCED 0–2 category shown in the shaded area. As mentioned before, the latter also includes those who completed primary or even a lower vocational school. The subgroup was nevertheless included to make the point that at the time the transitional crisis hit the CEE8 economies between 1990 and 1995, the group of older workers still included many who were unprepared for the skill-biased technological change the crisis brought forward. However, 10 or 15 years later such people were no longer among the new retirees.

In contrast, the share of people with completed secondary education almost quadrupled in the 20–29-year-old age bracket between 1950 and 1975. Among people in their twenties, twice as many did not complete primary school than those who finished secondary education in 1950. By 1975 the latter group reached 56 percent of the relevant population. In short, the effective retirement age could increase between the mid-1990s and the mid-2010s because the educational composition of the cohorts reaching retirement age improved, established by educational investments made in the 1960s and 1970s. The expansion of education produced a retirement-age premium many decades later.

ROOM TO RAISE THE EFFECTIVE RETIREMENT AGE GIVEN RECENT EDUCATIONAL INVESTMENT

Figure 16.4 extends panel a of figure 16.3 to the left, or back in time. Panel b of figure 16.3 makes a similar extension but this time to the right, to the future. The projection is based on observed educational attainment by age group in 2016 and an assumption that the achieved level will not change in the future. Accordingly, the composition of the 55–64-year-old age bracket by education in 2026 is supposed to be the age composition of the 45–54-year-old age group in 2016 and so on. The assumption of constant educational composition of an age group over time once the age group in question entered the labor market is conservative with respect to the point here. The educational composition usually increases during the active age of a cohort partly because a minority improve their educational level (whereas the individual level of highest education does not decrease) and partly because of education-specific mortality (survival rates of better-educated people are higher on average).

The projection shows a further decrease in the share of less-educated people (completing lower vocational school at most) from the current 13 percent to just less than 9 percent by the mid-2020s and stabilization beyond that point. The proportion of people with upper secondary education, whose spread among new retirees fed the increase of the exit age in the past decades, will peak in the mid-2020s and then start declining. However, this decrease will be more than compensated for by the growing share of tertiary-educated people. As above, panel a of figure 16.3 adds in the rate of people with a tertiary degree among the 25–34-year-old age group between the mid-1990s and 2016. It more than doubled, starting at 18 percent and reaching 40 percent, which will be mirrored in the educational composition of new retirees decades later. Recent investments in human capital can be expected to pay back with extended labor market careers in the future.

The analysis stops short of trying to predict how high the effective retirement age could grow in the future as a consequence of the recent expansion in human capital investments. That would require an explanatory model of the exit age, which is not presented here. Instead, table 16.1 shows how much the effective retirement age should grow by 2045 to keep life expectancies at exit age at the 2016 level.

On average an annual 1.7-month increase over three decades would keep retirement durations (that is, life expectancies) at the effective retirement age in 2045 at the 2016 level. This compares with the yearly 2.8-month increase between 2001 and 2016 actually achieved by the region. The regional average hides significant country variations. About one-half of the speed or even less of the past 15 years would be enough in the Czech Republic, Estonia, Poland, and the Slovak Republic; less than two-thirds is enough in Hungary; and about the same growth should continue in Latvia and Lithuania. Only in Slovenia should the growth of the effective retirement age accelerate.

TABLE 16.1 **Increase in effective retirement age required to keep retirement duration in 2045 at the 2016 level**

	CZE	EST	HUN	LTU	LVA	POL	SVN	SVK
Retirement duration (years), 2016	20.2	19.4	19.7	18.7	18.5	21.8	24.9	20.6
Effective retirement age, 2016	62.8	64.3	61.2	63.0	63.0	60.8	59.1	60.9
Required effective retirement age, 2045	66.5	67.7	66.4	68.0	67.8	64.9	62.2	65.5
Required increase in years	3.7	3.3	5.2	4.9	4.7	4.2	3.1	4.6
Months per year	1.5	1.4	2.1	2.0	2.0	1.7	1.3	1.9
Growth in months per year, 2001–2016	3.7	2.7	3.6	2.3	2.0	3.2	1.2	3.5

SOURCE: Original calculation based on Eurostat population projections (proj_15npms and proj_15nalexp).

NOTE: Country codes: CZE = Czech Republic; EST = Estonial; HUN = Hungary; LTU = Lithuania; LVA = Latvia; POL = Poland; SVK = Slovak Republic; SVN = Slovenia.

Robustness of the Results

The results are comparable to similar calculations by the OECD and Eurostat. Both institutions publish figures on effective retirement ages and length of working lives as well as expected retirement duration (Eurostat 2017; OECD 2017). Regular reports, such as the OECD's *Pensions at a Glance* series and the European Union's *Pension Adequacy Reports*, contain analyses similar to those presented above. This section briefly discusses (a) a methodological issue (the use of static instead of dynamic estimation of the effective retirement age) that distinguishes this chapter's results from those of the above institutions, and (b) the use of period instead of cohort life expectancies in the calculation of expected retirement duration.

STATIC ESTIMATION OF THE EFFECTIVE RETIREMENT AGE

The Latulippe (1996) formula, described in the text and endnotes, is applied to estimate the effective retirement age and the expected duration of retirement. The method is static in that the estimation is based on period values, meaning each entry in the time series is based on cross-sectional age profiles of participation rates. Scherer (2002) points out that a static indicator like Latulippe's is misleading because it mixes up genuine labor market trends with changing labor force composition. He uses demographic analogies, such as life expectancy or the reproduction rate, to prove his point. For instance, the reproduction rate describes period fertility, which is not informative about the expected completed fertility of cohorts currently in childbearing age.[5] Its variation indicates changes in cohort fertility as well as changes in timing of births. In the same vein, the actual Latulippe estimate of the effective exit age is exposed to developments other than retirement, such as labor market participation growing instead of decreasing by age in older working ages, which is not infrequent among women in some countries. Also, period fertility condenses information about 35 female cohorts whose lifetime fertility behavior may well prove to be very different in the end, for example, because of different labor market activities of the cohorts involved. Such a composition effect also distorts the Latulippe estimate because retirement behavior depends on, among other factors, the education of cohorts directly through skills and employability and indirectly through health status. Instead, based on recommendations by Scherer (2002), the OECD and Eurostat publish dynamic estimates of the effective retirement age, which are based on cohort activity measured at two consecutive timepoints (Keese 2012; Eurostat 2017; OECD 2017).[6]

Nevertheless, the static measure is used here for two reasons. First, the argument herein directly applies the changing composition of retirees—as the educational composition of the age group close to retirement changes so does the effective retirement age. A dynamic measure would filter out the very effect sought, as demonstrated by figure 16A.1 in annex 16A, which compares static and dynamic indicators by country and calendar year. In most cases the linear trend fitted to the dynamic time series of the OECD is flatter than the trend of the static one. This also suggests that a regression analysis of a time series of period measures of the exit age would probably find education an important explanatory variable.

The other reason for not working with the dynamic indicator is its volatility and the occasional difficulty of its interpretation. As figure 16A.1 shows, some developments are indeed hard to read in terms of effective retirement age, such as a 6.5-year increase in the course of only six years between 2003 and 2009 in Estonia (which in fact hides even more hectic but asynchronous shifts by gender, such as an 8.4-year increase in five years between 2005 and 2009 among men and a 7.5-year increase in an even shorter four-year period between 2001 and 2006 among women). The Estonian and the Latvian panels show similarly sharp decreases in the effective exit age. This is mostly due to the data source (Vogler-Ludwig and Düll 2008). The dynamic indicator is based on broadly independent samples of repeated labor force surveys, which are not designed for such direct time comparisons. The confidence interval around single-year age groups created from the sample is too large; and the five-year interval for comparison is too long in such surveys. In addition, the OECD dynamic indicator is more exposed to migration, especially temporary migration, than the static indicator (Keese 2012). Participation rates are gained from different types of data sources: population data come from censuses and activity data are from surveys. Surveys are conducted with higher frequency and reflect rapid changes in reality that are more difficult to follow by administrative population data that have no proper input on migration. This could be one reason why the curves of the Central European countries of figure 16A.1 are less hectic than those of the three Baltic states, which were more affected by migration during the period discussed here.

PERIOD ESTIMATES FOR LIFE EXPECTANCIES AT THE EFFECTIVE RETIREMENT AGE

The Latulippe (1996) measure for retirement duration (that is, life expectancy at the effective retirement age) is based on period figures. In this respect the static method does not differ from similar estimates by the OECD and Eurostat. As in the name, period life expectancy sums up information of one period of time, usually a year. It gives the expected remaining average lifetime of an age group as if its future mortality patterns over the years ahead are a perfect replica of mortality patterns of older age groups in the base year. In the age of falling mortality, such an approach systematically underestimates cohort life expectancies. Goldstein and Wachter (2006) find that in industrial countries period estimates of life expectancy at birth follow cohort estimates with a lag of 40–50 years: today's cross-sectional values are about the same as the cohort values were a half-century ago. In another study, period life expectancies at birth are 8–15 years shorter than cohort life expectancies in Australia, the United Kingdom, the United States, Portugal, and Spain; and even at age 65 the difference remains 2–4 years (Ayuso, Bravo, and Holzmann 2018).

Similar results are found here by comparing period and cohort life expectancies[7] at the effective retirement age (see the dashed and dotted lines, respectively, in figure 16.5) in the CEE8 countries. Cohort life expectancies are consistently higher by an average margin of 3.3 years, varying between the range of 2 and 4 years across countries, or 10–25 percent of the period values.

The deviation of cohort and period life expectancies has serious repercussions for the pension system. Since retirement is usually an absorbing state from which there is rarely a way back to the labor market, life expectancy at retirement can be considered the average duration of retirement, as assumed throughout this chapter. If retirement duration is based on period mortality data and consequently underestimated by 2–4 years, financial defined contribution (FDC) schemes collapse. Nonfinancial defined contribution (NDC) schemes, being based on the pay-as-you-go principle, would not literally go bankrupt but become unsustainable and require major reform at the cost of future pensioners. Ayuso, Bravo, and Holzmann (2018) find that a benefit formula based on period instead of cohort life expectancies can transfer as much as 30 percent of the pension wealth of the working-age population to current pensioners as an implicit subsidy.

However, devastating as it could be in a benefit formula, the period-cohort discrepancy does not directly affect this chapter's conclusions. The findings do not

FIGURE 16.5 **Period and cohort estimations for the expected duration of retirement in Central and Eastern Europe, 1996–2014**

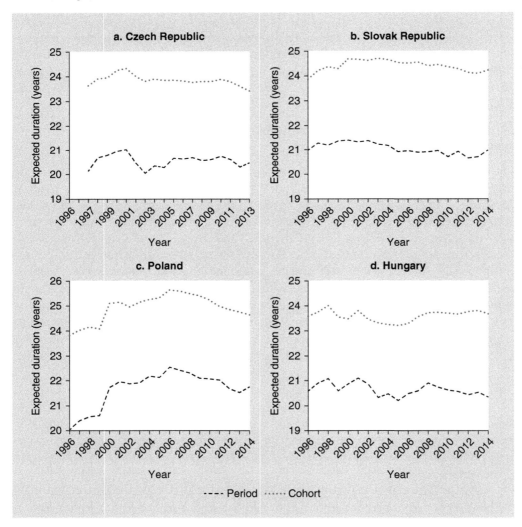

(continued next page)

FIGURE 16.5 **Period and cohort estimations for the expected duration of retirement in Central and Eastern Europe, 1996–2014 (continued)**

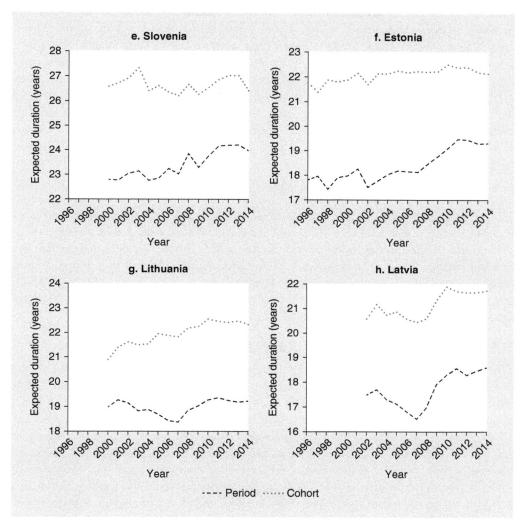

SOURCE: Period estimates: Eurostat (demo_mlexpec); Cohort estimates: original calculations based on mortality rates of the Eurostat population projection (proj_15naasmr).

NOTE: The ranges captured by the vertical axes are different but the scales are the same so the country panels can be directly compared.

include reference to the financial sustainability of the current length of retirement durations (an underestimation of this length would then be crucial, indeed), but to its relative invariability. This chapter does not assert that the CEE8 pension systems are sustainable because life expectancy at retirement is k years. Rather, it indicates that because life expectancies at the effective retirement age have not grown, falling mortality did not contribute to sustainability problems if there were any. It is not the difference between period and cohort estimates that affects these conclusions but potential changes in the difference. The use of period estimates would be misleading only if the gap between the results of the two types of mortality analyses diverged. If the gap is constant or grows narrower, these conclusions would remain unaffected or prove to be even stronger.

The empirical relationship between time series of period and cohort measures is not obvious. On a sample of industrial countries, Goldstein and Wachter (2006) find that although the lag with which period life expectancy follows cohort life expectancy grew as mortality fell, the actual gap between the two measures first grew and then declined. As the country panels of figure 16.5 show, the gap remained the same or even narrowed in most countries of the CEE8 region through the two decades between 1996 and 2014. The only place where the scissors somewhat opened is Lithuania.

A Wider Context

This section offers a wider context to the findings. It first shows that in most old member states of the European Union (EU), similar developments took place with growing effective retirement age and stagnating or even declining life expectancies. It then demonstrates how the results, based on the method of characteristic ages instead of the widely used predetermined demarcation ages, rewrite conventional wisdom on the effects of falling mortality. In addition, the outcome of the calculations is embedded in related research on the causes and effects of falling mortality.

THE CEE8 REGION VIS-À-VIS THE OLD MEMBER STATES OF THE EU

The chapter has shown that so far, the CEE8 countries were successful in fending off the potential threat of declining mortality in older ages on the pension system by postponing retirement from the labor market. In this respect the region is not unique, although it has done better than some other countries in Europe. Figures 16.6 and 16.7 show how the 15 old member states of the EU (EU15 hereafter) scored in terms of effective retirement age. For convenience the countries are split into three groups: quick improvers (2.7-month increase or more per year of the effective retirement age over the period 2001–16); average responders (within the range of a 1.8–2.3-month increase per year); and laggards (less than a 1.2-month increase, including two countries, Portugal and Greece, where the effective retirement age fell).[8] Figure 16.7 presents life expectancies at the effective retirement age, which almost perfectly mirror developments in the exit age: countries that produced rapid increases in the effective retirement age saw receding life expectancies at retirement, 0.6 months per year or more; countries with average exit age increments had stagnating life expectancies; and in the group of laggards life expectancies at the exit age increased. All in all, the expected retirement duration stagnated in the EU15, too, with an annual increase of about five days per year between 2001 and 2016 (versus a two-day decrease in the CEE8 region).

Against this background the CEE8 countries are not extraordinary. They increased their effective retirement age somewhat faster than the EU15 average but not as fast as the frontrunners of that group. Also, their stagnating or indeed slowly receding retirement duration decreased more rapidly than in the EU15 as a whole but lagged behind the drop in the quickly improving countries, especially the Netherlands.

The actual values of the ages of exiting the labor market make the frequently used indicator of the proportion of the 65-year-old and older population among adults an

FIGURE 16.6 **Average age of workers exiting labor market in pre-2004 EU member states, 2001–16**

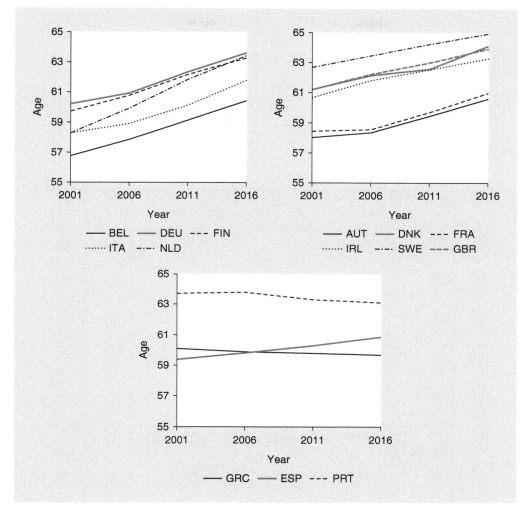

SOURCE: Original calculations based on OECD data on population and labor market participation.
NOTE: AUT = Austria; BEL = Belgium; DEU = Germany; DNK = Denmark; ESP = Spain; FIN = Finland; FRA = France;
GBR = United Kingdom; GRC = Greece; IRL = Ireland; ITA = Italy; NLD = Netherlands; PRT = Portugal; SWE = Sweden.
Luxembourg is not included.

unreliable proxy for measuring the effects of the aging process on the pension system. More importantly, their tendency to change over time renders any predetermined demarcation age, should it be 60, 65, or 70 years, dubious in cross-country comparisons as well as in longitudinal analyses.

PREDETERMINED DEMARCATION AGES VERSUS CHARACTERISTIC AGES

Instead of referring to old-age dependency ratios, which are based on predetermined demarcation ages between working age and old age, table 16.1 applies a measure based on the length of expected retirement duration as a fixed timespan. The analysis looks for the effective retirement ages carved out by this measure assuming further drops in mortality. In light of growing life

FIGURE 16.7 Expected duration of retirement in the pre-2004 EU member states, 2001–16

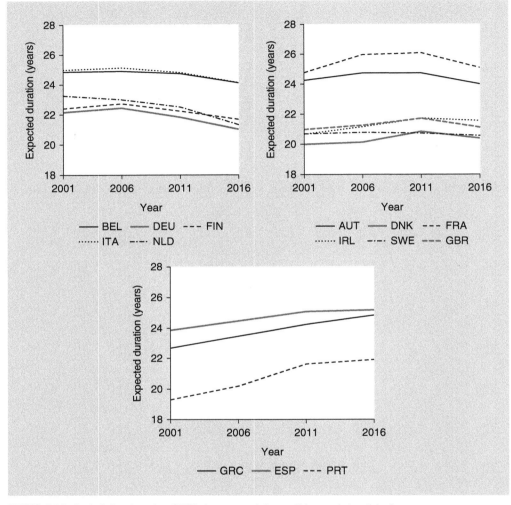

SOURCE: Original calculations based on OECD data on population and labor market participation.

NOTE: EU = European Union. Country codes: AUT = Austria; BEL = Belgium; DEU = Germany; DNK = Denmark; ESP = Spain; FIN = Finland; FRA = France; GBR = United Kingdom; GRC = Greece; IRL = Ireland; ITA = Italy; NLD = Netherlands; PRT = Portugal; SWE = Sweden. Luxembourg is not included.

expectancy among the old, the effective retirement age should be 4.2 years higher on average in the CEE8 region in 2045 to keep retirement duration constant at the 2016 level. The measure is based on the concept of characteristic age (Sanderson and Scherbov 2010, 2017), which is a general framework translating various characteristics of people to years of age. Such characteristics can vary over a wide range of frequently used measures of population aging, including (a) variants of remaining life expectancy, such as prospective old-age thresholds for the entire population or various social groups (the average age of a social group at which remaining life expectancy is a given threshold of years, usually 15 years) or the prospective median age (the age of a person in a population who sees as many people with higher and as many people with lower life expectancy than his or her own); (b) survival probabilities, such as the probability of surviving the next five years; or (c) health conditions of the population as a whole (such as the proportion of self-reported good or bad health) or that of various social groups (such as average hand-grip strength). The translation procedure requires two characteristic schedules. Average chronological ages of various social groups in a fixed age-specific characteristic schedule are related to chronological ages, called alpha ages, in another, variable characteristic schedule. With some simplification, this remapping creates iso-age contours by selecting the age equivalents of chronological ages in the variable characteristic schedule. Fixed schedules can be as different as some demographic characteristic of a reference group, such as one of the two sexes, a nation, a group with a given level of education, or a group in a given year; or a preset remaining life expectancy (such as a country-specific life expectancy at the average effective retirement age, as in this chapter). Variable schedules can be cross-country differences, changes over time, differences by age within one social group, or variation by the level of education.

The measure applied here, life expectancy at retirement as the fixed characteristic schedule, is a variant of the prospective age introduced by Sanderson and Scherbov (2013), except the country-specific retirement duration is used instead of a preset length of time, 15 years. It is used as a reference point not because it is a necessary or a sufficient condition of fiscal sustainability but for its salience in measuring the impact of falling mortality in older ages on the pension system. Nevertheless, it has a policy value, too. Linking the standard pensionable age to life expectancy is an increasingly frequent practice in the EU. Cyprus, Denmark, Finland, Italy, the Netherlands, Portugal, and the United Kingdom all apply it; in the CEE8 region the Slovak Republic has introduced it and the Czech Republic will follow suit in the future.[9] However, not all arrangements are designed to keep retirement duration constant. The Danish solution is (although the standard retirement age is linked to life expectancy at age 60, not at the effective retirement age), but Finland's incorporation of demographic change in the pension regulation will result in the standard pensionable age absorbing about two-thirds of the improvements in life expectancy (at age 62), keeping the proportion of retired and active careers, not the retirement duration, more or less constant (Lassila, Määttänen, and Valkonen 2014).

In fact, constant proportions of the active and retired sections of the life cycle are potentially more intergenerationally fair than the constant length of retirement if life expectancies are growing. Indeed, the proportion of life sections is the key issue of research on budgetary consequences of population aging. If declining mortality will extend the inactive period of life because of misguided policies or bad health or unemployability of older cohorts, aging will render the interage transfer system, and within that pensions, unsustainable at the cost of the future old. If instead the length of the healthy and productive period of life keeps up with longer life expectancies, population aging will not threaten budgetary balance.

POPULATION AGING AND THE PROPORTION OF ACTIVE AND INACTIVE LIFE-CYCLE SECTIONS

This chapter's analysis finds that falling mortality has not proved harmful for the CEE8 region's pension systems in the past 15 years and links this to past investments in human capital. This result fits well with other researchers' findings. As for the more general relationship, the positive effect of education on mortality (that is, better education decreases mortality and leads to longer lives), there seems to be a general consensus in the literature.

In some of the CEE8 countries the connection is particularly strong, as demonstrated in a simple cross-sectional design (table 16.2). Life expectancies at birth and at

TABLE 16.2 **Life expectancies at birth and at the average effective age of retirement by level of education in selected Central and Eastern European countries, 2016**

	CZE	EST	HUN	POL	SVK	SVN
At birth						
Less than primary, primary, and lower secondary (levels 0–2)	74.6	72.6	70.7	72.3	69.9	79.0
Upper secondary and postsecondary nontertiary (levels 3–4)	79.3	77.4	77.6	77.6	77.5	81.1
Tertiary (levels 5–8)	80.4	80.9	80.2	82.3	80.8	83.7
Difference between highest and lowest as % of lowest	*8*	*11*	*13*	*14*	*16*	*6*
At average effective retirement age						
Less than primary, primary, and lower secondary (levels 0–2)	19.4	18.5	17.2	20.9	18.8	24.2
Upper secondary and postsecondary nontertiary (levels 3–4)	20.0	18.9	20.5	21.4	20.7	24.7
Tertiary (levels 5–8)	20.3	20.1	21.2	23.7	22.2	26.1
Difference between highest and lowest as % of lowest	*5*	*9*	*23*	*13*	*18*	*8*

SOURCE: Original calculation based on Eurostat data (demo_mlexpecedu).

NOTE: Country codes: CZE = Czech Republic; EST = Estonia; HUN = Hungary; POL = Poland; SVK = Slovak Republic; SVN = Slovenia.

the effective retirement age are presented for the countries for which data are available. In the Slovak Republic, mortality rates draw a life expectancy of less than 70 years for a person with lower secondary education or less, 16 percent shorter than someone with a tertiary degree. Such differences, or even more (in Hungary as much as 23 percent), can be observed at the effective retirement age.

However, no consensus exists about whether the effect of education on mortality is causal or if it could be explained with other factors. Several studies argue that income is the primary determinant of current mortality trends (Bloom and Canning 2007; Mackenbach and Looman 2013; Preston 1975). Based on this logic, education is associated with health mostly because richer people can afford both better life conditions and health care and attain higher education. Another stream of research emphasizes the causal effect of education on mortality (Baker et al. 2011; Lutz and Skirbekk 2014). Lutz and Kebede (2018) even state that education could be more important in understanding mortality than the health care system. Quasi-experimental studies are also inconclusive. Although most demonstrate that education indeed has a causal effect on mortality (Gathmann, Jürges, and Reinhold 2012; Lager and Torssander 2012; Lleras-Muney 2005; Silles 2009), some find no significant effect (Albouy and Lequien 2009; Clark and Royer 2010). Despite the conflicting results, most studies agree that education helps individuals access resources (such as better life conditions and health care systems) or gain information about how to follow a healthier lifestyle (Caselli et al. 2014). Lutz and Kebede (2018) emphasize that the healthier lifestyle of more educated people is the reason for their lower mortality.

As for the more specific relationship between education and timing of retirement, the evidence is scarcer, although the hypothesis outlined in this chapter has been tested before and found support. Several researchers argue that higher retirement age is associated with education expansion (Loichinger and Weber 2016; Rehkopf, Adler, and Rowe 2016; Schirle 2008). This is due to higher work capacity, which makes more highly educated people more competitive in the labor market even in higher ages than their less educated peers (Boissonneault 2018; Monteiro, Ilmarinen, and Filho 2006), although Coile, Milligan, and Wise (2017) can support employability increasing with education only among women. The gap in work capacity between education groups can be mostly attributed to the fact that more highly educated people have better health, better work conditions, and less physically demanding jobs (Boissonneault 2018; Freedman and Martin 1999; Monteiro, Ilmarinen, and Filho 2006). However, no study establishes a causal relationship between education expansion and effective retirement age or working-life expectancy by using experimental or quasi-experimental design. Nevertheless, the association between having higher education and working longer is rather consistent across observational studies, which apply different sets of control variables in various countries.

Finally, another stream of research on the consequences of declining mortality on the proportions of life sections is the literature on healthy versus unhealthy aging: whether the healthy or the unhealthy periods of life will grow faster and whether the people who live longer remain healthy enough to work in the labor market. The first scenario, when healthy life expectancy follows life expectancy, is called compression of morbidity (Fries 1980); the second scenario is often referred to as the relative expansion of morbidity (Robine and Mathers 1993). Empirical research on this topic has produced mixed evidence so far. The results mostly depend on the choice of health measure applied (Ahacic et al. 2007; Parker and Thorslund 2007). Severe disability measures are found improving most of the time (Christensen et al. 2009), but the incidence of chronic disease and functional impairments often seems to be increasing (Chatterji et al. 2015; Crimmins and Beltrán-Sánchez 2010; Parker and Thorslund 2007). Also, results differ across countries. The review by Chatterji et al. (2015) finds that the compression of morbidity hypothesis is supported in high-income countries, which provide good-quality data on disability or impairment. In contrast, the paper by Salomon et al. (2012) on multimorbidities concludes that the number of unhealthy years has increased in most countries, which supports the expansion of morbidity hypothesis.

Concluding this short review of related research, there seems to be general support for the view that the demarcation line between active age and old age is moving and can be affected by policies such as health care and education. However, no general consensus exists on whether the line can be shifted fast enough to keep the proportion of active and retired sections of the life cycle unchanged.

Limitations

This chapter shows that the effective retirement age rose in the past decades in the CEE8 countries and connects it with the expansion of secondary education starting in the 1960s. The relationship between human capital investments and retirement is suggestive and supported by the available evidence. Yet reasons for concern arise even if retirement can be further postponed in the future. This section identifies three such issues. First, even if the average exit age increased given the recent expansion in tertiary education, an uncomfortably

TABLE 16.3 **Educational composition of 25- to 34-year-olds in Central and Eastern Europe, 2017**

	CZE	EST	LVA	LTU	HUN	POL	SVK	SVN
Less than primary, primary, and lower secondary	6	13	12	6	14	6	9	6
Upper secondary and postsecondary nontertiary	60	44	46	39	56	51	56	50
Tertiary	34	43	42	56	30	44	35	45

SOURCE: Eurostat (edat_lfse_03).

NOTE: Country codes: CZE = Czech Republic; EST = Estonia; HUN = Hungary; LTU = Lithuania; LVA = Latvia; POL = Poland; SVK = Slovak Republic; SVN: Slovenia.

wide section of the working-age population still has only a basic education. Second, the relationship between higher effective retirement age and past investments in human capital, convincing as it is, is not a one-way connection. The section shows that improving education can coincide with falling exit age, too. Finally, low contribution density, that is, the extent of tax evasion, is still a threat to future old-age income even if people can stay in the labor market longer.

AT THE LOWER END OF THE EDUCATIONAL HIERARCHY

To make the first point, table 16.3 presents the educational composition of the 25–34-year-old age group in the CEE8 region in 2017. Sizable segments of people still at the beginning of their labor market career, and 30–40 years from retirement, have only a lower vocational school education at most, which may prove insufficient to keep them working longer years. The Czech, Lithuanian, Polish, and Slovenian rates are among the lowest in the EU, but the Estonian, Latvian, and Hungarian rates (respectively, 13 percent, 12 percent, and 14 percent) are relatively high, even if such levels are still below the EU average (16 percent), which is pushed up by the Spanish, Maltese, and Portuguese rates (greater than 30 percent).

WHEN THE EFFECTIVE RETIREMENT AGE FALLS DESPITE IMPROVING EDUCATION

Another reason for caution is that the positive effect of improving education on the effective retirement age is far from automatic. So far, the focus has been limited to the past one or two decades. However, even if recent increases in the exit age can be traced back to past expansions in education, previous decreasing periods of the exit age are not associated with downward changes in the education level. This is illustrated using French data given that no sufficiently long time series is available for the countries of the CEE8 region. As figure 16.8 shows, between 2000 and 2015 France went through a development similar to that of the CEE8 countries. The educational composition of the 55–64-year-old age group changed for the better and the effective retirement age grew by 2.5 years over 15 years. However, the figure also reveals educational improvements among older working-age people between 1970 and 2000 (the rate of people with secondary education quintupled in the 55–64-year-old age group during these years), and yet the effective retirement age decreased by 5.6 years over this period. Clearly, human capital investment is not a

FIGURE 16.8 **Composition of 55- to 64-year-olds in France by highest level of education and effective retirement age, 1970–2015**

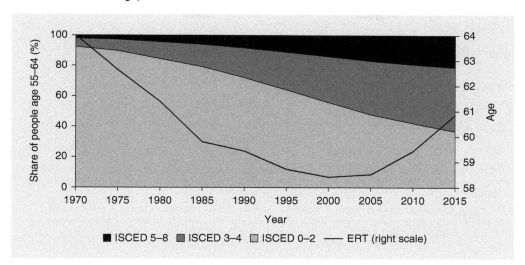

SOURCES: Education: Lutz, Butz, and KC (2014); Effective retirement age: original calculations based on OECD data on population and labor market participation.

NOTE: ISCED codes: 0–2 = lower secondary education or less; 3–4 = upper secondary and postsecondary nontertiary; 5–8 = tertiary; ERT = effective retirement age.

sufficient condition for postponing retirement. Misguided practices, such as the open-gate pension policies of the 1970s, inspired by the false expectation that the retirement of older workers would create employment opportunities for the young, cut the effective retirement age while the educational level of the relevant age groups kept increasing.

The CEE8 region is not immune to such policies, which could offer short-term political gains but are costly and difficult to reverse. Poland cut the standard pensionable age in 2016, reversing its gradual increase as foreseen by previous legislation. The new measure will increase retirement duration (European Union 2018, 109). Hungary introduced a service length–dependent component to its retirement process, which is otherwise solely based on age. Since 2011 women have been allowed to retire without restrictions if they collect 40 service years (which are not necessarily contributory). The provision caused the effective retirement age of women to deviate from that of men, breaking a convergence process. More importantly, both the Polish and the Hungarian measures will reduce future benefits despite the institutional differences between the two pension systems. Poland operates an NDC system and the benefit formula takes into account life expectancies at the age of retirement, so a lower pensionable age cuts benefits from the start. In the Hungarian defined benefit scheme, the consequences are not felt at entry to retirement. However, since indexation is price based, the longer the benefit duration the wider the gap between real wages and pensions. Because the preferential retirement applies only to women, whose pensioner career is longer on average, the service length–based retirement option will increase the poverty risk in old age and widen the pension gender gap.

TABLE 16.4 **Wage coverage in selected Central and Eastern European countries, 2016**

	CZE	LVA	LTU	HUN	SVK	SVN
Contribution rate (%)	6.5+21.5	23.86	3+23.3	10+21	4+14	15.5+8.85
Contribution ceiling	4 times AW	None	None	None	5 times AW	None
Pension contributions (€ millions)	12,534	1,432	2,625	9,858	3,999	3,293
Covered wage bill (€ millions)	44,765	6,004	9,980	31,345	22,214	13,522
Wages and salaries (€ millions)	55,230	10,160	13,258	41,723	25,869	17,204
Wage coverage (%)	81	59	75	75	86	79

SOURCES: Contribution rates: MISSOC (Mutual Information System on Social Protection); Pension contributions: HUN: Central Administration of National Pension Insurance, rest: Eurostat (gov_10a_taxag); Wages and salaries: HUN: Central Statistical Office national accounts, rest: Eurostat (nasa_10_nf_tr).

NOTE: AW = average wage; Covered wage bill = pension contributions/contribution rate; Wage coverage = covered wage bill/wages and salaries. Country codes: CZE = Czech Republic; HUN = Hungary; LTU = Lithuania; LVA = Latvia; SVK = Slovak Republic; SVN = Slovenia.

CONTRIBUTION DENSITY

Another threat to pension adequacy in the CEE8 region is low contribution density (Holzmann, Robalino, and Winkler 2018). Even if the expansion of education will allow people to work longer, sufficient old-age income will not be guaranteed unless they contribute to social security. Table 16.4 presents calculations of an indicator of contribution density—wage coverage—which is the rate of the covered wage bill and the actual wage bill. The covered wage bill is the actual amount of contributions collected over the official contribution rates and it shows how large the total wage bill would be if every cent of labor income paid contributions according to rules.[10] Wage coverage is an indicator of the reach of the pension administration to the taxable labor income of workers. The figures illustrate the difficulties administrations face: the Slovak Republic cannot tax about 15 percent of the wage bill; the Czech Republic and Slovenia about 20 percent; Hungary and Lithuania 25 percent; and Latvia as much as 40 percent (up from 20 percent in 2010).

In some cases, tax evasion means complete informality in transactions, which generate no eligibilities at all. In other cases, part of the wage (most often the mandatory minimum wage) is taxed, while the rest is informal. Long-term consequences for old-age income depend on the distribution of such informal arrangements among workers. If labor market careers are clearly distinguishable by spells of informality, and tax evasion is limited to cohorts, industries, or workers with poor education, poverty and inequalities in old age will be a real threat in these economies.[11]

Conclusions

This chapter shows that in the eight countries of Central and Eastern Europe, the effective retirement age (the average age of labor market exit) grew rapidly between 2001 and 2016, from 58.4 years to 61.9 years. The speed was more than three months per year on average in the the Czech Republic, Hungary, Poland, and the Slovak Republic;

between two and three months per year in Estonia, Latvia, and Lithuania (starting from a higher base in all three Baltic republics); and somewhat faster than one month per year in Slovenia. In the region as a whole, the increment was 2.8 months per year, or 7.1 days per month, or 5.6 hours per calendar day. Every day an average worker got closer to the effective retirement age by only 18.4 hours, instead of 24, because the effective retirement age was moving.

Retirement was so successfully postponed that in most observed countries life expectancies at the effective retirement age stagnated or even decreased. In 2001 the average life expectancy at the effective retirement age was 20.6 years; in 2016 it was 20.5 years. More or less mirroring developments of the exit age, it slightly decreased in the four Visegrad countries and in Lithuania, and it grew a little in Estonia, Latvia, and Slovenia. The effects of falling mortality were absorbed by the labor market, not the pension system. People could stay longer in the labor market as they stayed alive longer.

One possible reason for such a development is a replacement process. The cohorts in the age of retirement, the 55–64-year-old age bracket, were better educated in 2016 than were those who reached that age in 2001, let alone the years before. The rate of those who had lower vocational school as their highest level of education was nearly trisected (from 37 percent to 13 percent); the share of people with secondary education (holding more or less an equivalent of a *matura*, an *abitur*, or a *baccalauréat*) reached about two-thirds by 2016 (from 41 percent in 1996–98 and 49 percent in 2001). The wave of the expansion of secondary education of the 1960s and 1970s has reached the pension system. The CEE8 region invested in human capital and its pay-as-you-go schemes benefited decades later.

As a next step, the analysis fixes life expectancies at the effective retirement age at the 2016 level, looks for the effective retirement ages characterized by such life expectancies three decades later, and finds that those who will still have 20.5 years left will be 66.1 years old in 2045. In terms of life expectancies at the current effective retirement age, 66.1 will be the new 61.9. This gives reasons for optimism. Whereas in the course of 15 years between 2001 and 2016 the effective retirement age grew by 3.5 years across the region, it should increase only somewhat more, 4.2 years, in practically twice as many years between 2016 and 2045. In light of the expectable consequences of the rapid expansion of tertiary education, keeping life expectancies unchanged at the effective retirement age does not seem unattainable.

Falling mortality does not have to undermine the stability of the pension system if working-life expectancies grow, and the latter can be extended if older workers are better trained and more easily employable. Yet more education is not necessarily sufficient. Using French time series data that were long enough to cover the 1970s and 1980s, the chapter finds that even in times of improvement in the level of education of older working-age cohorts the effective retirement age could fall. The recent derailment of the process of raising the pensionable age in Poland and to some extent and indirectly in Hungary is menacing, with the prospect of upsetting the proportion of active and retired sections of the life cycle. Also, if the working life of better-educated cohorts is extended but the region's widespread tax evasion and tax avoidance are not contained, the CEE8's pension schemes will be ineffective in preventing old-age poverty in the future.

ANNEX 16A

FIGURE 16A.1 **Dynamic and static estimates of the time series of the effective retirement age in Central and Eastern Europe**

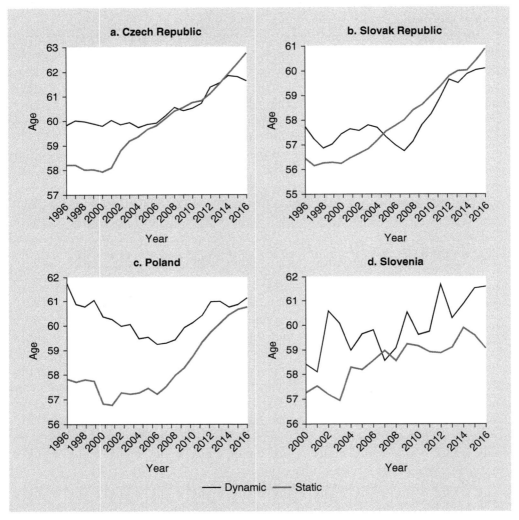

(continued next page)

FIGURE 16A.1 **Dynamic and static estimates of the time series of the effective retirement age in Central and Eastern Europe (continued)**

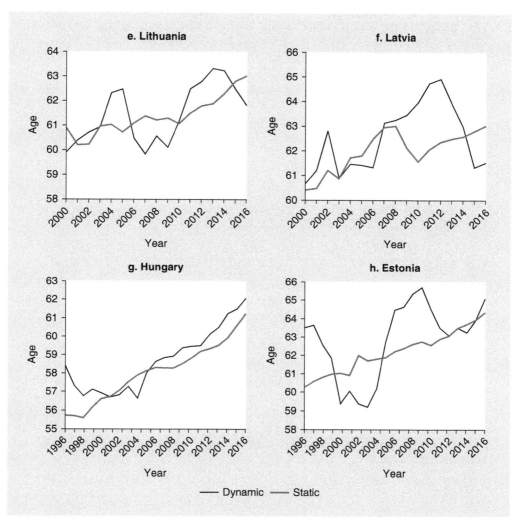

SOURCE: Dynamic estimates are original calculations based on gender-specific dynamic OECD estimates (http://www .oecd.org/els/emp/average-effective-age-of-retirement.htm) by applying gender- and age-specific population weights. The calculation of static estimates is described in the body text.

NOTE: Time series start in 1996 in the Czech Republic, Estonia, Hungary, Poland, and the Slovak Republic but in 2000 in Latvia, Lithuania, and Slovenia because of lack of data. The age span of the vertical axis is six years for all countries except Hungary and Estonia, for which it is eight years.

Notes

1. Population-weighted regional averages based on Eurostat's baseline population projection.

2. The Latulippe (1996) formula calculates the number of retirees by age group from period differences in participation weighted by population data. The estimated number of new retirees then serves as a weight for the age of the age group in the weighted average exit age. To assign a single age to a five-year age group, the formula applies the assumptions of identical cohort sizes (within an age group) and a linearly decreasing participation rate (also within an age group). This makes members of a single-year cohort who leave the labor market in the next five years do so at a steady pace, and it also makes the distribution of the exit age within an age group symmetric and centered around the lower age limit of the next age group. Accordingly, the average exit age is given by the following formula:

$$\overline{RA} = \frac{0.5 \times {}_5R_{40,44}^z \times 47,5 + \sum_{x=45,50...}^{75} {}_5R_{x,x+4}^z \times (x+5)}{0.5 \times {}_5R_{40,44}^z + \sum_{x=45,50...}^{75} {}_5R_{x,x+4}^z}$$

The function ${}_5R_{x,x+4}^z$ represents the number of people in year z of a given age group, x to $x+4$, expected to retire within the next five years. ${}_5R_{x,x+4}^z$ equals $(A_{x,x+4}^z - A_{x+5,x+9}^z) \times P_{x,x+4}^z$, where $P_{x,x+4}^z$ is the number of individuals of cohort x to $x+4$ alive in calendar year z, and $A_{x,x+4}^z$ is the average participation rate in cohort x to $x+4$ in calendar year z. Retiring 40–44-year-olds are assumed to retire at age 47.5 on average. Useful as it is, the Latulippe formula is not without its flaws, as discussed in "Robustness of the Results."

3. The OECD publishes labor force data only up to the age of 60–64 for the Czech Republic and Poland for the calendar years 1996–2001. Based on the assumption that the proportion of the participation rates of the 65–69 and 60–64 age brackets, those of the 70–74 and 65–69 age brackets, and those of the 75 and older and 70–74 age brackets are the same as in 2002, the right-hand tail of the participation age profile is estimated for these two countries for the years between 1996 and 2001.

4. Formally (also by Latulippe [1996]):

$$\overline{RD} = \frac{0.5 \times {}_5R_{40,44}^z \times e_{47.5} + \sum_{x=45,50...}^{75} {}_5R_{x,x+4}^z \times e_{x+5}}{0.5 \times {}_5R_{40,44}^z + \sum_{x=45,50...}^{75} {}_5R_{x,x+4}^z}$$

where e stands for life expectancy. $\overline{RD}$ can be interpreted as the life expectancy at retirement.

5. See Sobotka and Lutz (2010) on the total fertility rate, a related indicator.

6. Some differences arise between data of the two international agencies. The OECD uses five-year grouped data; Eurostat calculations are based on single-year age groups. The latter has a wider confidence interval but it can cover withdrawals in one year against the five-year interval in the OECD estimates. This makes the OECD time series more volatile. The retirement process starts at age 40 in the OECD but at 50 in the Eurostat. In principle, that should make Eurostat exit ages higher. The Eurostat time series is shorter, covering 2001–10. Even for that shorter period, one-quarter of the data points are not available for the CEE8 group.

7. Eurostat publishes complete life tables including period life expectancies by age (demo_mlex-pec) for a large number of countries. However, no comparable cohort life expectancies were found for the CEE8 countries. This chapter's own calculation is based on the assumptions on future mortality rates of Eurostat's 2015 population projection (proj_15naasmr). To capture all relevant cohorts, the estimation starts with l_x=100,000 at age 55.

8. Because of data problems, Luxembourg is missing from the comparison. In the OECD data set, the labor force in the 75 and older age group is zero in Finland and Sweden, possibly distorting the estimation in a conservative way, leaving the conclusions unaffected or even strengthened. In Belgium, Denmark, Germany, Greece, and Italy, the number of active workers in the 75 and older age group is calculated as the difference between the total and the 15–74-year-old workforce.

9. See the MISSOC collection of social protection rules at https://www.missoc.org /missoc-database/comparative-tables/.

10. The gov_10a_taxag data set of Eurostat distinguishes between pension and nonpension contributions for households but not for employees (so the figure on pension contribution includes amounts paid by the self-employed and the nonemployed). Data on employee-level contributions are available but they include health care and other payments, too. To separate pension contributions for employees from their other contributions, the household-level pension/nonpension rate is applied. Further data limitations arise, too. Estonian contributions are not split by function; Polish contributions are but not in the Eurostat data set; so, these two countries are missing from table 16.4. Hungarian data were collected from local sources. The estimation of the covered wage bill can be slightly distorted by potential ceilings on the tax base. National regulations on such ceilings were added to the table.

11. In addition, wage coverage is a measure of tax evasion (which is illegal) but not tax avoidance (which is legal). Undercontributing wages that legally circumvent taxation by exploiting regulatory loopholes can be found in the category of mixed income, too, in the national accounts, not only among wages and salaries.

References

Ahacic, Kozma, Ingemar Kareholt, Mats Thorslund, and Marti G. Parker. 2007. "Relationships between Symptoms, Physical Capacity, Activity Limitations in 1992 and 2002." *Aging Clinical and Experimental Research* 19 (3):187–93.

Albouy, Valerie, and Laurent Lequien. 2009. "Does Compulsory Education Lower Mortality?" *Journal of Health Economics* 28: 155–68.

Ayuso, Mercedes, Jorge Bravo, and Robert Holzmann. 2018. "Getting Life Expectancy Estimates Right for Pension Policy: Period versus Cohort Approach." IZA Discussion Paper 11512, Institute of Labor Economics, Bonn, Germany. https://papers.ssrn.com/sol3/papers .cfm?abstract_id=3177388.

Baker, David P., Juan Leon, Emily G. Smith Greenaway, John Collins, and Marcela Movit. 2011. "The Education Effect on Population Health: A Reassessment." *Population and Development Review* 37: 307–32. https://doi.org/10.1111/j.1728-4457.2011.00412.x.

Barro, Robert J., and Jong Wha Lee. 2013. "A New Data Set of Educational Attainment in the World, 1950–2010." *Journal of Development Economics* 104: 184–98.

Bloom, David E., and David Canning. 2007. "Commentary—The Preston Curve 30 Years On: Still Sparking Fires." *International Journal of Epidemiology* 36: 498–99. https://doi.org/10.1093 /ije/dym079.

Boissonneault, Michael. 2018. "Measuring the Impact of Health on Work in a Context of Delayed Retirement." Dissertation, University of Groningen. https://www.rug.nl/research/portal /files/62756519/Title_and_contents.pdf.

Caselli, Graziella, Sven Drefahl, Christian Wegner-Siegmundt, and Marc Luy. 2014. "Future Mortality in Low Mortality Countries." In *World Population and Human Capital in the 21st Century*, edited by Wolfgang Lutz, William P. Butz, and Samir KC, 226–72. Oxford: Oxford University Press.

Chatterji, Somnath, Julie Byles, David Cutler, Seeman Teresa, and Emese Verdes. 2015. "Health, Functioning, and Disability in Older Adults—Present Status and Future Implications." *The Lancet* 385 (9967): 563–75.

Christensen, Kaare, Gabriele Doblhammer, Roland Rau, and James W. Vaupel. 2009. "Ageing Populations: The Challenges Ahead." *The Lancet* 374 (9696): 1196–208.

Clark, Damon, and Heather Royer. 2010. "The Effect of Education on Adult Health and Mortality: Evidence from Britain." Working Paper 16013, National Bureau of Economic Research, Cambridge, MA.

Coile, Courtney, Kevin S. Milligan, and David A. Wise. 2017. "Health Capacity to Work at Older Ages: Evidence from the United States." In *Social Security Programs and Retirement around the World: The Capacity to Work at Older Ages*, edited by David A. Wise, 359–94. Chicago, IL: University of Chicago Press.

Crimmins, Eileen M., and Hiram Beltrán-Sánchez. 2010. "Mortality and Morbidity Trends: Is There Compression of Morbidity?" *Journals of Gerontology: Series B* 66 (1): 75–86.

Eggleston, Karen N., and Victor R. Fuchs. 2012. "The New Demographic Transition: Most Gains in Life Expectancy Now Realized Late in Life." *Journal of Economic Perspectives* 26 (3): 137–56.

European Union. 2018. *The 2018 Pension Adequacy Report: Current and Future Income Adequacy in Old Age in the EU*. Luxembourg: Publications Office of the European Union.

Eurostat. 2017. "Average Exit Age from the Labour Force—Annual Data (lfsi_exi_a)." (accessed January 6, 2018), http://ec.europa.eu/eurostat/cache/metadata/en/lfsi_exi_a_esms.htm) and Duration of working life—Annual Data (lfsi_dwl_a) (see https://ec.europa.eu/eurostat/cache /metadata/en/lfsi_dwl_a_esms.htm).

Freedman, Vicki A., and Linda G. Martin. 1999. "The Role of Education in Explaining and Forecasting Trends in Functional Limitations among Older Americans." *Demography* 36 (4): 461–73.

Fries, James F. 1980. "Aging, Natural Death, and the Compression of Morbidity." *New England Journal of Medicine* 303: 1369–70.

Gathmann, Christina, Hendrik Jürges, and Steffen Reinhold. 2012. "Compulsory Schooling Reforms, Education and Mortality in Twentieth Century Europe." SSRN Scholarly Paper No. ID 2020246, Social Science Research Network, Rochester, NY.

Goldstein, Joshua R., and Kenneth W. Wachter. 2006. "Relationships between Period and Cohort Life Expectancy: Gaps and Lags." *Population Studies* 60 (3): 257–69.

Holzmann, Robert, David Robalino, and Hernan Winkler. 2018. "NDC Schemes and the Labor Market: The Challenges of Formal Employment and Delayed Retirement." Revised paper presented at the 3rd NDC Conference, Rome, October 5–6.

Keese, Mark. 2012. "A Method of Calculating the Average Effective Age of Retirement." OECD Working Papers, OECD, Paris.

Lager, Anton Carl Jonas, and Jenny Torssander. 2012. "Causal Effect of Education on Mortality in a Quasi-Experiment on 1.2 Million Swedes." *Proceedings of the National Academy of Sciences* 109 (22): 8461–66.

Lassila, Jukka, Niku Määttänen, and Tarmo Valkonen. 2014. "Linking Retirement Age to Life Expectancy—What Happens to Working Lives and Income Distribution?" Finnish Centre for Pensions Reports 2014/2, Helsinki.

Latulippe, Denis. 1996. "Effective Retirement Age and the Duration of Retirement in the Industrial Countries between 1950 and 1990." ILO Issues in Social Protection Discussion Paper 2, International Labour Organization, Geneva.

Lleras-Muney, Adriana. 2005. "The Relationship between Education and Adult Mortality in the United States." *Review of Economic Studies* 72: 189–221.

Loichinger, Elke, and Daniela Weber. 2016. "Trends in Working Life Expectancy in Europe." *Journal of Aging and Health* 28 (7): 1194–213.

Lutz, Wolfgang, William P. Butz, and Samir KC. 2014. "*World Population and Human Capital in the Twenty-First Century.*" Oxford: Oxford University Press.

Lutz, Wolfgang, and Endale Kebede. 2018. "Education and Health: Redrawing the Preston Curve." *Population and Development Review* 44 (2): 343–61.

Lutz, Wolfgang, and Vegard Skirbekk. 2014. "How Education Drives Demography and Knowledge Informs Projections." In *World Population and Human Capital in the 21st Century,* edited by Wolfgang Lutz, William P. Butz, and Samir KC, 14–38. Oxford: Oxford University Press.

Mackenbach, Johan P., and Caspar W. N. Looman. 2013. "Life Expectancy and National Income in Europe, 1900–2008: An Update of Preston's Analysis." *International Journal of Epidemiology* 42: 1100–110. https://doi.org/10.1093/ije/dyt122.

Monteiro, Maria Silvia, Juhani Ilmarinen, and Heleno Rodrigues Corrêa Filho. 2006. "Work Ability of Workers in Different Age Groups in a Public Health Institution in Brazil." *International Journal of Occupational Safety and Ergonomics* 12 (4): 417–27.

OECD (Organisation for Economic Co-operation and Development). 2017. "Average Effective Age of Retirement." (accessed January 2, 2018), http://www.oecd.org/els/emp/average-effective-age-of-retirement.htm.

Parker, Marti G., and Mats Thorslund. 2007. "Health Trends in the Elderly Population: Getting Better and Getting Worse." *Gerontologist* 47 (2): 150–58.

Preston, Samuel H. 1975. "The Changing Relation between Mortality and Level of Economic Development." *Population Studies* 29: 231–48. https://doi.org/10.2307/2173509.

Rehkopf, David H., Nancy E. Adler, and John W. Rowe. 2016. "The Impact of Health and Education on Future Labour Force Participation among Individuals Aged 55–74 in the United States of America." *Aging and Society* 37 (7): 1313–37.

Robine, Jean-Marie, and Colin Mathers. 1993. "Measuring the Compression or Expansion of Morbidity through Changes in Health Expectancy." In *Calculation of Health Expectancies, Harmonization, Consensus Achieved and Future Perspectives*, edited by Jean-Marie Robine, Colin Mathers, Margaret R. Bone, and Isabelle Romieu, 169–286. Paris: Libbey.

Salomon, Joshua A., Haidong Wang, Michael K. Freeman, Theo Vos, Abraham D. Flaxman, Alan D. Lopez, and Christopher J. Murray. 2012. "Healthy Life Expectancy for 187 Countries, 1990–2010: A Systematic Analysis for the Global Burden of Disease Study 2010." *The Lancet* 380 (9859): 2144–62.

Sanderson, Warren C., and Sergei Scherbov. 2010. "Remeasuring Aging." *Science* 329 (5997/2010): 1287–88.

———. 2013. "The Characteristics Approach to the Measurement of Population Aging." *Population and Development Review* 39 (4): 673–85.

————. 2017. "A Unifying Framework for the Study of Population Aging." *Vienna Yearbook of Population Research* 2016 (14): 7–39.

Scherer, Peter. 2002. "Age of Withdrawal from the Labour Force in OECD Countries." OECD Labour Market and Social Policy Occasional Paper 49, OECD Publishing, Paris.

Schirle, Tammy. 2008. "Why Have the Labor Force Participation Rates of Older Men Increased since the Mid-1990s?" *Journal of Labor Economics* 26 (4): 549–94.

Silles, Mary A. 2009. "The Causal Effect of Education on Health: Evidence from the United Kingdom." *Economics of Education Review* 28: 122–28.

Sobotka, Tomas, and Wolfgang Lutz. 2010. "Misleading Policy Messages Derived from the Period TFR: Should We Stop Using It?" *Comparative Population Studies—Zeitschrift für Bevölkerungswissenschaft* 35 (3): 637–64.

Vogler-Ludwig, Kurt, and Nicola Düll. 2008. "Analysis of the Average Exit Age from the Labour Force." Research Report. http://ec.europa.eu/social/main.jsp?advSearchKey=lifelongapproachwork&mode=advancedSubmit&catId=22&policyArea=0&policyAreaSub=0&country=0&year=0.